"*Learning Messiah* by Edjan Westerman is a full scale biblical theology that is passionately Christian and passionately 'post-supersessionist' in equal measure . . . the contents of the book have impressed me as accessible, engaging, detailed, and often profound."

—**R. Kendall Soulen**
Emory University, Atlanta

"E. J. Westerman has written a very important book that revolutionizes our understanding of both Israel and the Church. In the case of the latter, a more deeply rooted Biblical identity of the Church arises on the basis of a new canonical approach to Biblical theology. This new canonical approach restores the ongoing meaning of Israel to God's purpose in creation and consummation and hence the unity of purpose for Israel and the Church."

—**Daniel C. Juster**
Director of Tikkun Ministries International

"Ever since the Holocaust Christian theologians have reexamined previous Christian thinking about Israel. Most have rejected one aspect of supersessionism, that which posited an end to God's covenant with the Jewish people . . . EJ Westerman provides us with a retelling of the biblical story in which Israel and her Messiah are at the center. This retelling sheds much new light on not only the Bible but the meaning of Israel and the nations. This is an important and helpful book for Christian theology, the Church, and Israel today."

—**Gerald R. McDermott**
Beeson Divinity School/Samford University, Birmingham, Alabama

"*Learning Messiah* is an important book. Edjan Westerman reads the Bible as a 'co-reader' with deep respect for Israel, the first reader. Starting from the belief that we received the Tenach and the New Testament from the beloved and elected people of Israel's God, he overviews and corrects the common Christian Biblical theology with his 'own' integral canonical approach . . . He wrote this book for the common, interested reader and invites them to react and to take a position. If we receive the Bible in modesty and in acceptance of the priority of God to Israel—what does this mean for our faith and our relation to the people of the Messiah?"

—**Bas Plaisier**
Former Vice President of the World Communion of Reformed Churches

"E. J. Westerman's book sets the standard for a new genre of theological literature—a post-supersessionist biblical theology which re-casts the biblical metanarrative along the lines of R. K. Soulen's *The God of Israel and Christian Theology*. His proposals will not be accepted by all, as they challenge a deep-rooted and prevailing paradigm. But anyone interested in a renewed biblical understanding of God's ongoing purposes through Jesus the Messiah with both Israel and the Church and all nations, and a detailed exposition of the whole of Scripture in support of such an understanding, will take serious note of this exciting and radical approach."

—**Richard Harvey**
Author of *Mapping Messianic Jewish Theology*

"This new volume by Edjan Westerman is an impressive and ambitious re-reading of the bible as a whole, with the aim of articulating its coherent narrative in a way that does justice to the enduring significance of the Jewish people and to the unique salvific role of Jesus. While demonstrating knowledge of scholarly currents, Westerman presents his material in a popular and accessible fashion."

—**Mark S. Kinzer**
President Emeritus of the Messianic Jewish Theological Institute

"This fascinating and revealing study is nothing less than a hermeneutical eye operation. It unveils the beauty of God's lasting covenant with Israel including the new covenant of the Messiah . . . Reading with new eyes yields a twofold fruit: the joy of a new understanding of God's way in this world, and tears of shame. Because we need to repent from using our traditional reading glasses that caused so much separation between the church and the people of God's original covenant."

—**Niek M. Tramper**
Pastor of the Protestant Church of the Netherlands

"I believe that this book provides a fresh and challenging new approach to the place of Israel in redemptive history. Proceeding from a post-supersessionist perspective, Westerman seeks to narrate the central message of the Tanach in such a way that the history of Israel as the people of God connects naturally to the coming of the Messiah and the foundation of the Church."

—**William T. Koopmans**
Dutch reading OT-scholar

"Westerman offers a lucid, comprehensive, and compelling treatment of Israel's indelible role in God's unfolding plan of blessing and redemption for the whole world. Written with a conscious eye to the dark shadow cast by the Holocaust (and the preceding centuries of erroneous Christian Israelology), Westerman's work contributes an important voice to the growing body of Christian scholarship reassessing Israel's significance in salvation history and her ongoing, unbreakable covenant with God."

—**Jennifer M. Rosner**
Fuller Theological Seminary

"[This] book is a Biblical Theology as I have never read before . . . It is a systematic theological study of the Bible starting from the conviction that . . . [God's] choice of Israel is still valid and is not in variance with the coming of the Messiah . . . Westerman shows that he can read the texts in a new manner from the perspective of a new canonical narrative . . . The book provides a good starting point to rethink the position of the nations in relation to Israel."

—**Ron van den Hout**
Roman-Catholic bishop of Groningen-Leeuwarden, the Netherlands

"This is a conscientious and thorough study of Israel's role in redemptive history. Though not being a fundamentalist myself, I became intrigued by the systematic patterns Edjan Westerman discovered through careful study of the texts. It gave me new insights in the continuing role of Israel and the relation between Israel and the Christians from the nations. This book certainly deserves a broad readership."

—**Dineke Houtman**
Protestant Theological University, Amsterdam

Learning Messiah

Learning Messiah

Israel and the Nations: Learning to Read God's Way Anew

EDJAN WESTERMAN

WIPF & STOCK · Eugene, Oregon

LEARNING MESSIAH
Israel and the Nations: Learning to Read God's Way Anew

Copyright © 2018 Edjan Westerman. All rights reserved. Except for brief quotations in critical publications or reviews, no part of this book may be reproduced in any manner without prior written permission from the publisher. Write: Permissions, Wipf and Stock Publishers, 199 W. 8th Ave., Suite 3, Eugene, OR 97401.

Wipf & Stock
An Imprint of Wipf and Stock Publishers
199 W. 8th Ave., Suite 3
Eugene, OR 97401

www.wipfandstock.com

PAPERBACK ISBN: 978-1-5326-5425-1
HARDCOVER ISBN: 978-1-5326-5426-8
EBOOK ISBN: 978-1-5326-5427-5

Manufactured in the U.S.A.   09/26/18

The original Dutch version was published in August 2015.

Edjan Westerman, *De Messias leren, Israël en de volken – Gods weg nieuw leren lezen*, Zoetermeer: Boekencentrum, 2015.

ISBN 978 90 239 7043 9
NUR 700,716

www.uitgeverijboekencentrum.nl
© Uitgeverij Boekencentrum

All Scripture quotations, unless otherwise indicated, are taken from the Holy Bible, New International Version®, NIV®. Copyright ©1973, 1978, 1984, 2011 by Biblica, Inc.™ Used by permission of Zondervan. All rights reserved worldwide. www.zondervan.com The "NIV" and "New International Version" are trademarks registered in the United States Patent and Trademark Office by Biblica, Inc.™

The image of painting The Shofar may not be reproduced or used in any way without the prior written permission of the painter Jip Wijngaarden. Copyrights © 2018 by Jip Wijngaarden | www.jipwijngaarden.com | All rights reserved

For *Coby*
loving companion, mother and grandmother

". . . we will tell the next generation the praiseworthy deeds of the LORD, His power and the wonders He has done."

Psalm 78:4

Contents

Preface to the English Edition | xvii
Preface: Understanding My Calling | xxi
Abbreviations | xxvi
Introduction | xxvii

    I.1 Learning to Read God's Way Anew

    I.2 Narrative

    I.3 Israel in Our Narrative

    I.4 Narrative and Paradigm

    I.5 A Life-endangering Paradigm

    I.6 Israel at the Foreground?

    I.7 Sketch of a Canonical Narrative

    I.8 Priestly Calling of Israel as Keynote of the Canonical Narrative

    I.9 Model of Interpretation and Understanding

PART I: THE CANONICAL NARRATIVE: THE TANAKH

CHAPTER 1

Creation and Waiting for Both the God of Israel and the Israel of God | 3

    1.1 Permanent Co-reading with Israel

    1.2 Genesis 1:1

    1.3 The Beginning of the Canonical Narrative

    1.4 Further Instruction Needed

    1.5 Humility

    1.6 Learning Tora

    1.7 An Unrelinquishable Position

    1.8 Waiting

    1.9 "The fear of the LORD is the beginning of wisdom"

    1.10 Israel as the Place of God's Self-Revelation

CHAPTER 2

Creation Awaits the Blessing of God | 11

    2.1 Blessing

    2.2 Blessed by God

Contents

    2.3 Earth Being Filled . . .

    2.4 And Yet Blessed Again

    2.5 Disobedience

    2.6 Blessing Out of Israel

    2.7 Mutual Blessing

    2.8 In the End

CHAPTER 3

The Creation of the Camp of Israel and the Priestly Nation: The Beginning | 19

    3.1 Creation of "The Camp of Israel"

    3.2 Creation of the People

    3.3 Abram the Blessing

    3.4 Dichotomy

    3.5 Contours of Priesthood

    3.6 Abram Waits

    3.7 Covenant

    3.8 The Binding of Isaac

    3.9 Blessing and Darkness

CHAPTER 4

The Creation of the Camp of Israel and of the Priestly Nation: the Sequel | 30

    4.1 Resistance against the Election

    4.2 Inheriting the Land Devoid of Human Strength

    4.3 To See from a Distance

CHAPTER 5

The Creation of the Camp of Israel and of the Priestly Nation: Waiting for the Tora | 36

    5.1 Tora in the Camp of Israel

    5.2 Instruction

    5.3 Expansion

        Excursus: Noachide Commandments

    5.4 Tora and *Tikkun Olam*

    5.5 Interpretation Key

CHAPTER 6

Liberated and Called: God's Treasured Possession and Nation of Priests | 41

    6.1 Imprisoned unto Death

    6.2 The Beginning of Redemption

    6.3 Resistance

    6.4 Night of Judgment and Deliverance

    6.5 Opposition Against the Exodus

6.6 Exodus and Destination
6.7 Prepared through Testing
6.8 The Calling

CHAPTER 7
Israel's Calling: Condition and Promise | 50
7.1 The Love of God
7.2 Two-sidedness
7.3 Treasured Possession
7.4 Kingdom of Priests
7.5 A Holy Nation
7.6 The Calling as a Possibility Today and in the Future
7.7 Once More: Two-sidedness
7.8 Priesthood as Model of Interpretation
7.9 Once More: Model of Interpretation
7.10 Waiting for . . .

CHAPTER 8
The Consecration of Priests and of Israel as a Priestly Nation: Waiting for the Eighth Day | 61
8.1 The Words and Covenant of God
8.2 I Will Dwell in their Midst
8.3 The Consecration of the Priests
8.4 Waiting for the Eighth Day
   Excursus: The Eighth day: Messianic Coloring of the Number Eight
8.5 The Consecration of Priests: A Model of Instruction for the Consecration of the People as a Whole
8.6 Toward the One Place of Worship and Toward the Eighth Day

CHAPTER 9
Priestly Nation around the One Sanctuary: Priests around the Dwelling | 73
9.1 Different Perspectives
9.2 Pure Service
9.3 A Holy Service Needs a Holy Fire
9.4 Priestly Distinctions and Priestly Separation
9.5 Be Holy
9.6 Structuring the Camp of Israel
9.7 The One Sanctuary
9.8 Toward God's Structuring of the Land
9.9 Toward the Indwelling in the Midst of the People and the Earth
9.10 Dwelling and Kingship of God

Contents

CHAPTER 10

Kingdom and Kingship of the People around the Dwelling of God | 83

    10.1 The Royal Perspective

    10.2 Kings

    10.3 Kingdom of Priests

    10.4 Jewish Interpretation of the Call to be a Kingdom of Priests

    10.5 Kingship as Model of Learning for Israel

    10.6 The Royal Calling: Promise and Obedience

    10.7 From Sinai Toward the Kingdom

    10.8 Learning and Waiting for the Eighth Son

    10.9 Paradigm of Suffering on the Road to the Throne

CHAPTER 11

The Calling Impeded by Israel's Disobedience and the Opposition of the Nations | 93

    11.1 A Dark Perspective

    11.2 Obstacles

    11.3 Two-sidedness of the Covenant

    11.4 Adulterous *Segula*-People

    11.5 Unholy (in the) Midst of the Nations

    11.6 Priestly Desecration

    11. 7 Royal Desecration

    11.8 Unholy Servant of God

    11.9 Unholiness and the Indwelling of God

    11.10 Divine Lamentation

    11.11 Toward the Day of the LORD and Waiting for the Eighth Day

CHAPTER 12

Learning about the Eighth Day: Prophetic Words about the Messianic Time | 111

    12.1 The End of the Canonical Narrative of the Tanakh

    12.2 Hopeful Prophetic Words: Puzzle Pieces of Blessing

    12.3 For the Sake of the Name

    12.4 Fulfillment of the Two-sidedness of the Covenant

    12.5 The Purification of the *Avoda* and the Servant of the LORD

    12.6 The Purification of the *Avoda* and the Servant as "Covenant for the People"

    12.7 The Messiah and the Calling of Israel

    12.8 God's Plans with Israel Realized

    12.9 The Gift of the Return of the People

    12.10 The Gift of the Unity of the People

    12.11 The Election of the Land and the City Confirmed

12.12 The Indwelling of God in the Midst of the Holy Camp

12.13 Around the Indwelling: A Kingdom of Priests

12.14 The Blessing for the Nations and the Service of the Nations

12.15 God's Intentions for All Creation Realized

12.16 The Tora and the Messianic Time

12.17 Finally, a Great *Sukkot*: A Thanksgiving Celebration of All Creation

12.18 The Canonical Narrative of the Tanakh

PART II: THE CANONICAL NARRATIVE: THE SCRIPTURES OF THE NEW COVENANT—THE NEW TESTAMENT

CHAPTER 13

Two-Part Canon, One Narrative? | 137

13.1 One Canonical Narrative?

13.2 New Testament: New Covenant

13.3 Two-part Canon: One God?

13.4 The Same God: A Different Story?

13.5 Replacement and Replacement Theology

13.6 Replacement of Israel and the Faithfulness of God

13.7 Structural Supersessionism/Replacement Thinking

13.8 Growing Chasm between Israel and "the Church"

13.9 The Traditional Canonical Narrative and its Conduciveness to the *Shoa*

13.10 Reconsideration Leading to a Confession of Guilt and Different Relations

13.11 A Jewish Reconsideration of the Chasm

13.12 Christian Reconsideration of the Interpretation of Scripture

13.13 Attention for the Jewish Context of the New Testament

13.14 Still Present: Structural Replacement Thinking/Supersessionism

13.15 Again: The Necessity for an Alternative to the Traditional Canonical Narrative

13.16 One-Canonical Narrative about Israel's Calling to be a Kingdom of Priests

13.17 Part II and Part III

CHAPTER 14

In the Camp of Israel: The Eighth Day Breaks | 154

14.1 Fourteen

14.2 Israel in the Center of the Earth

14.3 Israel Witnesses the Dawning of the Eighth Day

14.4 Celebrations of God's Deeds in the Camp of the People

14.5 Two-sided Character of the Eighth Day

14.6 The Eighth Day: The Compassion of God and Anointment of the Spirit

14.7 The Eighth Day: The Fire of Judgment

14.8 The Eighth Day: Salvation also for the Nations

Contents

CHAPTER 15

In the Camp of Israel: The Indwelling in the *Segula*-People | 163

15.1 God with Us

15.2 Incarnation in Israel: "Enfleshment" within the People of God

15.3 The LORD Is There

15.4 God Chooses His Own High Ways

15.5 "Who is This?"—Meeting the Presence of God in Jesus

15.6 The Messiah and the *Shekhina* of God

15.7 The Tanakh: Occasions that God Came Near and Revealed Himself

15.8 "One Is the LORD" and Immanuel

15.9 The Indwelling and the Deeds of God

15.10 The Scriptures of the New Covenant about this One

15.11 The Bodily Indwelling: A Desire Fulfilled

15.12 The Holy God Himself Performs the *Avoda*

CHAPTER 16

In the Camp of Israel: The *Avoda* Fully Lived and Perfectly Accomplished | 176

16.1 *Avoda*

16.2 The Enduring Two-sidedness of God's Covenants

16.3 God Provides: Covenantal Obedience and the New Covenant

16.4 *Avoda* Granted

16.5 The Messiah as *Brit Am*: Covenant for the People

16.6 The *Avoda* of *Yeshua*/Jesus: The Fulfillment of Israel's *Avoda*

16.7 Priest for Israel, Priest for the Nations: Adam in Israel

16.8 The Eighth Day: The Obedient One Enters Judgment

16.9 The Eighth Day: The Obedient One Enters Salvation

16.10 Preparation and Foretaste

16.11 The New Covenant: Inaugurated and Underway

16.12 The Blessings of the New Covenant and the Focus of the New Testament

16.13 In the Camp of Israel: The *Avoda* Fully Lived and Perfectly Accomplished

CHAPTER 17

In the Camp of Israel: The Priestly Nation Consecrated in the Sanctification of the Messiah | 192

17.1 Israel's Calling: The Eighth Day Dawns

17.2 The Essence of the Priestly Calling: The Tasks of the Priestly Nation

17.3 The Priestly Consecration of *Yeshua*/Jesus: The First One of the People

17.4 The Priestly Service of *Yeshua*/Jesus: The First One of the People

17.5 The Sacrifice Outside the City: Sacrifice of Israel, by Israel, and for Israel

17.6 The Sacrifice Outside the City: Also a Sacrifice of the World and for the World

17.7 Israel's Sacrifice Accepted: The Dawning of the *Olam Haba*

17.8 Israel's Priestly Service Sanctified: The Task Underway Toward the *Tikkun Olam*

17.9 The Priesthood of the Messiah Underway Toward the *Tikkun Olam*

17.10 God will not Rest until His Whole People are Priests

CHAPTER 18

In the Camp of Israel: The Royal Consecration and the Kingdom | 204

18.1 Kingship and Paradigms

18.2 Called to be a Kingdom of Priests: The Streambed of the Tanakh

18.3 Anointed to be a Priestly King

18.4 The Kingship of the Messiah: Preparation and Reminder

18.5 Royal Instruction

18.6 Royal Glory of the Messiah

18.7 The King of the Jews Guarantees the Kingship for Israel

18.8 The Hebron-Kingship and the Jerusalem-Kingship of the Messiah

18.9 A King in Exile

18.10 Kingship Understood from the Streambed of the Tanakh

18.11 Toward the Jerusalem-Kingship

CHAPTER 19

In the Camp of Israel: The Holy Nation Sanctified | 218

19.1 The Day of the LORD Breaks over the Holy Nation—the Eighth Day Dawns

19.2 Once More: Israel's Election and Calling to be a Holy Nation.

19.3 The Consecration of the Priests as a Model for the Messianic Sanctification of the People

19.4 Messianic Instruction

19.5 The Priestly Nation and Messiah "Unclothed": Entering the Day of the LORD and the Exile

19.6 The Priestly Nation and Messiah Anointed: Entering the Holy Life of the *Olam Haba*

19.7 *Am Kadosh* in the Messiah

19.8 Partial Sanctification: The Camp of Israel Enters the Judgment

19.9 The Darkness of the Day of the LORD Expands: Exile for the People, the Holy King, and the *Shekhina*

19.10 The Light of the *Olam Haba* Enters the World: The Calling of the *Am Kadosh* for the World Becomes Visible

19.11 Waiting for the Second *Pessaḥ* and the Unity and Return of the People

19.12 *Kedusha* in the Midst of the World: Blessing for the Whole Earth

CHAPTER 20

In the Camp of Israel: Blessing for the *Mishpaḥa* of Abraham and the Nations | 236

20.1 Salvation for the Nations in the Camp of Israel

20.2 Blessing for the Nations and the Election of Abraham's *Mishpaḥa*

20.3 The King of the Jews in Search of the Nations: The Blessing of the Exile

20.4 A Great Surprise

Contents

20.5 The Mystery of Ages Revealed: Ephesians 2–3
20.6 The Nations Come Flooding in: Probing Questions
20.7 The Mystery: The Messiah as Place of Salvation
20.8 Acts 15: The Council in Jerusalem
20.9 The Decision of the Apostles: Two Forms of Messianic Obedience
20.10 Two Callings: One Royal Priesthood
20.11 Israel, the Tora, and the Nations in the Dawning of the Day of the LORD and the *Olam Haba*: The Letter to the Romans
20.12 "The Works of the Law": The Letter to the Galatians
20.13 "Ready to Disappear": The Letter to the Hebrews
20.14 Reading from within a Different Paradigm: Circumcision, Food and Celebration
20.15 Israel's Calling in the Messiah Shared by the Nations: Branches on the Olive Tree
20.16 Resistance of a Part of Israel: Blindness and Deepening of the *Galut*
20.17 The Love of God and Hosea: Underway Toward the Jerusalem-Kingship
20.18 The King of the Jews Leads the Nations into Service and Pilgrimage
20.19 Together Abraham's *Mishpaḥa* and the *Mishpaḥot* of the Nations Grasp the Great Love of the Messiah

CHAPTER 21

The Camp of Israel: Waiting for the Return of the *Shekhina*—Israel and the Nations Advancing Toward the *Tikkun Olam* | 270

21.1 One Continuing Story
21.2 Return to Zion: Outlines and Fragments
21.3 The Simultaneous Approach of the Kingdom and Day of the LORD
21.4 Abiding Centrality: The Camp of Israel, the City of Jerusalem, and the Indwelling of God in Order to Bless
21.5 From Exile Toward the *Tikkun Olam*
21.6 The Safekeeping and Fullness of Israel
21.7 The Surrender and Resistance of the Nations
21.8 The Messiah at the Throne: The Lamb Opens the Seals
21.9 Ultimate Pride: The Antichrist and the Prostitute
21.10 The Kingship of God and His Messiah
21.11 The Kingdom in the *Olam Haze*: The Millennium, Gog, and Magog
21.12 The King of the Jews: Judge of the World
21.13 The New Heaven and Earth, and the New Jerusalem
21.14 What Will Come is Already on the Way: Mutual Blessing Between Israel and the Nations
21.15 God's Eternal Indwelling in Zion
21.16 The *Olam Haba*: *Kedusha* for the Whole of Creation
21.17 The Eternal *Shabbat* and the Messianic New Day

PART III: RETURNING AND RETHINKING: LIVING IN A "NEW" CANONICAL NARRATIVE

CHAPTER 22

To Repent | 293

22.1 "You Are the Man!"

22.2 A Shocking Discovery: The Tears of Joseph

22.3 Repenting of Our Role in the Ongoing Canonical Narrative

22.4 The Higher Thoughts and Ways of God

22.5 The Ways of God's Eternal Love for Israel: Contrition and Repentance

22.6 The Ways of the Messiah: Contrition and Repentance

22.7 The History and Future of the People, the City, and the Land: Contrition and Repentance

22.8 The Body of the Messiah: Contrition and Repentance

22.9 Reformation of Practice and Thought: Returning and Rethinking

CHAPTER 23

Returning and Rethinking | 301

23.1 The Holy One Chose to Be Defenseless

23.2 Called to *Kedusha* before God's Countenance

23.3 Called by the God of Israel Who Reveals Himself within the Camp of Israel

23.4 New Eyes Through the "Other" Canonical Narrative

23.5 A Lasting Central Place for Israel's Election and Covenantal *Kedusha*: The Messiah as the Obedient Firstling of Israel

23.6 An Identity that Remains Connected with Israel

23.7 Even "In The Messiah" All Israel Remains Connected to God

23.8 The Body of the Messiah: A Dual Structure from Israel and the Nations

23.9 The Mission of the Messiah among the Nations: Exaltation and Exile

23.10 Messianic Celebration with Israel

23.11 Underway Toward a Contested Zion: A Messianic Dispute Regarding the Land

23.12 The "Other" in the Canonical Narrative: Israel and "the Church" in the Jewish and Christian Canonical Narrative

23.13 New Eyes, New Words, New Actions

23.14 Ongoing Reformation of Thought and Practice

CHAPTER 24

Accompanying the Holy God Underway Toward the *Tikkun Olam* | 334

24.1 One Big Narrative

24.2 Toward the Completion of the Priestly People's *Kedusha*

24.3 The Fight Over God's Vine: Zion and the Tribulations of the Messiah

24.4 The Ways Toward Unity in the Time of the Hebron-Kingship

24.5 During the Hebron-Kingship: Israel Approaching the Second *Pessaḥ*

24.6 Underway Toward the Last Trumpet and the Fulfillment of *Yom Kippur* and *Sukkot*

24.7 Underway: The Body of the Messiah's Royal Prophetic Task

Contents

24.8 Temple Servants for the *Olam Haba*: The *Avoda* of All Israel—The Body of the Messiah Perfected—One *Kehilla* and the Twenty-four Elders

24.9 Threefold Reflection of the Self-Revelation of the Holy One of Israel

24.10 The Indwelling and the *Shabbat* of God

Epilogue | 348

List of Hebrew Terms | 353
Bibliography | 359
Index of Scripture | 365

Preface to the English Edition

THE BLESSING OF GOD—THAT is what this book is about.

That the Name of the LORD is praised "from the rising of the sun to the place where it sets,"[1] is certainly His blessing. A blessing of which Messiah Jesus—as is the conviction of His followers worldwide—is the pinnacle and embodiment, and which has been disseminated worldwide by the ministry of the Christian faith community. Even from a Jewish point of view, this worldwide dissemination of the knowledge of the Name of the God of Israel and His Scriptures is seen as a positive development.

Yet this book is also about *blindness*. Our collective Christian blindness. God's blessing does not exclude the possibility of blindness on our side. Though His faithfulness will surely overarch it, sometimes His blessing is interwoven with our blindness. To see this we only have to look—recently commemorating 500 years of Reformation—to the last years of Martin Luther. The blessing of a fresh reading of Scripture,[2] so much the hallmark of the Reformation, did not prevent him from taking a very anti-Jewish and even anti-Semitic stance in his last years. This severe blindness mingled with a true and fresh search of the revelatory ways of God, as we have seen so often throughout the ages, is an occurrence not just in Europe.

Learning Messiah, the English edition of the Dutch original *de Messias leren*, published in 2015, wishes to serve the worldwide Christian church. It is therefore written not only for a theologically-minded audience, and is not only meant to convey theological truths or to serve a theological debate. It is a book that invites Christians of whatever denomination or spiritual color to join looking in the mirror and to act upon what we see.

When, however, my Jewish friends or other Jewish readers might read this book, I would first of all regard—seen against the background of the very painful history of Christian-Jewish interrelations—their reading as an honor and token of a renewing mutual trust. Then I would invite them to see themselves as looking over my (and our collective) Christian shoulder, and to encounter and witness in this manner a

---

1. Ps 113:3.
2. Luther accepted only the Jewish canon of the Old Testament as Word of God, although the individual books kept their traditional (non-Jewish) place within the order of the Word of God.

Preface to the English Edition

thorough reconsideration happening on our side. So this book is first written for Christians, but my hope is that it will contribute to improving and deepening an encounter with Judaism and God's people Israel as a whole.

After all, this book is about the blessing of the God of Israel, His desire to and His actual blessing of the nations from the midst of His people Israel. The traditional narrative of the Christian church, so often lacking a clear vision that God has always been the God of Israel, eternally faithful to His once given word of love for this people, has had dire consequences. Christian readers are therefore in the first place invited to join in a quiet, long walk through Scripture in order to try to learn to read the ways of God anew.

The reception of the book in the Netherlands has showed that both theologians and non-theologically trained readers from all over the broad spectrum of the Christian faith community have begun this journey.[3] Both groups have had to adjust somewhat to the fact that this book desires to speak to a broad audience.

Learning Messiah is a book about our patterns of thought, and about our understanding of the various relationships within Scripture. It is a book about the deep, underlying, foundational relationships between God, His Messiah, and Israel. It is about God's intentions for creation, the relationship between God's salvific and redemptive work for both Israel and the nations, and the relationship between Israel and the nations and their respective existences. In one narrative this book attempts to bring together both the history narrated in Scripture and that which followed after the appearance of Jesus in the midst of Israel. In doing this it invites us to rethink in fresh ways—using sometimes words and expressions that at first may sound new or somewhat strange—the narrative we have lived with for so long, and that we ourselves have presented to others, both Jew and non-Jew.[4]

At the deepest level this book is about our knowledge and love of God. Therefore it speaks not just in rational manner, but also calls for love and a *return*-ing dedication to God. It calls for accompanying Him on His ways toward Zion, both in the present and in the future age to come.

This book would not have been translated and edited without the express support of the publisher of the Dutch edition, several Dutch foundations who financially supported this enterprise, and the encouragement of many friends. Especially I wish to thank Dr. Richard Harvey, Dr. Daniel C. Juster, Dr. Mark S. Kinzer, Dr. William T. Koopmans and Prof. Dr. R. Kendall Soulen, who, from the very beginning, have supported the translation and publication of the Dutch edition into English.

3. See www.messiasleren.nl .

4. Rosner gives a list of "examples of the theological work to be done" within the "Continued Recasting of Christian Theology in Light of Israel" (*Healing the Schism*, 294–295). Several of the points on that list have been addressed by me in this book (published in Dutch, also in 2015).

Preface to the English Edition

Not least I wish to thank Erin van Santen-Hobbie, (Badhoevedorp, the Netherlands; originally from Florida, USA) who has spent many hours editing the whole of the English translation and discussing many details. Thank you, Erin, for being a friend and co-worker in this effort; thank you for sharing your lingual sensitivity with me.

I would also like to express my gratitude toward Wipf and Stock Publishers for both their professional and personal involvement, while working together in bringing this book to life within the English speaking world. Thank you, Matt Wimer and Robin Parry, and many others I never met, but whose experience and dedication have contributed to the realization of this project.

Lastly, I wish to express my gratitude to my wife Coby, who for a considerably long period, again allowed me to dedicate myself in preparing the translation and publication of this book.

Finally, may the LORD, Israel's God, who also revealed Himself to me through His Messiah, and who granted strength and endurance, be honored by this book and the reading of it. May His Kingdom arrive speedily, and may we be found as "bound firmly together"[5] in His Zion.

Praying together with the people Israel, in this period of counting between *Pessaḥ* and the Feast of Weeks, from Psalm 67

> *May God be gracious to us and bless us*
> *and make his face shine on us –*
> *so that your ways may be known on earth,*
> *your salvation among all nations.*[6]

Edjan Westerman
2nd of May 2018 / the 32nd day of the Omer, 17 Iyar 5778
Aalsmeer, the Netherlands
www.learningmessiah.com

---

5. Ps 122:3 (RSV).
6. Ps 67:1–2.

Preface: Understanding My Calling

Goy

A GOY—THAT'S ME. THIS book has been written by a *goy*. A Hebrew word designated for someone from the nations. It is as a *goy* that I've become acquainted with the God of Israel.

Israel and the Nations

Such is the dichotomy that the Holy One of Israel brings into the world of the nations. As a *goy* I've learned that He continues to make a distinction between Israel and the nations. The Scriptures of Israel show this unchanging aspect of the God of Israel. How did I come to know this? I've learned this from One from Israel who has shown this to me in the Scriptures of Israel.

The Scriptures of Israel

The Scriptures of Israel—that is what they are. Yes, "the Church" did receive these Scriptures from Israel (I use this term to refer to the people of Israel whereby Scripture has been received and passed on), but, unfortunately, afterwards the Church "liberated" itself from the living context of Israel wherein the text has been and was meant to be heard. The Scriptures also received this same "treatment" and thus have been detached from this context. As a result, the line of vision has been changed, altering the understanding of the text. Israel's significance as the place and the people of the revelation became inconsequential, serving more and more as a secondary role in God's broader purposes. In the process of the interpretation of the Church, the very Scriptures written by and for Israel became above all the Scriptures *for* the world. And slowly these Scriptures thus became the Scriptures *of* the world. This occurred despite the apostle Paul's pronouncement that Scripture has been entrusted to Israel![1]

---

1. Rom 3:2.

Preface: Understanding My Calling

Christian

Christian, that is what I am. This book has been written by a Christian, a Greek word that marks a follower of Jesus Christ. Through meeting Him, thanks to the witness and the community of churches and Christians, and thanks to the power of the Spirit in His Body, I have come to read the Bible, a text I've known from since my youth, and experience it as the living word of God. I've learned that my whole life, including my reading and understanding of Scripture, is only possible by living in Him. To this day, the "apart from me you can do nothing"[2] has had a significant impact on my growth in the understanding of God's revelation.

As a good reformed Christian, I've always read the Old and New Testaments as one entity. I have been aware of the fact that it is the God of Israel who speaks to me through the Scriptures. I have, in service to the Word itself, tried to understand and carefully explain the Scriptures by giving special attention to the special place Israel has. I knew about the guilt of the Christian churches—"the Church"[3]—toward the Jewish people. I knew Israel's Messiah. I grew in the knowledge of Him as the One who has been named "Covenant for the people."[4]

Encounter

And then—around the turn of the century—I had a living encounter with Israel, its people and country, with living Judaism. Encircled by Jewish supplicants, I prayed at the Western Wall. A place of prayer certainly for Israel, and also a place of prayer for the nations. Deep relations grew. I also met Messianic Jews, in Israel as well as elsewhere. Their existence and their experiential presence opened my eyes to the fact that even within the Body of the Messiah, Israel comes first.[5] More and more my eyes were opened to the structural distinction that God makes between Israel and the nations. I learned to understand myself more and more as a *goy* with a calling.

---

2. John 15:5.

3. Within this book "the Church" is sometimes placed between quotation marks. The designation "the Church" as such could evoke an image of a centrally-organized unity to which all believers belong, with decisions centrally taken and applying to all. However, within this book it is in fact a manner to denote the totality of the Christian faith community through the ages, or in a specific time period. Although this "Church" has shown an image characterized by many differences, there also have been many commonalities. In a book like this, one can not help but speak in a somewhat general manner. No one should feel uneasy about this; how special or exceptional our specific part of the Church may have been in certain respects (and there have been exceptions in many areas that this book covers), yet as believers we are one in Israel's Messiah. For this see also Part III and the Epilogue.

4. Isa 42:6 and 49:8.

5. See my study *De Tora van de Messias en zijn twee kinderen*, 2004. I wrote this study after a period of study in Israel.

Goy with a Calling

I am a *goy* called by Israel's Messiah. As seen from the country of Israel, in a geographical sense living at the edges of the earth. In faraway coastal lands.

It is here that I am called to hear, understand, and proclaim the good news about the Messiah of Israel.

Structure

From the time I encountered the living Israel, I have become increasingly aware of the fact that Christian theology is often structured so that Israel has no permanent place in the systematic rendering of the intentions of God.[6]

I began to see that the structure of much Christian systematic theological thinking about Israel and the Tora is either based upon extra-biblical categories, or on a rendering of the Scriptural story where Israel has no permanent stage presence.

Reading and Learning Process

This book is an attempt to somewhat systematically define the fruit of my reading of Scripture. It is fruit in the midst of ripening, fruit that comes from continually listening. This is a learning process where I become more understanding of my role as a co-reader with Israel. "In Him"—there I'm referring to the Messiah of Israel—I read the Scriptures of Israel, by which I refer to both the Tanakh[7] and the Scriptures of the New Covenant.[8] I understand that I am connected to the part of Israel that confesses that He is God's Messiah. But I also wish to connect with the part of Israel that, due to two thousand years of Christianity, cannot see Him as the fulfillment of God's promises.

In this respect two words of Scripture are important to me, the first of which is:

> The secret things belong to the LORD our God, but the things revealed belong to us and our children forever, that we may do all the words of this law.[9]

Thereby, Israel has received God's Tora for all time. Co-reading—in Messiah Jesus—means searching with Israel to understand what the Holy God also discloses to the

---

6. See par example Soulen, *The God of Israel* and Drost, *Is God veranderd?*.

7. In this book I will use the expression "Tanakh" when referring to the Old Testament. TaNaKh is an acronym for *Tora* (the Pentateuch; the five books of Moses), *Nevi'im* (Prophets) en *Ketuvim* ("Writings"/the Hagiographa).

8. As designation for the New Testament I will often use "the Scriptures of the New Covenant," although I will sometimes alternate with the common expression "New Testament."

9. Deut 29:29. All biblical passages are taken from the New International Version, unless otherwise indicated.

Preface: Understanding My Calling

nations by the gift of His Tora as well as the other Scriptures He entrusted to Israel. Even Jesus Himself leaves no doubt that the Tora and the whole of the Tanakh are still in place as God's Word, pointing the way to God's future.[10] And both Moses and Jesus say that our reading should impact our doing.

The second Biblical text that is important to me in this context is the word of Jesus:

> Therefore every teacher of the law who has become a disciple in the kingdom of heaven is like the owner of a house, who brings out of his storeroom new treasures as well as old.[11]

What I see in this verse is that not only is there talk of new things, but also of old things. The Scriptures, entrusted to Israel and read by Israel for centuries, are a treasure from which these "old things" can and should be revealed. It is certainly true that God's light can come and shine forth over His words and deeds of old, illuminating new meanings! But for those who have become disciples of Messiah Jesus, the Scriptures also have their value as the treasure cove of the truth of old and revealed words of God.

This is about learning—*lernen*[12]—together with all Israel. How thankful I am for Jewish friends who have helped me on my path of learning.

Title

Learning Messiah
Israel and the Nations—Learning to Read God's Way Anew

At first sight *Learning Messiah* may seem a strange expression, but the title is meant to convey three things: First, the word "learning" evokes associations with the Jewish "learning" as I briefly referenced above. Next, together the title and subtitle refer to the requirement of a new reading of the Scriptures. God's way with Israel and the nations must be read and understood by us in a new manner. Also the Messiah must thereby be "learned and read" anew. Finally, this title calls attention to the fact that we are not only called to belief in the Messiah of Israel, but also to walk His ways. Even more: He wants to have *His* way in people.[13]

---

10. Matt 5:17–19.
11. Matt 13:52.
12. *Lernen* (a Yiddish word) is the Jewish designation for the process of reading and understanding that goes on and on and by which believers show that they want to live on the words of the LORD God (cf. Ps 119).
13. Having already traveled the road of writing this book for several years, I discovered that there is in the New Testament a parallel to the title of this book. Paul speaks in Eph 4:20 about the need to be instructed regarding the Messiah and uses then the expression "learning Christ/Messiah" (so also

Emuna

Judaism recognizes the concept of *emuna*,[14] a broad term which encompasses both trust and faith in God, but in such a way that it also includes the desire to follow Him in all His ways and to know Him in all His purposes. *Emuna* focuses on so much more than just fulfilling the commandments or on one's own life. It is comprehensive and its full meaning calls man to seek God fully,[15] focusing on God's ultimate kingdom and glory.

This book has been written from the same orientation. Keep in mind, therefore, that *Learning Messiah* is not written so that only theologically educated readers can benefit from these words. It is my hope and prayer that this book will be a blessing to many who desire to know the Holy God in all His ways, and desire His ultimate kingship. May the words of this book be read in this way.

> *May these words of my mouth*
> *and this meditation of my heart*
> *be pleasing in your sight,*
> *LORD, my Rock and my Redeemer.*
>
> Psalm 19:14

Aalsmeer, the Netherlands
11th of March 2015 / 20 Adar 5775

RSV; the rendering of NIV is more paraphrasing).

14. Trust, faith—the stem from which the word *amen* is derived.

15. HaRav Tzvi Yehuda HaCohen Kook: "*Emunah* isn't a simple proclamation of belief. Emunah is the greatest learning, the greatest wisdom, the profoundest thought, the broadest approach to the world, encompassing all of man, and all of the universe" (*Torat Eretz Yisrael*, 5). His father HaRav Avraham Yitzhak HaCohen Kook wrote: "*Emunah* encompasses all knowledge, creating a universal bond between all the different disciplines and fields, and this bestows eternal life to everyone who is blessed by its light. Its inner vitality brings life to society, to the foundations of ethical conduct, and to the life of the individual, in the same way that it infuses all of the universe with life..." (*Torat Eretz Yisrael*, 5).

Abbreviations

JANT The Jewish Annotated New Testament
JSB   The Jewish Study Bible
KJV   Holy Bible, King James Version
NIV   Holy Bible, New International Version
RSV   Holy Bible, Revised Standard Version

Introduction

I.1 Learning to Read God's Way Anew

WHAT IS THE WAY that God has chosen in relation to Israel and the nations? And what is the role of the Messiah? That is the subject matter of this book and a theme that has been reflected upon and written about for centuries. Isn't that what the Bible is all about? And yet!

This book appears more than seventy years after the horrors and darkness of the *Shoa* were revealed. It is a part of the reconsideration, which has since begun. This is not just a rational reconsideration. Much more is on the table. This is more like a Nathan[1]-confrontation. Through it both the Christian faith community and Christian theologians have had to ask themselves the question: did our reading of the Scriptures somehow contribute to the dark history of ages that culminated in the murder of six million Jews? Has our understanding of the Bible and the way in which God dealt with Israel and the nations served the God of Israel and reflected His faithfulness? Or has the "narrative scheme" we bring with us when we read the Scriptures and try to understand them already been severed from the fundament of God's faithfulness?

This introduction is not for all questions which have arisen and are still being asked regarding the reading and understanding of the whole of Scripture. The appearance of Jesus Christ and His message certainly leads to deep discussions within the Christian faith community over the question how these are related to the revelation within the Scriptures of Israel.

And yet in this introduction we will only take up the theme of our narrative and its structure and elaborate upon it a bit. And it is because of the fact that the appearance of Jesus Christ takes place, so to speak, within the streambed of the Tanakh—a setting fully prepared by God and His revelation—that this book presents a different order. It is only after having given thorough attention to the canonical narrative of the Tanakh in Part I, that we will deal with all questions which arose and are still being asked due to the appearance of Jesus Christ and the Scriptures of the New Covenant.

---

1. 2 Sam 12 tells about the confronting message which Nathan delivered to David after his adultery with Bathsheba and the murder of her husband Uriah.

Introduction

This structure does not originate from my wish to read the Tanakh at a distance from the Christian faith community, or even separated from Messiah Jesus. It has been chosen in order to gain a better understanding, in order to "learn Messiah" in a new way.

So first of all in Part I we will concentrate on the canonical narrative of the Tanakh, and then in Chapter 13—which forms the introduction to Part II—we will discuss extensively those questions related to the appearance and message of Jesus. But of course anyone who wants to allow the questions and answers which have been formulated throughout history to play a role in the reading of Part I, can read Chapter 13 directly following this introduction.

Because of the above-mentioned options we will turn now to the role of a "narrative scheme" and the expression "canonical narrative."

I.2 Narrative

Whether we are conscious of it or not we live as Christians with a structured narrative. Such a narrative consists of a more or less fully completed unity in which the broad thrust of the Bible is to be found. Such a schematic narrative helps us to deal with the multiplicity of Biblical data, persons and events. It could even be said that we live *in* this—our own—narrative. R. Kendall Soulen shows in his book, *The God of Israel and Christian Theology*, what influence our narratives have. He uses the expression "canonical narrative" to refer to such a narrative scheme.[2]

When one would ask an average group of Christians to summarize what the Bible is about, surely the narrative which is present in that group will show itself. Often that narrative will have as its key elements: the creation, the disobedience and fall of the first human couple, God's intervention unto salvation (from the start focused on and realized in the coming of Jesus Christ), and the future of the Kingdom of God. Very often the structure of that narrative will be the same as in the Apostolic Creed. Israel is absent in this and other ancient confessions of the Christian church.[3]

---

2. "*A canonical narrative is an interpretative instrument that provides a framework for reading the Christian Bible as a theological and narrative unity*" (Soulen, *The God of Israel*, 13; italics by Soulen). What is meant is that such a narrative summarizes, more or less extensively, the "story" that has been written down in the canon. Soulen uses the designation "canonical narrative" while referring to the complete canon of the Christian Bible. In this book I will also use this designation when speaking of and describing the narrative unity of the Tanakh (the Old Testament) as such, or the narrative unity of the New Testament in itself. The "canonical narrative" of the complete Christian canon is in every respect related to the internal unity of both parts of the Christian canon.

3. Soulen points to the fact that of all non recent confessions, only the Scottish Confession of 1560 deals in detail with God's history with the Jewish people although within the framework of the traditional narrative (Ibid., 181, footnote 77).

I.3 Israel in Our Narrative

The absence of Israel in itself shows already that such narrative does not equate with the Bible. It is a narrative based on a certain conviction of "how the Bible hangs together as a whole."[4] Whether or not this is consciously done, the use of such a narrative scheme shows what we believe regarding the unity of the story which the Scriptures tell us and what choices we make in interpreting it.

It is obvious that in the Bible a large place is given to God's dealings with Israel. When in our canonical narrative—in which we summarize in a schematic manner what the canon is about—Israel has "disappeared," then it can be said that apparently God's dealings with Israel have no structural meaning for our thinking.

Also very short summaries of the gospel can function as a summarizing narrative. That is the case with the Apostolic Creed, but also with summaries for teaching or evangelism purposes. For instance, whomever allows the gospel concur with the structure of misery-deliverance-gratitude[5], with the "bridge illustration"[6] or with the "four spiritual laws"[7], shows that obviously there is no need for Israel to play a real role in the (presentation) of God's purposes.

Soulen uses in this context the concepts of "foreground" and "background."[8] In his book he shows that during long centuries of Christian theological thinking, Israel disappears more and more into the background. The foreground is the place where, perhaps after a brief intermezzo of Israel having a part to play, the universal purposes of God appear which are spoken without reference to Israel. After having played its part—however perceived—Israel was removed from the stage and directed to the background. Only a few chapters of the Tanakh play a role; the biggest part of the Scriptures of Israel is not really needed on the stage.[9]

I.4 Narrative and Paradigm

An accepted narrative that makes its way into our thinking also begins to play a role of its own and influence us. It becomes a paradigm, the Greek word for a "scheme," which has two distinct meanings. First, it shows the many inflections of a verb in such a way that they can be learned more easily. It is a visual and mental scheme, which helps us to use the verb well. The word paradigm can however also be used to point to

---

4. Ibid., 13. See also footnote 2 in this chapter.

5. The structure of the Heidelberg Catechism (1563), one of the confessions of the Reformation churches.

6. A picture of a gap which separates God and man, bridged by God through the cross of Jesus so that God and man can be united again. Often used in evangelism and evangelistic literature.

7. A schematic reproduction of the themes of God the Creator—man—sin—salvation. Also often used in evangelism by certain parts of the Christian church.

8. Soulen, *The God of Israel*, 31–32 and passim.

9. Ibid., 31.

another understanding of "scheme," to a coherent system of beliefs, with which we try to understand and explain reality.[10] In that case the paradigm is a self-created frame of mind that can be laid over reality as some sort of grid. When this is the case, we are in danger of the paradigm becoming a worldview which determines not just our thinking, but also our behavior and in the end, reality itself.

The narrative that is being used in Christian theology and churches, consciously or not, has the role of an all-influencing paradigm. The narrative in which Israel disappears from the stage has contributed to the removal of Israel from our world of thought. And even more, it can be said that this has contributed vigorously to the attempts made to physically eliminate the Jewish people. After all, when God sends His people "from the stage" and replaces them, why should there be a need for a continued existence of Israel in this world? The "solution of the Jewish question"[11] in Christian theology through the ages has been interconnected with manifold attempts to end the existence of Israel in this world.[12] Sometimes Christian preaching has given impetus to anti-Jewish violence. Even age old anti-Semitism used Christian theological legitimation to undergird itself. The narrative that has been used for centuries within the Christian churches' reading of the Scriptures has shown to be a life-endangering paradigm for Israel. And where this narrative today is still active and undisputed, it continues to cause life-threatening situations for the people of God.

I.5 A Life-endangering Paradigm

A narrative in which Israel functions *only* as the "manger" from which the Christ has to appear—a crib that can be discarded afterwards when it is no longer needed—ultimately contributes to the discarding of the people of God. If the election of Israel as God's own people and God's choice of the land and the city of Jerusalem are not eternal

---

10. "A paradigm in science and philosophy is a coherent system of models and theories which form a conceptual frame with which 'reality' is analyzed and described. It also can be used in the sense of 'worldview.' For example, in social science, the term is used to describe the set of experiences, beliefs and values that affect the way an individual perceives reality and responds to that perception. Social scientists . . . (speak about, EJW) 'paradigm shift' to denote a change in how a given society goes about organizing and understanding reality. A 'dominant paradigm' refers to the values, or system of thought, in a society that are most standard and widely held at a given time." (https://en.wikipedia.org/wiki/Paradigm; accessed 11th of April 2016).

11. This expression—"the Jewish question"—was used within the anti-Semitism of the German empire to refer to the perceived unwillingness of the Jewish people to integrate and assimilate and the accusation of a Jewish striving for world dominion. Hitler and his National-Socialism wanted a definitive solution (*Endlösung*) to "the Jewish question" (see: http://de.wikipedia.org/wiki/Judenfrage; accessed 11th of April 2016). That this terminology shaped discussions shows the title *Die Judenfrage im Lichte der Kapitel 9–11 des Römerbriefes*. This little booklet of the *Bekennende Kirche*—a printed lecture (1942) by Karl Ludwig Schmidt discusses "the question" in the light of Romans 9–11. It unmasks the National-Socialist coloring of this question but leaves the terminology which in itself is already anti-Semitic unharmed.

12. Cf. Jansen, *Christelijke theologie na Auschwitz*.

and permanent, than of course the Messiah, Jesus Christ, also has nothing to do with the people, the land, and the city. In that case nations and also Christians until today can behave as they please with regard to the Promised Land and the promised city.[13] The return of God's people to the land is then not an act of God fulfilling His promises and there is no biblical fundament for Zionism.[14] Israel becomes just a people like all other peoples, although they had a special history. The Christian church and its theology has not made the realization that God Himself becomes untrustworthy when His faithfulness toward His people Israel can apparently be passé. Why then would He have to stay faithful toward the believers from the nations?

In such a narrative the prideful arrogance[15] can take its own course. The receiving of blessing out of Zion has given way to some sort of de-*Jew*-ized salvation. When the Christian confession of the incarnation means the end to the mediation of salvation through Israel and a new divine beginning of an universally oriented salvation, than the clinging of Israel to its own election is resistance to the Most High God Himself.

Such a narrative automatically brings with it a spiritualizing and universalizing exegesis of big parts of the Tanakh. The Christian church has mastered this extremely well. There is no real learning from Israel any more, since the Tora has more or less been emptied of its meaning. The grafting on the root of Israel[16] has been nullified one way or another. On the other hand, there is a permanent theological necessity for the Church to pursue its anti-Judaic path and its de-*Jew*-izing of Jewish believers in Jesus the Messiah.[17] After all, if the Messiah Himself has been severed from the context and the relationships in which He was placed by His birth in the midst of Israel, the totality of Christian thinking about God and His purposes has thus been removed from the revelation context of the people of Israel. For centuries the Church has thought that

---

13. Joel 3:1–3.

14. In such paradigm there certainly is no place at all for Christian Zionism.

15. Rom 11:20.

16. Rom 11:17–21.

17. The following text of John Chrysostom can serve as a saddening example and sort of culmination of this attitude: "As a preliminary to his acceptance as a catechumen, a Jew 'must confess and denounce verbally the whole Hebrew people, and forthwith declare that with a whole heart and sincere faith he desires to be received among the Christians. Then he must renounce openly in the church all Jewish superstition, the priest saying, and he, or his sponsor if he is a child, replying in these words: 'I renounce all customs, rites, legalisms, unleavened breads and sacrifices of lambs of the Hebrews, and all the other feasts of the Hebrews, sacrifices, prayers, aspersions, purifications, sanctifications and propitiations, and fasts, and new moons, and Sabbaths, and superstitions, and hymns and chants and observances and synagogues, and the food and drink of the Hebrews; in one word, I renounce absolutely everything Jewish, every law, rite and custom, (. . .) and if afterwards I shall wish to deny and return to Jewish superstition, or shall be found eating with Jews, or feasting with them, or secretly conversing and condemning the Christian religion instead of openly confuting them and condemning their faith, then let the trembling of Cain and the leprosy of Gehazi cleave to me, as well as the legal punishments to which I acknowledge myself liable. And may I be anathema in the world to come, and may my soul be set down with Satan and the devils" (taken from Parkes, *The Conflict*, 397–98).

Introduction

the God of the Bible was wholly as the Church itself was[18]—severed from its roots, severed from Israel—a God whose "image" could also be "formed" from un-Jewish thinking.

If such an extensive replacement paradigm determines life and actions, what stops the Christian church from halting the return of the Jewish people to the covenanted land in the name of Jesus, and in the name of universal human rights?[19] In this way the Church could again cooperate with the nations who would like to divide the land or place it at the disposition of "the common interest."[20] This takes away the need to comfort God's people[21] because of the suffering that the people Israel have had to endure throughout their existence. Then the suffering of Israel is no longer the suffering of "the apple of God's eye."[22] The followers of Jesus need not have a special connection of heart with this people for the Eternal One Himself has changed His own direction of heart.

The narrative in which Israel has been pushed to the background has shown to be literally a life-endangering paradigm. Even today such a narrative scheme is endangering the lives of God's people. Modern expressions of this paradigm will have the same results as the ones we know from history. Besides, such a replacement paradigm is a danger to the physical and spiritual life of who make use of it, its adherents. In the end it will surely mean death for the Christian church.[23]

I.6 Israel at the Foreground?

After the horrors of the *Shoa*, a theological reconsideration started within the circle of Christian churches. As a result a growing number of churches made statements denouncing replacement theology.[24]

Soulen, however, points out that even though Christian churches have stated that God's covenant with Israel is irrevocable and thus condemned replacement teaching, this does not mean automatically that Israel has made a definitive comeback at the foreground of the canonical narrative.

When Christians, churches, and faith communities state that God's plans with His people have not yet been completed and that God Himself is faithful to the covenant

---

18. Cf. Ps 50:21!

19. Sizer, *Zion's Christian Soldiers?* can serve as an example. The Ecumenical Liberation Theology Centre Sabeel in Jerusalem is one of the driving forces in this movement of thought and action within the Christian churches.

20. More and more a coalition of Christians, Muslims and human rights movements is forming itself which pleads for a non-Jewish status of Jerusalem and the land Israel.

21. Cf. Isa 40:1.

22. Zech 2:8.

23. Zech 2:9; Rom 11:22.

24. Cf. Aumann, *Conflict and Connection*. Chapter 6 gives an enumeration, which in itself is not complete.

Introduction

He once made with Israel, this does not guarantee that the structure of the canonical narrative they are using essentially has changed.[25] It is still possible that Israel stands backstage, waiting until it is time for a new role on stage. In the meantime, however, at the foreground another story is being presented. This story can be told in non-Israel categories. Very often it is a story predominantly about God's cosmic and universal purposes. In such representation of the Christian faith the background (and thus Israel) can be left out without hampering the logical unity of the salvation history.[26]

It is therefore necessary to present an alternative for the canonical narrative that has been prevalent during centuries. A narrative different in its basic underlying structures.[27]

I.7 Sketch of a Canonical Narrative

This book is an attempt to contribute to the aforementioned necessary theological rethinking. I will try to offer a sketch of a canonical narrative in which God's dealings with Israel are inseparable from His plan with the cosmos and in which the appearance of Messiah Jesus and the witness about Him stay inseparably connected with the covenant God made with Israel. A canonical narrative in which the ways of God with Israel are part of the "foreground" from the beginning until the end.

I speak about a "sketch" because elements of the canonical narrative will only gradually become more visible during the course of God's history with Israel and this world. This book will provide a view on the key features of the canonical narrative of Scripture, although some elements of this narrative have been elaborated upon in a more detailed manner.

As a starting point for my contribution to this process of rethinking, I will refer to both the text of the Tanakh and the Scriptures of the New Covenant as they have been handed down to us. I will not discuss questions related to the history of the origins and tradition of these texts. Because the Tanakh has been given to us as a unity, this unity has also been determinative in my reading and "use" of the texts. The same is the case regarding the Scriptures of the New Covenant. I want to read Scripture with the same reverence that Israel has, believing that it is the Word of the eternal God, who is revealing Himself in it. The Scriptures of the New Testament I also read believing that these words have been given to us by the Holy Spirit, who is also the Spirit of the Messiah.

---

25. Soulen, *The God of Israel*, 31.
26. " (. . .) without disturbing the overarching logic of salvation history" (Ibid., 32).
27. Soulen (Ibid., 109) offers in Part 2 of his book his "proposal" of an alternative canonical narrative. The mutual blessing of Israel and the nations is central in it. What the content of this blessing is according to the Scriptures has not been dealt with in a detailed manner. In later work he has elaborated upon this issue (based on personal information received, EJW).

Introduction

In the process of writing I have been conscious of the fact that words from the Tanakh can have more than one meaning and application. Words, which have been spoken in and to a special situation, can at the same time carry a meaning for other times. A Messianic interpretation of a text does not imply that there is no attention for the meaning of the text within the historical context in which the word has been spoken. For reasons of limitation these multi-layer meanings mostly have not been discussed.

In describing the canonical narrative of the Tanakh and the Scriptures of the New Covenant I have chosen to use a number of important Hebrew and Jewish concepts.[28] Although this can cause some feelings of estrangement in the readers, this inner alienation is meant to reveal the dominating paradigms of understanding that are active in us. I hope that through this revelation, a light will shine upon the ongoing Jewish character of the canonical narrative of the Tanakh and the New Testament. This also makes the bond with Judaism, which has been created by the ways of God's salvation, more visible. Sometimes I have chosen for a less usual terminology, so that some theological categories could be seen in a new light and might be freed somewhat from centuries old dominating paradigms.[29] Finally, above all I have chosen to narrate the canonical narrative and not to discuss at length every possible question or objection. The flow of the canonical narrative has value of its own. Discussion will certainly be needed but it should take place elsewhere.

I.8 Priestly Calling of Israel as Keynote of the Canonical Narrative

At the mountain Sinai Israel received its calling from God. The words of this calling from Exodus 19 resound till the last pages of the Scriptures of the New Covenant.[30]

> "Now if you obey me fully and keep my covenant, then out of all nations you will be my treasured possession. Although the whole earth is mine, you will be for me a kingdom of priests and a holy nation." These are the words you need to speak to the Israelites.[31]

Through these words Israel received its calling to be a kingdom of priests in the midst of the nations. The conviction which underlies this book is that this calling is "the interior," the content of the blessing with which the Holy God wants to bless His creation. In this calling also lies the unity of both the Tanakh and the Scriptures of the

---

28. See the list of Hebrew terms at the end of this book. In the book explanation of these words will be given when used for the first time. Hebrew terms are italicized with exception of Tanakh and Tora.

29. I regularly will use the expression "enfleshment in (the midst of) Israel" when speaking of the incarnation.

30. Cf. Rev 1:6; 5:10; 20:6; 21:3; 22:5 where these words or elements thereof can be found.

31. Exod 19:5–6.

New Covenant. When we give focused and sustained attention to this calling and its ongoing realization in the history of God with His people, we will be safeguarded from a theology in which Israel ultimately will be pushed to the background.

This priestly calling is the keynote of the canonical narrative.

I.9 Model of Interpretation and Understanding

At the same time this "priesthood of Israel" provides us with a model of interpretation in order to understand the relations between Israel and the nations both prior to the appearance of the Messiah, and in His coming as well as after His coming.

The royal priesthood of the people and the instructions concerning it given to Israel help us to understand and value the abiding, unique position of Israel even within "the Body of Messiah" and within the New Covenant. It provides us with a key to biblical interpretation, which helps us to grasp the deep unity between Jew and *goy* "in Messiah." It also helps us to understand the abiding singularity and the differences that go with it between Jew and *goy* "in Messiah."

When we pay attention to the abiding character[32] of this calling of Israel in the midst of the nations, we acknowledge the fact that we (as believers) from the nations want to receive the blessing through Israel. We acknowledge then also that we want to know ourselves as the Holy God names us. It is from Him that Israel and the *goyim* receive their name and with it their respective calling.[33]

---

32. Rom 11:29.

33. Cf. Eph 3:15. Paul described God's ways with Israel and the nations in chapters 2 and 3. In his prayer (3:14–21) he uses the word *patria*. In the Septuagint (Jewish translation of Tanakh in the Greek language) this word is very often used to translate the Hebrew *mishpaḥa* (= family, lineage, kinship). Both Israel and the nations can be designated in Tanakh with this Hebrew word. Given the link with the context it is logical to understand 3:15 ("from Him every *mishpaḥa* in heaven and on earth is named") to mean that this distinction is from God and brings its own calling. To be named is to be called to take one's own place in God's plan.

PART I
The Canonical Narrative: The Tanakh

Chapter 1

Creation and Waiting for Both the God of Israel and the Israel of God[1]

1.1 Permanent Co-reading with Israel

IT IS FROM ISRAEL that we Christians received the Scriptures. However, though being blessed by this gift, we behaved over time essentially as a band of robbers, plundering Israel of its God-given identity and prerogatives. For, receiving the Scriptures implies becoming *co*-readers. It asks for an attitude of respect for those who transmitted the Scriptures to us. It therefore asks for respect for Israel. It asks us to be conscious of the fact that the Scriptures were entrusted to that people in the first place, and that this is true until today. Therefore this situation asks for Christians to demonstrate a principled openness to *co*-reading with Israel. The coming of the Messiah meant no change with regard to this fundamental principle that learning from God implies co-learning with Israel. On the contrary, even in the circle of the Body of Messiah there has always been a God-given opportunity to first read and interpret together with Jews. But the gentile Christian church gave up its humility very quickly. And with this came an end to co-learning with Israel.

Pride caused this, along with the thought that above all God's purposes are ultimately oriented toward all nations and the whole of creation. In order to understand these universal intentions, non-Jews did not need to be disciples in a Jewish house of teaching. For knowledge and understanding we did not need to be dependent on Israel anymore. Having received the Scriptures from Israel, we gradually replaced Israel as co-reader and as living frame of interpretation. General human and non-Jewish ways of interpretation became prevalent and dominating. The Spirit of God, poured out on all flesh, no longer chooses the detour through Israel, so believers from the nations started to think. Was God Himself not back on His universally-oriented track

---

1. The title is partly based on a paragraph title in the discourse of Soulen (*The God of Israel*, 122).

which started with creation? Certainly, we read about God as Creator in the Scriptures of Israel, but between Israel and the creation there is no direct connection, we believed. The Creator certainly also became the God of Israel, but that He, the Almighty Creator, has been the God of Israel from the very beginning, has been unclear to us. The close connection between God as Creator and as the God of Israel has remained unnoticed by us.

1.2 Genesis 1:1

The traditional canonical narrative begins with Genesis 1:1. But according to this canonical narrative scheme, Israel is not yet present. In the beginning God created the heavens and the earth. All living creatures and the first human beings. Yes, we read about it in the Hebrew language, but that is of minor importance. Israel has served us and the world with the safekeeping and transmitting of this story of universal beginning. But because the exegetical line of vision is directed toward the universal, its seems fully logical that Israel is not yet to be found in Genesis 1.

What a difference there is in this respect with the exposition of Rashi[2] of Genesis 1:1. Rashi[3] joins the old rabbinic interpretation of the words *bereshit bara*.[4] Central to this interpretation is the fact that in the word *bereshit,* a reference can be found to the Tora as the beginning of God's ways[5] and to Israel as the first fruit of God's harvest.[6] In other words, the creation took place for the Tora and for Israel. The Creator created the cosmos for the sake of "the holy instruction/teaching,"[7] and for Israel's sake. In this canonical narrative, Israel is the focal point from the beginning. The cosmic purposes of God have to do with His Tora and His people.[8]

This interpretation of the first words of Scripture seems, from the viewpoint of the traditional Christian interpretation of these verses, rather far-fetched and even

---

2. Yohanan Petrovsky-Shtern, Professor of Jewish History (Northwestern University, Evanston, IL) pointed me to this interpretation during a bus ride in Jerusalem.

3. Rashi (Hebrew acronym for rabbi Shlomo Yitzchaki) was a French rabbi (1040–1105) and is one of the most authoritative commentators of Tanakh and the Talmud.

4. In elaborating comments in a digital version of Rashi's commentary reference is being made in this respect to Rabbi Akiva, Genesis Rabbah 1:6, and Lev Rabbah 36:4. (http://www.chabad.org/library/bible_cdo/aid/8165#showrashi=true, accessed 18th of April 2106). Besides referring to these old rabbinic interpretations, Rashi also speaks about the "simple meaning" of the text.

5. Prov 8:22. NIV translates, "The LORD brought me forth as the first of his works." The Hebrew speaks about "way." JSB (*The Jewish Study Bible*) translates, "the beginning of His course."

6. Jer 2:3 states, "Israel was holy to the LORD, the firstfruits of his harvest."

7. Rashi, ad Gen 1:1.

8. The Midrash (Genesis Rabbah 1: 4–8) names also the commandments regarding the tithes (Deut 18:4), the first fruits (Exod 23:19), and the first part of the dough (Num 15:20) as reasons for creation. This conveys the idea that honoring God with the first gifts of creation should be one of the reasons for creation. We even encounter the thought that the world has been created for the sake of the Messiah (b. Sanhedrin 98b, cited in Bialik and Ravnitzky, *Legends*, 481, fragment 117).

absurd. After all, in this traditional canonical narrative the election of Israel only occurs within God's intentions of salvation and thus most of the time has a place only within the boundaries of soteriology, the doctrinal teaching about salvation. From this viewpoint it is strange to think of Israel in these opening words of Scripture. Why and how is *Israel* mentioned even before sin, guilt, and redemption?

In this chapter I will try to show that the Scriptures can be read in such a manner that Israel does not only appear within a framework of universal salvation for the cosmos, but that instead from the beginning the cosmos waits for Israel. From the first moment of its creation, the cosmos is waiting until further notice for the instruction that God will give in the midst of creation—in the midst of His people Israel.[9]

1.3 The Beginning of the Canonical Narrative

The account of the creation of heaven and earth forms the beginning of the Scriptures of Israel and is therefore also the beginning of the canon of the Christian church.

Genesis 1 is the foundation for all that is to come in the history of Israel and the nations. This account has very often been read however, whether consciously or not, as a short introductory paragraph on the "actual" history of sin, its consequences, and the salvation which unfolds from Genesis 3 on.

And yet it is clear from Genesis 1–2 that God had specific intentions with His creation even before the disobedience of man. After the seventh day, another new day follows. Genesis 1 shows that creation is meant to have its own history. A history in which the earth shall become covered with crops[10] and in which day and night, months and years, will follow each other.[11] A history in which the sea and the earth will be filled with living creatures.[12] Man has a task even before he has been created.[13] He must live a life in relationship.[14] He must live his own history in which the whole earth will be his dwelling place.[15] It is for the sake of this history of heaven and earth that the LORD God bestows His blessing.[16] His blessing is directed toward the goal that He has set for heaven and earth. The creation was directed toward a history in which God's purposes would be realized in a process in which ever wider circles in time and place will be drawn. His blessing is the force which drives this development toward the future. The obedience of man is meant to be his answer to this calling.

---

9. I have been stimulated in this respect by the book of Soulen, although in elaboration and elemental implementation I have chosen an other route.

10. Gen 1:11–13.

11. Gen 1:14–19.

12. Gen 1:20–25.

13. Gen 1:26.

14. Gen 1:27.

15. Gen 1:28.

16. Gen 1:22 (animals) and 28 (man).

Part I: The Canonical Narrative: The Tanakh

1.4 Further Instruction Needed

Genesis 1–2 forms the introduction to all that follows. But this introduction already asks further instruction and explanation. A lot of questions arise. Who is this God? What exactly is "to bless"? What does "being created after God's image" imply? What does the sanctification and blessing of the seventh day mean? What is it "to be allowed to eat of the tree of life"? What is "to die"? In short, instruction is needed in order to be able to live according to God's will. This need for further teaching does not arise until after the Fall.

Two points become clearly visible here. First there is creation-unto-a-goal. "Creation-for-consummation."[17] Creation which is oriented toward the ultimate completion and perfection. The plans of God do reach further than the first phase of creation's call to being.[18]

This means that while reading Scriptures we should take into account the interrelationship between the intentions of God which are directed toward this "completion of creation" and His saving acts. God's revelation in the midst of Israel is not just marked by the resolution of the conflict that arose between Creator and His creation. The revelation given to Israel is as much revelation of the intentions for *consummatio* of the Creator.[19]

Secondly, there is the fact that creation needs further instruction from the Creator. This is the case right from the beginning. Creation awaits further instruction. Awaits meetings with the God who speaks to Adam and Eve in the garden. The need for growth in knowledge and wisdom also belongs to the good creation, just like the command to enter into history which is implied in "to fill the earth" and "have dominion over it."

That the first page of the Scriptures of Israel does not reveal directly all answers is a fact of creation and at the same time has deep hermeneutical implications. The creation and man will need to stay in the position of *learning*. We will have to learn from the Creator Himself. We will have to wait for His instruction, for His Tora.[20] The Scriptures show us the path leading toward this instruction that He wishes to give in

---

17. Soulen, *The God of Israel*, 16. This concept is fundamental to the thinking of Soulen. Creation happens with the eye on the goal of the ultimate perfection, the *consummatio*.

18. Soulen writes, speaking about the traditional canonical narrative, how this "coordinates God's work as the Consummator of creation with Adam and Eve, and tells how God having created the first parents initially proposed to consummate or perfect and fulfill them by bringing them to eternal life. The story than relates how God's consummating work suffered a calamitous setback in the event known as the fall" (Ibid., 15).

19. In Judaism the expression *tikkun olam* (the perfection/completion/full restoration of the world) is being used in this respect. See chapter 2, footnote 16.

20. The Hebrew word *tora* means in a literal sense "instruction/teaching." It can be used in many ways. It can indicate the whole of the revelation which God gave at Sinai and during Israel's time in the desert, but *tora* also can be used for one single stipulation or a set of commandments. Also the first five books of the Tanakh can be designated as the *Tora*.

the midst of the earth. The "path of man's learning" will have to be just like the path described by the Scriptures that God took toward the revelation of His Tora to Israel. In this there is no difference between Israel and the nations. Israel reads in Scripture that creation had to *wait* for the full revelation of God's Tora. The nations, co-readers with Israel, also learn that they (and therefore we) have to wait for further instruction from the Creator, who revealed Himself fully in the midst of Israel.

1.5 Humility

It is a token of wisdom to continue reading and wait for further information to be given when one does not understand a text in a book. Likewise, it is also a token of humility to exercise this waiting when reading Scripture. For myself, a member of the nations of this world, this path of humility in waiting for further instruction implies that I respect and honor the didactic method of the Creator.

1.6 Learning Tora

We may expect to find in God's Tora (used as designation of "instruction" as such) that His instruction is geared toward the *consummatio*, but also contains instruction related to the healing of the breach between the Creator and His creatures.

In every respect the teaching of the LORD is oriented toward the consummation. His Tora has been given in order to receive His blessing and is related to obedience to God's assignments and commandments. His blessing certainly has also as its goal the restoration and healing of what was damaged in the relationship between Creator and creature, but at the most fundamental level His blessing is oriented toward the end, the completion of His creation. However, His "rule" is that all instruction be given in the midst of the nations, "in the camp of Israel."

It is *there* that Israel itself may learn about these twofold purposes of the Holy One of Israel. It is *there* that the nations can learn about them. It is *there* that Israel and the nations learn about their respective callings on the path toward the consummation of heaven and earth. It is *there* that we both learn to await and receive the blessing. It is *there* that we also learn obedience in the fear of the LORD.

1.7 An Unrelinquishable Position

Israel "becomes" the God-chosen place of instruction and learning for us when we want to understand His ways. It remains clear that replacement and displacement is out of the question. In a newly-recovered canonical narrative, Israel has its unrelinquishable[21] place, a position in the foreground that has been chosen and established

---

21. The word "unrelinquishable" is used within the Protestant Church in the Netherlands. The

by God Himself. And it will have this position until the end of the "story."[22] Then it will become visible what the last pages of the Christian Bible put into words, namely that even in the new Jerusalem the nations will enter through the gates on which the names of the tribes of Israel have been written.[23]

1.8 Waiting

The title of this chapter refers to a twofold waiting. From the beginning the creation knows this twofold waiting. It awaits the God of Israel and the Israel of God.

Creation awaits the self-revelation of the Creator as the God of Israel. In His election of this people and His history with them, creation receives revelation about who He is, the Creator. As the God of Israel, the Creator acts to provide the blessing and salvation of Israel and the completion of the cosmos. In the midst of Israel, this God fights the gods of man. There in the midst of Israel, will be the one and only place that God has chosen for worship.[24]

When creation, or perhaps we who belong to the nations, would like to question: "Why this long waiting? Why waiting for the self-revelation of the God of Israel?" Then the answer is fitting:

> But who are you, a human being, to talk back to God?[25]

Or with the words of Jesus:

> It is not for you to know the times or dates the Father has set by his own authority.[26]

Creation itself had to wait a long time for the appearance of the Israel of God. It took another 430 years after Abram had been called before the people left Egypt en route for Sinai.[27] When creation would like to remark, "Why did I have to wait so long for the Israel of God?" then this answer is fitting:

> I am unworthy—how can I reply to you? I put my hand over my mouth.[28]

Church Order (Article I, 7) says (in the English translation), "The church is called to give expression to its unrelinquishable solidarity with the Jewish people." The Dutch text is even stronger and instead of "solidarity" uses the word "verbondenheid" (literally: connectedness). Also the expression "indissoluble bond" is used to render the Dutch expression "onopgeefbare verbondenheid."

22. See the Introduction.
23. Rev 21:12 and 22–27.
24. Cf. Deut 12.
25. Rom 9:20.
26. Acts 1:7.
27. Exod 12:40–41.
28. Job 40:4

After the appearance of the Israel of God in the midst of the earth, the waiting of creation was not over yet. The prophets spoke about the coming time when the nations would ascend to Jerusalem to receive the Tora of God out of Zion and to learn it from Him.[29] Creation is still awaiting that day. That is the case even as Jewish and non-Jewish believers in Messiah Jesus state that the fulfillment has begun in and through Him.

That the nations may share in the salvation that God promised to Israel is a mystery that for ages was kept hidden in God Himself.[30] Even if the Scriptures of Israel spoke to and continue to speak in many places about God's intentions of salvation for the nations, the bringing together of Israel and the nations in Messiah Jesus forms the revelation by the Spirit of God of a great mystery "which was not made known to people in other generations."[31]

Again it is befitting to be humble and acknowledge this truth:

> Your ways, God, are holy. What god is as great as our God? (. . .)
> Your path led through the sea, your way through the mighty waters,
> though your footprints were not seen.[32]

1.9 "The fear of the LORD is the beginning of wisdom"[33]

In the Scriptures of Israel we learn that a deep, humble reverence for the Holy One is the key to understanding and growing in knowledge.[34] God has often let creation, and later His people, wait for further revelation about Himself and His plans. This waiting and living with incomplete revelation is in itself not a result of sin, but is part of a humble life before the Holy God. We, who read from a long time distance and can speed back and forth between then and there, and here and now, should be as humble and willing to read on, guarding ourselves against quickly-attained (schemes of) interpretations. We live in a time in which knowledge seems to be easily attainable. Therefore we need faith and courage in order to continue living in dependence of the Eternal God. It takes courage to recognize His ways and timing without choosing our own paths to knowledge, as the first human couple did in the garden of Eden. We must learn to be content with the answer that times and dates are within the responsibility

---

29. Isa 2:1–5.
30. Eph 3:9.
31. Eph 3:5.
32. Ps 77:13, 19.
33. Ps 111:10; Prov 9:10; cf. Job 28:28 and Prov 1:7.
34. Prov 9:10.

of the Father[35] and to be willing to live with the "what is that to you?"[36] from the mouth of our Master.

1.10 Israel as the Place of God's Self-Revelation

The "new" canonical narrative thus begins with the waiting of creation for Israel's God and for the Israel of God. When creation has this inner orientation toward this goal, Israel is permanently on the foreground, right from the start. God chooses to reveal and explain Himself further in the midst of Israel. Israel is through the council of God and by His sovereign choice, therefore, an epistemological necessity. We need God's people in order to receive knowledge. In every respect Israel is His house of learning. Without Israel there would be no ongoing and deep revelation of God. At the same time, this self-revelation of God belongs to the blessing with which the Creator wants to bless the world.

All of creation and what belongs to it, awaits the blessing of the Creator. He will fully bestow this blessing in the midst of Israel and the blessing will flow from there. That is the quintessence of the canonical narrative that begins with the first verses of Genesis.

---

35. Cf. footnote 26 in this chapter.
36. John 21:22–23.

Chapter 2

Creation Awaits the Blessing of God

2.1 Blessing

THE BEGINNING OF THE canonical narrative tells us that the whole of creation waits for the blessing of the God who will reveal Himself as the God of Israel. He will bestow this blessing in the midst of Israel, and from there it will reach the world. His blessing is directed toward the goal that He had in mind from the beginning of the creation of heaven and earth and which He still wants to attain. Genesis 1–11 shows us a development which is oriented toward (the receiving of) this blessing.[1]

2.2 Blessed by God

First of all, on the fourth day of creation, the living "inhabitants" of sea and air are blessed.[2] The blessing they receive is given so that they will fill the sea and the air.

On the sixth day the animals which will live on the earth are created by God. They are created "according to their kinds."[3] Finally, man is also created on that same day. He has been created according to the image of God, in His likeness. Three times this making of man is described an act of creation by God.[4] This is followed by "man" (male and female) receiving God's blessing on that sixth day in order to fill the earth

---

1. I have been stimulated very much by the writing of Soulen in chapter 6 (*The God of Israel*, 114–140).

2. Gen 1:20–23.

3. Gen 1:24–25.

4. Gen 1:26–27. In these verses we find a remarkable alternation between singularity and plurality; that is the case in the words which God speaks about Himself as well as when man is the subject. In the rendering of NIV, this fact is obscured through the translation of "man," (*adam,* singular) as "mankind" (. . .) "they/them."

with His presence and to have dominion over it.[5] The animals of the earth do not receive this blessing. Man's mandate is to fill the earth: ". . . but the earth he has given to mankind."[6] The living space for the animals is limited for the benefit of man.[7] The blessing of the sixth day centers around man and his offspring. It is God's intention that His image bearer will fill the earth. When the earth is filled with the presence of man, the glory of God will be served, for then the image of God will fill the earth. The commandment to fill the earth shows that creation is geared toward the goal of being filled with the image of God. Even after the divide between creature and Creator, the Holy God does not give in. One day the earth will be full of "the knowledge of the glory of the LORD."[8]

The sanctification and blessing of the seventh day[9] also shows that creation is oriented toward a goal. The creation of the first six days enters the sanctified and blessed seventh day. The creation that heard God speak the word "good,"[10] has to enter into the sanctification—the *kedusha*.[11] All good things must be dedicated to Him. This dedication is the goal of creation.[12] God Himself performs this sanctification on the seventh day, but by doing this He makes clear that His image bearers are also called to this sanctification of all of life.[13]

Besides this orientation toward the *kedusha*—the sanctification of all of creation—the sanctification and blessing of the seventh day points also to the future, when all things will have come to their fullness and the earth will have reached its fulfillment. The seventh day celebrates the *Shabbat*[14] of God, His rest after the completion of His work, but it also looks for this *Shabbat* in the consummation. The creation of the first six days will enter into a future of sanctification and blessedness. It has an inner orientation toward this future.[15] It is geared toward the future blessing of the great seventh day, the *Shabbat* of the completion.

---

5. Gen 1:28.

6. Ps 115:16. Again the Hebrew has "man" (cf. footnote 4).

7. The threat of wild animals is a token of judgment and curse (Deut 32:24). For the opposite, see Isa 35:9.

8. Hab 2:14. This prophecy implies that the earth will be full with *people* who will know the glory of the LORD.

9. Gen 2:3.

10. Six times in Gen 1 we read that God saw that things were "good" (1:4, 12, 18, 21, 25, 31).

11. Derived from the Hebrew verb *kadash*, which has "to sanctify" as its meaning.

12. Thus Heschel, *The Sabbath*, 75–76. Heschel underlines the necessity of this sanctification. The "survival" of creation is dependent on the sanctity of the seventh day. God calls man to join in the sanctification which he Himself performs.

13. Hereby the blessing of God is joined to the *kedusha* that He asks from man.

14. Gen 2:2–3. The verb *shavat* (= to rest) is being used.

15. "God's Sabbath blessing forms the true climax of the passage and simultaneously points forward to God's history with Israel, for it is there that God's Sabbath will be first commanded and observed (Exod 16:23; 20:8–11)" (Soulen, *The God of Israel*, 118).

Also the Holy God Himself is directed toward this completion, this *tikkun olam*[16] and He awaits His future *Shabbat*.

It is clear that creation is still waiting for instruction about this seventh day. What do the sanctification and the blessing connected with it imply? In what respect is the celebration of the seventh day looking back, and in what respect is it looking to the future? What are the implications of the calling to and the living of *kedusha*, through which all good things will be dedicated to the LORD? This instruction the Creator will begin to give in the midst of Israel. This people will receive the gift of the *Shabbat* and the explanation of it. The creation of this people is already present, though in a hidden manner.[17]

2.3 Earth Being Filled . . .

The garden of Eden has been meant by God to be the place from which man and his offspring would fill the earth. This garden is the center. From this place, where the LORD walks and meets man,[18] God's blessing will be carried in to the world. Through his calling to guard[19] the garden, man is actually a temple guard.[20] Just as in the later Temple, so should man and his wife's service to the LORD in the garden be according to the regulations of God. Obedience to God's commandments is the way through which the sanctity of the garden will be guaranteed.

The opposite happens. The guard does not keep sentry, but lets un-holiness enter God's garden. The servants in God's "Temple-garden" doubt the truthfulness of the regulations of God. Man gives ear to God's opponent—who appears here without further explanation of his origins.[21] In the "Temple-garden," everything should circle around the word of God. By both listening to the other human[22] and becoming seduced by God's opponent,[23] man leaves the ways of God's commandment.[24] Deep down man does not wish to be a temple guard and servant to the holiness of God. Instead, he wishes to take the place of God Himself.[25] By this the *kedusha* of the garden is lost and death is the result of this desecration.

---

16. The Hebrew expression *tikkun olam* points to the perfection/full completion of the world. The expression is used in the Jewish prayer *Aleinu* where this perfecting of the world is connected to the kingship of God. See chapter 1 (1.4).

17. Cf. footnote 8 in this chapter.

18. Gen 3:8.

19. Gen 2:15.

20. Compare the role the gatekeepers play in the books 1 and 2 Chr, Ezra and Nehemiah. See par example 1 Chr 9 and 26; Neh 7:1.

21. Gen 3:1, 4, 14–15.

22. Gen 3:17.

23. Gen 3:13.

24. Gen 2:16–17; 3:6–7.

25. Cf. Gen 3:4–5.

Part I: The Canonical Narrative: The Tanakh

However, this is not the end. After the description of the beginning of the history of mischief that resulted from the disobedience of man,[26] the blessing of God is again being remembered. Man-with-his-blessing is being followed "in his generations."[27] The blessing of fertility allows man to multiply on the earth. By this will the "likeness of God"[28] also be multiplied on the earth?

But when the story of Noah and his descendants unfolds,[29] it becomes clear that this likeness of God does not multiply itself on the earth. Moreover, God sees exactly the opposite.[30] Injustice and violence are growing out of control. The man-woman relationship, meant to reflect the image of God, sinks into a sphere of injustice and violence.[31] There is no likeness at all with the Creator in good and just deeds. While all works of the Creator are only good, the works of men can only be called bad.[32] The earth is being filled with violence.[33] This is exactly the opposite of what the blessing of God was meant for. The LORD sees the earth and what he sees can not be called *tov*[34] any more, for the earth is full of wickedness.[35] All flesh on the earth,[36] the human family with its royal calling, has corrupted the way of life. The king drags his dominion along in his fall.[37]

But the eyes of the LORD find one righteous and blameless man.[38] One who walks with God[39] and who finds favor in the eyes of the LORD.[40]

It was God's intention that creation, in a process of ever wider circles in time and place, would live through a history of goodness and righteousness. That it would be filled with justice and knowledge of the glory of God. An utterly real physical extension of the garden of Eden. But the disobedience of men frustrates these intentions.

---

26. Gen 3 and 4.

27. Gen 5 shows the line of the generations from Adam until Noah. In verse 2 the blessing on being man and wife is spoken of. The "likeness" of God is being blessed.

28. Nachmanides (Ramban) characterizes the meaning of the word *demut* (translated as "likeness") as "similarity in form and deed," whilst *tselem* (translated as "image") means "appearance of (...) countenance." Ramban, *Genesis*, 53.

29. Gen 5:32.

30. Gen 6:5, 12.

31. Gen 6:1–2 tells about the injustice with which judges and office bearers take women ("any of them they chose") with violence and according to their whims (Rashi). Or it describes in a more general way the sin of Adam's offspring, the son of God (Ramban; cf. Luke 3:38).

32. Gen 6:5.

33. Gen 6:11.

34. Think of the repetition of this word in Gen 1.

35. Gen 6:12.

36. Gen 6:12; cf. "he is mortal," literally "flesh" in Gen 6:3.

37. Cf. Gen 3:17; 5:29.

38. Gen 6:9.

39. Gen 6:9; cf. 5:24.

40. Gen 6:8.

Evil does not hide itself anymore in the heart[41] of people, but it becomes fully visible. The opposite of *kedusha* happens. The heart of the Eternal God is filled with sorrow.[42]

2.4 And Yet Blessed Again

The administration of God's blessing does not stop, however. God wishes to bless the earth so that it will be filled with the knowledge of the glory of the LORD.[43] It will be both God's grace and the obedience of this one righteous Noah which will make the history of the blessing continue. At the same time creation waits for further instruction. One righteous man? A covenant[44] of life with him? What does this imply? Further instruction is needed.

The path that God's will-to-bless chooses leads through the judgment of the flood. But after the flood we find ourselves here again: "Be fruitful and increase in number and fill the earth."[45] Again we find here the correlation between this command and the fact that men have been created in the likeness of God. And, as a reaction of God in regard to the violence that has filled the earth, we hear from the mouth of the LORD an explicit threat that judgment will befall those who assault the image of God in threatening the life of another human being.[46] But this is very clear: God still wants to see His earth filled with His glory. His image must become visible wherever people are to be found. His blessing is intended toward this goal. Therefore, Noah and his family are saved.[47]

2.5 Disobedience

God's blessing wants the earth to be filled with His image, but for this to happen the bearer of His image must be obedient. Contempt for one another, for father Noah,[48] is exactly the opposite and causes a curse, exactly the opposite of blessing.[49] An earth that has been cursed is the abode for a people who have been cursed because of their disobedience to the intentions of their Creator.

Genesis 10 shows the growth of mankind in its different generations. At the same time it becomes clear that disobedience is also developing. Nimrod was the first ruler

41. Gen 6:5.
42. Gen 6:6.
43. Cf. footnote 8 in this chapter.
44. Gen 6:18.
45. Twice we hear this command from Gen 1 in the words God to Noah (Gen 9:1 and 7).
46. Gen 9:5–6.
47. "This blessing is the true cargo of the ark" (Soulen, *The God of Israel*, 119).
48. Gen 9:18–29.
49. After the cursing of the serpent (Gen 3:14), the earth (3:17; 5:29), and Cain (4:11) now follows the curse over Cham (9:25).

on earth, a man who ruled over others with power and violence.[50] There are good reasons to attribute the plan for the building of the tower of Babel to him.[51] Whoever the originator, the plan to build this tower meant direct opposition to God's commandment to fill the earth. Whether binding together out of fear, or out of motivation to become great, it is disobedience. In it direct resistance toward the Holy God becomes visible. "That we may make a name for ourselves"[52] is the opposite of the sanctification of the Name, which will be the essence of the *avoda*[53]—the service of worship of Israel.

Genesis 11 shows that there is more going on than just a building-enterprise. Here the desire to be as God, the One and only God, is at work.[54] "One earth" wants to be like the One God. This desire is being thwarted. For when God does not intervene, the monstrosity of the deified-man-society will be the result. The Babel of pride. The "one worship of prideful man" becomes frustrated. The "one place" thrown into the multiplicity of places. The history of separate nations that will become different more and more by geographical and linguistic barriers begins it course. But at the same time the Eternal God wishes His blessing to progress and acts toward this goal.

2.6 Blessing Out of Israel

God continues with His intentions, and Scripture shows that creation's waiting for the blessing out of Israel will not be in vain:

> When the Most High gave the nations their inheritance,
> when he divided all mankind,
> he set up boundaries for the peoples
> according to the number of the sons of Israel.
> For the LORD's portion is his people,
> Jacob his allotted inheritance.[55]

As a result of the dispersion of the nations, the people receive their own inheritance. The uniqueness and the distinctiveness of the nations are meant to not only contain evil, but to become a calling, an inheritance, a gift. Both the diversity and the dissemination that God intended become a reality through it.[56] Through this process God organizes the world of the nations to reflect the structure of Israel. The structure

---

50. Nachmanides (Ramban) writes, "Until his era there were no wars and no reigning monarchs; it was he who first prevailed over the people of Babylon until they crowned him" (*Genesis*, 147).

51. So Rashi.

52. Gen 11:4.

53. Literally *avoda* means "service"; it is used as the designation of the priestly (Temple) service for the Eternal God.

54. Cf. the repeated *eḥad* (one) in Gen 11:1 and 6.

55. Deut 32:8–9; cf. also Acts 17:26–28.

56. Soulen also points to this positive outworking due to God's acting (*The God of Israel*, 119).

with which God organizes His own people is the "measure" He uses for "measuring out" the world of the nations.[57]

Right from the beginning, the calling of Abram has been meant to further the advancement of the desire of God to bless all of creation. The LORD reveals this at once to His chosen one. Abram's call to leave *his* country[58] in order to go to the place which God will show him, makes it implicitly clear that his destination will be the place where God will let His blessing flow. The call to leave *his* people[59] also implies that the nations will be blessed out of a new family. Even more, this blessing will be out of a new House.

2.7 Mutual Blessing

It is important to recognize that Genesis 12:1–3 tells us that both Abram and his offspring and the nations are dependent on each other with regard to the receiving of blessing. Soulen speaks about "an economy of mutual blessing."[60] In the wisdom of His plans, God has chosen to bless people through a history of the receiving of mutual blessing. He therefore makes a distinction between Israel and the nations.[61] It will not be a hindrance for the blessing, but instead will be an essential part of the route by means of which people will receive God's blessing.[62]

Israel has to be blessed by the nations and the nations are dependent on the blessing that God wants to give them through Israel.

This mutual blessing has been God's original intention for creation. It is a fundamental principle not caused by the Fall, the original division between the Creator and

---

57. A relation of parallelism is noticeable between the "sons of Adam" (NIV: all of mankind; Deut 32:8) and the "sons of Israel" (so also NIV; Deut 32:9). The family of seventy members of Jacob (Gen 46:27) determines the structure of the seventy nations (Gen 10). The world of nations receives its order according to the "measure" of Israel, just as later on the ordering of the camp of Israel, in itself reflecting the structure of the Sanctuary, will be the model for the ordering of the world of the nations. Cf. chapter 9 (9.6 and 9.7).

58. Gen 12:1; this verse speaks about leaving land, family, and house.

59. This is the translation in NIV. The Hebrew word used means "family, clan, generation."

60. " (. . .) God's economy of consummation is essentially constituted as *an economy of mutual blessing* between those who are and who remain different" (Soulen, *The God of Israel*, 111). God works from the beginning "through economies of difference and mutual dependence, economies embodied in the distinction of humankind and the natural world, of male and female, of parents and children, of one generation and the next" (Ibid., 118).

61. It is with approval that Soulen refers to Fr.-W. Marquardt, who calls this distinction the basic structure of biblical ontology. Soulen writes, " (. . .) the Scriptures view the distinction between Israel and the nations as a part of the abiding constitution of reality in God, anticipated from the beginning and present at the end of all things" (Ibid., 121).

62. Following Dietrich Bonhoeffer, Soulen writes, "Difference and mutual dependence are not extrinsic to the supreme good that God appoints for creation but are 'intrinsic to the goal itself.' The Lord's blessing is available only through (. . .) the blessing of an other" (Ibid., 117).

His creation. However, due to the history of disobedience that occurs, the blessing of God will now also include the healing of this divide.

The extent of the blessing of God thus becomes greater. The same is true of the priestly calling of Israel. The priestly service to the LORD—the *avoda*—and the sanctification of life—the *kedusha*—can be characterized as goals of creation, but due to this rupture between God and His creation, the calling and task of Israel as a priestly nation becomes even more extensive. The priestly duties related to corrective teaching and purification, sanctification and atonement of people, altar and land, from now on shall necessarily be part of the assignments of the priests and the priestly nation.

2.8 In the End

The ultimate *shalom* is God's goal for His cosmos. Then Israel will be a blessing for the nations to the full, and the nations will be blessed out of, in the midst of, and together with Israel. But in this *shalom* the distinction between Israel and the nations will still exist. Even in the ultimate end of things, Israel and the nations will be distinctive entities. The nations will be blessed only when they will be "encamped around Israel." Blessing will flow when they enter and go out through the gates of Jerusalem.[63]

---

63. Rev 21:12, 24–26.

Chapter 3

The Creation of the Camp of Israel and the Priestly Nation

The Beginning

3.1 Creation of "The Camp of Israel"[1]

THE CALLING OF ABRAM inaugurates God's creation of the camp of Israel[2] in the midst of the nations, a real place that is a part of this created world.

Abram is called out of the lands of the nations to the land that God will show him and that he calls "my land."[3] He is being called out of the families of the earth in order to become a new family. Out of his father's house to a new home, where in the end the House of Blessing will be built.

In Genesis 12:1–3 it is remarkable that the place of residence is spoken of first. The words related to Abram becoming a great nation and the theme of blessing follow

---

1. In this book the expression "the camp of Israel" is used as the designation of the physical encampment of Israel (at first in the desert, and later in God's land in the midst of the nations), but also indicates certain developments that have taken place or started within the national community of Israel ("in the camp of Israel"), in its specific existence amidst the nations. This expression can also be used in different contexts to convey the direction *out of Israel* (out of/from the camp of Israel) or instead *toward Israel* (on the way to/directed toward the camp of Israel). The question can arise, against the background of the *Shoa,* if the use of the word "camp" is fitting. Negative associations can indeed hurt and hamper understanding. However the expression "camp" is in use in Jewish literature despite this dark history, and also in many Bible translations. Therefore, the expression "the camp of Israel" will also be used in this book.

2. The expression "camp" is based on the description of the encampment of Israel in the desert (Num 2). In Jewish literature we can also find a differentiation in this respect between the camp (*maḥane*) of the *Shekhina* and that of the Levites or the camp of Israel (thus p. xlviii of the general introduction to the Talmud tractate b. Yoma).

3. See Jer 2:7; 16:18; Ezek 36:5; 38:16; Joel 1:6; 3:2, and cf. Lev 25:23. Deut 11:12 tells that the eyes of the LORD are continually on the country, all year long.

Part I: The Canonical Narrative: The Tanakh

after this. The canonical narrative that is about the blessing for this real, created world focuses first on the place from where the blessing will be given. It is a specific place that God will point out. *He* chooses it, for all the earth belongs to Him.[4] Is the Almighty God thus beginning to show the way back to the garden of Eden?[5] Is the door to the garden opening a bit? Is Abram, at the deepest level, already being called from the house of his father to the place[6] of the House of God? On the way to the *tikkun olam*,[7] the restoration of all things,[8] the Eternal God directs Himself toward a very specific place, His own land.

> For the LORD has chosen Zion,
> he has desired it for his dwelling, saying,
> 'This is my resting place for ever and ever;
> here I will sit enthroned, for I have desired it. . .'[9]

The canonical narrative strongly emphasizes the reality of the chosen land. The Jewish order of the books of Scripture also points to the land as the place of blessing.[10] For centuries the Christian reading of the Scriptures of the Tanakh has interpreted this central place of the land either purely historically—as part of a bygone history—or has spiritualized the land and transformed it into a metaphor for salvation. But also within Judaism the influence of living in the diaspora is noticeable in regard to the position of the land. Although the land held an important place in the prayers and expectations of the people, the attention was predominantly focused on the pure fulfillment of the commandments. The land became a dream for the future. The chosen people and their Tora-obedient lives received all attention.[11] And yet within Judaism there have always been voices that strongly emphasized the election of the land and

---

4. Exod 19:5.

5. Jewish tradition localizes the place of the garden of Eden near mount Moriah, the Temple mountain.

6. Gen 22:3 speaks about "the place" in the land Moriah.

7. See chapter 2, footnote 16.

8. Acts 3:21.

9. Ps 132:13–14.

10. The Jewish sequence of the canon is that of Tora, Prophets and "Writings"/Hagiographa. The first book of the Tora ends with the waiting for the return to the *land*. The last book of the Tora ends with Moses looking out over the *land*. The Prophets end with Mal 4:6. There the call is heard to live faithfully with the LORD, so that He will not come and judge the *land*. The Writings end with 2 Chr 36:23. There the call is issued to return to the land to build the Temple of the LORD. And even the writings of the New Covenant bring us in the end to the (new) earth and end in the New Jerusalem.

11. This analysis can be found in the book *Orot* by HaRav Avraham HaCohen Kook. A part of this text has been made available (plus commentary) in Kook, *Lights on Orot*.

The Creation of the Camp of Israel and the Priestly Nation: The Beginning

the commandments that are connected to it.[12] The election of the land precedes the election of the people.[13]

The tent of Abram, later Abra*ham*, and in even latter days the camp of *all Israel* were stages on the way to the land and the city where the blessing for the world will come from. God acts for salvation "in the midst of the earth."[14] And there in God's land, the "*navel* of the earth,"[15] Israel will be a blessing.[16] There the LORD will dwell in the midst of the land and in the midst of the people.[17]

3.2 Creation of the People

With the calling of Abram begins the creation[18] of the people of God. This is the second element that comes to the fore in Genesis 12:1–3. God creates a people that only by His grace receives its existence in the world of nations. The Eternal God's choice of Israel is by His mercy.[19] The prerogatives of Israel are gifts of grace.[20] The greatness

---

12. An example is Nachmanides (Ramban; 1195– ca.1270), and also Juda Halevi (* ca.1080), who wrote the *Kitab al Kazhari*. In this dialogue between a rabbi and the king of the Kazhars, the rabbi says about the land, "It was appointed to guide the world" (2,16). He quotes the Talmud when he says, " (. . .) the atmosphere of the Holy land makes wise" (2, 22). The king of the Khazars then shows the rabbi that his high words about the land do not fit in with his existence in the diaspora (*Kuzari*, 92, 99).

13. Rav Tzvi Yehuda HaCohen Kook, commenting on a part of the morning prayers (*Torat Eretz Yisrael*, 160–161). Rav Tzvi Yehuda and his father Rav Avraham HaCohen Kook, who was the first chief rabbi of the state Israel, are the founders of the religious Zionist movement in Judaism.

14. Ps 74:12 (RSV; NIV is less clear).

15. Ezek 38:12. NIV translates this as "the center of the land," although it is better to interpret this verse as pointing to the dwelling place of Israel in the midst of the earth. In a translator's note, the NIV mentions that the "navel of the earth" is the literal meaning of the Hebrew phrase. Cf. Ezek 5:5.

16. Isa 19:24; cf. 10:23 and 61:9. When Abram leaves the land he is no longer the bearer of blessing; instead he causes non-blessing and heavy plagues (Gen 12:10–20)! That is also the reason why Isaac has to remain in the land (Gen 26:2).

17. Num 35:34.

18. Deut 32:6; Isa 43:6–7.

19. Rom 9:15–16. It is of course very possible that the life of Abram can also be designated as the life of a "righteous man." In Jewish tradition the opinion has evolved, based on certain exegetical arguments, that Abram fought idolatry in Ur of the Chaldeans. On the basis of a parallelism in the use of words in Gen 15:7 and Exod 20:2 (the verb translated as "bring out of"), and the fact that Ur means "fire," Ramban also concludes a miracle of deliverance out of captivity, possibly even deliverance out of the fiery oven of Nimrod (*Genesis*, 158–160).

20. Rom 11:29. Obviously there is a deep need in our human hearts to find reasons why God should want to have dealings with us. Both in the Christian world and in Judaism, a search for reasons (in ourselves) for God's calling and election exist. In an orthodox Jewish commentary on Gen 12:1–3 (Sherman, *The Torah*, 54) we read about Abraham that, " (. . .) after twenty generations of failure, the privilege of being God's chosen people was earned by Abraham and his offspring." In the comments the dedication to the name of the God of Abram and Sarai prior to their calling is mentioned. Also the opinion that Israel received the Tora because of its rejection by the nations (cf. Sifrei Deuteronomium 343) can be interpreted as originating from "seeking reasons for the grace of God." The flip side of the tendency to explain God's initiatives of grace is that there is a danger that Israel's calling by God could

and the name of Abram and his offspring are granted and guaranteed by God.[21] Here a sharp contrast is visible between Abram and his offspring, and the builders of the tower of Babel who wanted to make a name for themselves.

Abram will become a great nation, God promises. He fulfills within Abram and his offspring part of the intentions in existence since creation. In becoming numerous, this blessing of God becomes visible as was His intention. The initiative, however, lies only with God. Abram and Sarai do not have children. Their offspring, however, will be numerous as the stars of heaven.[22] This promise clearly shows that (this) offspring is not something natural, but a blessing from the Most High God. By giving children to the infertile women Sarai[23] and Rebekah,[24] God makes it clear that Israel has no natural human origin, but that the origin of the offspring of Abram is "from heaven."

Abram's faith in God's words, trusting this promise, is credited to him as righteousness.[25] Besides a name, Abram also receives righteousness out of God's goodness. As a gift from God, Israel, the father of the people, receives the status of a *tzaddik*, a righteous man. And what applies to the father of the people, applies of course also to the people itself. And so greatness, a name, and even righteousness become "goods" that have to be received as the blessings they are. Acts of God Himself, no work of man, and building blocks for the life of a priestly nation.

3.3 Abram the Blessing

The third element entailed in the promising words of Abram's calling, is the affirmation that Abram himself will be a blessing. Remarkably, this is the first time in the Tanakh that a person becomes a blessing through the will of God. Until now God bestowed His blessing upon man and animals. God now "places the blessing *in* Abram." Not only does he mediate the blessing, he *becomes* the blessing.

Abram becomes a blessing for God and also a blessing in the world of man. Abram will be a blessing for God because the LORD will be able to rejoice in him.[26] In Abram the outlines become visible of the priestly people that will glorify God and bless his name above all.[27] And as the man who blesses God and is blessed by God, he

---

be understood as something that God would recant (cf. Rom 11:29). Supersessionism, or replacement theology, is theology not based on the principle that God is faithful in and to His own initiatives!

21. Gen 12:2.
22. Gen 15:1–5.
23. Gen 18:10–15.
24. Gen 25:21.
25. Gen 15:6.
26. This interpretation of "and you will be a blessing" I also found in the commentary on this verse by Ovadiah ben Yaacov Sforno (born in 1470 or 1475 in Italy); see Sforno, *Commentary*, 62.
27. Cf. par example Ps 103:1, 2, 20–22. The command to bless God, however, has been rendered in NIV and many other translations as "Praise the LORD." This obscures the calling to be a blessing unto God Himself.

becomes the blessing that God deposits in the world. His existence, his life, is the place of blessing. In a very deep manner his life also becomes the content of the blessing. Concealed in his very loins[28] is the future existence of his offspring and the blessing for the world. Abram becomes a "person of origins,"[29] like Isaac and Jacob after him and later on also Moses. In this one man[30] the whole of Israel already has a share in the promise of God.

3.4 Dichotomy

Through the calling of Abram and later the people of Israel, a dichotomy develops within the world of nations. It is by the initiative of God and by His grace that from then on Israel belongs to God Himself in a special way. From that time on there are "children"[31] and "not-children."[32] There is "my people"[33] and "not-my-people."[34] At the same time, right from the start it is obvious that this calling is being issued in order to bless the nations. This one *mishpaha*—family—exists for all *mishpahot*,[35] the families of the nations. This one nation has been taken out of the nations but it also will belong to the nations. And so this people becomes the *place* of blessing and the *mediator* of the blessing, and in a deep sense will be the *content* of the blessing. In this the principle of "all-in-one"[36] is present. The contours of the priestly task of Israel are thus dawning, although it will take a time of humble waiting before the full clarity and realization of this priesthood of Israel arrives.

And yet Abram and his offspring are dependent on the blessing of "the others." God wants to bless all nations without any exception. All generations, all families of the earth, will be blessed. This promise is in itself the guarantee of the ultimate *tikkun*

---

28. Cf. Heb 7:10; see also chapter 12 (12.6).

29. This terminology stems from H. Ridderbos (*Paulus*, 439). Ridderbos (Ibid., 33, 60) refers to the thinking of H. Wheeler Robinson, who introduced the term "corporate personality" in describing the fact that a leader, king, family head etc. can function as the one in who many are (already) represented and present in a corporative unity.

30. This concept of "all-in-one" is important within the Tanakh. A patriarch, leader, king, and of course also a priest, can thus represent the whole of a people or community. The individual members of such a people or community can be identified with him in whom they are "condensed." Even a guilty person can be connected with the whole of the people in such a corporate unity.

31. Matt 15:26.

32. Cf. Hos 1:9; Rom 9:25–26 and 1 Pet 2:10.

33. Exod 19:5–6.

34. Hos 1:9; cf. Rom 9:25–26.

35. Gen 12:1–3 shows that God wants to bless the nations as families (*mishpahot*; NIV "peoples") through this one God-created family of Abram. See also chapter 9 about the order and regulation of the camp of Israel.

36. See footnote 30 in this chapter.

olam. It provides the certainty that the creation intentions of the Eternal One will become reality. In Abram, through him and with him, God will bless the nations.[37]

The receiving of this blessing of God by the nations, however, comes through the blessing of Abram and his offspring.[38] The obedience of the nations in this regard will be part of the dawning of the *tikkun olam*.[39] However, he who resists this election by God and curses the chosen one, cuts himself off from God's blessing and will be cursed.[40] In Lot we meet someone who cuts himself loose from the blessed Abram and thereby loses the blessing and the light.[41]

3.5 Contours of Priesthood

In the calling of Abram, the contours of the priesthood of Israel already become visible in several ways: set apart, called to a life before God with a God-given righteousness, and the bearer of blessing for others.

Pure priestly service is seen in Abraham's prayers for Sodom,[42] and his prayer for the healing of Abimelek, his wife, and all of their female slaves.[43] This priestly entreaty is in a remarkable way connected to the LORD's self-revelation to Abraham in which He appears almost incarnational in Abraham's life.[44] A type of indwelling in the life of the chosen, as later also will happen in the midst of the people.

This utterly real self-revelation of God in the life of Abraham is followed by a renewed promise of a son for Abraham and Sarah. And then God shares His deliberations about Sodom with Abraham. God shares His plans with Abraham and speaks, "I have known him."[45] God Himself is remembering what He wants to bring about in the world through Abraham and his offspring. Abraham is His chosen one and therefore He does not want him to stay ignorant. When Abraham hears about God's intentions, his pleading on behalf of Sodom begins. God's self-revelation to Abraham triggers priestly service. Again the structure of Israel's priestly calling becomes visible.

---

37. I interpret Gen 12:3 (with Ramban) as Paul (in Gal 3:8–9) interprets it. Rashi, however, thinks that the nations wish themselves to be blessed with (= as) Abram.

38. See chapter 2 (2.7; especially footnote 60–62).

39. See also chapter 12.

40. Gen 12:3.

41. Gen 13. Cf. Isa 59:9. We see that the life of Lot and his family is in danger already in chapter 14. Lot is taken captive by invading robbery groups from the East. Sodom does not provide safety. Abram becomes the "savior" of Lot. Lot, however, does not learn from it. Later he is being spared by (the prayer of?) Abraham. Gen 19:29 reads, "So when God destroyed the cities of the plain, he remembered Abraham and he brought Lot out of the catastrophe (. . .)."

42. Gen 18:16–33.

43. Gen 20:17–18.

44. Gen 18:1–15.

45. Gen 18:19; NIV renders the Hebrew with "I have chosen him."

The intercessory for healing of the house of Abimelek is performed by Abraham whom God called a "prophet."[46]

The priestly and prophetic task of instruction in the ways of God, which will have such a prominent place in the center of the people and in the Scriptures of the Tanakh, is part of what God intended for Abraham. "For I have chosen him, so that he will direct his children and his household after him to keep the way of the LORD."[47]

3.6 Abram Waits

And yet also in the life of Abram it is clear that he has to wait for the full realization of all promises given to him and his offspring. That includes the promise of a son and thus the creation of the people, but also includes all other promises. And waiting can be long, arduous, and done in the dark. Genesis 15 tells of Abram's experience.

It is here we see how the LORD, after renewing His promise to Abram about his own son,[48] makes a covenant with Abram. That covenant regards the promise of the land, and concerns the creation of the dwelling place, the encampment or "the camp" of Israel in the midst of the nations.

It is remarkable that Abram, after having prepared "the way of the covenant," a "path" between the halves of slaughtered animals, does not walk this path, although it was the custom that both parties in the covenant did so. Only the LORD walks the path, as a revelation of fire in the deep darkness between the halves. By this action Abram is ensured of the fact that the promise of the land is not dependent upon his own righteousness in fulfilling of the covenant. The LORD Himself—He alone—will live up to this covenant and fulfill His promise.

Abram, however, experiences[49] and hears[50] that waiting for the fulfillment will bring darkness and fear and sorrow. His offspring will live the life of slaves, far from their own[51] country. They will be oppressed for four hundred years.[52] It will be a time of waiting because of the righteousness of God, who does not want the death of a sinner, but waits a long time before He judges.[53] Abram's offspring will experience darkness during this long period of waiting until the measure of sin is filled. Darkness because of God's righteousness. Again we sense something of priestly suffering.

---

46. Gen 20:7; cf. also 1 Chr 16:19–22, where in a retrospect on this occasion Abraham and his companions are called "anointed ones" and "prophets." Has here the calling already become the "anointing" of priests and prophets? Also Jacob blesses Pharaoh twice (Gen 47:7,10).

47. Gen 18:19; cf. footnote 45 for the rendering of NIV.

48. Gen 15:4–6.

49. Gen 15:12; a thick and dreadful darkness comes over him while he sleeps.

50. Gen 15:13–16.

51. They will be "strangers in a country (that is) not their own" (Gen 15:13). For the people that would live in Egypt there was a land that could be called "their own."

52. Cf. Exod 12:40.

53. Gen 15:16; Ezek 18:32; cf. 2 Pet 3:8–9.

The election of God brings with it darkness, fear, ordeal, fight, and friction. Opposition is growing against this elective God. Struggle goes along with trusting. In the life of Abram there is famine,[54] living outside the Promised Land,[55] all too human attempts to beget offspring,[56] and the growing hatred against the God-elected heir[57] resulting from those attempts.

3.7 Covenant

But during the waiting periods there are also revelations from God. For Abram and, in him, also for Israel. After nearly twenty-four years[58] the LORD appears to Abram.

> When Abram was ninety-nine years old, the LORD appeared to him and said, "I am God Almighty; walk before me faithfully and be blameless. Then I will make my covenant between me and you and will greatly increase your numbers."[59]

"To walk before God and be blameless." Those are priestly commandments and such had to be the life of the people of Israel.

God confirms to Abram the promises He had given previously and he receives a new name. "Abraham," father of many nations. An eternal covenant is granted to him and his offspring. Forever. And the land is a gift of God for always.[60]

> Then God said to Abraham, "As for you, you must keep my covenant, you and your descendants after you for the generations to come. This is my covenant with you and your descendants after you, the covenant you are to keep: Every male among you shall be circumcised. You are to undergo circumcision, and it will be the sign of the covenant between me and you."[61]

Abraham receives the command regarding circumcision. It is for him and those who belong to him, now and always. With it he receives the *tora* regarding the circumcision,[62] for the future of Abraham and his offspring will not be the fruit of an uncircumcised life. God marks His people and those who stem from Abraham and

---

54. Gen 12:10–20.

55. Gen 20 and 21:22–34.

56. Gen 16.

57. Gen 21:8–10; see also 25:18, where it is said that the sons of Ishmael live (in hostility) opposite of (against) Israel.

58. Cf. Gen 12:4 with 17:1.

59. Gen 17:1–2.

60. Gen 17:2–8.

61. Gen 17:9–11.

62. Gen 17:10–14 entails the instruction regarding and the commandment of the covenant of circumcision.

belong to him.[63] The knife should cut the covenant in the flesh on the eighth day, an indelible sign of the covenant of God, a new symbol in the history of mankind. The begetting of offspring, in every respect belonging to Gods creational intentions and blessing, must be circumcised. A knife goes right past the source of life. A near escape. The line of generations is severed from the sphere of the natural.[64] God's covenantal plans can only be realized in the lives of renewed people, who have been freed from all barriers[65] which arise from man as he is in himself and from sin. From the beginning the existence of the future priestly people is marked by this sign of purification and being spared. In a certain sense this people will be "cut off from the land of the living."[66]

3.8 The Binding of Isaac

The culmination of the life of Abraham that Genesis draws toward is undoubtedly the "binding of Isaac"[67] in chapter 22. Here, all threads come together: the election by God of this one man and his offspring; the temptation and darkness that go with obedience; the calling to be a blessing unto God; the contours of the priesthood of the people of Israel which become all the time clearer; the choice of God for one specific place on the earth; the essence of the Temple service in this place; and again the promise of God that all nations of the earth will be blessed in Abraham's offspring.

"The LORD examines the righteous"[68]—here we see that happening. Shall the obedience of the chosen one be so unwavering that all wishes and longings will be centered on the ONE God? Will that be the case even when it concerns the only[69] son? And what if it seems by this as though all promises are coming to nothing? The command comes to Abraham in the night with its darkness and temptation. Will he then glorify God as a priest on this dark night?[70]

Not only is Abraham called to the task of sacrifice himself, but in him also his offspring. Never before he has received this calling.[71] It is the third time Scriptures tell about Abraham's priestly service in offering a sacrifice. The priest is summoned to

---

63. Ishmael has also been circumcised and possibly all his descendants. Can the same be said of the other nations which stem from Abraham (cf. Gen 25:1–6)? Even Abraham's slaves were circumcised (Gen 17:23).

64. The knife touches "the organ of continuity" (Sherman, *The Torah*, 74).

65. The Hebrew word for foreskin actually means "barrier" (Ibid., 74). Also Ramban speaks about "your flesh which obstructs" (*Genesis*, 220).

66. Isa 53:8.

67. In Judaism there is no talking about "the sacrifice of Isaac," but about "the binding of Isaac" (*akeda*).

68. Ps 11:5.

69. The stem of "only" is the same as of the word *eḥad* that we find in the *Shema* (Deut 6:4).

70. Cf. Ps 134:1.

71. Twice he builds an altar and places an offering on it (Gen 12:7–8).

Moriah.[72] There the House of the ONE God will be built in later times.[73] There he built *the*[74] altar. This altar is the beginning of the service of the altar on that place. This altar is the very beginning of the return to the garden of Eden.[75]

Abraham binds Isaac and lays him on the altar.[76] In doing this Abraham in fact lays everything on the altar. His total existence and even his God-promised future is committed to God. Therefore this mountain forms a great contrast with the self-built tower and the striving behind it. Here a man who focuses his life fully in total unity on Him who is ONE. He is obedient and walks blamelessly. And so he receives, very close to the place where child sacrifices later would be brought,[77] the revelation of the totally different character of the LORD. He does not wish the son's death, but wishes to receive from Abraham the blessing of total dedication. Answering to this dedication, the LORD Himself provides a vicarious burnt offering. In this lies the essence of the sacrificial service of Israel. The LORD *will see*.[78] He gives the sacrifices. He provides vicarious sacrifices. But He will also appear there and also man must appear there and will be *seen* by the LORD.[79]

Abraham "listened to the voice of the LORD." This expression summarizes everything.[80] Abraham does what Adam and Eve did not do. His obedience causes the blessing for the nations, which will be given on this mountain. This blessing will be "in" the offspring of Abraham,[81] and from this mountain the Tora of the LORD will go out over all the earth.[82]

3.9 Blessing and Darkness

The generations that came after Abraham also had to wait for the fulfillment of God's promise. This is the reason that we see the promise being repeated, the experience of darkness being multiplied and "accompanying" the people.

72. There is a connection between Moriah and *mor* (= myrrh), so Ramban, possibly also with *mora* (= fear).

73. 2 Chr 3:1.

74. The specific altar. In Jewish tradition there are voices which let this altar coincide with the altar of Cain and Abel and that of Noah.

75. In Jewish tradition Moriah, the place of the later Temple in Jerusalem, is situated on the place of the garden of Eden. Cf. chapter 12 (12.11).

76. In Jewish narrative exposition the binding is seen to happen on the demand of Isaac, who wanted to let the sacrifice take place unhindered.

77. Directly south of Moriah, later the Temple mount, lies the valley of Hinnom where Manasseh sacrificed his sons (2 Chr 33:6; cf. 2 Kings 23:10).

78. It is possible to render the name that Abraham gave along this line (Gen 22:14); cf. the use of the verb "see" in vss. 8 and 13 (NIV renders this verb in vs. 8 as "provide").

79. I have chosen to let all these nuanced meanings play their role.

80. Gen 22:18 (NIV renders "because you have obeyed me").

81. See footnote 37 in this chapter.

82. Isa 2:2–3.

Isaac is the heir of the promise instead of Ishmael.[83] Later it is Jacob and not Isaac's eldest son Esau who inherits the promise[84] and who receives God's explicit confirmation of it.[85] This inheriting of the election calls for the opposition of the sons of Ishmael and Esau. Dark clouds of conflict arise on the horizon of the election of Israel. A circle of enemy nations seems to be formed. The camp of Israel is not being pitched in neutral territory.

The creation of the priestly people and its dwelling place—its camp—is on the way and its contours become all the more clear.

---

83. Gen 17:18–22; 21:12; cf. 24:6–9, 27.
84. Gen 25:23–24.
85. Gen 28:13–15.

Chapter 4

The Creation of the Camp of Israel and the Priestly Nation

The Sequel

4.1 Resistance against the Election

THE CREATION OF THE priestly nation in the midst of the earth did not take place in a vacuum. The inhabitants of the earth would increasingly oppose this act of God. The world would not be cheering when Abram was elected and in him also the people of Israel.

In the dreadful darkness at "the covenantal path of blood,"[1] God had spoken of years of darkness that would come to Abraham's offspring. Because of God's righteousness, Israel would have to wait for its redemption. Only the fourth generation[2] would be allowed to return[3] to the land. God promised to give the land to His people only when the sin in the land had reached its full measure.[4] Israel may need to suffer because of the righteousness and patience of the Holy One in regard to the nations. A glimpse of the figure of the Servant of the LORD can be seen here already.[5]

In Jewish interpretation we find the idea that in the darkness Abram experiences in Genesis 15, four different stages (representing four periods of exile) are already hinted upon, which will befall the national existence of the people of Israel.[6]

---

1. Gen 15:9–20. See chapter 3 (3.6) and the footnotes 49–52 there.
2. So Rashi. Ramban interprets this expression as speaking about the Amorites.
3. The people will *return* to its place (Gen 15:16; NIV: come back here).
4. Gen 15:16.
5. Cf. Isa 50:5–6.
6. The different words in Gen 15:12 are interpreted in the Midrash Rabbah as pointing to the overpowering by Babel (*dreadful*), the Medes-Persians (*darkness*), Greece (*thick*), and Rome (*came over him*). The commentary also mentions that other interpretations conclude to different combinations.

The Creation of the Camp of Israel and the Priestly Nation: The Sequel

However, the obedience and the disobedience of Israel will have a role in this as well. In a mysterious way both the resistance of the nations and Israel's faithfulness (or unfaithfulness) are included in God's dealings with His people. The darkness of waiting will be caused by both opposition within the world of nations *and* by the opposition stemming from the uncircumcised heart of Israel itself.[7] In this context, it is remarkable that the Holy God passes through "the path of blood" alone. By this He makes the covenant regarding the land a fully one-sided covenant. Any unfaithfulness of Abram and his offspring becomes overshadowed by the one-sided faithfulness of God. In this case the LORD will provide,[8] making sure that one way or the other His promises will be fulfilled and the heart of Israel will be circumcised.[9]

The book of Genesis shows that the promise of God continues in a history in which both the faith and disbelief of Israel and the resistance of the nations are present, also after the life of Abraham. Under the arch of God's promise we encounter faithfulness and unfaithfulness, resistance and surrender.

The election of Isaac and not of Ishmael, Abraham's firstborn son, evokes jealousy and hatred.[10] The same occurs when God chooses Jacob, the younger son of Isaac.[11] Esau gets passed by and we hear explicitly that God's promises will be neither for Ishmael[12] or for him.[13] God chooses His own path. In both cases however, we see that sinful human behavior on the side of the bearers of the promise plays a role.[14] Through this God's election is effectuated. An element of this election is that God explicitly repeats the promises to Isaac and Jacob.[15] We also see how Isaac emphatically passes on this blessing—in speaking about the blessing of Abraham[16]—to Jacob.[17]

Ramban writes, "This experience came to Abraham because the Holy One, blessed be He, made a covenant with him to give the land to his children as an everlasting possession, He said to him, by way of a residuary of His gift, that during the four exiles the nations will subjugate his children and rule in their land, subject to the condition that they sin before Him" (*Genesis*, 201–2).

7. Lev 26:41; Jer 9:26; cf. Ezek 44:9.

8. See also chapter 12.

9. Deut 30. There the promise of circumcision of the heart (vs. 6) stands in a context of return to the LORD, but as such this circumcision of the heart is no human possibility.

10. Gen 17:18–22; 21:12; cf. 24:6–9, 27.

11. Gen 25:23, 24.

12. Gen 17:18–19. Abraham asks if Ishmael might live before God's countenance, meaning that he might live as the bearer of the promise. Gen 21:10 states, " (. . .) that woman's son will never share in the inheritance with my son Isaac." In this Sarah has spoken the words of God (vs. 12).

13. Gen 25:23.

14. We can think of the preference of Isaac and Rebekah for a specific child (Gen 25:28), the behavior relating to the red lentil stew (25:29–34), and the cheating of Jacob (27:1–40).

15. Gen 26:2–5, 23–24 (both times Abraham's obedience is mentioned as the reason) and 28:13–15.

16. Gen 28:4.

17. Gen 28:3–4.

Just as it was with Abraham himself, the election and blessing of Abraham's offspring is also meant to bless the world.[18] However, we see that receiving the blessing evokes jealousy and cheating. Even one's own relatives can resist God's choice.[19]

More and more we see that the camp of Israel will not be set up in neutral territory. A multitude of nations arises and surrounds the "nation-in-the-making."[20] For the first time we hear the names *Midian* and *Ashur* with all their frightful associations,[21] as they encamp opposite their brothers.[22] Increasingly it becomes clear that the world does want blessing, but has great difficulty receiving this blessing *in* Abraham and his offspring.

4.2 Inheriting the Land Devoid of Human Strength

God commands Jacob to return from exile to the land,[23] while around the land a circle of nations grows with an increasing aversion of the offspring of Abraham. Angels meet him on his way.[24] The army of the LORD is active in the return to the land of the promise. And yet it becomes clear that Abraham's offspring has no right of superiority, and therefore no right to enter the land. Without his knowledge, the house gods of Paddan Aram are stashed in Jacob's luggage.[25] Awhile later God has a fight with Jacob. Yes, the return and entrance into the land have been promised, but that does not mean that these promises are to be taken for granted. Jacob is already afraid of Esau, father of the Edomites and a threat to Israel, yet a far greater adversary is God Himself.

The history of the nocturnal struggle with the Angel of the LORD[26] shows that only the blessing of the LORD brings wealth.[27] Jacob realizes in a very significant way that the blessing of this ONE, who does not reveal His name, is life. He learns that

---

18. The election of Abraham and Israel happens *not* only for the purpose of blessing the world. So it is not just instrumental in character. God chooses His apple of the eye *and* wants to bless the world of nations.

19. Gen 29–31 mention the deceitful attitude of Laban and his growing aversion for Jacob.

20. Explicitly "nations" are mentioned in relation to Ishmael (Gen 17:20) and when the birth of Esau and Jacob is being narrated (25:23).

21. Gen 25:2–3.

22. Gen 25:18. What is being said about the numerous offspring of Ishmael applies also to the nations that originated from the sons of Abraham whom he sent away and who lived in the land of the East (Gen 25:1–6).

23. Gen 31:3; 32:9.

24. Gen 32:1–3.

25. Gen 31:30–35.

26. Gen 32:22–32.

27. Prov 10:22.

The Creation of the Camp of Israel and the Priestly Nation: The Sequel

living before the LORD is a dangerous calling.[28] To see His face and live is like being rescued from death.[29]

Jacob is allowed to pass through Peniel, but he is limping from his fight with the ONE. *Israel* will be his name from now on. Thus Israel enters the land, limping. Weak and wounded he must encounter his adversaries. Jacob and all his offspring must learn that only the Name of the LORD offers safety. In Shechem he erects an altar named, "The God of Israel is God."[30]

Still Jacob has not returned to Bethel. Finally he travels there, called by God in a situation of great fear.[31] Dwelling in a land that hardly can be called one's own[32] causes problems.[33] Amidst adversity and threats, God calls Jacob to deliver on his promise given in Bethel.[34] Perhaps made wise by his earlier encounter with the LORD, Jacob understands that he has to appear before the LORD and therefore is in need of preparation. The sanctification of this small, priestly, people-in-the-making consists of a radical break with all idols and the purification of body and clothing.[35]

Even before they arrive in Bethel, Jacob's offspring sees that sanctification is the road to safety. The Name of the LORD is a fortified tower.[36] God Himself frightens away possible pursuers by "the terror of the LORD."[37]

In Bethel God reveals Himself anew to Jacob. Only *then* has Jacob/Israel returned[38] from Paddan Aram. Returning without fulfilling the promises given is not returning at all. Only then and there Israel fully returns home. The LORD does not stay in heaven while angels climb up and down,[39] but comes to speak with Jacob/Israel himself.[40]

---

28. Cf. footnote 12.

29. Gen 32:30.

30. Gen 33:20. NIV interprets the Hebrew as "El is the God of Israel" or "mighty is the God of Israel."

31. See Gen 34:30.

32. Only the cave of Machpelah (Gen 23) and the piece of land in Shechem (33:18–20) have been paid for and can be called "property."

33. Gen 34 shows that dwelling near Shechem becomes impossible by the misconduct of Simeon and Levi as a reaction on the rape of Dinah (34:2). Their cunning and deceit, however, result in averting the threat of becoming "one people" (vss. 16, 22) with the inhabitants of Shechem (cf. 50:20).

34. Gen 28:20–22.

35. Gen 35:2; in the meantime the looted women, children, and possessions (and gods) of Shechem are part of this growing people.

36. Prov 18:10.

37. Gen 35:5.

38. Gen 35:9.

39. Gen 28:12.

40. Gen 35:13. Ramban writes that there the Divine Presence rested on Jacob, just as this was the case with Abraham (17:22). He cites a saying of the sages: "It is the patriarchs that constitute the Divine Chariot" (*Genesis*, 425).

Again we hear, "Your name will be Israel."[41]

4.3 To See from a Distance

Jacob lived as a sojourner in the land where his father had lived in the same way.[42] A permanent dwelling place for the people was something for which he and his family still waited. In sharp contrast was the ever increasing offspring of his brother Esau, "that is Edom."[43] When we read about Esau's offspring, we hear about "their settlements in the land they occupied."[44] It seemed as if the creation of the camp of Israel was not progressing much. It is even the other way around, the exile in Egypt appears on the horizon. More delay is to be expected.

Also the creation of the priestly people seems to be far from its ultimate realization. The murderous act of Simeon and Levi is no isolated incident. Even Judah, despite the feelings and expectations that his name evokes, is not truly focused on God's future.[45] Among Jacob's sons there is no unity; dissension marks their relationships. The holiness of the priestly nation is difficult to find. The history of Joseph[46] is a fabric in which human sin and unfaithfulness is woven into God's overarching actions.

> You intended to harm me, but God intended it for good to accomplish what is now being done, the saving of many lives.[47]

These words of Joseph in Genesis 50:20 form a sort of conclusion. Joseph's history turns out to be part of the greater plans of God. Joseph's pride, the evil scheming of his brothers, the eager but rather negative service of the offspring of Ishmael and Midian, the lies of Potiphar's wife, the unthankful obliviousness of Pharaoh's cupbearer, the famine that occurred, Pharaoh's dreams, everything had its place under God's overarching direction. God allows Jacob to leave the land another time.[48] God promises to bless him in Egypt and then bring him back to the land.[49] The creation of the priestly nation will surely take place and the dwelling place in the Promised Land will become

---

41. Gen 35:10; although also the name Jacob will be used in the remainder of Genesis.

42. Gen 37:1.

43. Gen 36:1.

44. Gen 36:43. There is an intended contrast visible between this permanent dwelling place of Edom that Edom possessed (the Hebrew speaks about "property"; cf. RSV: "the land of their possession") and the land where Jacob still lives as a sojourner (Hebrew: "the land where his father lived as a foreigner (*ger*)"; RSV: "in the land of his father's sojourning"). In fact 37:1 still belongs to chapter 36. In 37:2 a new section begins.

45. Gen 38.

46. Gen 37–50. The sheer extent of this history in my opinion shows that this history stands for much more. Such is the way how God creates blessing. In darkness He realizes the sanctification of His people and prepares it for its task of blessing.

47. Gen 50:20.

48. Gen 46:2–4.

49. Gen 46:4.

The Creation of the Camp of Israel and the Priestly Nation: The Sequel

reality. In a prophetic manner the land is already being allotted by Jacob to the tribes.[50] Even the dead Joseph is waiting for the fulfillment of this.[51]

But the fact remains, that while the earth is being inhabited and filled with all kinds of nations disposed to resist the intentions of God, the bearers of the promise do not live in the Promised Land. A grave is their only property, only the dead wait there for the LORD.[52] While the offspring of both Lot[53] and Abraham's concubines Hagar and Keturah[54] live in their own dwelling places together with Esau's descendants,[55] Israel is in exile in Egypt. In the beginning it was welcomed by Egypt, but more and more it comes under pressure. A nation-in-the-making with great promises. A people that expands under the blessing of God and multiplies greatly.[56] A nation that finds itself more and more in captivity. Centuries of darkness will follow. But just like Joseph's God-given dreams became reality after many years, the "Joseph-people" will also experience the fulfillment of this promise: "God will surely come to your aid."[57]

The world opposes Israel, the mediator of blessing, and yet it will be blessed in this people. Joseph's "store houses filled with life" stand as a model for the significance of this nation for the world. The blessing of Jacob for Pharaoh[58] functions as a model for God's intentions with the nations. And at the same time, the evil Pharaoh is a gloomy model of the world's opposition against God's election of Israel.

---

50. Gen 48–49.
51. Gen 50:24–26.
52. Besides the cave of Machpelah it also concerns the tomb of Rachel (Gen 35:19–20).
53. Gen 19:37–38.
54. Gen 25:1–18.
55. Gen 36.
56. Exod 1:7.
57. Gen 50:25.
58. Gen 47:7,10.

Chapter 5

The Creation of the Camp of Israel and of the Priestly Nation

Waiting for the Tora

5.1 Tora in the Camp of Israel

TOGETHER WITH THE INDWELLING of the Holy God, the Tora will be the center of the national existence of Israel, its people encamped around it. Physically and spiritually together with God, His *Tora*, His instruction, will stand in the midst of Israel[1] and thereby stand in the midst of his creation.[2]

Prior to the revelation at Sinai, we observe a development geared to this goal.

5.2 Instruction

Tora, understood as "instruction," belongs to the creation intentions of God. Creation was meant to be oriented toward this instruction of God.[3] The creation of man is also accompanied by *tora*. To live as image bearer of God and to fulfill one's own calling contains both instruction and commandment.[4] The command to eat and not-eat in the garden can also be called *tora*.[5] After the disobedience and the expulsion from the garden of Eden, the instruction of God and the *tora* of His commandments

---

1. The tablets of the Law, on God's command, were deposited in the ark of the covenant (Exod 25:21). The Tabernacle was the center of the camp of Israel.
2. See chapter 3 (3.1).
3. See chapter 1; also the footnote 20 about *tora* and *Tora*.
4. Gen 1:26–28.
5. Gen 2:16–17.

expand. After the flood, Noah receives a number of specific commandments.[6] Later Abraham receives the *tora* concerning circumcision.[7] At Sinai, God ultimately gives His Tora as the instruction and commandments to set Israel apart from the nations.

5.3 Expansion

We can conclude that the Tora of Sinai has not been given inside a vacuum, but rather is the ongoing expansion of revelation and earlier instruction. In the period prior to Sinai, within Judaism Abraham and his offspring are qualified as "children of Noah,"[8] who must live with the commands of God which already have been given. From the time of Noah, these commands can be characterized as Noachide commandments or laws.

The relationship between the Noachide covenant (based on God's creational intentions) on the one hand, and the covenant with Abraham and that of Sinai on the other, has been studied intensively within Judaism. The opinion is that the covenant with Abraham (and his descendants) does not nullify the covenant with Noah.[9] Abraham and his offspring prior to Sinai are therefore seen as Noachides. In the legislation at Sinai, commandments given to Noah are repeated, therefore both Israel and the nations are under these commandments. Therefore within the legislation of Sinai we find components normative for all nations.[10]

Excursus:[11] Noachide Commandments

What does the concept of Noachide commandments mean within Judaism?
Rabbinical thinking starts with the commandments God gave Adam. In Genesis 2:16–17 Adam and his offspring receive six commands dealing with (1) idolatry, (2) blasphemy, (3) jurisdiction, (4) murder, (5) illicit sexual relations, and (6) theft.[12] Af-

---

6. Gen 9:1–7.
7. Gen 17:9–14.
8. b Sanhedrin 58a–59b presents a discourse about this subject.
9. The covenant with Abraham does not nullify the covenant with Noah, but is intended "so that the divine rule may become manifest in history and eventually transform it" (Borowitz, *Renewing the Covenant*, 188). Cohen Stuart also has this opinion (*Joodse Feesten en Vasten*, 309–19). On the basis of Jubilees 14, he concludes that Gen 15 (the covenant with Abram still uncircumcised) actually means the renewal of the covenant with Noah. Gen 17 adds to this the covenant of circumcision (through Isaac with Israel, vss. 19–21).
10. This thought we also find with Paul in Rom 1. The nations stand guilty before their Creator because they did not live according to what He had commanded them. "He has shown you, O mortal, what is good. And what does the LORD require of you? To act justly and to love mercy and to walk humbly with your God" (Mic 6:8). The word *adam* is used here! b Yoma 67b links the Noachide commandments with the concept of a "natural law."
11. For this excursus I utilized what I wrote in my *De Tora van de Messias*, 41–42.
12. See par example Bockmuehl (*Jewish Law in Gentile Churches*, 151), and Cohen Stuart (*Joodse*

Part I: The Canonical Narrative: The Tanakh

ter the flood God again continues His dealings with His creation and gives Noah a covenant with two prohibitions: to eat flesh with its blood and regarding manslaughter/murder.[13] It is remarkable that God refers to His original creation intentions in this covenant with Noah. After all, humankind has been created according to the image of God.[14]

In rabbinical thinking a firm link was established between the covenant with Noah and the commands given to Adam, resulting in the further development of the concept of the Noachide commandments. Ultimately the Noachide covenant was thought of as consisting of the following seven covenantal stipulations, the first of these a positive commandment: (1) the creation of a system of jurisdiction. There then follow six negative commandments: the prohibitions concerning (2) idolatry, (3) blasphemy, (4) incestuous relations, (5) murder, (6) robbery, and (7) the eating of the flesh of a living animal.[15] All non-Jews are entitled to obey these commandments since they are all offspring of Adam. Whoever belonged to the non-Jewish nations and yet took upon himself these duties, was seen as a "foreigner residing among you"[16] or even as a "semi-convert."[17]

The stipulations concerning the "foreigner" in the Tora played a role in the creation of the definitive formulation of the "list" of Noachide commandments. We find three categories of commandments for foreigners in the Tora:[18] first, there are commandments relating to the service of the One God[19] followed by commandments that deal with the killing of people and the killing and eating of animals,[20] and finally commandments that have to do with illicit sexual relations.[21] They are commandments that concern the three domains (idolatry, the shedding of blood [murder], and sexual offences) where violation according to God's revelation is followed by the death

---

Feesten en Vasten, 311). Cohen Stuart cites rabbi Jehudah bar Shimon, who derives this from: Then *commanded* (1) *the Eternal* (2) *God* (3) *the man* (4) *saying* (5): *You are free to eat from any tree in the garden* (6)—Gen 2:16.

13. See Gen 9:1–7.

14. Gen 9:6; cf. Gen 1:26–27.

15. Here I follow the enumeration of Cohen Stuart (*Joodse Feesten en Vasten*, 313).

16. Hebrew: *ger-toshav*, "resident foreigner," see *Encyclopaedia Judaica*, www.jewishencyclopedia.com, sv. "Noachide Laws." Mention is made of the view of Maimonides, who viewed these heathens as the righteous from the nations, who will have a share in the world to come.

17. *Encyclopaedia Judaica*, sv. "Noachide Laws," presents this as the view which can be found in b Avoda Zara 64b. In the Second Temple period *ger* (= alien/foreigner) became the designation for a proselyte in the formal sense of a convert.

18. I follow the grouping given by Bockmuehl (*Jewish Law in Gentile Churches*, 153).

19. Lev 17:8–9; 20:2–5; 24:10–16. Foreigners in the midst of Israel were allowed to bring sacrifices (Lev 17:8); had to keep the *Shabbat* (Exod 20:10); were allowed (in the case of a man when he was circumcised) to celebrate *Pessaḥ*; and had to do away yeast and everything leavened (Exod 12:48 and 12:19). See also footnote 24 in this chapter.

20. Lev 24:17–22; 24:18; 17:10–16.

21. Lev 18 and 20.

penalty.²² Obedience to God's intentions in these three domains was the minimum requirement for those who lived in the land.²³ It is remarkable that we find these three domains also in the decisions of the meeting which we find reported in Acts 15.

5.4 Tora and *Tikkun Olam*

Thus the Tora of Israel consists of the revelation that God gave prior to the election and calling of Israel, with an expansion of components related specifically to Israel and what was necessary for the service of Israel, in a pure land,²⁴ in the midst of the nations. In this respect it is important to keep in mind that from the beginning of creation, God's Tora has been deeply oriented toward the *tikkun olam*, the consummation, the perfection and fulfillment of all things.²⁵ We must also acknowledge that both the instruction and the commandments have been expanded because of the restoration needed after disobedience.

5.5 Interpretation Key

The creation of this priestly people in the center of the earth provides us with a scripturally-interpretative key for understanding the difference and the relationship between the *tora* for all nations and the *tora* for Israel.

Israel will receive the calling to be a *nation* of priests.²⁶ At the same time God calls *one* family to be priests in the midst of the nation. They are a part of the people and yet are in possession of their own commandments, a priestly *tora*. The whole nation has a priestly calling, and yet the designated priests have this particular priestly

---

22. Since the second century, obedience and faithfulness in these three domains were considered as obligatory within Judaism. A Jew was expected to sacrifice his life rather than violate God's commandments. In the first centuries the Church has qualified violations in these three domains as "deadly sins."

23. Ezek 33:23–26. This section shows that eating flesh with the blood, the spilling of blood, idolatry, and adultery are the reasons why Israel cannot claim the possession of and the dwelling in the land. God's people did not even fulfill what was required of foreigners living in the land. I here follow Bockmuehl (*Jewish Law in Gentile Churches*, 154). b Yoma 9b utters the conviction that idolatry, incest, and murder formed the reasons for the destruction of the first Temple.

24. The necessity for a pure land caused the foreigners living in the land to also obey specific prohibitions. Just as was the case with Israel, they were threatened with death in the event of violation. See par example Lev 17:12–16 (relating to the eating of blood); 18:24–30 (relating to sexual impurity); 20:2 (relating to idolatry); 24:16 (relating to blasphemy of the Name of God); and 24:21–22 (relating to murder). Jacob Milgrom summarizes, "The *ger* is bound by the prohibitive commandments but not by the performative ones." The prohibitive stipulations had to guarantee the purity of the land. The foreigner was free to choose whether or not he would participate in certain elements of Israel's worship service; non-participation caused no pollution of the land (*Numeri*, 399, in: Excursus 34, *The 'Ger'*, 398–402).

25. See chapter 1, footnote 18.

26. See chapter 6.

tora. There is both a unity and diversity within the obedience to the laws that God commands.

It is here that we find the key to understanding the difference between Israel and the nations with regard to the *tora* of God that applies to each. Israel has been chosen out of the nations and yet is one of them. Israel, therefore, has a share in the *tora* given to all nations and yet receives a *tora* that is focused specifically on its own life as a priestly nation.

It is also important to remind oneself of the fact that the Tora of Israel (and by consequence the whole of the Tanakh) is not just meant to serve the process of reparation of what has been broken in an "universal" past. In other words it has not been given just to deal with the sin of universal mankind, but also *becomes* the "place" of God's new self-revelations. The covenant of Sinai (and by that reason also the Tora), therefore, has not just been given to restore the image of God in man. God's revelation in the Tora has no backward orientation or is just geared toward the salvation of a "return to Genesis 1" by a "reversal of Genesis 3." Revelation therefore is not simply focused on the "restoration" of Adam. In the revelation at Sinai (and by that reason also in the whole of Tora), new perspectives are opened up, and with it new riches are revealed: *this* Tora is the intention of creation.[27]

This fact affects the way we evaluate the "Jewish character" of the history of God. Since the history of Israel is focused on this future re-creation, the specific Jewish character of this history is not transient in nature. God's ways with Israel and His Tora reveal so much more about God and His salvation. Therefore the *tikkun olam*, the perfection and completion of everything, is by definition more than the beginning. This "added" value has a permanent character. The calling of Israel and the Tora are no workman's clothes that can be left behind when the work has been done. They are festive clothing, made to wear forever.

---

27. See chapter 1 (1.2).

Chapter 6

Liberated and Called

God's Treasured Possession and Nation of Priests

6.1 Imprisoned unto Death

ISRAEL'S EXILE IN EGYPT is covered in only a few chapters in Scripture, whereby the focus is on liberation from slavery. The long and dark centuries preceding largely remain untold. It is evident, however, that God fulfills His promises. In the long night of oppression Israel multiplies greatly. The darkness of this crucible of maltreatment and slavery culminates in the systematic murder of all newborn Israelite boys. The reigning Pharaoh hopes to keep the people of Israel small and powerless. When the midwives of Israel refuse to collaborate, all of Egypt becomes involved in the onslaught on this enslaved people.[1] But this causes Pharaoh and his people to collide with the God who promised that the offspring of Israel would be like the innumerable multitude of stars.[2] Egypt fights He who remembers His covenant. In this phase of Israel's history, Egypt is the representative of the nations who vehemently oppose the God of Israel.[3]

6.2 The Beginning of Redemption

However, hope dawns when all of Egypt is mobilized in the annihilation of newborn boys in order to stop the progression of Israel's future. It arises both from the house

---

1. Exod 1.
2. Gen 15:5.
3. Gen 10:6 shows that *Mitzraim* (Egypt) is one of the sons of Ham. He is the ancestor of Egypt but also of the Philistines (10:14). Canaan is another son of Ham and the progenitor of the nations who will populate the Promised Land (10:15–20). In "the root system" of the history of Israel, the curse fights the blessing (cf. also 10:25–27).

Part I: The Canonical Narrative: The Tanakh

of Levi,[4] meaning "one who is strongly attached/cherishes attachment,"[5] and by the mercy of the tyrannous Pharaoh's own daughter.[6] The child Moses is rescued and raised as the grandson of the Pharaoh. When he comes of age, he has to flee after his own attempt to intervene on behalf of his "own people."[7] A failed redeemer ends up a shepherd in the desert of Sinai. After the birth of Moses, for Israel there will be another eighty years[8] of groaning and calling on God for help. Their chilling lament will reach God.

> God heard their groaning and he remembered his covenant with Abraham, with Isaac and with Jacob. So God looked on the Israelites and was concerned about them.[9]

With these words the deliverance of Israel begins. God hears the lament, and remembers His covenant; He sees and He knows.[10] Thereby the deliverance of Israel is the result of the faithful heart of God. He lovingly knows the people that will be His treasured possession.[11] The redemption of Israel is grounded in God's covenant with the three patriarchs. He has promised them that He will bring their people into the land.[12] He is faithful to the covenant He has made, in which the inheritance of the land comes first.[13]

In a holy self-revelation of God, Moses receives his calling and the confirmation of all promises. He is allowed to know the Name of the LORD.

---

4. Exod 2:1. Cf. also 6:15–26 for the Levitical lineage of Moses (and also Aaron).

5. The name Levi means "One who is attached, who is strongly connected." Jacob himself gives this name to his third son and thereby declares his attachment to Leah. This attachment is a mutual bond in which both partners know that they are dependent on each other for their happiness. So Rabbi Samson Raphael Hirsch ad Gen 29:34 (*Bereishith/Genesis*, 474). The name Levi so surely becomes a God-given life goal (attachment to the LORD) for the tribe of Levi. The acts of the priest Phinehas show this clearly. He acts zealously for God when he pierces an Israelite man who had (sexually) cleaved/attached himself to a Midianite woman (Num 25:1–18); cf. Deut 10:20 where strong attachment to the LORD is asked from Israel (NIV: Hold fast to[the LORD, EJW]; the King James Version renders with "and to him shalt thou cleave"). Phinehas forms the culmination of the enumeration of Levi's offspring in Exod 6:15–26. Thereby the tone has been set: from now on it is about attachment to the LORD above all.

6. Exod 2:1–10.

7. Exod 2:11; literally "his brothers."

8. Exod 7:7.

9. Exod 2:24–25.

10. The NIV translates "was concerned." The Hebrew only says pithily, "and God knew." In Gen 18:19 God Himself remembers the fact that He has known Abraham (NIV renders "I have chosen him"). "To know" is also the expression that can be used in the Hebrew of the Tanakh for sexual intercourse (par example: Adam-Eve, Gen 4; Elkanah-Hannah, 1 Sam 1:19). The verb "to know" here expresses a deep comprehensive knowledge of the heart.

11. Exod 19:5; see below in this chapter.

12. Exod 3:17.

13. Exod 6:4; cf. chapter 3 (3.1).

> God also said to Moses, "Say to the Israelites, 'The LORD, the God of your fathers—the God of Abraham, the God of Isaac and the God of Jacob—has sent me to you.' "This is my name forever, the name you shall call me from generation to generation."[14]

Moses, and with him the people, are allowed to know the Name. This is the deepest blessing, in which the offspring of Abraham receives more than the patriarchs themselves received.[15] At the same time the deliverance of Israel thereby becomes a momentous opportunity of new self-revelation by God and of unknown blessing.[16]

The beginning of redemption is not just the ending of Israel's slavery in Egypt. It includes the will of God that His people will serve Him[17] because He wants to be their God.[18] In the center of the earth, God aims to create a people that will serve Him. A nation that will live in veritable *avoda*,[19] in the service of worship, for Him.

6.3 Resistance

At first, Moses's calling as redeemer meets resistance in his own heart.[20] Soon after the LORD Himself is Moses's opponent.[21] How could Moses deliver the message that Pharaoh's firstborn son would die[22] if he would not let God's own people go, while Moses's own firstborn son had not been touched by the knife of circumcision?[23] Surely redemption by the God of the covenant cannot be accomplished by he who omitted the sign of the covenant! Should Moses's feet not also stand on the path of the covenant?[24]

---

14. Exod 3:15.
15. Exod 6:2–3.
16. God's redemption is not only restoration of original intentions, but also progress and new revelation. Not just reparation of the past, but real restoration *and* new designing. It brings addition and enrichment. By definition the *tikkun olam*, the consummation, is more than the good beginnings. See chapter 1 (1.4) and chapter 5 (5.4 and 5.5).
17. Exod 3:18; 5:3; cf. 8:8, 25–28; 10:7–11, 24–26.
18. Exod 6:7.
19. *Avoda* is the Hebrew word for "service"; it has a special character because it is used for the service to the Holy God in and near the sanctuary. Cf. par example Lev 25:42, 55; Deut 32:36; Ps 134 and 136:22. The essence of Israel's life is that it should be such true servant (*eved*). Cf. the prophecies about the *eved* (Servant) of the LORD in Isaiah. *Avoda zara* ("strange service" = idolatry/service to idols) is the name of one of the tractates of the Mishna and the Talmud.
20. Exod 4:10–17.
21. Exod 4:24.
22. Exod 4:22–23.
23. Exod 4:25–26.
24. That is the reason why they are being touched with the foreskin of Gershom; Exod 4:25.

Part I: The Canonical Narrative: The Tanakh

At first the people believe,[25] though the signs had been given considering their unbelief.[26] However, when Pharaoh's opposition becomes real and makes their suffering harsher,[27] even the people join in the opposition against Moses and Aaron.[28] God's repeated[29] good intentions are met with unbelief and resistance. The redeemer experiences the harshness of his task.[30] God delivers an unbelieving and impatient people.

Pharaoh resists God's command to Israel to serve Him at a place which He will indicate.[31] The representative of the nations is not willing to contribute to the service of God through this people. He does want, however, to negotiate about an adapted form of this *avoda* on a place and time appointed by himself.[32] He demonstrates the utmost resistance, whatever the cost.[33] Therefore Egypt, together with Pharaoh, must learn that resistance to the Eternal God does not pay. On the contrary, it will result in a literal dead end—in the sea. Through this opposition the heart of Pharaoh is hardened, as part of the judgment of God.

When the plagues are announced and start to occur, Israel is spared but is not essentially different.[34] Scripture explicitly states that it is only from the fourth plague that Israel is spared in their place in the land of Goshen.[35] Therefore Pharaoh must know that the LORD God is present there, in the midst of the land, in the midst of the earth.[36] Time and again Scripture shows that God does not punish gladly, and therefore Moses, as a priest in Israel, prays for Pharaoh and all of Egypt.[37]

---

25. Exod 4:31.

26. Cf. Exod 4:1–9.

27. Exod 5:1–18.

28. Exod 5:19–21.

29. Exod 6:1–7.

30. Exod 6:9. Besides the suffering under the pressure of slavery, impatience (NIV: discouragement) is also designated as a cause for the resistance from the side of the people. See also vs.12.

31. Exod 3:18; 5:3; cf. 8:8, 25–28; 10:7–11, 24–26.

32. God chooses the desert (Exod 7:16). Pharaoh wants this service to God to take place in Egypt (8:25). God wants the whole of the people, including the livestock. Pharaoh only wants the adult men to go (10:11) and doesn't want to provide sacrifices and burnt offerings; he also doesn't want the herds and flocks to share in the deliverance (10:24–26).

33. Exod 12:29–30.

34. Cf. Deut 9:4–6. Notice that that we hear three times that the land is not given to Israel because of its own righteousness. Cf. also Deut 7:7–8: " not (. . .) because you were more numerous (. . .) it was because the LORD loved you (. . .)."

35. Ramban attributes the explicit mentioning of this from the fourth plague onward to the fact that the first plagues were not "migratory in nature" (ad 8:18; *Exodus*, 92).

36. Exod 8:22. It can refer to Egypt, but also to the earth, perhaps even to the midst of the earth (= the land of Israel).

37. Each time Pharaoh asks for prayer so that the plagues will end. Finally, in the night of the redemption he asks a blessing (Exod 12:32)—it is left untold if this blessing has been granted to him.

6.4 Night of Judgment and Deliverance

The last plague, coming in the night, will bring death and destruction to Egypt. This time Israel will be spared, but only if the people stay in homes marked with the blood of the *Pessaḥ*-lamb.[38] This night is just as dangerous for Israel as it is for Egypt. But there is a possibility of survival. Wherever the LORD sees the blood, He will pass by the doors. There the destroyer[39] will not enter and strike down. Israel learns this night that it is the mercy of the LORD that permits man to live.

On this night in Egypt, when the LORD causes the death of firstborn sons and the male firstborn of cattle and herds, then Israel must not think that its own firstborn sons have a right to live on their own accord, or that the firstborn male animals can be counted as part of its private livestock. All firstborn males belong to God and must be dedicated unto Him.[40] The animals shall be a sacrifice for Him,[41] but for the firstborn sons of Israel there will be a different way.[42] They must be "redeemed."[43] When God passes by in mercy,[44] this means grace for the offspring of Abraham.

On this night the LORD kept vigil, and from now on Israel must honor this night by celebrating it.[45] It is the night of redemption in the first month,[46] and begins with a meal of *Pessaḥ*-lamb and unleavened bread.[47] In the darkest night God strikes Egypt and spares Israel. The exodus is happening. Justice is happening. Overdue wages are being paid.[48]

---

38. Exod 12:22.

39. The angel who performs the judgment of God (Exod 12:23). Cf. 2 Sam 24:16. Ramban emphatically differentiates in this verse between the angel of destruction and the Eternal God Himself. His argument is based on the fact that the first half of this verse says that the LORD will strike Egypt (*Exodus*, 143–44).

40. Exod 13:12; 34:19.

41. Except the donkey fowls. Another animal should be sacrificed for them or they must be killed (Exod 13:13; 34:19–20).

42. Exod 13:13; 34:20.

43. The people received further instruction about this "redemption" only after the Exodus, in the desert (Num 3:44–51 and 8:5–22). It then becomes clear that the Levites form the substitutionary representatives of all male firstborns of Israel. Their existence is dedicated to God. They have to serve at the Sanctuary. Their service is an atonement for the Israelites, in the sense that when individuals of the nation violated the sanctity of the Sanctuary the life of the Levites functioned as atonement (8:19 and 18:23).

44. Exod 12:27.

45. Exod 12:42.

46. Exod 12:1–2.

47. Exod 12:8–11, 14–17, 39.

48. Exod 12:35–36; cf. 11:2–3.

Part I: The Canonical Narrative: The Tanakh

The LORD leads the way through a column of fire and clouds, preventing a return to Egypt. God knows the heart of His people.[49] His army[50] is not so trusting, faithful, or courageous.

6.5 Opposition Against the Exodus

Pharaoh's opposition shows itself again, but for the last time. His pursuit seems to be a success. In no time his armies, chariots, and drivers, will capture Israel back into captivity.[51] Israel itself is not filled with faith. The people start to doubt the beginning of the redemption. "It would have been better if Moses had not been called."[52]

The answer of God is powerful: the sea is parted in His Name and the heart of Egypt hardened.[53] The LORD Himself is fighting Egypt.[54] The opposition of the nations comes to an end in the sea.

> And when the Israelites saw the mighty hand of the LORD displayed against the Egyptians, the people feared the LORD and put their trust in him and in Moses his servant.[55]

6.6 Exodus and Destination

In the song of Moses[56] by the sea, the praise resounds for the LORD, who majestically has delivered His people from the chariots and horsemen of Pharaoh. Blessed is He, whose name is LORD. He shattered those who opposed Him. He leads His people in loving-kindness.

Prophetically Moses speaks about the new destination of the people, the dwelling place of God.[57] The mountain of God that is His own inheritance.[58] The place that has been prepared[59] to become His Dwelling, the Sanctuary.[60] God guides Israel to that place and there Israel will be planted.[61]

49. Exod 13:17.
50. Exod 12:41.
51. Exod 14:5–9.
52. Exod 14:10–12.
53. Exod 14:3–4, 15–18.
54. Exod 14:14, 25.
55. Exod 14:31.
56. Exod 15:1–18; cf. Rev 15:3–4.
57. Exod 15:13.
58. Exod 15:17.
59. Exod 15:17b. "The prepared place for your dwelling" (Hirsch, *Shemoth/Exodus*, 200) or "the foundation of your dwelling-place" (Sherman, *The Torah*, 381).
60. Exod 15:17.
61. Exod 15:17; cf. Ps 80:8–9.

Israel's destination is the Sanctuary of God. The service to the LORD in the Sanctuary is the destination of this redeemed people. The mountain of the LORD is the place where the people are planted, where they may grow up like a palm tree and grow as a cedar.[62] The real destination of the land of Israel is to be "a Home for the Presence of God on Earth."[63]

6.7 Prepared through Testing

The road toward the great encounter with the Eternal God is one of testing. God searches the heart and trust of His people. Water,[64] bread, quail,[65] and again water[66] form the theme of this testing. The trust of the people soon changes into rebellious unbelief, even threatening the life of God's servant Moses.[67]

Miraculous care alongside rulings and instructions[68] are provided by the hand of God. Receiving blessing and learning obedience, come together. Only in this way will Israel avoid the plagues with which Egypt is cursed.[69]

The opposition and resistance of the nations have not yet been shattered. Amalek appears on stage with his bands of robbers.[70] For the first time the armies of God have to fight.[71] The secret in overcoming the opposition lies in the "Hand on the throne of the LORD."[72] In this there is a lesson for the future, because enmity from the side of the nations will be experienced often.[73]

And yet, there is also an exception. Moses's father-in-law Jethro, the priest of Midian,[74] honors God and Moses.[75] The people of God are being blessed by the wisdom of this God-seeker from the nations.[76]

---

62. Ps 92:13–14. Every *Shabbat* this "Psalm for the *Shabbat*" voices anew the promise about being planted on this place.

63. Hirsch, *Shemoth/Exodus*, 200 ad Exod 15:17.

64. Exod 15:22–27.

65. Exod 16.

66. Exod 17:1–7.

67. Exod 17:4.

68. Exod 15:25–27; 16:23–24.

69. Exod 15:26.

70. Exod 17:8.

71. Exod 17:9–10.

72. Exod 17:16 (*JSB*); so also RSV, although RSV renders "banner" instead of Throne; NIV interprets as Amalek lifting up its hands "against the throne of the LORD").

73. Exod 17:14, 16.

74. Exod 18:1.

75. Exod 18:9–11.

76. Jethro helps Moses with his wisdom in ordering the people in a more practical way (Exod 18:17–23).

Thus after two months Israel reaches[77] the mountain in the desert of Sinai. There it pitches its camp and is being prepared for great things.

6.8 The Calling

It was here at this mountain that the LORD had appeared to Moses.[78] It was here that He had called Moses out of the fire of the burning bush. The sign He had promised to give to Moses was that the redeemed people would serve God at this mountain.[79] God had kept His word: the people He rescued were here! Moses climbs the mountain[80] and God calls to him from the top. God, calling![81] In imitation, what follows now, is worth calling from the rooftops! Moses must speak to the people about God's caring love[82] for Israel. And then the LORD proclaims their calling:

> This is what you are to say to the descendants of Jacob and what you are to tell the people of Israel: 'You yourselves have seen what I did to Egypt, and how I carried you on eagles' wings and brought you to myself. Now if you obey me fully and keep my covenant, then out of all nations you will be my treasured possession. Although the whole earth is mine, you will be for me a kingdom of priests and a holy nation.' These are the words you are to speak to the Israelites.[83]

Israel receives its calling to be, out of all nations, God's treasured possession. The people that is His, chosen from among the nations in order to be—in the midst of the earth—a kingdom of priests.

This is what creation has been waiting for. This was what God had intended. Within this calling of Israel also the blessing for all nations is contained. The time is now! The presence of the people at the mountain is a sign unto Moses. God is faithful, putting His words into effect. But also it is a sign for all creation, for all nations. Creation's house of learning is being constructed; it is the priestly dwelling of Israel. In it God will provide His salutary instruction, reconciliation, and self-revelation. With this calling of Israel God takes a decisive step on the road toward the *tikkun olam*, the consummation, the restoration of all things.[84] The earth will learn what serving the LORD, the Creator of heaven and earth, will mean. The priesthood itself, Israel, will

---

77. Exod 19:1.
78. Exod 3:1—4:17.
79. Exod 3:12.
80. We do not read about a commandment to do this. This shows Moses's eagerness to do what God wants (Sherman, *The Torah*, 401).
81. Exod 19:3.
82. Cf. Hos 11:1–4.
83. Exod 19:3–6.
84. Cf. chapter 1 (1.4); chapter 2 (2.2); chapter 3 (3.1); chapter 5 (5.4 and 5.5)

be the first to learn about its (priestly) task and what it implies. At the core is God's gift of an ever-deepening knowledge of the LORD.

This calling of Israel is all decisive in the Tanakh[85] and for the self-understanding of Judaism. In the Scriptures of the New Covenant the words of this calling play an important role. We will meet them again in the prophetic description of the restoration of all things.[86]

---

85. Cf. par example Isa 61:6.

86. 1 Pet 2:9–10; Rev 1:5–6; 5:9–10; 20:6. In many places we find individual elements of the wording of Israel's calling.

Chapter 7

Israel's Calling
Condition and Promise

7.1 The Love of God

BEFORE GOD REVEALS HIS purpose with Israel to the whole nation, He reminds "the house of Jacob and the sons of Israel"[1] of His love for all of them. He has surrounded the people with much care. He has brought them to Himself. And that is grace to the fullest! His love is the beginning, the origin of everything, including the calling which He will give to Israel. Israel has seen His love in its redemption from Egypt.[2]

God then invites Israel to accept the calling. Israel is invited to react, surrendering itself to God's plans by listening very carefully[3] to God's words and by keeping his covenant.[4] In this invitation God also shows His love. He does not place an unwanted burden on the neck of the people. When Israel walks in the ways of this calling, the people will see anew the love of God with their own eyes.[5]

---

1. This is the literal rendering of the Hebrew words in Exod 19:3. Hirsch interprets the expression "house of Jacob" as pointing to "the family, especially (. . .) the pillars of home life, the women" and "the sons of Israel" as pointing to the male Israelites. In this he joins Rashi, who, while referring to other sources, interprets the difference between the used verbs to show that the women had to be spoken to in a softer tone than the men (*Shemoth/Exodus*, 249). Also *Exodus Rabbah* (a narrative commentary from the eleventh/twelveth century) gives this interpretation. This manner of interpreting the text, based on close reading and giving attention to differences in meaning between used words, shows how our exposition can be enriched when learning together and from Judaism.

2. Also Exod 14:31 emphasizes the fact that Israel saw God's acts.

3. The verbal form used in the Hebrew points to a very intense action.

4. Ramban interprets "my covenant" in Exod 19:5 as pointing to the covenant made with Abraham mentioned in Gen 17:7 (*Exodus*, 273); others as pointing to the covenant made with Israel after the giving of the Tora (Exod 24:8). My opinion is that we do not have to choose; both meanings can be right at the same time.

5. An example is what the people saw happening in the giving of the Tora (Exod 20:18, 22).

7.2 Two-sidedness

The calling of Israel has everything to do with two-sidedness. The priestly nation itself will have to listen and keep God's covenant, that in itself is logical. After all, that is what serving God consists of. The garden of Eden has been closed and the earth has been cursed because of the disobedience of Adam and Eve.[6] Without attentive listening there will be no blessing for Israel and the world. "Disobedient priests" is a contradiction in terms. But when Israel hears and does,[7] all promising elements of God's calling will be fulfilled. And in a manner which will be both greater and more surprising than expected.

> "Now if you obey me fully and keep my covenant, then out of all nations you will be my treasured possession. Although the whole earth is mine, you will be for me a kingdom of priests and a holy nation." These are the words you are to speak to the Israelites.[8]

7.3 Treasured Possession

God wants Israel to be His most private "treasured possession." The Hebrew word used, *segula,*[9] designates something very valuable and precious, a personal treasure. Out of all nations of the earth this one nation receives this special position.[10] This loving choice of God calls Israel to make their own loving choice in order to be a treasured possession for the LORD.[11] In the words of Moses and Zechariah, Israel is "the apple of God's eye."[12]

---

6. "God did say" plays an important role in Gen 3:1–3. Listening to the woman instead of listening to God was Adam's sin (3:12–14) because of which the earth became cursed.

7. Exod 24:7. The Hebrew uses the verbs "do" and "hear." Note the sequence! In Judaism this sequence is emphasized very much. Even before the LORD has spoken there should be the willingness to do whatever He will say.

8. Exod 19:5–6.

9. Ramban asks himself for etymological reasons if *segula* could denote "attachment" (*Exodus*, 273). Rashi interprets the meaning to be "a cherished treasure" referring to Eccl 2:8 and writes "costly vessels and precious stones which kings store up. In the same manner shall ye be unto Me a cherished treasure more than other peoples" (http://www.sefaria.org/Rashi_on_Exod.19.5.3?lang=en&layout=lines&sidebarLang=all, accessed 16th of May 2016). HaRav Avraham Yitzhak HaCohen Kook, who can be named the spiritual father of religious Zionism, joins the etymological interpretation of Ramban when he speaks about "inner Segulot," unique spiritual bonds laid by God between Himself and the people and the land (*Orot*, 19 and passim). Mal 3:17 speaks about the salvation of Israel's pious faithful ones on the Day of the LORD: they will be His *segula* on that day.

10. In Deut 7:6; 14:2 and 26:18 Moses remembers the people of God's choice of Israel to be His *am segula*, His *segula*-people. In 26:18–19 this special position is being connected with a royal place of Israel among the nations. See also Ps 135:4.

11. So Hirsch, *Shemoth/Exodus*, 250. Deut 26:18 speaks about the acceptance of the calling to be *segula*.

12. Deut 32:10; Zech 2:8.

Part I: The Canonical Narrative: The Tanakh

God elects Israel from the nations, for "the whole earth is mine." Jewish scholars differ in their interpretation of these words. Do they mean that the whole earth falls under His dominion and that He chose Israel because the other nations were not worth being chosen?[13] Or do these words mean that God values all people as precious, and yet elects Israel?[14] Or even broader, does He elect Israel because He is thinking of reaching the whole earth?[15] When we notice the fact that the purpose of God's choice for Israel is elaborated in the concept of "priesthood," it becomes obvious that it is plausible to think of this broad, worldwide task of Israel within these verses. After all, priests are elected from a larger whole in order to fulfill their task on behalf of and with an eye on that larger whole.

7.4 Kingdom of Priests

Whatever may be said on behalf of a worldwide, nations-oriented task for Israel, the starting point is that Israel exists for the LORD. The people exist for Him, stand in His service whatever the task may be. "You will be for me. . ." The words of the *Shema*,[16] Israel's foundational confession of faith that ask for total love, correspond with these words.

"You will be for me a kingdom of priests." In this expression two elements come to the foreground: *kingdom* and *priests*. This combination has at least two different lines of interpretation. It can denote a kingdom in which the priests are kings,[17] or it could mean a kingdom in which (God is king and) the priests are His subjects.[18]

Again there is no need to choose. Scripture very often uses expressions with a multiple meaning. The earth has a need for priests.[19] God creates a royal priesthood

---

13. So Rashi. Perhaps the experience of the opposition of the nations, not only found in Scripture but so much a reality in centuries of hatred for the Jewish people, has darkened the interpretation.

14. Sforno writes, "Although the entire human race is more precious to Me than all other inferior creatures, for he alone (man, EJW) among them represents My intention (. . .) still you shall be to Me a treasure beyond all of them." Sforno cites in this respect also a saying from Pirkei Avot (3:14), "Precious is the man who was created in the Image." Thus he interprets this verse in a much more positive way (*Commentary*, 380).

15. See par example Hirsch, *Shemoth/Exodus*, 250.

16. Deut 6:4–9.

17. The so-called subjective genitive: the priests are the subjects in the kingdom. The meaning is in this case: the kingdom of the priests.

18. The so called objective genitive: the priests form "the content" of the kingdom. The meaning is than: the kingdom that consists of priests.

19. The far reaching implications of the use of the word *kohanim* (= priests) sometimes create an interpretative problem in Jewish interpretation of these words. See par example the translation and interpretation in the orthodox Jewish Ḥumash (Sherman, *The Torah*; Ḥumash is the designation of a printed copy of the first five books of the Tora). Thinking of the special position of the priests a rendition ("kingdom of ministers") is given and also an interpretation, which limits the task of the people to instruction analogue to the task of instruction of the priests in Israel.

in the midst of the earth. Also it needs priestly instruction[20] and the priestly service in the Sanctuary. It needs instruction in the ways of the LORD, specifically about the essence and the practice of serving Him. The service of sanctification and purification are needed, along with the service of reconciliation and forgiveness.

Israel does not yet understand its full meaning when God gives this calling from the mountain. But God will give a full instruction in the midst of the people. In His words about the calling, sanctification, task description and task fulfillment of the priests, God will implicitly reveal what His purpose is for Israel. He will teach the people what the priestly task He intended for them is all about. Even more, this priestly nation will also fulfill a royal task.[21] The Scriptures speak of the creation mandate, and man's reign over everything created is in fact already a royal task under God.

The other line of interpretation also shows itself in the calling and history of Israel: certainly God will be king over this people. And surely Israel will be God's kingdom and *all* the people a humble and obedient priesthood.[22]

Both the certainty of God's own kingship over His people, and the calling of the priestly people to be king itself are included in this calling of Israel at Sinai. In Israel's history these lines of God's own kingship and the kingship and priesthood of the people will be interwoven.

7.5 A Holy Nation

With the words "a holy nation," the national existence of Israel is called to holiness. In this characteristic expression God calls His people to share in the holiness that He commands, even to share in the holiness of God Himself. Just as the LORD speaks:

> Be holy because I, the LORD your God, am holy.[23]

There should be a holy people, living a holy life of a different quality, in the midst of the nations. It should be a life of cleaving to God[24] and of obedience to His Tora. It is thus that God also wants His people to be "a light for the Gentiles."[25] A nation where

---

20. Cf. Hos 4:1–10 and Neh 8:10.

21. See par example the prophetic-symbolic crowning of the high priest Joshua and what is said about it (Zech 6:9–15). Cf. also Dan 7:14, 18, 22, 27. Here we find an alternation between the kingship of the Son of Man (vs. 14) and that of "the holy people of the Most High" (vs. 18, 22, 27).

22. See Isa 61:6. Here the word "priests" is further qualified by the word "ministers." Yet a priestly future is promised to all Israel. Hirsch speaks in relation to this about the command for every Israelite to let all his actions be "regulated" by God and to take upon himself the yoke of the Kingdom of Heaven (*Shemoth/Exodus*, 251). Abraham Chill writes in his orthodox Jewish discussion of the God-given commandments ad Lev 22:32: "In the daily routine of his life, whatever he does and says and wherever he goes, the Jew must ask himself whether his deed will bring honor and add luster to the Name of God, or be profaning God's Name" (*The Mitzvot*, 275).

23. Lev 19:2.
24. So Ramban, *Exodus*, 273. Cf. Ps 63:8.
25. Cf. Isa 42:6; 49:6.

He can let His face shine, "so that your ways may be known on earth, your salvation among all nations."[26]

In the words about the holy nation, Jewish scriptural interpretation also finds the promise of eternal life for Israel. This because of the fact that God is holy and because He IS.[27] Or because of words in which a holy existence in Jerusalem is promised to Israel.[28]

7.6 The Calling as a Possibility Today and in the Future

The present and the future of the people are encompassed in this calling of Israel. It is precisely because of the conditions of "hearing" and of "keeping the covenant" that a history is beginning in which obedience and disobedience, trust and disbelief, are possibilities.

And yet, at the deepest level this history is embedded in the unconditional, God-given promise that the world will be blessed through the offspring of Abraham.[29] The covenant made at Sinai is "the more detailed content" of "the blessing of Abraham." Because of this, in one way or the other God's blessing will reach the world through the two-sided covenant of Sinai. Through the ministry of this "treasured possession" people, through this kingdom of priests and this holy nation, the world will be blessed with everything God has to "offer" through and in these priests.

7.7 Once More: Two-sidedness

Whoever reads the Scriptures of Tanakh and knows the history of the people of Israel and its God also knows that because of God's faithfulness, the way of God with Israel did not end. It, however, has also been a way in which the heart of Israel was revealed, revealing everything that exists in human hearts. The entirety of Israel's journey from Sinai until the Promised Land was a road to test the heart.[30] In every respect it was a learning process. All blessings along the road were meant to further trust and obedience. It was a road of hardship because God intended blessing.[31] In Deuteronomy Moses, on behalf of the LORD, exhorts the people to obedience more than once.[32]

---

26. Ps 67:2. This Psalm has a place in the Jewish prayers between *Pessaḥ* and the Festival of Weeks (*Shavuot*). Fifty times in this period of fifty days this Psalm is being recited. This makes visible what the ultimate goal is of the redemption celebrated on *Pessaḥ*.

27. Ramban: "Thus He assured them [of life] in this world and in the World to Come" (*Exodus*, 274).

28. Sforno refers to Isa 4:3 (*Commentary*, 381). In the Septuagint Ps 16:10 says that God did not let "his holy one" in the grave. Cf. the reference to this verse in Acts 2:27.

29. Gen 12:3.

30. Deut 8:2–3; the whole chapter is thus characterized.

31. Deut 8:16.

32. Cf. par example Deut 10:12–15 (following a recalling of a variety of disobedience), after these

He is recalling unfaithfulness and its consequences, along with God's goodness and promises. He tells them to *remember*. Blessing and curses are presented for the people.[33] A particular liturgy about this is taught.[34]

Even still Moses speaks prophetically about being driven away from the land, the exile,[35] but also about returning.[36] Moses, however, also prophesies about the mercy of God which will take form in the circumcision of the heart of the people.[37] God Himself will become Israel's *mohel*.[38] Ultimately, He will not let the hardness of heart win over His irrevocable will to bless the world.[39]

In his last prophetic song Moses looks back over the whole journey of Israel with his God.[40] The evil deeds of Israel are spoken of without any reluctance. They are not sons, but a corrupt nation.[41] Surrounded on all sides by the love of God, the people exchanged the *avoda*, the priestly service to the LORD, for the service to the idols.[42] Therefore God punishes His people severely. Jealous is He![43] He grudges the idols the love to which only He Himself is entitled. But again we hear: He will be merciful. He will not let His people die.

> See now that I myself am he!
> There is no god besides me.
> I put to death and I bring to life,
> I have wounded and I will heal.[44]

---

words the call to circumcise the own heart is heard (vs. 16).

33. Deut 11:26–28 and chapter 28.

34. Deut 27; cf. 11:29–32; Joshua 8:30–35.

35. Deut 30:1–2.

36. Deut 30:3–5.

37. Deut 30:6. The circumcision of the heart as an action by God stands here in the context of return to God. In the way of two-sidedness God will enable His people to become how He had intended them. The mercy that follows conversion ultimately takes away obstinacy that takes place time and again. Even within His mercy God leaves a place for a renewed life according to the covenant.

38. *Mohel* is a Hebrew word designating a person who performs a circumcision.

39. The orthodox Jewish author Michael Wyschogrod writes, "It cannot be denied that Israel's repentance would be very helpful in bringing this about. But in the final analysis it is not completely dependent on such repentance. In the Talmud, too, the desirability of repentance as a means of bringing redemption about is recognized. (But also there it is made clear that, EJW) (. . .) even if repentance is essential to the redemption, God can so arrange things that repentance will occur. (. . .) Exactly how this divine control is exercised cannot be known. Whether God turns the heart of Israel to repentance or whether He brings suffering on Israel which causes repentance (. . .) is immaterial. The point is that human free will cannot be the final determinant of the outcome" (*Abraham's Promise*, 65–67).

40. Deut 32:1–43.

41. Deut 32:5.

42. Deut 32:16–17.

43. Deut 32:21.

44. Deut 32:39.

Moses calls even the nations to rejoice, because God will not leave His downtrodden son under the might of enemies. The closing word is:

> ... he will (...) make atonement for his land and people.[45]

It is obvious that two-sidedness has very painful aspects, both for the people and for God Himself![46] God is journeying with a nation that very often will act contrarily to the characteristics of a priestly nation, a holy nation, a treasured and beloved possession of the LORD. Israel's righteousness is not convincing.[47] But the end will be atonement of/for God's land and His people. With the return of the people to God He will also grant the purification of His land and of the national existence. He will perform both priestly actions.

The book of Deuteronomy ends with a view over the land. The people have yet to enter it, still waiting for the fulfillment of God's promise. But in the way of two-sidedness of the relation between the LORD and His people, the return of Israel to God is also yet to come.[48]

The people that receive its calling at Sinai wait for the full realization of that calling. Yet only God can make this happen. Ultimately only God's own intervention will cause His land to be a blessing in the midst of the earth. Only by the intervention of the LORD Himself will His people be able to live and embody that calling. Only by the LORD Himself will there be blessing for the nations out of the land.

7.8 Priesthood as Model of Interpretation

In sketching out the ongoing canonical narrative, we now have arrived at Sinai. It is here that Israel receives its fully priestly calling. As was previously mentioned,[49] this characterization of the existence and task of Israel presents us with a biblical model of interpretation to first understand both the relationship between Israel and the nations. Second, it allows us to understand the relationship between the *tora* of Israel and the *tora* for the nations. We even find a key to better understand the relationship between the message of the Tanakh and that of the Scriptures of the New Covenant.[50]

When the LORD speaks about His people as a kingdom of priests, His people can not yet understand the meaning, the scope, and the implications of these words.

---

45. Deut 32:43. The LORD Himself will perform this priestly service of atonement.

46. The lamentations of God in Scripture show this undoubtedly. See par example Hos 11:8–9 and Jer 8:4—9:26. This last unit shows that the LORD Himself is lamenting intensely over His "daughter" Israel. The unit 8:13—9:24 forms in the synagogue service the reading from the prophets on the day of commemoration of all disasters that befell Israel (among others the destruction of both Temples), *Tish'a Be'Av* (the ninth day of the month Av).

47. Deut 9:6 concludes to obstinacy instead of righteousness.

48. See also footnote 39 in this chapter.

49. See the Introduction (I.8) and chapter 5 (5.5); see also 7.9 and chapter 8 (8.5).

50. See Part II of this book.

Although there were "priests" in their midst,[51] these men, whatever their task might have been, cannot yet be called priests for the LORD.[52]

First God gives His people His Tora and His covenant.[53] Then the primary command is to make the Tabernacle tent.[54] After all, the heart of Israel's existence and his camp is the Holy One Himself. At first, He gives orders about His own place and Dwelling.[55] After this, He designates the priests for Israel.[56]

It then becomes clear that within the wider circle of the whole people, smaller circles are being drawn.[57] The Levites are set apart from the nation.[58] And from the Levites God chooses Aaron and his sons to be priests before Him.[59]

In this way a visible and living "center of learning" originates in the midst of the nation, in the midst of the camp of Israel.[60] The House of God with its service. And around, it the house of Aaron is God's living "house of learning."

When the people humbly look and listen to this center, they would learn more about Israel's God and His priestly service. This instruction consisted in the life of the priests: their consecration and duties, the requirements that applied to them and their representative function. Of course this was necessary for the actual priestly ministry

---

51. Exod 19:22, 24.

52. Hirsch identifies these priests as the God-dedicated firstborns from the womb (Exod 13:2). Until Sinai their task was to represent their families when sacrifices were offered (*Shemoth/Exodus*, 256).

53. Exod 20–24.

54. Exod 25:1–9.

55. It is remarkable that in Exod 25, following the general command to make the Tabernacle, first of all the command is given to make the ark, the table, and the lampstand. Only then do instructions follow regarding the making of the Tabernacle. The three objects which are connected with the Presence of the LORD (in the Most Holy Place and in the Holy Place; in the inaccessibility of God and in the accessibility of this world) precede the House.

56. Exod 28–29 present the command thereof and the instructions for the consecration.

57. In his monumental commentary on Leviticus, Jacob Milgrom describes how several parallel circle structurings occur around and in the camp of Israel. They are the concentric circles of "*mankind—Israel—priests*"; connected with these the concentric circles (regarding permitted, edible animals) of "*all animals for mankind—few animals for Israel—the sacrifices for the LORD*" and the concentric circles of "*the earth* (for mankind)—*the land* (for Israel and the *ger* [= foreigner] who accepts God's laws and His claim on the land)—*the Sanctuary* (for the priests)" (*Leviticus 1–16*, 722–24). Milgrom describes several similarities between the commandments related to these different circle structurings. Par example: priests *and* sacrificial animals *and* the Sanctuary should be without defect and pure; he points to other similarities in the discussion of requirements for priests and animals in Lev 21 and 22. He also points to the fact that the outer circles are oriented toward the holiness of the center. The holy Presence of God in His Sanctuary asks from His people and the priests an attitude and behavior oriented toward His holiness.

58. See chapter 6, footnote 42 and 43.

59. Exod 28:1.

60. This was the case also in a literal sense. Surrounding the Sanctuary (the center of paramount importance) camped the house of Levi (priests and Levites). The house of Levi again was surrounded by the twelve tribes; three tribes on each side (Num 2).

Part I: The Canonical Narrative: The Tanakh

in the midst of the people, but it also formed one coherent program of instruction about the task of all Israel as the priestly nation in the center of the world.

And so the actual camp of Israel in the desert also became a model, a blueprint of the God-willed and God-ordinated mutual relations on His earth.[61]

At the center of it, visualized as the midst of the earth,[62] was the Dwelling of God. The inner circle of priests and Levites surrounding the Tent formed the utterly real image of the place of the priestly people Israel in the midst of the nations.[63] The outer circle of tribes, on each wind direction camped a group of three tribes,[64] provided an image of (the bridge to) the nations[65] around the chosen people.

The priests formed the link between God and the people, while the people as a whole were meant to be the connecting link to the nations. Therefore *taken* from the nations also implies *representative* of the nations. Taken from the people Israel therefore means: representative of the people. When there is pure service done in the centrally-placed Sanctuary, blessing shall go out to the people. Likewise, when pure service is performed by the priestly people, blessing, atonement, justification, and glory will go out to all the world.

Because of the priestly nature of the calling, the focus of this calling lies not just in Israel itself. The calling is also implicitly given with an eye to the nations.[66]

7.9 Once More: Model of Interpretation

When we recognize the God-intended priesthood of Israel, God provides us with a model of interpretation concerning our understanding of His Tora.[67] There is a visible structuring in "circles" within the Tora that parallels the structuring God ordained in the camp of Israel.

---

61. This desert blueprint stands also model for the future structuring of the land. Than the Temple in Jerusalem is the all-decisive center of the Promised Land. It is surrounded by Jerusalem, that, in its turn, is surrounded by the dwelling places of the tribes. Finally again the land is being surrounded by the nations. Cf. also Ezek 48:8, 15, 21; Zech 2:13.

62. Ps 74:12 (RSV).

63. Cf. Isa 19:24 where Israel is called a blessing in the midst of the earth (NIV: "a blessing on the earth").

64. That the wind directions are named (Num 2) makes clear that the world is envisaged. In Deut 32:8 we find a relation between the nations and the tribes. The four-times-three tribes form—also in the most literal, physical, sense—'the door' to the world of nations. Also in Acts 2 we see that Jews from all wind directions are addressed in the languages of the nations among which they lived or had lived. Obviously they are seen as "bridge head."

65. Also in the description of the Jerusalem from heaven in Rev 21:12 we read that the gates of the city bear the names of the tribes of Israel. The tribes of Israel form so to say the "entrance" to the city of God. Through the gates (= the tribes of Israel) the kings of the nations enter with their splendor the city of God (21:24–26). Also in Zech 2:11 we read that the nations seek God, who dwells in the midst of Israel.

66. See further chapter 8.

67. See the Introduction (I.8) and chapter 5 (5.5); see also 7.9 and chapter 8 (8.5).

At first there is the *tora*[68] for the priests[69] and the Sanctuary, with everything concerning the functioning of the priests and their duties.

Then there is the *tora* for all Israel. Through it the whole people, including the priests, is set apart in the circle of the nations.[70] In the God-ordained keeping of His laws, there is both a unity *and* a distinction between priests and the people as a whole.

Thirdly, there are the commandments which Israel shares with all nations. Because Israel has been chosen from the nations and yet it is one of the nations, it shares in the *tora* that has been given to all nations while at the same time receiving its "own" *tora*, one that focuses on its life as a priestly nation. Finally, there is for those from the nations who live in the land, the "foreigners among you," a small category of commandments and prohibitions relating to the shared life and the purity of the land.[71]

This biblical model of interpretation relating to the Tora is preferred by far to all other extra-biblical categories.[72] It is also helpful in understanding the relationship between the commandments of Israel and the Scriptures of the New Covenant.[73]

Above all, at the heart of these "circles," the self-revelation of God takes place: He is found dwelling in the midst of His people. His Presence in the Tabernacle and the Temple, the center of the national existence, creates a decisive difference between Israel and the nations. Of the LORD's self-revelation in the midst of Israel[74] (and thus in the center of the earth), it is written:

> For his compassions never fail.
> They are new every morning;

---

68. I use the word *tora* here as designation of a part of God's instructions dealing with special occasions or a special group of people. For the use of this terminology see Lev 6:9, 14, 25 (dealing with sacrifices) and Num 5:12–31 and 6:1–21 (concerning people).

69. Par example the commandments concerning the priestly garments, the marriage of priests and high priests, the honoring of priests, defects causing unfitness for priestly service, the blessing, the dwelling places, and all instructions concerning the service in the Sanctuary and the priestly share in the sacrifices.

70. Ps 147 speaks about the giving of the Tora and than says in verse 20, "He has done this for no other nation; they do not know his laws."

71. See chapter 5 (5.3), especially also footnotes 18–24.

72. Hays, ("Applying," 21–35), argues rightly the case for not using any more extra-biblical categories (i.e., differentiating between ceremonial, civil and moral laws) in the process of discerning (within the Christian community) the ongoing validity of the law sections from the Tora. However, he than again uses anew an extra-biblical terminology. Pleading the case for "principlism" (30) he looks for "universal, timeless principles" which lie behind "the Mosaic commands for the original audience" (31). Even when it concerns a general application of a section of the Tora, it still is something that has been revealed *within* the Tora. Because he does not consider the possibility of a difference in *tora* within the Body of the Messiah he can easily interpret "Mosaic Law" as something that belonged to a bygone era (and act accordingly). In his thinking there also is no place for an ongoing validity of the Tora in "the gospel of the circumcision" (this expression is used in Gal 2:1–10; NIV: "preaching the gospel to the circumcised"). See further chapter 20.

73. See the last paragraph (7.8).

74. See par example Joel 2:27; Zeph 3:15, 17; Zech 2:10–11.

Part I: The Canonical Narrative: The Tanakh

great is your faithfulness.[75]

7.10 Waiting for . . .

At Sinai Israel receives a comprehensive calling. It is embedded in the ways of obedience. God's choice to realize this priesthood of Israel through the obedient surrender of this people causes a history to begin: of hearing and not-hearing, of obedience and disobedience. And yet, the outcome is certain: this people will fulfill its calling to the fullest. Ultimately the sanctification of God's Name will be protected and realized by Himself.[76] If only because of His own Name and because of His promise given. This people will become and be a priestly blessing in the center of the earth. Israel and all the world can wait for it. That is why until today Israel prays:

> Bring us back, our Father,
> to Your Torah.
> Draw us near, our King,
> to Your service.
> Lead us back to You in perfect repentance.
> Blessed are You, LORD, who desires repentance.
> Find favor, LORD our God,
> in Your people Israel and their prayer.
> Restore the service to Your most holy House,
> and accept in love and favor
> the fire-offerings of Israel and their prayer.
> May the service of Your people Israel always find favor with You.
> And may our eyes witness
> Your return to Zion in compassion.
> Blessed are You, LORD,
> who restores His Presence to Zion.[77]

---

75. Lam 3:22–23.

76. See Ezek 36:22–23 and the promises connected therewith (vss. 24–38) of return, purification, giving of the Holy Spirit, repentance, living in the land, rebuilding and multiplication of the people.

77. The blessings "Repentance" and "Temple service" from the *Amida* (the standing prayer) also called the *Shemoneh Esrei* (literally: eighteen blessings), taken from Sacks (*The Koren Siddur*, 114 and 126).

CHAPTER 8

The Consecration of Priests and of Israel as a Priestly Nation

Waiting for the Eighth Day

8.1 The Words and Covenant of God

THE CALLING OF ISRAEL by God can be compared to a marriage proposal.[1] After a three-day period of preparation, the marriage covenant between God and His people is made. From beneath the *ḥuppa*, the bridal canopy of the dark cloud hovering over Sinai, the revelation of the marriage contract, the *ketuba*, takes place. When God utters the Ten Words not only Israel[2] but the whole world[3] witnesses the greatness of this revelation. Commandments are given by God, promises anew spoken by Him.[4] From beneath the overshadowing of God's Presence on the top of the mountain the covenant[5] is made at the foot of it.[6] Israel becomes God's *segula*, His most treasured

---

1. Cf. Jer 2:2–3. Also God's merciful and renewed salvation of His people has "the colors" of a marriage (Hos 2:14–16). Ezek 16:8 speaks in the same manner of a marital covenant between the LORD and Jerusalem.

2. Exod 20:18.

3. The Hebrew text speaks of "voices." In Jewish interpretation these voices are thought to be the seventy languages in which God announced the Ten Words to all the world. In Acts 2 we read about an audible and visible remembrance of the appearance of the LORD on Sinai. Also there and then the nations are spoken to in their own language while fiery languages ("tongues," vss. 3 and 4) are visible.

4. Exod 20:22—23:33.

5. Exod 24:3–8.

6. Milgrom joins Ramban (Nachmanides) in pointing out a parallel between the (theophany on) Sinai and the Tabernacle. He even points out more resemblances than Ramban does. The Sinai is "the archetype of the Tabernacle and is similarly divided into three gradations of holiness." The summit is the Most Holy Place. The part of the mountain which is clouded can be compared to the Holy Place of the Tabernacle. And the "foot of the mountain" is comparable with the courtyard of the Tabernacle which could be entered by all people if cleansed and sanctified. Milgrom respectively refers to Exod

possession. The people affirm their unconditional dedication.[7] Then a banquet of mercy and an encounter with God takes place on the mountain.[8]

After this celebration Moses receives the call to climb up to God.[9] The glory of God rests upon the mountain. Somewhere halfway the mountain Moses—Israel's representative—halts and waits. Six days of waiting. On the seventh day Moses is called.[10] At that moment he may enter the cloud.

Hidden by cloud and fire the LORD speaks to him.

8.2 I Will Dwell in their Midst

God speaks with Moses on the summit of the mountain, yet He does not dwell in their midst. But that will change.

> Then let them make a sanctuary for me, and I will dwell among them.[11]

The Presence of the LORD Himself will be the all-dominating center of Israel's camp, and later also of the land in the midst of the earth.[12] Therefore God, when the covenant has been made, speaks about the making of His Tabernacle first of all. He wants to dwell in Israel's midst, both in the darkness of the Most Holy Place and in the accessibility of the Holy Place. His Presence visualized by and connected with the ark, table, and lampstand. Israel has an opportunity to participate from their heart.[13] In the midst of the earth, life should be lived out of the center of life.

The priestly *segula*-nation learns that serving the LORD should be according to what God ordains and designates. No self-made design, no self-invented or self-willed service. Everything should be according to what has been spoken and after patterns

---

19:20; 20:21; 24:15–18, and to 19:17 and 24:4. Thus Moses is entering the Most Holy Place like a high priest (*Leviticus 1–16*, 142–43)! Cf. also footnote 52 of this chapter dealing with the non-Aaronic priesthood of Moses. See further chapter 7 (footnote 57) and chapter 9 (9.6) for the three grades/circles of sanctity in the camp and the land. Also in Jerusalem were three circles of sanctity, i.e., the Temple, the mountain and the city; so p. xlviii of the general introduction to the Talmud tractate b. Yoma, Schottenstein Edition; cf. also chapter 3 (footnote 1).

7. Exod 24:7. The sequence of the words used in Hebrew is remarkable and being emphasized within Jewish interpretation: first "do" and then "hear." Even before God is speaking the people is ready to "do." The "hearing" takes place within basic and fundamental dedication and obedience. NIV translates the Hebrew "we will hear" as "we will obey"; this has the effect that the distinction between "to do" and "to hear" is less clear.

8. Exod 24:9–11.

9. Exod 24:12.

10. Exod 24:16.

11. Exod 25:8. The heading of this paragraph is in line with the RSV. The dwelling of the LORD formed really the *midst* of the camp of Israel.

12. This theme will be discussed in chapter 9 (9.6).

13. Exod 25:1–2.

that have been shown.[14] This applies not only to the design and the making of the Tent,[15] but also to the consecration of the priests and their garments.[16] It applies to the sacrifices and the incense-offering for the morning and the evening,[17] and the choice of the men who will have to realize God's designs.[18] Furthermore God's *segula*-nation receives the *Shabbat* as token of its sanctification.[19]

Whilst the Holy One speaks from His heart in describing the Dwelling and the befitting service intended to take place there, something terrible happens at the foot of the mountain. The hearts of the people[20] turn away from the LORD. The covenantal love of God which they saw and heard with their own eyes and ears is not sufficient for them. Forty days without Moses is too long for Israel. The distance to the summit of the mountain—still enfolded in dark clouds—too great. In flagrant contradiction with the Ten Words a golden calf is made—possibly as symbolic visualization of the might of the LORD.[21] The whole procedure takes place under the guidance of Aaron.[22] Under the guidance of the chosen high priest the chosen priestly nation exchanged its Glory through this.

> At Horeb they made a calf
> and worshiped an idol cast from metal.
> They exchanged their glorious God
> for an image of a bull, which eats grass.
> They forgot the God who saved them,

---

14. Exod 25:9; cf. 1 Chr 28:19, also the building of the Temple should be according to the revelation (that David) received.

15. Exod 25:10–27:21; 30:11–38.

16. Exod 28:1—29:37.

17. Exod 29:38—30:10.

18. Bezalel and Oholiab; Exod 31:1–11.

19. Exod 31:12–17. *The Jewish Study Bible* points to the fact that the instructions for the making of the Dwelling are given in seven separate divine commands and that all culminates in the *Shabbat*, a structure which parallels the description of the creation in Gen 1–2 (*JSB*, 165).

20. It can be observed that the serious character of Israel's sin can cause some embarrassment in Jewish interpretation. According to the commentary of Raphael Pelcovitz in the edition of Sforno (*Commentary*, 451) the making of the golden calf was instigated by the leaders of the "mixed multitude" (Exod 12:38, RSV) and only a small part of the people was actually involved in it although the majority did not resist the plan.

21. We read that "a festival to the LORD" is celebrated (Exod 32:5). Was the golden calf meant to be a visible aid in the service to the LORD? Was it meant to be an other aid besides God, like the "disappeared" Moses had been?

22. Jewish interpreters can struggle with the involvement of Aaron. Sherman has the opinion that this could not have been a case of idolatry, or else Aaron would have died and he then certainly could not have become the high priest! If this should have been the case the first high priest of Israel would have sinned where innumerable thousands of Israel offered their lives in order not to sin in idolatry. Therefore Aaron one way or the other must have tried to correct the course of the people (*The Torah*, 493).

Part I: The Canonical Narrative: The Tanakh

who had done great things in Egypt.[23]

The heart of God has been hurt and offended. He wants, in a very literal sense, to get rid of the people and realize His promises otherwise. But Moses pleads with God. He pleads for the priestly people—he performs a high priestly task on behalf of the people including the intended/designated priests and high priest.

This priestly action by Moses has the effect that God retracts His threatening words.[24] Yet, the people are punished[25] and Moses climbs anew up to the LORD in order to plead for forgiveness and ask for God's abiding Presence.[26] For the Presence of God is at stake. Will the people have the privilege to know that God Himself is in their midst? Or shall only an angel be their company from now on?[27]

In a special tent, pitched far outside the camp, Moses meets the LORD. God speaks with him as with a friend. In this merciful confidentiality Moses cautiously touches on the essential question. Who will accompany the people? God gives a clear answer:

> My Presence will go with you, and I will give you rest.[28]

God will go Himself and give Moses rest. But does this also apply to the people? Moses, in his answer, makes it clear that only the very Presence of God makes Israel different from the nations. Oh, that the Holy One would accompany them and be in their midst! Had that not been God's intention when He thought of such special place for Israel?[29] Again Moses pleads as a high priest for the priestly nation. And again he is allowed to climb up to the Lord and even to see God's glory.[30]

A self-revelation of God is granted to Moses. The Holy One reveals Himself while Moses pleads on behalf of the stubborn people.[31] Again there are promises and words of the covenant written in a book and on two new stone tablets.[32] Again there is a forty day period; however the people now wait at the foot of the mountain.

Then Moses climbs down from God's Presence. He is the living proof that God does not want to withhold His Presence from the people. Moses's face is radiant because of God's glory.[33] Thus God's glory now shines at the foot of the mountain. The

---

23. Ps 106:19–21.
24. Exod 32:14.
25. Exod 32:25–29.
26. Exod 32:30–34.
27. Exod 33:2–3.
28. Exod 33:14. The "rest" can also point to the rest of entering the Promised Land (cf. Ps 95:11).
29. Exod 33:16.
30. Exod 33:18–23 and 34:4–7.
31. Exod 34:8–9.
32. Exod 34:10–28.
33. Exod 34:29–35.

making of the Tent takes a start.[34] God wants to dwell in the midst of the people. Out of pure mercy and goodness the Creator of heaven and earth wants to dwell in the midst of His creation. The earth is granted a place where God is coming near to His people and where the chosen nation may come near to Him. Here the service to Him may be performed.

The people willingly contribute[35] now that their hearts are directed toward the LORD. Men and women bring their personal treasures.[36] The book of Exodus further describes the making of everything that is part of God's Dwelling and ends with the consecration of the Tabernacle. In the account expressions are used which are also found in the account of the creation in Genesis 1–2.[37] The indwelling of the LORD is thereby designated as the beginning of the re-creation. A new creation begins on the first day of the first month with the setting up of the Tabernacle.

The Holy God dwells in the midst of His people. For the present moment they are still in the desert, but now underway toward the land in the center of the earth.

8.3 The Consecration of the Priests

It had been God's command, that when the Tabernacle was ready to be filled by His Presence, the priests should also be made ready for their service in that Dwelling.[38] The details of their own consecration had even been commanded.[39] No service to the LORD without preparations according to God's instructions!

All Israel was to gather at the entrance of the Tent[40] so that everyone could see how the priests were to be consecrated. The priestly nation, itself called by God, is shown how men from within their midst will become priests of the LORD.[41] Through this the people also receive fundamental lessons regarding the priesthood of all Israel. One of the main proponents of this book is to postulate that God wants to shape the priesthood of the whole people according to the model of the priesthood within Israel. By paying accurate attention to the priesthood of Aaron and his sons, Israel would learn God's intentions. Therefore it is important to give full attention to the different elements of the consecration of the priests.

34. Exod 35:4–29.
35. Exod 35:5, 21–22, 26, 29.
36. Compare with the contrasting Exod 32:2–3.
37. JSB, 200–202 draws attention to resemblances in the use of words in Exod 39:32—40:33. Parallel usage can be observed around: "the finishing of the work," the "see"-ing that everything is ready, the "sanctification" so that the Tent "will be holy," the sevenfold repetition "that everything had been made/done according to God's command."
38. Exod 40:12–16.
39. See Exod 29:1–37.
40. Lev 8:3.
41. The consecration of priests is spoken of and presupposed in Exod 40. The factual description we read in Lev 8–9.

Part I: The Canonical Narrative: The Tanakh

1. First of all Israel sees how Moses lets Aaron and his sons be brought to him in order to be consecrated. God's command is decisive. He calls His chosen ones "from among the Israelites."[42]

2. Then they are undressed and washed—immersed as in a bath of purification.[43] Naked for God. He sees and knows our lives and hearts. All distinctive differences are done away with. No approaching the Holy One without purification.

3. Subsequently Aaron receives from Moses his high priestly garments.[44] "God-fashion" with deep meaning in stead of human fashion.[45] For: ". . . as the LORD commanded Moses."[46]

4. Finally, after the anointing of the Tabernacle and all utensils thereof, Aaron is anointed.[47] Anointed unto sanctification[48] and dedication to God. In His power.[49]

5. The other priests are being clothed,[50] in pure linen garments,[51] ornamented with a pure head covering.

6. Moses then acts as a "non-Aaronic priest," who offers the sin-offering for the priests.[52]

7. The sin-offering consists in a bull—let no (high) priest think his own sin is light! The priests press their hands on the head of the bull and thus lay their own iniquity upon the animal.[53] Its blood purifies the altar. The bull is then burned outside the camp.

---

42. Exod 28:1.

43. Lev 8:6. Washed by immersion—as in a *mikva* (Jewish ritual bath). I follow in this Milgrom who concludes this, referring to the used Hebrew preposition (*in* water) and also to Lev 16:4 and 24, and joining Rashi and other interpreters (see Milgrom, *Leviticus 1–16*, 501).

44. Lev 8:6–9.

45. Exod 28; 39:1–31.

46. Lev 8:9, 13.

47. Lev 8:12.

48. Lev 8:12.

49. Cf. Zech 4:1–6.

50. Lev 8:13.

51. Exod 28:40–43.

52. Lev 8:15. Cf. Ps 99:6: "Moses and Aaron were among his priests." The sages of Israel have discussed the question how far this actual high priesthood of Moses went (see Milgrom, *Leviticus 1–16*, 555).

53. Lev 8:14.

8. Moses brings the burnt-offering for Aaron and his sons.[54] Again their hands are pressed on the animal's head. The burnt-offering also has an element of atonement[55] besides that of total dedication.[56]

9. Finally the ram of ordination is slaughtered, again after hands are laid upon its head.[57] In a certain sense this animal is (by this procedure) also representative of the priests.

10. With the ram's blood, the right ear, thumb and big toe of the priests are touched as a sign. The hearing, doing, and comings and goings of the new priests are being purified and dedicated to the Holy One.[58]

11. By a special ceremony, the life of Aaron and his sons is dedicated to the LORD as a wave offering,[59] where part of the meat of the ram of ordination is being placed on the hands of the priests and becomes presented to the LORD through a movement toward the LORD and back. Following this, it is placed on the altar as a symbol of their lives.

12. All priests are sprinkled with the holy anointing oil and with blood.[60]

13. They have to eat the meat of the ram of the ordination at the entrance to the Tabernacle.[61]

14. For seven days they must undergo this consecration liturgy.[62] Each day they become further removed from their former status, and each day they come nearer to the calling that God has intended for them.[63]

15. For seven days they must therefore stay at the entrance of the Tent.[64]

16. For seven days they wait for the eighth day. Only then, on the eighth day, may they begin to function as priests.

---

54. Lev 8:18–19.
55. Lev 1:4. Also Sforno draws attention to this (*Commentary*, 521).
56. Lev 8:20–21.
57. Lev 8:22–23.
58. Lev 8:23–24.
59. Lev 8:25–28.
60. Lev 8:30.
61. Lev 8:31–32.
62. Milgrom shows that the terminology used in Lev 8:33 points to a seven day repetition of the whole liturgy. He mentions that this is also the opinion of the sages of Israel and refers among other to Midrash Leviticus Rabbah 10:8. Possibly only the anointing of the Tent was excluded from this repetition (*Leviticus 1–16*, 538–40). Also Flavius Josephus (in his book *Antiquities of the Jews*, about the history of the Jewish people) mentions a seven-day consecration of the priests (III, 206).
63. The seven days form a time of transition. The sevenfold repetition was meant to underline the special character of the priesthood (so Milgrom, *Leviticus 1–16*, 538).
64. Lev 8:33–35.

Part I: The Canonical Narrative: The Tanakh

The phases of consecration enumerated here were and still are an opportunity for learning, both for Israel and the nations. Priesthood is being called by God, from a larger whole into service to the LORD. It is, in the first place, meant to honor the Holy God, but also a service considering that larger whole. It is first of all, by the service of God's servant,[65] to become purified and humbled. It is a call to the task of atonement in view of the adoration and worship of the LORD. To be a priest is to become a living wave offering. It is to live an existence that has been offered to God and has also been received back again. Near the Tent. Waiting for the Eighth Day.

8.4 Waiting for the Eighth Day

It is remarkable that as a community the consecrated priests must remain for seven days at the entrance of the Tent. To leave was asking for death.[66] Consecrated and yet waiting. Prepared, but not yet completely; the waiting for the eighth day completed the consecration. The people who attended the consecration ceremony were allowed to return to their tents,[67] the people, but not the priests. The priestly service in the Tabernacle was not yet allowed to begin. The altar was also waiting for the eighth day. For seven days in a row Moses offers a sin-offering and cleanses, atones, and anoints the altar.[68] Should the creation enter into a new existence? Is it only after the first seven days that the *avoda* can begin in the morning light of the eighth day?

Excursus: The Eighth Day: Messianic Coloring of the Number Eight

In the Tanakh the eighth day plays an intriguing role. The eighth day is the day of the coming of God in holiness and purifying judgment in the generation of Noah.[69] Also it is the day of promise, the day of the leaf of the olive tree.[70]

The first time that God explicitly underlines the special character of the eighth day, is when He commands Abraham (and his offspring) to circumcise the newborn

---

65. It is remarkable that the Aaronic priesthood in Israel itself has to be served by Moses. Priests never appoint themselves; they are prepared. In this first beginning the consecration is led and effectuated by a non-priest. Milgrom postulates that Moses as the leader of Israel—in fact as a king—is performing this consecration. He points to parallels in Mesopotamian documents where kings lead temple consecration ceremonies (*Leviticus 1–16*, 577). Cf. footnote 52 in this chapter.

66. Lev 8:35.

67. The people however had to appear all those seven days anew at the entrance of the Tent. See footnote 62 in this chapter.

68. Exod 29:37.

69. Gen 7:4, 10 speaks in fact about the eighth day: "seven days from now" (vs. 4), "after the seven days" (vs. 10).

70. Gen 8:11.

The Consecration of Priests and of Israel as a Priestly Nation

males on the eighth day:[71] "Every male among you who is eight days old."[72] Obediently Abraham circumcises Isaac on that day.[73] The firstborns of the cattle and sheep were also dedicated to the LORD on that day.[74]

On the eighth day the altar was consecrated and made ready for service.[75] We later read in Ezekiel of the same timing with respect to the altar when the LORD has returned to His Temple.[76]

On the eighth day the priests are allowed to begin serving God.[77] On that day for the first time the people receive the blessing of the high priest,[78] whose garments consist of eight different parts.[79] Later that day the people receive the blessing of both Moses and Aaron.[80] On that eighth day the glory of the LORD appears and touches the altar with fire.[81]

The eighth day also plays a role in the purification of a leper. On that day he is allowed to approach God with sacrifices. Just like the priests, he is then purified and sanctified in hearing, doing, and walking.[82] On the eighth day an unclean man or woman was allowed to once again enter the Sanctuary, after they had undergone a seven-day period of purification.[83] The same applies to a Nazirite whose Nazirite-ship had been defiled through contact with a dead body.[84]

The eighth day of the Feast of Tabernacles also received a special character from God,[85] which was loving intimacy and dedication to the LORD.[86] When the Temple had been built and consecrated, the people returned to their homes on that day; a new

---

71. Gen 17:12.

72. Gen 17:12; Lev 12:3.

73. Gen 21:4.

74. Exod 22:30.

75. Exod 29:37. Milgrom has the opinion that this eight-day period of consecration became a paradigm for later accomplished consecrations of the temple (*Leviticus 1–16*, 593). Cf. also 2 Chr 7:9 (a seven-day celebration because of the consecration of the altar).

76. Ezek 43:26–27.

77. Lev 9:1.

78. Lev 9:22.

79. Exod 28:4, 36, 42. In Jewish interpretation special attention is given to these eight different parts.

80. Lev 9:23.

81. Lev 9:24.

82. Lev 14:10, 23.

83. Lev 15:14, 29.

84. Num 6:10.

85. Lev 23:36, 39; Num 29:35; cf. 1 Kgs 8:66; 2 Chr 7:9; Neh 8:19.

86. Within Judaism this eighth day of the Feast of Tabernacles, *Shemini Atzeret*, has the character of a day of special intimacy and dedication to the LORD. It is also the day of *Simḥat Tora*, "Rejoicing of Tora," which celebrates the Tora.

situation had arrived: the Dwelling of the LORD in the midst of the land and of their lives.[87]

In Hezekiah's time the purification of the Temple was also completed in eight days.[88] And Josiah began to search the LORD earnestly in the eighth year of his reign.[89]

Also the number eight itself received a special Messianic coloring because of David's being the eighth son of Jesse.[90] The passing by of the first seven, these not-chosen sons of Jesse, served as a preparation for the appearance of the eighth son.[91]

Eight is also the number of those who survived the flood and were allowed to form the new beginning of humanity.[92]

Eight also rings of the Messianic salvation in the eight princely commanders who will stand up for Israel in the Messianic prophecy.[93]

It seems that the LORD God, in all sorts of ways, has marked the eighth day as a day of new beginnings, of completed purification and accomplished sanctification. A day of blessing, of new life spared in the covenant. Of dedication and Messianic blessing. A day on which the LORD appears with blessing and fire.

The "waiting for the eighth day" is then also a sign of the waiting for the full realization of the priesthood of Israel. Of waiting for the realization of everything that is implied in the calling of Israel. "Waiting for the eighth day" then means so much as "waiting for the *olam haba*,"[94] the world-to-come, the coming era of the kingdom of God. After the "first seven days of consecration and sanctification," the new era of God begins.

8.5 The Consecration of Priests: A Model of Instruction for the Consecration of the People as a Whole

When Israel is called at Sinai, it becomes clear that God intends a special task as kingdom of priests for His treasured possession. It also becomes clear that the realization

---

87. 1 Kgs 8:66; 2 Chr 7:10.

88. 2 Chr 29:17; cf. the eight day period of celebrations related to the sanctification of the Temple at the time of the Maccabees (1 Maccabees 4:56, 59), the origin of the Feast of Ḥannuka (the Hebrew word means consecration).

89. 2 Chr 34:3.

90. 1 Sam 17:12.

91. 1 Sam 16:10.

92. Cf. 1 Pet 3:20.

93. Mic 5:4, cf. the context of the whole of Mic 5. Cf. Rev 17:11 for the description of the pseudo-Messiah. The fact that he is also "an eighth king," shows that even the number eight is not safe for God's adversary.

94. In Judaism the distinction is customary between *olam haze* (the world that is now/the present era and reality) and *olam haba* (the world-to-come).

The Consecration of Priests and of Israel as a Priestly Nation

of this calling, throughout a history of faithfulness and infidelity, is secured. God Himself is guaranteeing this. Ultimately the whole of Israel will be a priestly nation in the midst of the earth.

By paying attention to the structure and meaning of the priestly consecration *within* Israel, we also gain insight in different aspects of the priesthood of *all* Israel. In a very detailed manner God has ordained the consecration of the priests. Therefore those details were and still are very meaningful; they are a message from God. In a prophetic way the structure of the priestly consecration teaches both Israel and us about God's intentions. It is also through this consecration that the God of Israel directs our attention and lives to the *tikkun olam*, the consummation of the whole of God's creation work.[95]

Just like the Aaronic priests in its midst, Israel will have a representative place in the midst of the nations. It will be oriented toward God and mediate blessing for the nations.

Israel as a whole will therefore have to be purified and clothed as priests.[96] But first it will have to be unclothed, stripped naked. Is there an indication of suffering implied, as Israel will have to be purified[97] as in a ritual bath of purification, a *mikva*? It will have to be clothed in "garments of salvation."[98] Israel as a whole will need the Messianic anointing. Through confession of sins and atonement, the burnt-offering of its life, and dedication to the priestly *avoda,* all Israel will be a wave offering for the LORD, both priest and priestly sacrifice.

Beginning with Sinai this has been anticipated. On "the Eighth Day" this all will come to pass. Can we hope that on that day, in that era, the *avoda* in Israel will be made completely perfect? And then, because of this, a fountain of blessing will be opened for the nations? Will this new era begin after "the first seven days"?[99]

This "waiting for the Eighth Day" creates room for Israel's history as a priestly nation. Seen in this light the "waiting" is also a biblical model of interpretation that helps

---

95. See chapter 1 (1.4) and 2 (2.2).

96. Deut 18:15–18 speaks of a Moses-like prophet who will be raised up by God. He will be "from among you" (vs. 15). In Jewish interpretation this implies a promise of the prophets designated as a special group (Rashi). Also that prophecy would only be given within the land or in relation to the land (Ramban), and that the Spirit would only rest on Israelites (Ramban). The Hebrew text however, speaks in the first place of *a* prophet (singular). Within the Judaism of the second Temple period (around the beginning of the Christian calendar era), therefore the expectation of "the Prophet" could also be found (see par example John 1:21, 25; cf. also 1:46 in that context).

97. Zechariah foresees such a purification of the whole nation (Zech 13:1). Cf. also Ezek 36:25 and the Mishnaic (Yoma 8.9) /Talmudic saying (b Yoma 85b) "The mikva of Israel is HaShem." This saying of Rabbi Akiva is based on a reading of Jer 17:13 ("LORD, you are the hope of Israel") whereby the word "hope" is interpreted as pointing to a ritual bath (in Hebrew the same word). Ezek 36:25 is then interpreted along this line.

98. Isa 61:10; see also vs. 6. There the whole of the people is designated as "priests of the LORD."

99. In the prophecies of Daniel we also read of "weeks" as designation of periods/era's. The rendering of NIV in Daniel 9 is "sevens" ("weeks" is mentioned as an alternative).

Part I: The Canonical Narrative: The Tanakh

us to grasp both the present and the future, the calling and its realization, the continuity and the expectation of the future of God's people. The "waiting for the Eighth Day" is a denominator under which the whole history of Israel can be captured. The whole of the history of faithfulness and infidelity, entry and conquest, of judges and prophets, kings and priests, of living in the land and exile, of return and waiting for the Messiah and the Messianic times.

It even can be postulated that the Tora is underway, together with the people. And that also the Tora looks for this "Eighth Day."[100]

8.6 Toward the One Place of Worship and Toward the Eighth Day

At Sinai God comes to dwell in the midst of His people. The life of the priestly people encamped around the Sanctuary and its priests begins. The camp is being structured around the all-dominating center.[101] Now the journey to the Promised Land can begin, a journey toward the one place of worship in the midst of the earth.[102] To the place where God's "kingdom of priests," with all its implications, will be fully realized.

---

100. See for this theme chapter 19.
101. Num 1–2.
102. Cf. Deut 12:1, 5.

CHAPTER 9

Priestly Nation around the One Sanctuary
Priests around the Dwelling

9.1 Different Perspectives

AFTER THE MOMENTOUS EVENTS at Sinai, the long journey toward the realization of the calling of Israel begins. And so ends chapter 8. In three chapters which deal with the same long period from a chronological viewpoint, we will now look at this long journey from three different perspectives.

The focus of this chapter will be the priestly nation[1] around the one Sanctuary. First we will look at specific aspects the calling of a priestly people encamped around God's Dwelling entails. God's Presence in the center of the nation requires both holy service and the sanctity of the whole people. In a special manner this people receives its place around God's Tent. And so it becomes a holy circle around this most holy center of all creation. The structure of Israel's camp in the desert is also maintained in the Promised Land. There the tribes receive their dwelling places around the city of Jerusalem, of which the Temple is the center. Time and again we meet the concentric circles of most holy, holy, non-holy or ordinary.[2] It is according to this structure that God orders His Sanctuary, His people, and also the world. And this structuring of Israel's dwelling place around the Dwelling of God also happens so that the world will ultimately be blessed from this center.

---

1. The royal aspect of Israel's calling comes forward only later in Israel's history. See further chapter 10.
2. See also chapter 8, footnote 6.

Part I: The Canonical Narrative: The Tanakh

9.2 Pure Service

The book of Exodus closes with the report of the set up and consecration of the Tent, as well as the altar and the priests. Within the Tora Leviticus then follows, dealing with the task of the priests[3] of Israel's God and the service and purity of the priestly nation.[4] In it, the God who dwells in the midst of the people, speaks of the service He desires in the Sanctuary.

The book of Leviticus begins[5] with instruction about the sacrifices; of those the burnt offering is discussed first. It is here that the tone is set: burnt offerings, with all implied meanings, form the primary task of all Israel. Burnt offerings burnt in totality;[6] they are an expression of the heart and life of the offerer,[7] and they also have an atoning function.[8] Nobody eats of them: this offering is a pure gift to God. This is the prescribed *avoda* for Israel.

9.3 A Holy Service Needs a Holy Fire

For the newly consecrated priests and the witnesses of this consecration, the death of two of Aaron's sons[9] was a grim reminder of the fact that Israel's service could not be self-invented or self-willed.[10] Precisely on the day their consecration was completed,[11] the eighth day on which the majesty of the LORD appeared and the fire came down on the altar, Nadab and Abihu bring "strange," or "unauthorized" fire.[12]

---

3. The name Leviticus, originating in the Septuagint, has nothing to do with the Levites. In Hellenistic times "Levites" was the designation for priests (Milgrom, *Leviticus 1–16*, 1). Milgrom mentions that "Leviticus" is an equivalent for the rabbinic designation *torat kohanim*, which he renders as "the manual of the Priests." The book Leviticus hardly pays any attention to the Levites.

4. From earliest rabbinic times Leviticus functioned as the basic teaching book of the Jewish "primary school" (Ibid., 3). Milgrom refers to a saying in Midrash Rabbah Leviticus (7:2) in which the purity of children is being connected with the purity of the sacrifices and where we hear: "Let the pure come and engage in the study of the pure."

5. The sequence in Leviticus is not necessarily chronological. According to a common Jewish hermeneutical principle there is no "earlier or later" in the Tora. The *tora* about the consecration of the priests in chapters 8–9 however certainly will have been given before this consecration—mentioned shortly in Exod 40—took place. This is also the opinion of Jewish interpreters. See also footnote 37 of this chapter.

6. Lev 1:9.

7. Lev 1:4. The laying on of hands makes the animal into the representative of the one offering.

8. Lev 1:4.

9. Lev 10:1–7.

10. Lev 10:1.

11. Lev 10:12–20 shows that the sacrifices presented to the LORD had not yet been eaten. Cf. the "today" in vs. 19.

12. "Strange" (in Hebrew *zar/zara*) meaning "unauthorized" (NIV) and thus "unholy" (RSV) we already met in the expression *avoda zara* ("strange service" = idolatry). The Hebrew text of Exod 30:9 mentions "strange incense" (cf. also vss. 34–38, especially vs. 37). Milgrom shows that "strange fire" has to mean that Nadab and Abihu did not use fire/fiery coals from the altar, but took their fire from

Instead of using the fire that has been ignited by the LORD,[13]—the fire that should not ever go out[14]—they create a new fire, made by human hands. It is then that the fire of the LORD hits them.[15]

> Moses then said to Aaron, "This is what the LORD spoke of when he said: "'Among those who approach me I will be proved holy; in the sight of all the people I will be honored.'" Aaron remained silent.[16]

Thus this eighth day brings Israel not only the Indwelling of God, God coming to His Dwelling in the midst of the people, but also judgment and sanctification of God's Name. Other places in the Tanakh also show these two sides of God's coming.[17] The eighth day, and everything this day represents prophetically, is also a "day of great holiness," on which God's great holiness is honored; if not by humans then by God Himself!

The reaction of the brand new high priest Aaron shows his humility. In remaining silent Aaron honors God. He and his remaining sons are not allowed to interrupt their priestly service in order to mourn. This is the price of their high calling. To be chosen implies that judgment hits the chosen ones first if needed.[18] In the lives of Aaron and his sons, the priestly nation sees how high and holy the priestly calling is. Only he who fulfills the prescribed service is allowed to come near to God. God Himself guards his Sanctuary and wants His people to live around it. In that manner He separates His people from the nations.

9.4 Priestly Distinctions and Priestly Separation

Priests must be able to distinguish between holy and unholy,[19] pure and impure.[20] It is because of this that they must always be clear-minded when serving in the Sanctuary.[21]

---

somewhere else (*Leviticus 1–16*, 598).

13. Lev 9:24. Also the fire upon the altar in the newly consecrated Temple built by Salomon was ignited by the LORD Himself (2 Chr 7:1–3). In the earlier times of David, on this same spot where the Temple would be built, God brought fire upon the altar (1 Chr 21:26). Cf. also 1 Kgs 18:20–46, especially vs. 24!

14. Lev 6:13.

15. Lev 10:2, 6.

16. Lev 10:3.

17. See par example Mal 3:1–5 and 4:1–2. In fact, here a coming of God "on the Eighth Day" is meant, the ultimate coming of God in the end.

18. With respect to this Ibn Ezra cites Amos 3:2, where the special calling of Israel also brings a special judgment (see Milgrom, *Leviticus 1–16*, 601). Cf. also 1 Pet 5:10. A striking parallel with Lev 10:3 (also with regard to the words used) has been found by others in Ezek 28:22 (Ibid., 601).

19. Lev 10:10.

20. Lev 10:10.

21. Hence the prohibition of alcohol during the period of priestly service in Lev 10:8–9.

They must be able to unequivocally instruct the people in all commandments.[22] Ultimately the people should learn to distinguish between impure and pure.[23] In multiple areas the life of the people around the Sanctuary receives a character different from that of the other nations. And as a nation of priests, Israel in particular should know this distinction.[24]

Therefore Leviticus continues with the *tora* about pure and impure animals.[25] Following all kinds of decrees are given relating to the purity and impurity of men and women,[26] of clothing,[27] and even of houses,[28] with the accompanying purification rituals.[29] Through all this a distinction is being made,[30] separating Israel from the nations surrounding it.[31] Israel learns that the Holy God wants all of life, starting from birth,[32] to befit His holiness. The body and its clothing, even including the place where one lives, has to be in accord with God's holy conditions. All decrees are intended to preserve the purity of the people around the Sanctuary. God's Indwelling in the midst of His people asks for purity and sanctity and is a matter of life and death. Whoever enters the House of the LORD in an impure state, pollutes it. The pollution of God's Dwelling causes death.[33] There will be life[34] only when Israel is distinct from the nation of Egypt and the nations of Canaan. Pollution of the Promised Land by unholy behavior will cause the land "to vomit out" the people.[35]

9.5 Be Holy

In the center of the book of Leviticus, and thereby in all of the Tora, God's command resounds:

> Speak to the entire assembly of Israel and say to them: "Be holy because I, the LORD your God, am holy."[36]

---

22. Lev 10:11.
23. Lev 11:47.
24. Lev 20:26.
25. Lev 11.
26. Lev 12:1—13:46 and Lev 15.
27. Lev 13:47-59.
28. Lev 14:33-53.
29. Lev 14.
30. Cf. also Exod 11:7 where the LORD says that through the tenth plague He will show the distinction He makes between Egypt and Israel.
31. Lev 20:24-26 explicitly states this.
32. Lev 12.
33. Lev 15:31.
34. Lev 18:5.
35. Lev 18:24-28 and 20:22.
36. Lev 19:2.

In Leviticus 19 the Holy God calls His people to be holy as He is. This chapter then fills in the details of this holiness through the Ten Words, which mark this chapter in several ways.[37]

Once a year the high priest has to make atonement for the sins of the people[38] and also atone the Most Holy Place, the Tabernacle and the altar, so that God's Dwelling will be sanctified again.[39] Thereby this Day of Atonement is marked by the command to be holy "as I, the LORD."[40] In the end all commandments are geared toward Israel's sanctification of God's Name, so that He will be "acknowledged as holy by the Israelites."[41] The priestly nation has to sanctify Him who wishes to dwell in their midst. Thus the people will continue to receive the favor of this Presence. After all, He Himself walks in their midst, and He moves about the camp to protect and deliver the people.[42] In this way the camp of Israel recalls the garden of Eden,[43] meant to embody in its present this "original future."

In the midst of creation and of the nations, God's people are called to be "a living reminder"[44] pointing to God's original intentions, which will be fleshed out anew in the future in an even more glorious manner. This is God's ultimate focus. The Redeemer-God[45] inhabits the Sanctuary in the center. In the decrees relating to the Sabbath Year and the Year of Jubilee,[46] He makes clear that the land in the midst of the earth belongs to Him. Israel's possession of the land will always be under His authority.[47] Ultimately He wishes the redemption of the people and the land.

---

37. Moshe Kline (www.chaver.com; last accessed 25th of July 2016), based on a plurality of arguments related to the structure of Leviticus, argues that this chapter is the center of the book. The whole of Leviticus has been ordered in circles around this center. Exodus and Numeri also received their place around this heart of the Tora. Kline postulates that the structure of Leviticus can be compared to the Tabernacle. He has the opinion that the reader, like the high priest, enters through the courtyard and the Holy Place to the Most Holy Place to find, in chapter 19, "the ark with the Ten Words." From the Most Holy Place the high priest then returns to the people and the world with the blessing of God's redemption, which is the shared theme of the chapters 25–27.

38. Lev 16:30. This only was possible after he made atonement for the sins of himself and his family (16:6, 11–14).

39. Lev 16:33.

40. We find these words 18 times in chapter 19.

41. Lev 22:32.

42. Deut 23:14.

43. Cf. Gen 3:8.

44. After Henri Nouwen's *The living reminder, service and prayer in memory of Jesus Christ*, 1977.

45. "Redeemer" is the equivalent of the Hebrew *go'el*. Redeeming/redemption is a central theme in the closing chapters of Leviticus. The meaning refers to a special legal redemption/buying out based on God's decrees.

46. Lev 25:8–55.

47. So Milgrom in his comments on Lev 25:23 (*Leviticus 23–27*, 2188).

There will be no perpetual slavery for people and land. The *tikkun olam*[48] resounds in the closing chapters of Leviticus.[49] If God wishes to be redeemer in the center of the earth, it will also reach the most faraway parts of the earth!

9.6 Structuring the Camp of Israel

It has been one month since the consecration of the Dwelling of God and His priests, when the command is heard to order to count the people and the camp.[50] The command to take a census of the people by their divisions[51] can be seen as the structuring of God's royal army. Following this the encampment, the camp of Israel, is arranged by God's command.[52]

The tents of the tribe of Levi, priests and other serving Levites will be arranged around the Dwelling of God.[53] Around these the twelve tribes,[54] in all four wind directions three tribes, put up their tents. It is an ordering whereby the priestly *mishpaḥa* around the Dwelling is encircled by the other *mishpaḥot* of Israel.[55]

The structuring of the camp begins by mentioning the position of the tribe of Judah on the east side.[56] The tribe of Judah thereby takes the place of the tribe of Jacob's firstborn son Ruben.[57] It is also from Judah that the princely ruler for Israel will come forth.[58]

The Tent of God thus is the physical heart of the camp of Israel. Even when the people traveled, the Tent had the central place in the marching order.[59] Around this holy center the circles of the holy Levitical servants of the Sanctuary and of the twelve tribes were drawn. The Indwelling of the Holy God calls first of all the priests and other Levites to their service. In turn they call the whole of the people to participate in the holy *avoda*.

---

48. See chapter 2 (2.2).

49. Also in Lev 26:12 God makes it clear that He wishes to walk in Israel's midst. See footnote 42 and 43 in this chapter.

50. Compare Exod 40:2, 17 with Num 1:1.

51. Num 1:2–3.

52. Num 2.

53. Num 1:52–54 shows that this position was also meant to guard the sanctity of the Dwelling.

54. See Num 2:2. Thus Levi is in fact a thirteenth tribe. The two sons of Joseph (Ephraim and Manasseh) fill up the number twelve. One and twelve—in this number we notice an image of the One God together with the people.

55. See chapter 3 (3.4).

56. Num 2:3–4.

57. 1 Chr 5:1–2.

58. Gen 49:8–10.

59. Num 2:17.

This call from the Sanctuary to turn oneself toward the Sanctuary does not stop with the circle of the twelve tribes. By their position[60] and by their number[61] they form the bridge the nations. Originating from this one priestly *mishpaḥa* of Israel there will be blessing for all *mishpaḥot* of the nations.[62] From this most holy center of creation an invitation goes out to all of creation. Ultimately the calling of Israel to be a priestly nation is geared toward the filling of the whole earth with the Name and service to the glory of God.[63]

At the same time it becomes clear that the one Dwelling of God can only be reached through the circles around the Sanctuary, through the service of the priestly people and their designated priests. The instruction of the priests and instruction from within the circle of Israel is needed.[64] Only within this community of people can the Holy One be known. Therefore Ruth says, "Your people will be my people and your God will be my God,"[65] and ten men from the nations say to this one man from Judah, "Let us go with you, because we have heard that God is with you."[66]

9.7 The One Sanctuary

The LORD at Sinai decreed the structure of the camp. He chose the center for His Dwelling and thereby revealed Himself as the center of all creation and of life, the One God who asks for one-hearted *avoda* in that place which He choses. He wills this in a world where humans have chosen and still want to choose their own service, their own gods, and their own places. Because of this, on their way to the land God gives His people the commandment regarding the one Sanctuary,[67] the place which He Himself will choose and reveal.[68] It will be to only that place that the people must go to bring sacrifices.

---

60. Toward the four wind directions: this opens up the view toward the nations

61. Four times three tribes on each side—all wind directions filled by the "green" of the knowledge of God (cf. Gen 1:11–13; Ps 1; 92:13–15).

62. See par example Zech 12:12–14 and 14:17–18 for the use of the terminology of "family and families" in the description of the future salvation.

63. The calling of Exod 19:5–6 is lived up to and becomes visible in the numerous calls to the nations to join in Israel's praise. See par example Ps 67. The people of Israel recites this Psalm in the fifty days between *Pessaḥ* and *Shavuot* (the Feast of Weeks; "the feast of seven weeks and one day" = the 50th day). The redemption from Egypt, the giving of the Tora at Sinai and the light of God's countenance among Israel (vs. 2), are instrumental to knowing God among all nations and for their praising God! Israel prays, "May God bless us still, so that all the ends of the earth will fear him" (vs. 8).

64. Cf. Hos 4:1–6.

65. Ruth 1:16.

66. Zech 8:23; see also Jer 12:16–17: " (. . .) then they will be established among my people."

67. Deut 12.

68. See par example Deut 12:5, 11, 14; 14:23–25, and 16:15–16.

In the Promised Land God wishes to adhere to this same structure: His holy Dwelling in the center where the service of the priests will take place.[69] Around it He gives the tribes their own dwelling places. And around that land will be the world of the nations.

9.8 Toward God's Structuring of the Land

Since their departure from Sinai, the history of the people can be seen as the journey toward "the structuring of the land" according to the blueprint of God's intentions. The entry, the conquest, and the following allocation of the dwelling places[70] are phases in that process. The (temporary) place for the Tabernacle in Shiloh,[71] the election of Jerusalem (realized over a longer period of time), and the designation of Mount Moriah as the place for the Temple,[72] were phases in the realization of God's plan for the midst[73] of the earth.

9.9 Toward the Indwelling in the Midst of the People and the Earth

The history of the people since their departure from Sinai can also be seen as the journey toward the Indwelling of God in the midst of the people and in the midst of the earth.

The God who visited His friend Abraham and was His guest, wishes to dwell in the midst of Abraham's offspring. In the midst of His *segula*-people.[74] He wishes to dwell with His beloved and treasured possession. To walk in the midst of His people and His camp.[75]

God's dwelling with them takes the form that fits the situation of His people. The itinerant nation receives a Tent-dwelling in which the Holy One time and again takes His lodging.[76] The nation that has (partially)[77] entered its rest in the land finally

---

69. In the land, Jerusalem will take the place of the first circle around the Tent in the desert, i.e., the circle of the priests and Levites.

70. Joshua 13–21.

71. Joshua 18:1, 8–10; cf. 1 Sam 1–3.

72. 1 Chr 21; 22:1 and 2 Chr 3:1. Cf. chapter 3, footnote 75.

73. Ezek 5:5: "This is what the Sovereign LORD says: this is Jerusalem, which I have set in the center of the nations, with countries all around her." Cf. Mic 5:7–8. Ezek 38:12 calls the land Israel "the navel of the earth" (RSV: "the center of the earth;" NIV: "the center of the land"). Also God's judgment over Israel will be executed "in the midst of all the earth" (Isa 10:23, RSV).

74. Exod 19:5. See chapter 7, footnotes 9–11.

75. Deut 23:14.

76. Cf. Num 10:33–36.

77. Cf. Ps 95:11 and Heb 4.

receives a permanent Dwelling of God where it can meet the Holy One.[78] This permanent Dwelling will be God's own resting place[79] forever.[80]

Out of this physical center, the heart of God's Indwelling, the living community of the nation has to become a "body of faith."[81] God's Presence wishes to "enflesh" itself in the people. In the Tanakh, however, we also find that the Indwelling of God wishes to journey even further into "the midst." When the ark is the Throne of the LORD[82] on earth, His footstool and the repository of the Tablets of the Law, then God's promise to put His Tora in the heart[83] is in fact a declaration of intention-to-indwelling directed to the people itself. Then the giving of the Holy Spirit in their inner hearts,[84] i.e., in the "midst,"[85] carries with it a promise of His Indwelling.

Ultimately God's choosing of people, land, city, and place is meant to lead to the reality of "the LORD is there,"[86] with which the book of Ezekiel ends. His goal is to ultimately dwell in the midst of Israel and Zion, in a time in which also many nations will seek the LORD and will be His people.[87] Jerusalem shall be visited and inhabited by the Holy God Himself, and there He will be king.[88] The heart of the land in the heart of the earth will be the place of the Throne of the king of the whole world.[89] Indwelling and kingship are closely related. Thereby, the themes of holy (In)dwelling, holy priesthood and kingdom of priests are also connected with each other.

9.10 Dwelling and Kingship of God

It is noteworthy that the consecration of the Temple at the time of Solomon takes place during *Sukkot*, the Feast of Tabernacles.[90] This celebration of thanksgiving for the experience of God's care at the time of the Exodus and every year since[91] has also an eschatological dimension in the Tanakh. The final deliverance from all distress and of all kinds of pharaohs is also being tasted in advance. The nations will seek the

---

78. 2 Chr 6:2. The Hebrew word for place is derived from a root which has the ring of permanency.
79. 2 Chr 6:41.
80. 2 Chr 6:2.
81. To the title of the book of Michael Wyschogrod, *The Body of Faith. God in the People Israel*.
82. 2 Kgs 19:15; Ps 80:1; Isa 37:16. Cf. Ps 22:3.
83. Jer 31:33.
84. Ezek 36:27.
85. The Hebrew word *qerev* also can be rendered as (the) "midst."
86. Ezek 48:35.
87. Zachariah 2:10–11.
88. Zachariah 14:4–5, 9, 16–17.
89. Zachariah 14:9.
90. 2 Chr 5:3; 7:8–10.
91. Lev 23:33–43. Verses 42–43 make the connection with the Exodus. Deut 16:13–15 shows the thanksgiving-for-the-harvest side of the Feast of Tabernacles.

Part I: The Canonical Narrative: The Tanakh

LORD and honor Him.[92] It thereby is also the feast of the king who will (have) cast down all other powers.[93] His name is (He who is) One[94] and He is the only One who remains.

The priesthood of the people of Israel is intended to serve and further the kingship of God and should show this. That is what the calling of the people to be "a kingdom of priests" is all about.[95] Here then also lies the connection with the next chapter, in which the kingdom of God, the kingship of the priestly nation, and the kingship within Israel will be discussed.

---

92. Zachariah 14:16–17. Rashi interprets the seventy additional sacrifices (Num 29:12–38) as the sacrifices which Israel offered for the nations (as atonement for their sins of ignorance) as long as the Temple existed. He also is of the opinion that the decreasing number of bulls points to the gradually decreasing power of the nations over Israel. The end will be that all nations will bow under the reign of God under the spiritual leadership of Israel (Sherman, *The Torah*, 895).

93. The Jewish celebration of *Sukkot* includes a meditation about the festive victory banquet. The Leviathan plays a role in it. His meat will be eaten!

94. Zachariah 14:9; ("and his name [will be, EJW] one," RSV).

95. Exod 19:5–6.

Chapter 10

Kingdom and Kingship of the People around the Dwelling of God

10.1 The Royal Perspective

THE JOURNEY OF ISRAEL'S calling to be "a kingdom of priests" began at Sinai. This designation demonstrates that this calling does not just involve the priesthood of this nation, but also the calling of kingdom and kingship. The priestly nation has to be God's kingdom, and must serve and promote the kingship of Israel's God. This perspective is central to this chapter.

10.2 Kings

When the LORD promised offspring to Abraham and Sarah, He used the words "nations" and "kings."[1] This promise carried a double meaning. It could mean that kings would arise from the offspring of Abraham and Sarah, but also that their whole offspring would consist of kings.[2] Abraham himself was called "a mighty prince among us"[3] by the Hittites of Hebron.

Remember that Abram's calling in Genesis 12 is directly related to the pride of the nations revealed in the building of the tower of Babel. According to Scripture and Jewish interpreters, the driving force behind this arrogant enterprise is Nimrod, the

---

1. Gen 17:6, 16.

2. Seen from this perspective, Gen 17:16 can already carry the meaning of "reigning over (the) nations."

3. Gen 23:6.

Part I: The Canonical Narrative: The Tanakh

first ruler[4] on the earth. Babel is called "the beginning of his kingdom."[5] Because of this context, Abram's calling receives a royal perspective. In the book of Genesis Nimrod has to make way for a "king" after God's heart, as King Saul must do in latter times. We already paid attention to the description in Genesis of the priestly calling of Abraham.[6] We now also see that in Genesis kingdom is placed in opposition to kingdom and king against king. Abraham is the first to receive this royal calling from God. It is God's will that his offspring will share in this calling.

In the life of Abra(ha)m we see how he defeats the kings of the nations.[7] He is the "mighty prince of God" who saves the life of Sodom and Gomorrah and their kings.[8] For this reason he is honored and blessed by the priestly king of Salem.[9] Abram then in turn "bows" for the royal priesthood of Melchizedek.[10]

The royal calling of Abraham has, just like David's calling, a somewhat hidden character that only occasionally shows itself. The same applies to Isaac and Jacob, who just like Abraham sometimes suffer from the kings of the nations.[11] But to Jacob God also reconfirms this promise: kings will come forth from him.[12]

Jacob's son Joseph embodies a clearly visible fulfillment of this promise.[13] This descendant of Abraham receives a salvific royal task for the whole world.[14] Yet this is only provisionally, for the dark years of the Egyptian exile will follow. Regardless, the figure of Joseph forms a significant, prophetic paradigm for the way of Israel with its calling.

When, at the end of Genesis, Jacob blesses his sons before he dies, Judah receives the promise that from his offspring a ruler will arise for Israel and the nations.[15] Im-

---

4. Nimrod is called a *gibbor* (strong, mighty man). RSV renders "mighty man," NIV "mighty warrior."

5. Gen 10:10 (RSV). NIV renders "The first centers of his kingdom were Babylon, Uruk, Akkad and Kalneh." The Hebrew word *reshit*, meaning "beginning/firstling," we also find in Gen 1:1. Opposite God's plan for His creation we see with Nimrod the beginning of a "grand work of man." See chapter 1.

6. See chapter 3.

7. Gen 14:1–17. The word kings (*melakhim*) is thematic in this chapter. The king of Sinear, the place where Babel had been built (cf. 11:2), is the first to be enumerated in Gen 14:1. The "kingdom of man" resurfaces, but counters resistance of Abram, the mighty prince of God.

8. Gen 14:11–17. Later (Gen 18:16–33) he will also be the priest who pleads for Sodom and Gomorrah.

9. Gen 14:18–20. Salem is the city which later will be named Jerusalem.

10. Abram gives him a tenth part of the spoil; cf. Heb 7:4–10.

11. See Gen 20 and 26 for troubles from the side of the Philistines. Also the fear of Esau (Gen 27 and 32) and the slavish serving of Laban (chapter 29–31) clearly show that the royal calling sometimes has only the character of a promise of something not yet seen.

12. Gen 35:11.

13. Gen 37–50. Appointed over all Egypt (41:41, 43) he feeds all Egypt, but also all the earth (41:57).

14. Cf. Poot, *Jozef*. This book presents much Jewish interpretation regarding the history of Joseph.

15. Gen 49:8–12; cf. especially verse 10! Cf. 1 Chr 5:2.

plicitly Genesis thus ends in anticipation of the fulfillment of this promise. However, when Joseph dies, the kingship of and for Israel seems to die with him. A new king of Egypt[16] arises and rules harshly. If left up to him and the land of Egypt, God's plans will never progress. Abraham's offspring has not become kings, but slaves.

10.3 Kingdom of Priests

After the darkness of the Egyptian exile, the night of the exodus arrives.[17] And in the end the army of Egypt's king lies debunked under the seas of God's might.[18] Abraham's offspring draws near to Sinai and receives its calling, which is at the same time a further elaboration of the promise given to Abraham:

> "Now if you obey me fully and keep my covenant, then out of all nations you will be my treasured possession. Although the whole earth is mine, you will be for me a kingdom of priests and a holy nation." These are the words you are to speak to the Israelites.[19]

"You will be for me a kingdom of priests"—these unique words, which we nowhere else find in the Tanakh, have a number of meanings which are all of fundamental importance in the history of the people called.

First of all the focus is on the kingship of God. God is king and Israel His kingdom.[20] "For me, your king, you are a kingdom of priests." God presents Himself as the king who claims this nation as His kingdom. The central question will be if He will be the real king of this nation.

Then two more lines of interpretation of the designation "kingdom of priests" present themselves to us. These have to do with the relations which are possible between the words "kingdom" and "priests."[21] First, the designation can denote priests

---

16. Exod 1:8.
17. Exod 12.
18. Exod 14:26–31 and 15:1–21.
19. Exod 19:5–6.

20. Deut 33:5 speaks about the appearance of God at Sinai as: "The LORD became king over Jeshurun" (RSV; NIV has: "He was king over Jeshurun"). Jeshurun is a name for Israel and means probably "the upright one" (cf. Deut 32:15; 33:26; Isa 44:2).

21. The genitive includes these two possibilities, Cf. "the son of David" and "the fear of the LORD." In the first instance David is the subject, the father of his son. In the second case the LORD is the "object" of our fear.

Part I: The Canonical Narrative: The Tanakh

who possess a kingdom and exercise the kingship.[22] In this case it speaks about God's intention that the priests, His people,[23] fulfill a royal task just like kings.[24]

The expression can also denote a kingdom of which the priests, the priestly nation, are the subjects[25] without further denotation to the king. God could be that king, but another king could also have power over the priestly nation. In that case here the possibility of a "king before God" opens up.

Therefore, the royal calling of Israel has three possible meanings: first, God is the king of His people; second, Israel is meant to be a royal people, a nation of kings; and finally, a king will rule over Israel. These three meanings simultaneously play a role in God's plan with His people. All three have a place in the continuing history and this history is about all three of them. The questions are then, will God be king? Will the priestly nation be king in the midst of the earth? And finally, will the kingship within Israel be focused on God, as "before the LORD"?[26]

In the desert the Dwelling of God was the center of the camp of Israel, and also in the land God's Indwelling would be the center of all of life. Therefore, the kingship of Israel and the service of its kings had to be oriented toward the kingship of God and His Dwelling.

10.4 Jewish Interpretation of the Call to be a Kingdom of Priests

The words of the calling in Exodus 19 are fundamental to Israel's self-understanding and for that reason have received much careful thought, and have been commented upon. In the exposition we find back all meanings mentioned above.

We find the kingship of God and the kingship of Israel combined in the *Mekhilta*.[27] In the *Kedushat Levi*[28] these words are related to the future priesthood of the

---

22. In fact the priests then form the subject. The interrelation between "kingdom" and "priests" is then that of the so-called genitivus subjectivus.

23. The identification of nation and priests is caused by the fact that in Exod 19:5–6 God addresses the whole nation. It would be possible however to think of the kingship of a priestly class, but there is no such thing in Israel. It is true, however, that Zechariah crowns the high priest Joshua as a prophetic token of the coming of the Messianic priestly king (Zech 6:9–15).

24. The Talmud (b. Shabbat 128a) cites R. Shimeon, who postulates that all Israel consists of royal princes. Rashi refers to 2 Sam 8:18 where David's sons are called priests; however he interprets the designation "priests" as meaning "princes."

25. The priests are then the "content" of the kingdom. In this case the interrelation is then the so-called genitivus objectivus.

26. 1 Chr 29:22 shows that both the anointed (high) priest and the king are living "before the LORD."

27. The facts related to the footnotes 27–34 I derived from Agnon, *Present at Sinai*. The Mekhilta is an early commentary on Exodus (dating from the first two centuries of our time reckoning), that has been edited after the fourth century.

28. Sermons on the Tora by the hasidic master Levi Yizhak of Berdichev, Poland (eighteenth to nineteenth century), published in Hrubishov (1818) and Lemberg (1850), (Ibid., 320).

whole nation.²⁹ This writing speaks in relation to this subject about three crowns: the crown of the Tora, that of the priesthood, and that of the kingship.³⁰ In *Torat Emet*³¹ the kingship of Israel is interpreted as implying having dominion over higher realms by which Israel will be able to chose from heavenly blessings.³² In *Avodat Yisrael*³³ the kingship and priesthood of Israel imply dominion over angels by Israel and its commandment and judgment of them.³⁴

10.5 Kingship as Model of Learning for Israel

As with the calling to be a priestly nation, the royal aspect of the calling of Israel has its focus both on God and on the nations. God also provides Israel with a "place and pathway of learning"³⁵ by which Israel can learn what God's kingship is about and how wise administration and human kingship are meant to be. God has given stipulations in the Tora meant for the future kings in Israel. The people receive a model of learning both by the model of their kings and in the laws meant for the kings. Through it Israel learns how it will be able to be a royal nation in the midst of the nations and in the center of the world. In Israel's midst the kings will be what the priests were also, a living reminder of God and of the holy calling of the nation. It is therefore that kings are commanded to permanently read, study, and apply the Tora.³⁶

By this paradigmatic existence of Israel's kings and of Israel as a royal nation, both Israel and the nations have the opportunity to learn about the future kingdom of God. As king God then will instruct the nations in His Tora,³⁷ and from Zion He will allow the nations to share in His *shalom*.³⁸

10.6 The Royal Calling: Promise and Obedience

Like the priestly calling, the royal calling of the nation calls for obedience. Obedience to God and His commandments will be the road which leads to the fulfillment of everything implied in the calling. At the same time, however, God promises that the

29. Ibid., 95.
30. Ibid., 95.
31. Hasidic homilies about the Tora and the feasts by Yehuda Leib Eger from Lublin, Poland (nineteenth century), (Ibid., 326).
32. Ibid., 96.
33. A homiletic work by Yisrael ben Shabtai of Koznitz, Poland (nineteenth century), (Ibid. 318).
34. Ibid., 104. Cf. 1 Cor 6:2 where the same is said about 'the saints' (NIV: "the Lord's people").
35. Cf. chapter 5 and 8.
36. Deut 17:18–20. A king must produce his own copy of God's law on a scroll and as a companion have it permanently with him. A sharp contrast forms king Johoiakim who burns the scroll with the words of Jeremiah (Jer 36).
37. Isa 2:1–5.
38. Isa 60:1–3.

royal calling will be realized fully[39] when the people will listen carefully and keep God's covenant.[40]

It is noteworthy that in the history of Israel the promise of a king from Judah[41] precedes the royal calling at Sinai. Through this the necessary obedience that God asks is placed under the arch of God's promise. Ultimately the obedience of the people will not be the all-decisive factor. God will surely give the kingdom He promised with the kingship of the nation and His king. Genesis ends with the unspoken question about the how and when of this king. The Tanakh shows what God's intentions are for this kingdom in the center of the earth and it tells the history of the royal nation. At the same time the final realization of God's kingship amidst Israel and amidst the nations is still awaited. The calling of the people of Israel also awaits the *tikkun olam*, the perfect completion of all God's purposes.

10.7 From Sinai Toward the Kingdom

Starting from Sinai the road that Israel will travel will also be the road toward the Kingdom. The calling is given and becomes more and more elaborated within the reality of life of the nation, with the Tora providing the direction. The instruction meant for the whole nation also applies to future princes and kings. In addition God gives specific commandments about the kingship in Israel.[42]

In the person of Moses, certain priestly, judicial, and royal[43] tasks are still combined. This combination cannot be a permanent one.[44] In God's Tora and the ordering of the camp we find in it, we learn that God wishes to bless the people by a distinct priesthood, a distinct judiciary,[45] and by the kings of Israel. Prophets are promised to the nation.[46] And there is yet the openness toward a future in which a second Moses will appear, in whom those many tasks will be brought together again.

---

39. Cf. Deut 26:19; 28:1, 13 where God promises Israel, if it is obedient, to set it high above the nations to be "the head, not the tail;" cf. however also vs. 44.

40. Cf. Exod 19:1–5.

41. See footnote 15 in this chapter.

42. Deut 17:14–20 mentions the appointment of the king of God's choice and gives several commandments and prohibitions for the king.

43. An example of a royal and at the same time priestly task before God is the raising of the staff of God in the battle with Amalek (Exod 17:8–16); cf. Ps 110:2 where also the staff/sceptre plays a role in the rule over the nations.

44. The sheer physical impossibility of this complex task is the theme of Exod 18. Already before the revelation at Sinai the (re)organization of the administration of the people has begun. The "heads" of the different subsections of the people are in their own way an expression of the royal calling of the nation.

45. Deut 16:18–20 and 17:8–13 respectively order the appointment of local judges and elders/rulers and of a national judicial institution.

46. Deut 18:15–22. This section speaks about a prophet who will be raised by the LORD. We can interpret this as a reference to the recurrent appearance of prophets, but at the same time this section

Kingdom and Kingship of the People around the Dwelling of God

Preceding the entry in the land, the nation lived in the desert together as a united organization of administration and justice with a somewhat simple structure. Upon entering the Promised Land, the structure of administration, justice, and instruction becomes more necessarily complex. The heads of the nation[47] and the leaders of the tribes[48] both have a role to play in this. Joshua is the designated successor of Moses.[49] Once in the land the judges appear in whom prophetic, judicial and royal-military tasks come together.[50] The prophetic books of Joshua, Judges, and 1 Samuel tell this history.

Samuel, the last judge[51] and prophet[52] who also performs priestly duties,[53] is called to appoint Saul as the first king over Israel.[54] The kingship as such certainly was intended by God and thereby permissible,[55] but in the demand for the first king resentment against God's kingship also raises its voice.[56] The nation does not long for the king of God's choice, but longs predominantly to be just like all other nations.[57]

When the first king of Israel is rejected because of his disobedience, God choses a new king for His people. In doing so He passes by the first seven sons of Jesse[58] and choses the youngest. The eighth son of Jesse will be Israel's new king.[59]

It is David who will be paradigm of the kingship of God amidst the people, although imperfectly. With his anointing a history of waiting begins for the realization of his kingship. The chosen one becomes king only through a path of suffering. This path and the waiting of the people for this king after God's heart do have a prophetic paradigmatic aspect. The waiting is for the complete kingship of God and for the

---

leaves open the expectation of a second Moses, in whom different duties will be combined. This special prophet has a place in later Jewish interpretation of these words. We also meet this interpretation in the New Testament (John 1:21; 6:14; 7:40; Acts 3:22 and 7:37). Cf. par example *JSB*, at Deut 18:15.

47. Cf. Exod 18:21–16.

48. Cf. Num 7:2–88.

49. Num 27:15–23. Verse 17 uses the metaphor of the shepherd for the task of Joshua. Ezek 34 connects the shepherding over Israel with the prince from the house of David (vss. 23–24).

50. Prophetic and sanctification duties go hand in hand with the military liberation by the judges.

51. 1 Sam 7:15.

52. 1 Sam 3:20.

53. Cf. 1 Sam 7:2–17.

54. 1 Sam 8.

55. See Deut 17:14–20. Jewish interpretation therefore views the commandment to appoint a king as one of the positive commandments which will apply when the whole congregation of Israel lives in the land. There is difference of opinion about the question if this commandment allows the wish of the people for a king to materialize, but in doing so in fact allows something which is contrary to "the spirit of Judaism" (see the enumeration of arguments in Chill, *The Mitzvot*, 428–429).

56. "(. . .) but they have rejected me as their king" (1 Sam 8:7).

57. Kahan points in his discussion of the 497th of the 613 commandments (based on Deut. 17:15) to the premature character of the demand and to the wish to be like the nations as reasons for disapproval of both Samuel and the LORD Himself (*The Taryag Mitzvos*, 294).

58. 1 Sam 16:10.

59. 1 Sam 16:1, 12.

Part I: The Canonical Narrative: The Tanakh

kingship of Israel in the world under the king after God's heart. The different layers of meaning within the royal calling from Exodus 19:5–6 all play a role in this history.

David receives the promise of a hereditary and eternal kingship for his family and his house. The prophet Nathan speaks:

> The LORD declares to you that the LORD himself will establish a house for you: When your days are over and you rest with your ancestors, I will raise up your offspring to succeed you, your own flesh and blood, and I will establish his kingdom. He is the one who will build a house for my Name, and I will establish the throne of his kingdom forever. I will be his father, and he will be my son. When he does wrong, I will punish him with a rod wielded by men, with floggings inflicted by human hands. But my love will never be taken away from him, as I took it away from Saul, whom I removed from before you. Your house and your kingdom will endure forever before me; your throne will be established forever.[60]

Not only does he receive the promise of the royal rule of his own son and his future offspring, but also an eternal throne of David. This promise implies that a son of David will sit on this eternal throne. Through it the prophetic blessing for Judah from Genesis 49 receives further elaboration. A prince from the house of Judah and the family of David will be of importance for all nations.[61]

In the midst of the nation of Israel, which can be called God's son,[62] there will be a kingship that stands under the promise a special son-ship of God. In the house of learning that God erects in the center of the earth, at the place He appointed for His people,[63] a visual instruction about the themes of kingship, son-ship, and obedience will take place. Just as David wishes,[64] the *avoda* of the king, his service, must focus at its deepest level on the (building of the) House of God. It is not without reason that David and Solomon and their service for the (building of the) Temple are extensively spoken about.[65] In this they are a model for all kings after them, with their service oriented toward the *avoda* of God in the center of the earth. Their faithful obedience was of fundamental importance in the plans of God. The kings were called to become receivers of the land by their faithful service to the LORD and to transmit this gift of God to their offspring.[66] Their calling was to sit on "the throne of the kingdom of the

---

60. 2 Sam 7:11–16.
61. Gen 49:10.
62. Cf. Exod 4:22–23 and Hos 11:1.
63. 2 Sam 7:10 connects the promise of the everlasting kingship with the place that God chose for Israel itself.
64. The wish to build the House of God "caused" the prophetic words of Nathan in 2 Sam 7.
65. In this God Himself is teacher and David and Solomon, the pupils. Just like the design of the Tabernacle (Exod 27:8) the design of the Temple is God's/ordered by Him (1 Chr 28:19).
66. 1 Chr 28:8. Dwelling and possession of the land thus are related to royal obedience.

LORD over Israel."[67] Their existence was paradigmatic for the people of God and for all nations.

God's promise to David also asks for the necessary obedience. Disobedience will have serious consequences,[68] and yet God will see His promise through. That will be His *chesed*,[69] His gracious and loving covenantal faithfulness toward David's offspring. The end will be the eternal steadfastness of the throne of David. And implied, a kingship that will make possible the dwelling in the land. The promise here is implicitly given of the needed royal obedience which will serve and contribute to the dawning of the *tikkun olam*.

Again the promise of God precedes the obedience and will create the obedience needed. In this manner the kingship of God will prevail. Will then, in this one Son of David, the kingship of God and that of Israel meet each other or even fully coincide?

10.8 Learning and Waiting for the Eighth Son

Both Israel and the nations receive instruction about God's kingship through the ordering of Israel's camp into God's house of learning amidst the nations. Yet, whoever follows the history of Israel's kings, becomes aware of the fact that the visual instruction given is just partial and far from perfect.

Even David himself discovers that the fulfillment of his royal calling lies in the future. He cannot build the Temple; his hands are too stained by blood.[70] His son Solomon is allowed to build the temple, but just like his father David and many kings after Solomon himself, he is a man that transgresses the commandments.[71]

The house of learning therefore is waiting for the "Eighth Son," the Messiah. It is He of whom the prophets speak when confronted with the kings on the throne in Jerusalem and the northerly kingdom of the ten tribes.

10.9 Paradigm of Suffering on the Road to the Throne

David had to wait long years for the consolidation of his throne in Jerusalem.[72] His election and anointing were followed by the persecution of Saul and his loyal followers

---

67. 1 Chr 28:5.

68. 2 Sam 7:14.

69. NIV renders "my love." The Hebrew word *ḥesed* has the ring of solidarity, friendship, and faithful (covenantal) love.

70. 1 Chr 28:3. We can think of all necessary wars, but also of the sin of murdering Uriah (2 Sam 11).

71. The multitude of horses and women of Solomon (1 Kgs 10:26—11:13) form together with his idol worship a transgression of God's specific command for the king in Deut 17:14-20. His disobedience causes Israel to be torn in two (1 Kgs 11:11-12). Because of his disobedience he is not able to transmit the land to his descendants.

72. Even when he is king, he is not yet king over the whole nation and not yet in Jerusalem.

Part I: The Canonical Narrative: The Tanakh

in Israel,[73] by the opposition of the surrounding nations,[74] and by treason and rebellion from his own family and inner circle.[75] The question arises if what could be seen in the life of the eighth son of Jesse, also revealed the road for and toward the kingship of God and of Israel as a whole? Will they also only be realized along roads of suffering? Is David's life also in this respect a model, a way of learning for them who follow after him?

The long road toward the full kingship of God and that of His people Israel has everything to do with sin in the life of Israel and with the opposition of the nations against Israel's calling to kingship and priesthood. Unwillingness from the side of Israel with respect to its calling and everything it implies, destroys much, barricading God's purposes. The resistance of the nations, with deep[76] and hidden origins, works against God's plans. This resistance to the election of Israel casts deep shadows of darkness and death over the people.

These dark sides of the way of God with His people, so extensively written about in the Tanakh, form the focal point of the following chapter.

---

73. See 1 Sam 18–31.
74. See 1 Sam 17 and 30.
75. See 2 Sam 15–20.
76. Cf. Ps 2.

Chapter 11

The Calling Impeded by Israel's Disobedience and the Opposition of the Nations

11.1 A Dark Perspective

THIS CHAPTER PRESENTS THE darker sides of Israel's long journey from Sinai toward the full realization of the calling received. It follows the path of the people from the covenant at Sinai to the partial return from exile. It is there the Tanakh ends. Throughout this journey we will focus on Israel's own disobedience, as well as on the nations that oppose the election and calling of God's people.

11.2 Obstacles

The words of the calling imply that obstacles may appear from different sides before it is fully realized.

> "Now if you obey me fully and keep my covenant, then out of all nations you will be my treasured possession. Although the whole earth is mine, you will be for me a kingdom of priests and a holy nation." These are the words you are to speak to the Israelites.[1]

First of all it is God's condition that the people will fully obey and keep the covenant. Israel is addressed, taken seriously as partner in the covenant. The flip side of the coin is that there is the risk that Israel will not listen and break the covenant. Such disobedience will not be without consequences, causing the path of the nation to be reversed, leading again into an "Egyptian darkness."[2]

---

1. Exod 19:5–6.
2. See Deut 28 for the blessing on obedience and the curse in case of disobedience. The chapter ends with the threat of a return to Egypt.

Part I: The Canonical Narrative: The Tanakh

At the same time it is obvious that God calls Israel from the nations. And prior experiences in Egypt show clearly that the nations will not unquestioningly resign themselves to the election of Israel. This hatred the nations have of Israel, and their resistance against Israel's election will regularly fall as a darkness of punishment over Israel.[3] Israel's calling, including the promised position among the nations,[4] becomes a reality only along the path of obedience.

Finally, in the very beginning of the Tanakh, it becomes clear that the pride and disobedience of mankind (and consequentially the resistance of the nations), are co-inspired by the opponent—*satan* in Hebrew—of the God of Israel.[5] Although most of the time the attention is focused on the human side of both Israel and the nations' resistance, this deep and revealing "diagnosis" reminds us that we must learn to observe this dark and demonic side of disobedient resistance in Israel's recorded history.[6]

11.3 Two-sidedness of the Covenant

The history recorded in the Tora[7] spanning from Sinai to the border of the Promised Land, circles around the instruction in God's commandments. Moses proclaims that how Israel chooses to relate to this instruction will be decisive:

> See, I set before you today life and prosperity, death and destruction. For I command you today to love the LORD your God, to walk in obedience to him, and to keep his commands, decrees and laws.[8]

Forty years spent in the desert was caused by the unbelief and disobedience of the people. Out of fear and unbelief the spies spoke evil words about the land, and by doing so they spoke badly about God.[9] The people followed them in this fearful unbelief and thus became "adulterous."[10] And yet the LORD wanted to forgive this breach of the covenantal love between Him and the people.[11] But His people would

---

3. See par example Deut 28:25–26, 28–29, 32, 36, 47–57, 63–65.

4. Cf. Deut 28:13: "The LORD will make you the head, not the tail. If you pay attention to the commandments of the LORD your God (. . .)."

5. Gen 3; behind the snake the *satan* is hidden; thus also Sforno, *Commentary*, 22. The Hebrew word *satan* is used for a human opponent in 1 Kgs 11:14.

6. Now and then this dark origin surfaces. Par example 1 Chr 21:1; cf. Job 1–2 and Zech 3:1, 2. Deut 32:17 and Ps 106:37 make a connection between idolatry and demon service. See also footnote 65 and 73 in this chapter.

7. Here, Tora designates the first five books of the Tanakh (the Pentateuch).

8. Deut 30:15–16.

9. See Num 13 and 14.

10. Num 14:33. NIV uses "unfaithfulness." The Hebrew word used has the connotation of disloyalty in a marital and sexual relation, adulterous behavior.

11. Num 14:20.

The Calling Impeded by Israel's Disobedience and the Opposition of the Nations

suffer the consequences, nevertheless.[12] The entry into the Promised Land is delayed by forty years, causing an entire generation[13] to miss out.

It is a new generation that stands at the border of the Promised Land, exhorted by Moses to stay obedient in keeping the covenant. But even the dedication and obedience of this new generation is diagnosed by Him as falling short. Even before the entry, Moses speaks about a heart without understanding and spiritual blindness and deafness.[14] With a God-given, somber clarity, he speaks about exile and dispersion among the nations.[15] Because of the God-ordained two-sidedness of the covenant, the disobedient will of Israel can grow to enormous proportions.

And yet these obstacles will not have the last word. Ultimately through a return to God,[16] a "circumcision of the heart"[17] promised by God, and obedient service, life for the nation will be realized.[18]

In the end God's will for His people will be realized. But the truth is that Israel's disobedience will cause every facet of its calling to suffer delay and frustration before its full realization.

11.4 Adulterous *Segula*[19]-People

As the bride who under the bridal canopy of the cloud at Sinai had made her marital covenant[20] with the Eternal God, Israel is called to exclusive love and attachment to its one, true Husband. The *Shema* can be seen as the daily expression of love of the people:

> Hear, O Israel: The LORD our God, the LORD is one. Love the LORD your God with all your heart and with all your soul and with all your strength. These commandments that I give you today are to be on your hearts. Impress them on your children. Talk about them when you sit at home and when you walk along the road, when you lie down and when you get up. Tie them as symbols on your hands and bind them on your foreheads. Write them on the doorframes of your houses and on your gates.[21]

12. Num 14:21–23.
13. Num 14:30–35.
14. Deut 30.
15. Deut 28.
16. Deut 30:2–3.
17. Deut 30:6. Cf. Ezek 36:25–27. The future return to God and the promise of a spiritual act of God are juxtaposed in Deut 30. A possible connection between them is not elaborated upon.
18. Deut 30:6.
19. Cf. chapter 8 (8.1).
20. See par example Jer 2:1–3 and Ezek 16:8: "I gave you my solemn oath and entered into a covenant with you, declares the Sovereign LORD, and you became mine."
21. Deut 6:4–9. This sections begins with "Hear," the Hebrew *Shema*, and is a regular part of the morning and evening prayers in Israel's liturgy.

Part I: The Canonical Narrative: The Tanakh

Central to this confession of faith and expression of love, is the oneness of God and an exclusive dedication to Him. This is precisely how the *segula*-people should be characterized,[22] and how the people of Israel should distinguish themselves from the nations with their many gods.

The dramatic truth, however, about the relationship between the people and their God becomes visible in the prophetic marriage of Hosea.

> The LORD said to me, "Go, show your love to your wife again, though she is loved by another man and is an adulteress. Love her as the LORD loves the Israelites, though they turn to other gods."[23]

Twice Hosea is commanded to give His love to an utterly adulterous woman. To love her who gives herself to others. Hosea had to experience what the LORD, God of Israel, experienced in that His tender love for His people was not reciprocated by faithful love. Time and again Israel's history will be characterized in this way.

Upon arriving in the land of her lover,[24] the new bride Israel turns away from her Husband and toward the attractive idols adored there. A divine warning causes tears,[25] but when a new generation grows up the first love[26] has been forgotten.[27] The bride is not committed to her lover in His own land.[28]

The book of Judges describes God's struggle with His people regarding its love for Him. Time and again there is adultery, each time answered by God with punishment and judgment. Out of compassion,[29] time and again God provides judges who act as marriage therapists to remedy the chaos caused by the adultery. It then becomes evident how idolatry and its practices have infiltrated the people's very existence.[30]

---

22. The exclusive love that the LORD asks from Israel is related to God's jealousy-out-of-love. In Exod 20:5 the jealousy of God and the exclusive dedication to Him are connected with each other. Perhaps it is for that reason that Num gives attention to jealousy between man and wife (Num 5:11–31) and the total dedication to the LORD of the Nazirite (Num 6:1–21) before mentioning the dedication of the people at the consecration of the Tabernacle. As if God, with an eye on the relationship between Himself and the people, refers to the absolute loyalty between man and woman and to the choice for total dedication out of love.

23. Hos 3:1.

24. Jer 2:7; Joel 3:2. The land has been chosen as a jewel (Ezek 20:6) for her!

25. Judg 2:1–5.

26. Jer 2:2.

27. Judg 2:10—3:5.

28. Cf. Ezek 20:40 " (. . .) there in the land all the people of Israel will serve me, and there I will accept them." God calls Israel to serve Him in the land and therefore also promises to bring them back to the land. This fact is related to His utter real wish to create a holy center in the visual reality of creation and bless the world from there.

29. Judg 2:18.

30. It becomes clear that Gideon's father has dedicated an altar to Baal (Judg 6:25). Also that Samson, the life long Nazirite (Judg 13:7), cannot live without heathen women who draw the heart away from God (Deut 7:3–4). In the end, Samson's life is a visible prophetic lesson that teaches Israel how difficult the way can be when disloyalty instead of obedience fills the heart.

The Calling Impeded by Israel's Disobedience and the Opposition of the Nations

Idolatry nestles itself within one of the twelve tribes.[31] The family of the high priest Eli is infected by it.[32] Later *terafim* will be found even in the house of David.[33]

The history of the kings of Israel also moves between the poles of faithful service to the LORD and involvement with idolatry. Already in the beginning of the age of the kings this contrast becomes visible. On the one hand we find Saul taking refuge in different sorts of idolatrous and occultist practices,[34] while on the other hand David as the king after God's heart prepares for the building of the Temple.[35] After David, the life of Solomon shows holy dedication to the service of God, while also defiling Jerusalem with the idolatry of his many wives and concubines.[36]

Ultimately, the divided heart of Solomon causes the division of God's nation,[37] occurring in the time of Rehoboam.[38] He who is ONE takes away the favor of the unity of the people because there is no one-ness in the hearts of those serving the ONE God.[39]

From then on, both the history of the kingdom of the ten tribes and that of the kingdom of Judah show a continuous conflict between the pure service (*avoda*) and the "strange" service (*avoda zara*) to the idols. Faithful and adulterous kings alternate, influencing their people, until both parts of the nation have ended up in exile. All the while the prophets champion the faithful marital covenant love for God. Their lives and wrestlings with the people show the wrestling of God with His beloved. In dramatic words and prophetic actions they make the love of God for His *segula*-people[40] visible and audible. God wishes to hear and see what was heard on Mount Carmel: "The LORD—he is God!"[41] But the times He experiences His beloved's forgetfulness and infidelity is often.[42] The prophets sing the songs of love which God sings to His

---

31. Judg 17–18 shows how the tribe of Dan became infected by a tenacious presence of idolatry that continued until the exile of the kingdom of the ten tribes (18:30).

32. 1 Sam 2:12–25. The introduction of a form of temple prostitution (vs. 22) is obviously related to assimilation to idolatrous practices. Later on even Samuel's sons show not to be reliable judges (1 Sam 8:1–3).

33. 1 Sam 19:13; cf. the history of Rachel and her theft of the family gods (Gen 31:30, 34; cf. also 35:2 for the presence of foreign gods in the house of Jacob).

34. 1 Sam 28; cf. Deut 18:9–22.

35. 1 Chr 22–29.

36. 1 Kgs 11:1–8; cf. Deut 17:17. Also by the many horses and great wealth of Solomon his life enters the danger zone that is pictured in "the *tora* for the king" in Deut 17.

37. 1 Kgs 11:9–13.

38. 1 Kgs 12.

39. In Ezek 37:15–28 the connection between the favor of the unity of the nation and the dedication of heart becomes visible.

40. See par example Jer 2–3; Ezek 16 and 23 and Hos 1–3 for the language of love, marriage, and adultery.

41. 1 Kgs 18:39.

42. Par example Jer 3:1 and Hos 2:4, 6.

Part I: The Canonical Narrative: The Tanakh

beloved, and they express His sorrow.[43] God's beloved is even worse than Sodom.[44] The "Song of Songs" does not at all resemble a rendition of the love of the nation for its God.[45] It looks as if the love for the Bridegroom of the nation[46] only keeps glowing in small circles,[47] whilst God (just like Hosea) feels obliged to keep himself at a distance for a long time.[48] Israel's calling to be God's most precious love seems impossible. Are God's ideals for His people too high?

11.5 Unholy (in the) Midst of the Nations

The structure of Israel's encampment in the desert shows what God had in mind regarding the placement of His people amidst the nations.[49] His holy nation was meant to be a holy center of the earth.

The command to execute God's judgment over the nations living in Canaan[50] and not to make covenants with them,[51] is in fact a command to cleanse the land[52] for the purpose of holiness. Israel's slothful disobedience in fulfilling this command,[53] means antagonism against its own calling and against God's wish to bless the world through His holy people living in a holy land.

Meanwhile, the ongoing threat from the surrounding nations is much more than a dispute about land and livelihood. It is a fact that God "planted"[54] Israel right in the middle of the trade route between Egypt and Mesopotamia, surrounded by jealous

---

43. Cf. par example the moving section Jer 8:13—9:24. This reading from the prophets for *Tish'a Be'Av*—the day of commemoration of the destruction of both the first and the second Temple (and many other disasters that came over the Jewish people)—makes the lamentation of the Eternal God audible. There is more to this section than that it would only show the laments of the prophet. Exegetically it is not possible to discern between different speakers in these utterances of pain and sorrow. On the contrary, it can be argued with many good reasons that the one who is venting his heart and showing his sorrow is the LORD Himself.

44. Ezek 16:46–52; cf. also Isa 1:10.

45. Cf. the statement "It is the duet of love between God and Israel (. . .) the literal meaning of the words is so far from their meaning that it is false (. . .)." (Introduction to Song of Songs in Sherman, *The Torah*, 1263).

46. Cf. Hos 2:18–19.

47. The "seven thousand" from 1 Kgs 19:18; groups of prophets, see par example 2 Kgs 4:38–44 and 6:1–7 and the "disciples" from Isa 8:16.

48. Hosea withholds Gomer the marital love (Hos 3:3) as token of the distance that God will let exist for a long time between Himself and the people.

49. See chapter 9.

50. See par example Deut 7:1–6; Joshua 23:6–13.

51. See also Judg 2:2; cf. Joshua 9 for the covenant with the Gibeonites; see also 11:19–20.

52. Lev 18:24–30; 20:23. Cf. Gen 15:16; Deut 18:12–14.

53. See Judg 1 and 3:5–7. In 2:1—3:4 we see that the results from this slothfulness and impotence are incorporated in God's plan as a test case for Israel's obedience.

54. Ps 80:8.

The Calling Impeded by Israel's Disobedience and the Opposition of the Nations

brother nations. But there is more to the ongoing raids by Philistines[55] and from the side of the brother nations Midian,[56] Amalek,[57] Moab,[58] Ammon[59] and Edom.[60] At the deepest level the ongoing attacks on the holy camp of Israel are for the purpose of destroying this place of blessing. The previous invasions by Egypt,[61] Aram,[62] Ashur,[63] and Babel[64] also have this dark, demonic background,[65] although God used these nations to punish Israel.

If only Israel would stay dedicated to God, it would be able to dwell in the holy, God-chosen midst of the earth.[66] Its desire to be like the nations,[67] including the adoption of idolatrous religious customs[68] and the search for political salvation from the powerful nations encircling it,[69] are all acts of unfaithfulness to God. By this adultery[70] Israel defiles the land of God, making it impossible for it to be the place of Indwelling and blessing it was meant to be.

Ultimately the whole people are exiled, only followed by a partial return from the nations.[71] The land falls prey to "the lust of dividing and scattering" of the nations,[72]

---

55. See Judg 13–16 for the fight of Samson with the Philistines. 1 and 2 Sam show the role of Saul and David in the struggle with this nation from the coast of the Mediterranean Sea.

56. Judg 6–8 picture the fight of Gideon with Midian and Amalek. The progenitor of Midian is a son of Abraham (Gen 25:1–4).

57. In the clash with Amalek, a confrontation with Esau takes place (Gen 36:12). Cf. also Exod 17:8–16.

58. Moab and Ammon are the sons of Lot born from incest (Gen 19:37–38). Cf. Deut 2:16–19. Ehud saves from the power of Moab (Judg 3:12–30).

59. Jephthah is called to fight Ammon (Judg 10–11). Cf. also 2 Sam 10; 11:1 and 12:26–31 for David's fight against Ammon.

60. Gen 36:1 has "This is the account of the family line of Esau (that is, Edom)."

61. See par example 1 Kgs 14:25–26 and 2 Chr 12 (Pharaoh Shishak); 2 Kgs 23:29—24:7 (Pharaoh Necho).

62. See par example 2 Sam 8:5–8, 10; 2 Kgs 16:5 and Isa 7:1. For the genealogy of Aram and Ashur, see Gen 10:21–31.

63. See par example 2 Kgs 17–19 for the destruction of the northern kingdom of the ten tribes and the siege of Jerusalem by Ashur.

64. 2 Chr 36:5–20.

65. Isa 10:5–19 mentions the pride of Ashur. Chapters 13–14 mention the pride of Babel that has almost "divine" traits (14:13–14). Ezek 28 shows how the same satanic pride is the force behind Israel opposing behavior of the commercial city Tyre (Ezek 26:1–2; cf. Isa 23).

66. Cf. Lev 18:28: " (. . .) if you defile the land, it will vomit you out." See also 20:22.

67. Ezek 20:32; cf. Deut 17:14 and 1 Sam 8:5.

68. 2 Kgs 16:10–18 shows how king Ahaz copies an altar from Damascus.

69. See par example Isa 30:1–17 and 31:1–9 for the judgment of God because the nation puts its trust in Egypt.

70. Ezek 23 also names "adultery" the political trust in foreign nations.

71. See the end of 2 Chr (with which the Jewish canon ends) and the books of Ezra and Nehemiah.

72. Joel 3:1–3.

and as the book Daniel shows,[73] also after the partial return to the land in the times of Ezra and Nehemiah. The prophets even foresee a massive attack on the people, the land, and the city.[74] The nations will resist until the end.

The calling of Israel to be separate from among the nations, receives much opposition from the side of both Israel and the nations, thereby receiving judgment from the LORD:

> The LORD Almighty has a day in store
> or all the proud and lofty,
> for all that is exalted
> (and they will be humbled), (. . .)
> The arrogance of man will be brought low
> and human pride humbled;
> the LORD alone will be exalted in that day,
> and the idols will totally disappear.[75]

11.6 Priestly Desecration

In the God-chosen land the priestly nation is expected to sanctify God's Name through holy service to Him. Therefore the people should learn about their own priestly calling by looking to the Aaronic priests in their midst, priests designated to point the people toward God's great acts and instruct Israel in the Tora. The service of the priests around the Sanctuary was meant to open up a fountain of blessing in the center of the earth. It was their task to teach the people how to live "around" God's Indwelling in the midst.

The unholy disobedience of the priests, however, will seriously hinder the realization of the nation's priestly calling, dragging the people after them. Many examples of this can be found in the Tanakh.

In the book of Judges we observe a direct connection between the disobedient and self-ordained priestly service of Micah,[76] in which an uneducated and unwitting

---

73. The book of Daniel shows that the nations will continue to attack God's land, city, and people. Behind the scenes a spiritual battle takes place around God's center of the earth (10:13, 20–21). In the closing visions the demonic attack that took place in the times of Antiochus IV Epiphanes is foretold. In 11:36 the unheard of pride against the God of Israel, "the God of gods," is again mentioned. The non-canonic books of 1 and 2 Maccabees describe this black period and God's deliverance.

74. Ezek 38–39 mention the attack of "Gog, of the land of Magog, the chief prince of Meshek and Tubal" (vs. 2). Zechariah describes the joint march of the nations against the city and the people of God (12:1–9 and 14:1–7).

75. Isa 2:12, 17–18. Both Israel and the nations will have to face this Day of the LORD. All prophets place both the nations and Israel under this judgment of God over all pride, ungodliness, and mercilessness.

76. Judg 17.

The Calling Impeded by Israel's Disobedience and the Opposition of the Nations

Levite plays a role, and the idolatry of the tribe of Dan[77] with the later kingdom of the ten tribes following suit.

Eli's sons present a terrifying example of the negative influence unholy priests can have on those entrusted to them.[78] Their behavior causes the people to despise the sacrifice of the LORD.[79] Instead of instructing the people in the Tora, they are reprimanded by the people.[80] Their father, the high priest Eli, is guilty of this because of his negligence and consumptive complicity.[81] He loves his sons first; the LORD is not above all.[82]

Later we see how the high priest Abiathar, stemming from Eli's family, choses against the God-ordained and anointed Solomon.[83]

After the splitting of the nation, within the kingdom of the ten tribes we see self-ordained, non-Levite priests leading an impure worship,[84] whilst the God-ordained servants of His Sanctuary are being impeded.[85]

The spiritual decline that becomes visible in the times of the kings certainly is related to the absence of pure and dedicated priests, although there are exceptions.[86] The amalgamation of the service to the LORD with every sort of idolatry[87] and the defilement of the Temple[88] and the land[89] with all sorts of idols have surely also been caused by priests who no longer knew,[90] lived, or taught the Tora.

---

77. Judg 18. Verse 30 shows that until the exile of the kingdom of the ten tribes, the Danites had descendants of Moses as priests instead of Aaron.

78. 1 Sam 2:12–25.

79. So 1 Sam 2:17 according to the Masoretic text. NIV interprets with the Dead Sea scrolls referring to the sons of Eli.

80. 1 Sam 2:16.

81. 1 Sam 2:29.

82. 1 Sam 2:29.

83. 1 Kgs 1:7, 19, 25; 2:26–27. From a human viewpoint this choice was most hurtful because David had protected Abiathar (1 Sam 22:20–23).

84. 1 Kgs 12:25–33; 2 Chr 11:15.

85. 2 Chr 11:13–14.

86. 2 Kgs 11–12 par example shows how the priest Jehoiadah plays an important role in the rescue of the Davidic monarchy and the following restoration of the Temple. See also 2 Chr 24:2–3, 14–16 for the influence he had during his life.

87. See par example 2 Chr 28 for the negative influence of Ahaz; 33:1–9 is about the idolatry of Manasseh.

88. Regularly we read that the Temple, the holy center, had been defiled and needed to be cleansed and purified again. See par example 2 Chr 29 and 33:15.

89. Josiah realized that not only the holy midst, but also the whole of the land had to be purified. See 2 Chr 34:1–7.

90. The discovery of the law scroll in the time of Josiah (2 Kgs 22–23 and 2 Chr 34) and what followed this, shows that sometimes a great (guilty) lack of knowledge regarding God's will and service existed.

Part I: The Canonical Narrative: The Tanakh

Hosea characterizes priests and prophets as leaders guilty of misleading the people. Dragging the nation along with them in sin, they do not teach the Tora.[91] They transform the sacrificial service in the Temple into something hypocritical and outwardly, as if God is interested in sacrifices without return and dedication to God.[92]

Hosea denounces the priests as the ones causing the land to be under God's judgment:

> Hear the word of the LORD, you Israelites, because the LORD has a charge
> to bring against you who live in the land:
> "There is no faithfulness, no love, no acknowledgment of God in the land.
> There is only cursing, lying and murder, stealing and adultery;
> they break all bounds, and bloodshed follows bloodshed.
> Because of this the land dries up, and all who live in it waste away;
> the beasts of the field, the birds in the sky and the fish in the sea are swept away.
> "But let no one bring a charge, let no one accuse another,
> for your people are like those who bring charges against a priest.
> You stumble day and night, and the prophets stumble with you.
> So I will destroy your mother—my people are destroyed from lack of knowledge.
> "Because you have rejected knowledge, I also reject you as my priests;
> because you have ignored the law of your God, I also will ignore your children."[93]

The center of the earth is no blessed place anymore, but a land full of disaster.[94] Priests are the main culprits. Jeremiah in his turn speaks in the Temple what the priests should have said.[95] Thus accused, the priests react furiously and instead of repenting pronounce a death verdict over Jeremiah.[96] Ezekiel, himself also a priest,[97] is shown by God how the Temple has been defiled and desecrated.[98]

Even after the return from exile and Ezra and Nehemiah's purification of the people,[99] the evil of unholy priests still exists. Even Malachi, chronologically the last prophet in the Tanakh, must denounce the priests of his time.[100] It is as if God Himself makes a final assessment regarding the priests in Israel when He compares the actual situation with His original intentions.

---

91. Or they "teach for a price (. . .) for money" (Mic 3:11) in order to please their "customers." Cf. also Isa 28:7; Jer 6:13.

92. Hos 6:6; cf. 1 Sam 15:22; Isa 1:1–17; Jer 7:3ff; Ps 40:6; 50:12–14.

93. Hos 4:1–6.

94. Hos 4:3; cf. Deut 28:15–63.

95. Jer 7:1–15; 26:1–24.

96. Jer 26:8–11. Lam 4:13 points to the sins of prophets and priests as the cause of the disasters that hit Jerusalem. They shed the blood of righteous people in God's city.

97. Ezek 1:3.

98. Ezek 8.

99. See Ezra 7–10 and Neh 8–13.

100. Mal 1:6–14; 2:1–9.

The Calling Impeded by Israel's Disobedience and the Opposition of the Nations

The LORD God thinks back to His covenant intentions with the priests from the tribe Levi:[101]

> My covenant was with him, a covenant of life and peace, and I gave them to him; this called for reverence and he revered me and stood in awe of my name. True instruction was in his mouth and nothing false was found on his lips. He walked with me in peace and uprightness, and turned many from sin. "For the lips of a priest ought to preserve knowledge, because he is the messenger of the LORD Almighty and people seek instruction from his mouth.[102]"

Such should have been the guidance of the priests for the people on the path of its the priestly calling. The opposite had been the case:

> "But you have turned from the way and by your teaching have caused many to stumble; you have violated the covenant with Levi," says the LORD Almighty. "So I have caused you to be despised and humiliated before all the people, because you have not followed my ways but have shown partiality in matters of the law."[103]

Therefore Malachi warns[104] that on the Day of the LORD there will be judgment for the priests. It was their God-given duty to prevent desecration of the Sanctuary,[105] yet through the centuries the priests themselves have contributed to its desecration and are guilty.[106] Because of them the center of the earth is no "delightful land."[107] And yet, even the last prophet in the Tanakh is allowed to proclaim a future turning of the heart to the LORD and a return to the Tora. There is still hope for the land.[108]

---

101. See Mal 2:4. Levi here is the designation of the priests. The covenant with Levi is mentioned in Num 25:12. Phinehas, champion for the sanctification of God's Name, receives an everlasting promise of God's blessing on his life and offspring.

102. Mal 2:5–7.

103. Mal 2:8–9; cf. Zeph 3:4.

104. Mal 4:1.

105. See Num 18:1 "The LORD said to Aaron, 'You, your sons and your family are to bear the responsibility for offenses connected with the sanctuary, and you and your sons alone are to bear the responsibility for offenses connected with the priesthood.'" This verse holds the priests responsible for possible desecration of the Sanctuary.

106. 2 Chr 36:14 (almost the end of Israel's canon) notices "Furthermore, all the leaders of the priests and the people became more and more unfaithful, following all the detestable practices of the nations and defiling the temple of the LORD, which he had consecrated in Jerusalem."

107. This designation can be found in Mal 3:12.

108. Mal 4:4–6. At the end of the three subdivisions of the Tanakh (Tora, Prophets and "Writings"/Hagiographa), the attention is focused on the (salvation of the) land of the promise.

11. 7 Royal Desecration

The kingship of Israel and the service of its kings must also be directed toward the kingship of God and His Indwelling in the midst of His people. The exercise of the royal duties by the kings were meant to be a visible lesson about the people's calling to live as a kingdom of priests amidst the nations.[109] But just like the priests, many kings were enormous hindrances on the road toward the realization of this calling.

The strong-willed and disobedient King Saul could serve as a model for the kind of resistance kings could show against God's purposes. Because he persecuted David, the man anointed by God, he thereby tore God's people in two.[110] In turn, in his pride David caused the plague in the land.[111] In his idolatry Solomon called over the people the judgment of the schism.[112] His son Rohobeam effectuated the schism between the kingdom of the ten tribes and the kingdom of Judah.[113] Nearly all of the kings of the kingdom of the ten tribes dragged those of the nation of whom they were responsible into idolatry.[114] Ahaz, Hezekiah's father, even models service to the LORD after an example of foreign idolatry.[115] Prideful Hezekiah[116] acts in such as way that "the LORD's wrath was on him and on Judah and Jerusalem."[117] His son Manasseh rules in such a way that Judah and the inhabitants of Jerusalem "did more evil than the nations the LORD had destroyed before the Israelites."[118]

These kings should have guided the people toward safety in the land.[119] Instead, the opposite happened. They dragged the nation after them in their sins, thereby driving the nation from the land promised.[120] Instead of blessing they brought disaster even to the land.[121]

---

109. See chapter 10.

110. "And the war between the house of Saul and the house of David lasted a long time" (2 Sam 3:1).

111. The census ordered by David was infringing the exclusive right of God on His people (see 2 Sam 24; 1 Chr 21).

112. 1 Kgs 11:11–13.

113. 1 Kgs 12; 2 Chr 10–11.

114. Most probably out of political motives even Jehu, who tried to extinguish the Baal service of Jezebel and Ahab, maintained the worship connected with the two altars in Bethel and Dan (2 Kgs 10:31).

115. 2 Kgs 16; 2 Chr 28.

116. After his deathly illness and his miraculous healing, Hezekiah does not speak to the Babylonian delegation about the LORD, but indulges in a focus on power and riches (2 Chr 32:25).

117. 2 Chr 32:25.

118. 2 Chr 33:9.

119. 2 Chr 7:19–20 shows that the people will be uprooted from the land when the kings (or: the king together with the people) will turn away from God. In line with this 2 Chr 33:7–9, in the context of a description of Manasseh's sins, reminds of the conditions God had set with respect to the dwelling in the land.

120. 2 Kgs 23:26–27.

121. Mic 2:10 shows that the defilement of the land caused the land to produce perdition. Cf. Hos

The Calling Impeded by Israel's Disobedience and the Opposition of the Nations

As history moves on the royal element from Israel's calling seems to be more and more of an illusion. Israel's kings are often a mockery of the Name of God. The kingship of the kings of the nations seems to trump the anointed kings of God. Instead of a "head," the royal nation becomes a "tail."[122] A source of mockery instead of head of the nations.[123]

11.8 Unholy Servant of God

At Sinai Israel was called to share in the holiness commanded by God; even more, to share in God's own holiness.[124] God spoke:

> Be holy because I, the LORD your God, am holy.[125]

A holy nation should exist among the nations. A nation with a different quality of life, cleaving to the LORD.[126] Obedient to His holy Tora. A nation as a light for the nations.[127]

The dwelling of the people in the land should, just like the camp in the desert, remind one of the garden of Eden where God walked and had communion with His holy servants.[128] But just like Adam and Eve were shut out of paradise because of their disobedience,[129] in the end the majority of Abraham's offspring ends up again outside the land.

Time and again, it becomes clear that Israel does not live its calling to be a holy nation to the fullest.[130] Israel frustrates that calling by not only unholy worship,[131] but also by unholiness in every area of life. And just as holiness in Leviticus 19 is defined by the Ten Words,[132] the unholiness of the nation violates all of God's commandments: the sin of Achan at the seizure of Jericho;[133] the domination of sexuality in the life

---

4:3; 1 Kgs 17–18 (the draught during Ahab's reign), and the message of the book of Joel with respect to the prophetically-interpreted locust plague.

122. Deut 28:13.
123. 2 Chr 7:20.
124. See chapter 7.
125. Lev 19:2.
126. Ps 63:8.
127. Cf. Isa 42:6; 49:6.
128. See chapter 9.
129. Gen 3.
130. Yet God's mercy always leaves a holy remnant. Par example the prophets hidden by Obadiah and the seven thousand whom God mentions to Elijah (1 Kgs 18:13–15; 19:18). Cf. also Ezek 9:4 "those who grieve and lament over all the detestable things."
131. See earlier in this chapter (11.4), (11.5), (11.6).
132. Cf. chapter 9, footnote 37.
133. Joshua 7.

of Samson;[134] the gang rape in Gibeah;[135] David's adulterousness and the subsequent murder of Uriah;[136] the treason and deceit at the royal court;[137] Ahab's greed;[138] and the murderousness of Athaliah[139] are all examples of an unholy life.

Isaiah, living from an experience of holy encounter with the LORD,[140] characterizes the leaders and inhabitants of Jerusalem as rulers and people of Sodom and Gomorrah.[141] The prophets pronounce God's judgments over every kind of injustice.[142] Life is not safe; justice is not just.[143]

Hosea sums up the violations on the basis of the Ten Words.[144] At that the people are blind in their own sin.[145] For one group there is superfluous prosperity[146] while the poor suffer from poverty and injustice.[147] Economic fraud is common.[148] The holiness of the marital covenant between man and woman is desecrated.[149]

Regularly the prophets remind the people of God's intentions:

> "These are the things you are to do: Speak the truth to each other, and render true and sound judgment in your courts; do not plot evil against each other, and do not love to swear falsely. I hate all this," declares the LORD.[150]

But it is an unholy nation that lives an unholy life in God's own land. Wherever the LORD looks, there is unholiness. Therefore He files a lawsuit against His people, with creation as His witness:

> Listen to what the LORD says:
> "Stand up, plead my case before the mountains;
> let the hills hear what you have to say.
> "Hear, you mountains, the LORD's accusation;
> listen, you everlasting foundations of the earth.

---

134. Judg 13–16.
135. Judg 19.
136. 2 Sam 11.
137. Par example the rebellion of Absalom and that of Sheba (2 Sam 13–20).
138. 1 Kgs 21.
139. 2 Kgs 11; 2 Chr 22:10—23:21.
140. Isa 6.
141. Isa 1:10; cf. also Lam 4:6. Ezek 16 calls Jerusalem more evil than her "sisters" Samaria and Sodom.
142. See par example Isa 5:8–25.
143. Mic 7:2–3; cf. Isa 5:7.
144. Hos 4:2.
145. Isa 29:9; Hos 4:11, 14.
146. See par example Isa 3:16–23 and Amos 3:15; 4:1 and 6:3–6.
147. See par example Isa 1:23 and Amos 5:7–13.
148. Amos 8:4–6; Mic 6:10–11.
149. Mal 2:13–16.
150. Zech 8:16–17; cf. par example also Isa 1:16–17 and Mic 6:8.

The Calling Impeded by Israel's Disobedience and the Opposition of the Nations

> For the LORD has a case against his people;
> he is lodging a charge against Israel.
> "My people, what have I done to you?
> How have I burdened you? Answer me."[151]

And as if the stock is being taken, the last prophet of the Tanakh speaks these words of God:

> "So I will come to put you on trial. I will be quick to testify against sorcerers, adulterers and perjurers, against those who defraud laborers of their wages, who oppress the widows and the fatherless, and deprive the foreigners among you of justice, but do not fear me," says the LORD Almighty.[152]

The people's desecration of every area of life appears to make the calling of the nation far from being realized. The holy center of the earth is impure.

11.9 Unholiness and the Indwelling of God

Israel received the calling to be a nation around the Dwelling of God. As God's *segula*-people, a people taken from the nations, the promise of the Indwelling of God is received. It applies to the camp in the desert. It also applies to the God-given land where the LORD let His countenance dwell within their midst.[153] The desecration of God's Name and of all His commandments causes Israel to lose this prerogative that came with the calling. The LORD removed His people from the land where His countenance dwelled,[154] to live in the impure lands of the nations.[155]

The Tanakh shows that prior to the entry of the people into their God-chosen land, this Promised Land had been made impure by the terrible sins of the nations that had lived there.[156] Yet the people were allowed to enter it, following the ark! God's very Presence and the holy *avoda* of His servant-nation would purify the land[157] and transform it into the holy camp of Israel around God's Dwelling. Ultimately His house would be erected in God's city in the midst of the nation. In this manner the people would be allowed to live around God's Indwelling, and thus a place of blessing for all nations would be created by Him.

---

151. Mic 6:1–3.

152. Mal 3:5.

153. Cf. 1 Sam 1:12, 15, 19, 22; 2:17–18.

154. 2 Kgs 17:18, 20, 23. Three times in these verses a removal from God's Presence is mentioned. Verse 23 mentions the land. Cf. also 23:27 and 24:20.

155. Amos 7:17; Ezek 4:13; Hos 9:3 (to eat "unclean food" refers to eating produce of a country that does not belong to the LORD but to the idols; so Wolff, *Hosea*, 199). Cf. Joshua 22:19; 1 Sam 26:19; 2 Kgs 5:17 also shows the relation between the purity of God's land and the service to Him. Also see Ezra 6:21.

156. See Lev 18:24–30.

157. Cf. 2 Chr 34:3, 5, 8; Ezek 39:12, 14, 16.

Not only does Israel's disobedience cause defilement for God's land, but also the nation, as mediator of Gods' blessing, must leave the land. As Israel is removed from purity into impurity, the world is further removed from the God-intended center of blessing.[158]

Even God's holy Presence wishes to stay no longer amidst the impurity of the people. God laments:

> Oh, that I had in the desert a lodging place for travelers,
> so that I might leave my people and go away from them;
> for they are all adulterers, a crowd of unfaithful people.[159]

Ezekiel, as prophet blessed with a vision of God's majesty and Throne-chariot,[160] observes how God's glory went into exile. The *Shekhina*[161] left the Temple[162] and the city.[163] What a disaster: the people sent away from the land and the Dwelling of God deserted by God Himself!

11.10 Divine Lamentation

The bridal phase between God and His people in the desert seems far away. The fresh moments of first love seem long ago.[164] Seemingly the people's calling has been derailed underway toward the *tikkun olam*. As if God's *segula* has completely become off track. The disobedience of God's people and the opposition from the nations have resulted in an impure and partially emptied land. Only jackals[165] inhabit the mountain of God's Dwelling and the place of God's House has become a stony field.[166]

Although there has been a partial return from exile and the Second Temple has been built, the *avoda* of the people remains essentially unchanged, as shown by the prophetic words from that period.[167]

---

158. Cf. footnote 155 in this chapter.
159. Jer 9:2.
160. Ezek 1–3.
161. The Jewish designation for the Presence of God.
162. Ezek 10–11. Chapter 10:15–22 mentions how in leaving, the glory of the LORD pauses for awhile at the eastern gate of the Temple. There is, so to speak (mentioned in chapter 11), a last round of inspection followed by the departure of the *Shekhina* from the Temple and the city. There is no longer a reason to stay!
163. Ezek 11:23; cf. Jer 8:19
164. Jer 2:2; Hos 13:5–6; cf. also 2:13.
165. Lam 5:18.
166. Mic 3:12; Jer 26:18.
167. Both Haggai and Zechariah act as prophets after the first return from exile. Both speak about the Day that will make Israel and the nations to tremble, but that also will bring salvation for God's people (see par example Hag 2:6–9, 20–23; Zech 13–14). Malachi also warns the people that they must prepare themselves for a day of fiery purification when the Angel of the covenant (to be identified with the Angel of the LORD; RSV and NIV "the messenger of the covenant") will come to His Temple. The

The Calling Impeded by Israel's Disobedience and the Opposition of the Nations

Therefore the journey of Israel toward the *tikkun olam* is accompanied by the lamentation of God until the end, where Jeremiah serves as the spokesman and which still today sounds in the synagogues on *Tish'a Be'Av*:[168]

> ". . . my heart is faint within me.
> Listen to the cry of my people from a land far away:
> "Is the LORD not in Zion? Is her King no longer there?"
> "Why have they aroused my anger with their images, with their worthless foreign idols?"
> "The harvest is past, the summer has ended, and we are not saved."
> Since my people are crushed, I am crushed; I mourn, and horror grips me.
> Is there no balm in Gilead? Is there no physician there?
> Why then is there no healing for the wound of my people?"[169]

11.11 Toward the Day of the LORD and Waiting for the Eighth Day

In His judgment of Israel, God's heart laments over His son and servant: "The whole house of Israel is uncircumcised in heart."[170] The prophets are very clear[171] that together with the nations, Israel must prepare itself for a day of judgment. This judgment will begin in the midst of the earth and will strike God's people first.[172] New waves of exile and threats will come over the people and as a result will bring forth purification.[173]

The judgment will not be the end, because God loves His people with an eternal love.[174]

> How can I give you up, Ephraim? How can I hand you over, Israel?
> How can I treat you like Admah? How can I make you like Zeboyim?

---

separation between those who fear the LORD and the godless people will also take place in Israel itself (Mal 3:1–2; 3:13—4:6).

168. See footnote 43 in this chapter.

169. Jer 8:18–22. The NIV mentions uncertainty regarding the meaning of the first half of verse 18 and interprets this as a call to God; RSV renders "my grief is beyond healing and my heart is sick within me" as other translations do.

170. Jer 9:26. These words are no part of the synagogual reading for *Tish'a Be'Av*, that ends with the positive admonition of 9:23–24.

171. Judgment prophecies for the nations are found with all prophets. "Collections" of such words par example can be found in Isa 13–23; Jer 46–51; Ezek 25–32 and Amos 1–2.

172. Cf. Ezek 9:6; cf. also Amos 1:2 (the judgment goes out from Jerusalem).

173. Zech 10:9 mentions a future (new phase) of exile. Also 14:2 foresees exile. In chapters 13–14 he speaks, *after* the return from exile, about future threats for Jerusalem with all accompanying disaster. The book of Daniel additionally shows that tribulations will come over the people, ultimately intended to bring about the purification of the people (Dan 12:1–3, 10).

174. Jer 31:3.

Part I: The Canonical Narrative: The Tanakh

> My heart is changed within me; all my compassion is aroused.[175]

God does not experience joy in His son and servant, but speaking words of judgment is not enjoyable either:

> "Is not Ephraim my dear son, the child in whom I delight?
> Though I often speak against him, I still remember him.
> Therefore my heart yearns for him; I have great compassion for him,"
> declares the LORD.[176]

Therefore, all disobedience and resistance of the priestly nation and all opposition of the nations are ultimately placed under a powerful reign of hope from the side of the Most High God. He will not give up until all His purposes have been realized.

Whatever may happen, the priestly nation, taken from among the nations in order to bless the nations, is on the way toward the full realization of its calling. Even the encircling nations, who are represented in this priestly people before God, are en route toward blessing which they will receive together with and out of Israel.

Israel and the nations are on the way toward the Eighth Day. This will be the theme of the next chapter.

---

175. Hos 11:8.

176. Jer 31:20. To speak *against* Ephraim hurts God. Jer 45 shows that not only the prophets (in this case Jeremiah's scribe Baruch) suffer by words of judgment, but also—and in the first place—the LORD Himself!

Chapter 12

Learning about the Eighth Day
Prophetic Words about the Messianic Time

12.1 The End of the Canonical Narrative of the Tanakh

HAVING SEEN THE DARK image of disobedience and resistance from the last chapter, one may ask, as the God-fearers in Israel did, if a time will ever arrive when Israel's calling will be fully realized.

Will there be an "eighth day"[1] for the calling to be God's *segula*-people and to be a kingdom of priests? A time when the nation will fulfill its task completely, just as the priests after their consecration on the eighth day[2] began their *avoda* in the Sanctuary? In that time will the *avoda* be perfect and complete, and usher into the midst of the earth a fountain of blessing? Will the priestly nation, as the center of the earth, minister atonement, holiness, and teaching to the nations? Will God permanently dwell in the midst of His people? Will the nations wish to be blessed from the Dwelling of God in the camp of Israel?

In short, what is the end of the canonical narrative of the Tanakh? Disobedience, resistance, and failure? Or will God's intentions from the first moment of creation and the very first words of the Tanakh become reality in the *tikkun olam*, once and for all?

12.2 Hopeful Prophetic Words: Puzzle Pieces of Blessing

God promised Israel prophets who would proclaim God's words to the people.[3] The structure of the Jewish canon makes this promise visible. After the Tora, the five books of Moses, the Prophets follow suit as second subsection of the Tanakh. Time and again

---

1. See chapter 8.
2. Idem.
3. See chapter 10 (10.7; footnote 46).

prophets accompanied Israel on its path with the calling, consistently challenging the people with God's final plans for His people and the world. No matter how many words of judgment were delivered, hope and salvation would have the final word.

The most foundational theme of the canonical narrative is found in this chapter. It is God's persevering, irresistible will to bless. From the beginning, both creation and the words of Scripture tell about the blessing that God wishes to give.[4] That blessing has been the driving force of the future-oriented history of Israel and the creation. The canonical narrative of the Tanakh ends with the final victory of the blessing of the God of Israel.

Just as in the last chapter, the structure of this chapter is determined by the different aspects of the calling Israel received at Sinai. This systematizing helps to categorize the many different aspects of the prophetic words of salvation. The blessing of God namely concerns different areas contained in the words of the calling. The words of the prophets are like "puzzle pieces of blessing." They are presented by the prophets, but not systematically laid out as a completed puzzle. Yet the "edge pieces of the puzzle" make it clear: God is moving toward the Eighth Day with His people, with His city, with His land, with His Tora, with the nations, and with creation. They are underway toward the final climax of the perfection, the consummation, in the *tikkun olam*.[5]

12.3 For the Sake of the Name

One thing Israel must know: God's salvation is not the necessary reward for its own merits. Ezekiel must speak:

> Therefore say to the Israelites, "This is what the Sovereign LORD says: It is not for your sake, people of Israel, that I am going to do these things, but for the sake of my holy name, which you have profaned among the nations where you have gone."[6]

The infidelity and disobedience of the nation[7] cause God to punish His people with exile. But precisely by this dispersion His name becomes profaned. The nations perceive God as the loser in the struggle with Israel's impure *avoda*.[8] Therefore God grants salvation and shows that He is the LORD, the Holy One.[9] Return, purification, the giving of the Spirit, renewing the land into the garden of Eden, rebuilding of cities,

---

4. See chapter 1.
5. See chapter 1 (1.4).
6. Ezek 36:22. Cf. verse 32 and 20:9, 14.
7. Ezek 36:18–19.
8. Ezek 36:20.
9. Ezek 36:23; 39:27.

the blessing to be a great nation, the privilege to be God's people,[10] all that God does, He does so that Israel and the nations

> . . . will know that I am the LORD.[11]

For the sake of His own Name, God does not rest before His people serve Him in a holy manner within the midst of creation, and so becoming a blessing.[12] The Holy One of Israel choses to reveal His greatness to the nations by having all His promises fulfilled in His land and people. From there until eternity God's revelation will take place.

12.4 Fulfillment of the Two-sidedness of the Covenant

Although salvation is realized by absolute, one-sided actions of God, the LORD does not annul the two-sidedness of the covenant. Unilaterally He realizes a perfect fulfillment of the two-sided covenant relation. By creating a pure *avoda* of an obedient people, He ensures that also the conditional aspect of Israel's calling remains valid. An obedient and dedicated priestly nation will enter into the Eighth Day.

From this hope, Moses speaks about a future divine circumcision of the heart of the people. The LORD Himself will be the *mohel*, the circumciser of His people. He will circumcise the hearts of the people so that the people will live[13] because they love Him, and so fulfill the *Shema*. He takes away the barrier created by deep disobedience by which love is hampered. On the LORD's command, Jeremiah promises:

> "The days are coming," declares the LORD,
> "when I will make a new covenant
> with the people of Israel
> and with the people of Judah.
> It will not be like the covenant
> I made with their ancestors
> when I took them by the hand
> to lead them out of Egypt,
> because they broke my covenant,
> though I was a husband to them,"
> declares the LORD.
> "This is the covenant I will make with the people of Israel
> after that time," declares the LORD.
> "I will put my law in their minds

10. For all these acts of salvation see Ezek 36.
11. Ezek 36:38.
12. Cf. Ezek 39:7, 25.
13. Deut 30:6. It is remarkable that Nachmanides (Ramban) positions the "circumcision" of this verse in the times of the Messiah. He will deliver the human family (thus not only Israel, EJW) from the desire to sin (*Deuteronomy*, 341–42). The New Testament also speaks about the Messianic circumcision that took place in Messiah Jesus and in which the nations can share (Col 2:11–12).

Part I: The Canonical Narrative: The Tanakh

> and write it on their hearts.
> I will be their God,
> and they will be my people.
> No longer will they teach their neighbor,
> or say to one another, 'Know the LORD,'
> because they will all know me,
> from the least of them to the greatest,"
> declares the LORD.
> "For I will forgive their wickedness
> and will remember their sins no more."[14]

God promises a renewed covenant,[15] the blessing of which consists in the placement of the Tora in "the ark" of the heart of the people.[16] This promise also implies that the heart of the people will be throne[17] and footstool,[18] in short the resting place[19] of the Almighty One.

God's Tora will be written on the tablets of the heart, resulting in a deep knowledge of God by young and old. There will be talk of forgiveness from all iniquity and a new obedience provided by God.

Also through the ministry of Ezekiel the LORD speaks about this purifying consecration and anointing of the people:

> For I will take you out of the nations; I will gather you from all the countries and bring you back into your own land. I will sprinkle clean water on you, and you will be clean; I will cleanse you from all your impurities and from all your idols. I will give you a new heart and put a new spirit in you; I will remove from you your heart of stone and give you a heart of flesh. And I will put my Spirit in you and move you to follow my decrees and be careful to keep my laws.[20]

God by His Spirit creates obedience and a pure *avoda*. A renewed creation "anointed" with the indwelling of the Spirit in the heart of men.[21] Just like priests were anointed for seven consecutive days, after having been purified for seven consecutive days.[22]

---

14. Jer 31:31–34.

15. Implicitly He promises here also a new *Shavuot* (the Feast of Weeks celebrated fifty days after *Pessaḥ* when Israel (among other aspects) celebrates the giving of the Tora at Sinai.

16. Cf. Exod 40:20. The ark formed the most holy center/heart of the nation.

17. Cf. Num 7:89; 1 Sam 4:4; 2 Kgs 19:15.

18. Cf. 1 Chr 28:2 In Ps 99 and 132 throne, footstool, resting place, ark, and Zion are mentioned together.

19. Cf. 2 Chr 6:41.

20. Ezek 36:24–27.

21. Cf. Gen 2:7 for the breathing of the breath of life; 1 Sam 10:9 for a new heart for King Saul following his anointing.

22. See chapter 8 (8.3).

Obedience of men, their *avoda,* is essential and necessary, following the task and the position God gives them. In this *avoda* Israel is called to dedicate its heart and soul, will and mind, its whole life to God. But just as its election and salvation, in the end even Israel's obedience is an act of God. The LORD Himself is the secret behind and within their dedication. The essence of this has been put into words by Isaiah:

> LORD, you establish peace for us; all that we have accomplished you have done for us.[23]

By the anointment of the priestly nation the LORD Himself is present and His Presence is the deepest secret of the service to Him. He Himself accomplishes the people's actions. Zechariah prophesies:

> So he said to me, "This is the word of the LORD to Zerubbabel, 'Not by might nor by power, but by my Spirit,' says the Lord Almighty."[24]

Not only will Israel's God give His Spirit in their hearts to ensure that His people will serve Him from the inside out, but He will also "become" in them the faithful service to Himself.[25] In the same vein the Talmud proclaims, "The mikva of Israel is HaShem."[26] God who purifies is Himself the purification.

12.5 The Purification of the *Avoda* and the Servant of the LORD

In addition the prophet Isaiah speaks about a pure *avoda* of Israel. As part of God's salvation His people will be named "priests of the LORD ... and ministers of our God."[27] Israel is God's elected and beloved servant.[28] Yet, at the same time God speaks:

> Who is blind but my servant,
> and deaf like the messenger I send?
> Who is blind like the one in covenant with me,
> blind like the servant of the LORD?[29]

---

23. Isa 26:12. This is the most obvious interpretation and translation. The Septuagint interprets in the same manner: "You have given us all." *JSB* interprets this verse as if it speaks about the giving of peace after God has requited the *mis*deeds of the people. The paradoxical character of this verse, however, is all too easily neutralized in this manner.

24. Zech 4:6.

25. Cf. Isa 28:5–6, where God promises that "He will be a spirit of justice to the one who sits in judgment, a source of strength to those who turn back the battle at the gate."

26. b Yoma 85b; see footnote 97 of chapter 8. *HaShem* is Hebrew for "the Name"; in Judaism this is one of the ways to speak about God or address Him. Cf. also chapter 8 (8.3; footnote 43) for the *mikva* of the priests. Cf. Jer 23:6 for the name of the Messiah: "the LORD is our righteousness" (NIV: "the LORD Our Righteous Savior").

27. Isa 61:6.

28. Isa 41:8–9; 43:10; 45:4; 48:20.

29. Isa 42:19.

Part I: The Canonical Narrative: The Tanakh

Yet God will redeem His messenger and servant Israel, causing the people to walk the pathway He has commanded.[30] Isaiah implicates God's intervention with regard to the pure *avoda* of His servant Israel. The servanthood of Israel is underway, standing under the promise of the Eighth Day.

In the direct context of these promises, however, Isaiah speaks words about a servant of the LORD who will perform a task on behalf of Israel. In these so-called sections about "the Servant of the LORD,"[31] a servant appears whose name is Israel and in whom God will glorify Himself.[32] He will restore the tribes of Jacob[33] and also be a light unto the nations.[34] He will be a "covenant for the people,"[35] resulting in an Israel that will be delivered and God's land rebuilt.[36] He will purify the people by his sacrificial death.[37] God Himself will ensure that justice is done to the servant.[38] He will purify many nations.[39] He will proclaim the Tora of God to the coastal lands.[40] The plans of God will prosper because of Him.[41]

The question regarding the identification of this servant receives different answers. Do we meet the *people* as God's servant,[42] or is this an *individual* sent by God, who will be a blessing for His people?[43] In identifying this servant, we do not necessarily have to chose between an individual or collective explanation. The servant who acts in relation to Israel has clear corporative traits. He seems to be somebody who represents the people and in whom the people are "present." Perhaps we must begin to realize that the individual and the collective interpretation are connected

---

30. In Isa 43:21 a proclamation of salvation ends with the word that God's people *will* glorify Him. In 44:3–5 we find that also Isaiah connects the gift of the Spirit of God with a renewed dedication to the LORD. In 59:21 we meet the promise of an everlasting Presence of God's Spirit and words.

31. Isa 42:1–7; 49:1–9; 50:4–16; 52:13—53:12.

32. Isa 49:3.

33. Isa 49:6.

34. Isa 42:6; 49:6.

35. Isa 42:6; 49:8.

36. Isa 49:8.

37. Isa 53:8–11. Also the translation of *JSB* goes in this direction ("if he made himself an offering for guilt") although the commentary distances itself from the notion of vicarious suffering.

38. Isa 50:7–9.

39. Isa 52:15; the Hebrew verb used points to a ritual cleansing by sprinkling (cf. Lev 4:6, 17; 8:11; 14:7; also see Milgrom, *Leviticus 1–16* on these verses; also NIV renders: "sprinkle"). When Jewish and non-Jewish interpreters can not understand the occurrence of this word in 52:15 and render as "startle" (RSV) or the like, the reason is not that the most obvious meaning is unclear to them. Much more the reason will be that in this section, which came to be contentious during the ages, there is speak of a ritual purification of the nations. See also Young, *Isaiah*, Vol. III, 338. Cf. also Zeph 3:9 for the purification of the nations.

40. Isa 42:4.

41. Isa 53:10.

42. As in Isa 41:8–10.

43. The servant in Isa 49:6 has a task to perform for Israel.

Learning about the Eighth Day

to each other, sometimes even playing their role together.[44] It may be that one time the attention is focused on the people as a whole, and then switches to focus on this one servant.[45] The relation between both becomes very clear when the servant of the LORD is named a "covenant for the people."[46]

12.6 The Purification of the *Avoda* and the Servant as "Covenant for the People"

Twice God proclaims His servant to be a "covenant for the people," a *brit am*.[47] God gives[48] this servant a place as a *brit am*. Because of the context we must conclude that this covenant is intended for the people of Israel.[49] The servant therefore can not coincide, at least not completely, with Israel. It seems that in the appointment of this one servant to be covenant for the people, all Israel is subsumed in this one man. He in himself is the covenant for Israel. God creates a "One-for-all-covenant-bearer." Just like Moses could function as the subsummation of the whole nation,[50] or the high

---

44. In the New Testament we also meet both interpretations. It is therefore obvious that in the first century the sections about the servant of the LORD could be interpreted both as speaking about the Messiah (Jesus) and about Israel (or at least about the Jewish disciples/envoys of Jesus). Cf. Luke 2:32 (Messianic interpretation) with Acts 13:47 (corporative interpretation).

45. The calling of a priest was in every respect connected to the priestly calling of the whole people. The servant as "light for the nations" (Isa 42:6; 49:6; NIV: "for the Gentiles") can point to the calling of an individual, but also refer to the task of the whole nation; cf. also 42:4.

46. Isa 42:6 and 49:8.

47. The rendering of these Hebrew words is "covenant of/for the people." It is noteworthy that in Jewish interpretation this designation is found puzzling (see par example *JSB* ad Isa 42:6). A choice is then made for what could be called more or less "a rendering of embarrassment" as "covenant people." Then, however, in fact the grammatical construction is turned upside down.

48. The Hebrew text of Isa 42:6 and 49:6 uses this verb ("give unto") in the sense of "to appoint."

49. In Isa 42:6 *brit am is* juxtaposed to "light for the nations"; this can mean that the verse mentions two different duties of the servant. In 49:8 the "content" of *brit am* in fact specifies what the first part of 49:6 mentions as the task of the servant with respect to Israel. The raising up and bringing back of Israel (49:6) receives elaboration in the task of restoring the land and the dwelling places (49:8). The task with respect to the nations is expressed again in 49:6 with the words "light for the nations."

I therefore interpret *brit am* as referring to the task of the servant for the people of Israel. So also Oswalt, *Isaiah*, 117. Oswalt postulates that those who identify the servant as the people Israel, often interpret *am* as referring to mankind. So par example Westermann, *Isaiah,* on these verses. Because of the parallelism in 42:6 he interprets *brit am* as "covenant-salvation for all mankind." Van de Beek, interprets the servant to be an individual but then says, " the Servant of the LORD has been appointed to a *Temple-berith* for the nations (translation EJW)" (*De kring om de Messias*, 191).

50. Cf. 1 Cor 10:2 for this New Testament concept.

priest and king as the representation of the nation,[51] this servant in some way is the embodiment of the covenant of God with Israel.[52]

In himself he will be, by reason of God's decisions and actions, a covenant for the nation. To understand, we can think of the covenant with Abram. In that time the LORD walked the path between the halves of the animals that had been slaughtered himself, and by doing so He founded the covenant upon Himself.[53] The LORD made a covenant *with* Abram, but Abram did *not* walk the blood-path of the covenant as covenant partner. Hereby God showed that only His own part in walking the path of the covenant was decisive. God's own covenant fidelity guaranteed the covenant. Therefore it would never be broken.

It seems as if God also appoints the servant about whom Isaiah speaks, to be a covenant-in-himself. The LORD makes him a covenant-path, which in itself brings with it unilateralism, thus creating in the servant a covenant that will not be broken and that results in salvation. With this servant, and with him as this covenant, salvation begins. God appoints him to be "my salvation."[54] This salvation has the color and the sound of the Year of Jubilee.[55]

It also is important to see that when this servant *is* the covenant, the total and perfect fulfillment of the covenant, he thereby also has obtained all covenantal blessings. For that reason, through him there is talk of the restoration of the land and salvation of the people.[56] His obedience obtains a right to all covenant promises. We must also understand his suffering to be the suffering of all covenant curses and the removal of them. Because of his listening to God and calling on Him, God delights in him and in those who are represented "in him."[57] By this, the future of salvation is a gift obtained through the way of the covenant. It is a gift of God, but at the same time a blessing merited by pure obedience.[58] In a miraculous manner the covenantal

---

51. Generations also could represent one another. Cf. Gen 17:7; we observe here how future generations, which will come forth from Abraham's offspring, are represented in Abraham and share in the promise through him. In Deut 29:14–15 we also see future generations represented by the people who are present.

52. Oswalt, "Somehow the Servant in himself will be the embodiment of God's covenant with his people" (*Isaiah*, 297). He also signalizes this same concept in the New Testament when he says, "The sense is almost certainly that the Servant represents the covenant, much as Jesus said, "I am the way, and the truth, and the life" (John 14:6)" (Ibid., 117). Oswalt holds the opinion that the servant (whom he interprets in an individual manner) as *brit am* will be the new form of the covenant foresaid by Jeremiah.

53. Gen 15:17–21.

54. With regard to the context it is more logical thus to render the ending of Isa 49:6: "The servant is My salvation, says the LORD" (so Young, *Isaiah*, 276).

55. Oswalt points to the "language of Jubilee" in the first three strophes of Isa 49:8 (*Isaiah*, 297).

56. Isa 49:8ff; Oswalt observes a "re-establishment of Joshua's work" (Ibid., 298). He interprets the expressions used in a spiritualizing manner, however.

57. See Deut 30:3–10 for the concrete blessing of circumcision of the heart, return, and living in the land, that is related to obedience.

58. Cf. Isa 53:11–12. The concept of the merits of the patriarchs is prominently present within

obedience of this one man and the covenant gift of the One God become connected in the servant as *brit am*.

The appointment of this servant to be a "covenant for the people" shows God's intervention very clearly. Like Jeremiah and Ezekiel, Isaiah hereby speaks of an overpowering initiative for the salvation from God. "Covenant for the people," "new covenant,"[59] "Tora in the heart,"[60] "a new heart and a new spirit/Spirit,"[61] and "circumcision of the heart,"[62] are all words that describe how God creates a pure *avoda* in the people. This servant, who is a "covenant for the people," naturally fixes our attention on the promises about Israel's Messiah.

12.7 The Messiah and the Calling of Israel

Long ago Moses spoke of the appearance of a prophet, like himself, who would proclaim the words of God to the people.[63] David received a promise from God about a son who would sit on his throne forever.[64] In the prophets' elaboration upon the theme of the coming of this Promised One, it becomes clear that royal, priestly, and prophetic duties coincide in him. In these prophetic words and therefore also in the expectation of Israel, the Anointed One, the Messiah,[65] takes shape, gaining clearer contours. God promises a son of David who will be anointed by the Spirit in a special manner.[66] The working of the Spirit will be upon and through him sevenfold.[67] He will act only in righteousness,[68] with his arrival signifying the end to all evil; he will

---

Judaism (founded among others on verses like Gen 15:6 and 22:16–18); still there has been a lot of discussion about this theme. As was the case with Abraham in Gen 22, so also in Isa 53 is the obedience of the servant the reason why blessing has become available.

59. Jer 31:31–34.

60. Jer 31:33. In Isa 51:4–7 we find a number of important concepts (the "Tora in the heart," the Tora as "Light for the nations" and "my salvation") mentioned together.

61. Ezek 36:26–27.

62. Deut 30:6.

63. Deut 18:18. See also chapter 10 (10.7).

64. 2 Sam 7:13–14. See chapter 10 (10.7).

65. Messiah is the rendering of the Hebrew *Mashiaḥ*, meaning the anointed (one). Anointment with oil was token of appointment and reception of authority by God. The high priest could be called *mashiaḥ* (Lev 6:22). The kings of Israel also were "anointed (ones)" (1 Sam 10:1; 16:6). The patriarchs could be named thus (1 Chr 16:22 = Ps 105:15; perhaps because of the Spirit of God leading them? Do these words in the historic context of Chronicles perhaps also recall the rushed and vagrant Israel?). Even the Persian king Cyrus could be named God's anointed (Isa 45:1).

66. Isa 11:1–2; cf. also 42:1.

67. In Isa 11:1–2 seven aspects of the work of the Messiah are designated with seven names of the Spirit. Jewish exposition compares these seven names with the seven arm of the *menora*.

68. Isa 11:3–5; 9:7.

fill the earth with knowledge of the LORD.[69] The nations will seek this son of David,[70] and he will restore the kingship in Israel, for Israel. God Himself will guarantee this.[71] God will keep His promises to David and give this king to His people and all nations.[72]

This pre-eminent Anointed One will perform more acts of salvation than all other anointed ones before him in a manner unmatched. He will bring God's words and Tora to the nations.[73] He will usher Israel into a year of Jubilee,[74] reviving the people and the land.[75] As a shepherd he will seek his sheep[76] dispersed in exile. He will bring them home and rule over them as a righteous king.[77]

In him royal and priestly duties coincide.[78] He will build the Temple[79] and be a royal priest.[80] In humility he will come to Jerusalem[81] and proclaim peace to the nations.[82]

In an unprecedented manner God is present and at work in him. His names make this visible as he has a sevenfold, nearly divine name.[83] He can be named Immanuel, God with us.[84] The name of this Branch[85] of David is "The LORD is our righteousness."[86] He is the exponent of God's power on earth and he therefore experiences the aggression of the nations.[87] His place is at the right hand of God.[88] Like Moses, he raises his scepter-staff.[89] A very special priest, he is appointed by God.[90] A

---

69. Isa 11:9.
70. Isa 11:10.
71. Isa 9:7.
72. Isa 55:3–5.
73. Isa 42:1, 4; 9:1–2 when read in the context.
74. In Isa 61:2 we find this designation.
75. Isa 66:10–24; cf. 49:8–9.
76. Ezek 34:23–24; Jer 23:1–8; in both sections acts of the LORD and the Branch are interwoven.
77. Jer 23:5–6.
78. The royal rule and the priestly instruction, mediation and leading the Temple service.
79. Zech 6:12.
80. Zech 6:13.
81. Zech 9:9.
82. Zech 9:10.
83. Isa 9:6.
84. Isa 7:14; the Messianic interpretation is possible even when a royal child in the time of Ahaz would have had this name.
85. Jer 23:5; Zech 3:8; 6:12. Cf. also Isa 11:1.
86. Jer 23:6 (RSV). NIV renders "The LORD Our Righteous Savior."
87. Ps 2:2.
88. Ps 110:1.
89. Ps 110:2.
90. Ps 110:4.

servant is he![91] He fulfills the calling of Israel[92] and allows Israel to fulfill its calling.[93] He will restore paradise once again on earth.[94]

In his existence Bethlehem and "eternal origins," "from of old, from ancient times,"[95] become connected. Suddenly various prophetic words resound. As puzzle pieces with the same color, words about the Son of Man[96] and the Servant of the LORD[97] begin to emerge from the prophetic books. In many sections the acts of God and the acts of the Messiah are shown in one panoramic view, and without a strict differentiation. Thus in different ways the *avoda* of the Messiah is connected with the acts of God by which Israel will be brought back to pure *avoda*.

12.8 God's Plans with Israel Realized

We have observed that for the sake of His Name, God's plans with Israel will be realized. In this fulfillment obedience, an essential element in the covenant, must play its role. God therefore creates a new obedience in His people and through the Messiah.

The prophets are very clear. Everything that God intended at the creation of heaven and earth will become reality in the end. God's Dwelling will be there, in the midst of the creation, in God's own land, a place of fellowship with the Holy One. The calling of the people will become a reality in the fullest sense. The blessing promised to Abraham will be distributed to the nations through Israel. This blessing will be royal and priestly, with His people as a "house of learning" for the nations.

It is good to remember that the prophets spoke about judgment and salvation in an all-encompassing panorama. The destruction of the first Temple, the first deportation from the land, and the violence of well-known enemies form the closest horizon. That the return from Babel and the rebuilding of the Temple are just the beginning of salvation is clear,[98] but which future deep and dark times are implicated, that remains hidden.[99] Also hidden are the moments of salvation that will dawn over the people.

---

91. Zech 3:8.

92. Cf. the preceding section about the servant as the *brit am*.

93. Isa 61:6; Ezek 37:24. Cf. also Dan 7:14 with 7:18, where the Son of Man seems to bring a people with him. We find the same congruence of the Messiah and "rulers" in Isa 32:1–2.

94. Isa 11:6–9.

95. Mic 5:2.

96. Dan 7:13–14.

97. Isa 42:1–7; 49:1–9; 50:4–11; 52:13—53:12.

98. Hag 2:1–9 shows that people were conscious of the fact that the rebuilding of the Temple did not bring the fulfillment of all promises.

99. To be sure, the book of Daniel asks our attention for different phases of the future. But the power of Rome, the destruction of the second Temple, the new exile, the desert of the nations, the *Shoa*, they all are phases of darkness implicitly present in the one panoramic view of judgment and salvation.

Part I: The Canonical Narrative: The Tanakh

These moments are implicated, but are not specifically named. Future deliverance and the creation of a new heaven and earth are found together in this panorama.[100]

We then must limit ourselves to summarizing the different parts of the future salvation God wishes to give.[101]

12.9 The Gift of the Return of the People

The dead will resurrect. So the prophet Ezekiel describes salvation that will be given to the dispersed people who resemble carelessly discarded corpses.[102] The grave of exile will not be the end. Hope that has died will be revived.[103] The LORD Himself will bring His people back to the land of Israel.[104] Miraculously the national existence will be restored, and it will be clear that the LORD has spoken and done it.[105]

This promise of the return of God's people to the land He chose and promised to the patriarchs and their offspring, we find often in the prophets.[106] Yes, the exile has been disciplinary,[107] but it will not be the end. The night of dispersion will be followed by a grand exodus[108] that will bring about a new *Pessaḥ* joy.[109]

In the end, the pain of dispersion will be replaced with God's healing. In the desert of the nations there will be mercy for the people.[110] Rachel's weeping will end:

> This is what the LORD says:
> "A voice is heard in Ramah,
> mourning and great weeping,
> Rachel weeping for her children
>   and refusing to be comforted,
> because they are no more."
> This is what the LORD says:
> "Restrain your voice from weeping
>   and your eyes from tears,
> for your work will be rewarded,"
>   declares the LORD.

---

100. Isa 66:22.

101. In the remainder of this chapter, a number of core sections will be focused upon. In the footnotes reference will be made in a limited way to other Scripture words.

102. Ezek 37:1–14.

103. Ezek 37:11.

104. Ezek 37:12.

105. Ezek 37:13.

106. Cf. Isa 49:8–13, 22; 60:4–9; Mic 2:12–13; Amos 9:11–15.

107. Jer 30:11; 46:28.

108. Jer 16:14–17(= 23:7–8).

109. Isa 12 refers to the song of Moses in Exod 15. See further Zeph 3:14–17; Isa 43:1–8; 52:12; 55:12.

110. Jer 31:2.

> "They will return from the land of the enemy.
> So there is hope for your descendants,"
> declares the LORD.
> "Your children will return to their own land."[111]

The nation's return to the Promised Land is intended to serve the LORD there under the leadership of the David whom the LORD would raise.[112] The exile and final return to the land are acts of the Shepherd of Israel, who sifts the nation and teaches it the covenant.[113] Therefore it is not strange to find the promise of the new covenant in Jeremiah chapters 30 and 31. Thereby the new covenant is placed within the context of the fulfillment of the promises to the fathers.[114] It can be argued that the structure of this salvation prophecy shows that a new covenant is necessary for Israel in order to be able to dwell permanently in the land. Only in this way can the people receive a new covenantal obedience.

Connected to the divine blessing of return is the gift of a prince and ruler for Israel who will be able to approach the LORD in a special manner.[115] The fulfillment of the promise to be God's people is connected to his appearance.[116]

12.10 The Gift of the Unity of the People

God who is One[117] creates a new one-ness in His people. Their previous disharmony, one that divided the kingdom and led to the "unity of exile," will be taken away. In a moving manner[118] Ezekiel prophecies about this new one-ness that will be given and closely connected with the service to the One God.[119] From the mouth of this prophet the word sounds,

---

111. Jer 31:15–17.

112. Jer 30:9.

113. Ezek 20:37–38. Chapter 34 speaks about the shepherding of God of His dispersed sheep. He gives in the Messiah a shepherd who will lead the flock; cf. also 37:24.

114. See Jer 30:3 and 33:25–26. Jer 30–31 continually mention (my servant) Jacob and (father) Israel. Cf. also Isa 41:8ff; Ezek 36:28.

115. Jer 30:21–22.

116. Ezek 11:20; 36:28; 37:27; Jer 24:7; 30:22; Zech 8:7–8.

117. Deut 6:4.

118. By means of a prophetic token of two pieces of wood, with the names of Judah and Ephraim written upon them, in the hand of the prophet (Ezek 37:15–28).

119. Ezek 37:22–23; see also 11:19 (RSV: "one heart"; NIV: "undivided heart"). Isa 11:13 also foresees a disappearance of the mutual jealousy and aggression between Judah and Ephraim. What this foretold harmony implies with respect to the extent of the return of the offspring of the exiles of the kingdom of the ten tribes is not elaborated upon.

> I will make them one nation in the land, on the mountains of Israel. There will be one king over all of them and they will never again be two nations or be divided into two kingdoms.[120]

Again we see how God places "one nation" under "one king" appointed by Him. This king is designated as "my servant David."[121] We observe each time that salvation for the people is connected with the divine blessing of leadership under the God-given king from the house of David.

12.11 The Election of the Land and the City Confirmed

The LORD will also comfort the land. In a moving way Ezekiel mouths the love of God for the land.[122] God will turn again to the land,[123] and the return of the people to its own land,[124] God's land,[125] is an act of God's mercy for the land. The mountains and hills, the ravines and valleys, hear God's word of mercy.[126] The land will again become like the garden of Eden.[127] The blessing for the land will be that it will be inhabited anew, tilled and built upon by the people of the LORD.[128] The defilement of the land by Israel's sin[129] has been taken away and is atoned for.[130]

In this context it can be stated that the promised purification and the gift of a new heart of the people is in the first place good news for the land.[131] The land clearly is more than just a piece of territory. It shares in the salvation just as it suffered under the defilement by sin.[132] It has also been mercilessly maltreated by the people of God.[133]

---

120. Ezek 37:22.
121. Ezek 37:24, 25; 34:24.
122. The whole of Ezek 36 is word of comfort for the land. This reality of God's special love for His land is the origin of the love for the land to be found in the prayers and writings of the Jewish people. The land is a spiritual entity. A place that is different from other places and that possesses its own holiness. It is the God-chosen "place" (*makom*, 2 Sam 7:10) for His people.
123. Ezek 36:9 (RSV).
124. Ezek 36:24.
125. Ezek 36:5.
126. Ezek 36:6.
127. Ezek 36:35.
128. Ezek 36:9–12, 33–38.
129. Ezek 36:16–18; Jer 16:18. Zech 13:2 shows that this purification also has a dimension in which spiritual powers are removed; cf. Hos 4:12.
130. Cf. Deut 32:43.
131. By its new heart and the new obedient life the people can remain in the land. Cf. Ezek 36:27–28. Cf. what has been written about Jer 30–31 in paragraph 12.9 of this chapter.
132. Cf. Hos 4:3.
133. Cf. 2 Chr 36:21; Lev 26:34–35.

Learning about the Eighth Day

By His love for this land, God confirms His election of the land. It will be His property in the midst of the world. His own House and a dwelling place for His people. God marries the land.[134]

Connected to the confirmation of the election of the land, is the everlasting and remarkable position of Jerusalem. Like the land, Jerusalem is comforted. The daughter of Zion has not been forgotten.[135]

> The LORD will surely comfort Zion
>   and will look with compassion on all her ruins;
> he will make her deserts like Eden,
>   her wastelands like the garden of the LORD.
> Joy and gladness will be found in her,
>   thanksgiving and the sound of singing.[136]

> "Comfort, comfort my people,"
> says your God.
> "Speak tenderly to Jerusalem,
>   and proclaim to her
> that her hard service has been completed,
>   that her sin has been paid for,
> that she has received from the LORD's hand
>   double for all her sins."[137]

God's love for the city is the love of a husband.[138] The city will again be His bride,[139] no longer abandoned, but beloved by Him anew.[140] God promises her a spacious dwelling; room must be made for the city.[141] She will be greatly filled with inhabitants.[142]

Her foundations will not be broken again. She will be founded forever.[143] The disaster of destruction will replaced by glory.[144] Judgment is over when God comes to His city,[145] and His Dwelling will be there forever.[146]

---

134. Isa 62:4–5.
135. Isa 49:14–16.
136. Isa 51:3; cf. 52:7–9.
137. Isa 40:1–2.
138. Isa 54:5.
139. Isa 49:18; 61:10; 62:5, here the land and the city are taken in marriage.
140. Isa 54:6–8.
141. Isa 54:2–3.
142. Isa 49:19–21; Zech 8:5; Mic 2:12.
143. Isa 54:11–12.
144. Isa 60:1–3, 15–18.
145. Isa 52:8; Ezek 43:1–5.
146. Ezek 43:7.

Never again Jerusalem will be plundered by the nations. On the contrary, the city will be built and blessed with the help of the nations.[147] The desert of her existence and appearance will become a garden of Eden.[148] God returns to this Eden to dwell there.[149]

12.12 The Indwelling of God in the Midst of the Holy Camp

Jerusalem will be God's city in the midst of the land, and within it the House of God and His Indwelling will be the all-dominating center. The name of the city will be "The LORD is there."[150] Mount Zion will have a special place within Jerusalem.[151]

God will forever keep to the structure of the camp of Israel. In a prophetic vision Ezekiel describes in a detailed manner the structuring of this holy camp of Israel.[152] All that lies around God's mountain will be blessed,[153] first the land, and from there the rest of the world.

The Sanctuary of the LORD, the place of His Throne and feet, will be the place of salvation for His people.[154] He Himself will be Sanctuary for His people,[155] and He will replace the sun and moon with the light from His radiant Countenance.[156] From His Sanctuary life will flow for the land[157] and the world.[158] Light and Tora will spread from the city for Israel and the nations.[159] The city will be filled with righteousness and justice,[160] as it shares in the holiness of God and bears His Name.[161]

---

147. Isa 60:4–11; 66:12.

148. Isa 51:3.

149. Jewish tradition holds that Jerusalem, and in it the Temple mount, is situated on the place of the garden of Eden. Will God's wish to "dwell and rest" here in this place (cf. Ps 132:13–14) be realized instead of "walking" in the midst of creation? (cf. Gen 3:8).

150. Ezek 48:35.

151. Ezek 34:26; cf. also Isa 25:6.

152. Ezek 40–48.

153. Ezek 40–48.

154. Ezek 43:7.

155. See Ezek 11:16. In Jewish interpretation, this verse is thought of as a denotation of the origin of synagogues ("little sanctuary" amidst the nations). The background of this thought is that the LORD has been "sanctuary" only in a limited measure (so also translator's note in RSV; NIV: "a little while") for the nation and that He wishes to be a sanctuary to the fullest. Cf. Ps 27:4–5.

156. Isa 60:19–20.

157. Ezek 47:1–12.

158. Zech 14:8.

159. Isa 2:1–5.

160. Isa 33:5.

161. Jer 33:16.

12.13 Around the Indwelling: A Kingdom of Priests

We have already observed the prophets speaking about a new obedience and the gift of a new heart by which the *avoda* of the people will be purified. Finally the priestly calling of the nation will become a reality. Isaiah prophesies:

> And you will be called priests of the LORD,
> you will be named ministers of our God.[162]

The context of these words makes it clear that the place of this people amidst the nations will be special. Its task is to be God's priests. All sons of Jerusalem will be taught by the LORD.[163] All the people will be righteous.[164] They will know the LORD from the least of them to the greatest.[165] A fountain of cleansing will be opened,[166] and supplication and contrition will arise.[167]

Joel prophesies about an anointment for the whole nation, even more, for all that lives.[168] Prophetic gifts will be given to the nation.[169] Ezekiel also speaks about the outpouring of the Spirit of God over His people.[170]

Finally Israel will be a kingdom of priests. God does not rest before the royal and priestly calling of Israel will have been realized in every respect by His election and faithful love. Blessing for the nations is also implied, for when Israel as the priestly representative of the nations has been made perfect, this has blessed consequences for the nations represented in Israel. The blessing for the nations is connected to this completed sanctification of the priestly people.

12.14 The Blessing for the Nations and the Service of the Nations

Israel had been called from the nations to be a blessing in the midst of the earth.[171] This blessing will start to flow when Israel receives the perfect fulfillment of its calling. Again we find promises relating to this in panoramic views. We find there diverse yet coordinated salvation affirmations, whilst the exact relationship is not elaborated upon.[172]

---

162. Isa 61:6.

163. Isa 54:13. In 50:4 also the servant of the LORD is taught by God, i.e., as a disciple. Could perhaps the images of this "disciple" and the whole nation as "disciple" blend with each other?

164. Isa 60:21.

165. Jer 31:34.

166. Zech 13:1.

167. Zech 12:10–14.

168. Joel 2:28.

169. Joel 2:28–29.

170. Ezek 36:27; 37:14; 39:29.

171. Isa 19:24.

172. See par example Isa 55:4–5; here the promise of the Messiah is juxtaposed with a verse

Part I: The Canonical Narrative: The Tanakh

We observe that the turning of God to His people is accompanied by salvation for the nations.[173] Judgment prophesies for the nations are alternated with affirmations of salvation.[174] The Messiah is named as the One who brings the nations salvation.[175]

It is obvious that God wishes to give also the nations purification of heart and lips to serve Him "shoulder to shoulder."[176] They also will be ritually cleansed[177] and be welcome in God's House,[178] and the covering will be taken away.[179] The nations will want to learn the Tora from the LORD,[180] wishing to be blessed out of and in the camp of Israel.[181] They will seek the God of Israel[182] and on Jerusalem's Mount Zion will receive salvation.[183]

By doing so they will submit themselves to the order God determined in His creation.[184] At last they will bless God's people.[185] They will want to be servants in the rebuilding of Temple, city and land,[186] and Israel's return happens through their service.[187] They will acknowledge and seek Israel's God and Messiah as king.[188] The Messiah will proclaim peace to them.[189]

A mission from God will be accomplished that is intended toward the proclamation of the message of Israel's God and His Glory to the nations.[190] Shall this mission

---

that describes how the nations will share in the salvation of Israel. Also a chapter as Isa 53 is actually juxtaposed to chapter 54. Is there a connection between the one and the other?

173. Cf. for this par example the two parts of Isa 25.

174. There is future salvation for Egypt and Asshur (Isa 19:23-25; Jer 46:26), Moab (Jer 48:47), Ammon (Jer 49:6), Elam (Jer 49:39).

175. Isa 11:10.

176. Zeph 3:9

177. Isa 52:15; cf. footnote 39 in this chapter.

178. Isa 56:7.

179. Isa 25:7.

180. Isa 2:3-5; Mic 4:2.

181. Zech 8:23; Jer 12:16(!).

182. Isa 55:6.

183. Joel 2:32.

184. Isa 60:14.

185. Gen 12:3; cf. chapters 2 and 3.

186. Isa 60:10.

187. Isa 49:22; 60:4, 8-9 (Jewish interpretation finds in vs. 8 both a passive, almost forced ["clouds"], and a voluntary, an active ["doves"], return foretold); Jer 16:16 (also this verse can be interpreted as meaning that the return is a promise that has both friendly ["fishermen"] and harsh aspects ["hunters"]).

188. Isa 11:10.

189. Zech 9:10.

190. Isa 66:18-19. "Survivors" (from the nations, see vss. 15-17) are sent to the nations to bring them the message about Israel's God.

Learning about the Eighth Day

be related to the Messiah?[191] The consequence will be that the nations will bring the dispersed Israel back home, to God's holy mountain.[192] In that context we hear:

> And I will select some of them also to be priests and Levites, says the LORD.[193]

The Holy One of Israel will take priests from the nations for Himself.[194] There will be a name for them in His House[195] and a place for them in the Sanctuary together with His people.[196] God wishes to give them joy.[197] If they keep His covenant, their *avoda* will be pleasing to the LORD.[198] For a special group there will even be a place and an inheritance amongst Israel in the land.[199]

The promise of the outpouring of the Spirit of God on all flesh,[200] implies that God will breathe again on everything. A new creation is given to all that lives. Ultimately the holy Breath of God will revive and permanently inspire His creation.

12.15 God's Intentions for All Creation Realized

The prophets are very clear: all creation will be blessed from within its midst. This will not just mean spiritual blessing for the nations, but also life in a physical sense. Salvation for all of creation.

And He, the LORD, will create a new heaven and a new earth.[201] Death will be destroyed forever and tears wiped away on the mountain of God.[202] The dead will live again,[203] and the righteous ones will "shine like the brightness of the heavens" and live forever.[204] When the earth is filled with the knowledge of the LORD, the animal

---

191. Isa 55:4–5; cf. footnote 172 in this chapter.

192. Isa 66:20.

193. Isa 66:21. Does the context imply that this "taking of priests" (from the nations) is related to the service of love the nations will render to Israel?

194. Isa 66:21. This verse can be interpreted in two ways. God takes priests from the nations who bring back the offspring of Israel to Jerusalem. Than an enlargement of God's priesthood with priests from the nations is meant. The other possibility is that God appoints priests in Jerusalem, taken from Israel that has been brought back by the nations. For contextual reasons (cf. vss. 18–24) I choose for the first possibility. The whole section is about God's plans with the nations, who will be blessed out of the blessed and preserved people of God.

195. Isa 56:5.

196. Isa 56:6.

197. Isa 56:7.

198. Isa 56:4, 7.

199. Ezek 47:21–23.

200. Joel 2:28.

201. Isa 65:17; 66:22.

202. Isa 25:8.

203. Isa 26:19; cf. Hos 6:1–3.

204. Dan 12:2–3.

world will change, down to the interaction between man and animal.[205] The nations will no longer learn war.[206] On the contrary, as guests of God they will celebrate a banquet together on the mountain of the LORD,[207] celebrating their fellowship with the LORD.[208]

12.16 The Tora and the Messianic Time

The promises of salvation for Israel and the nations show that the Tora for Israel and the nations is also underway toward the Messianic time. Even the Tora will "enter" the Eighth Day. Implied in the salvation promised, is a "renewal" of the Tora.[209]

There will be no more remembrance of the ark.[210] Emasculated persons will be welcomed in the congregation of the LORD.[211] A time will come when the curse over Ammon and Moab will belong to the past, and the salvation promises for these brother nations will be fulfilled.[212] The limitation measures for Egyptians will be annulled.[213] Of the new covenant it is said that it is not like that of Sinai.[214]

In line with these Scriptural facts, voices within Jewish tradition can be heard expecting such changes of the Tora in relation to the Messiah and the Messianic times.[215] Interpreters on the other side of the argument think that God and the Messiah will teach the already-given Tora in fullness, with its secrets explained and all questions answered. And if people have forgotten the Tora, the Messiah will teach them anew.[216] Be that as it may, Israel and the nations will finally receive God's instruction, possibly in a new way!

---

205. Isa 11:6–9; 65:25; Hab 2:14.

206. Isa 2:4; Mic 4:3. To "learn" meaning "learning the art of," "to become acquainted with."

207. Isa 25:6.

208. Cf. Exod 24:9–11, here a banquet and a vision of God on the mountain Sinai are mentioned.

209. The repetition of the Ten Words in Deut 5:6–21 in itself meant a "change" with respect to Exod 20. The motivation of the celebration of the Shabbat is here founded on the Exodus from Egypt and not on the creation.

210. Jer 3:16.

211. Cf. Isa 56:3–5 with Deut 23:1.

212. Cf. Deut 23:3–6 with Jer 48:47 and 49:6.

213. Cf. Deut 23:7–8 with Isa 19:23–25.

214. Jer 31:32.

215. All sacrifices, even the sin-offerings for there will be sin no more, will be discarded, except for the thanksgiving sacrifices. Also all prayers, except for the prayers of thanksgiving, will be discarded (Leviticus Rabbah 9:7—a narrating commentary from the fifth century.).

216. See Urbach, *The Sages*, 308–14. Kabbalists interpreted the sayings about a "new Tora" as pointing to the explanation of all esoteric secrets in the Tora.

12.17 Finally, a Great *Sukkot*: A Thanksgiving Celebration of All Creation

The end will be a great *Sukkot*, a great Feast of Tabernacles.[217] *Sukkot* forms the ending of Israel's God-commanded festival calendar.[218] Now fulfilled will be what had been indicated prophetically in this celebration. There will be a great thanksgiving celebration for God's care and sustenance in the desert of life. A thanksgiving for the fulfillment of His promises and for the renewed dwelling in the land. God will be king over Israel and all creation. Fountains of salvation will open up, never to thirst again!

Israel will be known and beloved by the LORD.[219] But the nations will also receive a blessing from Zion, allowing them to co-celebrate this celebration of God's royal care.

The prophecy of this great Feast of Tabernacles is part of a panoramic view of God's future and therefore can have different phases of fulfillment.[220] The center of it all is that the LORD is there[221] and that all is holy unto Him.[222] There will be healing,[223] tears will be wiped away,[224] and the blind, deaf, lame and mute will see, hear, dance and celebrate.[225] A road leads out of the world's desert to this feast and this future.

> And a highway will be there;
> it will be called the Way of Holiness;
> it will be for those who walk on that Way.
> The unclean will not journey on it;
> wicked fools will not go about on it.
> No lion will be there,
> nor any ravenous beast;
> they will not be found there.
> But only the redeemed will walk there,
> and those the LORD has rescued will return.
> They will enter Zion with singing;
> everlasting joy will crown their heads.
> Gladness and joy will overtake them,

---

217. *Sukka* (singular) means hut, tent/tabernacle; see Zech 14.

218. Lev 23; Num 28–29; Deut 16.

219. The celebration of the Feast of Tabernacles includes an eighth day, which in Jewish tradition has been interpreted as a day of loving intimacy between God and His people.

220. The description of the times and ways by which this all will become reality, falls out of the scope of this book.

221. Ezek 48:35.

222. Zech 14:20.

223. Mal 4:2.

224. Isa 25:8.

225. Isa 35:5–6.

and sorrow and sighing will flee away.[226]

God's own sorrow over His people will also be comforted. "In all their distress he too was distressed."[227] Even His sighs will be hushed. For Him there is no longer a need to speak to His people in judgment, by which His heart was distressed every time.[228] His heart needs not be anymore in anguish and pound of agony by what he sees.[229] The silence of love commences, also for the LORD.

> The LORD your God is with you, the Mighty Warrior who saves. He will take great delight in you; in his love he will no longer rebuke you, but will rejoice over you with singing.[230]

A new heaven and a new earth. The *tikkun olam*, the perfecting of the world, the complete restoration, commences. Out of Zion the Sovereign LORD will be king.[231]

The LORD will be One and his Name One.[232]

12.18 The Canonical Narrative of the Tanakh

The ending of the canonical narrative of the Tanakh can be characterized by the words from the Song of Songs:

> I am my beloved's and my beloved is mine.[233]

The narrative of the love of the God of Israel, the Creator of heaven and earth, ends with the embracement by the beloved.[234] Israel will be beloved eternally,[235] and also respond to that love.

The intentions of the Creator to dwell in the midst of creation and to reveal His love in a nation that loves Him, will be realized. Israel will be the center of God's

---

226. Isa 35:8–10.

227. Isa 63:9.

228. Jer 31:20. When God must speak judgment against Ephraim, His heart is always upset; see chapter 11 (11.11).

229. Jer 4:19–22. In this section we observe that the heart of God is restless because His tents are destroyed and His people are foolish.

230. Zeph 3:17. NIV renders "he will no longer rebuke you," the Hebrew meaning, 'he will be silent.'

231. Zech 14:16.

232. Zech 14:9 (my own translation, EJW); NIV renders, "On that day there will be one LORD, and his name the only name." Cf. Deut 6:4.

233. Song 6:3. It is not without reason that in Judaism, but also in the Christian interpretation of Song of Songs, the deepest meaning of this "Song of Songs" is found in the God-sought relation of love with His people.

234. Jer 31:22.

235. Jer 31:3.

creation. The house of learning for the nations it was meant to be, a place for communion with the Eternal God. It will be both a blessed nation and a fountain of blessing for the nations. By the disobedience that arose in creation, the blessing also would imply atonement, purification, and sanctification, showing God's love greater than ever before known or imagined.

Through eternity God will structure the world around His Sanctuary in the midst of Israel. Therefore the Tanakh looks longingly to the return of the people to God's land. It looks for the kingship of God served by the throne and the son of David. For the sanctification of God's Name by the service of the priestly people chosen for Himself, together with God-appointed priests from the nations. Psalms give words to the longing for this Eighth Day, this Messianic time. Lament, hope, and trust mingle together in the prayers.

We have arrived at the end of an account of the outlines of the canonical narrative of the Tanakh. Part Two of this book deals with the question whether the canonical narrative of the New Testament corresponds to the canonical narrative of the Tanakh. Is it a continuation and fulfillment? An ongoing interpretation and elaboration? An extensive excursus, perhaps? Or does a new story begin within the Scriptures of the New Covenant with new narrative structures, by which the old narrative has run out and must disappear from the stage?

May the Holy Spirit guide us, with humility shaping our listening. May we be reminded of the fact that God's thoughts are great and holy, as the psalm, which makes us long for the great rest—the great *Shabbat*—says:

> How great are your works, LORD
> how profound your thoughts![236]

---

236. Ps 92:5.

PART II

The Canonical Narrative: The Scriptures of the New Covenant—the New Testament

CHAPTER 13

Two-Part Canon, One Narrative?

13.1 One Canonical Narrative?

JESUS.[1] THAT HE PLAYS a central role in the New Testament is obvious to every reader. From the first sentences of the gospel according to Matthew, until the last chapter of the Revelation of John, we find his name.

The questions thereby put before us in the language of the theater, are these: is the New Testament the next act in the same play? Or is it the beginning of a totally new and different play?

Only two answers seem to be possible when we take in consideration the difference between the Jewish and the Christian canon. The reverence for the holiness of the Tanakh and for the one-ness of God in Judaism seems to make clear that as far as Judaism is concerned, the New Testament forms a totally different story.[2] There might perhaps be some familial relationship, but the Tanakh and the New Testament present essentially different—even alien—narratives.

The ready Christian answer seems to be implied by the fact that besides the Tanakh, the New Testament is also part of the Christian canon. Because of this it could appear as if Christians unanimously think that it is all about the same story on the same stage.

---

1. I use here the usual name, although a plea could be made for the use of the Hebrew form (*Yeshua*) in order to draw attention to the *Jew*-ishness of Jesus and His place in Israel. The estrangement that then can be experienced, at the same time may open up a new perspective. It is therefore that I will regularly use this Hebrew name, alone or in the form of a double designation *Yeshua*/Jesus. The use of the Hebrew name is customary in the Messianic Jewish movement and theology. So also Stern in his *Jewish New Testament Commentary*, 1. Stern has the same approach with regard to all Jewish names in his rendering of the New Testament.

2. Jews that have recognized Jesus as the Messiah during the centuries, form the exception to this unanimity.

Part II : The Canonical Narrative: The Scriptures of the New Covenant

The history of the Christian church and theology, however, shows that this appearance is deceptive. Yes, the Tanakh—designated as the "Old Testament" by the Christian church—for the greatest part speaks about God's dealings with Israel. But that did not mean, according to the Christian interpretation predominant for centuries, that God let His dealings with this people permanently play a role on the stage of His actions.[3] The opinion of large factions of the Church was that with the New Covenant, God returned to His original universal intentions, bringing an end to Israel's role in the foreground. At best Israel plays a secondary role, with long periods of waiting behind the wings.

13.2 New Testament: New Covenant

The designation of a "New Testament/Covenant"[4] in itself does not degrade the Tanakh as such, nor Israel as a primary actor on God's stage. In some way it is even logical to designate the writings, which originated around the appearance and the life and work of Jesus, as the New Covenant. After all it was Jesus's claim that the promise of the New Covenant, promised by God to Israel, would be fulfilled by Him. Quite naturally because of this the "New Covenant" became a focus of the gospel writings. But the designation as such did not indicate a totally new canonical narrative.[5]

In connection, however, with the fact that the designation of the Tanakh as "Old Testament" became more and more customary, the designation of "New Testament" appeared to indicate a new beginning. It seemed to be the beginning of a new dispensation, with different structures and a universal scope, where God chose new instruments and gave a new canon.[6] The Tanakh, in its capacity of the Old Testament, quite naturally became the canon of another people and meant for another time. Very soon after the period of the apostles, even the question posed was this: was the God of the Old Testament the same God who acted and revealed Himself in the New Testament?

---

3. See the Introduction.

4. In the Septuagint, the Greek translation of the Tanakh (around 200 BCE), the Hebrew *brit* (= covenant) is rendered as *diatheke*, a Greek word that originally referred to a testament initiated by one party. Via the Latin, the concept of *testamentum* then became customary. In Hebrew 9:15–22 both nuances of meaning are used. The use of blood at the inauguration of the covenant at Sinai is here brought in connection/relation with/to the death of a testator by which a testament receives legal effect. The connection then is made with the inauguration of the New Covenant by the sacrifice and the blood of the Messiah. For the terms Old and New Testament see further Paul, "Het Nieuwe Testament," 395–8.

5. Because of this I will also use the designation "Writings of the New Covenant." The contemporary (modern) Hebrew designation of the New Testament is *brit ḥadasha* (New Covenant). Paul prefers a characterization as "Former/earlier revelations/writings"—"Later revelations/writings," but acquiesces with the customary designations (Ibid., 398).

6. Tertullian (end second to beginning third century) designated the two parts of the Christian canon as the Old and New Instrument (Vos, *Biblical Theology*, 35).

13.3 Two-part Canon: One God?

In the midst of the second century, the novice Church was confronted with a radical answer to the question: did both parts of the Christian canon present one continuous narrative? Marcion[7] rejected this unity of the canon because he held the opinion that the Old Testament speaks about a different God than the New Testament. His opinion was that with Jesus, a total new story had begun. A "superior and other" God had revealed His intentions in Jesus.[8] Not only did Marcion discard the Old Testament as Holy Scripture,[9] but he then also purified the canon of the New Testament from what he thought breathed the spirit of the "inferior" God of the Old Testament.[10]

The developing Christian church and its theology radically rejected Marcion's thought of a divine battle between a lower and higher god. The Church held strongly to the conviction that only One God revealed Himself in the continuous history of the two-part canon of Old and New Testament.[11]

This profession of the unity of God and His revelation was of fundamental importance. It meant that the Christian church avowed that the Creator of heaven and earth and God of Israel was One and the Same as the God of the gospel of Jesus Christ. The same God acts and speaks in the Jewish canon, which had been adopted by the

---

7. Marcion was born as son of a bishop in Sinope, a city on the Black Sea coast. In 140 he joined a Christian congregation in Rome. In 144 he became excommunicated. Soon churches that adhered to his thinking materialized everywhere, which fact shows that his thoughts fit the spirit of the times. His opponents named themselves "catholic"; through this designation we are reminded until today of this serious theological threat in the second century.

8. Marcion was driven by the thought of a radical opposition between law and grace. He was an antinomist and fought what he considered as Judaistic tendencies in the Christian church. At the same time he was an ascetic, who despised the world. Because of this, Marcion fought against all gods active in nature (according to his reading of Gal 4:8) and the "terrible-righteous" creator-god of this world. He identified this world-god with the God of the Old Covenant and of the Jewish Scripture, so Von Campenhausen, *Die Entstehung*, 176. Marcion draws the utter consequences of a widely existing and gnostically inspired "moralischen und kosmischen 'Entweltlichung'" (Ibid., 176). By the way, the book by Von Campenhausen is determined in different ways by the traditional canonical narrative. The author interprets Paul from the opposition between grace and law and he interprets Paul as saying that a church that consists of Jews and gentiles formed a transitory phase and that these "branches" would not be permanent; the different communities would disappear into one "catholic community" (Ibid., 40, footnote 42; English rendering, EJW).

9. He rejected every form of allegory and typology (much used in a spiritualizing reading of the Old Testament) whilst interpreting the literal meaning of the Old Testament in the most carnal/fleshly manner and deprecate it with the lowest evaluation possible; for this see ibid., 177.

10. His canon—the first that originated in regards to the New Testament!—consisted of "the gospel" (a purified version of the Gospel of Luke) and ten letters by Paul. He made this choice because of his interpretation of Paul as a "freedom fighter" against the power of the law. According to Marcion, Jesus's first disciples already mixed Jesus's words with Jewish thinking. Paul's letters fought their message, so Marcion thought.

11. Already with Justin and later with Irenaeus, the unity of God formed the main argument against Marcion (Von Campenhausen, *Die Entstehung*, 195, footnote 82). This, however, did not mean that the words of the Tanakh had the same authority as those of the New Testament. In the process of the exegesis, in fact an actual/factual hierarchy between the two parts of Scripture could be introduced.

Church, and in the New Testament, which originated around the gospel. However, this profession did not mean that the two parts of the canon could expect to receive equal appreciation.

13.4 The Same God: A Different Story?

The growth, development, and final acceptance of the Christian church within the Roman empire was paralleled by a reverse development with respect to the position of Judaism. Once respected and privileged, Judaism became more and more a despised religion of a troublesome people.[12] Political reasons[13] and philosophical ideas[14] contributed to this development.

At the same time within the Church a growing distance on different levels toward the Jewish people began to develop. Jewish believers were the beginning of the community around Jesus and the gospel, holding onto their own identity for centuries.[15] But because of the tumultuous growth of the Christian church among the nations, they quite naturally became a minority, with all the consequences. Through the sheer power of numbers, they became invisible within the Church while the theological thinking of the developing Church began to distance itself more and more from its roots in Israel and Judaism.

Marcion had put the Tanakh and Judaism in opposition against Jesus and the gospel. In his eyes the New Testament spoke about a different God. In response to this thinking, the Church had professed the unity of both God and His revelation. There is no such thing as a different God! But those who think that thereby the unity of God's work of salvation would be guaranteed, are dearly mistaken.

More and more Christian theology began to emphasize that the One God who revealed Himself in the two-part canon, had changed His course with respect to Israel and the world, and in Jesus had come up with another plan of action. In fact, the New Testament had certainly become the canon of a *new* narrative.

The reason for this change of God's plans was credited to the behavior of the people Israel, but God's universal intentions then also necessitated this different route. On the stage of God's actions—so people started to think—a new act began with a change in primary actors.

---

12. In the Roman empire Judaism was valued and had certain privileges. Julius Caesar had permitted the Jews to live by their own customs and to collect money for their communal meals and religious celebrations (Josephus, *Antiquities*, Book XIV, 214 [see: http://www.attalus.org/old/aj_14b.html, accessed 16th of September 2016]).

13. The Jewish revolts and the resulting wars in 66–70 and 132–135 CE made the Jewish people into a difficult problem.

14. The thinking of Gnosticism caused people to think in antitheses between flesh and spirit, earth and heaven, rituals and spiritual truths etc.

15. See Skarsaune and Hvalvik, *Jewish Believers*.

13.5 Replacement and Replacement Theology

During those first centuries the central role of the people of Israel became thought of as more and more obsolete. In the developing narrative[16] of the Christian church, the election of Israel was increasingly perceived as having a temporary character. Salvation was interpreted as spiritual—heavenly spiritual and certainly less earthly—and received an anti-Judaic coloring.[17] The replacement of the people of Israel by the Church of Jesus Christ formed the goal and became the pinnacle of God's salvation acts.

The traditional narrative scheme begins with a good creation which found itself in a trouble caused by the disobedience of the first human beings. After God's choice of Abraham, a history followed that resulted in the election of Israel and the history of this people recorded in Scripture. In Jesus, however, the time for a new and different salvation than Israel possessed finally arrived. In the traditional canonical narrative, therefore, the emphasis is placed on the different phases of God's plan of salvation. Israel is replaced, superseded, because now is the time for a greater, universal salvation that is liberated from national limitations.[18] At that there is a version of the traditional canonical narrative which says that God's punishment of His people is the reason for God's rejection of His people.[19] This version tells that God's wrestling with His people's disobedience reached its culmination in the rejection of Jesus. His reaction to this was the judgment of rejection. But whether because of a new phase in God's dealings or as a part of God's punishing judgment, in both cases God rejects His people; He brings Israel's election to its end, and the Church takes Israel's place.

With the design of this canonical narrative begins a ripple effect: the history of supersessionism or replacement theology begins, and contributes to waves of hatred toward the Jewish people. The theological anti-Judaic orientation[20] leads in every

---

16. The traditional canonical narrative did not originate without cause. Soulen places the development of this narrative against the background of the battle of the young church in defining its own identity over against Jews, gentiles, and adherents of Gnosticism. Theologians as Justin Martyr and Irenaeus of Lyon can be named as the originators of this narrative. Because of the formation of the canon, an "interpretative framework or canonical narrative" was also needed in order to read and interpret the two-part canon. No later than the beginning of the third century, that canonical narrative was finished (Soulen, *The God of Israel*, 25).

17. "Anti-Judaic/Judaistic" meaning "the salvation is not Jewish or Israelitic anymore, but universal and spiritual."

18. Soulen speaks of "economic supersessionism" (derived from the Greek *oikonomia*), i.e., replacement because of God's economy of salvation, because of "God's saving management (*nomos*) of the household (*oikos*) of creation" (Soulen, *The God of Israel*, 27, 29).

19. Soulen speaks then of "punitive supersessionism," replacement as judgment of God (Ibid., 30).

20. Soulen describes how Justin, in interpreting the law, discerns between sections which are a prefiguration of Christ, sections which judge Israel or had to punish it, and universally-minded ethical sections. He also shows how Justin interpreted circumcision as the God-given means to distinguish Jews from other humans, as happened during the aftermath of the Bar Kochba revolt. Soulen writes: "Justin thereby chillingly transforms circumcision from a sign of election to an aid in extermination"

respect to an increasingly anti-Jewish attitude. As a result, people began to feel free to surrender themselves to the hatred of Jews present both inside and outside the Church.[21] In our times this deadly storm reached its most gruesome extent in the *Shoa*.

13.6 Replacement of Israel and the Faithfulness of God

For the Christian church, the thought that the Jewish people would have been set aside, was not interpreted as problematic. That Israel's election was promised by God to be forever[22] and that His love for this nation would be everlasting,[23] was of no importance. Instead, emphasis was placed upon the conditionality of the covenant and on Israel's disobedience. The element of the faithfulness of God, so fundamental to Paul, discontinued to be an aspect of the theological thought development. The traditional canonical narrative was not open to a correcting influence from a "theology of the faithfulness of God."

Yet, replacement theology can not be seen as an accidental and unhappy consequence within a further biblically-sound canonical narrative. Soulen shows that most replacement theology is enclosed in the structure of the thinking about and reading of the Scriptures.[24] It is so deeply interwoven as to be found in the "genes" of the traditional canonical narrative.

13.7 Structural Supersessionism/Replacement Thinking

It could be postulated that in the traditional narrative scheme, God's heart never really was with Israel. His love never was real love, at the utmost it was a form of instrumental involvement. At the deepest level He focused on something else.

In fact, the traditional canonical narrative revolves around God's focus on His creation, and His world, and His efforts to undo the history of sin.[25] His final goal is a general salvation of atonement, reconciliation, and eternal life. In this universally-interpreted salvation no place is left for individual nations, and especially not for *one*

(Ibid., 39).

21. For a catalogue of the hatred of Jews by the Church, see par example Jansen, *Christelijke theologie na Auschwitz*.

22. Only a few references here: Gen 17:7 and Jer 31:35–37.

23. Jer 31:3.

24. Soulen presents a concise summary of this problem. Among other things he says: "The standard model is structurally supersessionist *because it unifies the Christian canon in a manner that renders the Hebrew Scriptures largely indecisive for shaping conclusions about how God's purposes engage creation in universal and enduring ways*"(*The God of Israel*, 31; italics Soulen).

25. Soulen writes that there are four important episodes in the traditional canonical narrative, namely: God's wish to reach His goal with the first human couple created by Him—the Fall—the incarnation of Christ, and the inauguration of the Church—the final, perfect completion (Ibid., 31).

special nation, neither for ethnic customs or specific places, land or cities. The focus is on "man" and "mankind," on "the earth," and on the way of faith and obedience which every human should walk.

Scripture, interpreted from this traditional canonical perspective, hinges on the first chapters of Genesis, and because of this on the restoration of God's original intentions, as put into words by the prophets and the New Testament.[26]

We have seen already that the superseding replacement of Israel has its roots in the underlying structure of the canonical narrative. This was the case in the past centuries,[27] but it can also be found today in the work of contemporary theologians who have formulated their theology—including their Israel theology—after the gruesome event of the *Shoa*.[28]

In contemporary debates about Israel, the return of Jews to the land, the place of the city of Jerusalem and the land, we can observe many stances derived from this structural supersessionism.

The foundational presupposition of this structural replacement thinking is that God ultimately returns to His original intentions. He returns to man, created in His image in a good, new creation. In doing so He in fact distances Himself again from the special relation with the people and the land of Israel which He created during the history of salvation. In the traditional canonical narrative, the future is in fact a return to the beginning. Creation in itself was not geared toward a goal. In the traditional canonical narrative the history that began with creation serves only the purpose of reparation. But when we become aware of the possibility that right from the beginning creation was geared toward a goal, then we can learn to understand that the end never can be simply a return to the beginning.

The Scriptures show instead that God never retraces His steps, He never undoes His election of Israel, but instead allows the end to be richer than the beginning. Revelation from God made necessary by sin ultimately reveals more than in the beginning the greatness of God's holiness and mercy. The instruction of the Tora grants a deeper revelation of God's intentions, and will be God's abiding revelation on the road to go. Another example is how the incarnation of the Son in the midst of Israel is an act of God that lasts forever. This incarnation has not simply been an emergency

---

26. Ibid., 31–32. Soulen shows that this setting aside of the main part of the Hebrew canon also has an impoverishing effect. God's dealings with creation are only interpreted from the focus on sin and redemption. The versatility of the revelation in the Tanakh plays a role no longer. Besides this thematic narrowing, a temporal narrowing and shortening also take place (Ibid., 52–54). From the standpoint of the standard canonical narrative, the Hebrew canon no longer tells a story that "extends indefinitely into the future" (Ibid., 53). The story and the time period referred to that belongs to it in fact are already finished with Jesus Christ. See also the Introduction to this book.

27. Soulen describes the thinking of Justin and Irenaeus in the first two centuries, but also of Schleiermacher (Ibid., resp. 34–48 an 68–80).

28. Soulen shows this in a discussion of Karl Barth and Karl Rahner (Ibid., 81–106).

measure to be undone at some point in time.²⁹ In a great manner, this abiding act of God shows that God chose His Indwelling in the midst of His people, in the midst of creation. Until eternity this "enfleshment" in Israel will show itself to be a lasting revelation of God's love. An eternal confirmation of His election of Israel, of the covenant partnership of His people and also, because of the representative role of Israel, of the partnership in the covenant, the "co-worker-of-God"-ship of all creation.³⁰

13.8 Growing Chasm between Israel and "the Church"

In every respect the widening of the chasm between Judaism and "the Church"³¹ was connected to the gradual upgrading of the position of the Christian faith community and the simultaneous downgrading of the position of Judaism in the first centuries. Both faith communities quite naturally began to determine their identity as opposed and contrary to the other.

The fact that in the beginning a large community of Jewish followers of Messiah Jesus participated in the community around the Temple in Jerusalem,³² became more and more an anomaly. Even after the fall of Jerusalem,³³ the existence of all kinds of relations between Jewish Messianic believers and the rest of the Jewish population³⁴ was a reality, yet this reality disappeared from consciousness of both communities. As history progressed and the special position of Jewish believers within the Christian faith community increasingly came under pressure,³⁵ the Church became increasingly distanced from her Jewish roots. More and more, the Christian identity

---

29. So par example A. A. van Ruler. K. Blei writes about him: "Van Ruler concludes (in what he himself calls a 'giant swing on the horizontal bar' of systematic theology) that in the eschaton the incarnation will be annulled and that in the kingdom of God nothing remains than 'the triune God and things in their naked (although redeemed) existence'" (translation, EJW). This is the consequence of Van Ruler's fundamental thesis (against Barth) that the Christian faith "turns around Christ" (the atonement and justification), but "is not about Christ." See http://www.boekencentrum.nl/images/files/K.Blei-Recensie-Van_Ruler_Verzameld_Werk_IV.pdf (accessed 16–09–2016).

30. See further chapter 15.

31. The traditional contradistinction between Judaism on the one hand and "Church" on the other hand, is caused by a blind spot to the fact that through all ages a part of Israel has been included in "the Body of the Messiah." That contemporary churches and Christian theologians use the word pairs "Church and Israel" or "Israel and the Church" shows that very often no real theological place has been given to the fact that through all centuries a part of Israel has confessed Jesus as Messiah. See further Part III, chapter 23.

32. Cf. Acts 21:20.

33. In the year 70 BCE.

34. Besides the book named in footnote 15, see also Skarsaune's *In the Shadow of the Temple*. For a recent discussion of new insights relating to the relationship between Judaism and Jewish followers of Jesus, see Skarsaune, "Who Influenced Whom?," 35–52 and Runesson, "Who Parted from Whom?," 53–72. However this is not the place to describe the totality of the complex separation history with all factors involved.

35. Cf. the sad expression of this development in the quotation of Chrysostom (Introduction, footnote 17).

became shaped apart from Israel. The Church became a "new and spiritual Israel," often an opponent of the physical offspring of Abraham, the corporeal Israel, and the increasingly-developing rabbinical Judaism. Even the reading of the Scriptures failed to create fellowship and bridge the gap.[36]

Once Christianity became the state religion within the Roman empire, an amalgamation of the Christian faith with state power originated, lasting centuries and resulting in negative consequences for the position of Jews and Judaism within the diaspora. From that time emperors, kings, popes, and other rulers deepened the original theological gap, institutionalizing it and extending it to all areas of life.[37] In doing so they could easily make use of the pre-Christian anti-Semitism present since ancient times.

13.9 The Traditional Canonical Narrative and its Conduciveness to the *Shoa*

When, in the twentieth century, a massive number of the people of Israel perishes in the *Shoa*, churches and the world are confronted with the deadly outworking of Nazism and anti-Semitism. The question then arises: has the Church been accessory to this disaster? Did the message of the Church—based on the traditional canonical narrative—create a fertile ground for and stimulate the anti-Semitism present through the ages? Can one escape the conclusion that Christianity also shares responsibility in the death of millions of Jews throughout the ages?

The mirror of church history shows that the answer must be *yes*.[38] We must however also admit that there have been exceptions in the areas of theology and praxis.[39]

---

36. More and more the Christian church and rabbinical Judaism developed themselves along their own paths, partly also in opposition to each other. The Church read the Old Testament only as prefiguration of a Christ loosened-from-Israel. Jewish reading of the Tanakh understandably took a different route. Increasingly Judaism at that had to defend its identity against developing (and later state supported) Christianity.

37. One could point to anti-Jewish legislation of the Christian emperors and other rulers. By the introduction of an own (Christian) festive calendar, the relationship between Judaism and the Christian faith community is dissolved. On the 3rd of March 321 CE Constantine issued a Sunday law forbidding official persons and inhabitants of cities to work on Sunday. The development, started in the second century, to celebrate the Sunday instead of the *Shabbat*, took place in an anti-Jewish setting. The decision to not let the date of Eastern coincide any longer with 14 Nissan, taken by the council of Nicea (325) and confirmed at the council of Antioch (341), is "the first typical anti-Semitic decision that was taken at an official church gathering, a council" (Van Andel, *Jodenhaat & Jodenangst*, 27; translation EJW). In a personal conversation a Messianic Jewish leader once related the anti-Jewish and anti-Judaic decisions of emperor Constantine (with respect to the date of Eastern and Sunday) to the words from 2 Thess 2:3–4 and the person about whom Dan 7:25 says "He will (. . .) try to change the set times and the laws."

38. See footnote 21 of this chapter.

39. In the Netherlands one thinks of the Israel theology in circles of the Nadere Reformatie, a movement drawing on the Puritans, see Van Campen, *Gans Israel*.

Part II : The Canonical Narrative: The Scriptures of the New Covenant

But sadly, these were the exceptions. Replacement theology and anti-Semitism very often went hand in hand.

These dark consequences of an anti-Jewish interpretation of the gospel have not come to an end. It can be observed that in the last decennia the traditional canonical narrative fitted well to the feelings, thoughts, and needs of Christians and population groups that have great problems with the election of Israel and special promises for the Jewish people and the God-chosen land.[40]

13.10 Reconsideration Leading to a Confession of Guilt and Different Relations

Confronted with the bad fruits from the tree[41] of Christianity after the second World War, Christian theology and churches began reconsidering their positions. Christian theologians and churches of all denominations have confessed Christianity's complicity in the *Shoa*, giving declarations about their collective guilt and humbling themselves.[42]

At the same time a reconsideration began with respect to the basic foundations of Christian theology. The question was even asked if the New Testament itself has anti-Jewish sections and thereby contributed to hatred of Jews.[43] More than ever before, eyes were on the Jewish roots of the Christian faith and "the Church." New connections to Judaism were explicitly sought out.[44] Jewish interpretation of Scripture was brought to the table as these new relationships between Christians and Jews were formed. A critical dialogue was begun between church bodies and Jewish dialogue

---

40. Arabic Christians do not have to deal with the people of Israel within the setting of the traditional canonical narrative. Meetings with Palestinian Christians show the same. The Palestinian Ecumenical Center for Liberation Theology Sabeel in Jerusalem creates a theology in which the Old Testament and the election and position of Israel are interpreted in a way that from the side of God there is no longer continuity to the contemporary people and land of Israel. In Western countries we also observe that replacement theology is used in the process of "pacification" of and actions together with Islamic population groups with respect to the conflict concerning Israel and the land.

41. Cf. Mathew 7:16–20 and Jas 3:9–12.

42. Thankfully Moshe Aumann, appointed by the Israeli Foreign Ministry as Minister-Counselor for Relations with the Christian Churches, reports about this in his book (see Introduction, footnote 24).

43. The interpretation of verses and expressions which could be anti-Jewish (par example "synagogue of Satan" in Rev 2:9; 3:9) does not take place in a vacuum. On both sides, Christian and Jewish, the enlarged gap, the traditional narrative scheme, and the darkness of the *Shoa* play a role. On both sides, therefore, interpreters can be found who conclude an anti-Jewish character of some sections. But it can be equally postulated—thinking from one ongoing canonical narrative—that what appears to be anti-Jewish can also be interpreted as inter-Jewish prophetical critique, analogous to the "scolding" of the prophets in the Tanakh. Isaiah, Jeremiah, and Ezekiel, for example, do not hesitate to pronounce Israel and Jerusalem equal to Sodom and Gomorrah.

44. In the Netherlands the 'Interkerkelijk Contact Israel' (Inter-church contact group regarding Israel) started. The history of this contact group about Israel and Israel theology can be found in Van Klinken, *Christelijke stemmen over het Jodendom*.

partners that continues to this day.⁴⁵ New partnerships and projects of cooperation sprang up.⁴⁶

The establishment of the State of Israel and the return of the people of Israel from all parts of the world to the land played an important role with respect to the re-thinking in Christian circles. This sort of resurrection of the people of Israel put the question before us: is the traditional canonical narrative, including its disregard of this people, biblically sound?

13.11 A Jewish Reconsideration of the Chasm

Within the setting of a renewed relationship with Christianity, on the Jewish side a reconsideration also began. The origin and later development of the Christian faith became subjects of intensive study, including the New Testament. Jewish scholars like David Flusser⁴⁷ and Pinchas Lapide⁴⁸ found themselves with an attentive audience. In recent years even *The Jewish Annotated New Testament*⁴⁹ appeared, for the first time putting forth a publication of the whole New Testament annotated from a Jewish perspective.

This reconsideration on the Jewish side also showed that the movement beginning with Jesus was rooted in Judaism, and it drew attention to Jewish structures and elements within the Christian message. In a manner of speaking, Jesus was "brought home" again.⁵⁰ This renewed attention to the communal beginnings in the period of the second Temple and the gap that opened up later between Judaism and Church, naturally also influenced the subject matter of the growing dialogue. Less known is that in the same period, a reconsideration and resourcing from the Messianic Jewish side also began. More and more Jewish believers and theologians who confess *Yeshua* as Messiah, ask to be heard. For centuries their presence has been invisible and their voice nearly inaudible. It is true that from the nineteenth century on, fellowships of Hebrew Christians in different countries were formed.⁵¹ But from the 1960s and

---

45. The International Council of Christians and Jews (ICCJ) serves as an example. See: http://www.iccj.org/

46. *Christianity in Jewish Terms* edited by Tikva Frymer-Kensky and others can be named as an example of the fruit of those new relations and cooperation.

47. Among other subjects, Flusser studied the Jewish roots of Christianity. He considered Jesus to be a Jewish *tzaddik* (righteous one), completely fitting the Judaism of His time.

48. Lapide also authored some books about Jesus in His Jewish context. He was very much involved in the Jewish-Christian dialogue.

49. Levine and Brettler, *The Jewish Annotated New Testament* (*JANT*).

50. "Die Heimholung Jesus" (= the bringing home of Jesus) is the designation which characterizes the Jewish movement which studies Jesus in the context of contemporary Judaism and by that reason also studies the New Testament.

51. The Hebrew Christian Alliance of Great Britain is an example founded in 1866. Hebrew Catholic organizations also exist. For an overall introduction see Rudolph and Willitts, *Introduction to Messianic Judaism*. For a survey and introduction in Dutch one can find Van der Poll's *De Messiaanse*

Part II : The Canonical Narrative: The Scriptures of the New Covenant

70s onwards a new development takes place.[52] Autonomous organizations and the formation of Messianic Jewish congregations began. Related to this, the Messianic Jewish side began to catch up theologically.[53] As a result, the contemporary Christian church was increasingly confronted with her Jewish roots.[54] The structure of the traditional canonical narrative is placed under critique also from the Messianic Jewish side.

13.12 Christian Reconsideration of the Interpretation of Scripture

Within the Christian faith community, a reconsideration regarding the reading of Scriptures has begun.[55] In this process the Old Testament "became" increasingly Tanakh again—Tora, Prophets, and Writings: the (sequence of) the Jewish canon, honored also by Jesus and the apostles as the Word of God. In this process "Tora" became increasingly understood as "instruction" instead of as solely "law."[56] Christian interpretation revealed itself as having been very much determined by the antithesis between law and grace.[57] The relationship between the Tanakh and the writings of the New Covenant was again emphasized. The faithfulness of God and various aspects of the Old Testament which are not so dominant in the New Testament and which are still open to the future,[58] now receive more attention. The fact that Judaism and Christianity both wait for the full revelation of the kingdom of God was in some way "rediscovered" again.[59]

Beweging.

52. Especially the outcome of the Six Day War in 1967, and the fact that many secularized Jewish youth in the United States were touched by the message about Jesus, contributed strongly to this development.

53. See par example Harvey, *Mapping Messianic Jewish Theology* and Kinzer, *Postmissionary Messianic Judaism.*

54. For some time a yearly informal dialogue has taken place between the Roman-Catholic Church and a delegation of Messianic Jewish theologians and leaders. Also, (theological) dialogue is increasing between Jews within the Body of the Messiah. In the so-called Helsinki Consultation, both Jews who confess the Messiah and who participate in different Christian denominations dialogue with theologians and leaders from the Messianic Jewish movement (http://helsinkiconsultation.squarespace.com/). A movement like Toward Jerusalem Council II (TJCII) asks attention for the God-willed place of Israel within the Body of Messiah (www.tjcii.org).

55. For the Netherlands in this respect one can think of K. H. Miskotte, A. A. van Ruler en H. Berkhof (cf. also footnote 75 of this chapter). P. van Buren en F.-W. Marquardt can also be named in this respect.

56. "Houses of learning" start; places where Christians, whether or not helped by Jewish input, read the Scriptures with a new openness for Jewish interpretation.

57. Quite naturally the Jewish view of Christianity also became marked by this antithesis.

58. This is the analyzing opinion of K.H. Miskotte (*Als de goden* zwijgen, 145–229). Cf. also footnote 26 of this chapter.

59. As expressed also in Article 1 of the Church Order of the Protestant Church in the Netherlands.

13.13 Attention for the Jewish Context of the New Testament

Today eyes are opening to the Jewish context of the New Testament, with Jesus increasingly interpreted from the context of Judaism.[60] Paul is recognized more and more as a Tora-obedient Pharisee,[61] who when speaking about "the works of the law" predominantly thinks of the freedom of believers from the nations.[62] He was not the "champion of grace" and "opponent to the law." A "new perspective" on the message of Paul and his letters originated.[63]

Meanwhile, more insight is gained into the early history of Messianic Jewish believers in the land and within the setting of Judaism of the first centuries. Within Christian re-thinking the question increasingly is asked: do Jews and believers from the nations have different callings within the faith community around Messiah Jesus? Did not James and the apostles decide this?[64] All these elements are of importance for an alternative view of the great ongoing canonical narrative.

And yet the necessity for a "rewriting" of the traditional canonical narrative remains. Much of the Christian church is still marked by the traditional narrative structure. Even when the enduring election of Israel receives more attention, the phantom of replacement can still hide within the depths of the narrative structure. But very few people are aware of it.

13.14 Still Present: Structural Replacement Thinking/ Supersessionism

Replacement theology is still alive and well today within the international church.[65] Sometimes theologians and church councils are guides not followed by "all of the people." Sheer political and social motives can also play a role in the persistent holding to the old narrative structures.[66]

---

60. This "Heimholung Jesu" (the designation is by Shalom Ben-Chorin) came together—in time—with the attention for the Dead Sea Scrolls. Not only Flusser and Lapide have let their voices be heard, but also Messianic Jewish studies appear which show the Jewish context of the New Testament writings (Shulam and Le Cornu, *Jewish Roots of Romans*; Le Cornu and Shulam, *Jewish Roots of Acts*; Le Cornu and Shulam, *Jewish Roots of Galatians*).

61. His Tora-obedience is showed in Acts 21 then is not simply an adaptation to "perspectives outdated in Christ."

62. See par example Van Bruggen, *Paulus*. This book shows how also in reformed theological thinking new insights grow regarding "the meaning of the law in Judaism" and the exegesis that results from this.

63. In 1982 J. G. Dunn began to designate this new reading and interpretation of Paul and his letters as "the new perspective."

64. Acts 15 tells the story of the Apostolic Council in Jerusalem that dealt with this issue.

65. See footnote 40 of this chapter. This is also the case in Asian countries.

66. This becomes clear in the debate over Israel and the land, and about Zionism and Christian-Zionism.

Part II : The Canonical Narrative: The Scriptures of the New Covenant

But even when the New Testament (more specifically Jesus and Paul) are interpreted from the context of Israel, the underlying structure of the canonical narrative ultimately can result in a theological end for the elected and physical people of Israel. Consequently also a lasting theological place for particular promises regarding the land and the city of Jerusalem is lost.

Theologian N. T. Wright[67] can be named here as an example. He fully interprets the life and work of Jesus as the fulfillment of the calling of Israel, but it is precisely by this fulfillment that Jesus becomes "the end" of Israel in Wright's thinking.[68] According to Wright, with Jesus the special calling of Israel has been fulfilled and therefore comes to an end. Because of this thinking, Wright no longer gives the possibility for a particular position of an ethnic Israel, for a specifically-named land, for specific Jewish customs, or a specific city of God.[69] This conclusion is determined on the structural level.[70] The canonical narrative he finds in Scripture, brings him—and with him many—to a theologically-motivated choice against interpreting the return of Israel to the land as a prophetic fulfillment of God's promises. And as a result it is also a choice against Zionism and Christian-Zionism.[71] This stance, quite naturally, puts pressure on the renewed relationship with Judaism. Again it appears that the Christian message implies the ultimate superfluity of Israel. The unity of God and His faithfulness to His promises appear to have no lasting meaning.

It could be postulated that in the conflicting opinions within the Christian church regarding Israel and the actual conflict over the land, the traditional canonical narrative clashes with a canonical narrative that is fundamentally based on the faithfulness of God and on the lasting election and calling of Israel. At the same time it must be

---

67. Wright is a much read and influential author; he is a New Testament scholar and former bishop of Durham within the Church of England.

68. Wright considers the election of Israel within the canon of the Old Testament to be God's answer to the problem of evil. Israel's calling to a kingdom of priests is to show the nations "what it means to be truly human" (*Fresh perspectives*, 109). Jesus shows that in the highest form and with this Israel's calling is fulfilled. In Wright's thinking Jesus so becomes "the ending" (my designation, EJW) of Israel. He is not the Firstling of this people, who as such also is the guarantee and promise of the fulfillment of this calling by the whole of Israel.

69. " (. . .) in the life, death and supremely the resurrection of Jesus the promised new age has dawned. The return from exile has happened. (. . .) That, too, is the underlying rationale for the abolition of the food laws and the holy status of the land of Israel: a new day has dawned in God's purposes, and the symbols of the previous day are put aside, not because they were a bad thing, now happily rejected, but because they were the appropriate preparatory stages in God's plan, and have now done their work. When I became a man, I put away childish things. Lift up your eyes, says Paul in Romans 8, and see how the promises to Abraham are to be fulfilled: not simply by a single race coming eventually to possess a single holy strip of turf, but by the liberation of the whole cosmos, with the beneficiaries, the inheritors of the promise, being a great number from every race and tribe and tongue, baptized and believing in Jesus Christ and indwelt by his Spirit' (Wright, "Epilogue," 119–30; this article can be found at http://ntwrightpage.com/Wright_Holy_Land_Today.htm; accessed 19th of September 2016).

70. The beginning lies in the fact (see footnote 68 of this chapter) that Israel's election is thought to be sheerly therapeutic or instrumental in respect to evil and its atonement.

71. See Introduction (I.4). In his thinking, there is a christological end to Israel's election.

said that the theological consideration of this "alternative narrative" lacks depth and consistency. Very often in particular the place and meaning of the Messiah—Jesus, the Christ—in relation to the covenant with Israel remains unclear. This lack in the reconsideration makes it often seem that, with regard to Jesus, a choice must be unavoidably made between Israel and the world of the nations as if it would be a choice between specific salvation promises for a specific people and a universal salvation for humankind without distinction.[72]

13.15 Again: The Necessity for an Alternative to the Traditional Canonical Narrative

The New Testament "opens and closes" with Jesus. Does with Him a new chapter begin in the same canonical narrative that the Tanakh narrates? Is the narrative of the New Testament part of the canonical narrative of the Tanakh? Are big parts of the canonical narrative of the Tanakh discarded and declared of no use because of Him? Does the structure of the narrative of the Tanakh remain intact or is it changed by God? Does it revolve around the longing of God to bless the world from the midst of the earth, by means of His people and out of His city? With the appearance of the Messiah, shall Israel remain the primary actor, or must Israel as a people disappear from the stage? Shall the nations still receive knowledge of salvation, instruction and God's kingship out of Zion? In short, does salvation still come from the Jews?[73]

The history of the Christian church, of its theology and its relations with Judaism, shows that the question regarding the structure of our canonical narrative is not superfluous or redundant. First, the Scriptures themselves call out to us to learn anew the ways of God. Scripture does not surrender itself to the structure of the traditional canonical narrative. The very form and the content of the Scriptures collide with the thought that the lines drawn by the Tanakh would be erased by the appearance of *Yeshua*/Jesus, as the Messiah of Israel. It's out of the question that the narrative of the Scriptures would imply that the gospel—gone out from Zion to the nations—robs Israel from its election and its God-given prerogatives. When we carefully learn to read in a new manner, a narrative structure emerges that can be rightly called "canonical," a narrative structure that gives voice to the whole two-part canon. A narrative scheme that makes it possible to read and narrate that two-part canon in one continuing story.

---

72. Often it is postulated that based on Christology, there is no longer room for a special position for and treatment of a special nation.

73. John 4:22.

Part II : The Canonical Narrative: The Scriptures of the New Covenant

13.16 One-Canonical Narrative about Israel's Calling to be a Kingdom of Priests

Not only is a canonical narrative needed that honors the unity of the canon to the fullest, much more needed is one that renders the canonical narrative with the One-ness of God as its starting point. The fundamental confession that God is One[74] implies that His actions are one, and that He has not made mistakes, or spoken words or sworn oaths which have become null and void.[75] Within the traditional sketch of the canonical narrative, the episode of God's relationship with Israel has no lasting value. The love of God for the *physical* offspring of Abraham, Isaac, and Jacob—physical Israel—must make place for or was meant for the *spiritual* descendants of Abraham.[76] The calling of Israel to be a kingdom of priests in the center of the earth was only of a temporary nature,[77] or it only had a lasting meaning through typology,[78] or it came to an end with Jesus after all.[79] In every instance the One-ness of God, and with it His faithfulness, is at stake. The traditional canonical narrative can be considered substandard when one thinks of the faithfulness of God.

The conviction at the very foundation of this book is this: a canonical narrative can be read and narrated, that on the structural level confirms the work that God has begun in Israel. It is a narrative that, in a lasting way, underlines and makes the structure of the salvation work written about in the Tanakh visible.

It is not only needed, therefore, to read both the Tanakh and the Scriptures of the New Covenant with a non-superssesionist hermeneutical lense, but the traditional canonical narrative must be replaced. Even further, we need to read along with the Tanakh and so together with Israel learn to understand, think from the structures determined by the Tanakh, and in this way grasp the role and meaning of "actors and circumstances" which appear on the stage of the New Testament.[80] This new way allows the discovery of the different and ongoing canonical narrative that no

---

74. The *Shema* (Deut 6:4).

75. In footnote 6 of the Preface the book by Drost is mentioned (mind the title: Has God Changed? [*Is God veranderd? Een onderzoek naar de relatie God-Israël in de theologie van K. H. Miskotte, A. A. van Ruler en H. Berkhof*]). In this book theological structures of actual replacement are shown to be present in the theological thinking of those named in the title.

76. With many so Wright, see footnote 69 of this chapter.

77. In a system of dispensations in which the Church replaces Israel as primary actor.

78. I mean that form of typology which notices prefigurations of a Christ-loosened-from-Israel, who only brings salvation for all people alike. There is, however, a legitimate form of prophetic typology which notes in the Tanakh prefiguring reminders which relate to the Messiah of Israel—redeemer of Israel—and therefore redeemer for the nations.

79. Cf. my earlier remarks about Wright (13.14).

80. For example, the instruction of the Tanakh about God differentiating between Israel and the nations, about the meaning of God's land as center of His creation, the relation between the commandments for Israel and those for the nations, about covenant and priestly representation within Israel and the nations, is presupposed and determining for the interpretation of what in the canon of the New Testament is presented about those themes.

longer (both theologically and physically) threatens the Jewish people and Judaism. The dialogue between Jews and Christians will be served by this. After all, the Jewish understanding of "the Christian narrative" has been necessarily determined by the story Christians told themselves. Therefore Jewish thinkers have not been able to understand the New Testament as otherwise than a fully anti-Jewish message at the deepest level. A message that *had* to be rejected by them because of the faithfulness the LORD asks of them.

The Tanakh and the Scriptures of the New Testament, however, present one canonical narrative that keeps circling around the God-chosen path to bless the world out of and by Israel. A canonical narrative that, with the appearance of *Yeshua*/Jesus, still revolves around the God-intended and God-wished Israel as kingdom of priests, that will mediate His blessing amidst the nations. The remainder of this book is dedicated to making this clear.

13.17 Part II and Part III

As in Part I we followed the lines of the canonical narrative presented by the Tanakh, in Part II we will focus upon the description of the New Testament part of the canonical narrative. This chapter forms the introduction to Part II. Our starting point will be the text of the New Testament canon as we have it, just as the text of the Tanakh that has been transmitted formed the starting point for Part I.[81] The themes of the different chapters have been defined following the different elements of Israel's calling received at Sinai.

In Part III we will focus on the implications of the alternative to the traditional canonical narrative sketched in Parts I and II. As mentioned, every canonical narrative creates its own world of consequences.[82] Furthermore, those who narrate and adhere to that canonical narrative naturally start living in the narrative as understood by them. It becomes an all-dominating paradigm that determines life, understanding, and actions.

In this manner the traditional canonical narrative has been the determining factor in the thinking about God, the relation between Israel and the nations, and the created world. Systematic theology, but also ethics, the teaching about the Church (ecclesiology), and eschatology have been stamped by it. Until today the attitude of "the Church" toward Jews—even to Jews who confessed Jesus as Messiah—has often been determined by it. Hermeneutics—the interpretation not only of the Scriptures, but also of the God-started history—has also been deeply influenced by the traditional canonical narrative.

In Part III, therefore, we will dwell on the different implications and consequences of the sketch of the canonical narrative offered in this book.

81. See Introduction (I.7).
82. See Introduction (I.4).

Chapter 14

In the Camp of Israel

The Eighth Day Breaks

14.1 Fourteen

FOURTEEN. THIS IS THE numerical value of the Hebrew letters which together form the name of David.[1] Three times fourteen generations are counted by Matthew.[2] "Three times David." In this manner he makes the connection between Abraham and *Yeshua*, Jesus. Whomever might think that a new story begins with the gospel is immediately corrected. In fact, what now follows is an intensification of the canonical narrative of the Tanakh. In every respect the lines are extended, as Matthew emphasizes with his three counts of fourteen.

We still find ourselves in the priestly camp of Israel, in the midst of God's people. We are witnessing what happens *there*. That is what the writers of the gospel narratives want to make clear. The Messianic Day—the Eighth Day[3]—breaks in the camp of Israel. Although part of the people lives in the diaspora,[4] there is certainly a camp of Israel where the people in the land around the Temple and the city of God form the nucleus of it. This chapter presents a short introductory description of the dawning of

---

1. In a Jewish manner Matthew uses the numerical value of letters and words in the exposition of the Scriptures. Also in other places in Scripture we come across this hermeneutical method (called gematria—from the Greek *geometria*). An example is the messianic interpretation of Gen 49:10: the numerical value of Shiloh is the same as that of Messiah. (KJV renders the Hebrew as: "The sceptre shall not depart from Judah, nor a lawgiver from between his feet, until Shiloh come; and unto him shall the gathering of the people be." NIV and RSV render differently.) Gematria was/is one of the thirty two interpretative methods enumerated by the wise of Israel. See http://www.jewishencyclopedia.com/articles/6571-gematria; accessed 22nd of September 2016.

2. Matt 1:17.

3. See chapter 8.

4. Cf. par example the description of the diaspora in Acts 2:9–11.

this Eighth Day. In the other Part II chapters, the salvation of this Messianic Day will be described on the basis of themes related to Israel's calling.

14.2 Israel in the Center of the Earth

Like the Tanakh, the gospel writers think and speak based upon the God-ordained structuring of the world of the nations. Israel is God's royal priestly nation and remains the middle of the earth. This nation and this land form the center from which God wants to bless the world. First of all, both the salvific appearance of Jesus and His message are intended for Israel.[5] The choice of twelve special disciples—His later emissaries—also shows that Israel receives attention and salvation from the Messiah first and foremost.[6] The nations may pour in to see, hear, and taste what happens here,[7] but they also must wait.[8] Only when in Israel's midst a fountain of salvation has sprung up, the light will enter the world.[9] The nations shall not be forgotten, but will hear the word of the Messiah through His people,[10] out of His land[11] and from "the city of the Great King."[12] The Light of the world shall shine forth from this center of the world of nations.[13]

The Messiah will also return to His city.[14] This city stays bearer of promises, even if it can appear otherwise during the prolonged oppression by the nations.[15]

Israel's calling, promised to Abraham and given at Sinai, is confirmed by the evangelists. In doing so they, along with the whole of the New Testament, presuppose the God-ordained structure by which the world of the nations is ordered.

---

5. Matt 1:21 only speaks of the people of Israel. This nation will be shepherded by Him (2:6). Cf. also the meeting with the Greek woman from the region of Tyre and Sidon (Mark 7:24–30).

6. Mark 3:13–19; Acts 1:2.

7. See par example Matt 4:24–25. The Magi, wise men from the east, also are an example of this (Matt 2:1–2).

8. John 12:20–32 describes how Greek men wish to meet with Jesus, but hear that He will "draw" (12:32) them when His death and resurrection will have become a liberating victory over the power of "the prince of this world" (12:31).

9. Cf. John 12:31; 14:30; 16:11.

10. Matt 28:16–20 shows how the twelve apostles—in a bodily manner, but also by their number, the representatives of Israel—will instruct the world about the Messiah and His teachings.

11. Acts 1:8 describes how the path of the preaching begins in the center—God's city—and reaches from there the whole land, and then leads to the surrounding nations. This structure we find elaborated upon in the whole of the book of Acts.

12. Jesus in Matt 5:35 designates Jerusalem with this expression from Ps 48:2.

13. Matt 5:14; cf. John 8:12; 9:5 and Isa 42:6; 49:6; Luke 2:32.

14. Matt 23:39.

15. Luke 21:23–24 connects people, land and city. The trampling upon of the city will not be forever. The diaspora and the disasters for the land are thereby implicitly terminated.

14.3 Israel Witnesses the Dawning of the Eighth Day

Yet something new is happening. The Eighth Day dawns. "The kingdom of God has come near," preaches John the Baptist and later, Jesus of Nazareth.[16]

> The Spirit of the Sovereign LORD is on me,
> because the LORD has anointed me
> to proclaim good news to the poor.
> He has sent me to bind up the brokenhearted,
> to proclaim freedom for the captives
> and release from darkness for the prisoners,
> to proclaim the year of the LORD's favor.[17]

These words from Isaiah 61 are proclaimed by Jesus to be fulfilled at the moment He speaks in the synagogue of Nazareth.[18] He is the messenger of the Messianic time. His preaching is part of the dawning of that great eschatological moment.
About Him the angel Gabriel had spoken to Mary:

> He will be great and will be called the Son of the Most High. The Lord God will give him the throne of his father David, and he will reign over Jacob's descendants forever; his kingdom will never end.[19]

This great son of David would be king over Israel until eternity. The royal element of the eternal calling of Israel would arrive at fulfillment through Him. The promised sanctification would be also be realized by Him. The same angel spoke to Joseph:

> She will give birth to a son, and you are to give him the name Jesus, because he will save his people from their sins.[20]

When these words are read within the context of everything the Tanakh teaches of the calling, tasks, assignments and promises for Israel, we begin to understand that implied in this promise of the redemption from sins is the complete realization of everything that God has promised to His people. This word of Gabriel implicitly speaks of the ultimate fulfillment of the priestly task of Israel, the preservation of the people, the return from the diaspora, the dwelling in the land, and the full knowledge of the LORD.

---

16. Matt 3:2 and 4:17.
17. Isa 61:1–2.
18. Luke 4:21.
19. Luke 1:32–33.
20. Matt 1:21.

In the Camp of Israel: The Eighth Day Breaks

He is the promised Comforter. The *menaḥem* who is not far off, but near.[21] Simeon expected the consolation of Israel.[22] The praise he gives to God, as the infant Jesus lies in his arms, identifies Jesus as the God-given Comforter.[23] Jesus later points to Himself as Comforter when He speaks about the Spirit as the *other* Comforter.[24] By this denotation He also implicitly indicates Himself to be the Messiah.

Therefore His name must be *Yeshua*, a name in every respect related to the salvation He will bring. "He will save"[25] will be His name, commanded by God Himself. He is God's salvation and redemption.[26]

Mary's song of praise shows clearly that the salvation she sings about first of all means compassion for Israel.[27] Zechariah's song is also about the "horn of salvation" God has raised up in the house of David.[28] The redemption of Jerusalem is at hand.[29] Out of Bethlehem God's *shalom* will touch the earth.[30] The Messianic time, the Eighth Day, is dawning. As this day breaks, at the same moment we observe the beginning of the nations' opposition as God's salvation comes near.[31]

14.4 Celebrations of God's Deeds in the Camp of the People

The one who reads, trying to interpret the narrative of God's deeds in the Scriptures of the New Covenant, is shown that it is a narrative about the deeds of God which He performs in the midst of His people Israel.

---

21. Lam 1:16 speaks of a "comforter" (*menaḥem*) who is far off. Jewish interpretation links this expression to a name of the Messiah. For references see Bialik and Ravnitzky, *Legends*, 197–8.

22. Luke 2:25; cf. also Isa 40:1 and 66:13 for God's consolation for Jerusalem and His people.

23. Luke 2:29–32.

24. John 14:16–17, 25–26. The designation of the Holy Spirit as "Comforter" (as KJV) should not be interpreted from the Greek word meaning (this is the background of the rendering of NIV as "Advocate"), but from the Jewish background of Lam 1:16. Against the background of the comforter being "far off" in Lam 1:16, also the "coming near and abiding with you" of the Comforter about which Jesus speaks (John 14:16) receives a deep meaning.

25. "He will save" (*yoshia* in Hebrew) is from the same stem as the name of Jesus (*Yeshua*). "Jesus" is the Greek form of the Hebrew name and is a contraction of the name *Ye(ho)shua* (Joshua) which means "the LORD saves." (See Stern, *Jewish New Testament Commentary*, ad Matt 1:21). Through His name there is a link with Moses's successor Joshua (whose name was Hosea, Num 13:16) and the prophet Hosea. According to David Flusser, *Yeshua* was pronounced as *Yeshu* in Galilee (cf. *Iesous* in the Greek); see Flusser *Jesus in Selbstzeugnissen*, 13.

26. As a noun the Hebrew word *yeshua* also has the meaning "salvation" (as in Isa 49:6).

27. Luke 1:46–55.

28. Luke 1:68–75.

29. Luke 2:38.

30. Luke 2:14.

31. Herod the Great, the child murderer of Bethlehem and as an Edomite an embodiment of age old resistance (cf. the role of the Edomite Doeg in 1 Sam 22), and later also Pilate and the Roman soldiers make this visible.

It is during *Pessah*, the celebration of the exodus, that *Yeshua*/Jesus dies and is raised from the dead. It is at *Shavuot*, the Feast of Weeks that occurs on the fiftieth[32] day after *Pessah*, that the Holy Spirit is given. God acts on His appointed feasts. Even more parallels can be observed between the journey of Israel from the exodus to Sinai and the period between the resurrection of Jesus and the giving of the Spirit.[33]

Also the way Jesus spoke about the New Covenant shows that God performs His salvation acts first of all within the circle of Israel and for Israel. After all, the promise of this New Covenant was in every respect related to the eternal calling and position of Israel amidst the nations.[34]

The texts in the New Testament show in many different ways that with the appearance of Jesus in Israel's midst, the canonical narrative of the Tanakh is continued. It is precisely this canonical narrative that enters into the last days.

14.5 Two-sided Character of the Eighth Day

From the beginning it is clear that the times of the Messiah will have a two-sided character. Not only was the eighth day of the consecration of the Tabernacle a day of joy and of the Indwelling of the glory of God, it also was a day of judgment fire that meant death.[35] The preaching of John the Baptist, continued by Jesus, preaches of baptism with the Holy Spirit, but also of an all-consuming fire.[36] The LORD God comes near,[37] but this intimacy also requires sanctification.[38] The axe is at the root of the trees.[39] The kingdom of God has come near, but with it also the Day of the LORD, in which God will purify and sanctify His priestly people.[40]

---

32. "Fifty" in Greek is *pentekoste*. From this "Pentecost" is derived.

33. Exod 17:8–16 narrates how Moses, while standing on a mountain, raises his staff over his enemy Amalek and creates a parallel between his action and the ascension of Jesus in order 'to raise the scepter/staff over the nations' (Acts 1:6–11; cf. Ps 110; Dan 7:14). The ordering of the nation prior to their appearance at Sinai (Exod 18) parallels the ordering of the number of the apostles in Acts 1:12–26.

34. See chapter 12 (12.9)

35. See chapters 8 and 9.

36. Matt 3:11–12.

37. Matt 3:3; cf. Isa 40:3.

38. The call to return to the LORD (*teshuva*) precedes this nearing (Matt 3:2 and 4:17). It is remarkable that the preaching of John the Baptist and Jesus happened in a time in which Judea and Galilee experienced an "outburst of purity" (the designation is based on a Jewish text). The lives of great segments of the population were influenced by a longing for purity. The community of Qumran can serve as an example, but Pharisees and Sadducees also strived for this purity. Laws that originally applied to priests were soon followed outside of Jerusalem and outside the circle of priests. The remains of countless ritual baths over all of the country are proof of this, according to Jensen, "The Galilean Cradle of Jesus," 1–21.

39. Matt 3:10.

40. Mal 3:1–6.

In the Camp of Israel: The Eighth Day Breaks

Simeon had already spoken of the appearance of Jesus in Israel as having these two sides.[41] On the one hand, there was compassion, blessing, and an anointing for the nation called to priesthood. On the other hand, there was necessary judgment, and the putting away of the unholy *avoda*, like Aaron's sons experienced on the eighth day of the consecration of the Tabernacle.[42]

14.6 The Eighth Day: The Compassion of God and Anointment of the Spirit

The coming of Jesus means God's compassion for His people, for His "daughter Israel."

In the gospels we find a combined report of the healing of the woman suffering from hemorrhage and the raising of the daughter of Jairus from the dead.[43] This section characterizes Jesus as the healing answer of God to the lamentations uttered in Jeremiah 8 and 9.[44] It is noteworthy that here Jesus comes to the aid of two daughters of Israel, both distinguished by the number twelve.[45] It is important to note in this context that Jesus actually never addresses a woman as "daughter."[46]

In Jeremiah 8–9 God Himself laments over His people Israel, His daughter.[47] Why has His daughter not been healed? Why is there no physician, no medicine for her?[48] Why has all hope of life for His daughter vanished?[49] God's lamenting simultaneously communicates that it would be better if He should leave His people to look elsewhere for a lodging place for Himself.[50]

Against the background of this section from Jeremiah, the actions of Jesus show that *in* Him God looks after His people, His own daughter. He is the physician for what is incurable and brings hope where there is no longer hope. The Eighth Day, the Messianic time, is about compassion. Jesus's other healings also show that God's

---

41. Luke 2:34 ("destined to cause the falling and rising of many in Israel").

42. Lev 10:1–7.

43. Matt 9:18–26; Mark 5:21–43; Luke 8:40–56.

44. Jer 8:4—9:26. The section 8:13—9:24 is the reading from the prophets for *Tish'a Be'Av* (the ninth day of the month of Av), the day of mourning and sorrow in Judaism. In Israel's history on that day great disasters came to pass. See chapter 11, footnote 43.

45. The woman is suffering for twelve years; the girl is twelve years old. Both times the number twelve points to Israel.

46. Only in Luke 23:28 the women of Jerusalem are addressed like that as a group. In a descriptive manner Jesus can speak about "daughter of Abraham" (Luke 13:16).

47. The lamentation about "the daughter of my people" (so the Hebrew, 8:11, 19, 21, 22; 9:1, 7) mouths God's own lamenting voice. God calls the people "my daughter, my people." So Westerman, *Hoofdlijnen*. It is to be lamented that NIV renders solely as "my people." This obscures deep Scriptural connections which could enrich our understanding.

48. Jer 8:20–22.

49. Jer 8:18–20.

50. Jer 9:2.

promises of salvation are being fulfilled.[51] The people, unclean as if by leprosy, encounter a living "fountain of purification" and thus experience new life.[52]

The "salvation from sins" announced by Gabriel[53] and mentioned above, means the redemption of everything that got in the way of God's nearness and blessing in the history of God with His people.

The calling of the people to be a kingdom of priests, however, is also not forgotten. Jesus's designation by John the Baptist as the Lord who will baptize with the Holy Spirit is related to this calling in every respect. Jesus's preaching is the preparation for the anointing He will give. The *mikva* of immersion in the river Jordan (located not by chance on the threshold of the Promised Land[54]) resembles the action of the stripping naked and washing of the priests during the days of their consecration.[55] This purification is only completed when the anointment of the Spirit takes place, making the Spirit-worked *avoda* possible.

Jesus will consecrate the people as a non-Aaronic high priest,[56] just like Moses did. He therefore leads in this repentance and turning toward God, being immersed just like Israel in the *mikva* in the river Jordan.[57] As the first one of the people it is there He receives the priestly anointing.[58] As the Son[59] He thus walks the way of God's son Israel—also the way through the desert.[60] When He has been tested and proven righteous in the temptations, He walks His path under the people. He sanctifies Himself for the people in order that they also may be sanctified in truth.[61] Through this walk of sanctification the God-sought covenant obedience is lived out by Him and the covenant promises become to be received.

---

51. See the quotation from Isa 53:4 in Matt 8:17.

52. Against the background of Lev 13–14 the healings of the lepers receive a deep meaning.

53. Matt 1:21.

54. The preaching and the baptism/immersion of John took place on the threshold of the Promised Land, there where Israel had entered the land (over against Jericho). This call to return to God brings the people back to the very beginning of their dwelling in God's land.

55. See chapter 8.

56. Also for this parallel to Moses, see chapter 8.

57. Matt 3:13; Mark 1:9; Luke 3:21.

58. Matt 3:16; Mark 1:10; Luke 3:22; John 1:32–33. Simultaneously the baptism/immersion and anointing of Jesus can also be seen as the inauguration of a king; cf. the anointing of Solomon at the Gihon well (1 Kgs 1:33–34, 45).

59. As in Ps 2:7. After Jesus's immersion in the river Jordan God called out him to be His beloved Son (Matt 3:17; cf. 17:5).

60. Jesus's forty days in the desert (Matt 4:1–11 and parallels) resemble the time of desert temptations of Israel in which the people so often were disobedient.

61. John 17:19.

14.7 The Eighth Day: The Fire of Judgment

With salvation's approach also comes darkness and threat. The kingdom of God and the Day of the LORD are connected to each other. Malachi spoke of the coming of the LORD to His Temple,[62] describing how that event would bring about a process of purification.[63] John the Baptist also spoke about the fire wherewith the coming One would burn everything that was not bearing fruit and resembled chaff.[64]

When Jesus later enters the Temple and cleanses that place of prayer,[65] He thereby becomes the one who enters into the fulfillment of these words. His words of invitation can also become hidden when they are not really heard.[66] Jesus confronts Tora scholars and other Tora-abiding people with the hidden depths of their hearts.[67] Cities and villages that witnessed His words and miracles but did not react to them are placed under judgment.[68] Jesus brings separation to families and causes divisions within the circle of the people.[69] His own heart is torn by it, just as the heart of Israel's God is torn on the inside when He has to announce judgment.[70]

At the same time He also is the first one who enters the judgment of the Day of the LORD. In His immersion in the water of the river Jordan He surrenders Himself, with an eye on the future, to the God-ordained way of repentance and sanctification for all Israel.[71] He is the shepherd of Israel who as the first one must receive the judgment for the herd.[72] The darkness which will characterize the Day of the LORD, as Amos spoke,[73] spreads itself like an Egyptian darkness,[74] covering the place and the land where Jesus dies.[75] The judgment of the LORD's abandonment, a night without vision, without a word from God,[76] comes over Him. He enters that forsakenness as

---

62. Mal 3:1–2.
63. Mal 3:3–5.
64. Matt 3:10–12; cf. for this fire also Mal 4:1.
65. Matt 21:12–17; John 2:13–25.
66. Matt 13 shows that speaking in parables also is a form of judgment.
67. See par example Matt 23.
68. In Matt 11:20–24 Jesus mentions Chorazin, Bethsaida and Capernaum.
69. Matt 10:34–36.
70. Luke 19:41; cf. the texts from Jer 8–9 and Jer 14:17; 31:20; 48:30–32.
71. Matt 3:15; it is the way by which all righteousness will be fulfilled.
72. In Matt 26:31 and Mark 14:27 Jesus describes His nearing death with the words from Zech 13:7.
73. Amos 5:18–20 and 8:9–10.
74. Cf. Exod 10:21–23.
75. Mark 15:33.
76. Mic 3:6–7; cf. Amos 8:12 and Isa 59:2, 9.

the first of all[77] and dies the death of the first-borns.[78] The theme of "entering the Day of the LORD as the first one" will regularly return in the next chapters.

14.8 The Eighth Day: Salvation also for the Nations

The coming of the Messianic time, as pictured in the Scriptures of the New Covenant, follows the patterns of the Tanakh, also when it concerns the nations. From Zion the salvation will go forth;[79] it is a salvation from the Jews.[80] First of all Jesus is sent to the sheep of Israel.[81] The shepherd of Israel, however, has a heart for the sheep of an other fold.[82] And yet, they must wait until the prince of the world is overthrown.[83]

The ending of the Gospel according to Matthew[84] is a model for what we meet in all of the New Testament, namely that the king of Israel also wishes to be the Lord of the nations. This invitation for the nations does not disqualify the disciples' question regarding the kingship for Israel.[85] The kingship for Israel and the promises connected with it are not passé. However the words of Simeon, when he holds Jesus in his arms, may reveal a certain order in time:

> For my eyes have seen your salvation,
> which you have prepared in the sight of all nations:
> a light for revelation to the Gentiles,
> and the glory of your people Israel.[86]

In the next chapter we will first focus on the heart, that which is most central to the Messianic time: the coming of the LORD and His Indwelling in the *segula*-people.[87]

---

77. Matt 27:46; Mark 15:34. Jesus expresses this abandonment with the words of Ps 22.
78. Exod 12:29–30; cf. Amos 8:10 and Zech 12:10.
79. Acts 1:8 shows that Jerusalem is the starting point.
80. John 4:22.
81. Matt 15:21–28.
82. John 10:16. The expression "the scattered children of God" in John 11:52 can both point to the Jewish people in the dispersion as well as to believers from the nations, so par example *JANT* on this verse. Cf. also footnote 4 of this chapter.
83. John 12:30–31.
84. Matt 28:16–20.
85. Acts 1:6; see further chapter 18.
86. Luke 2:30–32.
87. Cf. chapter 8 and 12.

Chapter 15

In the Camp of Israel
The Indwelling in the Segula*-People*

15.1 God with Us

SIMILARLY TO ISRAEL BEING blessed with the Dwelling and the Presence of God in the midst of the camp at Sinai, in the coming and appearance of *Yeshua*/Jesus, God's "treasured possession"-people, His *segula*, receives the mystery of "God with us."

The name Immanuel, meaning God with us, we find in the beginning of the first gospel.[1] The mystery of the mysterious origin and birth of Jesus, begotten by the Holy Spirit,[2] is put into words by John:

> The Word became flesh and made his dwelling among us. We have seen his glory, the glory of the one and only Son, who came from the Father, full of grace and truth.[3]

With these words John shows that the mystery of the person of *Yeshua* has been revealed through the experience of His presence. The "dwelling" and the "seeing" allow insight to grow. In the center of the nation, marked by God's revelation, someone appeared who spoke and acted in a manner that aroused a sense of more.

In the streambed of Israel, formed by the confession of the *Shema*, someone appears who speaks "I am" words[4] and who performs deeds in which the Presence of the Name of God is illuminated. His appearance creates division within the people until today. Does the narrative about Him still fit the streambed of the canonical narrative

---

1. Matt 1:23; cf. Isa 7:14.
2. Luke 1:35.
3. John 1:14. The Greek word rendered as "dwell," literally means "to dwell in a tent."
4. See par example John 4:26; 6:48, 51; 8:12; 10:7, 11; 15:1.

of the Tanakh? Or did a new story begin with Him that runs counter to the central confession of Israel?[5]

The conviction foundational to this book is that there is one story told, one ongoing canonical narrative. But we also should interpret the writings of the New Covenant from the streambed of the Tanakh. Therefore this chapter will not present a systematic theological discussion of the person of Jesus, nor will it dogmatically discuss the doctrine of God in relation to Jesus. Our focus still is on the description of the canonical narrative. The "letters" of the Tanakh and the revelation granted there, help us to "spell" the mystery of the Indwelling John speaks about.

15.2 Incarnation in Israel: "Enfleshment" within the People of God

The words of John, cited above, speak of the "incarnation" of the Word. Often this "incarnation," literally "enfleshment," has been interpreted from within dogmatic categories marked by the antithesis of God and man, Spirit and flesh. John, however, speaks of an "enfleshment" within Israel. God's *segula*-people is the place of His Dwelling. He wishes to be there and to reveal His glory in their midst. At Sinai He uttered this wish and granted His people His Presence. In a manner unknown until now, the *segula*-people again receives the Indwelling of God: the flesh of Israel, in the actual body of *Yeshua*/Jesus, is the place of His indwelling. This "enfleshment" shows that God did not choose a totally different route with respect to the gospel of *Yeshua*/Jesus. God would never walk in ways that invalidated His previously-spoken words. This "enfleshment" in Israel means that both Israel's election and calling are completely assumed[6] and confirmed. The manner of God's dealings with Israel remains valid.

His way is still the two-sided relationship in which both God's faithfulness and mercy play a role, as well as the obedience of His people. Israel remains the royal priesthood in the midst of the earth. In this nation—at the deepest level—the other nations are represented. God continues to make a distinction between this people and the other nations. It still revolves around God's wish to bless the world from the center of the earth. All structures revealed in the Tanakh: priestly representation, blessing for obedience, and judgment for disobedience are maintained. The self-revelation of God to Israel and in Israel is not replaced, but confirmed and continued.

The God of Abraham, Isaac, and Jacob makes His glory to dwell in the flesh of Israel. This is Immanuel in the most literal sense.

---

5. John 10:30–31 shows that opponents perceived such a clash occurring.

6. In the traditional theological discussion of the incarnation, the term "assume" (meaning: acceptance of) is used.

15.3 The LORD Is There

The book of Ezekiel ends with the words, "The LORD is there."[7] Israel's prophets spoke about a time in which God's Presence would be in the midst of the people.[8] A time, in which not only the people would live in the land, but also God's glorious Presence would be there. The *Shekhina*[9] would return to the Temple in the center of the city and the land.[10] At that time the Temple would be the place for the feet of the Eternal God.[11] Zephaniah prophesies:

> The LORD, the King of Israel, is with you;
> never again will you fear any harm.
> On that day
> they will say to Jerusalem,
> "Do not fear, Zion;
> do not let your hands hang limp.
> The LORD your God is with you,
> the Mighty Warrior who saves."[12]

In meeting *Yeshua*/Jesus, people in some way or another became conscious of the incomparable. This man was so different. The task even of carrying His sandals or untying their straps would be too holy.[13] It was extraordinary to even welcome Him in one's home.[14] His nearness resembled a holy fire threatening to consume.[15]

Time and again the question "Who is this?"[16] was asked. Could Israel's God grant His Presence in this dawning Messianic Day in such a manner that prophetic words could be realized in a more literal and utterly corporeal way; in a manner in which all anthropomorphisms[17] became reality? Would in this time expressions

---

7. Ezek 48:35.
8. See chapter 12.
9. *Shekhina* is a Hebrew word, stemming from *shakhan* (meaning: to sit down, to dwell). In Judaism it became the designation for the revelation of the Shining Presence of God. In the long run it came to replace the designation "the glory of the LORD" (Hebrew *kavod*). The word usage is based on verses like Exod 25:8, in which the dwelling of God is designated in this manner.
10. Ezek 43:1–5; cf. 1:4–28; 10:1–22 and 11:22–25.
11. Ezek 43:7 and Isa 60:13.
12. Zeph 3:15–17.
13. Matt 3:11; Luke 3:16.
14. Matt 8:8.
15. Luke 5:8.
16. Luke 8:25; cf. Matt 8:27.
17. Anthropomorphic (human-like) expressions used in speaking about God, i.e., God's hands, eyes, feet, face, etc. Greek philosophy held big disdain for anthropomorphic speaking about the gods. In Christian theology, this manner of expression was disdained. The Jewish sage Maimonides thought this manner of expressing to be of lesser value and held the opinion that all thinking about God should be freed from it.

like "dwelling"[18] and "entering,"[19] "coming"[20] and "sitting,"[21] but also "to be distressed,"[22] "yearning,"[23] and "taking delight"[24] describe the Presence of God in a non-metaphorical way? Would it then be possible to hear, see, and touch the Presence of God in a manner unsurpassed and unimagined?

John, the disciple at the bosom of Jesus,[25] describes in such a manner the deep mystery that was heard, tasted, and touched in the relationship between the disciples and Jesus.[26]

The LORD Himself, present in Abraham's tent said, "Is anything too hard for the LORD?"[27]

15.4 God Chooses His Own High Ways

Through the service of Isaiah God makes clear that His ways and thoughts are higher than the thoughts and ways of human beings.[28] He is free and does not consult humans for His plans and deeds. No human is His counselor.

> Who can fathom the Spirit of the LORD,
> or instruct the LORD as his counselor?
> Whom did the LORD consult to enlighten him,
> and who taught him the right way?
> Who was it that taught him knowledge,
> or showed him the path of understanding?[29]

This confession of the sovereign freedom of God is important in Judaism. The Jewish author Wyschogrod,[30] therefore, holds the opinion that nobody—not even a Jew—can postulate *a priori* that with respect to Jesus, the thought of an Indwelling of God

---

18. Ezek 43:7.
19. Ezek 43:4.
20. Isa 40:10; Mal 3:1.
21. Mal 3:3.
22. Isa 63:9.
23. Jer 31:20; see chapter 12, footnote 228.
24. Zeph 3:17.
25. John 13:23 (KJV; RSV: "close to the breast"); cf. John 1:18 (both KJV and RSV: "the only Son, who is in the bosom of the Father").
26. 1 John 1:1–3.
27. Gen 18:14.
28. Isa 55:8–9.
29. Isa 40:13–14.
30. Michael Wyschogrod is an orthodox Jewish author who intensively studied themes related to the dialogue between Judaism and Christian theology.

In the Camp of Israel: The Indwelling in the Segula-People

in the flesh of Israel *must* be out of the question. This only could be the case when the incarnation in Jesus implied that God retracted His promises to Israel.[31]

The narratives of the gospel are characterized, so to speak, by the simple overwhelmingness of the experiences narrated. Only witnesses are given, without explanation, as if it is out of the question to enter into discussion with God about the ways of His revelation. A humble reading of Scriptures asks for surrender to God who walks His own high ways. Therefore we should read the Scriptures of the New Covenant from the context of God's revelation in the Tanakh. When we stay in this streambed, we can also learn to expect the unexpected. At the same time this means that we should not try to understand the mystery of *Yeshua* while using extra-biblical categories. We should also remind ourselves of the fact that in Israel in the first centuries, the thinking about God and the Messiah was not yet as strictly formulated as it later would be.[32]

15.5 "Who is This?"—Meeting the Presence of God in Jesus

When people met Jesus they regularly asked, "Who is this?"[33] Even His mother Mary and Joseph only gradually understood the mystery of this Son.[34] The fact of Mary treasuring moments quietly in her heart at the time of His birth[35] and the years in Nazareth[36] contributed to silence around Jesus. This only changed with His first public appearances.

His words and deeds caused people to talk. The fact that He spoke with authority,[37] performed healings,[38] delivered people from demons,[39] and resurrected the dead[40] caused people to think about Him. This rabbi forgave sins, something only God could do.[41] He spoke like a second Moses.[42] He provided food for many,

---

31. His views on this are summarized in Soulen, "An Introduction to Michael Wyschogrod," 14–16.

32. See par example Roukema, *Jesus, Gnosis & Dogma*. In chapter 8 ("Does Jesus as LORD and Son of God Fit into Early Judaism," 145–63) he summarizes his studies. He postulates that early Judaism was not so exclusively monotheistic, that there was no place for the acknowledgement of other heavenly and divine figures within the beliefs and the worship of Israel.

33. See footnote 16 in this chapter.

34. See par example Luke 2:40–51.

35. Luke 2:19, 51.

36. Matt 2:22–23.

37. Mark 1:22.

38. Mark 1:29–34; cf. Matt 8:14–17.

39. Mark 1:27.

40. Matt 9:18–26 and parallels; Luke 7:11–17.

41. Mark 2:1–12.

42. The Sermon on the Mount (Matt 5–7) can be seen as a parallel with the giving of the Tora at Sinai.

like manna in the desert.[43] The wind and the sea obeyed Him.[44] He walked on the waves.[45] People thought Him to be the son of Joseph,[46] but He spoke about Himself as the Son of Man.[47] "Who is this?" "Is he the Messiah?" "Are you the one who is to come?"[48] Dissension began to grow around Him.

In His life the *kedusha,* the sanctification of the Name of God, was central.[49] At the same time He could speak words which seemed to be blasphemy. "Before Abraham was, I am."[50] "I and the Father are one."[51] It was not surprising that after those words stones were picked up to throw at Him.[52] Reverence for and dedication to the One God who had revealed Himself to Israel are found in His life and prayer. At the same time He speaks of the position He had with God before the world had been created.[53] Is not God making it too hard for His people by this puzzling appearance?

"The fear of the LORD is the beginning of wisdom."[54] Therefore God had prepared the people through the preaching of John the Baptist.[55] Whoever learned this fear of the LORD anew from John, received an inner preparation for the meeting with this special teacher in Israel.[56] He who had put aside this call in preparation to return to God, had to experience that God could use hiddenness as a form of judgment.[57]

All the people and their leaders were confronted by this question: "Who is this?" Even the Roman governor had to react.[58]

Finally this Son of Man dies and the meeting with and recognition of the resurrected *Yeshua*/Jesus takes place, hidden from the eyes of many.[59] After a time of hidden instruction He is lifted up to the Throne of God.[60]

---

43. John 6:1–41; Mark 6:30–44; 8:1–10.
44. Mark 6:45–52.
45. Matt 14:22–23.
46. Luke 4:22; Mark 6:3.
47. Mark 2:10.
48. Matt 11:3.
49. John 17:6. Jesus speaks here about Himself as revealing the Name of God (NIV: "I have revealed you;" RSV: "I have manifested thy name").
50. John 8:53 (RSV).
51. John 10:30.
52. John 10:31.
53. John 17:24.
54. Ps 111:10; Prov 1:7.
55. Luke 1:16–17, 76.
56. Luke 7:29; Matt 21:31–32.
57. Luke 7:30.
58. Matt 13 shows that the parables also imply a judgment of hiding as a reaction to the opposition of groups of teachers of the law and Pharisees (see Matt 11–12).
59. The gospels show that only the circle of disciples meets with the resurrected Lord.
60. Acts 1:11.

In the Camp of Israel: The Indwelling in the Segula-*People*

Then, at *Shavuot* and by the giving of the Spirit, He is shown to be God's appointed Messiah. It becomes all the more clear that He is confirmed and appointed as Messiah.[61] Just like Moses was honored by God and confirmed in his office at Sinai.[62]

15.6 The Messiah and the *Shekhina* of God

As is the case in Genesis 1, in the introduction to his gospel John establishes a connection, between on the one hand God and His Word by which all has been created, and on the other hand the created world and Israel in its midst. Just as the word of God awakened man to life in Genesis, now the Word becomes flesh in Israel's midst. The *Shekhina* of the Word, His glorious appearance, has been seen and gives life.[63] It was the *Shekhina* "as of the only Son of the Father."[64] John then calls His name Messiah Jesus,[65] joining all of these designations together: God, the Word, the *Shekhina* of the Word, the only Son of the Father, and the Messiah. In Luke 1 it is the Spirit of God who overshadows Mary and begets the holy Son of David. John 1 tells about the Word from eternity, that was with God and was God, that enters the world.

In the expectation of the Messianic time, among other things, it revolved around an intervention by God Himself,[66] by which He Himself would accomplish the deeds of the people.[67] It revolved around the sovereign God who does not share His honor with another[68] and around deeds performed by God which at the same time would be deeds of the people. In his prologue John announces that this time of the Messiah has arrived. God is here, and the Messiah of the people!

As for God, the Messiah, and the Messianic time, in Jewish thinking at that time, more room existed for the unexpected and never-imagined than in later periods when boundaries were drawn partly in reaction to the ever-growing Christian community. The *Shema*[69] was certainly the fundamental confession of faith, even more so after the exile because of idolatry[70] and after the difficult period under Antioch Epiphanes IV.[71] And yet, there was an ongoing reflection about the self-revelation of God and

---

61. Acts 2; see vss. 33–36 for this appointment as Messiah by God.

62. Exod 19:9! Cf. 34:29–35.

63. John 1:4–5.

64. John 1:14 (RSV). NIV leaves out "as"; but the use of "as" reminds of the repeated use of "as" in Ezekiel, but also in the description of the visions in Daniel and Revelation.

65. John 1:17.

66. See chapter 12.

67. Isa 26:12; see chapter 12 (12.4).

68. Isa 48:11.

69. The confession of Deut 6:4: "Hear o Israel (. . .) the LORD is one."

70. 2 Kgs 24:3–4 mentions the sins of Manasseh including the shedding of blood as its cause. Cf. 2 Chr 36:11–21.

71. This Syrian king wanted to Hellenize Jerusalem and Israel. Because of his desecration of the Temple, the revolt of the Maccabees begins (167–164 BCE).

His *Shekhina*,[72] also in relation to contemporary religious philosophies. After all, even the Tanakh contributed to this reflection.

15.7 The Tanakh: Occasions that God Came Near and Revealed Himself

Clearly God speaks His "I am" in relation and in opposition to the gods of the nations surrounding Israel.[73] The people learn to reverently fear Him as the One God and at the same time to tremble at His greatness and majesty. The times when he reveals Himself can have a overwhelmingly crushing effect on the people.[74] Sometimes His glory may be seen, although to see His majesty in every respect is too much for man.[75] His appearance transcends all seeing and understanding.[76] Ezekiel's visions of the *Shekhina* of God illustrate this very clearly.[77] Their interpretation is very often counted too wonderful for a human being to grasp.[78]

However, in this self-revelation of the One God and His drawing near, Israel is regularly surprised by what transcends human thoughts. The Tanakh opens our eyes to see these wonderful manners of self-revelation. A few examples can be mentioned: In the creation story of man being made in the image of God, we find a remarkable alteration between God, the LORD and a "we/us," not further defined.[79] We find the same kinds of words at the building of the tower of Babel.[80]

In the description of various occasions that God draws near to human beings, we find a wonderfully, non-differentiating manner of speech. Many times "the Angel of the LORD"—clearly he is a special messenger of God—appears in the life of humans.[81] We then observe that this messenger can speak as the LORD Himself.[82] These appearances sometimes also happen in such a way that it seems God Himself is

---

72. For a summary of thought relating to the *Shekhina* see par example: http://www.jewishencyclopedia.com/search?utf8=%E2%9C%93&keywords=shekinah&commit=search (accessed 02-10-2016).

73. Exod 3:14.

74. See par example Exod 20:18–21.

75. Cf. Ezek 1:28; Dan 10:7–9.

76. Cf. Elijah covering his face (1 Kgs 19:13).

77. Ezek 43:1–5; cf. 1:4–28; 10:1–22 and 11:22–25.

78. According to Jewish sages the exposition of Ezek 1 could only take place in a very small circle of initiated people.

79. Gen 1:26–27.

80. Gen 11:6–7.

81. "Angel" is the rendering of the Hebrew word for messenger. See par example Gen 16:7–13 (Hagar); 22:11, 15 (Abraham); Exod 3:2 (Moses); 23:20–23; 32:34; 33:2 (Israel in the desert); Joshua 5:13—6:5 (Joshua); Num 22:22–35 (Balaam); Judg 2:1–5 (Bokim); 6:11–24 (Gideon); 13:3–23 (parents of Samson); Mal 3:1–5.

82. See par example Gen 22. "Angel of the LORD" can be alternated with "the LORD."

In the Camp of Israel: The Indwelling in the Segula-People

present.[83] As if this messenger mediates or embodies the Presence of God,[84] bringing the Countenance of God near[85] while sharing in the pain and hardship of the people.[86]

In the Psalms we sometimes find a remarkable manner of expression when speaking of a king.[87] In Psalm 45 a king is even called God.[88] We can also think of the manner of speaking about the Wisdom that was present before creation and which accompanied God in His work of creation.[89] Sometimes the manner of speaking about the Word of God seems to suggest a separate entity.[90]

All of these Scriptural particulars played a role in early Judaism's reflections.[91] In the midst of the people of Israel, also influenced by these reflections, Jesus appears. Against this background of the Tanakh and within the openness in reflection these scriptural particulars created, the recognition of the mystery of the Messiah took place.

15.8 "One Is the LORD" and Immanuel

Jesus's disciples were confronted with the deepest truths about His life and person through meeting with Him in person and witnessing His deeds, His death and resurrection, His exaltation to heaven, and the giving of the Spirit at *Shavuot*.

In line with His own words and deeds, the Spirit has given clarity, as promised.[92] Amidst the God-beloved people One appeared whom God Himself had called His beloved Son.[93] This One taught and lived the fear of the LORD. He honored God as His Father and God.[94] He prayed the *Shema* with all of His heart.[95] At the same time He spoke about His one-ness with the Father in such manner that it resembled

---

83. This is the case when Gideon and the parents of Samson meet the Angel of the LORD (Judg 6 and 13).

84. See par example the meeting of Moses with the Angel of the LORD/the LORD in the burning bush (Exod 3–4). Joshua's meeting is marked by the same holiness (Joshua 5–6).

85. Cf. The "the angel of his presence" (Isa 63:9, [NIV, RSV]; the Hebrew has: "of his Countenance").

86. Isa 63:9.

87. Ps 2:6–7; 89:27–28; 110:2–4. See Roukema, *Jesus, Gnosis & Dogma*, 150.

88. Ps 45:6–7.

89. Prov 8:22–31. A lot of thinking has been given to the theme of "Wisdom" or the "Word" (*memra* in Hebrew; *logos* in Greek); cf. also Prov 30:4!

90. Roukema points to Ps 33:6; 107:20 and 147:15 and Isa 55:11 (*Jesus, Gnosis & Dogma*, 149).

91. See footnote 32 in this chapter.

92. John 14:25–26; 16:12–15.

93. Cf. Matt 3:17.

94. Matt 11:25–27; John 20:17.

95. Mark 12:28–34.

blasphemy.[96] He designated His existence with words that went above every concept of time.[97] Meeting Him could be overwhelming.[98] He did not reject honor seen as only befitting to God.[99] Against disparaging descriptions attributed to Him, He qualified His existence and actions as "the Wisdom."[100]

Overwhelmed by His resurrection and convinced in the power of his Messianic Spirit the conviction is this: He is the God-raised and God-enthroned Messiah. At the same time there is an even deeper consciousness of the mystery of this Anointed One. At the end of the gospel of John, Thomas confesses:

> My Lord and my God.[101]

Jesus does not reject these words, but blesses whomever arrives at this belief without "seeing," without encountering Jesus physically like Thomas has.[102]

The canonical narrative of the New Testament holds the knowledge of a deep confirmation of the Messiah-ship of *Yeshua*/Jesus, but also of the fact that in the most literal sense He is *Immanuel*. In Him the *Shekhina* of God has become visible. In this One who stood in the midst of the people, loving and serving them, fully belonging to them, God's glory was simultaneously bodily present among the people. John tells that God's Presence has dwelled among us, in the midst of Israel, in the center of the world.[103]

15.9 The Indwelling and the Deeds of God

The expectation of the Messianic time, the Eighth Day, revolved around God Himself, first and foremost. He would show His Presence anew and perform deeds of salvation. Isaiah spoke about a time in which God Himself would accomplish the deeds of the people. He Himself would fulfill the covenant obedience requested.[104] The canonical narrative of the New Testament is marked by the merging of God's initiative-taking

---

96. See par example John 10:22–39; but Matt 11:27 also can be interpreted in this manner.
97. John 8:38.
98. John 18:6.
99. John 5:23; 20:28.
100. Matt 11:19; Luke 7:35.
101. John 20:28.
102. John 20:29.
103. John 1:14. Wyschogrod (see footnote 30 and 31 in this chapter) postulates that Christology "is the intensification of the teaching of the indwelling of God in Israel by concentrating that indwelling in one Jew rather than leaving it diffused in the people of Jesus as a whole," (*Abraham's Promise*, 15). The first edition of the *Encyclopedia Judaica* speaks (in the article "Shekinah," see footnote 72 above) from the same viewpoint: "The idea that God dwells in man and that man is His temple (*e.g.*, Col. ii. 9; II Cor. vi. 16; John xiv. 23) is merely a more realistic conception of the resting of the Shekinah on man."
104. Isa 26:12; see chapter 12 (12.4).

In the Camp of Israel: The Indwelling in the Segula-People

Presence and the covenant-fulfilling work of the Messiah. It is therefore that we meet both lines in the person of Jesus Christ, the Messiah *Yeshua*. He is the One "whose origins are from of old, from ancient times"[105] and who at the same time serves as the representative mediator between God and men.[106]

15.10 The Scriptures of the New Covenant about this One

The prologue of the gospel of John begins in "the ancient days" when the Word coming near is described. There are also other places in the New Testament that the "the days from of old" of the Messiah are mentioned. As is the case with John, these descriptions show that the Messiah is more than a heaven-sent servant or a special God-created human being.[107]

Paul calls Him "the one" in whom the fullness of God is present bodily.[108] He is the one in whom God has made His fullness dwell.[109] Paul, however, is clear that this Indwelling of God is an honor granted to someone who already was before creation.[110] By this prerogative He who is the image of the invisible God,[111] has become the reconciler of all that exists.[112] He who stood at the beginning of everything and holds everything together still[113] has also become the firstborn from among the dead and head of the Body, the Messianic community formed in Him and through Him.[114]

Paul describes how this salvation has been thought of and prepared by God throughout eternity.[115] In His teaching he uses verses of ancient hymns that sing out this mysterious and wonderful coming of the eternal Son.[116] Paul has also discerned the presence of the Messiah in the past history of the people of Israel.[117]

---

105. Mic 5:2. RSV has "ancient days;" KJV renders "whose goings forth have been from of old, from everlasting."

106. 1 Tim 2:5.

107. Jewish sources present (based on Ps 72:17) the Name of the Messiah as one of the things that God thought of prior to creation.

108. Col 2:9.

109. Col 1:19.

110. Col 1:15 ("firstborn over all creation" in a temporal sense "before creation came about") and vs. 17.

111. Col 1:15.

112. Col 1:20.

113. Col 1:17.

114. Col 1:18.

115. Eph 1:3–14.

116. Phil 2:5–11 and 1 Tim 3:16.

117. 1 Cor 10:4. The Messiah accompanies here the people in the desert. Jewish tradition both knows the thought that the Messiah existed prior to the foundation of the world, as well that He will come to the people in a natural way.

Part II : The Canonical Narrative: The Scriptures of the New Covenant

The letter to the Hebrews also begins with "the days from of old" of the Messiah. In these last days[118] he is the highest word of God.[119] The Son has appeared.[120] He is the one for whom everything was created and who will receive all created reality as a gift.[121] He has been God's partner in creation[122] and upholds everything by His word.[123] He reflects the glory of God[124] and now sits, after the atonement of sin, at the right hand of God.[125] The prophets and the psalms have also spoken words designating Him as the Son[126] and even God.[127]

In this letter salvation is covenantal salvation too, consisting in the fulfillment of all covenant obligations,[128] and accomplished by an initiative from heaven. God Himself provides the obedience required with respect to the atonement of sins.

In the Revelation to John the risen Messiah Jesus appears as the one who bears the names and rights of God. His appearance is as God's appearance.[129] While He has authority to command life and death,[130] it is obvious that He honors His Father and confesses the One God.[131] He is the servant who is called the Word of God.[132] Yet songs are sung to Him and honor is received by Him which God is worthy of.[133] We read how God shares His Throne with the Lamb, the Lion of Judah.[134] We also read that this will be an eternal reality in the New Jerusalem.[135]

The canonical narrative of the New Testament still takes place in the streambed provided by the Tanakh, but in a manner unthought-of, the Name of God appears to be present in the midst of His people in the midst of the earth.

---

118. Heb 1:2.
119. Heb 1:2.
120. Heb 1:2.
121. Heb 1:2.
122. Heb 1:2.
123. Heb 1:3.
124. Heb 1:3.
125. Heb 1:3.
126. Heb 1:5.
127. Heb 1:8–9.
128. See par example Heb 9:15.
129. Rev 1:12–20.
130. Rev 1:18; see also the seven letters in chapters 2–3.
131. Rev 1:6 shows that the work of *Yeshua*/Jesus is focused on His God and Father. Also see 2:27 and 3:12, 21.
132. Rev 19:13.
133. Rev 5:12–13; cf. 7:10–12.
134. Rev 5:6.
135. Rev 22:1, 3.

In the Camp of Israel: The Indwelling in the Segula-People

15.11 The Bodily Indwelling: A Desire Fulfilled

Within the context of the traditional canonical narrative in which the election and calling of Israel ultimately disappear from the stage, playing no lasting role, often the incarnation is seen solely as an act of God motivated by the Fall.

When, however, it is a narrative about God's creation being oriented toward a goal[136] (as in the alternative narrative presented in this book), and about God who journeys with His creation toward the *tikkun olam*, then a different light is shed on the incarnation. Then God's Indwelling in the flesh of Israel might express an eternal desire to "embrace" His people, and thereby the whole of creation, literally "pressing His people to His heart." Then the incarnation is the deepest form of *kedusha* by which the people and the world are sanctified. Then the incarnation—the "enfleshment within Israel"—is not only instrumental or therapeutic.[137] Then it is a revelation of the desire of God, expressed earlier at Sinai, to press in the first place His *segula*-people Israel to His heart.

In this context we must remember the first words in Genesis 1, which can be read through the lens of the purpose of creation. Namely, when creation happens with an eye on the firstling, we can also think of the Messiah as we interpret these words. He can be seen as this first one for whom the world has been created.[138]

We again observe the structure of the three circles of holiness in everything. In this case, the center is the Indwelling in the Messiah, the beloved Son. He then stands in the circle of the beloved people, which in its turn is surrounded by the nations. In the Messiah those who are called from the nations may also share in the love of the Presence of God.

15.12 The Holy God Himself Performs the *Avoda*

Central to this chapter is that in the Indwelling in the flesh of Israel, the truth and promise of "God-with-us" has become a bodily reality in this Immanuel. It also has already been indicated somewhat that through Immanuel God has fulfilled the covenant Himself, and walks the path of both covenant partners, which in itself is a mystery.[139]

The next chapter will look more closely at this fulfillment of the *avoda* requested from Israel.

---

136. See chapter 1 and 2.

137. Cf. chapter 13, footnote 29.

138. See chapter 1, especially also footnote 7. Then the Messiah as the firstling/first one is the goal of creation. In the interpretation of the first verses of Gen 1 we then make a connection with the involvement of this firstling in the creation process, as Paul says in Col 1:15–18; cf. footnote 89 of this chapter. See chapter 16, footnote 117.

139. Cf. Gen 15:17.

CHAPTER 16

In the Camp of Israel

The Avoda *Fully Lived and Perfectly Accomplished*

16.1 *Avoda*

IN THIS BOOK *AVODA*[1] is used to designate Israel's service as requested by God, the totality of a fully sanctified life that is focused on the honor of God. The use of this word is deliberate, meant to convey that everything around Messiah *Yeshua* is still focused on Israel's life *as* priestly service to God. Additionally, the use of this word also fits Paul's characterization of a God-requested life for Messianic believers as "worship."[2]

This chapter looks to the coming and life of Messiah *Yeshua*/Jesus from the viewpoint of the God-requested *avoda*. At first we will focus upon some foundational structures from the Scriptures. Thereafter we will divert our attention to a variety of textual particulars.

16.2 The Enduring Two-sidedness of God's Covenants

The description of the canonical narrative of the Tanakh shows that God's dealings with His people were characterized by a clear two-sidedness.[3] The coming of the Messiah in the flesh of Israel—His "enfleshment within Israel"—does not nullify this, but on the contrary implies that this is still the case. The canonical narrative of the Scriptures of the New Covenant has everything to do with this two-sidedness of God's

---

1. The designation points to the priestly service of God. Serving idols is designated in Hebrew as *avoda zara* ("strange service").

2. In Rom 12:1 he uses the Greek word *latreia*, which he also uses when characterizing Israel's worship as a gift from God (Rom 9:4).

3. See chapter 7 (7.2 and 7.7) but also chapter 12.

In the Camp of Israel: The Avoda *Fully Lived and Perfectly Accomplished*

covenant with Israel. It revolves around the demand for the God-requested obedience, the demand for the sanctified *avoda*.

We have already seen that God, even when He promises that *He* ultimately will realize salvation, does not repeal the two-sidedness of the covenant.[4] Obedience is a necessity, the flipside of the coin of creation, the calling of man and of Israel. He thereby takes the partnership in the covenant seriously. Obedience has power and is rewarded by God with blessing and promises. It could be postulated that obedience results in "receiving."[5]

16.3 God Provides: Covenantal Obedience and the New Covenant

The calling Israel received at Sinai was still valid with the appearance of *Yeshua*/Jesus. This calling had to be lived out in the midst of the earth. Together with the Tora of Sinai, Israel was making its way toward the Eighth Day. The promise given was that God Himself would provide a New Covenant whereby the Tora would be placed in the hearts of His people.[6] Israel's heart of stone would be removed, and by the Spirit of God Israel would receive an inner desire to walk the ways of the LORD.[7] Forgiveness and purification of all iniquities and idols would be its foundation and starting point.[8]

The narrative of Jesus tells about the fulfillment of this promise. He has been given to bring about this New Covenant. The manner of His appearance among Israel was that of the ram in the thicket of Moriah[9] and of the silver coin from the mouth of the fish in Galilee.[10]

Abraham was called to the highest sacrifice whereby his utter willingness to serve God was tested.[11] In the binding of Isaac[12] he shows God that he is willing to give everything. After the binding God Himself provides for this sacrifice of love. Abraham thus brought the sacrifice requested by God and at the same time Isaac—and in him Israel—was spared. The LORD provides[13] and the sacrifice of ultimate love could be offered.

---

4. Chapter 12 (12.4).
5. Cf. Heb 10:36.
6. Jer 31:33. See chapter 12 (12.4).
7. Ezek 36:26.
8. Ezek 36:25; Jer 31:34.
9. Gen 22:13.
10. Matt 17:27.
11. Gen 22:16.
12. Judaism speaks about this history as "the binding of Isaac" (see chapter 3, footnote 67).
13. Gen 22:14.

The history of the silver coin in the mouth of the fish also shows that provision is granted from heaven.[14] Peter is asked if Jesus will pay the Temple tax, a payment which implied that belonging to God's people was not a right, but an undeserved prerogative.[15] The Tora shows that this tax was a kind of "atonement money" for a man numbered in the census. To belong to the circle of God demands purification and atonement.[16] "Will rabbi Jesus pay this tax?" Peter thinks so, but hears from Jesus that *sons* are exempted.[17] When it concerns *Jesus*, the Son and the son of Israel, it really is an unnecessary payment. But Jesus speaks about "sons," thereby raising the question: how can *Peter* be a son and therefore exempted from paying? Again the answer is: provision will be made, this time by a coin worth double the atonement money.[18] This is enough for Jesus, who does not wish to cause offense and submits to the stipulations of the Tora. This is also enough for Peter. On the basis of the "atonement money of the Messiah" provided for by heaven, a new communal life around Messiah Jesus can commence.[19]

16.4 *Avoda* Granted

God provides from heaven the *avoda* requested in the obedience of Jesus. Peter says that by His obedience, the crucified and resurrected Lord has obtained the promise of the Holy Spirit.[20] The coming down of the Spirit in fire and wind at *Shavuot*[21] is the new *Shavuot* that was implicitly spoken of in the promise of the New Covenant. The gift and promise of the Holy Spirit, who purifies,[22] indwells[23] and circumcises hearts,[24] has been received by Messiah *Yeshua*/Jesus because of His complete obedience to God. Moses already stated that God Himself would be the *mohel*, the

---

14. Matt 17:24–27.
15. Exod 30:11–16.
16. Exod 30:15; cf. also 38:25–26.
17. Matt 17:26; the Greek has "sons" (RSV so renders also); NIV has "children," this rendering par example obscures the relations and associations with the son-ship of Israel and of Jesus (Matt 2:15; cf. Hos 11:1), the designation of Jesus as the "Son, whom I love" (17:5) and the mentioning of "the Son of Man" in 17:22.
18. Matt 17:27 mentions a *stater* worth double the Temple tax.
19. The whole of Matthew 18 deals with the communal life around Jesus, and the section (17:24–27) about the atonement money, that originally was related to the numbering of God's people, is the introduction to it.
20. Acts 2:33; cf. Ps 68:18.
21. Acts 2:1–3.
22. Ezek 36:25–26.
23. Jer 31:33.
24. Rom 2:29.

In the Camp of Israel: The Avoda *Fully Lived and Perfectly Accomplished*

circumciser, of the people,[25] when the people would repent, turn to God, and take everything that God ordained to heart.[26]

The canonical narrative of the New Testament tells about the obedience of the One in whom the people was represented.

16.5 The Messiah as *Brit Am*: Covenant for the People

In chapter 12 we paid extensive attention to the prophetic promise of the servant of God who would be *brit am*. The prophecy spoke of an "One-for-the-whole-covenant-bearer" in whom Israel would be encapsulated. One by whom Gods salvation not only would reach Israel, but also all nations.[27]

The Tanakh, therefore, has different ways of speaking about the salvation God wishes to give His people. Salvation can be named, but also the bringer of salvation. As *brit am*, both the gift and the bringer of the gifts, the servant of God Himself becomes the place of salvation. The Messiah becomes the salvation.

The following words of Paul must be read against this background:

> It is because of him that you are in Christ Jesus, who has become for us wisdom from God—that is, our righteousness, holiness and redemption. Therefore, as it is written: "Let the one who boasts boast in the Lord."[28]

Here we read that by a decision of God, Messiah Jesus Himself has become salvation. It is because of this that the New Testament so often speaks about "being in Him" and "being in Christ/Messiah."[29] This also forms the background of the word of Jesus:

> I am the way and the truth and the life.[30]

In the context of offering an alternative to the traditional canonical narrative in which Israel is driven of the stage, it is important to remind ourselves of the fact that the prophets speak about the Messiah as covenant for the *people*. He is the covenant for Israel. He is certainly also a light for the nations.[31] However, as the one who brings about the New Covenant, He is first of all God's gift to Israel. Within the God-ordained structure of priestly representation, He also represents the nations, something that we will elaborate upon later.

---

25. Deut 30:6.
26. Deut 30:1–2.
27. Isa 49:6.
28. 1 Cor 1:30–31. RSV renders "whom God made our wisdom, our righteousness, and sanctification and redemption." NIV interprets "wisdom" to be explained by what follows. RSV juxtaposes four blessings to be received in the Messiah.
29. In numerous places, see the text quoted; also par example Romans 6 and 2 Cor 5:17.
30. John 14:6.
31. Isa 42:6; 49:6; Luke 2:32; Acts 13:47; cf. John 8:12.

Within the traditional canonical narrative, this element of substitution and representation predominantly and sometimes exclusively is related to "mankind" in general. This relates to the fact that very often the incarnation is interpreted only in a universal-human manner, and not as "enfleshment within Israel."

However, when Jesus during the *Seder*-meal[32] identifies the third cup[33] with the New Covenant in His blood,[34] He does so at a feast of Israel's God, in the circle of Israel, and in the context of God's covenant renewal with Israel. This also shows that the New Covenant is first of all oriented toward salvation for Israel, stemming from God's eternal love for Israel.[35]

As *brit* for *this* people, the Messiah has fulfilled all obedience of Israel and also suffered the covenant curses.[36] He thereby is "the place" and "the cause" of salvation that does not just concern the inner and spiritual life of the people, but is "the cause" of the salvation of survival and the return to inhabit the land again. Isaiah makes this clear,[37] Jeremiah's words about the New Covenant also stand in this context.[38]

Therefore, even the words Jesus speaks at the third cup may hint that the Messiah Himself is both the covenant and the summation of God's salvation. Namely, it is possible to interpret Jesus's words, "this is my blood of the covenant"[39] not only as meaning "this is my blood that I give as the blood by which the covenant is made," but also it could mean "this is my covenant blood," more or less identifying it as "the blood of the covenant that I am."[40]

16.6 The *Avoda* of *Yeshua*/Jesus: The Fulfillment of Israel's *Avoda*

Israel was called to perform the service of *kedusha* in the midst of the earth, to sanctify God's name and live the totality of life in the holiness of full obedience to Him. Their task was to live this way as the heart of all of creation, and thereby leading the way for others to follow. This was the priestly duty of God's people. The fulfillment of this service was the God-appointed path toward God's future of salvation, the coming age, the *olam haba*.[41] For this reason Israel was taken from among the nations with an

---

32. *Seder* (= order); the (partly) liturgical meal with which the celebration of *Pessah* begins.
33. Luke 22:20; the third cup is "the cup of redemption."
34. Matt 26:28; Mark 14:24; Luke 22:20.
35. Jer 31:3; this is the same chapter in which also the New Covenant is mentioned.
36. Cf. Deut 28.
37. See par example Isa 49:8–12.
38. See chapter 12 (12.4).
39. Mark 14:24.

40. In this case the genitive expresses more a substantive relationship (genitive objectivus). The rendering "the blood of my covenant" can also be found.

41. *Olam haba* is the Hebrew designation for "the coming age"/the world-to-come, meaning the kingdom of God that will replace the present era (*olam haze* = this age).

In the Camp of Israel: The Avoda Fully Lived and Perfectly Accomplished

eye unto those nations.[42] This was already present in the calling received at Sinai. Just like the priests in Israel's midst represented the whole people, so the priestly people as a whole also in a certain sense represented the other nations.[43] At the same time, however, this priesthood for the nations was waiting for the completed sanctification of the Eighth Day.

When Jesus begins to fulfill His task at the age of a royal priest,[44] it is clear from the start that He fully surrenders to God's direction for His people.[45] He also submits to the call to repentance, and is immersed on the threshold of the Promised Land.[46] He thereby also surrenders to the threat of the judgment for the people. He sanctifies Himself with an eye on the Day of the LORD.

In the same manner as "God's son"[47] Israel, as the Son He suffers the temptations Israel suffered in the desert, the temptations Moses refers to in Deuteronomy 8.[48] But in these He remains obedient, carrying the incomplete[49] son-ship of Israel into the Messianic time.[50] He pays "atonement money" for Himself.[51] He obeys the God-given Tora, having come not to abolish it by His behavior or by His teaching.[52] The reverse is true: its final fulfillment is His mandate.[53]

He has been "born under the law."[54] Paul says to believers from the nations in Rome that he

> "... became a servant to the circumcised (...) in order to confirm the promises given to patriarchs ..."[55]

He has served Israel. He was the gift of the true and trustworthy God. His service was meant to confirm all promises given to Abraham, Isaac, Jacob, and their offspring. His

---

42. See chapter 7 (7.4).

43. See chapter 7.

44. Luke 3:23. At the age of thirty a priest was allowed to perform his duties (Num 4:3). David also was thirty years old when he became king (2 Sam 5:4). The same applied to the Levites, cf. Num 4:2, 23, 30.

45. Matt 3:15. He speaks of "to fulfill all righteousness." Righteousness meaning "everything that God wishes." A man who fully walks the ways of God and does His will, is a *tzaddik*, a righteous man.

46. Matt 3:13–17.

47. Hos 11:1.

48. There is a significant relation between the description of Jesus's temptations and Deut 8.

49. See par example Jer 3:19–22. Speaking from disappointment about Israel as a people of sons God promises a time of return to Him as Father.

50. Matt 4:11 and Mark 1:13 describe how Jesus as the Son who remained obedient, is served by angels and was "with the wild animals." He makes the Messianic Day dawn over Israel's son-ship. In Him Israel's sons-ship enters the eschatological fulfillment.

51. Matt 17:24–27.

52. Matt 5:17.

53. Matt 5:17–19.

54. Gal 4:4.

55. Rom 15:8 (RSV); NIV renders "a servant of the Jews."

service also took place on the threshold of the Day of the LORD. By His preaching He prepared the people for the nearing of the kingdom of God, while His disciples baptized people, immersing them in water as part of this preparation.[56]

He fully walked the way of Israel described in Psalm 80. He became a man over whom strife began.[57] He was one with Israel in the deepest sense: the vine planted by God in the land,[58] the root planted by God's right hand.[59] Although He could be named "the son,"[60] "the man at your right hand,"[61] and "the son of man,"[62] He was gnawed at by the "boars from the forest."[63] Even He had to call out for deliverance and life by asking for the light of God's countenance to come over Him.[64] One with the people, He prayed out of the suffering of dispersion and looked for consolation for Jerusalem. At the same time He was the One who would come near to deliver the people.[65] He shared in the lament and the suffering *and* He was the God-given mediator of the redemption.

Like Moses he was an extraordinarily-appointed high priest,[66] who wished to sanctify the priestly people in their totality and draw them nearer to their calling.

He was simultaneously a member of the priestly people *and* the One who had to sanctify them.

He belonged to the people called God's servant, *eved*,[67] while He was also the Servant par excellence. Interwoven were the *avoda* of *Yeshua*/Jesus *and* the *avoda* the people owed God. Also interwoven, therefore, are the suffering of this holy servant *and* the judgment that falls upon unholy *avoda*.

In Isaiah 52:13–53:12 we observe this interwovenness, while at the same time see what effect pure *avoda* has had and continues to have. In the New Testament this chapter is quoted regularly in the interpretation of the mystery of the life and service of *Yeshua*/Jesus.[68] In this chapter, the fourth Song of the Servant of the LORD,[69]

---

56. John 4:1–2; this "baptism" in fact was an immersion as in a *mikva*, a ritual bath. Very often the word "baptism" carries associations which mask the original context.

57. Ps 80:6.

58. Ps 80:8–11; cf. John 15:1–8.

59. Ps 80:15.

60. Ps 80:15.

61. Ps 80:17.

62. Ps 80:17.

63. Ps 80:13. NIV uses the verb "ravage"; "gnaw" is the rendering of *JSB*.

64. Ps 80:19.

65. When Jesus in speaking about Himself uses the designation "Son of Man" (par example Mark 2:10), He chooses a name which includes both the suffering of Ps 80 and the victory described in Dan 7:14.

66. See chapter 8.

67. *Eved* and *avoda* stem from the same Hebrew root.

68. See par example Matt 8:17; 1 Pet 2:21–25.

69. See the discussion of this section in chapter 12.

In the Camp of Israel: The Avoda Fully Lived and Perfectly Accomplished

the nations are encamped in a circle around the camp of Israel, so to speak, and together with Israel witness what is happening there.[70] Not only they are astonished and appalled, but they—many nations[71]—are also ritually purified by this servant. The priestly calling of Israel for the nations becomes reality through this servant. His life amidst the people Israel was a path of suffering. In his death, as says the LORD,[72] a sacrifice took place that purifies Israel. It is by his knowledge of God[73] that this righteous[74] one will justify many. This one (man) bore[75] the sins of the many, as a sacrificial animal over which guilt has been confessed and sins have been lain.[76]

All of this happened in Israel's midst with Israel as witness.[77] Through an unholy disobedience of the people, His death became a reality. The voluntary service[78] of this servant, however, opened up a fountain of righteousness. God's plans will prosper by His service.[79] After his sufferings and his death, he will live a joyful and victorious existence.[80] By the *avoda* of this one, salvation is from God for the many inside the camp of Israel, but also outside the camp of Israel.[81]

The canonical narrative of the New Testament testifies to the service of Jesus: He is that Servant![82] By His hand[83] the will of the LORD will prosper[84] and be fulfilled. All promises are confirmed and will be fulfilled,[85] even those who await completion.[86]

Israel was called to perform the service of *kedusha* in the midst of the earth. It has happened. One has accomplished it. He sanctified God's Name and lived all of His life in sanctification before Him. In this He led the way as the heart of Israel and as such also as the heart of all creation.

---

70. Isa 52:15.
71. Idem; see chapter 12 (12.5; footnote 39).
72. Isa 53:8 mentions "my people."
73. Isa 53:11.
74. Isa 53:11.
75. Isa 53:6.
76. Cf. Lev 16:21.
77. Cf. the repeated use of "us."
78. Isa 53:10.
79. Isa 53:10–12.
80. Isa 53:10–12 mentions "see," "prolong his days," and "divide the spoils."
81. Isa 53:5 speaks of God's *shalom* for Israel. The "nations" and "many" will share in this salvation.
82. This does not exclude that simultaneously the *eved*-ship of Israel will play a role.
83. Isa 53:10; cf. Num 36:13.
84. Isa 53:10.
85. 2 Cor 1:20.
86. Rom 9:4.

16.7 Priest for Israel, Priest for the Nations: Adam in Israel

Throughout eternity God desired to place Israel as a living house of learning in the midst of creation.[87] It is there Adam and his offspring were meant to learn about God's purposes and the sanctification of all of life. And when sin necessitated the priestly service of atonement and sanctification, Israel remained the place of this atonement. Adam and the nations, however, also remained represented in the priestly people Israel. They awaited the completed sanctification of this priestly nation in the Messianic Eighth Day.

Israel's calling from within the nations, but also for the sake of the nations, only became fully effectuated in "the Day" of Messiah Jesus. The "ministry of reconciliation"[88] could only begin when, for the first time, the *avoda* of Israel had been completely lived in the center of the earth. The openness of *Yeshua* and His disciples toward the nations is not founded on a change of plans by God, neither is it caused by a rejection of His people in favor of universal salvation. That the nations may share in the salvation of God in the New Testament has nothing to do with a change "in" God, or points to a "different god." Even more, this does not signal that from now on the focus is on "spiritual" salvation, versus an "earthly" salvation still bound up with one specific nation and one specific land.[89] The Scriptures of the New Covenant still stand in the streambed of the canonical narrative of the Tanakh. This stands, even when the Eighth Day has dawned and for the first time, in the Messiah, the holy *avoda* of the priestly nation has been fulfilled. Therefore, what the prophets spoke of while searching "intently and with the greatest care,"[90] now unfolds, and what at the same time "has been kept hidden for ages and generations"[91] has now been disclosed.[92] Because of God's mercy made visible in Israel, the gentiles too will glorify God.[93]

16.8 The Eighth Day: The Obedient One Enters Judgment[94]

Because the Day of the LORD and the Kingdom of God were nearing, the people were called to repentance, a core element of the preaching of Jesus.[95] Israel's camp, and also the nations surrounding it, must enter the judgment of God, a judgment over all

---

87. See chapter 1.
88. This designation is found in 2 Cor 5:18.
89. Cf. chapter 13 (13.14) for N.T. Wright postulating the opposite.
90. Cf. 1 Pet 1:10.
91. Col 1:25–26.
92. Eph 3:4–6.
93. Rom 15:9.
94. Also see chapter 14.
95. Matt 4:17.

In the Camp of Israel: The *Avoda* Fully Lived and Perfectly Accomplished

iniquity and idols.[96] This judgment begins with Israel, the household of God.[97] The coming of the Messiah will also bring the fire of judgment.

The message of the New Testament about the death of the Messiah doesn't just arise from an abstract context of cultic technical or systematic theological categories of guilt, acquittal and forgiveness, sacrifice, atonement, and reconciliation.

The fire Jesus spoke about, referred to the fire of the Day of the LORD against all "the proud and lofty"[98] as did the altar fire in the Temple. It is the fire that will consume all idols,[99] that will do away with all disobedience, and will end the demonic darkness behind every disobedience—both in the people Israel and the world.[100] It is also the fire of judgment for the nations that threaten and hate Israel, and for him who inspired their resistance, God's opponent.[101] It is the "judgment on this world" and on "the prince of this world."[102]

Only when the fire of the Day of the LORD has burned, purity will be a reality, and a new future for Israel and the nations a possibility. The judgment on the present world with all its unholiness—the *olam haze*—clears the way for the coming era, the *olam haba*.

The canonical narrative about *Yeshua*/Jesus makes clear that, as the First One of Israel and so also as the First One of the world, He has entered the fire of this Day of the LORD. In this fire He has been "cut off from the land of the living" as if by the circumciser's knife.[103] Made "to be sin for us" by God,[104] He disappeared in the darkness of that Day.[105] His death outside the city was the most definitive form of exile.[106] Relinquished to a distant country.[107] Burnt like trash.[108] Just as Israel was ravaged by the nations—gnawed at by the boars from the forest.[109]

---

96. Ezek 36:25; Zech 13:2.

97. Cf. Exod 32:26–29; Ezek 9:4–7; 1 Pet 4:17.

98. Isa 2:12.

99. Isa 2:18.

100. Zechariah mentions "the spirit of impurity." Cf. also Jer 23:13 and the description of the spiritual powers at work in and behind the nations which are dealing with Israel (Dan 10:13–21).

101. Cf. Matt 16:23.

102. John 12:31.

103. Isa 53:8. Here the death of the servant of the LORD is denoted as "to be cut off."

104. 2 Cor 5:21.

105. Amos 5:20; cf. Matt 27:45.

106. Heb 13:12–13.

107. Isa 22:17; Jer 10:18; 16:13.

108. Ps 80:16.

109. Ps 80:13.

At the same time, as shepherd He has been betrayed by one of His own, the sheep of Israel.[110] Exchanged for a murderer by the majority of the people.[111] The fire on this altar, however—ignited by Israel—will cleanse and purify Israel.

Because of this astonishing substitution it could be said:

> God made him who had no sin to be sin for us, so that in him we might become the righteousness of God.[112]

16.9 The Eighth Day: The Obedient One Enters Salvation

The raising[113] of Jesus from the dead is in itself not just a happy end for the life of one individual. This resurrection is the honor of God for this One,[114] and by it God declared Him to be righteous.[115] In breaking forth from the grave, it became overwhelmingly clear that He was God's Son in power.[116]

But the resurrection of Jesus means still more. He is the First One[117] who enters the salvation of the Eighth Day, the First One of Israel in the midst of the world who will experience the fulfillment of everything God promised. As the first gift of the *olam haba*, the nearing Messianic age, He receives both the Holy Spirit and the authority to bestow the Spirit.[118]

Knowing this we must keep in mind that His resurrection from the dead, being seated at the right hand of God, and the giving of the Spirit at *Shavuot* are to be seen and understood in one breath. This is the path of this First One of Israel toward the promised future, which He wishes to bring his people into as a *Yehoshua*, or Joshua.

He has completed the *kedusha*. In every respect was His life holy. By reason of that holiness He received a share in the holy life that remains eternal,[119] and is able to give life to whom He wishes.[120] He has been granted authority over death,[121] entering

---

110. Matt 26:14–16.

111. Acts 3:14.

112. 2 Cor 5:21.

113. The New Testament has both the designation "raised (from the dead) to life" (Acts 2:32) and "resurrection" (Acts 2:31).

114. Cf. John 5:41.

115. Acts 3:14–15.

116. Rom 1:4.

117. One of the designations (and names) of the Messiah in Judaism is "the First One" (*rishon*), so Strack and Billerbeck, *Matthäus*, 65.

118. Acts 2:33; cf. Rom 8:23 for the designation of the Sprit as the first gift, the "firstfruits" of the coming age.

119. Cf. chapter 7, footnote 27–28.

120. John 5:21, 26.

121. 2 Tim 1:10.

God's Presence and receiving gifts of salvation.[122] All authority in heaven and on earth has been given to Him:[123] authority over the powers of darkness;[124] authority to grant salvation to the nations.[125] In His death the judgment came over the world and the prince of the world was driven out.[126] The idols and the demons behind them[127] have no choice but to give way to the glory of the LORD, which will cover the earth.[128] Rulers will bow down before the majesty of God's reign over the nations.[129]

In all things[130] He is the Firstling. Before anything else He is the Firstling of Israel, the firstling of the "harvest" of *Pessah* in the land.[131] His resurrection means that on His behalf there is also passage for Israel, a passage from the death of sin to life. This also implicates the fulfillment of the promise of the return from the diaspora to the land. His resurrection means an exodus from impurity to the full *kedusha*, and a nearing to the complete fulfillment of the calling the people received at Sinai. Here everything hinges on a full understanding of the meaning of the "enfleshment in the flesh of Israel." In this He has been appointed by God as the First one, the Firstling and substitute for Israel. By it He ultimately draws the whole people after Him as he breaks through before them.[132] In Him the fulfillment of all promises for Israel precedes the fulfillment of all promises for the nations and creation. Here also it is "first the Jew and then the Gentile."[133]

As the Firstling of the nations,[134] however, as Israel-in-One He also is the representative of the offspring of Adam, that is, the nations. As Lord who has been enfleshed in Israel He also is the last Adam,[135] the second man.[136] Therefore to the

---

122. Ps 68:18; Eph 4:7–13.

123. Matt 28:18.

124. Col 2:15.

125. Matt 28:18–20; Luke 24:46–47.

126. John 12:31.

127. Cf. 1 Cor 8:4–6 and 10:19–22.

128. Hab 2:14.

129. Luke 1:52.

130. Col 1:15–20 emphasizes this.

131. See Lev 23:9–11. The firstfruits/firstlings of the harvest in the land (!) have to be brought before God during the days of *Pessah*/the Festival of Unleavened Bread "on the day after the Sabbath" in order "that you may find acceptance" (so the rendering of 23:11 in RSV; NIV has "so it [the offering, EJW] will be accepted on your behalf"). "Firstling" as designation of the Messiah in this context also implies that the (coming of the) Messiah does not mean that Israel's history is coming to an end or that Israel's role has been played out.

132. Mic 2:13.

133. Cf. Rom 1:16.

134. "so that in everything he might have the supremacy" (Col 1:18).

135. 1 Cor 15:22, 45.

136. 1 Cor 15:47.

Part II : The Canonical Narrative: The Scriptures of the New Covenant

nations He too can show the way to their required *avoda*. In Him they can learn and receive this *avoda*.[137]

16.10 Preparation and Foretaste

The entrance of the Messiah both in the Day of the LORD and the Eighth Day, as described above, plays a role in the teaching and ministry of Jesus preceding His death and resurrection. His teaching was both preparation for the judgment as well as preparation for the entrance in the kingdom of God in the Messianic day. Both lines can be found in it: "Repent" and "the kingdom has come upon you."[138] His preaching was a part of God's approach unto judgment and salvation.

Besides preparation, in a tangible manner the reality of God's judgment over sin and disobedience[139] as well as the foretaste of the *olam haba* (in healings, deliverance from demons, and the raising of the dead[140]) was present.

Wherever He came, He drew people into the nearing of the Day of the LORD *and* into the connected nearing of God's kingship. How the people lived with their God-given calling came to light. All that was hidden was revealed in this nearing of the Day of the LORD and the Reign of God.

16.11 The New Covenant: Inaugurated and Underway

The gift of the New Covenant, promised by the prophets, turns out to be made possible and inaugurated by the *avoda* of *Yeshua*/Jesus. He characterizes His death and His blood and "this cup" as the consecration of this covenant.[141] His blood is "poured out for many."[142] Those "many" who were not present at that *Pessaḥ* meal also will share in it, including future generations.[143] At the same time this announcement and inauguration of the New Covenant exists in the context of waiting for the fulfillment.[144] Paul sees himself to be minister of this New Covenant and he lives and acts out of the expectation of the full realization of everything implied in that covenant.[145]

---

137. Cf. Eph 4:21–24; Col 1:28.

138. Matt 12:28; Luke 11:20 and 17:21.

139. We can observe this happening par example in the judgment over the fig tree, the cleansing of the Temple (Mark 11:11–26), and in the aspect of "taking away" which is one of the reasons for Jesus to speak in parables (Matt 13:11–15).

140. Cf. Matt 11:2–6.

141. Matt 26:28; Mark 14:24; Luke 22:20.

142. Mark 14:24; cf. 14:25.

143. Deut 29:15.

144. Luke 22:16.

145. 2 Cor 3:6; for his expectation, see 3:7–18.

Additionally, the letter to the Hebrews also speaks about the sacrifice of Jesus taking place to deliver from the sins committed under the first covenant.[146] His *avoda* took place "under" the Tora of Sinai. He fully lived God's Tora, as He had said He would.[147] On that account His obedience covered all Israel's sins and gained entrance into the Covenant of the Eighth Day. The New Covenant is indeed the Covenant of the Messianic time and becomes a possibility through the firstfruit gift of the Holy Spirit. This also implies, however, that the blessings of this covenant share both in the "already" as well as in the "not-yet" of the Messianic time. Those who participate in this covenant have a share in a new blessing, but at the same time they still live with a partially-realized promise.[148]

The "new-ness" of the New Covenant is connected to the newness of the Messianic time. It is related to the new creation, which opened up in the resurrection of Jesus from the dead.[149] In the camp of Israel death has been conquered in the raising of the Firstling, and immortal life has been brought to light.[150] Eternal salvation from death has appeared on the horizon.[151]

16.12 The Blessings of the New Covenant and the Focus of the New Testament

There is one ongoing canonical narrative. Messiah *Yeshua*/Jesus appears and acts within the streambed of the Tanakh. He realizes all of God's promises and inaugurates the Messianic time. It is fundamentally important to remain thinking—in every respect—within the framework of the God-ordained structures revealed in the Tanakh.

The traditional canonical narrative, however, where Israel disappears to the background and the incarnation is interpreted in general human terms, presupposes a totally new beginning with the appearance of Jesus. That new beginning then is not the dawning of the Eighth Day. It is not the newness of the *olam haba*, but the newness thereof is predominantly understood as a change in regard to what preceded. It is the beginning of something totally different, creating a breach between what was before and what came after. It then relates to a different, a universal orientation of God's purposes. From that moment on God is interested in a spiritual salvation that consists in knowing Him, and attention to a God-given future of Israel as a people, for Jerusalem and (the return to) God's land, disappears.

---

146. Heb 9:15.

147. Matt 5:17.

148. Heb 9:15 speaks of "the promised eternal inheritance." "Eternal" then should not be interpreted as antagonistic to "earthly," but in relation to the abiding character of God's kingdom in the *olam haba*.

149. 2 Cor 5:17.

150. 2 Tim 1:10.

151. Heb 2:15; Isa 25:7–8; 1 Cor 15:25–27.

Part II : The Canonical Narrative: The Scriptures of the New Covenant

The reasoning leading to this interpretation hinges on the fact that the New Testament predominantly appears to focus on the knowledge of God and life through the Spirit. Eternal life is then interpreted as a contrast to everything "earthly." It indeed appears as if there has been a change of focus, resulting in a visible shift of subjects wherein the revealed Tora has been overshadowed by universal commandments.

In regard to this interpretation it has been postulated by those emphasizing the fidelity of God, that everything that has not been clearly retracted by God—namely the election of Israel and the promises spoken—may be presupposed to be still valid. This certainly is the case, but there is more to be said. When we recognize the Messianic character of the New Covenant, we understand from that viewpoint that with respect to this covenant and its blessings there are things which come first, and things which follow suit.[152] The blessing of the New Covenant is given in the form of a first gift by which the life-underway-to-the-fulfillment can be lived. This covenant is given in the form of an "already" *and* a "not-yet." This takes form in "tasting the Eighth Day" *and* in waiting for the full revelation of the salvation of God.

We need to realize that there are themes and subjects which are elaborated upon and thereby become highlighted, and those which are implied and presupposed. We have to pay attention to both groups.

Salvation for the nations, their God-given access to it, and their path of faith obedience[153] receive much attention in the New Testament. Many of the epistles have been written to congregations mainly consisting of believers from the nations. What these first readers needed is extensively written about. But does this mean that we have to conclude that God made a change in His plans? Or, does this observation only teach us that we, in the process of interpretation, also have to take into account the fact that by the fulfilled *avoda* of the Messiah—underway toward the full salvation of the Eighth Day—a period of mercy for the nations has begun? We have to reckon with the fact that a quest of the Lord of lords is taking place among the nations! A quest caused by a partial rejection by Israel, but also taking place while the full salvation for Israel is still awaited!

Even the treatment of the commandments—the ethical appeal—is determined by the structure of representation of Israel and the nations in the Messiah, as well as by this special period of creation's journey toward the Eighth Day.[154]

Therefore, the New Testament appearing to have a different focus is more related to "times or seasons"[155] than to God's plans altering. We will pay attention to this theme in the remainder of this book.

---

152. Cf. for this terminology (in a different context) 1 Tim 5:24–25.
153. Rom 1:5 and 16:26.
154. See for this chapter 20.
155. Acts 1:7 (RSV).

16.13 In the Camp of Israel: The *Avoda* Fully Lived and Perfectly Accomplished

The title of this chapter calls attention to the fact that Israel's calling has been lived and fulfilled in its midst by Messiah *Yeshua*. Jesus lived and taught this calling. By His *avoda* He obtained the authority to let His people Israel and the nations of the world share in the *yeshua*—the salvation—of God.

In this chapter we predominantly paid attention to the streambed of the Tanakh and the structures found in it, which have to be taken into account when interpreting the appearance and the meaning of the service of this One.

In the following chapters the *avoda* of the Messiah and the reactions to it within the camp of Israel and surrounding nations will be elaborated upon with respect to the different elements, which constitute the calling Israel received.

CHAPTER 17

In the Camp of Israel

*The Priestly Nation Consecrated
in the Sanctification of the Messiah*

17.1 Israel's Calling: The Eighth Day Dawns

THE NEXT THREE CHAPTERS will focus on what the dawning of the Messianic time in the appearance of Messiah *Yeshua*/Jesus meant to the different aspects of Israel's calling.

Due to the fact that they are aspects of *one* calling, some overlapping will take place. A logical interweaving of the themes discussed has been attempted within these chapters.

The starting-point is that the canonical narrative of the New Testament is a narrative that still takes place in the streambed of the canonical narrative of the Tanakh. Israel is, with its calling, on its way to the full sanctification and fulfillment of this calling in the Eighth Day of God. The nation as *segula*—God's treasured possession—and because of this the nation as a son, is on its journey to the time of Messianic love. As a *kingdom of priests* (and thereby also servants), Israel is on its way toward a full realization thereof. The people as *holy nation* are moving toward the full *kedusha*, in which life will be fully dedicated to God.

The Messiah both enables this Messianic sanctification and is the first one to enter into it, enabling His people to share also in the authority and privileges of this Messianic time. He leads His people on the road toward the full realization of all God's intentions. On this road, in the light of this beginning but not yet perfected Eighth Day, the nations are also invited to salvation. They even are invited to share in aspects of Israel's calling. This chapter's focus is on the consecration of the priestly nation in the sanctification of the Messiah.

17.2 The Essence of the Priestly Calling: The Tasks of the Priestly Nation

As outlined within the canonical narrative presented in this book, the calling of Israel was one of God's intentions when He created the cosmos. God created the cosmos in such manner that His creation would be dependent on further instruction about its own essence and purpose. The name of the house of learning in which this instruction would be provided is Israel.[1] Therefore instruction is the primary task for priests and the priestly nation. Instruction in God's Tora remains essential in God's future for His people and the cosmos. The Tora will go out from Zion and the nations will want to learn it there.[2] About Jerusalem we read, "All your sons will be taught by the LORD."[3] Priestly instruction is thereby a creational intention of God and will have a permanent place in the Messianic Day.

From the beginning of creation, priestly blessing also is a God-intended task for His people in the center of creation. Not only must everything good be placed under God's blessing, as God Himself shows in the blessing of the seventh day,[4] but first and foremost the goal must be (the) blessing (of) God, the honor and praise of His Name, which belongs to the good creation and is the logical[5] *avoda* from the very first beginning into all eternity.[6]

The *kedusha* of the totality of life is also a priestly calling for creation, which was intended to be taught in Israel's house of learning.

As a result of man's disobedience to God's intentions—and creation taking part in it—the "ministry of reconciliation"[7] with all its aspects and instruction became necessary, a part of the task and calling of God's priestly people.

In all this, it revolved around obedience to the God-given calling, which stems from being God's image-bearer and a partner in His covenant(s). Due to the breach caused by sin the necessity of obedience is emphasized even more. Now needed is a new path of repentance, returning to God, and sanctification.

In the canonical narrative of the Scriptures, God's people are underway—as His intended priests—toward both the dawning and the completion of the Eighth Day. The full revelation of God's creational intentions is awaited, along with the shining glory of God extended through the ways of redemption. The nations "encamped around Israel" wait for the blessing from the midst of the earth. Creation also awaits this resplendent moment.

1. See chapter 1.
2. Isa 2:3.
3. Isa 54:13 (RSV). Meant is "all who live in Jerusalem."
4. Gen 2:3; cf. also 1:22, 28.
5. Rom 12:1; see chapter 16, footnote 2.
6. For that reason *Berakhot* (= blessings) is the first tractate of both Mishna and Talmud. This tractate deals with the blessing of God and His Name.
7. The designation stems from 2 Cor 5:18.

17.3 The Priestly Consecration of *Yeshua*/Jesus: The First One of the People

When speaking of the priesthood of *Yeshua*/Jesus we have to keep in mind that Jesus did not *genealogically* belong to the priesthood within Israel. He did, however, live the priestly calling that concerned the people as a whole.[8] His life was a fulfillment of the promise that one day all of Israel would be called priests and priestly servants of God.[9]

His immersion in the river Jordan can therefore be understood as the *mikva* of the priestly consecration. He underwent this immersion as *one* of the people, but also as the *first one* of the nation. Members of priestly families, for various reasons, sometimes could be prevented from serving as a priest.[10] Jesus, however, is designated as "the holy one" even before His birth.[11] This again is confirmed powerfully by His resurrection from the dead.[12]

Simultaneously, it can be postulated that His whole life has been a priestly consecration in anticipation of His "priestly officiating" in the Eighth Day. After all, just before He dies he speaks of His path toward death as a sanctification in order that those who are His own will be sanctified by it also.[13] His raising from the dead by God and the implied declaration of His righteousness is therefore the prelude to His exaltation and priestly service. The "glory" which had to be entered through suffering, of which Jesus speaks while walking to Emmaus, can also be interpreted as indicative of the glory of His royal and priestly service.[14] In this manner there is a similarity with the path of Israel receiving at Sinai its royal-priestly calling and task among the nations following the redemption from Egypt. Following the *Pessaḥ* in Egypt, the service of the people begins at *Shavuot* at Sinai. The same structure can be observed in the existence of Jesus. By His death and resurrection—His *Pessaḥ*—and His exaltation to the Throne of God, He received the glory of His Messiah-ship. This becomes visible on the fiftieth day after *Pessaḥ*, on *Shavuot*. Through this way God has made Him both Lord and Messiah.[15] It is against this background that the Letter to the Hebrews

---

8. See chapter 7. Also chapter 14, footnote 38 about the widespread longing for purity that existed within the nation at the time of the appearance of Jesus.

9. Isa 61:6.

10. Cf. Lev 21–22.

11. Luke 1:35.

12. Rom 1:4.

13. John 17:19 mentions this sanctification. This "sanctification" then pertains to both the sanctification of the (Messiah as) priest for His service and of (Himself as) the sacrifice for the altar.

14. Luke 24:26.

15. Acts 2:36. Just like David (as the one who was anointed for kingship) became the anointed king through waiting and obedience. Promised Messiah-ship becomes realized and authority-invested Messiah-ship.

puts that Messiah *Yeshua* has "received" the priestly ministry.[16] Through His death He received an eternal priesthood and thus became "the source of eternal salvation."[17] He has also received the promised Holy Spirit[18] and lets His people share in this blessing.[19]

Like Moses who had to sanctify the priests of the nation, Jesus is a non-Aaronic high priest who performs and fulfills the consecration of the priestly nation.[20] In contrast to Moses, who had to die because of his disobedience,[21] *Yeshua*—His name connecting Him to Joshua[22]—receives an eternal high priesthood on behalf of His holy and immortal life.[23] It is the priesthood of the *olam haba*, which will never pass away.[24]

At the same time this priestly consecration of the Messiah also is the consecration of the First One of the priestly nation. He Himself is the guarantee that ultimately the whole people will become priests for God. Just as counting the *Omer*[25] connects *Pessaḥ* to *Shavuot*, so the Firstling of the redemption guarantees that God "keeps counting" until ultimately His Spirit will be on all the people and all flesh.[26]

17.4 The Priestly Service of *Yeshua*/Jesus: The First One of the People

Instruction in the Tora, blessing, the *kedusha* of God's Name and of life, and the mediation of forgiveness, reconciliation, and healing were the tasks of the priests.

In the New Testament we see how Jesus lives this calling in a perfect and complete manner. In His teaching He is the Teacher who teaches God's Tora,[27] without abolishing or altering a minute detail.[28] His instruction in the Tora is not just an alternative voice within Israel. He is the promised Teacher, who is both announcing and a part of the *olam haba*.[29]

16. Heb 8:6.
17. Heb 5:4–10.
18. Acts 2:33.
19. Heb 6:4–5.
20. Cf. chapter 8, footnotes 6 and 52. Milgrom signalizes that Moses also acts as a king who appoints priests (see chapter 8, footnote 65). Consecration of priests then also is a "royal" task and privilege.
21. Num 20:12; cf. Deut 34.
22. Cf. chapter 14, footnote 25 about the name *Yeshua*/Jesus—*Yehoshua*/Joshua.
23. Heb 7:28 shows both elements (holiness and immortality).
24. Heb 12:27.
25. *Omer* is the Hebrew word for "sheaf." From *Pessaḥ* onwards Israel has to count fifty days (following the command in Lev 23:9–16; Deut 16:9). From the first sheaf till the in-bringing of the full harvest.
26. Joel 2:28–29.
27. Matt 5–7 shows the central place the Tora has in Jesus's instruction.
28. Matt 5:17–18.
29. Cf. Joel 2:23. The Hebrew word rendered as "rain" can also mean "teacher." Therefore also the rendering "teacher for righteousness" is possible (*JSB*, 1172; commentary ad Joel 2:23).

He blesses both the people as a whole and as individuals.[30] He sanctifies the Name of God.[31] He dedicates His whole life to God.[32] In the authority that He received He mediates God's forgiveness.[33] He is God's living Temple,[34] not only by reason of His miraculous birth, but also because of His holy life in the Spirit of God.[35] Through His pure life He enables the Indwelling of the Holy One. In the most literal way, in Him the God of Israel dwells and walks amidst the people.[36] He is both the Dwelling—*Shekhina*—of God and a servant in that Dwelling.

As a servant He brings the sacrifices of Israel in the House of God, but does not offer the sacrifices Himself. Although as a son of Israel He participates in the sacrificial services in the Temple, He teaches and exemplifies that this sacrificial service symbolizes the sacrifice of man's own life. After all, the Tanakh teaches that obedience is better than sacrifices[37] and that God does not want sacrifices—ritually pure as they might be—when the heart of the people is distanced from Him.[38] As Teacher of Israel, Jesus teaches this at various occasions.[39]

He fulfills—so says the writer of the Letter to the Hebrews—the words and the service of Psalm 40.[40]

> Sacrifice and offering you did not desire –
> but my ears you have opened; –
> burnt offerings and sin offerings you did not require.
> Then I said, 'Here I am, I have come –
> it is written about me in the scroll.
> I desire to do your will, my God;
> Your law is within my heart.'[41]

The Letter to the Hebrews shows that this prophetic psalm speaks of an individual who, just like David, would desire (with the Tora in his heart) to do the will of God. One who carried the blessing of the New Covenant in Himself and in this manner serves.

---

30. Mark 10:13–16; Luke 24:50–51.
31. Matt 6:9; John 17:6.
32. John 5:30; Luke 22:42.
33. Mark 2:1–12.
34. John 2:21; cf. also Matt 12:6, "something greater than the temple is here."
35. Rom 1:4.
36. Cf. Exod 25:8.
37. 1 Sam 15:22–23.
38. Hos 6:6; cf. Mic 6:8.
39. Matt 12:7. In Matt 23:23 Jesus shows that He creates no contradistinction between "meaning" and actual fulfillment of sacrifice related commandments.
40. In Heb 10:5–10 parts of Ps 40 are discussed.
41. Ps 40:6–8.

In the Camp of Israel: The Priestly Nation Consecrated in the Sanctification of the Messiah

In the New Testament we see how people, confronted with the way of Jesus and God's response to Him, begin to realize that for the first time Someone has lived and obeyed the totality of the covenant of Sinai. The sins committed under the first covenant have been atoned for.[42] This also implies that the reality of the forgiveness, which Israel received through all ages and the sacrificial legislation is related to the sacrifice of this One. The Messiah appears to not only have been Israel's companion[43] in a mysterious way, but also the fountain from which forgiveness has flown to the people for centuries. In some way He always has been "the way."

As was customary within Jewish interpretation of Scripture, in the New Testament various typological connections[44] are clearly pointed out between both elements of the sacrificial service and the God-ordained feasts, and the salvation of Messiah *Yeshua*/Jesus.[45] In various ways the Tanakh pointed toward what would happen in the fullness of time.[46]

The canonical narrative of the New Testament is deeply influenced by the awareness that the death of this High Priest meant atonement and reconciliation. The Tora had already determined that the death of a "normal" high priest could accomplish atonement for someone guilty of unintentional killing.[47] By virtue of the death of Jesus there is forgiveness, according to Paul, for everything that could not be atoned for under the Law of Moses.[48] The death of this High priest is the fulfillment of the annual *Yom Kippur*, the Day of Atonement.[49] Hebrews further shows how various elements of this holy day received their deepest fulfillment in the sacrifice of the life of High Priest *Yeshua*/Jesus.

The Day of Atonement was for every high priest the eighth day after a seven-day period of preparation.[50] Just as on every Day of Atonement the high priest walked

---

42. Heb 9:15.

43. 1 Cor 10:4 ("the spiritual rock that accompanied them, and that rock was Christ"); cf. Isa 63:9.

44. The conceptual designation "type" in this context means that certain things, persons, and occasions can have a God-intended pre-figurative character pointing to things, persons, and occasions occurring at a later time.

45. Par example Jesus is called "the Lamb of God, who takes away the sin of the world" (John 1:29). He also is the "Passover lamb" (1 Cor 5:6–8), and various elements of the celebration of *Pessaḥ* receive their fulfillment in relation to Him. In Heb 9:1–10 we observe how various details of the Tabernacle and priestly service have a meaning which is related to "the time of the new order" (9:10); cf. also 9:23.

46. Gal 4:4.

47. Num 35:25, 28, 32. Both Mishna and Talmud discuss this theme; see Milgrom, *Numbers*, 294.

48. Acts 13:38–39.

49. See Lev 16 for the liturgy of this day. The Talmud (tractate b Yoma 39b) mentions how in the last forty years prior to the destruction of the temple some remarkable changes took place with respect to certain tokens, which until then had occurred during the liturgy of *Yom Kippur*.

50. The Mishna describes in tractate Yoma the preparation for and the service of the Day of Atonement. In m. Yoma 1,1 this seven-day period of secluded preparation is mentioned.

the way to the Throne of God,[51] *Yeshua*/Jesus became "the way"[52] on "His Eighth Day." He became the living way.[53] He accomplished the nearing to God and the related Messianic forgiveness, as well as also the son-ship of the *olam haba* for the people. The faithful service of this son of Israel made the New Covenant possible. His blood inaugurates this covenant.[54]

His obedient and perfect[55] priestly service is the initiation and the dawning of the promised Messianic time in which the Spirit of God will perfectly complete the son-ship of the people.[56] It is this eschatological son-ship John speaks of.[57] Through the death of this Firstborn, the sons of Israel have been redeemed and are no longer slaves.[58]

The healings and deliverances, which take place prior to and following the resurrection of Jesus, are tokens of what He has accomplished. Isaiah 61 was the portion of Scripture that sounded when His ministry began,[59] now even more it tells how as priest He will work to bless God's people. This chapter of Isaiah tells that as the First One He will also draw the whole of God's people Israel with Him into the priesthood.[60]

17.5 The Sacrifice Outside the City: Sacrifice of Israel, by Israel, and for Israel

According to God's commandment the slaughtering of a sheep or goat as burnt offering of Israel took place on the north side of the altar.[61] It is very possible that the dying of Jesus also took place at the north side of the Temple and the altar.[62] When Jesus dies on Golgotha, outside the city—just like the scapegoat on *Yom Kippur*;[63] as if driven out in exile—it is there the slaughtering of Israel's sacrifice takes place. In the midst of the earth, amidst the people of God, the Firstling of this people dies. He

51. Cf. Heb 8:1–2; 9:12; 10:20.
52. John 14:6.
53. Heb 10:20.
54. Cf. Heb 10:18; 9:18.
55. Heb 7:28.
56. Rom 8:15; Gal 4:6.
57. John 1:12; 1 John 3:1.
58. Cf. John 8:30–36. Jesus does not deny Abraham's sons to be sons of God. The background of this discussion is the fact that this son-ship of Israel was not complete and perfect. See par example Jer 3:19–22.
59. Luke 4:14–30.
60. Isa 61:6.
61. Lev 1:11; see Milgrom, *Leviticus 1–16*, 164–65.
62. Golgotha was situated outside the city. It is traditionally identified as the place of the Church of the Holy Sepulcher in Jerusalem. It was situated north of the historical city at that time.
63. Cf. Lev 16:22.

In the Camp of Israel: The Priestly Nation Consecrated in the Sanctification of the Messiah

undergoes the night of the Day of the LORD. And represented in Him, the people are with Him in that night of death.

Even though He is alone in His death, all of this is about the sacrifice *of* Israel. He has been left alone by His twelve disciples, representing the twelve tribes of Israel, His most dedicated circle of followers. None of His disciples probed the depth of Mary's anointment, a token of love like the love of the Song of Songs, an image of Israel's calling to love the LORD; they even deemed it inappropriate.[64] One of them even betrayed Him. Those who were asked to keep vigil slept. All abandoned Him.

In this *Pessah* night of keeping vigil[65] this little band of disciples slept, a miniature version of Israel. On this night before *Yom Kippur*, the friends of this High Priest should have kept vigil.[66] In this night of covenant making, *Yeshua*/Jesus is the only one who keeps vigil. In staying awake, He is more than Abram;[67] He keeps vigil over the path by which the New Covenant will be made.[68] He sacrifices Himself,[69] but He is also given unto sacrifice.[70] In the Tanakh it was already made clear that within Israel the death of the sinner could cover willful evil deeds.[71] But also the death of a high priest could bring atonement in cases of unintentional evil.[72] Now the First One of Israel dies *in* Israel *by* Israel *for* Israel. He dies as one cursed,[73] as a scapegoat,[74] and as a High Priest who by His death brings atonement.

The canonical narrative of the New Testament follows the line of the prophetic words of Caiaphas:

> "You know nothing at all! You do not realize that it is better for you that one man die for the people than that the whole nation perish." He did not say this on his own, but as high priest that year he prophesied that Jesus would die for the Jewish nation, and not only for that nation but also for the scattered children of God, to bring them together and make them one.[75]

---

64. Matt 26:6–13; John 12:1–8.

65. Exod 12:42.

66. The companions of the high priest were obliged to keep him awake during his nightly preparation for the service of *Yom Kippur* (m. Yoma 1,6–7).

67. Gen 15:12.

68. Cf. Gen 15:10, 17.

69. John 10:18.

70. Rom 3:25; 2 Cor 5:21.

71. Cf. Lev 18:29–30.

72. See footnote 47 in this chapter.

73. Deut 21:22–23.

74. See Lev 16.

75. John 11:49–52; see also chapter 14, footnote 82 about the interpretation of "the scattered children of God."

17.6 The Sacrifice Outside the City: Also a Sacrifice of the World and for the World

The words of Caiaphas cited above show that the death of *Yeshua*/Jesus belongs within an even wider perspective. It can be said that His life and death also form the sacrifice *of* the world and *for* the world. That Jesus within the gospels implicates salvation for the world is not a radical course correction by God. Although there is a deep awareness of a hidden mystery that has been revealed,[76] it is a continuation of the developments implied in the structure of God's salvific actions.

From the beginning and throughout the ages across many generations,[77] God's intentions remained hidden. Israel's existence as a blessing in the midst of the world, as promised to Abraham, was also meant as blessing for the nations. This much had been clear. How this would be realized and what the character and content of this blessing would be had remained hidden, although alluded to in numerous places in the words of the prophets.

Yet at the deepest level salvation for the nations was implied in Israel's calling to be a kingdom of priests. Called from among the nations with an eye on those nations. Priestly nation representing the other nations, just as the Aaronic priests within Israel represented the whole people.[78]

The mystery of why it took so long before the mystery was revealed—nations being included in the sacrifice of the Messiah—remains with God, who chooses His "times and seasons." It also has to do with the full realization of Israel's priesthood in the Messiah. In His Eighth Day the priestly consecration of the people was complete and the curse that covered the world could be removed, the power of sin broken and God's opponent defeated.

In a prophetic way, spoken but not yet understood, there is talk of one who dies for all. At Jesus's entrance in Jerusalem the "the whole world" seemingly follows Him,[79] after which John speaks of a few Greeks' (re)quest to meet Jesus.[80]

When there are many references in the New Testament focusing on these wide circles of salvation, the presupposition is always that this salvation has been accomplished in the midst of Israel. Jesus's life, death, and resurrection have been a "path" on which the nations were also present. They were present as represented by Israel and consequently by Him who is Israel-in-One. In Israel and in Israel's Messiah, even Adam and his offspring were present. This is the thinking Paul elaborates upon in a number of places throughout Scripture.[81]

---

76. Eph 3:1–12; cf. also 1:9, 17–18; Gal 1:16; 2 Cor 4:6.
77. Rom 16:25–26; Eph 3:5, 9; Col 1:26–27.
78. See chapter 7.
79. John 12:19.
80. John 12:20–21.
81. Rom 5:12–21; 1 Cor 15:20–22, 45–49.

The involvement of Herod Antipas,[82] Pilate, and the Roman soldiers in the enactment of the execution of Jesus very clearly shows that the death of Jesus is a death in the center of the earth, in which both the nations and God's people Israel are involved. Therefore after His resurrection the apostles refer to Psalm 2,[83] concluding a communal responsibility.[84] Together with Israel's evil, the evil of the nations came upon His head. Thus from the midst of Israel the Lamb of God carried away the sins of the world.[85]

17.7 Israel's Sacrifice Accepted: The Dawning of the *Olam Haba*

The resurrection of Jesus from the dead shows that Israel's sacrifice has been accepted. God does not leave this Firstling in death.[86] It becomes clear that He meritoriously received the first gift, the gift of the Spirit of the coming age. The Eighth Day is dawning over Israel and the world. The first gift of the *tikkun olam*, which is not yet fully realized, is given.

It is important to note this difference between beginning and fulfillment. The New Covenant would indeed enable obedience and make the blessings and promises of the covenant given at Sinai accessible in a new way.[87] Nearing God in the Messiah, however new it might be, would not be the one and only gift.

The covenant at Sinai was certainly given within the streambed of the election of Israel and the promises made to the patriarchs. Considering that election and those promises God would enable the required obedience in a New Covenant. This "better"[88] way consisted in placing the Tora in the heart of the people. In this manner the required obedience would be granted and made possible. The promised New Covenant did not mean abolishment of everything pre-existing. It "just" meant that a new way of nearing to and knowing God would be given, founded in the forgiveness of all sins.[89]

The Firstling-Messiah would include the people of Israel in His own approach of God and by His Spirit enable this new nearness to God. But this would all happen in the streambed of the election and the promises. The focus on the new way that opened

---

82. Cf. Luke 23:8–12. This verse mentions Herod (Antipas), the son of Herod the Great, the Edomite, who converted to Judaism.

83. Acts 4:25–26.

84. Acts 4:24–28; cf. also 2:23; 3:13–14.

85. John 1:29.

86. Cf. Rom 1:4; the resurrection is a divine declaration with regard to Jesus's holiness.

87. So also James G. Dunn, who with reference to Jer 31:33 speaks of "the promise of a more effective implementation of the earlier covenant by divine initiative" (*The New Perspective*, 443).

88. Cf. Heb 6:9; 7:19, 22; 8:6; 9:23.

89. Jer 31:34; cf. Heb 8:12.

up,[90] on Messianic son-ship[91] or on forgiveness and salvation[92] does not mean that the promises made to Israel were suddenly invalidated, limited, or spiritualized. It only shows that what comes first, also first receives attention. When it concerns the fulfillment of all other promises given to Israel as a people in the center of the world, there are seemingly other "times and seasons" in God's agenda.

17.8 Israel's Priestly Service Sanctified: The Task Underway Toward the *Tikkun Olam*

It is clear that Messiah *Yeshua* does not discontinue the priesthood of the people (and of the priests within the people). He respects and recognizes the authority of the priests as God-ordained ministers.[93] We also see that He engages His disciples in the priestly calling of the whole nation that is preached and lived out by Himself. Several times He sent out groups, which should represent Him in this priestly calling,[94] a calling which includes instruction, blessing, prayer, healing, and redemption.

This also is the case after His resurrection. As yet He still directs His voice to the people Israel regarding its calling. But the nations also appear in sight.[95] They too must be instructed in all that Jesus has taught, and be baptized.[96]

Just as Jesus Himself has been the living "Temple of God" among the people,[97] so God's Spirit makes Israelites and now also people from the nations into dwelling places of God.[98] This does not imply disrespect for the physical Temple. We see that this House of God also has that meaning amongst the disciples of Jesus.[99]

Many priest-sons of Aaron—*kohanim*—also accompany the people on this path of Israel's priestly calling.[100] And from the nations people are called, as foretold,[101] to share in this priesthood of the people of God.[102]

---

90. Heb 10:19–20.

91. See par example Rom 8:14–17.

92. Cf. par example Rom 3:23–24; 5:1; 8:1; 2 Cor 5:20.

93. Matt 8:4; Mark 1:44; Luke 5:14; 17:14.

94. Matt 10:1–11:1; Luke 10:1–20.

95. This already was also the case in the period preceding His death and resurrection. See par example Matt 4:23–25.

96. Matt 28:19–20; Luke 24:46–47.

97. John 2:21.

98. 1 Cor 3:16–17; 6:19; Eph 2:22.

99. Luke 24:53.

100. Acts 6:7. So there were amongst the first followers of Messiah *Yeshua*/Jesus many who knew the Temple service from the inside (like the writer of Hebrews?).

101. Isa 66:21.

102. Cf. the use of the words of the calling of Israel in 1 Pet 2:9–10.

17.9 The Priesthood of the Messiah Underway Toward the *Tikkun Olam*

The Messiah has not been a priest briefly, in order to perform a one-time priestly act of atonement. He is the First One who in fullness obtained this enduring and eternal calling of Israel, and as the First One remains serving in this capacity. This one Jew performs this service at the Throne of the Almighty One, exalted to the place at God's right hand.[103] Through this service salvation remains "from the Jews." Through Him believers from Israel and the nations can approach the Throne.

This priesthood of the Messiah also implies, as long as the *tikkun olam* has not been perfected, a suffering and groaning. This will be extensively elaborated upon in following passages.[104]

Believers from Israel and the nations not only receive blessing by the Holy Spirit through this priesthood of the Messiah, but the Spirit draws them *into* the priesthood of the Messiah. This also is the case with the groaning and tribulations on the way toward perfection.[105] This also will be discussed later.[106]

17.10 God will not Rest until His Whole People are Priests

The New Testament makes clear that only part of Israel has recognized the ways of Messiah Jesus as the ways of God. This has also been the case in the centuries following the closure of the New Testament canon. We, however, must keep in mind that this later rejection also has been motivated by the fact that the gospel became a message in which God's faithfulness toward His people had disappeared. At that, the age long hatred and persecution from the side of the Christian church also contributed even more to the hiding of the face of the Messiah. Yet He is the Firstling of Israel. Thereby He is the guarantee of the fulfillment of all God's promises. Because of Him, and because of His own faithfulness, God will not rest until all of His people are priests.

In the following chapters this expectation, arising from the Tanakh and the Scriptures of the New Covenant, will be discussed. But first we will turn to the royal aspect of Israel's calling in the work of the Messiah.

---

103. Ps 80:17; cf. Acts 2:34–35.
104. See chapter 19–21.
105. Cf. Rom 8:23–26; 2 Cor 1:5–6; 4:7–15; Col 1:24.
106. See chapter 19–21.

Chapter 18

In the Camp of Israel

The Royal Consecration and the Kingdom

18.1 Kingship and Paradigms

NOWHERE ELSE THE INFLUENCE of hermeneutical paradigms reveals itself so clearly as in relation to the royal aspect of Israel's calling. We have seen that in the traditional canonical narrative, Israel more or less fades into the background with the appearance of Christ. The kingship of the Messiah in that narrative is solely interpreted in an universal manner, and no longer leaves room for a kingship within and over Israel.

A section from Acts can serve as an illustration. In the opening chapter of this book, the disciples of *Yeshua*/Jesus address the theme of kingship explicitly, and there we also find Jesus's own answer.

> Then they gathered around him and asked him, "Lord, are you at this time going to restore the kingdom to Israel?" He said to them: "It is not for you to know the times or dates the Father has set by his own authority. But you will receive power when the Holy Spirit comes on you; and you will be my witnesses in Jerusalem, and in all Judea and Samaria, and to the ends of the earth."[1]

Within the reading of the traditional canonical narrative, this question of the disciples is often interpreted as showing their incomprehension, their unspiritual human desires and expectations. Obviously they are still focused on earthly salvation for Israel, whilst salvation with the coming of Christ would have become universal, and above all spiritual and heavenly. A kingship over and for Israel does not fit this narrative. Within this model of interpretation, the designation of the Messiah as "king of Israel"

---

1. Acts 1:6–8. The Greek word rendered as "kingdom" also can mean kingship.

In the Camp of Israel: The Royal Consecration and the Kingdom

becomes a designation of His spiritual kingship over believers.[2] The words of Gabriel about the eternal reign on the throne of David[3] then speak of an everlasting kingdom of the Christ. That the gospels tell about the wise men,[4] and later Pilate, calling Jesus "king of the Jews," no longer has real meaning.[5] Yes, the people thought of an earthly kingdom, but Jesus meant a spiritual kingdom. Jesus's answer, seen from the perspective of this traditional paradigm, is interpreted as a rebuke of their earth-focused incomprehension. Jesus is perceived as emphasizing the spiritual reign of Church and mission over the longing for an earthly kingdom.

Yet *Yeshua*'s reply to their question about the time of the restoration of the kingship/kingdom only means that God alone can answer it. He is the One who knows "the times or dates." His disciples do not need to know these; they receive a commission. They are not allowed to know God's timing, but receive a promise and a mission that must be obeyed.[6] There are things that come first—in this case the promise of the Spirit and the assignment to witness—and things that will follow suit.[7] The wish to know the exact time of God is inappropriate, but the question about the kingship in itself is neither strange nor wrong. Jesus, however, still stands in the streambed of the whole of the Tanakh. And yes, these Scriptures certainly speak of a kingdom and kingship for Israel.

18.2 Called to be a Kingdom of Priests: The Streambed of the Tanakh

Israel at Sinai was indeed called as people of God to be a "kingdom of priests." We have seen that this unique designation carries various meanings.[8] First of all, these words point to the kingship of God over Israel. Then, this designation focused our attention to the royal task of the priestly nation as a whole. Finally, we saw that also the possibility of kingship within Israel was indicated. It is this calling, carrying these three directions of meaning, which is present in the streambed of the Tanakh, when Jesus appears amidst the people.

At the same time, it is clear that the fulfillment of this calling is dependent on the God-required obedience, but simultaneously stands under a promise.[9] The royal as-

---

2. Cf. F.F. Bruce, "This interest in the hope of an earthly and national kingdom (cf. Mk. x. 35ff.) gave place after Pentecost to the proclamation of the spiritual kingdom of God, into which men might enter through repentance and faith in Christ' (*The Acts of the Apostles*, 70).

3. Luke 1:32–33; Matt 2:2.

4. Matt 2:2.

5. John 19:14–15; Matt 27:37.

6. John 21:22 mentions how Peter receives a somewhat identical answer to an "inappropriate" question.

7. See also the end of chapter 16.

8. See chapter 10.

9. See chapter 10 (10.6).

pect of Israel's calling is thereby subject to the same structures we discussed earlier.[10] Obedient *avoda* as part of the two-sidedness of God's covenants, the promise of God-given obedience, and a servant as *brit am*, these are the ways by which God ultimately realizes Israel's calling. The promises of the covenant made at Sinai were not retracted by the promise of a New Covenant. On the contrary, in a very special manner they were underlined and brought near to realization by the promised renewal of the Sinai-covenant, which would be the essence of the announced New Covenant.

It is for this reason that in the context of God's eternal love for Israel[11]—the same context in which also the promise of the New Covenant is found—Jeremiah speaks about a ruler who will arise in Israel and will be allowed to come close to God.[12] Pondering this, we realize that the promise that a son of David, who will sit eternally on David's throne, was given unconditionally.[13] Certainly the obedience of the king formed an important factor.[14] A king could be either a curse or a blessing to his people. Therefore Jeremiah's words about a prince and ruler who will be able to approach God implies that it will be an obedient king. Even a king who will be allowed to near to God as a (high)priest,[15] without risking death.[16]

All of this belongs to God's revelation in the Tanakh. This is the streambed, the context in which *Yeshua*/Jesus appears.

18.3 Anointed to be a Priestly King

In relation to the fact that even before His birth *Yeshua* already had been designated as the great son of David and king of Israel, His immersion in the river Jordan can be viewed as the consecration of His (priestly)[17] kingship. This immersion has the characteristics thereof. Just like Solomon was anointed and proclaimed king at the Gihon well,[18] now at the Jordan the Almighty God Himself, following the descent of the Holy Spirit, proclaims the just-baptized Jesus as His Son.[19] God too had spoken

---

10. See chapter 12 and 16.
11. Jer 30–31; cf. 31:3.
12. Jer 30:21.
13. 2 Sam 7:13.
14. 2 Sam 7:15 shows that God will not leave the disobedience of the king unpunished.
15. The verbs in the sentence "I will bring him near and he will come close to me" (Jer 30:21) are respectively used in Num 16:5–7 for the nearing to God of the God-appointed high priest and in Exod 24:2 in relation to Moses approaching God on mount Sinai.
16. Num 8:19 and Exod 19:21, 34:3 show that the people risk death when approaching the LORD. King Uzziah wished to enter the Sanctuary to burn incense like a priest, and was punished for it with leprosy (2 Chr 26:16–21).
17. See chapter 16 for His immersion in the Jordan as the *mikva* of His priestly consecration.
18. 1 Kgs 1:38–39, 45.
19. Matt 3:17; cf. also 17:5.

In the Camp of Israel: The Royal Consecration and the Kingdom

of Solomon in this way.[20] Among the many meanings this proclamation has, is the connection with Psalm 2. There the Messianic king by the LORD God Himself is proclaimed to be His "son,"[21] whilst the nations witness this.

In His immersion Jesus was also the First One of the people, and therefore His consecration as king over God's people implied a consecration of the whole of the people unto a collective kingship, a royal nation. He would be the king who would let His people share in this Divine kingship.

Israel's kings—the life of Solomon shows this especially[22]—knew themselves to be called as first ones of the nation to build the Temple of the LORD. The people, at Sinai, received the assignment to build God a House.[23] At first, this task had been executed under the supervision of Moses, as priestly king over Israel.[24] Later on David was allowed to make preparations for the building of the Temple by his son Solomon.[25] Later kings were involved in the conservation of the Temple, its sanctification and restoration activities.[26] In the times of the rebuilding, following the exile, God gave a promise about the Messianic king—the Branch from the house of David[27]—who would build the Temple of the LORD and who would reign as priest-king.[28]

Seen from this perspective, it can be said that the royal consecration of Jesus forms the beginning of the building, sanctification, and restoration of the House of God. His cleansing and clearing of the Temple makes this visible. This Son of David wishes the House of God to be as intended by God.[29] However, the people also were intended as a Dwelling place of God. The promise that the people would be a living ark of the LORD, was part of the promised Eighth Day.[30] Precisely the preparation for this Day formed the heart of Jesus's preaching. Just as the kings of Israel, He is

---

20. See 1 Chr 22:10; cf. also Ps 89:27–29.

21. Ps 2:7. The "begetting" of which this verse speaks (so RSV "I have begotten you"; NIV renders "You are my son; today I have become your father"), is seen as pointing to Jesus's resurrection from the dead in Acts 13:33. Possibly there are interpretative connections to the inauguration celebration of a king (cf. Ps 2:6) and to the "pouring out" (meant as "formation") of the Wisdom in Prov 8:23. See chapter 15, footnote 89.

22. See 2 Sam 7; 1 Kgs 7. 1 Chr 22:6–10 mentions the reason why David was not allowed to build the Temple. Verse 10 connects the "son-ship" of Solomon very closely with the building of the House of God; this connection we also find in other places.

23. Exod 25:8–9.

24. See par example Exod 40:1–2, 33.

25. 1 Chr 22–26. Besides, also "the bringing home" of the ark of the LORD to Jerusalem (2 Sam 6 and 1 Chr 13 and 15) shows this involvement in the building of God's House.

26. Par example Hezekiah (2 Kgs 18; 2 Chr 29–31) and Josiah (2 Kgs 22–23; 2 Chr 34–35).

27. Zech 6:12; cf. also 3:8 and Jer 23:5; 33:15.

28. Zech 6:9–15. It is noteworthy that this "building" also takes place with the cooperation of those "who are far away" (vs. 15). Are these people Jews who returned and/or also people from the nations? Cf. Isa 66:21.

29. John 2:13–23; Matt 21:12–16; Mark 11:11–25; Luke 19:45–48. Time and again the gospels also relate the Temple service with the inner attitude of the people.

30. Jer 31:33 implies that the heart of the people will become an "ark of the LORD."

made responsible for the conscientious and obedient *avoda* of the people.[31] At that, He Himself is first of all a holy Temple for Israel's God.[32] It is God's intention that *Yeshua* will be the cornerstone[33] within the process of building of the Temple, whereby the people will become House of the living God.[34] It is noteworthy that Peter will later see a connection between the themes of the building of the living Temple and of the royal priesthood.[35]

18.4 The Kingship of the Messiah: Preparation and Reminder

Israel's kings exercised their royal power before God and were intended to be "a living reminder"[36] of the kingship of God. Likewise, Jesus's message was unified with His life. He was a living paradigm by which people could see how preparing for God's kingship unified with the exercise of God-given royal authority. That this "*Yehoshua* (Joshua)"[37] combined the tasks of king and priest in a deep unity,[38] therefore makes a sharp distinction between both somewhat artificial.[39]

That the nations gather around *Yeshua*/Jesus,[40] the One who has been given resurrection authority over the nations,[41] shows that the canonical narrative of the New Testament paints Him as the fulfillment of the promises Israel had received. In Him Israel is "head of the nations,"[42] and therefore salvation goes to the nations from the Jews.[43] He is the son of David who as king would be "the most exalted of the kings of the earth."[44]

At the same time His authority over demons clarifies that the spiritual powers behind the visual reality also have been subdued and accordingly must submit to

---

31. Deut 17:14–20 shows that the king was made responsible for the keeping of the Tora.

32. John 2:19, 21.

33. Cf. Ps 118:22 and the role this section plays in the preaching of Jesus and the apostles (Matt 21:42; Mark 12:10–11; Acts 4:11; 1 Pet 2:7).

34. Eph 2:20.

35. 1 Pet 2:4–10.

36. See for this expression chapter 9, footnote 44. See further also chapter 10.

37. Jesus bears the name of the high priest in Zech 6:11.

38. High priest Joshua from Zech 6:9–15 receives *one* crown and the promise of (both; so RSV and footnote NIV) a royal and priestly ruler (NIV) who will cooperate in a council of peace. A promise of Messianic cooperation between two aspects of one calling or of two persons.

39. For the priestly aspect of Jesus's ministry see chapter 17.

40. See par example Matt 4:23–25.

41. Matt 28:16–20.

42. Deut 28:13.

43. Cf. John 4:22; Isa 2:3.

44. Ps 89:27. This psalm connects the themes of God's kingship and the kingship of David and his offspring. We also find the theme of the son-ship of the kings from David's family there.

Him.[45] He determines their "living space" and power range.[46] He delivers from the power of the "gods,"[47] a prerogative that has been *given*, as made clear in the Scriptures of the New Covenant. His perseverance and faithful *avoda* force Satan and the demons to obey Him.[48]

It becomes clear that Jesus's disciples, a subsummation and vanguard of Israel, may share in His authority.[49] Messiah *Yeshua* shares His kingship with the people of God.[50] He is the First One who engages the whole people in His fulfillment of the calling of the people. He also is the First One who, because of His obedience, obtains the kingship and therefore also this prerogative for the people.[51]

18.5 Royal Instruction

Together with His words the presence of Jesus among the people formed a living entity of instruction. His teaching circled around the kingship of God[52] and the preparation for His kingdom.[53] The presence of God's kingdom[54] and the wait for its full realization[55] were themes in His teaching in addition to the kingship of the Son of Man[56] and the participation of God's people in this kingship.[57] His words themselves were part of the coming of God's kingship.

He also made the royal power of God visible in such manner that God's reign, and Israel's participation in it, were seen as connected. Authority over wild animals,[58] the sea, wind,[59] food shortage,[60] sickness and death[61] were a reminder of the power of God as well as tokens of the significant place of (the First One of) Israel in God's plans.

---

45. Mark 1:27.
46. Mark 5:6–13.
47. Cf. 2 Sam 7:23–24.
48. Matt 4:10–11; Col 2:13–15 also makes this relation visible.
49. Matt 10:1; Mark 6:7; Luke 9:1; see also 10:1, 17.
50. Cf. the alternation between the king and the royal people in Dan 7:14, 18, 22, 27.
51. Cf. Acts 2:36.
52. He proclaims "the good news of the kingdom" (Luke 4:43).
53. The nearing of the kingdom of God asks for repentance (Mark 1:14–15). It is a matter of "entering the kingdom" (Mark 9:47; 10:14–15). However the parables also address themes dealing with this preparation. All of them circle around the theme of the kingdom of God (Mark 4:10–11; Luke 8:10).
54. Matt 12:28; Luke 17:21.
55. Luke 19:11–27.
56. Mark 8:38; Matt 25:31–46; cf. Heb 2:5–9.
57. Matt 19:28; Luke 22:30; cf. for the same thought 1Cor 6:2.
58. Mark 1:13; cf. Isa 11:6–10.
59. Mark 4:35–41.
60. Mark 6:30–44.
61. Mark 5:21–43.

Part II : The Canonical Narrative: The Scriptures of the New Covenant

Simultaneously, it was also here that the fulfillment took place—through the ways of the representation of Adam in Israel—of the calling of Adam and His offspring![62]

By predominantly designating Himself as "the Son of Man,"[63] Jesus taught in a somewhat hidden manner about His own role as the God-given king. By using this designation Jesus references both Daniel 7 and Psalm 80, thereby giving His words about Himself double meaning.[64] Royal glory *and* suffering are implied. At some point in His instruction the suffering of the Son of Man receives special attention.[65] Thereby Jesus makes clear that His Messiah-ship will be of a different kind than what was accepted in His contemporaries' expectations of the Messiah.[66] It was precisely this combination that caused His disciples to misunderstand.

After His resurrection he says to two disciples on the road to Emmaus:

> "How foolish you are, and how slow to believe all that the prophets have spoken! Did not the Messiah have to suffer these things and then enter his glory?" And beginning with Moses and all the Prophets, he explained to them what was said in all the Scriptures concerning himself.[67]

He shows that the Scriptures of Tanakh also foretell a journey of suffering for the Messiah, as the glory of the Messiah only can be obtained through suffering.[68] His ministry as Messiah only can fully begin when He has walked this path of suffering to its end. Thus only he will obtain this glory.[69] Besides previously-mentioned qualities,[70] His kingship will show parallels with the ways of Joseph[71] and David. A king He would be, who just like Joseph, had been sold as slave. A king who, just like David, had to wait for the realization of God's promises.[72] A king who also was driven from His throne.[73] A king who would suffer by the hands of His own people.[74]

---

62. See chapter 16 (16.7 and 16.9). For Adam's calling we can think of Gen 1:26–28 (the mandate to rule over the earth) and of Gen 4:7 (the command to rule over sin).

63. See par example Mark 2:10; 8:31, 38.

64. See chapter 16 (16.6).

65. Mark 8:31–38; cf. also 9:30–32; 10:32–34.

66. Cf. John 6:15.

67. Luke 24:25–27.

68. We need not interpret this "glory" only as heavenly glory, we also can interpret it as "the glory of the accession to his office and the ministry thereof by the Messiah."

69. Cf. the use of "receive" in Acts 2:33 and "God made this Jesus (. . .) both Lord and Messiah" in 2:36.

70. See chapter 16.

71. See chapter 4 and 10 (also footnote 14 in that chapter).

72. As the anointed one of God, David waited for his kingship and underwent sufferings from the side of Saul.

73. 2 Sam 15–20 tells about the rebellion of Absalom and various kinds of opposition by which David has to flee.

74. Cf. John 19:15.

In the Camp of Israel: The Royal Consecration and the Kingdom

Therefore the theme of waiting for His kingship also played a role in His teaching. Knowing that the multitudes around Him as well as His disciples expected a speedy revelation of the kingdom of God,[75] He spoke of waiting.[76] He also taught the necessary life attitudes for this waiting time. Summarizing His teaching in a narrative manner, Matthew 25 shows that keeping vigil, serving faithfully, and sharing in His suffering[77] belong to the waiting for the ultimate kingship.

Like the parables, *Yeshua*'s life and preaching have a double structure. Revelation and concealment. The title "King of the Jews" is rightly above His head on the cross, but on the other hand, His kingship is confronted by unbelief and mockery.

18.6 Royal Glory of the Messiah

That the royal glory of the Messiah is something that must still be realized, is predominant in Jesus's teaching. In the Scriptures of the New Covenant, Jesus's exaltation after His resurrection from the dead is "realized" divine salvation history. This act of God has obtained Him the glory of the Messianic office. By it the greatness of the Messiah was revealed. His exaltation to kingship at the right hand of God then became starting point for faithful living and thinking in the growing community of followers of Messiah Jesus.[78]

Like Moses ascended the mountain to raise his staff in the battle with Amalek after the deliverance from Egypt, as the appointed holy Messiah *Yeshua*/Jesus was exalted to the Throne of God. By this exaltation everything was subjected to Him. Psalm 8, the psalm which speaks of the high position of man, appears to speak also of Him.[79] Various psalms suddenly reveal, in unsuspected depth, elements of the mystery of the Messiah.[80]

In the Messiah the lines of priesthood and kingship prove to converge in an unsuspected, yet divinely foretold, manner. The priesthood after the order of

---

75. See par example Luke 19:11.

76. See par example the teaching about the future at the Mount of Olives (Matt 24; Mark 13; Luke 21).

77. The three parables in that chapter address these three themes. Matt 25:31–46 moreover shows that surely the Messiah will be present in the waiting time (which also applies to the nations), but He will be so in the form of His brothers who suffer. This designation does not refer to all who suffer in the world, but to "brothers" who are part of His Body (with in it the first circle of Israel and the second circle from the nations; cf. "brothers" as designation for Jesus's disciples in Matt 28:10 and 12:49) and possibly also to the persecuted people of Israel, with whom He, as king of the Jews is connected (cf. "brothers" as wider designation for fellow Jews, Matt 5:22–24, 47 and 23:8; see also chapter 19 and 20.

78. The account of the evangelists naturally also has been determined by their faith in *Yeshua*'s exaltation to receive His Messiah-ship in the fullest sense. Cf. Acts 2:33–36.

79. Heb 1:5–9 cites this psalm and relates it to Jesus.

80. See par example Heb 1–2, where Ps 2, 45, 110, 8 and 22 are quoted.

Part II : The Canonical Narrative: The Scriptures of the New Covenant

Melchizedek[81] in Him proves to become reality.[82] In Messiah *Yeshua* the lines of non-Levite priesthood,[83] kingship over Jerusalem,[84] a wonderfully unknown descent and eternal life,[85] converge. Psalm 110 reveals unsuspected depths in the light of the appearance of Messiah *Yeshua*.[86] This great priest-king sits at the right hand of the Eternal One.

The glory of His royal ministry not only consists in the place at the right hand of the Almighty God,[87] but implies a promise of much more. Following this exaltation, Psalm 110 indeed says that the LORD God Himself shall make all enemies "a footstool" for the feet of the Messiah.[88] According to these words His exaltation is not yet complete. He still waits until the fullness of His kingship is given to Him.

At the same time we also see that the Messiah Himself plays a role in this. Just as Moses must raise his staff, He will do this in a prophetic fulfillment of this psalm.[89] We observe that Paul connects this active side of the kingship of the Messiah with God's all-subjecting power.[90]

Yeshua/Jesus had spoken of the power of judgment that had been given to Him.[91] Just as in Daniel 7 the Son of Man nears the Throne of God, which also serves as the judgment seat,[92] He will be the God-appointed judge over His people and the whole of the world.[93] Paul speaks of "the judgment seat of Christ"[94] and of the judgment that

---

81. Ps 110:4 mentions a word of God that promises the Messiah an eternal priesthood "after the order of Melchi'zedek" (RSV), "in the order of Melchizedek" (NIV).

82. Heb 7 gives an extensive study of the high priesthood of the Messiah in relation to Melchizedek. Astonished the author delves various hidden treasures from the concise history narrated in Gen 14:17–20.

83. Heb 7:11–14. Besides the analogy with the non-Aaronic priesthood of Moses (cf. paragraph 8.3 in the discussion of the priestly consecration in chapter 8) there thus also is the typological connection between Melchizedek and Messiah *Yeshua*.

84. Melchizedek is king of Salem (Gen 14:18; cf. Heb 7:2), a different name for the later Jerusalem.

85. Heb 7:3, 16–28 shows that the brief mentioning of Melchizedek (we know nothing of his descent or prior history) contains a typological pointing toward the eternal descent and the eternal life of the Messiah. The themes of chapters 14–19 of this book converge in the typological connection between Melchizedek and Messiah *Yeshua*.

86. Reflection on the figure of Melchizedek we also find in one of the Dead Sea scrolls and in early-Jewish and early-Christian literature.

87. Eph 1:20; Col 3:1; Heb 10:12.

88. Ps 110:1; cf. Heb 1:13.

89. The kingship of God is related to the judgment of the nations. God's Messianic king shares in that divine prerogative; cf. Ps 72, 89, 96, 97, 98, 99.

90. In 1 Cor 15:23–28 Paul brings to the fore both these lines from Ps 110.

91. John 5:26–29.

92. Dan 7:14; see also verse 10.

93. The Son of Man receives at the judgment Throne His authority and glory, the office of judgment is implied in it. Also see Dan 7:10, 22 for the judicial aspect of this nearing to the Throne.

94. 2 Cor 5:10.

In the Camp of Israel: The Royal Consecration and the Kingdom

will be spoken by Him.[95] In Athens Paul makes clear that Jesus's resurrection from the dead is the very proof of His appointment as judge over the whole world.[96] The First One of Israel,[97] within the God-given structure of representation, is also is the First One of all creation. In this way He receives and fulfills Adam's highest calling: to rule over creation. The First One of Israel fulfills both the calling to rule over everything created,[98] and the calling to rule over sin that wants to enter the heart of man.[99]

Just as God redeemed Israel from Egypt, the nations and their gods,[100] so Messiah Jesus has disarmed the powers and authorities. He has broken their might.[101] Because of this, the power of demonic darkness is broken, and a new freedom has become possible.[102] Jesus indicated this earlier when just before His death, He spoke about the coming confrontation with the prince of this world, which would drive him out. Jesus connected this to the possibility for Greeks to come to know the God of Israel and His Messiah.[103] Yet the Messiah had to also deliver Israel from the power of sin.[104] That such a redemption had to happen for God's people also was indicated in both the promise of a divine circumcision of the heart and that of the New Covenant. The power of sin, by which death ruled as king both over Israel and the nations, had to be broken within the camp of Israel in the center of the earth.[105] The Messiah, king of Israel, realized this by giving His life as ransom.[106] Isaiah 53, often cited in the New Testament as prophecy about *Yeshua*/Jesus, foretold that the servant of the LORD, following His death, would receive a long life, "offspring," and "spoils."[107] Paul observes that Psalm 68 receives fulfillment in the life of Messiah *Yeshua*: as victor He receives riches and apportions them.[108]

The royal glory of the Messiah at the Throne consists in the fact that He, as the First One of Israel, has fully lived the *avoda* and obtained for Himself the royal blessing and the kingship for Israel. One Jew has become king over the cosmos. At the same

---

95. Rom 2:16; cf. also 1 Cor 4:5.

96. Acts 17:31.

97. Cf. also Ps 89:27. God promises in this verse to appoint David "to be my firstborn"; in the second half of the verse this expression is explained as "the most exalted of the kings of the earth." Also see Rev 1:5 where both designations are found together.

98. Gen 1:28.

99. Gen 4:7.

100. See 2 Sam 7:23; cf. Ezek 20:7–8.

101. Col 2:15.

102. Col 1:13; cf. Acts 26:18.

103. John 12:30–31.

104. John 8:31–36; cf. also Eph 2:1–3 where Paul implicitly reviews his life prior to his encounter with the Messiah, and describing himself as a Jew imprisoned in sin.

105. Cf. Rom 5:12–21. Also see Paul's use of Hos 13:14 in 1 Cor 15:54–55.

106. Mark 10:42–45.

107. See Isa 53:10–12.

108. He cites Ps 68:18 in Eph 4:8.

time, this kingship is still contested. The exalted king waits for *and* is involved in the subjugation of all enemies and enmity, including that of death.[109]

In Revelation we see again how His kingship is in fact the driving force behind the progress of history, while also waiting for the beginning of the definitive kingship of God and His Messiah.[110] As Psalm 2 shows, there will be resistance against the God-appointed king until the end of history.[111] This is the reality reckoned with in the New Testament.[112] In Revelation we see also the theme of the enormous confrontation of the powers of the nations with God's kingship reoccurring, as found in the Tanakh.[113] A triumphalist understanding of the kingship of the Messiah, in the sense that there will be no more struggle, suffering, and waiting, is made impossible by this "revelation from Jesus Christ"[114] given to John. On the contrary, through the acceptance of the kingship by the Messiah, an intensification of the physical and spiritual opposition against it has indeed begun.[115]

18.7 The King of the Jews Guarantees the Kingship for Israel

The disciples' question about the restoration of the kingship[116] is not only a question about the kingship of the Messiah over Israel, but also about the kingship of Israel itself. In accordance with the Tanakh, in His teaching Jesus spoke of Israel sharing in the eschatological kingship of the Son of Man.[117] *Yeshua*'s answer[118] to the question of His disciples implies that in God's time, Israel's participation in the kingship of the Messiah will also become reality. The Messiah indeed is the Firstling of all Israel. The First One who fully lived the covenant and therefore merited and received the blessings of the covenant, including the position as head of the nations.[119] Although the New Testament predominantly focuses on the Messianic kingship of *Yeshua*/Jesus over all authorities and powers, this does not mean that the kingship of the priestly nation is out of the picture. Even though believers from the nations share in the royal

---

109. 1 Cor 15:25–26.

110. Rev 5–8 shows how the Lamb, the Lion from Judah (5:5), opens the seals of the scroll of God's plans. This opening of the seals culminates in the kingship of God and His Anointed One (11:15–19).

111. Ps 2:1–3.

112. Cf. Acts 4:25–28, where the apostles identify the opposition by using Ps 2.

113. Rev 20:7–10.

114. Rev 1:1.

115. Cf. Rev 12–13, where it becomes clear that all powers of hell have broken loose against "the kingdom of our God and the authority of his Messiah" (12:10).

116. Acts 1:6 (also see 18.1).

117. Matt 19:27–28; 20:20–28; Mark 10:35–40; Luke 22:29–30.

118. Acts 1:8 (also see 18.1).

119. Deut 28:13.

calling of Israel,[120] the promises of God for all Israel as royal nation still stand.[121] This stands true, even as the realization of it is hidden in the "times and dates" of God.

18.8 The Hebron-Kingship and the Jerusalem-Kingship of the Messiah

The kingship of Messiah *Yeshua* is a reality now, but still awaits its full realization. Already He is king over Israel, but there is still a "not-yet." Likewise, as king of the Jews, He already is "the ruler of the kings of the earth,"[122] even as a "not-yet" is present. He awaits the final full revelation of both these aspects of His kingship.[123]

A remarkable parallel can be observed in David's journey toward his full kingship over Israel. At first, following the death of Saul, David only was recognized as God's anointed king by part of the people. He was a king of only a part of Israel.[124] On God's command[125] he reigned in Hebron, and only over time the other tribes came and also recognized him as their king.[126] It was only after him becoming king over all Israel, and following the capture of Jerusalem,[127] in the eighth year of his kingship,[128] that his kingship-from-Jerusalem commenced.

The Scriptures of the New Testament show that indeed there is a kingship of the Messiah over Israel, but also that it has an aspect of "not-yet." This is a "Hebron-kingship" of the Messiah. It is in this "capacity" that He, at the same time, awaits the definitive kingship from Jerusalem. His "Jerusalem-kingship" is still hidden in the "times and seasons" of the Father.

By characterizing the kingship of the Messiah as "Hebron-kingship" in this outline of the canonical narrative of the Scriptures, it remains clear that it is still a kingship over *Israel*, although partial and incomplete. And because we speak about the "not-yet" of the Jerusalem-kingship, it becomes clear that also in this waiting the Messiah still is and remains connected to the whole of Israel.

---

120. Cf. 1 Pet 2:9–10; Rev 1:6; 5:10.

121. Rom 15:8; 2 Cor 1:20.

122. Rev 1:5.

123. The traditional canonical narrative only knows of a waiting for the realization of the kingship over the whole earth.

124. 2 Sam 2–4 tells about the long "war between the house of Saul and the house of David" (3:1).

125. 2 Sam 2:1–4. God orders David to go to Hebron. This name means "joint-together-ness," "be-friend-ness" (association, company, connectedness) from a verb that means "to join." A significant name! See chapter 19 (19.9).

126. 2 Sam 5:1–3; 1 Chr 11:1–3.

127. 2 Sam 5:6–10; 1 Chr 11:4–6.

128. 2 Sam 5:5.

18.9 A King in Exile

It is obvious that the New Testament speaks of the exalted Anointed One, the king who sits at the right hand of God. At the same time, it is clear that there is still a journey of waiting and even tribulations[129] for the Messiah.

David first had to wait long years in Hebron, as disunity and division characterized the one people of God. Jesus also shows that the division within the people of Israel with respect to His Messiah-ship, as seen from the perspective of the "Jerusalem-kingship," necessitates His exile.[130] This aspect of the "not-yet" of the kingship over Israel receives further elaboration in the next chapters.

In Jesus's parables we meet a man, receiving kingship in a "distant country."[131] This phrase refers to a country overseas, far away from the country promised by God. Although at first the parable conveys that there will be a long time of waiting with the appointment of king to be received elsewhere, we also hear in it that there will be a dark side to this kingship-reception taking place in the "distant country." Here there is a certain parallel with Joseph, who also became king out of sight of his family,[132] in exile, far away from God's country. It certainly stems from a biblical background, that within later Judaism we encounter a *Mashiah-ben-Josef* who would suffer for the salvation of the people during a period of seven years prior to the revelation of the *Mashiah-ben-David*.[133]

18.10 Kingship Understood from the Streambed of the Tanakh

When Israel's calling to be a kingdom of priests and its fulfillment by Messiah *Yeshua* are interpreted within the framework of the Tanakh, it is obvious that the kingship of God and His Messiah appears even richer and more multifaceted. When we remain standing in the streambed provided by the Tanakh, we find that the New Testament texts imply much more than first appears. "The credit balance of the Old Testament"[134] also implies the restoration of Israel and the kingship for Israel. The kingship of God

---

129. Cf. Col 1:24.

130. Matt 23:37–39.

131. Luke 19:11–12; cf. also 15:13. The Hebrew expression underlying this use of "distant country" refers to a country on the sea shore or overseas. Herod the Great received his kingship in Rome.

132. Joseph's elevation to his high position took place in Egypt; cf. Gen 37–50.

133. An extensive quotation about this Messiah (who is son of Joseph) from the Pesikta Rabbati (a Midrash on the Jewish festivals from the early Middle Ages) can be found in Bialik and Ravnitzky, *Legends*, 396–97.

134. The Dutch theologian K.H. Miskotte coined this expression (in Dutch: Het tegoed van het Oude Testament), using it to point to various aspects of the Old Testament, which come less to the forefront in the New Testament and were neglected in Christian theology and the Church (*Als de goden* zwijgen, 145–229).

In the Camp of Israel: The Royal Consecration and the Kingdom

and His Messiah over the *world* does not exclude the kingship of God and His Messiah over *Israel*. On the contrary, the former is indeed the result of the latter.[135]

18.11 Toward the Jerusalem-Kingship

When we begin to see the full, though partly implicated, richness of the expectation of the kingship of God and His Messiah, we also begin to understand the waiting of God and His Messiah for the full realization of the Jerusalem-kingship. We then also slowly begin to understand something of the ways by which the Messiah wishes to let Israel and the nations share in this eschatological kingship. In the next chapters we will pay attention to the way the Messiah will walk toward this kingship of the full Eighth Day.

In doing so we will see that He both is the exalted king and shares the way of His people Israel. We also will note His exaltation to be "the ruler of the kings of the earth" and His journey through the world of nations.

Meanwhile, we have seen something of the structures, which give guidance and direction to our understanding. From both the fact that the Jerusalem-kingship was granted to David after the people had again become one entity,[136] to the idea that the restoration of Israel's unity is part of the Messianic prophecy,[137] we can infer that the Messiah will wish to realize this unity on His way toward the full Eighth Day.

At the same time we discover more of the importance that the full *kedusha* of His people has in the eyes of God. In the midst of the earth and in this era, in the *olam haze*, true sanctification should take place if the future age, the *olam haba*, will come to pass. But this brings us to a new chapter in this account of the canonical narrative of the New Testament.

---

135. Further see chapter 20.

136. Cf. what the tribes of Israel say to David, coming to him in Hebron: "We are your own flesh and blood" (2 Sam 5:1; 1 Chr 11:1).

137. Ezek 37:15–28; cf. Isa 11:13; Mic 5:2.

Chapter 19

In the Camp of Israel
The Holy Nation Sanctified

19.1 The Day of the LORD Breaks over the Holy Nation—the Eighth Day Dawns

THE DARKNESS OF THE Day of the LORD begins to fall over Israel, over the people called to be a holy nation in the midst of the nations. "The Day of the LORD against all unholiness" first comes over the people who had received the calling to live the *kedusha*. These people are summoned to prepare. The First One of the people sanctifies Himself and enters this night of judgment. On the third day it appears that "the Spirit of holiness"[1] has been in Him, and He is raised from the dead. In Him dawns the Messianic time of holiness and eternal life: the Eighth Day.[2]

The canonical narrative of the New Testament tells how the calling of the *am kadosh*—the holy nation—has been lived obediently by Jesus in the camp of Israel, and what blessing resulted from it. A fountain of *kedusha* opens in the midst of the earth from which Israel and even the nations may draw. The path of the sanctification of God's Name together with the sanctification of all of life, which God Himself showed on the seventh day of creation,[3] appears to be the way by which the holiness of the Eighth Day dawns.

This short sketch asks for further elaboration, which the remainder of this chapter will provide.

---

1. Rom 1:4.
2. Cf. paragraph 7.5 for the connection between holiness and eternal life. In John 6:68–69 we also find both concepts closely related.
3. Gen 2:1–3, cf. chapter 2 (2.2).

19.2 Once More: Israel's Election and Calling to be a Holy Nation.

When we think of the God-required *kedusha*, deserved by the LORD and worthy of Him, we once more "encounter" Israel's God-given calling to be an *am kadosh*. When the New Testament speaks of holiness and sanctification, we still find ourselves in the streambed of what has been written, promised, and required in the Tanakh.[4] We still find ourselves in the camp of Israel, and the sanctification of Messiah *Yeshua* takes place in the context of God's way with Israel. The canonical narrative of the New Testament unfolds itself from within the progress and continuity of the canonical narrative of the Tanakh.

The structure of the two-sidedness of God's covenants is still determining when the narrative is about *kedusha*. Based on this structure there is the necessity of obedient *avoda*, but on the other hand there also is, with respect to *kedusha*, the promise of God-given obedience. Here again there is a role for the servant of God to play as *brit am*. Lastly, the principle is still valid that obedience will be blessed and that the receiving of the mercy of holy life follows proven faithfulness. God realizes Israel's calling to be a holy nation within the covenantal structure outlined here.

19.3 The Consecration of the Priests as a Model for the Messianic Sanctification of the People

We have learned that the priests in the midst of God's people were to be a model of priestly living for the whole of the people.[5] The seven-day period of their sanctification in relation to taking up service also then shows the structure of the sanctification of the whole nation.[6] Related to this, the description of what happened on the eighth day of the consecration to two sons of Aaron,[7] shows also that the sanctification of the people in relation to the Messianic era has two sides. The nearing of the Messianic time means that the judgment over all unholiness of the *olam haze* is nearing. Yet at the same time the door is opened to the anointing enabling life in holiness.

With God's revelation at Sinai we observe that Israel's calling to be God's holy nation has these two elements: sanctification preceding the revelation of the LORD,[8] and God's descent and nearing to His people, with an "anointing" of the people through His words and commandments.[9] When God subsequently reveals the Tora to Moses, the calling to holiness is articulated in concrete commandments. The rulings and

---

4. See chapters 14–18.
5. See chapters 7 and 8.
6. See the discussion of the priestly consecration in chapter 8.
7. Lev 10:1–7; also see chapter 9.
8. Exod 19:10–15, 21–25.
9. Exod 19:17–20; 20:1–21.

instructions[10] teach the people the way of sanctification. This *kedusha* is necessary for the LORD Himself is holy.[11] The canonical narrative of the New Testament tells about the Messianic fulfillment of the calling of the holy people. Both the nearing of the judgment and the sanctification of the *olam haba* happen in and around Messiah *Yeshua*/Jesus.

19.4 Messianic Instruction

The preaching of *Yeshua* is preparatory teaching. It prepares for both the nearing judgment and the dawning era of salvation. It is good to remember, therefore, that His words not only *speak about* but also are *part* of both "approaches of God." It is not just an alternative voice in Israel that speaks, or just a different sort of rabbi that appears, making His voice heard within the rabbinic debate. The teaching of *Yeshua*/Jesus is the voice from God's Presence. His words and signs show that salvation is beginning to spring up. It is the blossoming staff who points to Him,[12] and the blossoming almond branch that shows that God is watching over His Word.[13] Before the ears of the people, the Word of God is being fulfilled.[14] Their eyes behold the glory of the LORD.[15]

In this instruction Jesus remains standing within the streambed of the Tanakh. There is no way that He would bring a new message with a new ethics of some higher order.

> "Do not think that I have come to abolish the Law or the Prophets; I have not come to abolish them but to fulfill them. For truly I tell you, until heaven and earth disappear, not the smallest letter, not the least stroke of a pen, will by any means disappear from the Law until everything is accomplished. Therefore anyone who sets aside one of the least of these commands and teaches others accordingly will be called least in the kingdom of heaven, but whoever practices and teaches these commands will be called great in the kingdom of heaven. For I tell you that unless your righteousness surpasses that of the Pharisees and the teachers of the law, you will certainly not enter the kingdom of heaven.[16]

He preaches what the Tanakh preached. He confronts the people with what God had, in the Tanakh, asked from His people. He does not devalue what has been previously

---

10. Exod 15:25; 16:28; 20:6; Lev 19:37; Deut 4:1–10.
11. Lev 19:2; also see chapter 9.
12. Cf. Num 17:1–9.
13. Jer 1:11–12.
14. Luke 4:21.
15. John 1:14; 1 John 1:1–2.
16. Matt 5:17–20.

revealed and spoken. When He summarizes God's intentions in a few words,[17] this is not meant to reject God's revelation in the Tanakh. In doing so He does what the prophets did when they proclaimed the words of God in summarized form.[18] He indeed makes the deepest intention of God's words clear. When He references Hosea 6:6, He does so in order to both confront His listeners with God's most fundamental intentions and to expose the unholy depths in their lives.

> On hearing this, Jesus said, "It is not the healthy who need a doctor, but the sick. But go and learn what this means: 'I desire mercy, not sacrifice.' For I have not come to call the righteous, but sinners."[19]

When in a different setting He quotes this same passage, He does not intend to do away with the very concrete commandments of God, but to highlight the intentions of the commandments.

> "I tell you that something greater than the temple is here. If you had known what these words mean, 'I desire mercy, not sacrifice,' you would not have condemned the innocent. For the Son of Man is Lord of the Sabbath."[20]

At the same time He speaks with God-given authority.[21] He is the God-appointed Son of Man. He is the Lord over all of life. In His presence one experiences the holiness of God and His revelation.[22] Through His words and life sons and daughters of Abraham discover how deeply present unholiness is in their lives.[23] In His rigor He does not differ from the previous messengers of God, but brings all words of God—without leaving out one or denigrating another—to full power. His words to scribes and Pharisees are not meant to undermine their authority or to ridicule their intentions.

---

17. See par example Matt 22:40.

18. Par example Hos 6:6, Mic 6:8, and Zech 8:16–17. The Talmud presents a section in which the many commandments are seen as already summarized in Scripture. "Rabbi Simlai said: "Moses gave to Israel six hundred and thirteen commandments. David came and comprehended them in eleven (Psalm 15). "Isaiah came and comprehended them in six: 'He that walks righteously, and speaks uprightly, he that despises the gain acquired by oppression, that shakes out his hands from holding bribes, that stops his ears from hearing of blood, and shuts his eyes from looking upon evil, he shall dwell on high' (Isaiah 33:15). "Micah came and comprehended them in three: 'He has told you, O man, what is good and what God requires of you–only to do justice, love mercy and walk humbly with your God' (Micah 6:8). "Isaiah further comprehended them in two: 'Observe justice and do righteousness' (Isaiah 56:1). "Amos came and comprehended them in one: 'Seek me and live'" (Amos 5:4). "Another finds the one comprehensive word in Habakkuk: 'The righteous man shall live by his faithfulness' (Habakkuk 2:4)" (Talmud b. Makkot 24a, cited in Isaacs, *Mitzvot*, 59–60).

19. Matt 9:12–13.

20. Matt 12:6–8.

21. Matt 7:28–29; Mark 1:22.

22. Luke 5:8.

23. John 8:31–36.

> "Woe to you, teachers of the law and Pharisees, you hypocrites! You give a tenth of your spices—mint, dill and cumin. But you have neglected the more important matters of the law—justice, mercy and faithfulness. You should have practiced the latter, without neglecting the former. You blind guides! You strain out a gnat but swallow a camel."[24]

For Him it is about the essence of all commandments and the inner side of Israel's *avoda*. Through Him and around Him what is in the heart becomes visible.[25] His sometimes shocking and confronting manner of speaking[26] is the shuddering of the Day of the LORD which begins to fall over God's people. It is the words of the Awesome God,[27] who should be feared. His teaching is also simultaneously inviting and full of love, the welcoming salutation into the *olam haba*.

> "Come to me, all you who are weary and burdened, and I will give you rest. Take my yoke upon you and learn from me, for I am gentle and humble in heart, and you will find rest for your souls. For my yoke is easy and my burden is light."[28]

This invitation is no downgrade of the Tanakh. Nor it is a rejection of the yoke of the commandments of the kingdom.[29] In and through Him the Tanakh enters the Eighth Day, with all commandments and promises. He *is* the beginning of the Eighth Day and speaks *from* the anointing of the *olam haba*. His words are full of its power, full of the Holy Spirit. The people are invited to enter into this reality.

As the Messianic Teacher who explains and applies the commandments in the power and authority of a heavenly appointment to office,[30] there is no way that He would pridefully exalt Himself above what had been revealed in the Tanakh. When there appears to be a difference in regard to what has been revealed, this is "the difference of the deepest intention"[31] or "the difference of fulfillment."[32] There is no such

---

24. Matt 23:23–24.
25. John 6:64.
26. See par example Matt 23.
27. Exod 15:1; Deut 7:21; 10:17.
28. Matt 11:28–30.

29. Cf. the use of the word "yoke" in Matt 11:30. Taking up the "yoke of the kingdom" is a Jewish expression for the obedient life according to God's commandments. In Acts 15:10 it is used by Peter in a somewhat negative sense.

30. Matt 11:27; John 8:26; 14:24.

31. See par example the manner in which some of the Ten Words are discussed in Matt 5. Cf. also Matt 19:8; 23:23. Mark 7:10–13 shows that Jesus discerns between what God has ordained and what people have added to it in the course of time and in the developing of tradition.

32. John 7:53—8:11 shows how Jesus grants forgiveness from the dawning of the *olam haba*—and out of the year of God's favor (= the year of Jubilee [Isa 61:2; Luke 4:19])—and leaves out the death sentence. Cf. Zech 14:11, we there hear that there is no room for *ḥerem* ("death penalty," so Milgrom, *Leviticus 23–27*, 2035; "curse" [RSV], "utter destruction" [KJV], NIV uses in its rendering the verb "destroy") any more in the Messianic future.

In the Camp of Israel: The Holy Nation Sanctified

thing as a New Testament revelation of love over and against a revelation of rigorous righteousness in the Old Testament. With Jesus there is no fundamental distinction between spiritual service to God and outward cultic service.[33] When He speaks it is the Messiah speaking, in whom all longings and requirements and promises of the Tanakh are fulfilled.[34] Jesus lived and taught the full *kedusha*.

At the same time His instruction is the living encounter with the salvation from the glory of the *olam haba*. Words that demand everything from God's people, seemingly no longer minding brokenness and imperfection,[35] are words originating from the new possibilities of the future that has been opened up in Him. He does not teach newer and better ethics that still belong to the *olam haze*. He is the vine of fulfillment, in whom and by whom Israel definitively can bear fruit in "the last days."

He is the full Nearing of God *and* the complete *avoda* of Israel. His appearance and speech, His life and death and resurrection together as a whole, embodies the eschatological fulfillment of the words from the Song of Songs: "My beloved is mine and I am his."[36] This eschatological mutual knowledge of God and this First One from Israel determines His teachings. The Tora of the Messiah is the Tora of the Eighth Day, and for that reason in some points different and new. Not because the old was bad, but because the new has come.

His resurrection from the dead is the Divine affirmation of the instruction of this Teacher of Israel.

19.5 The Priestly Nation and Messiah "Unclothed": Entering the Day of the LORD and the Exile

At Sinai the God-called priests were unclothed every day during the period of their consecration.[37] These men stood uncovered before God, without the possibility of hiding. That is also what happened to Israel within the encounter with *Yeshua*/Jesus. "The thoughts of many hearts" became revealed.[38] His preaching also calls for (immersion in) a *mikva* as a response.[39] Following an acquaintance period, resistance grows. Saturated with miracle bread,[40] but with aversion against the explanation in

---

33. Matt 23 shows that *Yeshua*'s/Jesus's concern is for obedience to the commandments with a heart that is fully dedicated to God. Cf. the ending of verse 23: "You should have practiced the latter, without neglecting the former."

34. Matt 5:17–18. The Messiah is the goal (*telos*) of the Tora (Rom 10:4).

35. We can think of Jesus's words about forgiveness in Matt 18:21–35 and the section that follows about divorce (19:1–12).

36. Song 2:16; cf. 6:3; 7:10.

37. See chapter 8 (8.3).

38. Luke 2:35.

39. John 4:1–3.

40. John 6:1–15.

which He designated Himself as the bread of life,[41] many of His disciples turn away from Him.[42] Experiencing this, He even asks the chosen twelve if they also want to leave.[43] If those happening to accompany them had left them, it is then not astonishing that those in charge of the people perceived Him to be a danger from the devil,[44] threatening the pure *avoda* of the people? His appearance and preaching require that people must choose.[45] The kiss of Judas[46] is the opposite of what Psalm 2 calls for.[47] In a time where Israel is characterized by a desire for ritual purity,[48] whole villages and small towns[49] cannot bear to hear that Israel must be redeemed at still a deeper level than they could imagine themselves.[50] For many, the hour of the Son of Man's approach was hidden.[51] All hearts were revealed when He appeared, and thoughts and obedience were searched and tested, as was prophesied.[52]

This wasn't only occurring within the circle of the people, but also within the circle of the twelve disciples, the likeness of the whole of Israel. Their lack of understanding also has a satanic background.[53] What Jesus's companions are shown within themselves, occurs on a bigger scale with regards to the nation as a whole. Both Peter's denouncement[54] of Jesus and the consenting call for His death from the multitude[55] stem from the same root. It is the God-ordained and necessary unclothing of the priestly people. It is God, who within Israel, calls Adam from his hiding place. This is also worked out by the Tora of the Messiah.[56]

Yeshua/Jesus's cleansing of the Temple points to the unholy *avoda* of Israel, and shows that *kedusha* is absent from the heart of God's land in the center of the earth.[57] The chief priests and scribes' reactions to it shows that even their hearts are contaminated.[58] Jesus shows how their attitude is in line with a history of ignoring and

---

41. See the discussions and the rejection described in John 6:22–66.
42. John 6:60.
43. John 6:67.
44. Matt 9:34; 10:25; 12:24.
45. Matt 10:34–36.
46. Luke 22:47–48.
47. Ps 2:12.
48. So Jensen, "The Galilean Craddle," 1–21.
49. Cf. Matt 11:20–24 were judgment words are addressed to Chorazin, Bethsaida and Capernaum.
50. Cf. Matt 9:12; John 8:34–36; 9:40–41.
51. Matt 11:25; Luke 19:42.
52. By Simeon (Luke 2:35).
53. See par example Matt 16:23.
54. Matt 26:69–75.
55. Matt 27:23; John 18:39–40.
56. Cf. what Paul says in Rom 3:20 and 7:7.
57. Matt 21:12–17; also see John 2:13–24.
58. Matt 21:23–27.

In the Camp of Israel: The Holy Nation Sanctified

hardening against God's warnings,[59] warnings which continue in the Dwelling of God until the last moment.[60]

It is irrevocable that the judgment of the day of the LORD will come over people, land, and city.[61] Therefore when Jesus leaves the Temple He goes to the Mount of Olives, where He sets Himself down.[62] Whoever reads this from the streambed of the Tanakh, inevitably must remember what Ezekiel described when he saw the *Shekhina* of God leave the Temple and setting itself on the Mount of Olives.[63] That Jesus leaves the Temple and sets Himself down on the Mount of Olives is therefore a significant act! He will only enter the Temple again when He is welcomed again.[64]

His words from the Mount of Olives are the announcement of and preparation for entering into the Day of the LORD. They also mark the beginning of the exile of this Holy and Righteous One.[65] Somewhat later He will also die outside the city.[66] This also implies the beginning of a new phase of the exile of the people.[67] And it is *Yeshua* who, as the First One, will also enter that judgment over God's people and share in it. When He is unclothed and nailed to the cross,[68] He suffers the same judgment that the people and land will suffer. The dividing of His clothes and the casting of lots over them by the Roman soldiers are a token of what the nations will do to God's people and land. The nations will disperse the people of Israel, divide the land, and cast lots over God's people.[69] The First One of the people undergoes this as a token, tasting the bitterness of the Day of the LORD. As the holy supplicant He asks for forgiveness for what in the midst of the earth is done to Him.[70] The holy priest leads the way, entering into the night of judgment.

---

59. Matt 21:33–41.
60. Matt 23 is Jesus's last speech in the Temple. After it He leaves the House of God (24:1).
61. Luke 21:23–24.
62. Matt 24:3.
63. Ezek 11:22–23.
64. Matt 23:38–39.
65. Peter thus designates *Yeshua* in Acts 3:14.
66. John 19:20; Heb 13:12; cf. Luke 23:48.
67. It is noteworthy that *Yeshua*, underway to the Mount of Olives (see par example Matt 26:30–32), says that all His disciples will fall away on account of Him, and, in that context, then quotes Zech 13:7. In this verse the death of the shepherd is connected with the dispersion of the sheep! On His way to Golgotha—the way out of the city—*Yeshua* is accompanied by a diaspora-Jew (Simon of Cyrene). He simultaneously warns the bystanders for what will befall them (Luke 23:26–31).
68. As Ps 22:18 foresaw with prophetic depth.
69. Joel 3:2–3.
70. Luke 23:34; cf. Isa 53:12.

Part II : The Canonical Narrative: The Scriptures of the New Covenant

19.6 The Priestly Nation and Messiah Anointed: Entering the Holy Life of the *Olam Haba*

The sevenfold unclothing of the priests opened up the way to a sevenfold priestly anointing,[71] and with it entrance was allowed into God's Dwelling on the eighth day. The same happens to this very first holy and righteous one from Israel. Previously we saw that the complete fulfillment of the priesthood and kingship was granted to Him.[72] Through His *kedusha*, *Yeshua*/Jesus was also granted to share in the holiness of the *olam haba*. God is holy, and therefore holiness also is the key to receiving the life of the Eternal God Himself.[73] We already observed that Jewish interpretation makes a clear connection between the holiness and imperishable life of the LORD Himself and of His *olam haba*.[74]

At *Shavuot*, the feast of the harvest, the feast of first fruits, and the celebration of the descent of God's fiery Tora, it becomes clear that the Messiah as the anointed Holy One of God, allows Israel to also participate in the anointing that He obtained to holiness and holy service.[75]

The *Ruaḥ HaKodesh*—the Spirit of the Holiness—is granted in order to give holiness, and guides God's people further into the holiness of God and in "the life of firstfruits/firstlings."[76] Paul will further elaborate on this firstfruits-life by speaking about the "sanctifying work of the Spirit," for example.[77] Messiah *Yeshua* did not come to replace the way of obedience by a way of grace, but instead to enable obedience in a new manner to let man live fully for God! Just as man at creation came to life by the breath of God, the Messiah now gives the *Ruaḥ HaKodesh*—the holy Breath of God[78]—unto obedience.[79] Now the way of life can be walked!

19.7 *Am Kadosh* in the Messiah

When in Jerusalem at *Shavuot* the Spirit falls upon the vanguard of the people of Israel, gathered by *Yeshua*—in the God-intended sequence of His feasts,[80]—the focus is still the calling of *Israel* to be a holy nation. This "Pentecost" is not "the birth of the Church," but God's gift to His people Israel, so that they can be a holy nation amidst of

71. See chapter 8 (8.3).
72. See chapter 17.
73. See chapter 7 (7.5).
74. 2 Pet 1:4 also links (holy) obedience with participation in imperishable divine life.
75. Acts 2:33.
76. Heb 12:10, 14.
77. 2 Thess 2:13.
78. Gen 1:2; see 2:7 for the breathing of life into man; cf. also 6:3. The Hebrew word *ruaḥ* can mean both "spirit" and "wind."
79. Matt 28:19–20 shows that it is about keeping what Jesus commanded. Cf. Rom 1:5; 16:26.
80. Also see chapter 21.

In the Camp of Israel: The Holy Nation Sanctified

the nations. The canonical narrative of the Scriptures of the New Covenant still stands in the streambed of the Tanakh. Firstlings of the firstling-nation participate in the firstling gift of the *olam haba*, which is obtained by the First One of Israel. The blessing of a new *kedusha* for the whole of creation is given first to the nation in the midst of the earth. Only out of this fulfillment of the Sinai-revelation, within the existence of God's chosen holy nation,[81] *kedusha* flows for all the world.

With regard to Israel's calling to be *am kadosh*, it is also clear that God does not wish a holiness disconnected from the obedience of His people. The newly-created possibility of sanctification and holiness on Israel's part, also as representative of the nations, shows God fully engaging with the covenant partnership of Israel. This also shows that God does not wish to redeem the concrete reality of creation in just a *spiritual* manner, but that He wishes it to enter also *physically*, in a complete creation-befitting sanctification. The way of the holy nation is granted certainly in the Messiah, but even so remains a way which should be *walked*. The God-intended *kedusha* consists of works which have been prepared by Him and in which people may "walk."[82] Therefore it is neither strange, nor a token of ignorance or darkness,[83] that we find the Messianic vanguard in the Temple[84] and witness their zeal for God's Tora and its commandments,[85] including the commandment of circumcision.[86] That is exactly why the Spirit of *kedusha* had been given, for both an imputed holiness[87] originating from the Messiah as *brit am*, and for the enablement to walk a "holy walk on the path of holiness." The canonical narrative of the New Testament is totally misunderstood; even worse, it is being falsified when we interpret "grace" in such manner that there is no longer need for an obedient life. Through the blessing of *Shavuot*, when God's Tora was laid in the heart of His people, obedience became rather a new possibility, with no distinction between faith and obedience to be found.[88] Even though the nations have their own particular way of *kedusha*, this does not mean that they are free from having to walk in a way of obedience. Even stronger, it also does not mean that Israel's own way of *kedusha* should be considered archaic or obsolete.

---

81. Chapter 20 elaborates upon this blessing for the nations and the world.
82. Eph 2:10 (RSV).
83. Within the paradigm of the traditional canonical narrative, their dedication to the way of the commandments by the Jewish disciples of Jesus was interpreted as "transition situation" or as token of "not-yet-fully-understanding."
84. Luke 24:53; Acts 3:1, 8; 5:12, 20–21, 42; 24:17–18.
85. Acts 21:20.
86. Acts 16:3 shows Paul circumcising Timothy.
87. Cf. Gen 15:6; Rom 4:3; Gal 3:6; Jas 2:20–26.
88. Jas 2:20–26.

19.8 Partial Sanctification: The Camp of Israel Enters the Judgment

It is obvious that division within God's people arises around Jesus and because of Him. Jesus Himself predicted this.[89]

And yet, in Israel's history partial sanctification happened earlier. In Hezekiah's time, only a part of the priests sanctified themselves,[90] causing the celebration of *Pessah* to be postponed.[91] Even during the postponed celebration, exceptional measures had to be taken because a large percentage of the people had not yet sanctified themselves.[92] Initially it was also only a percentage of the people that recognized the God-anointed David as king and subjected itself to him.[93]

Thus was also the case around Jesus. Only partial acceptance of Him occurs. And so only a partial sanctification of the people takes place. Only a part of the nation of Israel accepts the Messianic *mikva* of the nearing of the Day of the LORD and of the *olam haba*, although there is talk of significant numbers of Jewish disciples who believed the message regarding Him.[94]

This dissension within the people of the One God also tears the heart of the Messiah.[95] Just as Moses suffered because of the disobedience of the people, and Aaron because of the judgment over his disobedient sons, so *Yeshua*/Jesus suffers because of the divide within His people. Just like David long ago, His kingship is still only partial. It is a Hebron-kingship and not yet a Jerusalem-kingship.[96] In His waiting for the completion of His kingship, He also reveals the heart of the One God.[97]

Just as the people were torn apart by brotherly disputes during the kingship period in Hebron, so it occurred in the narrative of the New Testament.[98] The unity of the people of God is broken because of the Messiah's message. This causes the darkness of the Day of the LORD to fall over the camp of Israel in vehemence. The message of *Yeshua* was indeed a *mikva* of purification by which judgment could be averted. But God's offer, that would serve *shalom,* had been hidden for the eyes of many in that

---

89. Matt 10:34–36.
90. 2 Chr 30:3.
91. 2 Chr 30:15–20.
92. 2 Chr 30:17.
93. 2 Sam 2–5 describes this state of affairs.
94. Acts 21:20 shows—whether or not the Greek *muriades* should be rendered as an unspecified "thousands" or as a specified "tens of thousand"—that the total numbers are in fact, in the thousands (cf. also 2:41 and 4:4).
95. Luke 19:41.
96. See chapter 18 (18.8).
97. Cf. John 1:18 and also the "Anyone who has seen me has seen the Father" in John 14:9.
98. Matt 10:17–31; John 16:1–3. The book of Acts too shows in many places that because of Jesus a rift developed within the people.

moment.[99] Now a perfect, consummate judgment would fully come.[100] God's people must enter the full Day of the LORD only partially protected, and the people and the House in the midst of the earth will be the first to be affected.[101] In this night of judgment, the House of God is to be destroyed, God's city trampled on, and the land laid waste. The people would have to enter into an even deeper exile.[102] Even so, this would not be the end. There is still an "until."[103]

19.9 The Darkness of the Day of the LORD Expands: Exile for the People, the Holy King, and the *Shekhina*

In the traditional rendering of the New Testament canonical narrative, Israel and the Messiah often part ways following Jesus's ascension into heaven. The Messiah, exalted as king, goes toward glory and authority while Israel follows a way toward dispersion and God's wrath.[104] There is often no attention for the fact that part of Israel has already entered the Messianic *kedusha* of Israel. Often there is also no attention given to the fact that the way of all Israel stands under the arc of God's faithfulness, as the streambed of the Tanakh shows. If only because of His own Name, He has promised that the election and calling of Israel will be completely realized. The end will be that *all* of Israel will be *am kadosh*!

Often there was also no real understanding of the fact that *Yeshua*'s life and preaching and His resurrection and exaltation did not prevent the Day of the LORD from coming. Both John the Baptist and Jesus had announced this Day. It would certainly come, and it did come. And as the First One of Israel He entered that judgment, as He also entered the dawning *olam haba*. But with His exaltation, the nearing of that Day is not over.

It is therefore that, around Jesus, the judgment over the *olam haze* and the dawning of the *olam haba* overlap,[105] making it important to always speak these two words: "already" and "not-yet." In the farewell speech on the Mount of Olives—even before His death and resurrection—it becomes clear that the kingship of the Messiah does not imply that the Day of the LORD has been revoked. It will come, not in one moment but in successive waves,[106] until the Son of Man arrives in glory.[107] All Israel will

---

99. Luke 19:42.
100. Matt 23:35–36.
101. Cf. Ezek 9:1–7; 1 Pet 4:17.
102. Luke 21:20–24.
103. Luke 21:24.
104. Luke 21:23–24.
105. Dunn speaks in another context about "a period of overlap" (*Romans 1–8*, 468).
106. Matt 24:3–14.
107. Matt 24:30–31.

end up in these waves of tribulation.[108] The whole people called to be *am kadosh*, even the part that had entered into the *kedusha* of the Messiah.[109] The whole earth will also be included.[110] For the people of God this means that a new phase of exile will begin, driven out of God's city and land as a part of this approach of the Day of the LORD.[111] From the Mount of Olives, Messiah *Yeshua* prophecies this way for all Israel. The "already" of the sanctification of a part of Israel does not prevent them from undergoing the "not-yet" of persecution and dispersion together with the whole of the people.[112]

We have seen before that with regard to the kingship of the Messiah there is an "already" and a "not-yet," both occurring simultaneously. Until His kingship is complete, designated by us as "Jerusalem-kingship," both the "already-kingship" and the "not-yet-kingship" continue. The kingship of the Messiah at the Throne of God is still incomplete and waits,[113] like the Hebron-kingship of David. Seen from the perspective of Jerusalem, the Messiah king is still in exile and shares in the darkness of the tribulations of the Day of the LORD.

This resembles the kingship of Joseph, that as seen from the Promised Land, was also a kingship in exile. The setting of Jesus's farewell speech also carries the theme of exile. Indeed, Jesus speaks of the tribulations that will come after He leaves the Temple and sets Himself down on the Mount of Olives, where the *Shekhina* has also set itself upon leaving the Temple.[114] The Mount of Olives is the same mountain that for David, driven from Jerusalem, formed the first stage of his exile outside the land.[115] Perhaps even the conclusion of the Gospel of Matthew, situated in Galilee, in some way sketches a setting of exile. For Galilee was the place of refuge confronted with the enmity of King Herod against the newborn King of the Jews.[116] It certainly is also the bridge to the nations,[117] but possibly both elements can be found there.

The Hebron-kingship of Messiah *Yeshua* brings with it the suffering of the not-yet-arrived Jerusalem-kingship. The New Testament knows of the Messiah's sufferings

---

108. Luke 21:23–24.

109. Jesus speaks about His disciples in Matt 24:3–28; Mark 13:4–23, and Luke 21:12–24.

110. This "beginning of birth-pains"(NIV), meaning "the beginning of the sufferings" (RSV), does not pass over the nations and the whole earth.

111. Luke 21:23–24.

112. Matt 24:3–14 shows that Jesus prepares His disciples and followers for the dark ways they will have to walk.

113. 1 Cor 15:23–28 shows that the kingship of the Messiah is not yet complete. Rev 19:6–21 also shows that in a certain sense the kingship of God has to be established.

114. Ezek 11:22–23; cf. 43:1–4.

115. 2 Sam 15:30, 32. Matt 25:14–15 tells—following chapter 24!—about a person's abrupt departure for a foreign country. The "at once" (verse 16, NIV) can best be taken together with verse 15 (with most handwritings, and also KJV), so Van Bruggen, *Mattheüs*, 431. The whole of Matthew 25 circles around the theme of "waiting" and "serving the absent and yet also present hidden Son of Man."

116. Matt 2:22.

117. Matt 4:15; cf. Isa 9:1–2.

In the Camp of Israel: The Holy Nation Sanctified

which are not yet completed.[118] There is talk of the Messiah's suffering in which His followers will participate.[119] They will enter "through many hardships" the kingdom of God.[120]

In Romans 8 we find, in one broad view, the groaning of the whole of creation, the groaning of believers, and the groaning of the *Ruaḥ HaKodesh*—the Holy Spirit.[121] In this, the groaning of the Spirit becomes a prayer on earth that is shared by the exalted Messiah and brought to the Throne of God.[122]

In chapter 9, after Paul has joined personally in the groaning of the creation and the Spirit and the pleading of the Messiah,[123] he begins to discuss the way that God goes with the whole of Israel.[124] The whole discourse of Romans 9–11 is therefore embedded in a deep longing and at the same time a painful anticipation of the *tikkun olam*, when all of God's plans will be completed.[125]

The kingship of the Messiah at the Throne of God *and* its yet far-off completion are simultaneous realities, as are the exaltation *and* the exiled existence of this king. The exile of the king, the "not-yet" of His Jerusalem-kingship, not only is deeply grievous for Himself, but at the same time for Israel is part of God's judgment of abandonment, as was the case with the exile of the *Shekhina* in Ezekiel. The tears of *Yeshua* accompany the judgment of abandonment.[126] We find the same in Jeremiah 8–9, where God's lamentations and His judgmental words are interwoven. In this section the LORD even wishes that He would find a place in the desert to escape His people.[127] At the same time these chapters are the LORD's painful lament over His daughter Israel,[128] specifically because He will disperse her among the nations,[129] and because her land will be destroyed.[130]

Earlier we observed that the streambed of the Tanakh has been absent very often in the process of interpretation leading up to the traditional canonical narrative. Therefore in this narrative there is little awareness of the abiding engagement of God and His Messiah with the people, that must enter into the darkness of the Day of the LORD. The emphasis on the triumph of Jesus on the one hand, and the judgment over

---

118. Col 1:24.
119. Rom 8:16–17, 36; 2 Cor 1:5–6; 4:7–15. Cf. Matt 10:24–25.
120. Acts 14:22.
121. Rom 8:18–27.
122. Rom 8:34; there is a close connection with verse 27.
123. Rom 9:1–2.
124. Rom 9:4 speaks about Israel as a whole; so also 11:26.
125. Matt 24:3 speaks about "the end of the age," the completion of this world.
126. Luke 19:41.
127. Jer 9:2.
128. See chapter 14 (14.6).
129. Jer 9:16.
130. Jer 9:10–12.

Israel on the other hand, has cut off the King of the Jews from His people, a people over which He will exert His Jerusalem-kingship in the most literal sense.

As explained above, in Him the *olam haze* and the *olam haba* overlap. The "already" and the "not-yet" come together while He waits for His full kingship. He is the First One of the *am kadosh* and He has already drawn part of the people after Him into His *kedusha*. But at the same time He suffers still because the unity of the people has been broken and the darkness is therefore deepening. In all this He is both the living *Shekhina* of God and the First One of Israel. Thus also in Him the exile of the *Shekhina* and Israel come together. The painful waiting, the participation in the tribulations, *and* the exaltation of the Messiah are present together at the right hand of God.[131]

As the First One of His people, and because of His total *kedusha*, He both received the imperishable life and revealed it. He also goes, as the First One of His people, alongside His people through the night and even death, toward the nearing Day of the LORD. This is the way for that part of the people that is *am kadosh*-in-Him, but also for the part that has not yet recognized and acknowledged Him as the Holy One of God.

In the brotherly fight that takes place when one part of Israel persecutes the other, the Messiah is present in a suffering manner.[132] The King of the Jews is and remains engaged with the whole of His people, just as Isaiah speaks of when he speaks of God:

> In all their distress he too was distressed,
> and the angel of his presence saved them.[133]

In a way the First One of Israel co-suffers and undergoes exile because of the "non-unity" of His people, and at the same time He is the one who will ultimately restore the unity of the people.

19.10 The Light of the *Olam Haba* Enters the World: The Calling of the *Am Kadosh* for the World Becomes Visible

The exile of this people called to holiness means that the nation will again be dispersed under the nations.[134] Therein the *am kadosh*-in-*Yeshua* leads the way.[135] The exile of all Israel will only follow later.

---

131. Cf. Rom 8:34.

132. Saul hears: "Why do you persecute me?" (Acts 9:4).

133. Isa 63:9.

134. Acts 8:4 and 11:19. Again we see here the Divine principle at work that "judgment begins at the House of God," in this case at "the house of the Messiah," who/that forms the center of Israel.

135. Luke 21:23–24.

In the Camp of Israel: The Holy Nation Sanctified

The flipside of the coin, however, is that the Word of God goes through the land[136] and into the world.[137] Although it still is a small beginning, the glory of God begins to fill the earth. Starting from the midst of the earth, an *am kadosh* (the twelve special emissaries of *Yeshua* show in their number the number of Israel's tribes) carries the glory of God into the world.

This blessing for the nations from the midst of Israel will be the central theme of the next chapter.

19.11 Waiting for the Second *Pessaḥ* and the Unity and Return of the People

It is obvious that for the holy king and the holy people there still is a waiting for the ultimate *kedusha* which will belong to the *tikkun olam*. There is a "not-yet." There is a waiting near the Throne of God and an exile on earth.

The death and resurrection of *Yeshua* during *Pessaḥ* have not been recognized or acknowledged as acts of God by the whole of the people of Israel. It could therefore be said that a second *Pessaḥ* is expected. In the Tora the LORD opened up a possibility for the celebration of a second *Pessaḥ*.[138] A second possibility to celebrate this feast was given to whomever was unclean through contact with a corpse—Jewish interpretation applied this to all kinds of impurities[139]—or to whom because of a distant journey had not been able to celebrate at the first set date. Therefore a second possibility was given. We have seen how in the time of Hezekiah this occurred when a large percentage of the priests and the people had not sanctified themselves.[140] By analogy it can be said that the Messiah waits until all Israel will accept His *kedusha* and then, clothed in His *kedusha*, will celebrate *Pessaḥ* in a perfectly and completed manner. In His discourse about Israel, Paul refers to this kind of purification when he speaks about the Redeemer/Deliverer[141] who will "turn away" the godlessness from Jacob. He then cites a verse from Isaiah found in the context of the gift of the Spirit in the hearts of the whole people.[142]

---

136. Acts 8:4–40 describes par example the preaching of Philip among the Samaritans and to the treasury official of the queen of the Ethiopians.

137. See Mark 13:9–11; Luke 21:10–19 and connected with it Matt 24:14; also see Acts 8:4 and 11:19.

138. Num 9:1–14.

139. Milgrom, *Numbers*, 68–69.

140. 2 Chr 30. Verse 2 and 13 speak about the *Pessaḥ* in the second month.

141. In Rom 11:26 Paul cites Isa 59:20. There is God the *go'el*—the redeemer—who redeems the people as was the duty of the *go'el* (Lev 25:25; cf. the book of Ruth, in which Boaz acts as redeemer). There is a connection with the year of Jubilee (see Lev 25) in which all debts were forgiven and property was given back to the original owners.

142. Isa 59:20. Shulam and Le Cornu commenting on Romans 11:25–26 draw attention to the combination of forgiveness and the gift of the Spirit in these verses (*Jewish Roots of Romans*, 397).

Part II : The Canonical Narrative: The Scriptures of the New Covenant

Perhaps we might even see, from a prophetic depth, a connection between the "distant journey" that hinders the celebration of *Pessaḥ* and the "far away" of the exile in which even the LORD is forced to keep a distance from His Sanctuary.[143]

The unity of the people is also awaited. Interpreted from the streambed of the Tanakh, the canonical narrative of the New Testament expects all of Israel to unite around Messiah *Yeshua*.[144] As a gift from God He will ultimately restore the unity of the people,[145] finally welcomed in the city of God.[146] Considering the parallel with David, it is not strange to think that the Jerusalem-kingship will begin when unity within the people is restored. Then Jerusalem will be a city of unity, "bound firmly together"[147] as a "Hebron,"[148] that is a "unification," where the people became again one under David. Just as the tabernacle, which was made into one whole.[149] Just as Jerusalem, after the restoration of unity, was given by God as capital and place for the Temple,[150] so it will happen in the future to the city of the great King and the kingship of God's Messiah.

We saw that the nearing of the Day of the LORD would also mean exile for the people, the king, and the *Shekhina*.[151] This fact especially makes us aware that the canonical narrative of the Scriptures of the New Covenant continues to stand in the streambed of the Tanakh. The promise given to Abraham about the land still is part of God's election and intent with the people. When we again hear, around Messiah *Yeshua*, about an exile for the whole people, and in a certain sense also for the king, this shows that the way of God with His people still is the way toward the land in the midst of the earth. Messiah *Yeshua*/Jesus and His realized *kedusha* have everything to do with the land. The judgment of exile is part of the "not-yet," is only judgment because living in the God-promised land still is God's blessing for His people. The

---

143. Ezek 8:6. There is a word usage relationship between the distant journey and God's kept distance from the Sanctuary.

144. Rom 11:26 speaks about "all Israel."

145. See chapter 12 (12.10).

146. Matt 23:39.

147. Ps 122:3 (RSV). In Jewish interpretation this is seen as a designation of the connectedness of people (not stones).

148. Hebron (Hebrew: *Ḥevron*) stems from the Hebrew verb *ḥavar* that means "to unify." In Ps 122:3 it is used together with a word that is related to the Hebrew word for "one" (*eḥad*) and also is found in the *Shema*. See chapter 18 (18:8).

149. In Exod 26:11 also the same combination of words is used as described in footnote 148 of this chapter. Reference found in Kidner, *Psalms 73–150*, 433.

150. See 2 Sam 5:1–12; 1 Chr 11:1–9. Jewish interpretation has that the first Temple (built by Solomon) has been destroyed for reasons of idolatry of the people, and that the second Temple (built after the partial return from Babel, later extended and beautified by Herod the Great) has been destroyed because of the disunity, hatred and lack of love amongst God's people.

151. See 19.10.

repeated "until" from the mouth of Jesus[152] and Paul[153] makes it clear that the exile for people, land, and city will not be forever. In accordance with the prophetic promises and because of the *kedusha* He lived, the Messiah will ultimately lead His people into the *kedusha* that belongs to the *olam haba*. Thereby the people will be able to finally return and live in safety at the God-chosen place in the midst of the earth.[154] Because of Him there will be no talk anymore of the curse of dispersion among the nations.[155]

When we see the canonical narrative of the New Testament as in every respect standing in the streambed of the Tanakh, it becomes clear that God is ONE in all His works and also faithful to His promises.[156] No different story was begun with Messiah *Yeshua*, in which God would distance Himself from the ways He walked within Israel's history. If that was the case, this First One of Israel would no longer show the face of the Father of Israel.[157] At the deepest level, the Messiah then would issue a call to serve an other god than Israel's God.[158]

However, it is indeed from the *kedusha* of the NAME[159] and all of God's words by this First One from Israel by which the *olam haba* has begun. By this *kedusha* He obtained blessing for God's people and the world.

19.12 *Kedusha* in the Midst of the World: Blessing for the Whole Earth

Central to this chapter was the *kedusha*, completely perfected by the Messiah in the center of the earth. Israel had been chosen by God from all nations to be His holy nation. This election showed God's love for His people, and was not just a means to bless the nations, although God certainly also conceived of them in His heart. God had indeed promised to let Abraham and his offspring be a blessing for the nations in the midst of the world.[160] The *kedusha* into which the world would be able to enter, and which had been the goal of creation, had been lived out and revealed in the midst of the camp of Israel. Now this *kedusha* could be learned and received by the nations too, together with the *am kadosh*.

This blessing for the nations and the world from the midst of the camp of Israel will be the subject of the next chapter.

---

152. Matt 23:39; Luke 21:24.
153. Rom 11:25.
154. In John 10 Jesus designates Himself as the good Shepherd; read against the background of Ezek 34 this eschatological shepherding implies more than just spiritual salvation.
155. Cf. Deut 28:63–64. Further see chapter 21.
156. Ps 33:4.
157. John 14:9.
158. Cf. on the other hand Mark 12:29–31 where *Yeshua* cites the *Shema*.
159. Luke 11:2; John 12:28; 17:6, 26.
160. Gen 12:3; 18:18; 22:18; 28:14; Gal 3:8; see chapter 3 (3.3).

Chapter 20

In the Camp of Israel

Blessing for the Mishpaḥa *of Abraham and the Nations*

20.1 Salvation for the Nations in the Camp of Israel

ALTHOUGH OF FOREMOST IMPORTANCE, yet Israel's life in the midst of the earth was not intended only as a blessing for God by means of the *kedusha*,[1] neither was Israel's existence meant to only revolve around itself. What is again confirmed, particularly through Messiah *Yeshua*'s pure *avoda*, is that the intentions of God's heart also meant blessing for the nations. This has always been the case, but now these intentions become visible in the camp of Israel in an overwhelming way. In the camp of Israel a well of salvation is opened up from which the nations, together with Israel, may drink. The news about these wells of salvation must be told to the nations.[2]

On the last and greatest day of the Feast of Tabernacles, *Yeshua*/Jesus speaks in the Temple of Himself as the one who will make the people themselves wells from which rivers of living water will flow.[3] This was the day that the *hoshana*[4] resounded a thousand times against the walls of the Temple, and the day that, as on the other days of the feast, water was brought joyfully from Siloam and poured out on the altar.[5] The nations were also in sight at this *Sukkot* celebration. In Jewish tradition

---

1. Cf. chapter 3 (3.3).
2. Isa 12.
3. John 7:37–39.
4. The last—seventh—day of the Feast of Tabernacles is named *Hoshana Rabba* (= the Great Hosanna). On that day the multitude went seven times around the altar in the Temple, while the refrain of the prayers was *Hoshana* (meaning an emphatically: Save [us]!). In the liturgy of the synagogue we also find these elements. According to some there is a relation to the sevenfold circling of Jericho. *Sukkot* envisions the final victory over all opposition against God's plans (see Goldwurm, *Succos*, 67–72).
5. Together with wine the water was poured out over the altar following the morning sacrifice

In the Camp of Israel: Blessing for the Mishpaḥa *of Abraham and the Nations*

the seventy added festive offerings of the seven days of the feast were interpreted as offerings for the nations.[6] This salvation for the nations asks for our attention now. The title of this chapter reminds us of the fact that this blessing for the nations has already been promised to Abraham.

20.2 Blessing for the Nations and the Election of Abraham's *Mishpaḥa*

When God elects Abraham to become the father of God's own people, the other nations also come quickly into view. Abraham himself will become a fountain of blessing from which all nations may draw salvation. The election of Abraham and his offspring—his *mishpaḥa*—is accompanied by a promise of blessing for all *mishpaḥot* of the earth.[7] The Scriptures of the New Covenant show that in Messiah Jesus this promise for the nations has become reality. The blessing of Abraham is now available and reaches the nations.[8]

It is important to note that the election of Abraham and his offspring preceded the giving of the Tora. God's instruction and laws are given at Sinai to the nation that had been elected long before.[9] When, for whatever reason, there would be talk of a change in "law," this would still leave Israel's election intact. Even if in "the Messianic Day" any aspect of the Tora would change, God's election of Israel would remain irrevocable,[10] something He would never disavow.

This point of God's election is an important one. In the traditional canonical narrative, marked by replacement thinking, the theme of "the law" was strongly connected to Israel's election. Based upon expressions like "the fulfillment of the law"[11] and Christ as "the goal of the law,"[12] it often was concluded that the role of the Tora

---

(Ibid., 59–60). More connections between the celebration of *Sukkot* in the Temple and John 7:10–8:20 can be pointed out.

6. Par example see Goldwurm, *Succos*, 47. In a row of diminishing numbers seventy bulls were sacrificed during the seven days of *Sukkot*. Jewish tradition interprets these sacrifices as offerings of atonement for the nations. On the last day of the feast thus the expectation of the final victory over all opposition (see footnote 4 of this chapter) and the atonement for the nations came together. After the seven days of the feast, an eighth day of rest followed (Lev 23:39) that had a special character and was thought of as a day of intimacy between God and His people. Against this background John 8:1–11—the adulterous woman who is not sentenced—gets a special meaning.

7. Gen 12:1–3. See chapter 3 (3.3 and 3.4).

8. Gal 3:8–9, 14.

9. For this see Gal 3:17–19 (although in a slightly differently-oriented discourse).

10. Rom 11:29. For the Tora in the Messianic times see chapter 12 (12.16) and chapter 19 (19.4).

11. Rom 13:10.

12. Rom 10:4. The Greek *telos* (goal) has been rendered by NIV as "culmination." The rendering of the used expression by "end of the law" (RSV; KJV and other older translations) is completely misleading and reveals a different interpretative paradigm.

had been played out for the biggest part, and that with it the special election of Israel would have also come to an end.

This chapter certainly will also discuss the place of God's Tora in the lives of the Messiah's followers, both from Israel and the nations. The Scriptures clearly reveal to us, however, that the nations will receive God's blessing and instruction within the streambed pictured by the Tanakh. Within this streambed Israel remains the God-chosen place of salvation, where blessing is available for the nations.

20.3 The King of the Jews in Search of the Nations: The Blessing of the Exile

We have already observed that the brotherly dispute within the people of Israel over Messiah *Yeshua*/Jesus opens up a new phase in the exile. The whole people will enter the darkness of the Day of the LORD. The "firstlings of Israel" who accepted the *kedusha* of the Messiah lead the way, and the whole of the people will follow. In a certain sense, as King of the Jews, even Messiah *Yeshua* accompanies His people into exile. His kingship seems to be even further off.[13]

It is clear, however, that at the same time this dispersion of the Messianic firstlings[14] of the priestly nation will also mean blessing for the nations of the world. The salvific message of the God of Israel is now carried into the world, exactly as Jesus had said it would.[15]

The darkness of the nearing Day of the LORD, with God's purifying judgment, first falls over the Messianic first ones of Israel when Stephen is killed.[16] Beginning with His death, the "afflictions of the Messiah"[17] begin to affect the physical existence of the Body of the Messiah. His death is the signal for the beginning dispersion of these firstlings of Israel.[18] Again "a Saul" persecutes "a David."[19] At the same time, Messiah *Yeshua* once again walks in His followers the way of the grain of wheat, pointed

---

13. See chapter 18 (18.8 and 18.9) and 19 (19.8–19.10).

14. As firstlings of Israel they are "a kind of firstfruits of all he created" (Jas 1:18). Cf. the expression "redeemed from mankind" (Rev 14:4, RSV. NIV has "purchased from among mankind"). The presupposition is the priestly representation of the whole creation by Israel.

15. Par example see Matt 24:14, 28:18 and Acts 1:8.

16. Acts 6–7.

17. This expression we find in Colossians 1:24. The Greek word rendered as "afflictions" (*thlipsis*) points to hardships, tribulations, persecutions, Cf. par example Acts 14:22; Matt 24:9 (RSV: "tribulation").

18. Acts 8:1, 4.

19. Acts 8:1–3.

In the Camp of Israel: Blessing for the Mishpaḥa *of Abraham and the Nations*

out by Himself to be the way to a rich harvest.[20] The Psalm for the Counting of the *Omer*[21]—Psalm 67—speaks of the harvest in the world of nations.[22]

The expulsion of the Messianic firstlings from Jerusalem disperses them over the regions of Judea and Samaria, resulting in the good news spreading throughout the whole of God's land. Wherever they meet fellow Jews, they tell about the things that had happened in Jerusalem.[23] Jews from both within the country and outside of it—Lebanon, Cyprus and Syria appear on the scene[24]—hear about God's actions in and through Messiah *Yeshua*/Jesus.

But non-Jews also receive the salvation, with Samaritans leading the way. From Zion the message descends to the city of Samaria.[25] The inhabitants hear "the good news of the kingdom of God and the name of Jesus Christ,"[26] and are immersed/baptized in the name of *Yeshua*.[27] When the apostles in Jerusalem hear of this, Peter and John are delegated. By their laying on of hands and prayer, the Messianic blessing poured out at *Shavuot* in Jerusalem, is now received by Samaritans.[28] These people, who from Jewish religious perspective are evaluated as bastards, receive the *Ruaḥ HaKodesh*. These non-Jews receive the Indwelling of God's Spirit. As a result, Peter and John proclaim the gospel to many Samaritan villages on their way back to Zion.

The Samaritans still lived in God's land, but now wide circles began to be drawn toward distant countries. A high-ranking Ethiopian experiences the fulfillment of prophecies of the Tanakh.[29] Even Imperial Rome comes into view when Peter is sent by God to the house of the Roman Cornelius.[30] Roman non-Jews (*goyim*, who in Jewish perception were so much connected to idol service that often all contact was avoided), must be visited at the Holy Spirit's command.[31] They also receive the Spirit of the Messiah.[32] This again proves that, by means of His emissaries, the Shepherd of Israel is also in search for sheep which do not belong to the flock of Israel.[33]

---

20. John 12:24–26.

21. See chapter 17 (17.3).

22. Israel prays this Psalm in the period of counting the days from *Pessaḥ* till *Shavuot*. Ps 67:7 shows that the blessing in the midst of the camp of Israel ultimately will lead to the recognition of the LORD God by the nations.

23. Acts 8:4.

24. Acts 11:19.

25. Acts 8:5.

26. Acts 8:12.

27. Acts 8:12.

28. Acts 8:14–17.

29. Acts 8:26–40.

30. Acts 10.

31. Acts 10:19–20.

32. Acts 10:44–46.

33. John 10:16.

Part II : The Canonical Narrative: The Scriptures of the New Covenant

By means of ordinary dispersed firstlings of Israel, even those without a commission as apostle, God searches the nations. The exalted King of the Jews, who at the same time wanders on a path of exile through the world, searches for inroads in the Hellenistic culture. In the Syrian city of Antioch, Greeks[34] hear from Jewish men about the Lord *Yeshua*.[35] A great multitude of them believes the message and turns to this Lord.[36]

The exile of the king and the expulsion of some of His followers from Zion do not make His word a powerless invitation. Amidst the persecution of the Messiah and His firstlings, it suddenly becomes clear that it is precisely in this manner that the power of the royal word reveals itself. The word of Jesus strikes Saul blind.[37] It becomes clear that also in other places within this dispersion a royal struggle takes place with disbelief and satanic resistance.[38] In a powerless manner the Holy One of Israel reveals the power of the Messiah and the Spirit. The Shepherd of Israel, like His forefather David, defeats lion and bear "at His choosing."[39]

Meanwhile, the circles around Jerusalem grow wider and wider. The missionary journeys of the obedient-made *Shaul*/Saul carry the message further in the direction of Turkey and Europe.[40] The letters of this *Shaul*—Paul[41]—show this dissemination, Rome also being found on the travel agenda.[42] The end of Acts shows us Paul in this capital of the empire, as both prisoner of the emperor and prisoner of the Messiah.[43]

The Scriptures of the New Covenant illuminate the promise that all nations on the whole earth will hear the Word of God *from* Zion. It simultaneously becomes clear that, by the Spirit of the Messiah, the nations will also become oriented *toward* Zion. The exile of the firstlings, and somewhat later of all Israel, and the "not-yet" of the Jerusalem-kingship of the Messiah will not be the end. The Spirit wishes to teach

---

34. The designations "Greeks" is not so much geographical. It designates the cultural embedding of various people and language groups. The Hellenistic culture left its mark on the life of all nations in the contemporary Roman empire. Nations outside of it could be designated "barbarians" (cf. Col 3:11).

35. Acts 11:20.

36. Acts 11:21–26. Here the designation originates of *christianoi* for the disciples of the Christ/Messiah. The rendering "Christians" nowadays regrettably carries the association of "disjoined-from-Israel" or of "totally-different-from-Jewish" and of "Churchly-Christian." At that time it meant something like "Messianics."

37. Acts 9:8–9.

38. See Acts 8:9–11, 18–24; 13:6–12; 16:16–18.

39. 1 Sam 17:37.

40. His missionary journeys are described in Acts 13–14; 15:36—18:22 and 18:23—21:14.

41. It was very customary that Jews sometimes had two names (a Hebrew/Aramaic one for use amongst Jews and a Greek/Latin name for use in a gentile context). The name Paul could have been chosen because of a sound resilience with *Shaul*/Saul, because of being named after someone else, or because of the meaning "the small one" (Le Cornu and Shulam, *Jewish Roots of Acts*, 439–43).

42. Rom 1:13.

43. Acts 28:16.

In the Camp of Israel: Blessing for the Mishpaḥa *of Abraham and the Nations*

the nations to search for salvation from Zion and to orient themselves toward this center of the earth. Jerusalem remains the midst of God's work on earth, not only for the Jew *Shaul*/Saul,[44] but also for the believers from the *goyim*.[45] At the same time, the surrender of this Jewish Saul to the Son of David could be seen as a prophetic sign for the unity that some day will be granted to Israel, and which will end up in the Jerusalem-kingship.[46]

The Messianic filling of the earth with the knowledge of the Name of the LORD[47] is accompanied by the longing of the Spirit for Zion. Just as the Spirit, as the eyes of the LORD ranging through the world[48] in the times of the first return to Jerusalem was restless in the diaspora,[49] now with pain and groaning the Spirit of the Messiah longs for the end of this dispersion and for the *tikkun olam*, the completion of all God's plans.[50] This completion of God's plans with Israel and the nations is indeed connected to the appearance of God's Deliverer from Zion. And the *olam haba* also has Jerusalem, the imperishable city of God, as its center.[51]

The words "from him . . . through him and for him,"[52] found at the end of Romans 11, must be interpreted still from the streambed of the Tanakh. Therefore they are interwoven with the final words from Ezekiel, "The LORD is there."[53]

20.4 A Great Surprise

When a new reality becomes clear: that non-Jews are sought out, privileged by God Himself with the salvation that Messiah *Yeshua* has worked in the midst of Israel, it is overwhelming and confusing. The God-fearing Roman Cornelius in Caesarea receives a God-arranged visit by Peter.[54] During the preaching of God's deeds in

---

44. Paul stays focused on Jerusalem as the city of God and the Temple as place of prayer (Acts 15:2; 19:21; 20:16, 22; 21:17, 26).

45. Acts 11:29–30 shows that the believers in Syrian Antioch give financial support to "the brothers and sisters living in Judea." Later on we see that the congregations in the diaspora again express their connection to the believers in Jerusalem by means of a collection (1 Cor 16:1-3).). Paul gives it a deeply spiritual meaning. It is only logical that *goyim* who have come to share in the spiritual richness of Jerusalem let their love return toward Jerusalem (Rom 15:25–26). Jerusalem also is the place from which spiritual oversight over the Body of the Messiah flows forth (Acts 15:1–2).

46. Further see chapter 21.

47. Ps 113:3; Isa 59:19; Mal 1:11.

48. Zech 4:10 (cf. 1:11); Ps 11:4; 2 Chr 16:9.

49. Cf. Zech 6:8.

50. In Romans 9–11 Paul voices his grief over Israel. Thereby a connection is made between the groaning of creation and the Spirit in 8:18–39. The future of "all Israel" (11:26) is closely connected to the groaning and pleading of the Spirit on earth (8:22–23) and of the Messiah at the Throne (8:34).

51. Isa 54 and 60; Rev 21–22.

52. Rom 11:36.

53. Ezek 48:35.

54. Acts 10.

and through the Messiah, the Holy Spirit falls on the household of this God-fearing Roman. There is no longer a position of exception for this God-fearing man.[55] The Indwelling of the LORD is audible, experienced as the *Ruaḥ HaKodesh* fills all who hear the word. As at *Shavuot* in Jerusalem, a Roman household is now immersed in the baptism of conversion and fulfillment with the Spirit.

Peter's preaching in Caesarea has the same structure as it did earlier in Jerusalem.[56] He describes how God in the Jewish land[57]—the midst of the earth—has acted within the life and death and resurrection of Jesus. How subsequently the Messiah Himself commanded the witnesses of His resurrection to proclaim to Israel that He had been appointed to judge over the living and the dead. How the prophets show that *everyone*—the circles are drawn wide here!—who believes, will receive forgiveness of sins.[58]

The nearing of the judgment of the Day of the LORD, and the call to repentance and turning to God in order to be able to enter the Kingdom of the *olam haba*, still form the background. The structure of the preaching of both John the Baptist and of *Yeshua*/Jesus forms the structure of the preaching we meet in Acts.[59] It is a good message in view of the nearing Day of the LORD. Together with Israel, the nations are also placed under the nearing of the Day and summoned to prepare to render an account to the judge.[60] "The culmination of the ages has come."[61]

The great surprise is that many within the circle of nations believe this message, taking leave of their own ways to repent and turn to the God of Israel.

20.5 The Mystery of Ages Revealed: Ephesians 2–3

The unexpected acts of God—the giving of the Holy Spirit to *goyim*—suddenly cause a new light to shine over words, revealing textual associations within the Tanakh. Peter points the God-fearing Cornelius to "all the prophets."[62] And James too cites "the words of the prophets" in order to show that "from long ago" God had planned to "choose a people for His name from the Gentiles."[63]

Paul characterizes the message he proclaims with the words:

---

55. God-fearing *goyim* participated to a certain extent in Jewish life, but were closed out at other points. Par example they were not allowed to participate in the bringing of prescribed sacrifices; voluntary sacrifices however they were allowed to bring (see Le Cornu and Shulam, *Jewish Roots of Acts*, 549–50).

56. Cf. Acts 2:14–40.

57. Twice Peter mentions the land (Acts 10:37, 39).

58. See Acts 10:34–43.

59. See par example Acts 13:23–41; 14:14–17; 17:22–31; 26:19–23.

60. Acts 26:17–18.

61. 1 Cor 10:11.

62. Acts 10:43.

63. Acts 15:14–15, 18.

In the Camp of Israel: Blessing for the Mishpaḥa *of Abraham and the Nations*

> ... the mystery that has been kept hidden for ages and generations, but is now disclosed to the Lord's people. To them God has chosen to make known among the Gentiles the glorious riches of this mystery, which is Christ in you, the hope of glory.[64]

Paul too invokes the Tanakh time and again. Every element of the good news was "according to the Scriptures."[65] Yet, it is only after the resurrection and exaltation of the Messiah that the time has come for God to reveal this (already-written) mystery to His "saints"—meaning in the first place to His people Israel and then also to the believers from the nations.[66] It seems as if the time of insight and understanding has only arrived when the actual turning of the LORD toward the nations has been enabled and begins to take place. No less than a revelation was needed for this understanding to begin.[67] In a special manner Peter and Paul, and with them the Messianic firstlings from Israel, received a new understanding of ancient words and their textual connections.[68]

For generations it had been possible to read the Scriptures and not to understand what was read.[69] Paul uses the expression "mystery of Christ"[70] in this context. Apparently the Messiah is a great mystery. Unexpected and never imagined, He appears to also be the hope of the glory of God for *goyim*.[71] It is about "boundless riches"[72] and the love of the Messiah that surpasses all understanding.[73]

It also is a mystery[74] that Samaritans, and now Romans and Hellenistic *goyim* may be "fellow citizens with God's people" and "members of his household,"[75] "heirs together with Israel," "members together of one body," and "sharers together in the promise in Christ Jesus."[76] Firstlings from Israel, and *goyim*—who also can be named

---

64. Col 1:26–27. The Greek *en humin* can be rendered "in you" as well as "among you." By the Holy Spirit the Messiah makes His dwelling in and thus also among the *goyim*. Cf. Luke 17:21 where we also find such possibility of double meaning.

65. 1 Cor 15:3–4. Cf. also chapter 17 (17.16).

66. Eph 3:5; Col 1:26; cf. 1 Cor 2:10.

67. Eph 3:3; cf. 1 Cor 2:10–12; Eph 1:17.

68. God's special way toward the *goyim* has remained hidden for ages (Eph 3:4–5; Rom 16:25; 1 Cor 2:7) and has yet been according to the Scriptures (Rom 1:1–2) and for that reason everywhere substantiated with words of Scripture from the Tanakh.

69. Cf. Acts 8:30–31.

70. Eph 3:4.

71. Col 1:27.

72. Eph 3:8.

73. Eph 3:19.

74. Col 1:27.

75. Eph 2:19.

76. Eph 3:6.

firstlings[77]—are built together into a dwelling of God.[78] The God of Abraham, Isaac, and Jacob appears to bestow His love to the nations in an unsearchable manner. Together with Israel they will be blessed in the Messiah.

20.6 The Nations Come Flooding in: Probing Questions

Luke's report shows that in Antioch God Himself commissions the work of preaching the word of God in ever widening circles around the center of the earth.[79] Paul and Barnabas obediently begin travelling, first visiting the synagogues in the places where they arrive.[80] Only when Israel has heard the message do *goyim* have their turn.[81] Astonished and thankful, Paul and Barnabas conclude that God Himself has "opened a door of faith to the Gentiles."[82]

Yet not everyone has had a personal vision like Peter,[83] or has been sent by *Yeshua* Himself like *Shaul*/Paul.[84] Both men received an overtly clear revelation about the participation of the *goyim* in salvation. They witnessed how the *Ruaḥ HaKodesh* fell on *goyim* in Caesarea[85] and how the Messiah's authority over satanic practices brought a Roman governor to faith.[86] The strange turn toward the *goyim*, however, had already raised questions in relation to Cornelius in Jerusalem,[87] and here we now see the same happening in Antioch in Syria.[88]

By means of Paul and Barnabas's journey begun in Antioch, congregations of disciples have originated in various other places. There Jews and *goyim*[89] share the same faith in Messiah Jesus, both having repented and purified themselves in view of the nearing Day of the LORD and the life of the *olam haba* received in the Holy Spirit.[90] But as a result, it is precisely these previous questions and anxieties which rise up again. Participation in the blessing of Israel's God, this is not so obvious, is it? Shouldn't this then be followed by a conversion to the Jewish people? A physical transition to Israel would be needed, correct? According to Moses, wouldn't the

---

77. 2 Thess 2:13; cf. Rom 16:5; 1 Cor 16:15.
78. Eph 2:22.
79. Acts 13:2–3.
80. Acts 13:5, 14; cf. also the "to you first" in verse 46.
81. Cf. Rom 1:16.
82. Acts 14:27.
83. Acts 10:9–16.
84. Acts 9:15–16; 26:12–18.
85. Acts 10:44–45.
86. Acts 13:12.
87. Acts 11:1–18.
88. Acts 15:1.
89. Acts 11:20–21.
90. Cf. Eph 1:13–14.

In the Camp of Israel: Blessing for the Mishpaḥa *of Abraham and the Nations*

men need to be circumcised? Is partaking in the salvation of Israel's Messiah possible without walking the special way of Israel's physical offspring? It is people from Judea who ask these questions in Antioch, and they themselves formulate an unambiguous answer. Connected to the movement of the Pharisees, they argue that *goyim* should be circumcised and keep the law of Moses.[91] The unclean Gentiles should undergo further purification. After all it is about *kedusha* for God.

It is important to remember that this discussion is not about the validity and need of "law" within the salvation of the Messiah. There is no contradistinction between "the mercy of Christ" and "the law" at work here. It is about if *goyim* without obedience to the *tora* for Israel (and thus in principle without becoming Jew) may belong to Israel's God. Implicitly the question is also on the table: what lasting status and meaning is there for the *kedusha* that is specifically required from the priestly nation Israel? If *goyim* without a valid Jewish conversion—without circumcision and the taking on of the yoke of the law—are allowed to come near to the Holy One, what then does that ultimately mean for the special calling of Israel amidst the nations?

The questions are raised from a deep desire for the *kedusha* unto which Israel is called. Ultimately it is about the Indwelling of God in His people Israel in the midst of the earth, is it not?

20.7 The Mystery: The Messiah as Place of Salvation

It is not surprising that these probing questions are being asked. A mystery was being revealed about something foresaid by God, but not foreseen by His people. This revelation was about undiscovered truth within Israel's own election and calling. About undreamed of depths and realities regarding the *avoda*—life as worship ministry in and around the Indwelling of God in Israel. The mystery of *goyim* coming near has everything to do with the mystery of the Messiah:

> For he himself is our peace, who has made the two groups one and has destroyed the barrier, the dividing wall of hostility, by setting aside in his flesh the law with its commands and regulations. His purpose was to create in himself one new humanity out of the two, thus making peace, and in one body to reconcile both of them to God through the cross, by which he put to death their hostility. He came and preached peace to you who were far away and peace to those who were near. For through him we both have access to the Father by one Spirit.[92]

In this description of the salvation of the Messiah for Israel and the nations, various lines of the Tanakh coincide: the Indwelling of God in the Temple and the culmination

---

91. See Acts 15:1, 5.
92. Eph 2:14–18.

Part II : The Canonical Narrative: The Scriptures of the New Covenant

thereof in the Messiah;[93] the priestly calling and separation of Israel amidst the nations and the perfect obedient fulfillment of this calling by *Yeshua*/Jesus;[94] the "presence" of all creation and of Israel by representation in this One from Israel;[95] the necessity of the God-commanded *kedusha* and *avoda* in relation to the blessing of the nations;[96] the overlap between the judgment over the *olam haze* and of the beginning of the *olam haba* in the Messiah;[97] the connection between the building of a Dwelling of God and a/the new creation;[98] and the desire of God who is ONE for unity and peace in His creation.[99] All these lines concur in the Messiah and form the background of this section from Ephesians.

In this description Paul fixes our attention on the mystery of the Messiah to the fact that He has been, has become, and remained the living Temple. *He* is the place of the Indwelling and of the nearing to God. As the Temple of God resurrected from the dead, He also is the beginning of the new creation.[100] In the second Temple in Jerusalem the *goyim* and Israel were separated by the "dividing wall of hostility" between the courtyard of the Gentiles and the courtyard of the (Jewish) women. *Goyim*, and whoever had been defiled by a corpse, had to stay behind this wooden partition and thereby were the furthest from the altar and the Temple and its Most Holy Place within.[101] Through the Torah of Sinai Israel, meant to be a holy nation in the world of nations, was separated from the other nations. The God-required purity of the *avoda* in the whole of life and in the Temple caused *goyim* to keep at a distance. "The law with its commands and regulations" created separation, so that the one creation was divided the way light and darkness were on the first day.[102] This separated the people who were "near" and the people who were "far" away.[103] Israel was near to God and the *goyim* far away.[104]

---

93. The mention of the Temple and the placement of the Messiah as "location of salvation" in contrast have to do with this. See chapter 8 (8.2), 9 (9.9), 12 (12.12 and 12.13) and 15.

94. See chapter 8, 9, 12 (12.7) and 16.

95. This becomes visible by the emphasize on the unity of "the two" in the one Body of the Messiah. See chapter 3 (3.3 and 3.4), 16 (16.7), 17 (17.6) and 18 (18.6).

96. See chapter 9 and 12 (12.13 and 12.14).

97. See chapter 17 and 19 (19.9).

98. The mentioning of the Messiah as place of salvation and of the "creating" of the Messiah shows this. See chapter 8 (8.2). The recreation of mankind by means of the recreation of Israel also plays a role in the background. See chapter 16 (16.7) and 17 (17.6).

99. See chapter 12 (12.7).

100. Cf. John 2:13–22 for a discussion about the resurrection of Jesus's body as sign of (His right to and the beginning of) the eschatological cleansing of the Temple. Also see chapter 8 (8.2).

101. Violation of this rule was punishable by death. An inscription on stone with this warning has been found.

102. Gen 1:3–5.

103. Isa 57:19 uses the designations "far" and "near." Cf. the "far away" in Eph 2:13, 17.

104. Eph 2:11–12 sums up the differences between Israel and the *goyim*.

In the Camp of Israel: Blessing for the Mishpaḥa *of Abraham and the Nations*

But now—in the culmination of time[105]—a mystery has become reality and been revealed. Together with Israel *goyim* are allowed to come near and partake in the one Spirit of God. How that has come about? Paul shows how Messiah *Yeshua*/Jesus as living Temple *and* as Most High priest *and* as executioner of the judgment of God, has also become messenger of peace for Israel and the nations. In Him the judgment over the *olam haze* has been executed and the *olam haba* has dawned. The eschatological *shalom* has begun, for the *kedusha* both *for* and *from* all the earth has been perfected in the Messiah. Israel has been sanctified in Him and the *goyim* have been declared pure and righteous, because He also completed the righteousness and *kedusha* required from them. The eschatological *shalom* brings a unity that comes forth from God and is befitting to Him. The "division of two" of the *olam haze* becomes the "connectedness of two" that belongs to the *olam haba*.[106] The eschatological son-ship of Israel of the *olam haba* and the fulfillment of all promises, the gift of the Spirit and the Indwelling of God that comes with it, have been made available for Israel as priestly nation between the *goyim*. From the midst of this nation *goyim* are now blessed, participating in this salvation and becoming confirmed in their own calling.[107]

It is this mystery that gradually determined the thoughts and actions of the firstlings of Israel. But the understanding of this revelation and its implications did not come at once. Therefore in Antioch probing questions are asked and insufficient answers given by the followers of the Messiah from Judea, followers with ties to the Pharisees.

Because Paul and Peter had received special revelation of God regarding the mystery of the Messiah in relation to the salvation of the *goyim*, they strongly protest. Therefore a delegation is sent off to Jerusalem in order to receive answers from there.[108] This being the case because *Yeshua* had given authority to His apostles to make decisions regarding the law.[109] The nations should indeed receive instruction from Zion.

20.8 Acts 15: The Council in Jerusalem

There are great differences of opinion also at this council in Jerusalem, regarding the question of conversion: should *goyim* make an actual religious transition to the Jewish people in order to be able to partake in the salvation of the Messiah?[110] What is the

---

105. Heb 1:2.
106. Eph 2:15–16.
107. Cf. 1 Cor 7:17–24. See in this chapter 20.9
108. Acts 15:2–4.
109. Matt 16:19 and 18:18 speak about this commission of authority. Cf. Deut 17:8–13.
110. Acts 15:5. The difference of opinion was about the question in what manner the *goyim* would be spared and saved in the judgment of God.

Messianic *halakha*[111]—the way of obedience—for the *goyim*? To what law and commandments is obedience required from them? Not only the question regarding the obedience of believers from the nations is on the table. Implied in it, is the question regarding the specific place of Israel. Also implied are the questions regarding the abiding meaning of Israel's election, and the special promises and task for Israel in God's plans.

In the end, only Peter's recollection of God's deeds silences the council. God had indeed given the Holy Spirit without making any distinction, purifying the hearts of the *goyim* by faith. If this first gift of the *olam haba* had been granted without any formal conversion to Israel, then this brought consequences for the *halakha* of the *goyim*. Therefore, they should not be placed under the yoke of the *tora* that was given to Israel. For them also there is salvation in the Day of the LORD through mercy just as there would be for Israel.[112] It is only after everyone present has been reassured, that there is time to listen to Paul and Barnabas's recollection of the acts of God worked among the *goyim*.[113]

James then draws a conclusion and gives the final decision regarding the *halakha* for the *goyim*. He notes that God has decided to gather a people for His Name also from the *goyim*,[114] and bases his conclusion on the prophets.[115] Amos had spoken earlier about the restoration of the fallen booth—*sukka*—of David. Here James points to the restoration of the house and the kingship of David.[116] This Messianic restoration of the house of David would take place so that God would be sought from the circle of the nations too. He says that these things have been decided upon by God from the beginning, even before there were prophets who would proclaim them.[117] Therefore *goyim* will be allowed to partake in the realm of the exalted Son of David. God Himself let them enter into it, without a conversion to Judaism.

If the LORD Himself allowed *goyim* to participate as *goyim* in the salvation of the Messiah, who then, says James, will ask more from them? They must be told that the apostles ask nothing more from them than this:

111. *Halakha* (plural: *halakhot*) is derived from the verb *halakh* that means "to walk, to go." In Judaism *halakha* is the designation for the God-required way of obedience to His commands.

112. Acts 15:11.

113. Acts 15:12.

114. Acts 15:14.

115. James herein surely weaves together elements from Amos 9:11–12 and Isa 45:21; the interpretation of the Greek translation of the Tanakh (Septuagint) plays a role too.

116. Amos 9:11–12 even caused some to call the Messiah "son of the one who is fallen." Johannes Jacobus Oosterzee (nineteenth century Dutch theologian) asks himself if the mentioning of the restoration of the booth of David also points to a time in which Israel, after returning to the land, will taste the full blessing of the Messianic reign under the Messiah king (cited in Dächsel, *Bijbelverklaring*, Vol. 5, 715; commentary ad Amos 9:11–16). The opinion that the *sukka* of David is a designation of the eschatological Temple in which the believers from the nations too would be enclosed, can be found in Le Cornu and Shulam, *Jewish Roots of Acts*, 883–884.

117. So Le Cornu and Shulam (Ibid., 834).

In the Camp of Israel: Blessing for the Mishpaḥa of Abraham and the Nations

> ... to abstain from food polluted by idols, from sexual immorality, from the meat of strangled animals and from blood. For the law of Moses has been preached in every city from the earliest times and is read in the synagogues on every Sabbath.[118]

This halachic decision of James is characterized by the core commandments within Judaism that were seen as obligatory for "the foreigners in the land."[119] These consisted of commandments that dealt with the service to the One God,[120] commandments regarding the killing of humans and the killing and eating of animals,[121] and commandments regarding illicit sexual relations.[122] Violation thereof would be followed by the death penalty.[123] James points to precisely the same three subjects.

The way of the *goyim* now becomes a way of *goyim*-in-the-Messiah. He represented Israel, but in that capacity also the nations. By His *avoda* He lived the *kedusha* required from Israel, but at the same time in this way He also fulfilled the commandments applying to the nations. In the Tora of Sinai there were also the commandments deeply enclosed that were meant for all nations. If Israel as a priestly nation has both a more extensive calling and a more specific obedience required from it, then we now see that the Spirit is given so that the nations can also live their own calling in the Messiah.

The *goyim* who received the Spirit of the Messiah are called to live in the power of the Messiah in what had already been, from early times, their own calling and way. The *Ruaḥ HaKodesh* wishes to lead them on a threefold path: a path of dedication to the God of Israel and of breaking with all forms of idolatry; a path of respectful behavior with respect to sexuality and thus, of a loving behavior toward fellow human beings who are God's image bearers; and finally a path of abstention from food in which blood still can be found. Implied there is the command not to kill, but to honor and bless the life of man and animal. These are in fact the areas pointed out in the summary Jesus gave to all of the commandments.[124] Note that these commandments for the *goyim* also form the background of the ethical appeal in the letters of the Scriptures of the New Covenant.[125]

James concludes with the remark—possibly meant to address the fear that Israel's God-given Tora would disappear from view—that everywhere in the cities of the world

---

118. Acts 15:20–21.
119. See chapter 5 (5.3).
120. Lev 17:8–9; 20:2–5; 24:10–16.
121. Lev 24:17–22; 24:18; 17:10–16.
122. Lev 18 and 20.
123. In these three subject areas, Judaism knows of the obligation to remain faithful whatever the cost. A Jew should sacrifice his life rather than sin in these areas. In the first three centuries the Church has also dubbed violations in these areas as "deadly sins."
124. Mark 12:29–31.
125. For this see also Bockmuehl, *Jewish Law in Gentile Churches*. Also see chapter 16 (16.12).

this Tora was taught to Israel.[126] Within the priestly nation, disseminated throughout the world, this instruction will keep its place of permanence, even when a "people"[127] with a somewhat different way of obedience originated. In this way the *goyim* would be able to receive instruction everywhere regarding the character and essence of the way that God pointed out to them: what is commanded to them is indeed a kind of synopsis which asks for further instruction.[128] This further instruction too the *goyim* should receive "out of" Israel and from the Tora given to Israel. Thereby the *goyim* also continue to be permanently dependent on God's revelation in the Scriptures of Israel.

20.9 The Decision of the Apostles: Two Forms of Messianic Obedience

The decision, spread by letter to the newly-formed faith communities among the nations, shows that in the Messiah there are two kinds of an "obedience of faith."[129] These are two kinds of *halakhot*[130] based on the Tora God gave to Israel. And this decision in no way invalidates the Tora. What it means is that there are two peoples in the Messiah: one people from Israel, and one from the *goyim*. Each is addressed in a different manner,[131] and both must live their own calling and walk their own path.[132] Both of them have their own *tora*—meaning instruction[133] with respect to what specific obedience is expected from them.

The traditional canonical narrative—wherein Israel was left with no or little permanent meaning—has always been based on a contradistinction between the mercy of God on the one hand and the law on the other. Consequently, the law as concept and reality, received a less prominent place, and because Israel as nation had been

---

126. Acts 15:21.

127. Cf. Acts 15:14. The Greek word for people (*laos*) is used in 10:2 (see RSV) and 42 for the chosen people of Israel. In the Septuagint, the Greek translation of the Tanakh, *laos* was the usual rendering for "the people" Israel. In the New Testament it is used in various places as designation of the Messianic faith community (par example Acts 18:10 and Titus 2:14; see Strathmann and Meyer, "*laos*," 29–57.

128. See Le Cornu and Shulam, *Jewish Roots of Acts*, 838–39. Some understand this halachic decision to be the mentioning of a minimum-beginning, that later on will be added upon when more instruction will follow. Sometimes the—more or less openly worded—purpose thereof is that *goyim* in the end will observe the whole of the Tora. Thereby however this interpretation joins the way of the men from Judea (Acts 15:1) and of the people in Jerusalem who felt encumbered (15:5). Cf. also chapter 19 (19.4, footnote 18) for other summaries of God's commandments.

129. For this expression see Rom 1:5 and 16:26 (RSV).

130. See above footnote 111 in this chapter.

131. Paul speaks in Gal 2:7 about "the gospel to the uncircumcised" and about "the gospel to the circumcised"(RSV).

132. See 1 Cor 7:21–24. This verse shows that to be circumcised and to be not-circumcised both imply a calling from God.

133. Also see chapter 1, footnote 20.

In the Camp of Israel: Blessing for the Mishpaḥa *of Abraham and the Nations*

removed from the stage, it was only logical that there was no longer a place for Israel's Tora in the lives of the followers of the Messiah.

A consequence of this opinion is that the Tora obedience of Jewish followers of the Messiah was seen as belonging to a transition situation.[134] Later, Jewish followers were denied the right to let the Tora play a role in their life altogether. Jewish life was seen as incompatible with Christ and therefore cursed.[135] The decision of the apostles was understood less and less, and ultimately it was "translated" into the opposite of its intended purpose.[136] The possibility of two kinds of *tora*—two specific forms of God-required obedience in the Messiah—was banned in both theology and praxis. Only an obedience based on Gentile-Christian—*goy-ish*[137]—thinking and praxis was deemed right and possible.

The decision of the council in Jerusalem no longer played a role in the interpretation of the various writings of the New Testament. Sections dealing with elements of Jewish obedience to the Tora were read from this Gentile-Christian perspective.

Therefore there was no longer an understanding that the Jewish Messiah would actually bring Israel to its full and perfected destination in the Messianic time, in the Eighth Day. And also the completion of the calling of the nations—given with their creation—did not receive a place in theological thought. Within this thinking it was as if the *tikkun olam*, the restoration and perfecting of all things, would erase the special character of both Israel and the nations.

20.10 Two Callings: One Royal Priesthood

Yet this question arises: how does this "two-one-ness in the Messiah" relate to the "one-ness in the Messiah" mentioned in various texts? How can words about "fellow citizens with God's people," "members of his household,"[138] "heirs together with Israel," "members together of one body," and "sharers together in the promise in Christ Jesus"[139] be used, when there yet appears to be a specific path of obedience for Jews and *goyim* in the Messiah? What is the meaning of words about the unity in Christ of Jew and Greek, slave and free, man and wife, with respect to this?[140] What does it im-

---

134. It was thought that during this period, in which old thought patterns were still active, the ritual aspect of following Christ as saying would fade away and disappear as a result of further instruction.

135. See the Introduction (I.4, footnote 17).

136. For centuries "the Church," mainly consisting of believers from the nations (that is Gentile Christians), has required and forced Jewish followers of the Messiah to give up their Jewishness and to become equal to the Gentile believers.

137. *Goyish*—here used in a traditional Jewish manner meaning "non-Jewish" and not at all befitting to Judaism.

138. Eph 2:19.

139. Eph 3:6.

140. Gal 3:28–29; Col 3:11; Rom 10:12.

ply that Jew and Gentile in the Messiah have been created to form "one new man?"[141] And even more, can we still speak of a continued specific calling of Israel, when it appears that the words with which Israel was called at Sinai can also be applied to the *goyim* who came to believe in Messiah *Yeshua*?[142] Does this not mean that there is an end to the specific ways and calling of Israel and the nations in the Messiah?

The answer to these questions can only be found when we remain standing in the streambed of the revelation given in the Tanakh. And this answer is enclosed in "the mystery of the Messiah." The Messiah is Israel-in-One. As priestly representative of all Israel, He also is additionally the representative of the *goyim* who are represented by this priestly nation. In His *kedusha* He fulfills the totality of the calling of Israel received at Sinai. In His obedient *avoda* He fulfills all commandments of the Tora, including the *tora* for the nations enclosed in it. In His death He suffers the judgment of the Day of the LORD over Israel and the nations, including the judgment over the hostility between both. In the sacrifice of His life He receives the purification of all iniquity of both Israel and the *goyim*. The enmity between Jew and *goy*, because of God, is taken away. Also through His resurrection from the dead, the Messiah is the firstling of Israel *and* the nations. He therein becomes the beginning of the new creation. In His body, Israel and the nations were present by means of priestly representation. In the body of the Messiah as the first one of the new creation, both of them are connected again to each other in a new unity.[143] In Him—through His resurrection, He is the restored living Temple—there is a new possibility for Jew and *goy* for a holy drawing near to God.[144] In Him, as the beginning of the new creation, these two become one—as "one new man"[145]—in a reconciled relationship with God. Israel's priestly calling is completely realized, and blessing is made available for the nations. *Goyim* may be included—as priests from the nations—participating in the royal priesthood of Israel, as Isaiah already prophesied.[146]

Peter sees the fulfillment of Israel's calling occurring in the Messianic community of believers:

> But you are a chosen people, a royal priesthood, a holy nation, God's special possession, that you may declare the praises of him who called you out of darkness into his wonderful light. Once you were not a people, but now you

---

141. Eph 2:15 (RSV).

142. As par example in Rev 1:5–6.

143. The "body-language" has to do with the bodily reality of the representation in the Messiah. At the same time it is also "creation-language" and thus points to the creation of man in Gen 1–2 and to the new creation.

144. See above in this chapter (20.7). Both are built together into a Temple in the Lord (1 Cor 3:16–17; 2 Cor 6:16; Eph 2:22; cf. John 14:23).

145. As in Gen 1:27, where "man" appears to consist of man and woman; the one man becoming visible in two!

146. Isa 66:21; see chapter 12 (12.14).

are the people of God; once you had not received mercy, but now you have received mercy.[147]

It is possible that here he is yet only addressing a Messianic *Jewish* community.[148] This is certainly not the case when John in the opening words of Revelation says:

> To him who loves us and has freed us from our sins by his blood, and has made us to be a kingdom and priests to serve his God and Father—to him be the glory and power for ever and ever! Amen.[149]

What this suggests is that the Messianic confirmation of Israel's calling does not exclude that possibility that sanctified and called *goyim* may also participate in it. At the same time, it is clear from the whole of the Tanakh that this Messianic fulfillment does not at all imply an exclusion of Israel, or a retraction of the special position of God's *segula*-people.

Indeed we begin to understand the "one-ness of the two" and the "two-ness within unity" when we note the God-ordained structure within the model character of Israel as a priestly nation. The whole nation of Israel received this royal and priestly calling, yet within the people there were God-chosen priests and kings with specific commandments and rules. The perfect fulfillment of Israel's calling by the Messiah confirms Israel's calling and at the same time engages priestly *goyim* in this calling. But just as the whole nation at Sinai could be called a priesthood, even while *kohanim* were among the people, so is it "in the Messiah" too. This model structure of Israel helps us to understand that "in the Messiah" Israel can also maintain the position of the *kohanim*, while the whole Messianic community in a more general sense can be called "a royal priesthood." It also helps us to understand that—analogous to the situation of the priestly nation at Sinai—there can be two kinds of specific rules within the Messianic community.

The creation of the "one new man"[150] in the Messiah does not imply a "return to Adam" accompanied by a "declaration of obsolete-ness" of Israel's special position as a chosen nation. On the contrary, it shows that only in Israel's midst—more specifically: in the Messiah—the nations are redeemed and called to their God-intended status of priests before God.[151] This new creation in the Messiah has "the color of Israel," and is taught by the Messiah in "the camp of Israel." It is this instruction from Zion for which the nations will wish to search.[152] Ultimately the depths of the Tora will be fulfilled

---

147. 1 Pet 2:9–10.

148. 1 Pet 1:1–2 can be interpreted as denoting dispersed Messianic Jewish believers.

149. Rev 1:5–6. In other places in Revelation too reference is made to the words of the calling that sounded at Sinai; see 5:10, 21:3 and 22:5.

150. Eph 2:15 (RSV), "that he might create in himself one new man."

151. See chapter 16 (16.17).

152. Isa 2:1–5.

in the Jerusalem of the *olam haba*.[153] That is the *tikkun olam* the Tora is pointing toward. And it is for this reason that Paul directs the *goyim* in love and service toward Jerusalem.[154]

20.11 Israel, the Tora, and the Nations in the Dawning of the Day of the LORD and the *Olam Haba*: The Letter to the Romans

When the guidance of the Spirit of the Messiah has been received at the council in Jerusalem, we find His emissaries again entering into the world of the nations. In ever-widening circles beginning with Jerusalem, the King of the Jews searches for the nations. Unfailingly the Shepherd of Israel first looks for the sheep of Israel before the *goyim* of new cities and regions hear the message of the nearing of the Day of the LORD and of the dawning of the *olam haba*. It is like a pond, rippling by a stone thrown.

The history of God's love for Israel and all nations goes on. It is His love that conceives of the newly-formed communities of believers. The letters and other writings of the New Covenant originate from this quest of love, with the intention of "presenting a pure virgin to Christ."[155] This is a quest throughout foreign countries for the preparation of a bride. We should remember this when we read and interpret these passages.

The purpose, therefore, is not "pure and theoretical" theological science centering around themes like faith and "law."[156] The meaning centers around Israel and the nations preparing for the Day of the LORD and beginning to live in the sanctification, the *kedusha* of the Messiah, which is the *kedusha* of the *olam haba*. All is on its way toward that future of God. Israel forever remains God's beloved *segula*-people, and the nations are invited to share in the salvation that has begun to break through in Israel's Messiah. They are invited to take their own place in the worship—the *avoda*—of the God of Israel.[157]

The letter to the Romans, meant to give the congregation in Rome insight in the message Paul preached, shows that the gospel is proclaimed against the backdrop of the nearing judgment of the Day of the LORD. Now God's judgment is becoming

---

153. Isa 54:11–14; Rev 21–22.

154. See above in this chapter (20.3, footnote 44 and 45).

155. Paul thus describes his pastoral compassion for the congregation in the Greek harbor city Corinth (2 Cor 11:2).

156. It also is a fact that the letters in the New Testament always have been written for a specific reason and that this context determines the word usage. Identical designations therefore can have differing meanings in different letters.

157. Rom 12:1–2.

In the Camp of Israel: Blessing for the Mishpaḥa of Abraham and the Nations

visible.[158] Heaven[159] itself is wrathful about all iniquity of all people,[160] and nobody must think that he will escape it. Not only does this apply to every *goy*, but equally it applies to every Jew.[161] God will judge according to works.[162] *Goyim* will be judged according to what they have known, taught others, and done themselves.[163] And this is the case with Jews too. Israel dispersed among the nations has the Tora, God's instruction. But the question will be: did it also live what the Tora asks of God's people? Israel can not hide itself behind the Tora or the sign of the covenant.[164] Whoever has the Tora but does not live it, is deemed guilty by this Word of God.

Just as John the Baptist called all Israel to return to God, Paul shows from the Tanakh that Israel is ready for punishment. Together with the *goyim*, even God's own people are in danger from the nearing judgment.[165]

But there is more to be said: God has revealed[166] a new way to receive the righteousness of God for Israel and the nations, as the Tora and the prophets have spoken.[167] A way by which Israel and the nations can become righteous ones in the eyes of God—*tzaddikim*.[168] For all trespassers, namely Israel and the *goyim*, God has given a means of atonement: the Messiah.[169] Because of their belief in the God-wrought redemption in Messiah Jesus, God will declare Jews and *goyim* righteous. In the death of the Messiah God's righteousness punishes the sins of Israel and the nations. Whoever believes this good message, will be declared righteous by grace—"for free"[170]—and may live in peace with God.[171]

Let nobody think, however, that the Tora is thereby invalidated.[172] It is this very Tora that shows Abraham, at the time still uncircumcised,[173] declared a *tzaddik* by God because of his trust in God. His faith was credited to him as righteousness.[174]

---

158. Rom 1:18.

159. "Heaven" is a Jewish way of alluding to God. Cf. "kingdom of heaven" (Matt 4:17) and "kingdom of God" (Luke 4:43).

160. Rom 2:1.

161. In these chapters of Romans we observe how in Paul's thinking about the world too the distinction between Israel and the nations forms the structuring principle. See chapter 3 (3.4).

162. Rom 2:6.

163. Rom 2:1–3.

164. Rom 2:17–29.

165. Rom 3:9–20.

166. Rom 3:21.

167. Rom 3:21.

168. Rom 3:22.

169. Rom 3:23–26.

170. Rom 3:24.

171. Rom 5:1; 8:1.

172. Rom 3:31.

173. Rom 4:9–10.

174. Rom 4:3.

Abraham and his offspring only later received the gifts of the covenant, circumcision and the Tora.[175] No one in Israel can enter the nearing judgment on the basis of his own obedience to the Tora. Just as Abraham trusted God's promises, now everything also hinges on believing and trusting in God's action in the death and resurrection of the Messiah. In this there is no difference between Israel and the *goyim*.

In this present age, through the Messiah there is peace and atonement, hope in tribulations, and a certainty of salvation even when the wrath of God will fully come.[176] In the overlap between this time and God's future, even now the Holy Spirit fills people with the love of God,[177] ensuring them of the fact that they both are and will be redeemed unto obedience.[178]

For indeed it is also about obedience in the Messiah.[179] In the Messiah and by the indwelling of God's Spirit, the eschatological son-ship of the *olam haba* has indeed begun and is made available for all of Israel and the nations who have been declared righteous by God.[180] The obedience of the Messiah, which belongs to and is part of the *olam haba*, will characterize the life of His brothers[181] from Israel and the *goyim* in every respect.[182] Through their obedience He will accomplish within them "the righteous requirement of the law."[183] Each in their own way, Jew and *goy* will live in obedience according to the Spirit.[184]

Because of this the path of His followers is just like that of the Messiah Himself: a path through tribulations while the first gift of the *olam haba* has been received.[185] Sons from Israel and the nations walk together along with the Messiah as if through the pains of childbirth.[186] They await the day that this eschatological son-ship is a full reality, visible to everyone.[187] On their way they participate in the suffering of the Messiah and in the groaning of the Spirit,[188] sharing also in the Messiah's grief and

---

175. Cf. Rom 4:13 and chapter 3 (3.2).
176. Rom 5:1–11.
177. Rom 5:5.
178. Rom 6–8.
179. Cf. Rom 6:15–23.
180. Rom 8:14–15.
181. Rom 8:29.
182. Rom 8:1–17.
183. Rom 8:3–4.

184. In the congregation in Rome the emphasis lies upon the unity of Jews and *goyim*. In Rom 13:8–10 it is therefore the second table of the law, which binds both communities together, that has a central position and is valued as a summary and fulfillment of the Tora.

185. Rom 8:23; cf. Eph 1:13–14.
186. Rom 8:22.
187. Rom 8:23.
188. Rom 8:17, 23, 26, 34.

In the Camp of Israel: Blessing for the Mishpaḥa *of Abraham and the Nations*

longing for the whole of Israel.[189] For indeed the *olam haba* will not and cannot come without "all Israel."[190]

In the letter to the Romans there is no contradistinction between grace and Tora.[191] The contradistinction which is there, is the one between trusting the obedience of the Messiah and trusting the own obedience of Jew or *goy*.[192] Also the question of the need for circumcision, and thus of a formal and ritual transition to Judaism—the reason for the meeting in Jerusalem of Acts 15—, only indirectly plays an role.[193] We encounter a totally different situation in the letter to the Galatians.

20.12 "The Works of the Law": The Letter to the Galatians

The traditional rendering of the canonical narrative caused the interpretation of the letter to the Galatians to suffer the same fate as the decision of Acts 15. Although this decision of the Spirit and the apostles left room for two distinct forms of Messianic obedience, Christian theology and praxis very soon declared the Jewish Messianic *halakha* to be an impassable and forbidden way for Jews-in-the-Messiah. The interpretation of Galatians has also been distorted by this same perspective.

Also in the congregations in Galatia[194] the problem existed that previously had been the reason for the council in Jerusalem. *Goyim*, those converted to the God of Israel and His Messiah, were confused by a specific message from Jewish preachers. This message could be summarized as the importance for believing *goyim* to be circumcised, also implying this as just a first step.[195] Paul, however, opposed this preaching that asked necessary "works of the law" from *goyim*.[196]

The calling of *goyim* to walk their own way in the Messiah was declared impossible by this preaching.[197] According to these preachers within the Galatian congregations, there was no place for a distinct Messianic *halakha* for *goyim*. They proclaimed that God also asked the same obedience from the *goyim* as from Israel. This brought great unrest.

First of all this negated the fact that *goyim* had been represented in the Messiah as simply themselves, receiving the Spirit in an unconditional way as *goyim*.[198] But that wasn't all. To the believing Galatians this preaching focused again on the impor-

---

189. Cf. Rom 9:1–2. For this see also in this chapter paragraph 20.17
190. Rom 11:26.
191. Rom 7:12.
192. Rom 9:30–10:3.
193. For Rom 14–15 and the discussion about the weak and the strong, see paragraph 20.14.
194. Gal 1:2.
195. Gal 5:2–3; 6:12–13; cf. 2:3–5.
196. Gal 3:2–5.
197. 1 Cor 7:17–20.
198. Gal 3:2; cf. Acts 11:16–17.

Part II : The Canonical Narrative: The Scriptures of the New Covenant

tance of "works," which had held such weight in the gentile religious environment in which they grew up.[199] Although in this case they would be "works of the law," works derived from the Tora of Israel, this would deter the *goyim* from trusting the substitutionary obedience of the Messiah. In this manner, however, they would stand unprotected in the judgment of the Day of the LORD. They would even live under a curse.[200] For them, just as for Israel, no shelter was to be found in one's own *kedusha* and in one's own obedience.[201]

Paul has to again remind the Galatians of the fact that the Scriptures show that Abraham too was declared righteous on the basis of his faithful trust.[202] The blessing promised to Abraham will be received in the same manner: through the way of faithful trust in God.[203]

In the traditional canonical narrative, Galatians has been a sort of key witness in a trial against Israel as a whole, and the Tora in particular. A trial in which the verdict was clear from the start. From this perspective, Israel no longer held a special calling or mandate. Within this thinking, the unity through baptism and the "clothing" of oneself 'with Christ'[204] is interpreted as a unity that replaces Israel's calling with a universal "son-ship of God," no longer leaving a place of distinction and particular prerogatives for Israel.[205] This stands in clear contrast with what Paul himself says in other places within Scripture.[206]

20.13 "Ready to Disappear": The Letter to the Hebrews

While the quest of the Messiah and His emissaries for Israel and the nations continued in the diaspora, it is possible that the daily worship (liturgy) in the Temple in Jerusalem still took place and daily sacrifices were offered.[207] At the same time, Messianic-Jewish

---

199. In this interpretation from the gentile background of the letter to the Galatians "works of the law" gets the ring of "exerting efforts (as you were used to perform for your gods, but which you now want to perform) for God (based on the Tora)," so Van Bruggen, *Paulus*, 202–5.

200. Gal 3:10.

201. Gal 3:11.

202. Gal 3:6.

203. Gal 3:14.

204. Gal 3:26–29; verse 27 uses the metaphor of clothing oneself with the Messiah; cf. Rom 13:14. Jewish tradition knows of "the garments of the Messiah" and "the garments of God." The wise of Israel described God's way through the history of salvation as "God clothing himself with various garments." From creation until the victory over evil the Holy One successively clothes himself with seven garments, "the garments of salvation" (Shulam and Le Cornu, *Jewish Roots of Romans*, 447); also see Le Cornu and Shulam, *Jewish Roots of Acts*, 486–87.

205. In this interpretation "the Israel of God" in Gal 6:16 can not designate the people of Israel.

206. Rom 9:4–5 mentions a series of prerogatives still belonging to Israel. Amongst them the giving of the Law.

207. Heb 8:3–5 and 13:10 could be named as arguments for this possibility.

In the Camp of Israel: Blessing for the Mishpaḥa of Abraham and the Nations

believers were under pressure to give up their faith in the Messiah.[208] It is in this context that the letter to the Hebrews has been written.

In Hebrews the central question is whether *Yeshua*/Jesus is the promised Messiah, the bringer of the New Covenant and the starting point for the *olam haba*. This is a question asked within a Jewish context. Messianic-Jewish believers, belonging to the covenant people, asked themselves if they had made the right choice and were walking on the right path. Yet they and their opponents are still standing in the streambed of the Tanakh. When we interpret this letter from this same perspective, we begin to understand that this letter is not about a contradistinction between Judaism and Christianity. The discussion is about the Messiah: is He the reality foreseen and foretold by the Tanakh? In various ways the writer affirms this and makes his position clear by contending that the New Covenant has been mediated by the service of the Messiah, a service higher than that of an Aaronic priest. And yes, since the dawning of the *olam haba*, there surely is a change of Tora with respect to the Temple service, as was also expected in other Jewish circles.

However, what is not being discussed is the election and special calling of Israel. The writer possibly recalls words about the destruction of the Temple, while looking forward to a quickly-arriving beginning of the unshakable Kingdom.[209] Both elements may be present in the verse:

> By calling this covenant "new," he has made the first one obsolete; and what is obsolete and outdated will soon disappear.[210]

The interpretation is stretched too far when these words are read with the implication that from now on the focus is on heaven, whereby the true religion is freed from external, national, and racial limits.[211] The gift of the New Covenant still is in the first place the gift of the Bridegroom of Israel.[212] It is still about belief in and an avowal of the revealed *kedusha* and *avoda* of the Messiah to be the *kedusha* whereby the sins under the Sinai covenant have been atoned,[213] making the eschatological nearing to the Throne of God possible.[214] It is a question of being faithful in the expectation of the

---

208. Par example see Heb 3:6–19; 4:11; 6:9–12; 10:19–39; 12:1–17.

209. Heb 12:28.

210. Heb 8:13.

211. So Bruce, *Hebrews*. When dealing with the quote from Jer 31 he remarks that the reality of the New Covenant implied that "national origin and racial descent must also be included among those externalities from whose control true religion is released by the new covenant" (Ibid., 178). He cites with approval H.L. Ellison, who postulates that God does not dispense with physical Israel, but "in saving it transcends it" (Ibid., 179). In this manner, and by all contradistinctions that Bruce creates, the abiding position and meaning of the people Israel within the New Covenant is undermined.

212. It is even possible to observe in Jer 31:32 reference to a marital relation, so *JSB*. NIV renders: "though I was a husband to them." So also Bruce, *Hebrews*, 176, footnote 63.

213. Heb 9:15.

214. Heb 10:19–22.

Redeemer coming soon.²¹⁵ Followers of the Messiah from Israel are exhorted to stay on the path of their conviction that Jesus is the Messiah.

Questions regarding the abiding obedience to specific commandments of the Tora hardly play a role in this letter.²¹⁶ Jewish faithfulness to God's commandments was indeed presupposition and played no role in the discussion; it simply belonged to the life of the Messianic firstlings of Israel.

20.14 Reading from within a Different Paradigm: Circumcision, Food and Celebration

For centuries the Christian reading of the New Testament has been determined by the conviction that there was no longer an abiding place for Israel within the universally-oriented salvation of the Messiah. Texts about circumcision, food, and feasts were interpreted from within this paradigm. While a different way of reading these texts is possible, an interpretation was chosen that befitted this paradigm. When the starting point for the interpretation is that God's choice for and His promises about His people have not changed, the text is illuminated in a new way. Therefore he who wishes to remain standing in the streambed of the Tanakh must learn to read old texts with new eyes.²¹⁷

Then it can be understood (and even expected) that the Messiah, as the Firstling of God's people, does not wish an end to Israel but rather that He wishes to secure the whole of Israel in its own calling. As priestly nation Israel was distinct from the other nations. Circumcision, dietary laws, and God's feasts played an important role, and also meant to serve the separation of this nation.²¹⁸

We can clearly see from the New Testament that these commandments did not stand by themselves, but were related to the coming of the Messiah and the times of restoration.²¹⁹ They can be called "shadows" of the reality to come.²²⁰ This clarified that external obedience was not the intention, as already could be known on the basis of the Tanakh alone.²²¹

215. Heb 10:37–38.

216. Heb 13:9 mentions in a very general sense "foods" (so RSV; the rendering of NIV, "ceremonial foods," is more interpretative). It is not exactly clear what is thought of. Has it do with Jewish dietary laws, is it about food that has been offered to idols or about a gnostic mix of several elements? It is clear that God's mercy should be the surety for the heart of man.

217. The growing attention and appreciation for, and study of Judaism contribute to this process. Also the developing Messianic-Jewish movement and theology show that a different reading of the texts is possible. For this paragraph I gratefully used the insights of the Messianic-Jewish theologian Mark S. Kinzer (in his book mentioned earlier).

218. Gen 17:9–13; Exod 31:12–17; Ezek 20:12; Lev 23:44; cf. chapter 9 (9.4).

219. Heb 9:10.

220. Col 2:17. RSV renders "only a shadow," by adding "only" it is clear that in the RSV interpretation there is no room left any longer for an abiding place of these "shadows."

221. Rom 2:28–29.

In the Camp of Israel: Blessing for the Mishpaḥa of Abraham and the Nations

With respect to circumcision, a circumcision of heart was meant; Moses and Jeremiah had both spoken of this earlier.[222] Therefore Paul could say too that the ultimate question is whether someone is a new creation.[223] Nowhere, however, does Paul draw the conclusion that Israel's special election and its covenantal sign has been nullified.[224] Viewed from this angle, circumcision is a prerogative,[225] and it was therefore that Paul circumcised Timothy.[226] In Jerusalem this question is explicitly posed to Paul: did the circumcision command still have a place in his message? Paul honors this request and shows the whole Jewish community that the distinction of the covenant people by circumcision did have a place in his message.[227] The sign in the flesh is for Israel, but at the same time this sign refers to the reality of the inclusion in the death and resurrection of the Messiah, which has become available for both Israel and the nations.[228] Just as the *kohanim* had a token function within the people, the circumcised Israel has "in the Messiah" a similar function for the believers from the nations within the Body of the Messiah.

It is only within a narrative scheme, in which God does *not* wish to let His people exist as His *segula*-people, and in which He *no longer* has need for it in His plans, and whereby He will *retract* His prior promises (even giving them a different interpretation), that it is understandable that God would allow His people to lose their identity within the multitude of the nations. When such a narrative scheme stands in full conflict with the real canonical narrative of the Tanakh and *Yeshua*'s place in it, however, as postulated in this book, then we may assume that God still wants Israel to remain distinct from the nations.

In this context the dietary laws must also be addressed. In Mark's gospel we find a section which reports on a teaching of *Yeshua* with respect to food. Here it is clear that He asks obedience to what God has commanded and that He does not tolerate human tradition that undermines God's command. The implication that this underlining of God's commandments would also apply to the dietary laws, appears however to be undermined by these words: "In saying this, Jesus declared all foods clean."[229] Is not this verse then showing that Jesus declares all dietary laws—and not just human tradition relating to it—to be obsolete? A superficial reading of the text could lead to this thought, but a different explanation, reassuring for *goyim*, is also possible.[230]

---

222. Rom 2:29; Deut 30:6; Jer 4:4.

223. Gal 6:15.

224. Rom 9:4–5 speaks of prerogatives that remain, not of prerogatives that have been declared obsolete. Cf. Rom 11:29.

225. Cf. also Phil 3:5 where Paul sums up such prerogatives.

226. Acts 16:3. Titus however was not circumcised (Gal 2:3)!

227. Acts 21:20–26; we find the explicit question regarding circumcision in verse 21.

228. Col 2:11–14.

229. Mark 7:19.

230. I follow Kinzer, *Postmissionary Messianic Judaism*, 52–58 in his interpretation of this section.

Part II : The Canonical Narrative: The Scriptures of the New Covenant

Believing *goyim* (Mark's gospel is addressed to them) hear that they do not become impure when they eat what Jews are not allowed to eat. The source of impurity does not lie in the food itself. Unclean food is this solely by the fact that God has declared it forbidden to Israel. When a Jew would eat it anyway, his disobedience would make him unclean. The source of impurity therefore doesn't lie in the food, but in the heart of one who eats such forbidden food.[231] When God does not limit *goyim* with respect to food, He thereby does not condemn them to a life of objective impurity.[232] They are called to live in the freedom God gives them.

Something similar applies to the feasts of God, with the *Shabbat* heading the list.[233] We see that the feasts too were (and still are) reminders of the expected and realized appearance of the Messiah.[234] Believing *goyim* must know that their being "in Christ" lets them share in that reality of the Messiah. The token character of the feasts is confirmed by Paul without the feasts themselves being a point of discussion within the Jewish Messianic *halakha*. What we do see however, is that Messianic *goyim* must not let themselves to be unsecured by the various themes related to the celebration of God's feasts.[235] Again we observe the teaching that their being-included-in-Christ means the certitude of their salvation. The adding of conversion conditions, this time related to the feasts, draws the trust of the believing *goyim* away from the Messiah.[236] It is of this that Paul warns them.

At the same time we observe Paul celebrating the feasts of God and honoring the *Shabbat*.[237] Here too it shows that "the reality," the deepest meaning and fulfillment, of the feasts is to be found in the Messiah, and refers to the salvation in which the nations may also participate. At the same time, because of the token character of the life of Israel, it is also that "in the Messiah" the celebration of the feasts by Israel has an abiding place. If the Messiah Himself is indeed the fulfillment of the feasts of God,

---

231. Kinzer (Ibid., 55, footnote 11) finds—referring to the Dutch scholar Peter Tomson who elaborates on this point in *Paul*, 247–49)—in Jewish tradition an answer to the question if unclean foods were unclean in themselves or if they only were so because of the LORD God's command. *Goyim* could have the feeling to be condemned to a second rate purity. They now however hear that foods are not unclean in themselves, but only because of the command of the LORD. When He permits *goyim* to eat such foods, He does not put uncleanness in their mouth.

232. Kinzer (Ibid., 55, footnote 11) also interprets Romans 14:1—15:1 against this background. The weak think that foods are in themselves unclean and cannot be eaten (not even by *goyim*). An identical background would play a role in the observance of special days.

233. Lev 23 opens with the mentioning of the *Shabbat* (verses 1–3).

234. Col 2:17.

235. Col 2:16.

236. Col 2:19. Further see chapter 23 (23.10) for a limited discussion of questions that are at the table related to the theme of co-celebrating with Israel.

237. Paul wishes to celebrate *Shavuot* in Jerusalem (Acts 20:16) and always goes to synagogues and places of prayer on *Shabbat* (and this certainly not only out of missionary motives). See par example Acts 13:14; 16:13; 17:2–3; 18:4; 19:8.

In the Camp of Israel: Blessing for the Mishpaḥa *of Abraham and the Nations*

how could it be otherwise? How could He turn His back on the streambed in which God has acted?

Even the gathering of believing *goyim* and firstlings of Israel on "the first day"[238] has in itself a Jewish character. The Jewish designation clearly implies that believing *goyim* are included in the world of Israel's celebrations and remembrance days. Gathering together on the first day is a recognition of God's new salvation acts, as that was the case on the days of *Purim* and *Ḥanukkah*. Those feasts were also not commanded at Sinai, but came forth from the experience of new salvific acts of God.[239] The fact that during history this "first day" has become a purely Christian day and has replaced the *Shabbat*, tells more about the spirit that has been active for centuries than that it tells us about the remembrance and celebration of this Jewish day as such.[240] In the beginning, anchored in the Jewish calendar, on this day the salvation that God had accomplished in Israel's midst by the resurrection of the Messiah was celebrated.

20.15 Israel's Calling in the Messiah Shared by the Nations: Branches on the Olive Tree

In a variety of ways the Scriptures of the New Covenant show that Messiah *Yeshua* fulfills Israel's calling as the First One, and that He thereby enables the fulfillment of this calling for all Israel. God chooses no other priestly people. Israel remains called, intended to be God's kingdom of priests. The new thing, however, is that God adds *goyim* to this priesthood of Israel.[241] *Goyim* too become redeemed and are called to be priests for the God of Israel.[242]

Goyim are added to Israel, but they do not replace Israel. In the letter to the Romans Paul uses the metaphor of wild olive branches being grafted on the "cultivated" olive tree.[243] This emissary of *Yeshua* wants to thereby make it clear to the believing *goyim* that they have no reason to be proud of their own obedience of faith. He warns them about pride over Israel.[244] The metaphor of the grafting of wild olive branches *between* the natural branches, shows the believing *goyim* that their participation in the salvation is a result of God's active intervention. It is God who has grafted them into the cultivated olive tree;[245] it is the root that carries these wild branches and not

---

238. Acts 20:7. The designation "first day" is the Jewish designation for Sunday.

239. For *Purim* see Esther 9:18–32. *Ḥannuka*—the feast of the consecration of the Temple (164 BCE) after prior desecration by Antioch IV Epiphanes—is mentioned in John 10:22.

240. The Sunday law, issued during the reign of Constantine the Great, was related in many respects to the growing anti-Jewish sentiment at that time and the growth and development of the Christian church and theology.

241. Cf. Isa 66:21. See chapter 12 (12.14).

242. See in this chapter paragraph 20.10.

243. Rom 11:17–24.

244. Rom 11:20.

245. Cf. Rom 11:23.

the other way around.²⁴⁶ Wild branches receive life from the root, they do not have it within themselves.²⁴⁷ If necessary, they can be broken off.²⁴⁸

From the very beginning the seduction of a prideful self-made wisdom is a temptation, luring *goyim* to conclude that God's dealings with Israel have ended.²⁴⁹ Even as they partake in the salvation of the God of Israel, Roman *goyim* must be warned to not become enemies of God's people. Even though they might suffer hatred and persecution from the side of the Jewish community in Rome, they are not more than their Master and are to dedicate themselves as sacrifice to God.²⁵⁰ They are urgently admonished not to live in pride toward Him who has the power "over the clay."²⁵¹ God's dealings with Israel must bring them to a humble acknowledgment of His wisdom and to worship His greatness.²⁵²

This warning of Paul was a necessary one, but we later see that it has not been heeded. The necessity of a book like this shows that the pride of the nations has made itself at home in the community of believers, and for centuries has determined the interpretation of Scripture and the thought and lives of believers from the nations.

20.16 Resistance of a Part of Israel: Blindness and Deepening of the *Galut*

Only part of Israel believed the message about the Messiah in relation to the Day of the LORD, the beginning of the *olam haba*, and God's merciful inclusion of the *goyim*. This message about the gift of salvation to the nations certainly also caused much opposition.²⁵³ In his body Paul experienced persecution from the side of his own flesh and blood,²⁵⁴ like *Yeshua* had foresaid.²⁵⁵ This resistance against the Anointed One of God is characterized in the manner of the prophets, with its deepest origins put into words.²⁵⁶ This sharp language, however, is in no way related to anti-Semitism. It is

---

246. Rom 11:18.
247. Rom 11:17.
248. Rom 11:21–22.
249. Rom 11:25.
250. Rom 12:1–2 (and verses 9–12) are the concrete summary of the life (by the Spirit) of the Messiah as put into words in Rom 8 and 9:1–3.
251. Rom 9:20–21.
252. Rom 11:33–36.
253. Paul tells about it in Acts 22:21–23. 1 Thess 2:14 also shows that the preaching to the nations was a source of nuisance and anger.
254. 1 Thess 2:15; Acts 9:23; 13:45; 14:2; 18:12 and the description of the process of his arrest and trial in Acts 21–26.
255. Luke 21:12; John 16:1–2.
256. 1 Thess 2:15; Rev 2:9; 3:9 (for "synagogue of Satan" cf. John 8:44).

In the Camp of Israel: Blessing for the Mishpaḥa *of Abraham and the Nations*

the language that, like the prophets before, sounds out the depth of the resistance. It is language that gives utterance to the heart of God as the heart of a rejected lover.[257]

Even in this resistance, Divine judgment takes place,[258] analogous to the speaking in parables of *Yeshua*.[259] It is there that unsearchable ways of God are revealed,[260] ways in which He blesses the faith of part of Israel and reaches the nations by the resistance of the other part of Israel. Through the exile of the King of the Jews and the firstlings of His people, word of Him goes out into all the world.[261] His intention, however, is ultimately to return to Zion after the entry of the fullness of the nations, and to fulfill His purposes for all Israel.[262]

The exile, the *galut*, of Israel is deepening in this nearing of the Day of the LORD. Ultimately Jerusalem will be destroyed and be laid waste. The word about the wrath coming "unto the end"[263] does not imply a rejection of Israel, but speaks about the measure of this judgment. All of this still takes place within the streambed of God's revelation in the Tanakh, with the Messiah appearing within God's unfolded intentions. Within this streambed the word applies:

> for God's gifts and his call are irrevocable.[264]

Therefore God continues his purposes with Israel's election. He will never allow the whole of Israel to resist Himself. In the times of Elijah God found a faithful rest. In the era of the letter to the Romans, He found a part of the people on the side of the Messiah.[265] And even the resistance of another part of the people exists within His sovereignty, for in His judgment they are blinded, as in the times of Isaiah.[266]

---

257. Cf. chapter 11 (11.4).
258. Rom 11:7–10; cf. Acts 28:24–27.
259. See par example Matt 13:10–17.
260. Rom 11:33.
261. Rom 10:18; 11:11.
262. Rom 11:26–27.
263. The Greek text has "*eis telos*" (literally: unto the goal/end). KJV interprets these words as speaking of the measure of the judgment ("the wrath has come upon them to the uttermost"). NIV and RSV give a temporal interpretation ("at last"). The influential Dutch Statenvertaling (seventeenth century) and the widely used Dutch translation of 1951 render "tot het einde" (till the end) which would be misinterpreted when thought to imply a final judgment dealing of God with Israel, as is the opinion held by the seventeenth century Annotations to the Dutch Statenvertaling.
264. Rom 11:29.
265. Rom 11:2–5.
266. Rom 11:8.

It is with a deep sorrow and with deep humility that Paul describes these ways of God.[267] Yet he is deeply convinced that God's Word has not failed,[268] certain that there is no trace of untrustworthiness and injustice in God.[269]

Finally, it is important to note that the words, whereby the Scriptures of the New Testament designate the unbelief of part of Israel, have been spoken in a specific historical context. Therefore they should not be interpreted in a generalized way apart from that context.[270] This applies in the same way to the announcements of judgment by Isaiah. Although this prophet announced the judgment by the hand of Ashur/Assyria,[271] Assyria did not receive freedom to act as it wanted.[272] The God of Israel indeed calls Israel His *segula*-people and the apple of His eye and stays faithful to this name. The resistance of part of the people in a specific period against the Messiah of God takes place in that same streambed of the Tanakh. Therefore the judgmental words in the New Testament about part of Israel should be read out of the longings and sorrow of God, just as *Yeshua,* and Paul too, make this visible.[273]

20.17 The Love of God and Hosea: Underway Toward the Jerusalem-Kingship

In the "Israel chapters" of his letter to the Romans, Paul quotes the prophet Hosea.[274] Hosea particularly speaks of the Holy One of Israel as both judge and lover, and how He keeps loving even when He has to send judgment. If God's mercy gifts and calling do not change, than how much less does He Himself change.[275] When we remain persevering, living and reading within the streambed of the Tanakh, we must open our eyes to God's unrelinquishing love for Israel in good days and evil days.

We must confess that *He* is the God who, just like Hosea, continues to love His own wife, although this sometimes can be, literally or figuratively, "from a distance." On God's command, for a time Hosea too had to love his wife from a distance. She needs to be accustomed to his love:

---

267. Rom 9:1–3.

268. Rom 9:6. The Greek verb literally means "to fall off/from." God's word has not fallen (away), thus not "failed" (NIV and RSV).

269. Rom 9:14.

270. Also see Part III of this book.

271. Par example see Isa 8:5–10.

272. Isa 10:5–19 shows that Ashur behaves haughtily while executing this judgment, and therefore will be judged itself. Zech 1:12–17 shows that God will punish the nations who, full of pride, did evil against Israel, whilst God Himself was "only a little angry" (verse 15).

273. See Luke 19:41–44 and Rom 9:1–2.

274. Rom 9:25–26.

275. Rom 11:29; cf. Ps 102:27; Isa 43:10, 13; 48:12.

In the Camp of Israel: Blessing for the Mishpaḥa *of Abraham and the Nations*

> Then I told her, "You are to live with me many days; you must not be a prostitute or be intimate with any man, and I will behave the same way toward you." For the Israelites will live many days without king or prince, without sacrifice or sacred stones, without ephod or household gods. Afterward the Israelites will return and seek the LORD their God and David their king. They will come trembling to the LORD and to his blessings in the last days.[276]

Of course these words began to be fulfilled in the period following the Babylonian exile. But this was only a small beginning. The prophecy reaches altogether to the eschatological appearance of the Messiah and thus draws the lines toward the *olam haba*. Therefore it is fully in line with the Tanakh to see this Hosea-love of God continuing forever. The "wife" of God is His "wife," even when there should be love "from a distance." Based on the Tanakh, there is every reason to count on the loving and wise dealings of God with (the history of) the whole of His people through the ages.

Moreover the kingship of Messiah *Yeshua* is like the "Hebron-kingship," as He is on His way toward the "Jerusalem-kingship." Both His exaltation to the Throne and His simultaneous exile, as viewed from Jerusalem, will ultimately come together in His kingship in Jerusalem. Then He will be king over Israel in the midst of the earth, and reign together with His kingdom of priests over the earth and cosmos. On His way to this goal He is connected to the whole of His people in the "not-yet" of His Jerusalem-kingship. He prepares the whole of His people for an eternal covenant in love.[277] He watches over His people with this goal in mind. While on His way He still endures tribulations, shared by those who are joined with Him.[278]

20.18 The King of the Jews Leads the Nations into Service and Pilgrimage

In the Scriptures of the New Covenant, we see how the apostles as the first emissaries of the Messiah, and how the communities of firstlings from Israel and the nations, later become involved in the "discipling" of all nations. We also observe, however, that the believing *goyim* become oriented toward Jerusalem and God's people Israel.

In the various journeys of Paul, from the diaspora back to Jerusalem, we find a prophetic beginning modeling an attitude of blessing from the side of the nations toward Israel. We see how believing *goyim* join the Jewish *Shaul*[279] and bring gifts with them for the community of firstlings of Israel in Jerusalem.[280] This then fulfills what

---

276. Hos 3:3–5.
277. Hos 2:19–20.
278. Col 1:24.
279. Paul's Hebrew name, used in Acts 7–13; from Acts 13:9 onwards the name Paul is used. In this chapter see footnote 41.
280. Rom 15:25–28; cf. also Acts 11:29–30.

the prophets have foretold: *Goyim* go with a Jewish man.²⁸¹ They have become disciples of the First One of Israel.²⁸² They learn about service to God, intended to make all Israel jealous.²⁸³ In these firstlings from the *goyim*, the nations begin to understand and fulfill their calling toward God's people. They have been blessed from Zion and partake in the blessing of Israel.²⁸⁴ In their care and love for the firstling-community, they bless the whole of Israel. Through this service they contribute to the restoration of God's people, although in the limited manner of a prophetic sign.²⁸⁵

In their turning toward Zion it becomes clear that ultimately the Messiah, the First One, will also return there with all Israel. And at the deepest level the nations will join in this return home, co-travelling and serving Him, as they enter God's city and future.²⁸⁶ In Zion they will celebrate the feasts of God.²⁸⁷ From the desert of this world they will turn themselves to Zion and the Messianic Eighth Day. On this way they too suffer with Israel and the King of the Jews. In them the Spirit groans for the rest of the *olam haba*.²⁸⁸ Their ascent to Zion with the Messiah is caused by and an expression of the longing of the *Shekhina* for Zion.

20.19 Together Abraham's *Mishpaḥa* and the *Mishpaḥot* of the Nations Grasp the Great Love of the Messiah

The nations are blessed by the service of the eternally elected Israel. This becomes visible when the twelve apostles, as prophetic token of the whole of Israel, are sent into the world of nations. The nations serve and bless Israel and become priests for the Most High God together with Israel. This also becomes visible as a prophetic sign when a little band of *goyim* travels to Jerusalem together with Jewish brethren and the gifts from the nations. The *kedusha* out of Zion, from the camp of Israel, has begun to bless the world and the world begins to walk before God in this *kedusha*. The Name of the LORD of Hosts is praised from the East to the West.²⁸⁹

Paul sees how God confirms each *mishpaḥa*, every "family" called to existence by Him,²⁹⁰ in its own calling and grants them the gift of the Indwelling of the Spirit of the Messiah.

281. Zech 8:23.
282. Matt 28:19; Isa 2:3.
283. Rom 11:11.
284. Rom 15:27.
285. Acts 11:29–30; Rom 15:25–26; 1 Cor 16:1–4.
286. Ps 87; Rev 21:24.
287. Acts 20 and 21 show how Paul's travel company of Jews and *goyim* is heading for Jerusalem in order to co-celebrate *Shavuot* there.
288. Rom 8:26–30.
289. Mal 1:11; Ps 113:3.
290. The word *patria* that Paul uses is used as the rendering of the Hebrew *mishpaḥa* in the Greek translation of the Tanakh (the Septuagint). These words show that God has thought of and created

In the Camp of Israel: Blessing for the Mishpaḥa of Abraham and the Nations

> For this reason I kneel before the Father, from whom every family in heaven and on earth derives its name. I pray that out of his glorious riches he may strengthen you with power through his Spirit in your inner being, so that Christ may dwell in your hearts through faith. And I pray that you, being rooted and established in love, may have power, together with all the Lord's holy people, to grasp how wide and long and high and deep is the love of Christ, and to know this love that surpasses knowledge—that you may be filled to the measure of all the fullness of God.[291]

He also describes how all saints,[292] the *mishpaḥa* of Abraham together with the *mishpaḥot* of the nations, have been gathered *and* must be joined in a love that belongs to the *olam haba*. And he makes clear how they need each other in order to grasp the unsearchable love of the Messiah, even if their understanding is incomplete. By this they will grow toward receiving the fullness of God's salvation and Presence.

By sharing in the salvation from Zion, the Messiah brings blessings into the world of the nations. By these blessings Israel also will be enriched in turn, being blessed with an ever-increasing knowledge of the all-surpassing love of the God of Abraham, Isaac, and Jacob. An eschatological and mutual *learning* begins to take place. The blessing of Abraham multiplies itself as it moves toward the *olam haba*. The end, the theme of the next chapter, will be much more than the beginning.

> Now to him who is able to do immeasurably more than all we ask or imagine, according to his power that is at work within us, to him be glory in the church and in Christ Jesus throughout all generations, for ever and ever! Amen.[293]

---

various "families" on earth (and even in heaven: of angels?).

291. Eph 3:14–19.
292. This designation here point to the sanctified believers from Israel and the nations.
293. Eph 3:20–21.

CHAPTER 21

The Camp of Israel

Waiting for the Return of the Shekhina—*Israel and the Nations Advancing Toward the* Tikkun Olam

21.1 One Continuing Story

THIS CHAPTER WILL BRING the description of the canonical narrative of the Tanakh and the Scriptures of the New Covenant to an end. The coming of Messiah *Yeshua* and the message proclaimed in His command to Israel and the nations are rooted in the streambed of the Tanakh, taking place within it, and also are in every respect related to it. What has been written about the Tanakh's expectation of the *tikkun olam*[1] also forms, therefore, the streambed of the New Testament's expectation of the dawning of the *olam haba*. The "ending" of the New Testament canonical narrative is identical to the "ending" of the narrative presented within the Tanakh.

Surely with the appearance of the Messiah, some aspects of the eschatological expectation in the Tanakh have begun to be fulfilled, or have been further elaborated, or better understood. The Messiah has received "a face." The undreamed of depth and range of "the mystery of the Messiah" have been revealed, and it yet remains the story of the Song of Songs.[2] The Almighty God still groans in anticipation of the end of the exile. Together with His beloved people, God longs to return to Zion in order to reveal the *tikkun olam* there. At the same time the mystery of His love has only become greater. Because in the Messiah God's Indwelling has been granted to Israel, the Presence of God now also shares the exile of His people and the nations in this First One of Israel. In the Messiah, the Holy One of Israel also wishes to bring His sheep home to Himself and lead their return to Zion.

---

1. See chapter 12.
2. See chapter 12 (12.18).

The Camp of Israel: Waiting for the Return of the Shekhina

Just as the appearance of *Yeshua* brought deeper insight in the ways of Israel's God toward the *tikkun olam,* what has happened since then in relation to Israel and His Messiah is relevant for understanding God's ways and intentions. By means of our shuddering over Israel's *galut* and the dark pride of the nations, under the guidance of the Holy Spirit, new insights in Scripture and unexpected footsteps of the Holy One can be revealed.

The canonical narrative of the Tanakh and the New Testament does not just exist on paper or in the mind. It took place and it still works itself out in this world! It encompasses the cosmos and the centuries. It continues today. All of humanity, we too, stand in the streambed of this ongoing canonical narrative, and we have been called by God to read His Scriptures from here. The centuries of ongoing history around Israel and the Messiah therefore also play a role in our interpretation and understanding. The Scriptures want to open our eyes to the things God has done and that He in His faithfulness will do.

Therefore, in prayer to the Spirit who reveals, we may try to "go along" with what took place and still takes place in this streambed. We will look from the circle of the nations to what God has done and still is doing in and out of the camp of Israel. Therefore this chapter forms the transition to Part III and is part of it already.

21.2 Return to Zion: Outlines and Fragments

God Himself wishes to return to Zion, that much is clear, and His longing is for His people to return there. Once again Jerusalem will be the God-indicated center of the world. The nations will wish to go there and be welcomed. In the present time, the *olam haze*, God will make His way there in order to allow the beginning of the *olam haba* for the whole cosmos from within His city.

The final words of the Scriptures of the New Covenant speak of the city of God as the heart of the new heaven and earth, descending from above. This new shape of God's Jerusalem is the place of Indwelling, the heart of the new creation. She is both the essence of the *tikkun olam* and the fulfillment of the Tanakh.

In this chapter we will only be able to focus on the outlines of the Divine returning to Zion. Only fragments of the eschatological expectation of the Scriptures can be discussed, like small pieces of a far bigger puzzle, yet unfinished and still missing the final picture. Therefore, certain interpretations will be indicated in a questioning tone.[3] There are big differences of opinion both in Jewish tradition and in Christian theology regarding eschatology. Therefore, it is essential to be modest and humble. The *tikkun olam*, the restoration of all things, belongs to what God will create anew

---

3. The specific character of the Book of Revelation with its mixture of metaphorical language and concrete designations (par example of Jerusalem in chapter 11:8 and 20:9) makes humility in the process of interpretation very important.

and for that reason alone surpasses our understanding and imagination.[4] This does not, however, need to be a hindrance to a passionate longing for the full revelation of the Messianic Eighth Day. Just like Daniel, we may expect that the LORD God will give more insight as the time nears.[5]

21.3 The Simultaneous Approach of the Kingdom and Day of the LORD

We saw earlier that in and around the Messiah, the approach of the coming age and the reality of the present age overlap.[6] The Kingdom of God and the judgment of the Day of the LORD both come near. Through the ever growing darkness of the exile, God and His *Shekhina* are advancing toward Zion. In the metaphor of "pains of childbirth," both the pain of the present time and the expectation of what will come exist side by side.[7]

In the New Testament sections describing this path to the future, both aspects come to the foreground. They describe both the pains of childbirth and the dawning of the *olam haba* in the coming of the Messiah.[8] Together with the Messiah and the Spirit,[9] creation[10] and believers-as-firstlings[11] long for the end. Together the Spirit and the bride call for the coming of the Messiah.[12] The Spirit is also waiting for the restoration of the city of God.

We see that heaven itself opens, allowing God's sovereign power to be seen.[13] We also see that judgment multiplies on the earth, allowing dark sources of satanic opposition to break open.[14] Amidst this darkness the Messiah walks the path of exile with His followers among the nations.[15] Thus the nations hear the good message about Israel's God and His Messiah,[16] while at the same time He participates in the exile of all Israel.

---

4. Cf. 1 Cor 13:12: "For now we see only a reflection as in a mirror."
5. Dan 12:4; cf. John 14:26; 16:13.
6. See chapter 17, 19 (19.9) and 20 (20.7).
7. Rom 8:22.
8. Rom 8:17–39.
9. Rom 8:23–27, 34 mention the groaning of the believers, the pleading with unutterable groanings of the Spirit and the pleading of the Messiah; cf. also Rev 5:6, where the Spirit (seven spirits of God) is mentioned as sent out into all the earth, and Zech 6:8 where "giving rest to the Spirit of God in the land of the north" is mentioned.
10. Rom 8:19–22.
11. Rom 8:23.
12. Rev 22:17.
13. Rev 4–5.
14. Rev 6 and 8–9.
15. Matt 24:8–13; cf. chapter 19 (19.9).
16. Matt 24:14.

Resistance increases as the Day of the Last Judgment nears. The opposition against God takes on flesh,[17] and organizes itself in the city of man against the city of God.[18] God's faithfulness overcomes and guarantees what He has promised: the great *Shabbat* of God, His Messiah, and the Spirit is on its way and with it the end will come.

21.4 Abiding Centrality: The Camp of Israel, the City of Jerusalem, and the Indwelling of God in Order to Bless

On the road toward the restoration of all things, the camp of Israel, the Promised Land, and the city of Jerusalem remain the center of all. It is here that the *tikkun olam* will dawn. The focal point is still the return to Zion. In every respect salvation will be from the Jews.[19] Therefore the opposition of both Satan and the nations will also direct itself against Jerusalem and the land.

In the "Mount of Olives-speech" about the last things,[20] there still is a central place for "the city of the Great King."[21] Jesus speaks of the desecration and destruction of the Temple,[22] of the flight from the city and the land,[23] and the related great tribulation[24] which implies exile and subjugation to the power of the Gentiles.[25] At the same time the context of Jesus sitting on the Mount of Olives reminds us in a hopeful manner of the return of the *Shekhina* to the Temple and city.[26] The restoration of the land, the people, and the city of Jerusalem is, in Luke's rendering, consequently the other side of the coin: the defeating crush of God's city will only be permitted for a limited period of time.[27]

The resistance against God and His commandments will also manifest itself in a physical manner at a given time in the midst of the earth, according to Paul. As an enfleshed token of all resistance to God, "the man of lawlessness"[28] will set up his throne in the Temple.[29] It seems as if the confrontation between this anti-messiah[30] and Messiah *Yeshua* will take place in Jerusalem, the heart of the physical creation.

---

17. Rev 13; cf. 2 Thess 2:3–10.
18. Rev 14:8; 17–18.
19. Cf. John 4:22.
20. Matt 24; Mark 13; Luke 21.
21. Cf. Matt 5:35 and Ps 48:2.
22. Matt 24:15; Luke 21:20–24.
23. Matt 24:16–20; Luke 21:21.
24. Matt 24:21–22; Mark 13:18–19.
25. Luke 21:24.
26. Matt 24:3; cf. chapter 19 (19.9).
27. Luke 21:24.
28. 2 Thess 2:3.
29. 2 Thess 2:4.
30. 1 John 2:18, 22.

Part II : The Canonical Narrative: The Scriptures of the New Covenant

In Revelation, the land, the people of Israel, and the city of Jerusalem also have a central position. Jerusalem is the city trampled upon, but this will not last forever.[31] God's wrathful judgment will take place there.[32] It is within this city that God will reveal Himself to both Israel and the nations.[33] It will be here that the Messiah, together with His people, will stand on the mountain of Zion.[34] It is here He will be welcomed.[35] From here He will lead all Israel into His love.[36] In an attempt to collectively obstruct God's plans, the nations will march there, unaware of the fact that they have been summoned to appear there on the great Day of God.[37] Out of "the city he loves,"[38] God's reign will cover the earth.[39] And the final attack of the nations, Gog and Magog,[40] will be against "the camp of God's saints and the beloved city."[41]

Thus the camp of Israel will be the center until the end, and there the revelation of the *tikkun olam* will take place. There the New Jerusalem will come down.[42]

The prophets continually spoke of the salvation that would be revealed in Jerusalem. Daniel received his visions during his Jerusalem-oriented prayers.[43] Just like the Tanakh, the Scriptures of the New Covenant focus our attention on what is happening in Jerusalem, and on what yet will take place in God's city amidst His people in the midst of the earth.[44] In Jerusalem blessing will well up for all nations.[45]

21.5 From Exile Toward the *Tikkun Olam*

In every respect the return to Zion is a return from exile. For all Israel it is a return to the Promised Land, but first of all it is a return of the Holy One Himself. It is an ascent from the desert of the world to the city of God. *Yeshua* Himself also expects a welcome by and physical reunion to Jerusalem.[46] He even alludes to returning to the Temple.[47]

- 31. Rev 11:2.
- 32. Rev 14:10.
- 33. Rev 11:3–10.
- 34. Rev 14:1.
- 35. Cf. Rev 1:7 and Matt 23:39.
- 36. Rom 11:25–27.
- 37. Rev 20:8; cf. 16:14–16 and 19:19.
- 38. Rev 20:9.
- 39. Rev 20:16.
- 40. Rev 20:8.
- 41. Rev 20:9 (RSV).
- 42. Rev 21–22.
- 43. See Dan 6:10–11.
- 44. In the Dead Sea Scrolls too we find this orientation toward the city and the Temple.
- 45. Rev 22:1–2.
- 46. Matt 23:39; Luke 13:34–35.
- 47. Matt 23:38 mentions the "house" of Jerusalem. Possibly Jesus thinks of the destruction of the

The Camp of Israel: Waiting for the Return of the Shekhina

John's exile at Patmos is not incidental, but stands as a model for the way that the Messiah, in and with His Body of firstlings from Israel and the nations, walks together with all Israel. As previously mentioned, this path of the Messiah should be spoken of in two ways: with the "already" in regard to His ascent to the throne, but also with the "not yet" of His kingship in Jerusalem. The overlap between the misery of the *olam haze* and the dawning of the *olam haba* in the Spirit of the Messiah can be found in the life of John. This disciple of Jesus knows these two sides in his own life as he participates both in "the kingdom" and in "the suffering."[48] In the power of the Spirit he lives on the earth where the devil still furiously roams.[49] In John's exile the Messiah lives in exile too, as *Yeshua* mentioned earlier.[50]

As the Lion of Judah, the way of the Messiah is the way of the Lamb.[51] This also characterizes His way with His people: Israel is "a mother's womb" from which the Messiah comes forth, and she is the exalted woman in Revelation 12 who must flee and is safeguarded in the desert until the appointed time.[52] God's enemy cannot harm her in this safe position, and so focuses on her offspring, and directs himself to the nations.[53] The sea of the nations will vomit out onto the earth the fleshly incarnation of the resistance against God.[54] The world of nations will rise in rebellion against God, a rebellion also directed against God's Tent, His Dwelling.[55] But through all of this the return of the Messiah to Zion, accompanied by all Israel, will take place.[56] It makes one wonder if this return is also partly the result of the man of lawlessness's anti-God campaign.[57] No matter what, toward the end the Lamb will stand on Mount Zion and with Him the 144,000 from the tribes of Israel.[58]

In this period in which the *olam haze* and the *olam haba* overlap, there is opportunity for both increasing sanctification—*kedusha*—and falling away and resistance.[59]

Temple which He has foretold in 24:1–2. Cf. Mal 3:1.

48. Rev 1:9.

49. Rev 12:12.

50. Matt 25:31–46 shows that at some point of time it will show that the Messiah has been present amidst the nations in a manner which implied hunger, thirst and nakedness, imprisonment, or being a foreigner.

51. Rev 5:5–6.

52. Rev 12:13–14.

53. The expression "the rest of her offspring" (literally: of her seed) in Rev 12:17 reminds of Gen 3:15, where the seed of the woman is mentioned that will crush the head of the serpent. In Rev 12 the dragon goes after those who belong to this remaining offspring, and in doing so he heads for the sea. This gives the impression that we should interpret this to point to the believers from the nations who have come to follow Israel's God and Messiah.

54. Rev 13:1.

55. Rev 13:6.

56. Rev 14:1.

57. Does the sequence of chapter 13 and 14 possibly show this too?

58. Also see Rev 7:1–8.

59. Matt 24:12; 2 Thess 2:3; 1 Tim 4:1–3; 2 Tim 3:1–5.

The desert of the world is also a place of temptation. The exile can cause not only the Body of the Messiah, but also all Israel, to forget God.

Like Joshua, the Messiah will come to judge the nations and punish their rebellion.[60] The land will be the center of God's reign, and ultimately God's renewed Jerusalem will come down there to be established.[61] Then the return to Zion will be complete, and the exile—along with all first things—will pass away.[62]

Then God, the Almighty One Himself, will be the Temple for the city,[63] a city with the same measurements as the Most Holy Place.[64] In this Jerusalem-Temple, the city will dwell "in God" and in the Lamb.[65] God will be "all in all."[66]

21.6 The Safekeeping and Fullness of Israel

In the Scriptures of the New Covenant, God's faithfulness to His most treasured possession, His *segula*-people,[67] is fundamental to the salvation of the whole world[68] from the beginning until the end. Paul speaks of "all Israel" that will be saved in the judgment of the Day of the LORD.[69]

John explicitly speaks of Israel's recognition of the Pierced One, as foretold by Zechariah.[70] Further on in John's visions we observe how, as in Egypt, the fullness of Israel is spared in the judgments preceding the Day of the LORD.[71] Accompanied by the fullness of the hosts of Israel,[72] the Lamb confronts the great seducer of the nations. As an unforeseen threat to the enemy, this Lamb will stand on Mount Zion.[73] This implicates not only the return to Zion of the Messiah, but also the return to the land of Israel's fullness. For readers who are acquainted with the streambed of the Tanakh and its role in our interpretation, it is clear that in these few designations in Revelation, much can be found that is foretold in the Tanakh.

---

60. Rev 19:11–16.
61. Rev 21:2.
62. Rev 21:1, 4.
63. Rev 21:22.
64. Rev 21:16. The Most Holy Place of the Tabernacle also had this cubic shape.
65. Rev 21:22.
66. Cf. 1 Cor 15:28.
67. See chapter 7 (7.3).
68. See chapter 19 and 20.
69. Rom 11:26.
70. Rev 1:7; Zech 12:10.
71. Rev 7:1–8.
72. This fullness of the hosts of Israel is designated by the number 144,000 (12 x 12,000; cf. Num 31:5; 2 Sam 17:1; 1 Kgs 4:26).
73. Rev 14:1; cf. Zech 14:3, 4; Mic 5:4 ("He will stand").

The Camp of Israel: Waiting for the Return of the Shekhina

The themes of safekeeping of Israel through the ages, God's last Elijah-call to the nation and the world,[74] the recognition of the Pierced One and the contrition of Israel accompanying it,[75] the fulfillment of the Day of Atonement for the people,[76] the gift of the unity of the people,[77] the return to the land, the LORD's standing on the Mount of Olives,[78] the kingship of the LORD,[79] and the celebration of the completely perfected Feast of Tabernacles in the eschatological *Sukkot*[80] are presupposed as knowledge. The Messiah, who gives His revelation to John and calls Himself "the Word of God,"[81] does not explain it all. There is no need to. John was the "bosom-friend" of the Master who said that He would not do away with "the smallest letter, nor the least stroke of a pen."[82]

In Revelation the *tikkun olam* is sketched with restored Israel in the midst of the new creation, and the city of God as a place of salvation for the nations. Such is the full picture of the restoration of all things.

21.7 The Surrender and Resistance of the Nations

Clearly in also Revelation, Israel and the nations are distinguished from each other. We meet both the fullness of Israel and the great multitude from all nations.[83] And against the new city of God stands the city of man, the prostitute Babylon.[84]

Jesus has already foretold that the nations will hear the gospel, but would also react with hatred.[85] Paul describes how preceding the Day of the LORD "the rebellion" must come and "the man of lawlessness" has to reveal himself.[86] In pride he will exalt himself against God and His Messiah. Even the Temple is not safe from him.[87] John also describes the anti-messiah and his forerunners who will appear.[88] In Revelation

---

74. In Matt 17:10–13 and Mark 9:11–12 Jesus speaks about Elijah's coming to restore everything. He also said that John the Baptist formed a fulfillment of the words of Mal 4:5. In Rev 11 we observe a kind of Elijah-call to Israel and the nations that precedes the end.
75. Zech 12:10–14; cf. Hos 3:5.
76. Zech 3:9; 13:1.
77. See chapter 12 (12.10).
78. Zech 14:4.
79. Zech 14:9.
80. Zech 14:16–19.
81. Rev 19:13.
82. Matt 5:17–18.
83. Rev 7:9–17.
84. Rev 17–18.
85. Matt 24:9.
86. 2 Thess 2:3.
87. 2 Thess 2:4.
88. 1 John 2:18–27.

Part II : The Canonical Narrative: The Scriptures of the New Covenant

we see the movement of resistance and pride against God culminating under the guidance of this "man" of lawlessness who is the opposite of the Son of Man.[89]

En route to the *tikkun olam* it is possible that the nations will behave like the Pharaoh of Egypt and the Amalekites,[90] or as Haman[91] and Antioch IV Epiphanes,[92] or as those haughty builders of Babel.[93] The spirit of the prostitute of Babel is the opposite of the Spirit which forms "the bride,"[94] "the wife" of God's Messiah.[95] The believers from the nations are also warned by Paul[96] against the pride which seems to be in the genes of the nations from the beginning.[97] John mentions that anti-messiahs will arise from within the circle of the followers of the Messiah.[98] Even within the Body of the Messiah, sinful pride can raise its sinister head, opposing God's election and His ways—as indeed has happened.[99]

21.8 The Messiah at the Throne: The Lamb Opens the Seals

Although there still is a way through the desert on the earth, in heaven there is sovereign action. John learns repeatedly to watch what is happening on earth from a heavenly perspective.[100] The seven churches do not have to stand alone. The resurrected Son of Man walks among them.[101] A door in heaven is opened up for John, and the highly exalted Messiah invites him to enter the Throne room of the LORD God.[102] John will be shown what is to come.[103]

---

89. Rev 13:6, 18.

90. Cf. Exod 17:8–16.

91. Esther 3–8.

92. The Syrian king whose Hellenizing and anti-Jewish policy (culminating in the desecration of the Temple) induced the revolt of the Maccabees (167–164 BCE). See chapter 11 (11.5).

93. Cf. Gen 11:1–9.

94. Rev 19:7–8; cf. 22:17.

95. Rev 21:9.

96. Rom 11:20–21.

97. See chapter 11 (11.5).

98. 1 John 2:18–19.

99. See Introduction (I.4), chapter 13 and Part III.

100. He may look from the perspective of the opening vision (Rev 1:9–20) to the situation of the seven congregations (2:1—3:22; the rendering "churches" may carry some negative associations, in stead of conveying that they were gatherings of Messianic believers). The judgments which will follow stand in the light of what he was allowed to see in the heavenly Throne room (4:1—5:14) The rise of the anti-Godly powers stands in the light of the great sign in heaven (12:1–12). The last plagues (16:1—18:24), including the judgment over the whore Babylon, are introduced by the vision from chapter 15 in which heaven opens up.

101. Rev 1:12–13.

102. Rev 4:1.

103. Rev 4:1.

The Camp of Israel: Waiting for the Return of the Shekhina

In the setting of a worship service of angelic beings and twenty-four elders,[104] he beholds the Throne and Who is sitting on it. In the hand of the Almighty One there is a sealed scroll. Nobody may look inside. Only "the Lion of the tribe of Judah" has the prerogative to break the seals.[105] The Lion has walked the way of the Lamb.[106] As partner in God's reign, thereby fulfilling Israel's calling to be king before God,[107] He may both open God's decrees and execute them. For He has fulfilled Israel's calling and thereby also the command given at creation to rule before God's countenance.[108] He has led God's people to its calling to be a kingdom of priests, and by doing so He has added a great multitude of royal priests from all nations.[109] Because of Him, Israel's calling to bring the nations to *kedusha* of the Name has been made into reality. Therefore He is worthy of all honor.[110]

John observes that the opening of the seals by the Lamb calls for judgment over the world, bringing the wrath of God and the Lamb.[111] God and His Messianic partner from the tribe of Judah order this, as Egypt once experienced in plagues.[112] Like Moses once did in Egypt, the God of Israel allows the First One of Israel to execute the judgments.

At the same time we see that God reigns sovereignly, right through the night of judgments. The fullness of Israel is now also spared, as it once was in the land of Goshen through the night of *Pessah*.[113] And God simultaneously redeems and sanctifies an innumerable multitude from all nations and languages of the earth, which together with the fullness of Israel is spared through "the great tribulation."[114] It is clear, therefore, that these travel companions do not form a "mixed multitude,"[115] as was the case in the time of the Exodus.

Against the subjugation of the whole earth to the power of the devil, together with His Israel God reveals the Messiah in the midst of the earth on Mount Zion.[116] The final judgment will be executed there, outside the city, by this Son of Man.[117] Through

---

104. Twenty-four in the first place is the number that has everything to do with the structuring of the Temple service by David (see 1 Chr 24–25). Besides this, are the elders at the Throne also representatives of Israel and the nations?

105. Rev 5:5.

106. Rev 5:6.

107. See chapter 10 and 18.

108. Gen 1:26–28.

109. Rev 1:5–6 and 5:9 connect the multitude from the nations to Israel's calling.

110. Rev 5:11–14.

111. Rev 6:1, 3, 5, 7, 9, 12; 8:1.

112. Cf. Exod 7–12.

113. Exod 12.

114. Rev 7:14.

115. Exod 12:38 (RSV).

116. Rev 14:1–5.

117. Rev 14:14, 20; cf. Matt 24:30–31, 37–42.

all judgments God accomplishes "the mystery of God . . . as he announced to his servants, the prophets."[118] We are approaching the accomplishment of this mystery.[119] The story does not end in the judgment, but rather in the salvation of Israel and the nations by the Lamb.[120] The story does not end with the prideful and promiscuous city of Babylon, but with the bride of the Lamb.[121] Just as the utterly humble Moses,[122] following the Exodus, led Israel to the wedding ceremony under the *ḥuppa* at Sinai,[123] so now the Lamb leads His *segula*-people to the wedding banquet,[124] at the same time drawing a multitude from the nations to Him under the wedding canopy of God's eternal love.

21.9 Ultimate Pride: The Antichrist and the Prostitute

Yet this revelation of God's highest love will not take place until the pride and idolatry of man ultimately is incarnated. The drawback of God's creation of man as a partner in His reign over creation is the possibility of rebellion. Indeed, a "palace rebellion" has taken place. In Revelation we observe that with the nearing of the *olam haba*, powers of prideful resistance will rise up from both the caverns of the world and from within the human heart,[125] leading to "the rebellion."[126] False teaching will regularly raise its head.[127] False messiahs will appear.[128] In the end, a pseudo-lamb[129] and an anti-anointed-one will seduce the whole earth and, if possible, even the followers of the Lamb.[130] People will become detached from God's commandments, and lawlessness will make life unbearable.[131]

Throughout Israel's history, coalitions of nations have regularly tried to torment God's people and plague the land.[132] As the end nears, a league of nations and their leaders, expressing themselves in the form of a city, will oppose God and His saints.[133]

---

118. Rev 10:7; cf. Amos 3:7.

119. Is the mystery mentioned here the same as the mystery that Paul describes in Eph 3 and Col 1:24—2:3?

120. Rev 15:2-4.

121. Rev 19:6-10; 21:1—22:5.

122. Num 12:3. The Hebrew word used designates humility and modesty.

123. See chapter 8 (8.1).

124. Rev 19:7, 9.

125. Rev 9 and 13.

126. 2 Thess 2:3.

127. 1 Tim 4:1-5.

128. Matt 24:4-5, 23-24.

129. Rev 13:11.

130. Matt 24:24.

131. Matt 24:12.

132. Rev 14:8; 17:1—19:5.

133. See chapter 11 (11.5).

This demonic rebellion against God leads to a conspiracy against Him.[134] By designating this rebellion as "the prostitute Babylon," it becomes clear that, from the beginning, this resistance is directed against the Holy Lover. It yet still is about the love of the Song of Songs, a love that wishes for the *huppa* of the Eternal God to be the end of all. The designation "Babylon" points to the former pride of the nations, countered by God through the confusion of the languages and the election of Israel.[135] That the power of the Roman empire was thought of as "the prostitute Babylon" in the interpretation of John's visions is only logical. However, an exclusively historical interpretation in which Revelation speaks only of a spiritual confrontation with historic Rome, would not be sufficient. As the revelation of the *tikkun olam* in Zion approaches, the Messiah will wish to open eyes to recognize the resistance against the Most Holy God. This resistance will increasingly manifest itself throughout history, increasingly "taking form and face" in two extreme forms of rebellion: the "man-of-lawlessness,"[136] and a rebellious center of power: the city that is the prostitute.

21.10 The Kingship of God and His Messiah

The judgment over "the great Babylon" forms the introduction to the kingship of God Almighty over all the earth.[137] Now God's kingship is no longer contended. The Great King is now the one, true King. God's royal rights have been defended and reclaimed by the Lamb. Israel's Messiah is the King of kings and Lord of lords.[138] And so the kingship of God and His Anointed One has begun.[139]

Again we observe a close connection between the kingship of God and the union of the Messiah with His bride.[140] The kingship of God will indeed be exercised by the Messianic king, the First One of Israel, who grants His people to participate together with the added multitude from the nations. God and His Messiah obviously will not rest before the kingdom of priests has become reality in Israel.

The fulfillment of Israel's calling *and* the blessed effects of it in the adding of the multitude of priests from the nations both precede and are conditional to the dawning of the *olam haba*.[141] From this we can conclude how much the Eternal One longs for the *kedusha* of His people. At the same time we see how the obedience granted by the

---

134. Rev 16:13–14; 17:12–13; 19:19–20.
135. Gen 11:1–9.
136. Characterized by the number 666 (Rev 13:18).
137. Rev 19:6.
138. Rev 19:16.
139. Rev 11:15.
140. Rev 19:7 (mentioning the marriage and the bride) gives substance to verse 6 (mentioning God's kingship). The welcoming of the Bridegroom/King as described in 1 Thess 4:13–17 is implicit, as is the resurrection of the dead, and their change into a state of imperishable immortality at the last trumpet (1 Cor 15:51–53) lies hidden in what Revelation describes.
141. See chapter 7 (7.2 and 7.5); 12 (12.4) and 16.

Messiah results in the preparation of "the bride of the Lamb" for the royal task.[142] Again it shows that God is asking for obedience, but at the same time provides this obedience Himself.[143] Here the word of Isaiah is being fulfilled:

> LORD, you establish peace for us;
> all that we have accomplished you have done for us.[144]

When the bride has clothed herself with fine (priestly) linen garments and the marriage can be celebrated, the world will see that the *kedusha* of all Israel has been completed. Here is also implied that the entire people of Israel will have learned that they are the bride of the Lamb. The recognition of the Pierced One and the repentance of past sins are naturally implicated as well.[145] Previously, *Yeshua* clearly taught that the opening of the eyes of all Israel would lead to *shalom*.[146]

The kingship of God that begins with the marriage of the Lamb is the fulfillment of the ongoing line of God's feasts. It carries traits of the Feast of Tabernacles, as a great *Sukkot*.[147] The last trumpet[148] announcing the coming of God's judge,[149] and the *Yom Kippur* for those who return to God, have preceded this great *Sukkot* of God's kingship. The exile of the *Shekhina* and of Israel, and yes, even the exile of the nations, which were estranged from God and His salvation, will come to an end.

21.11 The Kingdom in the *Olam Haze*: The Millennium, Gog, and Magog

Yet it appears that the kingship of God will first begin in the present age and only later will be fully realized in the coming of the Kingdom of the *olam haba*. Revelation 20 appears to say that God will give the world a chance to be reigned by His city in the midst of the earth.[150] It's as if the LORD takes mankind so seriously that the world, yet in this present age, receives an opportunity to let itself be reigned by the Messiah King

---

142. Rev 19:7-8 shows both sides: the priestly bridal garments are a gift, and she has clothed herself with them. Clearly the righteous deeds of the saints have been given to them; cf. also Eph 2:10.

143. See chapter 12 (12.4).

144. Isa 26:12.

145. Zech 12:10-14.

146. Luke 19:42.

147. Rev 7:9-17 mentions palm branches, the Tent of God and fountains of water; cf. John 7:37-38. Also see Rev 21-22. The presence of the Lamb as "its lamp" (21:23) reminds of the great illumination in Jerusalem during *Sukkot*; cf. in this context also what Jesus says in John 8:12 on the eighth day (following the seven days of *Sukkot*; cf. Lev 23:36).

148. Rev 11:15; cf. 1 Cor 15:52 and 1 Thess 4:16. The days preceding *Sukkot* begin with the Day of trumpets; then follows on the tenth day *Yom Kippur*; finally *Sukkot* begins on the fifteenth day (see Lev 23:23-36).

149. The kingship of God and the judgment are connected with each other; see par example Rev 11:17-18; cf. also 20:4.

150. Rev 20:4-6.

The Camp of Israel: Waiting for the Return of the Shekhina

and His fellow-kings.[151] It seems that the LORD God is providing an opportunity for the nations and creation to learn God's Tora in the house of learning, as it has been intended right from the beginning.[152] Could it be for a test that is still to come?[153]

In this manner will the nations receive a new opportunity to not rise up against God, to bless Him, His city, and His people? Whatever it might be, we see that deception is needed to bring the powers of Gog and Magog together.[154] A moment of choice will again come for the world of nations. And for the last time there will be a siege of the camp of Israel and of Jerusalem.[155] The choice must be made whether or not to join this campaign.

When interpreting these series of events in Revelation 20 (so briefly indicated and yet so much discussed), we must keep in mind that this section also stands within the streambed of the Tanakh *and* must be interpreted as such. The structure of God's actions, which He revealed in the camp of Israel, should be leading our interpretation. In this context we must think of the God-intended and required *kedusha* of the concrete creation. God desires His intentions to be realized *within* this creation. Thereby God adheres to the two-sided character of His covenants, including the obedient *avoda* (of his people); God deems that *avoda* as necessary.

This interpretation of Revelation 20 is fathomable when we see it as the result of God's will to give the obedient Messianic kingship its place amidst the nations. After all, it is His will that a holy kingship will be realized in the midst of creation. The coming of the *olam haba* also waits for real *kedusha* to become visible in the *olam haze*. The resulting consequence, however, is that there will be an opportunity to choose again. The choice will be to obey the dragon—the seducer and murderer from the beginning[156]—or to live according to the royal *Tora* of God's Messiah.[157] Could this be why the dragon is released once more?[158]

Does God wish to give creation one more opportunity to show its deepest loyalty? Is the obedience of mankind, created to be God's image and intended to be partner in the covenant, so important to God that the *olam haba* does not come down from heaven just like that, but involves man's obedience? Is this the beginning—still within the present era, the *olam haze*—of the times of salvation for and from Zion of which the prophets spoke?[159] Does "the bride of the Lamb" receive the opportunity

---

151. There is a community of believers participating in the kingship, priesthood and judgment (Rev 20:4, 6).
152. See chapter 1.
153. Rev 20:7–8.
154. Rev 20:8.
155. Rev 20:9.
156. Rev 12:9; John 8:44.
157. Isa 42:4.
158. Rev 20:7.
159. See chapter 12 (12.17).

to execute the reign of *kedusha* in the center of the earth together with her Messianic Bridegroom? Do the nations receive grace by showing their dedication to the God of Israel? Will it be a thousand years long or an era symbolized by that number?[160] New perspectives of understanding open up from the structures revealed within the streambed of the Tanakh.

At the same time the implication is that there will be an opportunity for a massive rebellion against the Holy One and His saints—this at least is made clear in this context by the mention of "Gog and Magog."[161] It will be a final attempt by the nations and the darkness of the dragon to take possession of the midst of the earth, a place newly inhabited by God's people.[162] A final attack on Zion, His king, and His community of kings will take place. Will this attack show once and for all that the hatred of the rebellious prince of darkness and his army is, at the deepest level, a hatred against the God of Israel and His people, His land and His city? From the beginning, has the wish to frustrate the God-intended structuring of the world around the camp of Israel as house of learning and place of salvation, been the ongoing line in the resistance against God? This rebellion, however, will never succeed.

21.12 The King of the Jews: Judge of the World

The King of the Jews, the First One of His people and the nations, will appear.[163] That will be the end of the *olam haze*. He will be the God-appointed Judge over the world,[164] Ruler over all rulers.

A white Throne appears. Heaven and earth flee from His presence.[165] In God there is no trace of darkness.[166] He who sits on the Throne sentences all darkness to death and brings an end to death itself. The dead stand before the Throne, and books are opened.[167] In a concise manner, John describes how a great separation takes place before the judgment seat of God[168] and His Messiah seated at His right hand.[169]

---

160. Rev 20:6–7.

161. Rev 20:8.

162. Cf. for this also the sequence of the chapters in Ezekiel. In chapter 37 at first the resurrection, the return and the new unity within the people are described. Then follows in Ezek 38–39 a description of the massive attack on God's returned people and the victory over Gog and Magog.

163. Rev 19:16.

164. Acts 17:31; see chapter 18 (18.6).

165. Rev 20:11.

166. 1 John 1:5.

167. Rev 20:12.

168. God is the One who is seated on the white Throne (Rev 20:11); cf. Rom 14:10 and Heb 12:23.

169. See Acts 10:42; 2 Cor 5:10; Jas 5:7, 9.

The Camp of Israel: Waiting for the Return of the Shekhina

A lake of fire is Satan's certain future. Death and its realm (*She'ol*), the antichrist and his divine idol power share the same fate.[170] Life is for whoever is written in the "book of life."

21.13 The New Heaven and Earth, and the New Jerusalem

The resurrection of *Yeshua* as Firstling of both Israel and creation helps us understand the essence of the new creation and the New Jerusalem which is sketched in Revelation. His resurrected body implied a continuity with His life preceding His death, while at the same time it was a redeemed and renewed existence.[171]

In the same manner, the new heaven and earth are the redeemed and renewed form of existence of the first creation: a redeemed and renewed heaven and earth. The canonical narrative does not end with the fiasco of creation, but with its redemption. Death, tears, mourning, and sorrow will be no more.[172]

The New Jerusalem is likewise the resurrected form of the earthly Jerusalem. In the renewed creation Jerusalem will finally be the redeemed and renewed center of the whole cosmos. Only when this holy midst is again inhabited by the people of God, the world is restored. When the priestly nation has come home there, then creation will not be out of lead any more. The *tikkun olam* has begun.

Seen from this perspective, it should not be perceived as strange that Jewish tradition maintains Jerusalem as the holy location of God's salvation. Why would it not be possible that this continuity in location of the paradise, Mount Moriah, the Most Holy Place in the Temple, and the new city would be renewed and confirmed in the resurrection form of the city?[173]

Also in the *olam haba* the city of God appears to be the center for the nations. God's Tent stands in the midst of mankind.[174] They will be His nations.[175] Starting from the outside and moving toward the center, it seems that first of all the attention is focused on the location of the city in the midst of the nations, and on the salvation that can be found there.[176] Subsequently the attention is focused on the heart of this new earth itself: the city of God that is the bride of the Lamb.[177] It is then that the

---

170. Rev 20:10, 14 (the Greek uses *Hades* for the realm of death; the Hebrew equivalent is *She'ol*, verse 14).

171. Cf. 1 Cor 15:42–44.

172. Rev 21:4.

173. See chapter 3 (3.8) and 12 (12.11).

174. Rev 21:3.

175. Rev 21:3.

176. Rev 21:1–6.

177. Rev 21:9–21.

Indwelling of God in this "Most Holy Place-city" receives attention, along with His Throne and the river that wells up there.[178]

Still the distinction between Israel and the nations remains clear. The nations may enter through the twelve gates[179] on which the names of Israel's tribes are written.[180] Their exile too, seen from the perspective of this city, comes to an end if they are willing to encamp around the city and the camp of Israel. The city itself is both Temple and the holy camp of Israel. The city is "in God," because He is her Temple.[181]

Does the distinction between the bride-city and the nations[182] also show that God rewards the *kedusha* of the bride with a place of honor in the *olam haba*?[183] And that the nations, which have become obedient in the final period of mercy,[184] have a place in the *tikkun olam* distinct from that of the bride?

Just as Jerusalem was illuminated in a grand manner during *Sukkot*, the bride-city is illuminated by God Himself.[185] He will be king, along with the Lamb! And His servants will participate in that kingship.[186] What has been celebrated in the feasts of God for centuries and what they referred to, has fully been realized.

21.14 What Will Come is Already on the Way: Mutual Blessing Between Israel and the Nations

Just as there is a simultaneous approach of the Kingdom and the Day of the LORD,[187] there are also two simultaneous interactions between Israel and the nations underway toward the *tikkun olam*: on the one hand, a multitude from the nations accompanies the King of the Jews and His people; on the other hand, an ever growing antagonism between the nations and God's *segula*-people becomes visible. Previously, we spoke of the growing hatred of the nations, and now we will focus shortly on the positive interactions—the mutual blessing[188]—between Israel and the nations.

Through His Jewish apostle, Israel's Messiah reveals Himself to the seven churches in Asia Minor.[189] In doing so He speaks the language of the Tanakh. For this reason

178. Rev 21:22–25.
179. Rev 21:24–25.
180. Rev 21:12.
181. Rev 21:22.
182. Rev 21:22—22:5 shows a clear distinction between the bride-city and the nations.
183. Cf. Rev 14:12–13.
184. Rev 20:3.
185. Rev 21:23; cf. Isa 60:19–21. For the extraordinary illumination of Jerusalem during *Sukkot*, see Goldwurm, *Succos*, 63, where this illumination is discussed, based on Mishna tractate Sukka 5, 2–3. This context of *Sukkot* is also present when Jesus speaks "I am the light of the world" (John 8:12).
186. Rev 22:5.
187. In this chapter see paragraph 21.3.
188. See chapter 2 (2.6 and 2.7) and 12 (12.14).
189. Rev 2–3. These cities were situated in the Roman province of Asia.

The Camp of Israel: Waiting for the Return of the Shekhina

alone, through their Jewish Messianic fellow believers, the non-Jewish members of these Messianic congregations need to learn from Israel in order to understand words and images.[190] We observe that Israel and the nations are spoken about in a unifying manner, just as Paul travelling with his companions to Jerusalem is a such a prophetic sign.[191] Together they will see the coming of the Son of Man, and together they will mourn.[192] Royal priests from the nations will be added to the royal and priestly community of Israel.[193] For the nations too there will be a place in the Temple of God.[194] Following the description of Israel spared in a perfect *Pessah*, an innumerable, festive and *Sukkot*-celebrating multitude from the nations is sketched.[195] Clearly they are celebrating *Sukkot*, and in doing so are dependent on and co-celebrating with Israel.[196] Together the nations and Israel are spared by God and the Lamb in the day of judgment.[197] Although Israel and the nations remain distinct until the end, they are still spoken of in the language of unity in discipleship and obedience.[198] Both the fullness of Israel and the great multitude from the nations are shown to John as a sort of calm within the storm of God's judgments.[199] They are thereby joined together, both dependent on God's safekeeping. We notice what the Spirit of the Messiah wishes to make complete as the *tikkun olam* approaches: the unity which is a condition to the revelation of the Jerusalem-kingship of the Messiah.

Is the Lamb's return to Zion with His people Israel,[200] in every respect the opposite to the idolatry of the nations,[201] an occasion to proclaim an "eternal gospel" among

---

190. An other example: In 1 Cor 10:18 Paul refers to the Temple service and thus also to the Tora regarding this service. His non-Jewish audience here receives instruction of the Lord by means of reference to the Temple service and what is shown in it.

191. See chapter 20 (20.3 and 20.18).

192. Rev 1:7.

193. See chapter 12 (12.14) and 20 (20.10).

194. Rev 3:12.

195. Rev 7:9–17. The mentioning of palm branches (vs. 9), the shouts of joy because of salvation (vs. 10), the Tent of God (vs. 15; the expression rendered as "shelter them" [NIV and RSV] has as its root the Greek word for "tent") and the springs of living water (vs. 17) give this section the color of *Sukkot*; cf. Isa 4:5–6 (in Jewish tradition interpreted against the background of *Sukkot*, for this see also Bacchiocchi, *God's Festivals*).

196. Cf. also the singing of the song of Moses by all believers, thus by those from the nations too (Rev 15:3–4).

197. Rev 6:16–17.

198. In Rev 5:9–10, 14:12–13, 15:2–3 and in the mentioning of "the bride" the language of unity (of Israel and the added multitude from the nations) is used.

199. Rev 7 interrupts the opening of the seals and thus places both spared communities in the midst of the series of judgments.

200. Cf. what has been written about this in paragraph 21.5.

201. Rev 14:1–5 forms a conscious contrast with the nations as depicted in chapter 13.

the nations?[202] Does the sequence of various visions in Revelation point to deep connections between Israel and the nations within the execution of God's council?[203]

In its completed form, we see the mutual blessing between Israel and the nations in the description of the New Jerusalem. The city of God and her inhabitants form the bride of God.[204] Whereas the bride consists of the fullness of Israel with the multitude from the nations added to it, the bride herself is already place of unity and mutual blessing. She is a place of learning and understanding together.[205] At the same time, we see that this Divine bride-city has a blessed relationship with the nations. Her gates are open and the nations in turn bring their splendor to her.[206]

Because this New Jerusalem embodies the perfection and continuation of what has already begun in the present age, in this end we are able to see the outlined form of the road leading toward it. The mutual blessing, observed around the bride-city Jerusalem, shows what the Spirit and the bride long for in the *olam haze*.[207] In this present age the Spirit is actively preparing the bride of the Lamb.[208] In this age the Spirit is also actively involved in bringing about the mutual blessing between Israel and the nations, and thereby also brings the *olam haba* closer. What will come is already on its way.

21.15 God's Eternal Indwelling in Zion

The canonical narrative that began with the Tanakh originated from the desire of the Eternal God to dwell in the midst of His creation.[209] It was in view of this original intention that God granted Israel the prerogative to build Him a Dwelling.[210] He wished to live in a Dwelling erected by the obedient *kedusha* of Israel. We observed how Moses and later David, Solomon, Zerubbabel, and high priest Joshua led the people in the raising of God's Dwelling.[211]

The end of the canonical narrative, as sketched in the Scriptures of the New Covenant, also shows that ultimately One from Israel has prepared the Dwelling and led

---

202. Rev 14:6–7.

203. Some examples: at first Rev 11:1–14, then followed by 11:15–19 (= at first a last Elijah-call from Jerusalem, then follows the announcement of the kingship of God). First Rev 12–13, then thereafter 14:1–5, 6–13 (= at first the persecution of the Messiah and Israel and the rise of the reign of the beast with its anti-king, then following this the standing of the Messiah on Mount Zion).

204. Rev 21:2 and 9–10.

205. Cf. Eph 3:14–21; this section describes the grasping to understand together the love of the Messiah by believers from Israel and the nations.

206. Rev 21:24–26.

207. Rev 22:17.

208. Cf. the mentioning of the speaking of the Spirit at the end of all letters in Rev 2–3 and Rev 14:13.

209. Cf. chapter 3 (3.1), 8 (8.2), 9 (9.9), 12 (12.12).

210. See chapter 8 (8.2).

211. See chapter 10 (10.7).

His people in accomplishing this. The Messiah has prepared the bride-city, and He "created" the city-as-bride unto a Dwelling for the Eternal God. The bride is clothed with her righteous deeds, these garments have been given to her. The *kedusha* of the Messiah is the essence of the *kedusha* of the bride.

The New Jerusalem as Dwelling of God is given by God, and at the same time it is obtained by the merits of the *kedusha* of the Messiah. He has obtained and "built" her,[212] just as He also obtained the kingship of God *for* God on earth and realized it fully.[213] The new city which is the center of the *olam haba* comes down on the basis of the *kedusha* the Messiah accomplished in the midst of Israel. God's royal and priestly covenant partner is God's co-worker to the fullest in the realization of God's creational intentions.[214] Therein it becomes clear how much God values and honors the obedience within and from the midst of His people, and how deep the ways have been that He chose to go in order to make this covenant obedience possible.

The King dwells forever in the midst of Zion. His intentions with creation and His salvation will converge in an unexpected manner in the midst of the new creation.

The exile for the *Shekhina* will come to an end. The Holy God and His shining Presence on earth will dwell as *one* in this new Zion.

21.16 The *Olam Haba: Kedusha* for the Whole of Creation

The sketch of the canonical narrative of the Scriptures is as good as completed. The question on the table has been: is Israel as the people of God His beloved nation forever? Does this nation remain on stage or has it, by some action of God, been sent behind the stage? It is clear, however, that Israel's calling to be a kingdom of priests has never been retracted by God. And it also became clear that He has kept this calling safe in an unexpected manner, allowing it to become a blessing for creation and the nations of the earth.

The restoration of all things as part of the *olam haba* has been accomplished and obtained by the obedience of the One from Israel. He has sanctified Israel. He has accomplished everything that belonged to the calling of a kingdom of priests. In this way He also let the nations share in the *kedusha*. The restoration of all things has been obtained by Him and will commence. The whole of creation healed by the obedience of One Jew! By Him Jerusalem is both comforted and built for eternity. The obedience and sanctification that has been accomplished by Him in those who belong to Him,

---

212. Cf. also John 14:2–3.

213. Cf. also what 1 Cor 15:21–28 tells about the Messiah as the King who will vanquish all resistance against God. The humble transfer of power from the side of the Messiah (15:28) seems to be implied in the sequence of the words in the designation "the throne of God and the Lamb" (Rev 22:1, 3) and in the closing verse of John's vision of the New Jerusalem (22:5), in which only the LORD is the light wherein all and everyone will live eternally.

214. This is also shown by the fact that the names of the apostles, the emissaries of the Lamb, are written on the foundations of the city (Rev 21:14).

will appear to be included in overthrowing the dragon and sanctifying the world.[215] Here too it becomes clear how much God values the obedience of His people, including it in His works.[216] The last offer of mercy and the last victory over the resistance of Gog and Magog do not take place without the obedient and holy service of the bride of the Messiah. The *kedusha* of Israel-in-Messiah and of those who have been included, are involved in ushering in the dawning of the *tikkun olam*.

In this consummation[217] of creation, this *tikkun olam*, the original intentions of God become reality in a much more glorious manner. The calling to be God's priestly nation received at Sinai is also Israel's calling in the *olam haba*. The New Jerusalem will forever be God's house of learning in the center of creation. In this all-determining center of the camp of Israel, a permanent fountain of salvation and new life for all nations will be opened up.[218]

21.17 The Eternal *Shabbat* and the Messianic New Day

Just as in the beginning the LORD entered, on the seventh day, into the rest of the *Shabbat*,[219] so will it be in the end. In His return to Zion the God of Israel enters His rest. What Israel's Messiah near the Throne[220] and the Spirit on earth both still groan for[221] will have been realized. It will be *Shabbat* for God and His *Shekhina*, and it will be *Shabbat* for the Spirit. The joy of the Indwelling in Zion will be tasted by the Eternal One and His creation. The eternal *Shabbat* will in a certain sense also be a fully Messianic first day—the Eighth Day—following the passing away of the old creation. To grasp and experience this Messianic reality will at the deepest level be a learning—*lernen*[222]—of the Messiah. His *kedusha* forms the two-sided mystery that consists of the mysterious converging of the actions of the Holy God with the full obedience of Israel.

Yet this is being awaited.[223] Yet we are approaching this day. The canonical narrative sketched in Part I and II is still on God's stage. And what about us? We are part of it; we live right in the middle of it. The question, however, that confronts us now is what role we as believers from the nations shall play. The question we have to ask ourselves is: where have we stood on God's stage through the centuries? And where do we stand now?

---

215. Rev 12:11; cf. 1 John 5:4–5; Rom 8:37–39.
216. Rev 22:5.
217. See chapter 1 (1.4).
218. Rev 22:1–2; cf. Ezek 47:1–12.
219. Gen 2:2–3; see chapter 2 (2.2).
220. Rom 8:34.
221. Rom 8:26–27.
222. Cf. Preface, footnote 12.
223. Rev 6:9–11; 22:17.

PART III

Returning and Rethinking: Living in a "New" Canonical Narrative

Chapter 22

To Repent

22.1 "You Are the Man!"

WITH THESE WORDS THE prophet Nathan named King David as a murderer and confronted him with God's judgment over his deeds.[1] In an identical manner, the *Shoa* showed the world of nations its hatred of Jews with its gruesome, violent, outworking. Western culture, much influenced by Christianity, was confronted with an evil that lingered in its own bosom. Exposing this deadly anti-Semitism also brought the Christian contribution into the spotlight.[2]

It then became apparent that the *Shoa* was no tragic accident, but that many centuries of anti-Semitism prepared for the *Shoa*. A poisonous mixture of age-old hatred of Jews had been strengthened by an age-old anti-Jewish (and sometimes also anti-Semitic) thinking in Christian theology and within churches.[3] This thinking caused many to "willingly cooperate"[4] in one way or the other. The fact that these masses were in part "Christian" and "belonging to the Church" made no difference whatsoever. Christian-motivated hatred of Jews had actually been a reality for centuries.[5] This book is part of the necessary reorientation that has begun. Finally within the circle of Christian theology and churches, the prophetic verdict of "You are the man!" has been taken to heart.

1. 2 Sam 12:7.

2. See Introduction and chapter 13.

3. David Nirenberg describes in his *Anti-Judaism* the history of anti-Jewish thinking in Western culture, wherein ancient (Egyptian and Roman) hatred of Jews and later originating Christian anti-Jewish thinking have led to ("handy and useful," EJW) anti-Jewish thought and language pattern that has been applied in innumerable ways in Western (political and philosophical) culture, and still is present there.

4. So Daniel J. Goldhagen, *Hitler's Willing Executioners*. Extensively he describes the willing cooperation of ordinary Germans.

5. Par example see Jansen, *Christelijke theologie na Auschwitz*.

Part III: Returning and Rethinking: Living in a "New" Canonical Narrative

22.2 A Shocking Discovery: The Tears of Joseph

Joseph's brothers suddenly discover that the brother they had sold into slavery had a special place in God's plan.[6] When Joseph finally makes himself known, it is a shock that causes his brothers, the perpetrators, fear and sorrow.[7] When today's Christian faith community begins to discover the real ongoing structure of Scripture's canonical narrative, something similar happens: we discover that we have been blind to God's eternal love for His people Israel and that we have contributed to the "slavery" of His people.

It is noteworthy that in fact it is Joseph who weeps when he reveals his identity to his brothers.[8] Only Benjamin, his one full brother, weeps with him.[9] The shocking confrontation with their blindness could easily cause a new division between them,[10] since seemingly there is more fear of the consequences than real contrition about what they have done to Joseph.[11] The tears of Joseph, however, first reveal his suffering and then also his longing.

Perhaps this story can be a reminder of the fact that the LORD God Himself has been the First One who suffered from our self-willed distortion of the canonical narrative. His sorrow about it is greater than we are conscious of. His longing for our repentance is more intense than we realize.

22.3 Repenting of Our Role in the Ongoing Canonical Narrative

When Nathan finishes speaking, David reacts with these words: "I have sinned against the LORD."[12] We must learn to speak these words when we learn our own history of the distortion of God's canonical narrative. And even when certain faith communities or individual believers have held more scriptural different opinions, and have acted differently, in connectedness with the whole Body of the Messiah, the Church of all ages, we must learn to confess what Daniel confessed in connectedness with the whole of Israel:

> "Lord, the great and awesome God, who keeps his covenant of love with those who love him and keep his commandments, we have sinned and done wrong. We have been wicked and have rebelled; we have turned away from your commands and laws. We have not listened to your servants the prophets, who spoke in your name . . .

---

6. Gen 45:7–8.
7. Gen 45:3, 5.
8. Gen 45:2, 14–15.
9. Gen 45:14.
10. Cf. the "Don't quarrel on the way!" (Gen 45:24).
11. Cf. Gen 50:15–21.
12. 2 Sam 12:13.

> "Lord, you are righteous, but this day we are covered with shame—the people of Judah and the inhabitants of Jerusalem and all Israel, both near and far, in all the countries where you have scattered us because of our unfaithfulness to you."[13]

It appears that for centuries, the community of believers from the nations who have entered "into the Messiah"[14] in some way has been a "community of robbers" too, often adopting this characteristic from the nations.[15] In some way we as the community of believers from the nations have both robbed God of His people Israel and Israel of its birthright.[16] We have taken away the Messiah's Jewish identity, and from the King of the Jews His nation and land. We even considered ourselves blessed while deconstructing the God-ordained connections and structures discussed within this book. For centuries this influenced not only our thought, but also our faith traditions and therefore our actions.

Today when we wish to be pleasing to the God of Israel, following the *Shoa*, we must wholeheartedly pray in the manner of Psalm 51[17]:

> "Create in me a pure heart, O God,
>   and renew a steadfast spirit within me.
> Do not cast me from your presence
>   or take your Holy Spirit from me."[18]

22.4 The Higher Thoughts and Ways of God

The prophet Isaiah speaks of the higher thoughts and ways of God,[19] which are not like those of man. God is characterized by faithfulness to what He promised, manifold forgiveness, and determination to do whatever He has spoken.[20]

In the traditional canonical narrative, the faithfulness of God is limited. Within that narrative the people of Israel find themselves outside the reach of God's mercy because of stubbornness. As seen from the traditional interpretative paradigm, also God's words about His people, city, and the land remain unfulfilled because people,

---

13. Dan 9:4–7.
14. Cf. chapter 20.
15. Cf. chapter 11 (11.5) for the greed of the nations; also see Zech 2:8–9. In Westerman, *The Messiah and His two children* the names of the two sons of Isaiah are interpreted in relation to the two communities which have been brought into the Messiah. Also see Westerman, *De Tora van de Messias*, 6–12 and passim.
16. Cf. Rom 3:1–2; 9:4–5.
17. The heading (not numbered in NIV) connects this Psalm of David to the appearance and words of the prophet Nathan.
18. Ps 51:10–11.
19. Isa 55:8–9.
20. Isa 55:3, 7, 11–13.

Part III: Returning and Rethinking: Living in a "New" Canonical Narrative

city and land have no lasting and individual position within the salvific actions of God.

The traditional canonical narrative, therefore, is an expression of human thinking about God.[21] It is unmasked as something human and prideful, a stubborn resistance to His revelation. We have been blind while seeing, and deaf while hearing.[22] When we discover this, only one response is possible: we must mourn and repent.

22.5 The Ways of God's Eternal Love for Israel: Contrition and Repentance

The way of God's eternal love for Israel is the way by which He wishes to bless the world. This has been His intention from the beginning of creation. So much has become clear in the rendering of the canonical narrative presented in this book. The traditional view on the narrative of the Scriptures whereby the people of Israel disappeared to the background after their role was fulfilled, meant that we as community of believers from the nations did not follow God in His ways.

The way of God toward the midst of creation, toward the house of learning as He intended, toward His indwelling amidst His people in order to ultimately bless the whole world from there and to usher in the *olam haba*, has largely remained unknown by us. Consequently we did not "accompany" the God of Israel by longing for what He longs for or walk with Him in His ways.

Because we often read the Scriptures of the New Covenant as if they were removed from the streambed of the Tanakh, we have not recognized the love of God for his people as the love Hosea was commanded to show:[23]

> I will betroth you to me forever;
> I will betroth you in righteousness and justice,
> in love and compassion.
> I will betroth you in faithfulness,
> and you will acknowledge the LORD.[24]

We have not read these words as originating from this "Hosea-love" of God. From the love of a God who will, if necessary, wait and who will do anything in order to prepare His wife for love again.[25] Thereby we often have separated God and Israel in our thinking; we have "cut-them-loose" from each other in our thought. In this manner we were not able to see God acting in a manner that was directed—although perhaps invisible

---

21. Cf. Isa 55:8 and Ps 50:21.
22. Cf. Isa 6:9–10; John 9:39–41.
23. Cf. chapter 20 (20.17).
24. Hos 2:19–20.
25. Hos 3:5.

and unrecognizable to us, and sometimes in judgment[26]—toward all of Israel's ultimate embrace of God.[27] Not only did "the Church" often not show reverence for the apple of God's eye,[28] but even became a sort of "bird of prey," hunting God's speckled bird Israel.[29] Therefore, we as "believers from the nations," "the Church," must take the judgment of the LORD into account for ourselves.

But above all, as believers from the nations, we have not known God Himself fully. Through our blindness, our knowledge of Him was only partial. In our communion with Him we lacked the knowledge of His first love.[30] We made the LORD into the image of ourselves,[31] and we left Him alone in His love for His people and His desire to bless the nations and creation from the midst of this people. Our heart was far away from Him instead of cleaving to Him.[32]

22.6 The Ways of the Messiah: Contrition and Repentance

In the same way, we have removed the Messiah from the streambed in which God planted Him. Therefore we have had no perspective of the various dimensions of His *avoda* in Israel's midst. Seldom have we seen that His life, in the obedience of His holy priesthood and kingship, really implied the fulfillment of Israel's calling.

Therefore we have also not understood what blessing for all Israel His covenant fulfillment brought. We have not recognized His kingship over all Israel, even if it (for the time being) yet has the shape of the Hebron-kingship. We have not recognized the participation of the Messiah in Israel's exile, part of the "not-yet" phase of His kingship, even though our recognition of this aspect of His Messiah-ship could have meant mutual recognition together within the encounter with Judaism. Messiah *Yeshua* certainly mirrors the suffering *Mashiaḥ-ben-Yosef* from Jewish tradition,[33] and indeed is found "at the gates of Rome."[34]

---

26. Even the judgment of partial blinding (Rom 11:1–10) is oriented toward the future of God's compassion (Rom 11:32).

27. Jer 31:22.

28. Zech 2:8.

29. Jer 12:9.

30. Cf. Jer 2:1–3.

31. Ps 50:21.

32. Ps 63:9.

33. Judaism knows of both a conquering form of the Messiah (the Messiah, son of David) and a suffering form of the Messiah (the Messiah, son of Joseph). Par example see Bialik and Ravnitzky, *Legends*, 395–97 (Fragment 56). Also see chapter 18 (18.9).

34. The Talmud has a discussion about the recognition of the Messiah. In it the prophet Elijah says that the Messiah can be recognized by the fact that he can be found among the sick at the entrance of Rome, where he cares for them; for this section from tractate b. Sanhedrin 98a see Bialik and Ravnitzky, *Legends*, 390 (Fragment 18).

Part III: Returning and Rethinking: Living in a "New" Canonical Narrative

We as the "Church of the ages" have loved Jesus Christ and wished to follow Him; at the same time we have made Him unrecognizable to His people. And because of our ignorance we have not been able to accompany Him on His ways with His people. Like His disciples left Him alone in His wrestling on the Mount of Olives,[35] we are also guilty of such behavior. In a certain sense His loneliness which began there has continued through the centuries, without understanding from His disciples from the nations, and the Messiah of Israel has continued wrestling for His people and for the world.

22.7 The History and Future of the People, the City, and the Land: Contrition and Repentance

The Jewish scholar Maimonides[36] placed the history of Christianity within the framework of the sovereignty of the God of Israel. From his perspective of rabbinic Jewish orthodoxy, and despite his critique on Christianity and the Christian message, he yet observed a Divine intention. According to him the LORD served His own purposes with this "instrument" in order to bring the nations to monotheism and to spread the knowledge of the Name of Israel's God among them.[37]

On the Christian side, the traditional canonical narrative has often negatively affected the perspective on the ongoing history of the people Israel, the city of Jerusalem, and the land. The leading ideas and arguments in the Christian evaluation included God's denouncement and rejection, ultimately declaring the nation of Israel expendable. These thoughts naturally led to a process of theological de-Judaizing the city of Jerusalem and the land, replacing God's love for His city and His land with a universally-oriented "*sanctus*-fication" of the land and Jerusalem.[38]

However, when the people, the city, and the land are so intensely connected to the *avoda* of the Messiah, as this book shows, and thus have a God-intended future, a light of hope shines from Messiah *Yeshua* over this priestly nation, the city of Jerusalem, and the land in the center of the earth. We can discern and should expect

---

35. Matthew, Mark, and Luke emphasize that Jesus, following the celebration of *Pessaḥ* went to the Mount of Olives; Luke does not even name Gethsemane. Cf. chapter 19 (19.5) and (19.9).

36. Moses ben Maimon or Maimonides (also known as Rambam) lived between 1135–1204. Born in Cordoba (Spain), he later studied and worked in Morocco and Egypt.

37. "And all these things of Jesus the Nazarene, and of (Muhammad) the Ishmaelite who stood after him—there is no (purpose) but to straighten out the way for the King Messiah, and to restore all the world to serve God together. So that it is said, 'Because then I will turn toward the nations (giving them) a clear lip, to call all of them in the name of God and to serve God (shoulder to shoulder as) one shoulder.' (Zephaniah 3:9) . . . (*Hilkhot Melakhim* 11:10–12)," https://en.wikipedia.org/wiki/Judaism's_view_of_Jesus (accessed 27th of February 2017).

38. The attention that the Promised Land and the city of Jerusalem received within the framework of Christian pilgrimages and the crusades was de-Judaized. Only in a general and universal way they were "Holy land" and "Holy city." Also see chapter 23 (23.11).

therefore the footsteps of the Holy One around the camp of Israel—designation of the people and the God-intended home of Israel.[39]

Then, filled with shame, we will remember how "the Church" together with the nations has often cast lots for God's people, traded it for slavery, and divided up the land.[40] Without really grieving over "the ruin of Joseph,"[41] we thought of ourselves as the rich, and we have dishonored the poor, sending poor Israel away without caring for its needs.[42]

22.8 The Body of the Messiah: Contrition and Repentance

"The Body of the Messiah" has often been equated to "the Church," which in its turn had been ripped of the rootedness in the Jewish Messiah, who appeared in the streambed of the Tanakh and therein still stands with all His *avoda*.

When, however, the canonical narrative as sketched above is our starting point, we learn to think differently about the Body of the Messiah. Believers are then grafted into Israel from the nations, as it has seen its calling fulfilled and obtained in the Messiah. Fundamentally it is about being blessed with and from Israel. From the beginning the Messiah then connects us, believers from the nations, with Israel. The firstlings of Israel form the first community of believers in the Messiah. The faith community from the nations is added later. Then there is no room for pride, not even against the part of God's people who have, for whatever reason, not yet recognized and embraced God's fulfillment of Israel's calling in the Messiah.

Instead of self-exaltation, we then learn to rejoice in the fact that we might become co-heirs.[43] Before God we become aware of the fact that we have been invited, in a certain sense, to leave our own tribe, language and people, and to join in the way toward the camp of Israel in the midst of the earth, toward Zion, where the LORD wishes to dwell.[44] We then learn to see how our own calling remains indissolubly connected to the eternal election and calling of God's people. Before God's countenance we then become conscious of the depth of our resistance against joining with this one Jewish man.[45]

---

39. For "the footsteps of God" cf. Lev 26:12; Deut 23:14 and Ps 77:19.
40. Joel 3:2–3.
41. Amos 6:6.
42. Jas 2:6, 15–16.
43. Eph 3:6.
44. See par example chapter 9 (9.8 and 9.9), 12 (12.12 and 12.13) and 15.
45. Zech 8:23.

Part III: Returning and Rethinking: Living in a "New" Canonical Narrative

22.9 Reformation of Practice and Thought: Returning and Rethinking

Contrition and repentance form the first step in this new beginning. It will include a (re)turn of our hearts with much prayer and tears. All tribes of the earth will mourn together with Israel because of the Pierced One,[46] because of Him who suffered once outside Jerusalem, but who also so often has been thrown out and pierced anew. Our repentance can be part of this mourning.

But whoever repents, must also return and reconsider our thinking. The Hebrew *teshuva*—meaning 'return'—connects returning to God with practical and concrete returning: the returning from ways we have chosen to walk. Different ways and thoughts need to well up from a different inner life. Nothing less than a reformation of life and thought around Israel and Israel's God and His Messiah needs to take place amongst us.

This is the theme of the next chapter.

---

46. Rev 1:7.

CHAPTER 23

Returning and Rethinking

23.1 The Holy One Chose to Be Defenseless

SEEMINGLY DEFENSELESS, THE HOLY One of Israel allowed Himself to be robbed by "the Church" and "theologically transformed" by human thinking, as was briefly discussed in chapter 22. In this manner the God of Israel and His Messiah put into practice what *Yeshua* taught in the Sermon on the Mount.[1] It appeared that, besides "the coat of the Messiah" being willingly parted with, so too could "His shirt" be freely taken away.[2] It's as if He simply chose to continue walking "a second mile" with His followers from the nations, people often blinded in pride and yet often very dedicated.[3] For the Body of the Messiah, the Holy One of Israel has responded to curses with blessing, and there has even been prayer in heaven for those who shamefully abused Him.[4]

Now, however, not only is it time for repentance, but also for a concrete return from the paths that we have chosen. We finally begin to realize just how far we have gone astray. Returning from a long distance along the wrong path takes time and effort. It asks for humility and perseverance. It calls for concrete actions inspired by a different way of thinking, a thinking that wishes to align with God's own thoughts. This chapter, therefore, hopes to be a small contribution to this reformation.

---

1. Matt 5–7; Luke 6:20–49.
2. Luke 6:29; Matt 5:40.
3. Matt 5:41.
4. Luke 6:27–28; Matt 5:44.

Part III: Returning and Rethinking: Living in a "New" Canonical Narrative

23.2 Called to *Kedusha* before God's Countenance

It is foundational to realize that the God of Israel has called us to *kedusha*, together with His people. He has called us to the sanctification of the Name of God and to the sanctification of life and the world in the way of His commandments. The coming of the Messiah and the gift of the Holy Spirit have been oriented to this; from the very beginning this has been God's will and intent.[5]

The *avoda* of Israel was not primarily intended for the receiving of blessing, as was the case in the service of Baal. This idol-god was served in order to obtain "blessing."[6] Unfortunately, in many Christian circles (at least in the average preaching and faith practice) this focus on the receiving of God's blessing has been prevalent.

Kedusha is also the focal point in the gospel of the Messiah and the Kingdom. Therefore this message is not only or predominantly about forgiveness, reconciliation and salvation (Western Christianity), or about the obtaining of immortality (Eastern-Orthodox Christianity). It is even less about obtaining some kind of prosperity (through the preaching of a so-called prosperity-gospel),[7] or about obtaining spiritual authority over other powers or gods.[8]

Israel was called to the sanctification and worship of God's Name, even in the night and in times of shortage and lack of blessings.[9] The prayer book of the Psalms, the prayer of Israel so much lived by the Messiah, and Judaism's intense focus on "blessing God" remind us of this original intention of God.[10]

As believers from the nations, we too have been called to stand before the countenance of the God of Israel, who also is the God and father of *Yeshua*, King of the Jews, and honor Him. Even in the darkness of the times.[11]

To discover this calling anew also requires a massive reorientation of our prayer and song. Prayer life and habits, prayer and song texts will not automatically change. The realization that, by this calling, we are beckoned to join in the prayer of the camp of the priestly Israel, comes through knowledge. Only teaching and learning will bring about a fertile soil for the reformation of which this chapter speaks.

At the same time our reading and application, both collectively and individually of Scripture, here the Tanakh in particular, should be marked by the perspective of "sharing together with Israel" in its salvation. The traditional manner of spiritualizing-focused reading must make way for a manner of reading that attempts to learn the totality of God's intentions. We must learn reading habits characterized by modesty,

---

5. See chapter 2 (2.2)
6. Cf. Hos 2:5.
7. Various shapes thereof can be observed within the world-wide Christian faith community.
8. Cf. for this Acts 8:9–25 (Simon the sorcerer).
9. Cf. Hab 3:17–19.
10. The very first tractate of both Mishna and Talmud is *Berakhot* (Blessings).
11. Cf. Ps 134:1.

in which we remain discerning between what God promises and asks of His people Israel, and what revelation and salvation He thereby also gives to those of us called from the nations to share in.

23.3 Called by the God of Israel Who Reveals Himself within the Camp of Israel

The revelation of God in the camp of Israel, as en-*Scripture*-d in the Tanakh, has a somewhat casual character within the traditional canonical narrative, as the Apostolic Creed[12] and the Confession of Nicaea[13] show. In these confessions of the ancient Church, which can be seen as a kind of summary of the traditional canonical narrative, Israel is nowhere to be found. The Tanakh, for the greatest part, does not play a role in these ancient confessions.[14] Therefore the incarnation, death, and resurrection of the Son form an event without a real prior context, a heavenly "stray stone" or "Fremdkörper," one that seemingly could be understood without the Tanakh.

These confessions of faith show how, right from the beginning, the growing faith community of the Christian church had difficulty understanding itself as positioned in the streamed of the revelation within the Tanakh which the God of Israel had given to Israel. For the Church, its own robust growth and the ever-troublesome fate of Israel became divine "road signs" pointing to a canonical narrative in which the lasting election of Israel had no place anymore. The confession of God as Creator was upheld against those such as Marcion,[15] but the remaining part of the Old Testament only functioned as a prophetic pointer to Christ and the salvation for all people. In "passing by" one could also learn from it how incomplete and earthly (and therefore not heavenly and eternal) Israel's religion was. Also in the debate of the Christian theologians with contemporary philosophical schools the growing distance toward the Jewish people and the Tora of Sinai played a helpful role. Insights of Greek philosophers were directly connected to the activity of the not-yet-incarnated Son of God,[16] thereby devaluating the revelation granted to Israel. When these philosophers had indeed been inspired by the not-yet-incarnated Son, God's way of revealing Himself in Israel's camp could be thought of as a "detour."

---

12. This confession of faith is dated around the midst of the second century CE.

13. The full name of this creed is the creed of Nicaea-Constantinople (after the councils of 325 and 381 CE at which the themes were discussed which we find in this creed).

14. See the Introduction.

15. See chapter 13 (13.3).

16. Therein the concept of *logos* (meaning "word") was useful. Both in Greek philosophy and in Christian faith this designation played a role. Greek philosophy used *logos* for the divine reason that was thought as foundational to everything. See also John 1:1–5, 14; here *logos* is the name of the Son of God who was involved in creation and is incarnated. Besides also Judaism knows of a similar concept, namely the *memra* (= word) who was with God from the beginning. Also see chapter 15, footnote 89.

Part III: Returning and Rethinking: Living in a "New" Canonical Narrative

The triumph of the Christian message became visible, so many thought, when Christianity became the state religion of the Roman empire.[17] Quite naturally the Christian churches in the East and the West took on the allure of a triumphant religion. The Church was "the new Israel," and sometimes even identified itself as "the new Jerusalem." In this de-*Jew*-ized and sometimes even fully anti-Semitic[18] context, the religious practice of the Christian churches developed, including theological thinking, and new manners of reading Scripture. The result was that an all-determining theological replacement-DNA was formed, which naturally determined thinking and practice more and more. The structures of thinking about God and His revelation, His promises and commandments, His salvific intentions and ways, came to be marked by it. This traditional canonical narrative became "truth" more and more, heavily influencing the life of the Christian faith community. On a large scale today's Christian church still carries these deeply-etched markings, being influenced by this de-*Jew*-ized DNA.

The reconsideration of the traditional canonical narrative and a sketch of the "alternative" canonical narrative, as presented in this book, also originate from a previous reconsideration of the doctrine of faith and of scriptural interpretation begun earlier.[19] In an ever-deepening process of rethinking, this "new" canonical narrative continues to contribute to a "cycle" of reconsideration.

Our learning about God and His ways begins with astonishment and humility. It should come forth from a deep awareness that a knowledge of God is only possible because the Most High God has wished to make Himself known to us as the God of Israel, in and out of the camp of Israel. Our systematic theology must be willing to stand in the streambed of the "other" canonical narrative, a streambed of the canonical narrative in which God chooses to dwell and act from the God-chosen midst of creation. A narrative in which He structurally remains faithful to His election of Israel. A canonical narrative in which Israel's calling is the continuing theme, and in which the Scriptures of the New Covenant are read as situated within the streambed of the Tanakh. A narrative that is told in such manner that the meaning of God's revelation for believers from the nations is exclusively categorized as "sharing in the salvation that has been granted to Israel." And finally, this ongoing canonical narrative must not be invalidated again by our systematization of themes.

When all of these things are being reconsidered, our reading of the Scriptures will naturally find itself more and more in the streambed of the Tanakh. In humble openness to what we, connected to Israel's Messiah, can co-learn together with all Israel.

---

17. This was the consequence of emperor Constantine I (ca. 280–337 CE) accepting the Christian faith.

18. Cf. the quote of Chrysostom in the Introduction (I.4, footnote 17).

19. See chapter 13.

23.4 New Eyes Through the "Other" Canonical Narrative

The traditional canonical narrative not only places the biblical history and its interpretation within its own framework, it also caused church fathers and later interpreters to interpret Church and world history from the perspective of the traditional narrative. The alternative canonical narrative within this book not only presents an opportunity to read the Scriptures of the Tanakh and the New Covenant as one ongoing narrative, but also gives us new eyes; it offers a different perspective on the (ongoing) history of Israel and "the Church" in the world of nations. Through it, the historical reconstruction and interpretation of the "parting" of Judaism and Christianity is also changed.

"The parting of the ways"[20] has indeed partially materialized through convictions foundational to the traditional canonical narrative. The Christian church, increasingly consisting of non-Jews, believed it essential to cut ties with Israel for the sake of the gospel of Christ. In this manner the Church believed to follow God self and to obey the message of the New Testament. This being the case, it was only logical for the Jewish side to conclude that with Jesus and His message a new religion, alien to the Tanakh, had begun.[21]

The result of this development was that Judaism, in its evaluation of Christianity in a certain sense actually "took over" the traditional canonical narrative, and its structure determines the Jewish view on the history of Israel and "the Church" until today. As a result, the Jewish reading of the New Testament has been stamped by the conviction that these writings can in no way be part of the narrative of the God of Israel.[22]

The "other" canonical narrative brings with it a different way of looking and evaluation. It therefore contributes to a different dialogue with Judaism, because it reveals a deep and lasting connectedness.

23.5 A Lasting Central Place for Israel's Election and Covenantal *Kedusha*: The Messiah as the Obedient Firstling of Israel

While the traditional canonical narrative separated Israel and "the Church" by means of the contrast between "law and grace," among other things, the "other" canonical narrative demonstrates that there is no such distinction between (works of) obedience

---

20. This expression is sometimes used to designate the separation between Judaism and Christianity.

21. The conceptual pairing of "Israel-Church" or "Church-Israel," often used to designate the historically-developed contradistinction, is at the deepest level not really helpful when we on the one hand want to honor the difference between Judaism and the Christian faith community, and on the other hand do not wish to come to the conclusion that there are two separate religions, each with its own way. The presence of Jews, who confess *Yeshua* as Messiah, is made invisible by this conceptual pairing.

22. This is still the case in *JANT*.

and grace. Even further, the *kedusha* God required from His people Israel still forms the heart of the covenant He granted to Israel and of its election also in the New Testament.

It is precisely *because* of the necessity of obedient sanctification of the covenant by Israel, that the LORD chooses a way in the midst of Israel that makes this obedience possible. A way which includes a new self-revelation from God Himself.[23]

The message of the Messiah as the obedient Firstling of Israel,[24] will certainly raise questions within the circle of the Jewish people. However, it should also be clear that the message about this Firstling in no way discharges Jews who believe in Him of their calling to live the *kedusha* to which Israel has been called. And at the same time it must be clear that *goyim* too in Him are called to their own Messianic *halakha*, the way of obedience specifically commanded to them, which lies enclosed in the Tora that has been given to Israel.[25]

This must be clear: the all-dominating center remains the self-revelation of the God of Abraham, Isaac and Jacob, who remains eternally faithful, and does not annul Israel's election and calling, but confirms it and thus brings creation to its goal.

23.6 An Identity that Remains Connected with Israel

The traditional canonical narrative and the practices related to it caused a deep separation between Judaism and "the Church." Each identity, on both sides, has predominantly been determined by a contradistinction considered irreconcilable. Today when the community of the followers of Messiah *Yeshua* begins to realize that its identity has been determined by the anti-Judaic scheme of the traditional canonical narrative, then a re-evaluation of this identity can begin on a path of repentance and reconsideration.

What follows is that the strange identity of the "other" will then not be so unfamiliar. Through Messiah *Yeshua* the community, comprised of both His followers from Israel and the nations, remains connected to all Israel. The "big multitude from all nations"—so the rediscovered "other" canonical narrative tells us—is being gathered around the King of the Jews, who within His Hebron-kingship, gathers all Israel and the nations around Himself. He gives the multitude a drink from a well, where salvation granted to Israel wells up.

We must learn to confess that we did not live in accordance with what we at the deepest level were and are meant to be: co-sharers in Israel's salvation, and that we have hated and rejected those who were and are loved by the Holy God. Such repentant confession will cause churches and Christian faith communities to recognize humbly, as Peter was humbled after three times disowning Jesus, that the encounter

---

23. See chapter 12 (12.4) and chapter 15.

24. Par example see chapter 16 and 17.

25. See chapter 20 but also paragraph 23.7 in this chapter for the specific callings of Israel and the *goyim* "in the Messiah."

with Judaism is not something to be taken for granted. And that the Church can claim no rights whatsoever within these encounters.[26]

We must also learn to recognize that the boundless disunity that is present within the Body of the Messiah is based on a "writing-off-the-other" principle that resurfaces again and again. This process started with the "writing off" of Israel's abiding place in our narrative of God's plans. As a further consequence, there was no longer a place for the firstlings from Israel within the Body. This first rupture has been repeated again and again.[27] Without repenting of those repetitive fractures in the Body of the Messiah, a discussion about the first rupture is actually impossible. Without repentance, we as believers in Israel's Messiah—in all our disunity—are not an attractive dialogue partner for the whole of Israel.

23.7 Even "In The Messiah" All Israel Remains Connected to God

Within the traditional narrative scheme, after the coming of Jesus only a severed relationship with God remains for the majority of the people of Israel. If there is a relationship at all, it is a relationship of judgment. "Exiled," "rejected," "objects of God's wrath," "abandoned"—such was the terminology used when it concerned the Jewish people as a whole. There was no understanding of "the two languages" that God uses when referencing His people. We've observed that concerning the Messiah the language of His triumph was predominantly used, and that the language of His exile and the "not-yet" of His kingship was unknown.[28] The situation was exactly the same when it concerned our thinking and speaking of the ways of God with all Israel. The fact that in that first period a majority of the people did not accept the message about *Yeshua* led to the conclusion that God had rejected them. In this manner, however, God's eternal love for His people was not credited. Paul also shows that we need at least "two words." There may be "enmity" when it concerns the message of the gospel, but all Israel consists of people who are "loved on account of the patriarchs."[29]

We previously learned that that God's connection to His people is never broken, even on the night of judgment. God's faithfulness is foundational. It might be possible that there is "distance" in some respect, as with Hosea, but it is that "distancing" that is preparation for love.[30] The Messiah still awaits the complete surrender to Him as King of the Jews, just like David waited for the realization of His kingship.[31] There is

26. As a negative example can serve the forced Jewish participation in doctrinal debates, or the Jewish audiences that were forced to listen to Christian sermons in cities and villages.

27. The insight in the relationship between the first rupture and the pattern of repetition I gained from the thinking within the international reconciliation movement Toward Jerusalem Council II (also see 23.8).

28. See chapter 18 (18.8 and 18.9), 19 (19.9), 20 (20.3), 21 (21.5).

29. Rom 11:28.

30. See chapter 20 (20.17) and 22 (22.5).

31. See chapter 18 (18.8 and 18.11).

Part III: Returning and Rethinking: Living in a "New" Canonical Narrative

in a certain sense, abandonment by God and exile, but at the same time there is the presence of the Messiah as God's *Shekhina* sharing in the exile and pain of all Israel.[32] There is suffering for Israel because of sins, but there is also the "Comfort, comfort my people"[33] from the mouth of the LORD. There is punishment because of disobedience, but there is also the fact that God—even if only for His own honor[34]—will not allow the possibility for His words and promises to remain unrealized.[35]

"In" Messiah *Yeshua* God remains unchanged. He is and remains the Same.[36] He still is the God of Israel, even in the history following the parting of the ways between Israel and the community that confessed Jesus to be Messiah. Because of this we may know that He remained active in and around His people. We must recognize the fact that He, even if His "feet" walked sometimes incomprehensible paths,[37] has safeguarded His people for Himself and that He slowly and relentlessly works toward the day of the full return to Zion, both His own and the nation's.

Paul discovered that the Messiah was with the people in the desert following the exodus.[38] If indeed the whole of the cosmos is sustained by Him,[39] how could Israel's national existence and faith then fall outside of His reign! The Messiah, however, does not act outside of what God wishes. On the contrary, He reveals the Father.[40]

From the viewpoint of the "other" canonical narrative, we also learn to look at "the history of Judaism" differently. Israel's history is a history geared toward a goal. A history where the LORD works toward His abiding Indwelling in Zion. Instead of contempt, love for those "loved on account of the patriarchs," and hope must color our view.[41]

The safekeeping of Israel's existence in the exile—*galut*—and the gradual, and in our times big-scale, return to the land are not facts within themselves, separated from Divine action. This being the case even if the enigma of the *Shoa* thereby becomes even more pressing.

---

32. See chapter 19 (19.9).
33. Isa 40:1.
34. Cf. Ezek 36:22.
35. Isa 55:11.
36. Jas 1:17.
37. Cf. Ps 77:20; Isa 55:9.
38. 1 Cor 10:4.
39. Col 1:15–17; Heb 1:3.
40. John 1:18; 14:7–10.
41. In a certain sense there is a chiastic connection between the exaltation of the Messiah and the path of suffering of all Israel, and between the exile of the Messiah and God's faithful dealings with His people. The "already" of the kingship of the Messiah is related to the "not-yet" of the dedication of all Israel. The "not-yet" of His kingship is related to the ever abiding "already" of God's Presence and care for His people.

Neither have spiritual developments within the people taken place outside of His reign. The codification of tradition in the Mishna and later the Talmud,[42] the further development of rabbinic Judaism, the rise of Jewish mysticism and Chassidism, but also Zionism (both secular and religious), have in some way or another, even if we do not know exactly how, a place in the mystery of the Messiah's connection to the whole of Israel. This is even the case with Jewish atheism as a response to the pain of the *Shoa*.[43]

As seen from the perspective based on the "other" canonical narrative, the centuries-long, internally-Jewish discussions about the essence of Judaism and the path of the Tora ultimately stand in the context of the return to Zion and the self-revelation of both God and His Messiah there.

Just as on the Christian side there has been deformation of the thinking about God and His purposes in Christ,[44] this possibility also has been present on the Jewish side. This deformation of thought on both sides was much stimulated by the fact that the "own identity" was very much formed in confrontation with and rejection of "the other." So also within the circle of Israel it was possible to think that God is like man,[45] and to misunderstand Him.

Yeshua/Jesus Himself, however, shows that in no way does He categorically reject traditions within Israel. Tradition could count on His critique[46] only in so far the intentions of the Tora got lost by it. Also the words of the teachers of the Tora were not rejected by definition.[47] His preaching, like that of the Scriptures of the New Covenant, is based on the Tora and the whole of the Tanakh, and thus presupposes the abiding Divine revelation in this Scripture. In the treasure storeroom of Israel there is much to be found, also for the disciples of Messiah *Yeshua*.[48] This includes the internally-Jewish reflection on historic and contemporary developments within Judaism (with respect to Israel's calling and its required *avoda*), the *halakha*, Zionism, living in the land, the attitude toward the state of Israel, and the attitude toward secularization, to name a few. This reflection also takes place, in some way or an other, within the mystery of the Messiah's connection to all Israel, and therefore can serve our thinking as well.

A renewed learning from and with the whole of Israel is the desperately-needed answer to the de-*Jew*-izing of thought and practice that has been prevalent within

---

42. Respectively around the end of the second century (CE), and in the sixth century (CE) and later.

43. This short characterization I owe to Dan Juster.

44. See chapter 22 and in paragraph 23.1 in this chapter.

45. Cf. Ps 50:21.

46. See par example Matt 23:23; Mark 7:7–13.

47. See par example Matt 23:3.

48. Matt 13:52. The connection between the weekly reading of the Tora and sections from the prophets in itself can already be a revelation to non-Jews.

Christian faith communities. A renewed perspective of Messiah *Yeshua* will lead to new discoveries in the treasure room from which He Himself learned and taught. The blessing of learning is also "in the Messiah" from the Jews.[49] This stems from a certain overlap in identity between Judaism and the Body of the Messiah. The Spirit who, on God's command, will reveal everything,[50] does this as the Spirit of the God of Israel and of the King of the Jews. He makes us aware of this connectedness and uses it in His work of instruction.

All this means that also within faith communities—the churches—formed around Messiah *Yeshua*, a deep encounter with Judaism and with a Jewish reading of Scripture should not be an exception.[51] Even more, it is an indispensable *necessity* on the path of following Israel's Messiah, who wishes to reveal His Tora also to the nations.[52]

23.8 The Body of the Messiah: A Dual Structure from Israel and the Nations

Within the traditional narrative scheme "the Church" became antithetical to Israel. Israel certainly was "the manger of the Messiah," but with Him something completely new began, causing a rupture of the continuity with "the old Israel." In fact, this implied that God's way with Israel had simply been an intermezzo, meant to show the necessity of a different kind of salvation. A salvation intended for all people, not limited to one nation and land. A salvation that was less earthly, suitable to a more spiritualized reading of the Tanakh. According to this view the Messiah appeared for no other purpose.

We have, however, already discussed that through the enfleshment in the midst of Israel, something totally different was illuminated:[53] the *kedusha* and *avoda* of the Messiah confirmed and fulfilled Israel's calling. The gift of the *Ruaḥ HaKodesh* at *Shavuot* in Jerusalem[54] did not mean, as often stated, "the birth of the Church." This (mis)interpretation separates Israel and the Messianic fellowship from each other. It is true that something new has begun, but the newness lies in the fact that the God of Israel is beginning to realize His promises in Israel's midst. Through His *avoda* the

---

49. John 4:22.

50. John 14:25–26; 16:12–15.

51. Naturally this asks for knowledge of the Hebrew language, familiarity with Jewish ways of reading of Scripture, and up to date knowledge of Judaism and its history. Perhaps special institutes of study concentrating on the theme of the "old" versus the "new/other" canonical narrative could contribute. (Thereby then being the total opposite of the program of de-Judaizing of the Christian faith in Nazi-Germany. See on this Heschel, *The Aryan Jesus*). Learning from Jewish scholars who study the New Testament and the church fathers would then be normal.

52. Isa 42:4; cf. Matt 28:19.

53. See chapter 15 (15.2).

54. Acts 2.

Messiah has obtained the promise of the Spirit for God's people. Within the circle of His people, the complete *kedusha* becomes available for the priestly nation. By the Spirit the firstlings of Israel become a living "ark" and "temple."[55] In the camp of Israel, the perfect sanctification begins, allowing the people to mediate priestly blessing. The consecration of the people takes place, causing it to become a "temple" by the gift of the Spirit, a "temple" in which the nations will be welcomed. By means of the priestly people, now the nations begin also to be invited to receive the blessing of this *kedusha*.

The salvation for the nations becomes available within the camp of Israel. And the nations become invited to celebrate these acts of God together with Israel, while the distinct callings of Israel and the nations remain in place. Analogous to the special position of the priestly sons of Aaron within Israel, "in the Messiah" a special calling also remains for that part of Israel that as firstling is sanctified in Him while awaiting the eschatological *kedusha* of all Israel.[56]

The blindness to this dual structure of calling caused "the Church" to develop more and more into a gentile-Christian direction. "The Church" not only thereby found itself in a position opposite Israel, but the continuity with Israel found itself under more and more pressure, also within the Body of the Messiah. Jewish life "in the Messiah" was seen as a theological impossibility, a *contradictio in terminis*, instead of the logical consequence of God's eternal faithfulness. The "doctrine of the Church," ecclesiology,[57] was fully de-Judaized. The firstlings from Israel were robbed of their God-intended position and silenced. Thereby the memory of the rootedness-in-Israel was also erased. The Jewish presence and life within the Messianic fellowship could not function anymore as a reminder of this rootedness-in-Israel.

In this manner the Messianic firstlings from Israel were banished from both sides. They were seen as traitors in the eyes of Judaism,[58] and viewed as theologically substandard in the eyes of gentile-Christians. For Jewish believers, even the Body of the Messiah was a dangerous place at times.[59] As a consequence of this structural exclusion, for centuries there has been no real reflection on Jewish-Messianic life and thought, or on the corresponding *halakha* within "the Church" and the circle of Jewish followers of *Yeshua*. The standard became assimilation to the prevailing theo-

---

55. For this cf. respectively Jer 31:33 (the heart of the people becomes "ark") and Ezek 36:27 (the heart of the people is inhabited as "temple"; also cf. 39:29).

56. See chapter 19.

57. Derived from the Greek word *ekklesia* (literally: [a body] called from/out of) that we find in the New Testament and is rendered as "church/congregation." The rendering "church" carries a lot of associations. In the Greek translation of the Tanakh it is used for the assembly/congregation of the people of Israel.

58. "Traitors" because of the accusation that they fled Jerusalem prior to its fall. Messianic-Jewish believers are further seen as having succumbed to a different (idolatrous) religion, because of the profession regarding the divinity of Messiah Jesus.

59. We can think of the Roman-Catholic way of dealing with the Marranos (Jews who had been baptized, often by force, and their offspring in Spain, Portugal and Latin-America) in the sixteenth and seventeenth century, who were persecuted and tortured on the suspicion of secret loyalty to Judaism.

Part III: Returning and Rethinking: Living in a "New" Canonical Narrative

logical convictions and life practices. Despite exceptions, voicing different convictions through the ages,[60] sometimes within Christian churches there was even a forced assimilation of Jewish believers.[61]

Today within the circle of Jewish followers of *Yeshua*, we see a remarkable reconsideration beginning. This reconsideration deals with both theology and practical life,[62] and is the result of a renewed consciousness among Jewish believers of their own Jewish identity. This reconsideration is tremendously stimulated by the rise and growth of newly-formed Messianic-Jewish faith communities, but takes also place within the circle of Jewish believers within existing denominations. Communal reflection from both of these groups has been taking place for some time.[63]

It should be noted, however, that this reflection on the Jewish-Messianic side is still nearly invisible to the majority of Christian churches and their theologians. It is only where churches and theologians have paid attention and are able to relate to the Messianic-Jewish movement, or to Jews professing *Yeshua* as Messiah within the different denominations, that we find knowledge of and participation in this new reflection.[64] After all, the special position of Jewish believers has been an unknown and sometimes uneasy phenomenon for many theologians and churches.

When, in the years following the *Shoa*, a renewed encounter between churches and Judaism began to take root and grow, the presence of Jews who professed *Yeshua* as the Messiah[65] appeared to be problematic. Their existence ran counter to the (conceptual) rift that had developed between Israel and "the Church." Therefore, they were often kept outside of these encounters, again resulting in pain for them.[66]

Today we see that because of the development of identity within the Messianic-Jewish movement and theology, both worldwide and in the state of Israel, new discussions take place at different levels. This can vary from yearly meetings for dialoguing[67] to scholarly attention.[68] Consequently, when it becomes clear that the eternal elec-

---

60. The Moravians were involved in efforts to establish special congregations for Jewish believers.

61. See the quote in the Introduction (I.4, footnote 17).

62. A survey and introduction can be found in (the dissertation of) Harvey, *Mapping Messianic Judaism*.

63. In the meetings of the so-called Helsinki Consultation (so named after the first place of convening) intensive communal consultation takes place. See http://helsinkiconsultation.squarespace.com/ (accessed 26th of March 2017).

64. The Caspari Centre for Biblical and Jewish Studies is one of the institutes contributing. See: https://www.caspari.com (accessed 26th of March 2017).

65. Hadderech, the Nederlandse Vereniging van Jesjoea HaMasjiach Belijdende Joden (the Dutch association of Jews who profess *Yeshua* as Messiah, EJW) characterizes itself with this designation. See www.hadderech.nl (accessed 26th of March 2017).

66. For the Dutch situation see Van Klinken, *Christelijke stemmen over het Jodendom*.

67. The Vatican has already for years an informal dialogue with the Messianic-Jewish movement. Alternately delegations of Roman-Catholic and Messianic-Jewish leaders and theologians meet each other in Rome and Jerusalem.

68. In 2009 and 2013 the World Congress of Jewish Studies paid attention to questions regarding

tion of Israel is part of the gospel of Messiah *Yeshua*, a reconsideration of positions earlier adopted could also possibly take place within the encounters with Judaism.[69]

The history of the two communities, found "in" Messiah *Yeshua* and consequently also in His Body, has been characterized by pride, "crowding-out" (in a very literal sense) and identity theft from the side of the gentile-Christians. This history, in regards to the Messiah, has been one of "maltreatment." Behind this is a history of "mal-thinking," wrong thinking about the Messiah and His salvation. Parallel to the repentance and turning back within the relationship to Judaism, repentance and turning back is therefore also needed with respect to the community of Jewish believers within the Body of *Yeshua*. It is God's mercy at work that this reconciliation is starting to receive more attention, both in various Christian denominations, and worldwide.[70]

This reorientation toward God and each other in the Body opens the eyes to the history of pride and its consequences. Genuine repentance and reconciliation will lead to a new sense of unity in which the specific callings of Israel and the nations remain valid. This renewed unity must also lead to a different thinking on the following subjects: the organization of "the Church," i.e., the different respective denominational families; the mutual (power) relations between the parts of the Body; the specific calling of Jewish followers of the Messiah within the Body of the Messiah,[71] including their specific *halakha*; parallel to this the specific calling of *goyim*-in-the-Messiah with their *halakha*;[72] the re-interpretation of church history; and the attitude toward the Messianic-Jewish movement and Jewish believers within the churches.[73] These are just some of the subjects which will have to be addressed within the new context of repentance and rethinking.

Essential to this is humility, especially theological humility, which recognizes the fact that from the side of the Messianic-Jewish theology and movement, an enormous effort to make up for lost time is taking place. It's as if an unknown land has been entered, a *terra incognita*, with all the discussion, confusion, insecurity, unclear formulation, etc. that will come with it.

> Break up your unplowed ground
> and do not sow among thorns.

Messianic Judaism.

69. This is shown by positive reactions from the Jewish side to Soulen's *The God of Israel*, and to Kinzer.

70. Here the international reconciliation movement Toward Jerusalem Council II plays a leading role (www.tjcii.org).

71. See about this Harvey, *Mapping Messianic Judaism*, and par example also Kinzer, *Israel's Messiah*.

72. See par example chapter 20.

73. In the Church Order (Ordinance 1, article 2.2) of the Protestantse Kerk in Nederland (Protestant Church in the Netherlands, EJW) this church speaks of the need of more special attention for the place of Jewish members of the church.

Part III: Returning and Rethinking: Living in a "New" Canonical Narrative

> Circumcise yourselves to the LORD
> circumcise your hearts.[74]

This was God's appeal to Israel. No less would do in regard to the reconsideration taking place within the Body of the Messiah.

23.9 The Mission of the Messiah among the Nations: Exaltation and Exile

History tells of various motives that have been leading the missions of the Church. Expressions such as "expansion of the Church," "saving souls for the Lamb and eternity," and also the more biblical expression "proclamation of the Kingdom" show some of these motivations.

The way of the gospel has sometimes been characterized as the triumph tour of Jesus Christ throughout the world. The triumphant Savior of the world (to whom all authority has been given, according to Scripture[75]) subdued the nations to His power and teaching often helped by the strong hand of the Church or state. This characterization implied, however, that the bond between Christ and Israel was severed. And sometimes the Redeemer was thought of as making His way, together with the multitude of His followers predominantly toward heaven, with the creation of a new heaven and earth out of the line of vision.

And even when the motive of "the preaching of the Kingdom of God" is predominant, as we often see now, it does not mean that the kingship of God and His Messiah are interpreted as originating from and still standing in the streambed of the Tanakh. Even then, the kingdom of God is often interpreted in a way that pictures it in "universal colors," leaving no special position for the royal priestly people in the midst of the earth. Within this interpretation there is no longer room for *one* specific people, land, or city.

Additionally, the missions based upon the traditional canonical narrative have often been a threat to the special identity of the Jewish people. The bond between God and His land, city, and people was often seen as something from a bygone period. From this perspective, God Himself left the earthly Zion, intending a better place. God's faithfulness to the world no longer left room for His faithfulness to Israel. The designation as "King of the Jews" for the exalted Lord Jesus at most referred to His origins, but did not say anything essential about the character and the realm of His kingship.

Based on the Scriptures, however, the "not-yet" of the kingship of the Messiah can be interpreted as His sharing in the exile of all Israel, and as His accompaniment with His people into the darkness of the approaching Day of the LORD. His entrance

---

74. Jer 4:3–4; cf. Hos 10:12.
75. Matt 28:18.

into the world of the nations is then oriented both toward the dispersed Israel, and toward reaching the nations with the message of the "already" of God's kingship, begun in Jerusalem. He points the multitude from the nations, who believe this gospel, toward Zion. In this manner the believers from the nations are "reached" from Zion, and are actually "returning" with Him to Zion.[76] In this mission of God[77] and His Messiah, Israel and the nations become and remain deeply connected. Reaching the nations with God's message, and the fellowship with all Israel, are then two sides of the presence of the Messiah among the nations.

Part of this "alternative" gospel is that the (believers from the) nations learn to seek the nearness of Israel[78] while learning to love this people of God. In humility, they are called to be willing to learn from the treasure storeroom of Israel. They are mobilized as comforters of God's people, a people that walks its path in exile.[79] In this way they also comfort the Holy God in His sorrow and as He longs for Zion.[80] It is on this path that they bless Abraham's seed, and are therefore blessed themselves, as God promised.[81] This is the manner in which they have been called to make all Israel jealous.[82]

We must face the fact that, contrary to the message that is determined by the paradigm of the traditional canonical narrative, this "alternative" gospel will meet opposition from an ethnic and religious contextual background. We can think of the preference of Christians in Islamic or Asian cultures for a proclamation of the gospel along the lines of the traditional canonical narrative, in which Israel ultimately has no lasting place.[83] Such proclamation confirms existing prejudices. In Islamic countries the traditional narrative scheme fits well to the prevailing anti-Jewish attitude of Islam, and thereby avoids conflict with the surrounding culture. Additionally, also a culture marked by Christian nationalism can lead to an identical predilection for the traditional canonical paradigm.[84]

The reflection on the mission of the Body of the Messiah in this world also asks for a reformation of thought and practice. A reformation that includes both the gospel

---

76. In missiology the designations "centrifugal" (coming from the center) and "centripetal" (oriented toward the center) are used to designate these both directions.

77. Meaning the task that God has put before Himself. The designation *Missio Dei* is used in missiology to express that—when it concerns "mission"—God Himself is the First One. *His* mission is the beginning and the essence of what people accomplish in "missions."

78. Acts 15:21 can be interpreted in such manner that believers from the nations are referred to further Jewish instruction.

79. Isa 40:1–2.

80. Ps 69:20.

81. Gen 12:3.

82. Rom 11:11, 14.

83. Often then this is the case with Christians belonging to traditional (Roman-Catholic and Orthodox) churches.

84. Here one can think of Orthodox churches which show that the Christian message in thought and practice often is strongly interwoven with nationalism and patriotism.

message that is preached to the nations, as well as the contribution to the "dialogue with Israel" from the Christian side. One could question what would have happened if the Christian faith community would have read the Scriptures from the beginning in the light of God's eternal love and faithfulness for His people Israel, in the light of His longing for Zion. But this has not been the case. Therefore, the only way before us is a way of repentance and "renewed thinking."

23.10 Messianic Celebration with Israel

We have seen that Messiah *Yeshua*/Jesus celebrated God's feasts in the midst of Israel.[85] We have also seen that God Himself characterizes the Messianic salvation as an ongoing fulfillment of these feasts, and establishes His salvation during those feasts.[86] God thereby honors His once-given feast calendar. The appointed feasts of God therefore maintain their central place within the camp of Israel, even when Jews, who recognize *Yeshua* as Messiah, experience and celebrate these feasts with new light shining over them, and added depths of understanding. At the deepest level these Messianic Jewish celebrators share in the *avoda* of Messiah *Yeshua*, who commemorates God's salvific acts in the midst of Israel.

We observed how Paul, as a prophetic sign, orients believers from the nations to Jerusalem, also taking them there.[87] Thereby he follows the direction pointed out by the Tanakh to the nations. The nations are called to join Israel in its songs of praise, and to be astonished together with Israel about the great deeds that God has performed in "His camp" amidst the nations.

The traditional canonical narrative has been blind to this Messianic co-celebrating with Israel by believers from the nations. From the replacement paradigm point of view, this co-celebrating has even been consciously obstructed. By choosing a fixed date for Easter, the Christian church (that had become state church), deliberately created a distance between itself and the feast calendar of Israel.[88] The effect was that a distinct church calendar of Christian feasts evolved, with specific customs, including the re-interpretation of Jewish names and customs. This is just one of the ways the Christian church has tried to end every form of "co-celebrating with Israel."[89] Although, through all ages, there have been counter-voices on this point as well.

---

85. See chapter 16, 17, 18.
86. See chapter 14 (14.4).
87. See chapter 20 (20.18).
88. This occurred at the council of Nicaea (325), that was convened by emperor Constantine I. Until then the Eastern churches still celebrated Easter on the first Sunday following the Jewish *Pessaḥ*, and thereby still had a connection to the Jewish celebration. The Western churches had by then long followed their own dating system. From then on Eastern was celebrated on the first Sunday after the first full moon in Lent. Every "celebrating" with Jews became forbidden (Van Andel, *Jodenhaat & Jodenangst*, 27).
89. Parkes, *The Conflict*, 394–400, presents various confessions of faith, obligatory for Jews who

Returning and Rethinking

In detaching itself from Israel, the resulting liturgical structure and design of church life has become so deeply ingrained within Christian life that it has become the backbone of Christian life. A new and distinct identity, over and against Israel's identity, was created. Therefore, even the idea of reforming thought and practice alone would bring much opposition, as we can see also today.

And yet today we see more and more the beginnings of reconsideration, in the first place from within Jewish-Messianic circles. Because of their unique and important perspective of continuation of the distinct calling of Israel "in Messiah," a Messianic-Jewish way of celebrating Israel's feasts has originated.[90] At the same time there is also a movement amongst believers from the nations intending to restore the connection to Israel in this area of celebration.[91]

Many new questions are now raised. Should there be room for, or even more poignantly put, must there be two kinds of *halakhot* regarding the feasts of God within the Body of the Messiah? A distinct way of obedience for Jewish followers (in a Messiah-confirmed fellowship with all Israel) *and* a distinct way of obedience for believers from the nations? What is "God's command for this moment" for the believers from the nations? A total reformation of the liturgical structuring of life? A Messianic co-celebration with Israel, but in such manner that Israel will not feel robbed again? Or a Spirit-led acceptance of the differences that have evolved, but within the framework of an "ultimate return to Zion?"[92] Or a combination of both?

This not only concerns the celebration of *Pessaḥ*/Easter, *Shavuot*/Pentecost, and the very much prophetic-eschatological oriented *Sukkot*/Feast of Tabernacles, although this feast has no place in the Christian feast calendar.[93] It also touches the question of the place of the *Shabbat* in relation to Sunday as a day of rest within the life of believers from the nations.[94] There has always been an ongoing discussion, however, about the place of the day of rest within the Christian life, even after the introduction of Sunday. That discussion, however, mostly focused on the meaning and the implica-

---

wished to be baptized, in which in a shocking manner every form of Jewish faith and thinking was rejected.

90. For this see Van der Poll, *Sacred Times For Chosen People*.

91. In certain parts of the Body of the Messiah there is much attention for the "Jewish Roots." For an example, see Juster, *Jewish Roots*. There also is a Messianic movement of non-Jews that wishes to align in thought and practice with (Messianic) Judaism. Along the lines of study of sections about the resident foreigner in Israel (the *ger-toshav*) biblical direction and principles are sought for living and co-celebrating with Israel. Janicki, *God-Fearers* can serve as an example of this search. This is not the place for an intensive discussion of this theme, but such discussion will have to take place within the Body of the Messiah.

92. Also anithin Judaism voices can be heard saying that, if the people are not ready for a certain (new) element of the *halakha*, it would be unwise to declare such element as binding.

93. It also concerns the totality of the so-called Fall feasts, and therefore also *Rosh HaShana* (Jewish New Year) and *Yom Kippur* (The Day of Atonement). Also Ḥannuka (celebrated too by *Yeshua*; John 10:22–39) and *Purim* can be named. Cf. for further information regarding the Fall feasts see Bacchiocchi, *God's Festivals*.

94. See chapter 20 (20.14). Cf. the Dutch study: Locht, *De Sabbat*.

Part III: Returning and Rethinking: Living in a "New" Canonical Narrative

tions of the fourth commandment of the Decalogue.[95] The present attention for the place of the *Shabbat* within the life of believers from the nations stands in the context of "co-celebration with Israel" and the search for "the Jewish roots." This renewed attention is therefore connected at the structural level to God's revelation in the camp of Israel, and originates from a different view on the canonical narrative.

The choice for Sunday as a Christian replacement of the *Shabbat*, supported by imperial authority, took place in a setting that can be called anti-Jewish. Anti-Judaic theology joined hands with anti-Jewish sentiments.[96] The Scriptural statement that the Messiah was and still is the reality that the *Shabbat* referred and refers to, does in itself not require an abrogation or replacement of the seventh day. The Messiah Himself lived the *Shabbat*, even in His death.[97] Believers from the nations, *goyim*, certainly do not need to be bogged down by condemnation because of rules related to the celebration of the *Shabbat*, as Paul writes.[98] Certainly the celebration of the resurrection of the Messiah on the first day asked for a place in the sanctification of time, and in the feast calendar.[99] But that is something different than what happened: the combined introduction of Sunday and the new feast calendar created a radical division with Israel as a whole. Instead of celebrating *together with* Israel, a weekly celebration *without* Israel originated, whereby the Jewish Messianic believers were forced to assimilate to the majority of the believing *goyim*. The acts of God to be celebrated on the first day, Sunday, were no longer related to Israel. Also the prophetic reference of the *Shabbat* to the great *Shabbat* of the *tikkun olam*,[100] the restoration of all things, was lost, together with the prophetic reminders present within the feasts of Israel.

The question again confronts us: will it be possible that, apart from a Messianic-Jewish celebration of the *Shabbat*, there also can be a Messianic co-celebration of the *Shabbat* by believers from the nations in such manner that Israel does not once again feel robbed? Or must a Spirit-led acceptance take place of the differences that have evolved, but then within the perspective of an ultimate return to Zion?[101] Or perhaps also a combination of both?

It already requires much prayer, courage, and patience just to confront these questions, let alone to answer them in a way that deviates from what has evolved.

---

95. Within thinking that is severed from Israel the *Shabbat* commandment is related more to creation.

96. See par example Bacchiocchi, *From Sabbath to Sunday*. He postulates that the Christian church of Rome (marked by a very anti-Jewish sentiment) contributed decisively to the introduction of the Sunday.

97. The resurrection took place after the fulfillment of the command of the *Shabbat* (cf. Luke 23:56).

98. Col 2:16–17.

99. See chapter 20 (20.14).

100. Cf. Heb 4:9.

101. M.J. Paul writes about the acceptance of grown differences in his introduction to Locht, *De Sabbat*.

Therefore, we must develop a real openness to listen to other voices within the Body of the Messiah.

23.11 Underway Toward a Contested Zion: A Messianic Dispute Regarding the Land

Within the "other" canonical narrative, as put forth in this book, God has been underway toward Zion from the very first beginning in order to dwell there in the midst of His creation. "In the Messiah" this Indwelling becomes very concrete, as the Holy God takes steps toward His definitive return to Zion. In this return He involves Israel, the nation intended to be the first circle around His Indwelling. For ages the Messiah has been working toward the return of His people to Zion, within the land in the center of the earth. Also Zionism, both religiously and nationally motivated, therefore cannot be interpreted as severed from these footsteps of the Holy One toward Zion.[102]

The safekeeping of the people and the return to the land from the darkness of the *Shoa* despite anti-Semitism and anti-Zionism, still very much alive even after that gruesome event, are therefore to be interpreted—together with Israel itself —as "the first flowering of redemption."[103]

However, within the prevailing orthodox Christology based on the traditional canonical narrative, there is in fact no connection between Christ and the land promised to Israel. This fact plays an important role in the discussions within the Christian churches with regard to the significance of the land, and the conflict over it. Christians who interpret the return of God's people to the land as fulfillment of prophecies and contribute to it in different ways, are accused of adhering to an unorthodox Christology.[104] Their "Christian-Zionism" is seen as a relapse in an ethnically-determined faith.[105] God's faithfulness in His promises to Abraham is then re-interpreted from the lens of Christology, in such manner that there is no longer a special position for the land and the nation in the midst of the earth. The New Covenant, in this view, implies an end to all old promises. The Body of the Messiah, interpreted from this perspective

---

102. See in this chapter 23.6.

103. "The first flowering of our redemption" (Sacks, *The Koren Siddur*, 522). This expression is used in the synagogual morning prayers for *Shabbat* and festivals. The prayer for the State of Israel was added after the foundation of the State of Israel in 1948.

104. This occurs from the side of Palestinian Christians, and also from the side of denominations strongly represented in the Middle East; but such voices are heard also within more traditional churches in the West.

105. This is the position of Sabeel, the Ecumenical Liberation Theology Centre in Jerusalem, and its leader Naim Ateek. Par example see Ateek, *A Palestinian Christian Cry*. But also in the thinking of the influential NT-scholar N.T. Wright there is no room left for a special position for a specific people or land.

Part III: Returning and Rethinking: Living in a "New" Canonical Narrative

as "ongoing meaning"[106] and as replacement of the old Israel, no longer has a specific connection to the land. The land only refers now to *all* lands, to the whole earth.[107]

As argued above, this Christology derogates the fact of the incarnation in the midst of God's people, the "enfleshment" of the Messiah within Israel.[108] Also this Christology has no real understanding of the significance of the *kedusha* and the *avoda* of the Messiah, His complete sanctification and obedience accomplished in the midst of the people, and on behalf of the people.[109] Thinking from the perspective sketched here, there certainly are connections to Israel, people, and land,[110] not only from a theology of God's faithfulness, but also from Christology.

Thus there is not only a divine dispute about the land from a Jewish perspective, but also from a Messianic (or Christological, one could say) perspective. God and His Messiah wish to, together with all Israel, return to the land in order to usher in the dawning of the *olam haba* and realize the *tikkun olam* there.[111] The deep resistance of the nations and their gods in our day becomes visible in the Islamic opposition against this "Zionism" of God Himself. In this context, within the Christian churches, international law is often seen as the "solid ground" in the swamp of big religious narratives and claims, a position motivated by a desire for an end to the conflict. This position is in accordance with a de-*Jew*-ized Christology. Fear of religious-based claims, wars, and new crusades leads this argument.[112] As a result, sometimes a Christological based anti-Zionism goes hand in hand with an outright anti-Semitic anti-Zionism.[113]

---

106. For this characterization of the continuity within a replacement-theological scheme I owe Juster.

107. So par example Munayer, "Theology of the Land," 234–64. Yohanna Katanacho designates Christ as the Owner of the land, but within his thinking this designation also stands in the context of an universalization of salvation in Christ (at the expense of the connection with Israel or a special significance of the physical offspring of Abraham), and of the universalization of the significance of the land. Christ and Israel are sharply opposed in his thinking. Only he, who is spiritually connected to Christ, belongs to the seed of Abraham and shares in the promises given to him. See Katanacho, *Christ is the Owner of Haaretz*. http://katanacho.com/datadir/en-events/ev30/files/Christ%20is%20 the%20Owner%20of%20Haaretz.pdf (accessed 4th of April 2017).

108. See par example chapter 15 (15.2).

109. See chapter 16 and 18 (18.2).

110. After the title of an important declaration of the Nederlandse Hervormde Kerk (1970): *Israël, volk, land en staat. Handreiking voor een theologische bezinning* (to be found in: Van Campen and Den Hertog, *Israël, volk, land en staat*, 53–78).

111. See chapter 12 and 21.

112. This opinion has been leading in the positioning of the Protestantse Kerk in Nederland in the document *Het Israëlisch-Palestijns conflict in de context van de Arabische wereld van het Midden-Oosten. Bijdrage tot meningsvorming in de Protestantse Kerk in Nederland* (The Israeli-Palestinian Conflict in the Context of the Arab World. Contribution to the Formation of Opinion within the Protestant Church in the Netherlands, EJW), accepted by the General Synod of this church on the 11th of April 2008. This document, that is based on the acknowledgment of the right of a safe and recognized existence of the State of Israel, postulates that solving the conflict over the land will only be possible on the basis of international law.

113. Sometimes anti-Zionist Christians join hands with par example Islamic anti-Zionists for

The believers from the nations, however, called by God to His Messiah, are the firstlings from the nations. These believers are called to live a priestly life both in relation to the people of Israel as well in relation to the nations they belong to. Their calling thereby also implies that they must be the first ones to humble themselves under the nations' resistance against God's election of His people, land, and city. At the same time they are called to call on the nations to comply with God's will.

Very concretely, the implication is that these believers are to summon the nations as watchmen of God, whether or not this is politically opportune or feasible, to submit to God, who wishes to let His people return to His land. This remains true even when God speaks of places and territories which fall outside human-drawn boundaries.[114] In doing so they also should speak of the promises that God's Word speaks over the Arab nations.[115] It is possible that this seems a foolish mission in the eyes of many, even of the faith communities they belong to. Regardless, this actual calling is to be obeyed.

As members of the Body of the Messiah, however, we as believers from the nations are called to simultaneously walk a path of priestly humility while not passing by the pain suffered in the dispute over the land. Deeply connected to God's desire to return to Zion, under His guidance we must learn to seek ways of reconciliation, truth and healing, how provisional they might be for the present.[116] Neither our thinking nor our lives should be determined by a deficiency in our Christology and nor should they predominantly be driven by pain or frustration.[117] We should, however, realize that reconciliation will never happen on the basis of denying Israel's God-given special identity.

Today, within the Hebron-kingship of the Messiah, both the Messianic firstlings from Israel as well as those from the nations are called to be the firstlings seeking fellowship with the King of the Jews, who is actively gathering all Israel and a multitude from the nations in preparation of His Jerusalem-kingship. This future Jerusalem-kingship implies that many names from the circle of the Arab nations will be also "inscribed" in Jerusalem.[118] The present dispute over the land, therefore, stands in the perspective of hope, although it remains an expectation that requires Israel and the nations to recognize the structures and paths that God wishes to walk in order to also bless the world of nations from Zion.

---

whom the Jewish state as such is an abomination.

114. Here a contradistinction becomes visible between God's right on the land and "international law." Besides, there is also discussion going on about the meaning of the concept of "international law" in relation to the conflict over the land. Cf. for this De Blois, *Israël: Een staat ter discusie?*

115. See par example Isa 19:23–25, where God promises blessing to Israel, Egypt and Asshur together.

116. See par example Loden, "Towards Reconciliation," 217–25 en Harvey, "Towards a Messianic Jewish Theology of Reconciliation," 82–103.

117. The discussion should also not be determined by caricatures of the different stances.

118. See Ps 87.

Part III: Returning and Rethinking: Living in a "New" Canonical Narrative

23.12 The "Other" in the Canonical Narrative: Israel and "the Church" in the Jewish and Christian Canonical Narrative

A canonical narrative as a coherent survey and description of what the Scriptures wish to say shows what "role" various groups of people have within that narrative. Both the place of "the own" and the "the other" who appear in it becomes clear. Naturally, this is also the case with the rendering of the canonical narrative of the Tanakh and the Scriptures of the New Covenant, as presented in this book. After all, these Scriptures show us how God Himself moves toward His future, a future He intends Israel and the nations to enter into.

The Jewish canonical narrative is only based on the Tanakh. And yet we can find a reflection on "the role of the other."[119] Maimonides[120] viewed both Christianity and Islam as instruments in God's hand in order to bring the nations to a monotheistic religion, for the propagation of the Name of Israel's God to the nations, and as preparation for the coming of the Messiah.[121] However, he qualified Christianity as idolatry because of the profession of the trinity. Islam as religion was not evaluated by him as "idolatry," but because of the fact that Islam dismisses the Tora as a forgery made by Israel, Maimonides held the opinion that no discussions should be held with Muslims. Discussions with Christians, however, were permissible as Christianity had always recognized the Tora as the Word of God. In Maimonides's thought there is no room for a specific position of Jewish believers in *Yeshua*. They were no longer viewed as Jews, but as converts to a different religion.[122]

This radical distinction between Israel and the community that originated around the message of God's acts in *Yeshua*, formed the basic presupposition of both the Jewish canonical narrative as well as of the traditional Christian canonical narrative, with both assuming a basic incompatibility.[123] God's election and abiding faithfulness toward Israel and "the gospel of Jesus" thereby stand in radical opposition to each other.

---

119. Non-Jews par example receive a place in the ongoing narrative by means of the designation Noachide/Noachidic (see chapter 5).

120. See chapter 22 (22.17).

121. Yanover, "Maimonides. Islam Good, Christianity Bad, Muslims Bad, Christians Good," writes: "In his legal opus Hayad Hachazaka, Maimonides states that thanks to both these religions 'the world has become full of the ideas of the Messiah, the ideas of the Torah and the ideas of the commandments, so that these have spread to faraway islands and to many dim hearted nations, and they now discuss these ideas and the commandments of the Torah.'" See: http://www.jewishpress.com/indepth/opinions/maimonides-islam-good-christianity-bad-muslims-bad-christians-good/2013/11/15 (accessed at 3d of April 2017). In December 2015 a group of orthodox Jewish rabbis issued a statement that, while referring to the thinking of Maimonides, Yehudah Halevi, Jacob Emden, and rabbi Samson Raphael Hirsch, speaks of "the ongoing constructive validity of Christianity as our partner in world redemption." See: http://cjcuc.org/2015/12/03/orthodox-rabbinic-statement-on-christianity/ (accessed 28th of July, 2017).

122. This because of the profession of the trinity and the divinity of *Yeshua*.

123. Also the Islamic narrative presupposes an incompatibility with the Jewish narrative.

Additionally, the traditional narrative of the churches also became a powerful factor contributing to widespread anti-Judaism, sometimes with deadly consequences.[124]

Within this traditional canonical narrative, Israel and Jews who had not recognized *Yeshua* as the promised Messiah, held a position that forced them to the background.[125] In their miserable existence they formed the living proof of the superiority of "the Church." The devastation of Jerusalem functioned as additional confirmation:[126] Israel was outdated. God had begun something new in Jesus Christ, and God was now punishing this people because of its unbelief regarding Jesus. Actual relationships with Jewish people could differ in different times or places, but within the paradigm of the traditional canonical narrative there was no longer room left for Jews and their God-given election. That meant there was no future left for Israel as nation, and even Jewish believers in *Yeshua* no longer had a special position.

Within the "alternative" canonical narrative that this book presents, there is an abiding role for Israel at the "foreground," also "in the Messiah." Within this narrative, the totality of the history of Israel as a whole remains connected to God, His Messiah *Yeshua*, and the Messiah's priestly kingship. The Messianic firstlings of Israel therefore have their own place too, both in relation to the whole of Israel as well as to the community of believers from the nations.

Although many hold the opinion that "big narratives" are outdated, the Scriptures do certainly present us a "big narrative" that does not contribute to anti-Jewish thought and hatred of Jews, but is a narrative that helps correct centuries of supposed superiority within "the Church." A narrative that calls us to share in the desires of God, who wishes to return to Zion. Despite centuries of blindness, He prepares for this return within Israel and within the nations. Sometimes He awakens faith and then acts in response, on other occasions He acts and thereby awakens faith and expectation.[127] He is underway toward the fulfillment of all promises and prophecies.

This "new" narrative is not a new form of old theological imperialism, one that again subdues Israel, but is a divine call to believers from the nations. This "new" narrative gives us fresh eyes and calls for new words and actions. It is possible that there are elements in this narrative that still seem strange to the "other," to Judaism in all its variety. We may hope, however, that this "new narrative" also provides safety within the encounter with all of Israel.

---

124. See the Introduction to this book and chapter 13.
125. For the concepts of "foreground" and "background" see the Introduction (I.3 en I.6).
126. This thought was present within both the old-Christian and the Islamic tradition.
127. In Ezek 36–37 both the return and the spiritual renewal of the people of Israel are spoken of. In chapter 37 the Spirit is given following the restoration of the bones to bodies. Also HaRav Avraham Yitzhak Ha Cohen Kook, the first Chief rabbi of the State of Israel, spoke of restoration of the national existence as part of the coming to full knowledge of God by the whole of the people. Acts of God sometimes precede the recognition thereof. Also see Kook, *Orot*.

Part III: Returning and Rethinking: Living in a "New" Canonical Narrative

23.13 New Eyes, New Words, New Actions

The new paradigm, resulting from the canonical narrative presented in this book, helps us look with new eyes to discover new relationships. It involves us in the ways that God still walks with His people and the world. It therefore also asks for a very concrete new vocabulary, and the resulting actions. The following summary presents nothing more than a global overview in light of this.

Dual Humbling Before God

The believers from the nations, or "gentile-Christians," are doubly related to the suffering of Israel. Israel suffered from the actions of the nations of the world *and* it suffered from the actions of "the Church," consisting of mainly gentile-Christians. Therefore, the believers from the nations who entered "into the Messiah" are first of all called to a dual humbling before God.

Just as Daniel humbles himself under the guilt of all Israel,[128] gentile-Christians are called to humble themselves under the guilt of the total Christian faith community toward God's people Israel. This form of humbling concerns all thoughts and actions of "the Church" by which Israel's life as a whole has been threatened throughout the centuries.

Additionally, the believers from the nations also are in a certain sense firstlings of the nations,[129] and as such are called to stand before God as priests from their nations, confessing their guilt toward God's people Israel before God, and to humble themselves before the people of Israel.

Although steps in this direction have been made by churches and Christian faith communities,[130] this broad priestly humbling seems more of an exception than the rule, both within the churches, but even more within the nations to which the churches belong.[131] For many, the time is coming for the chapter of the *Shoa* to be closed. When believers from the nations really wish to participate in the priestly task of the Messiah among the nations, they should distinguish themselves also in this respect. Before God and because of the suffering of His people Israel, remembering the *Shoa* and humbling ourselves under the guilt of it can never cease.

---

128. Dan 9.

129. Rom 16:5; 1 Cor 16:15; cf. also Jas 1:18; Rev 14:4.

130. This refers to both theological reflection as well as to liturgies of humbling before God (services of repentance and humbling before God with respect to the guilt in relation to the Jewish people in various circumstances and countries during the ages).

131. A radical manner of going back to misdeeds from the past can be observed in Spain and Portugal, where descendants of Jews, who were expelled in the fifteenth and sixteenth century, can obtain citizenship anew. Economic motives, however, play a role in this too.

Ways of Reconciliation within the Body of the Messiah

We have already concluded that also within the Body of the Messiah reconciliation is needed.[132] In addition to the mutual disunity of the churches, the oldest division in the Body of the Messiah is still present, the rupture between Jewish believers and the believers from the nations. When unity is concerned, the Body of the Messiah needs Christian churches, predominantly consisting of believers from the nations, to be concretely involved in ways of reconciliation with the Jewish part of the Body. This asks first of all for a Church-wide awareness of the dual character of the faith community around Messiah *Yeshua*.[133] But also, with God's guidance, steps need to be taken for the Church to humble themselves in response to historic sins, as the Roman-Catholic church has done a number of times in reference to the atrocities committed against the Marranos.[134]

A second "Council of Jerusalem" is the a goal of an international reconciliation movement from both Messianic-Jews and Christians from all traditions[135] which, in alignment with the first council of apostles,[136] will revoke the history of identity theft and forced assimilation of Jewish believers. Such official recognition of the twofold structure of the Body of the Messiah implies at the deepest level a *teshuva*—a thorough turning back—to God who elected Israel for eternity.

These ways of reconciliation consist of many small steps, varying from biblical instruction and knowledge of history to loving relationships with Jewish believers, as well as practical support in the processes of reconciliation between these two faith communities within the one Body of the Messiah.

"Comfort, Comfort My People"

In Isaiah 40 the LORD calls to comfort His people.[137] Here God is focused on salvation for His people, and promises an end to the exile in Babylon. A perspective opens wider until it reaches the imperishable Jerusalem.[138] Not only the prophet, but also

---

132. See paragraph 23.7 in this chapter.
133. See chapter 20 and paragraph 23.8 in this chapter.
134. See for this Hocken, *The Marranos* (published by TJCII; see www.tjcii.org). Within the context of reconciliation conferences in Latin-America delegates of the Roman-Catholic Church have confessed the guilt of the Church, and made steps of reconciliation toward descendants of the Marranos. Cf. footnote 59 in this chapter.
135. Toward Jerusalem Council II (www.tjcii.org).
136. Acts 15.
137. Isa 40:1–2.
138. Cf. Isa 54:11–17; 60; 66:10–14.

the nations (as belonging in God's audience)[139] are called to praise God for what He will do for His people, and to bless His people.[140]

After centuries of blindness and bitter contempt for God's people, now is the time of comfort for Israel. The love of the Comforter-Messiah[141] must reach through His Body all Israel. Our humility can show itself therein.

In the story of God's love for His people, it is the duty of the faith community sharing in the salvation that welled up in Israel to reveal the image of the Messiah. Just like the Good Samaritan's wine and oil, this comforting of Israel is the expression of love for a people maltreated by thieves and murderers.[142] For this to happen, the Church must draw near to Israel in her pain, following the example of the Holy One Himself.[143] This could become very real by sharing in the pain of all Israel on *Yom HaShoa* or other mourning or remembrance days.[144]

We must note, however, that the task of comforting God's people is mostly only obeyed where people view Israel as God's *segula*-people. It is the same with respect to the dual humbling before God, and some more themes addressed below. It is often pioneering-communities that have the heart for this task. This assignment, however, must be understood within the whole of the Body of the Messiah as coming from God Himself.

Called to Be Watchmen: Praying Together with Israel

Isaiah 62 speaks of God-appointed watchmen on the walls of Zion. They must "give him no rest" until He, in His mercy, has completely accomplished His purposes for Zion, His land, and His people.[145] Simeon and Anna were such watchmen.[146] And the Messiah Himself another, praying and calling out to God. The Body of the Messiah is called to join Him in His prayers.

The prayer for Israel is one of the first responsibilities of the Body of the Messiah. Here too the word is valid: first the Jew and then the Greek.[147] The prayer for the peace of Jerusalem[148] is the heart of the prayer for the Kingdom.

---

139. Isa 41:1; 43:9; 49:1.
140. Cf. Isa 49:22–23.
141. Cf. chapter 14 (14.3) for "Comforter" as name of the Messiah.
142. Luke 10:34.
143. Isa 63:9.
144. *Yom HaShoa* is the Hebrew name of the Jewish remembrance day of the *Shoa*.
145. Isa 62:6–7.
146. Luke 2:25–38.
147. Rom 1:16.
148. Ps 122:6.

Here the *kehilla*, the "called-together" congregation[149] of the Messiah, prays together with the *kehilla* of Israel. The process of removing our blindness to God's desires regarding Zion may be partially due to the prayers of Israel. Israel has prayed tenaciously and persistently for the fulfillment of God's promises regarding Zion. In her prayers the Christian church was oriented toward the de-*Jew*-ized, universal, heavenly Jerusalem. The prayer "your Kingdom come," however, has everything to do with what must happen in the midst of the earth.

Also here, churches and faith communities can learn from various prayer movements, which fulfilled and still fulfill a task as frontrunner in this respect.[150]

Ministry of Service to Israel: A New Task

That Paul taught the believers from the nations the ministry of service to the Messianic *kehilla* in Jerusalem,[151] was also a prophetic sign. In these firstlings the nations learned to bless Israel. After all, that was the way by which the LORD wished to bless the nations. By blessing Israel they too would be blessed.[152] The Body of the Messiah is called to lead the way in this blessing of Israel, as Messiah *Yeshua* also did Himself. This calling applies even more after centuries of contempt for and robbing of Israel.

This "serving-without-something more," this serving of God's people without other motives than showing loving involvement, might seem a new task within the life and thought of many churches. This ministry, however, requires its own place beside the traditional ministry of helping those in need. Here churches and Christian faith communities can learn from movements and individual Christians, who already practice this ministry of service. This service of love can focus on the totality of the life of the Jewish people, both in the diaspora and in the land Israel, and therefore can have many faces.[153] At the deepest level it is, however, an expression of comfort for God's people, and also an expression of real repentance.

Service without a hidden agenda is the only manner in which the circle of all Israel becomes aware of real and devotedly-connected fellow travelers.

---

149. *Kehilla* is derived from *kahal*, meaning "to call." The Greek word *ekklesia* is derived from the verb *ekkaleo* that means "to call out, to call out from." In the Septuagint, the Greek translation of the Tanakh it is used for the *kehilla*, the congregation/community of Israel.

150. As an example can be named the Evangelical Sisterhood of Mary (Darmstadt-Eberstadt, Germany). This evangelical monastic sisterhood is a clear example of the ministry of reconciliation and love toward, and prayer for Israel. Also within the Roman-Catholic Church there are communities that have the prayer for Israel on their hearts. At that, a variety of mostly evangelical-charismatic (low-church) prayer movements with a focus on Israel can be found worldwide.

151. See chapter 20 (20.18).

152. Cf. Gen 12:3.

153. This can vary from the care for Jewish cemeteries (as the Dutch Christian organization, Stichting Boete & Verzoening, provides in close cooperation with Jewish authorities in the Netherlands), and Jewish schools, to the involvement with many aid projects in Israel.

Part III: Returning and Rethinking: Living in a "New" Canonical Narrative

Watchmen Against Hatred: Anti-Semitism and Anti-Zionism

The hatred of Jews and Israel as a people is age-old, and is a hatred that deeply injures God as Israel is the apple of His eye.[154] Believers from the nations are called to oppose this hatred of the Most High God Himself, and to surround Israel as watchmen. Anti-Semitism is incompatible with a belief in the God of Abraham, Isaac, and Jacob. It also runs contrary to obeying Messiah Jesus, making the concepts Christian *and* anti-Semite incompatible with each other before God. The Body of the Messiah, therefore, must fight every kind of anti-Semitism and lovingly surround Israel as watchmen.

This also applies to anti-Zionism, which often is anti-Semitism in modern form.[155] Because of the *Shoa*, particularly in Western countries and in international politics, an old-fashioned hatred of the Jews is not politically correct and no longer "does the job." Therefore, although a form of Jewish anti-Zionism exists,[156] along with a humanistic variant that does not identify itself as specifically anti-Jewish,[157] the old hatred of Jews clothes itself today in the garments of anti-Zionism. The role of the Jew as the cause of all evil that befalls countries, sadly a well-known theme,[158] is then given to the State of Israel, whose sheer existence is an abhorrence to millions of people, both Islamic and non-Islamic.[159] Various international organizations that join hands and vigorously oppose "Zionism," in reality are opposing Israel and all that is related to Israel. The public opinion in Western countries is moving more and more in this direction. The presence of massive groups of Muslims in Western countries, openly-menacing or not, contributes to this. International political interests clash with each other in relation to the land of Israel in the center of the earth. The popular suggestion is that the world will finally move toward peace when the "conflict over the land" is solved.

Consciously or unconsciously, people have been blinded to the intended de-*Jew*-izing of the land (and thus also the State) of Israel, and to the often openly-voiced Islam-inspired determination to exterminate the Jews in the land.[160]

---

154. Zech 2:8–9.

155. For this, see par example Yakira, *Post-Zionism, Post Holocaust* and Rosenbaum, *Those Who Forget the Past*.

156. A certain segment of Orthodox Judaism—Neturei Karta can be named here—is anti-Zionist because of religious motives (and therefore sometimes a fierce opponent of the State of Israel) and out of fear to act as humans where God alone must act.

157. The convictions regarding the people of Israel, the land and the return to the land within this humanistic anti-Zionism, however, clash at the deepest level with the election of the people and the land by the Eternal One.

158. Through all centuries Jews have been "identified" as the cause of various disasters and accused of acts that made the life of other people impossible (par example: poisoning of wells, etc.). This phenomenon can be observed also in the adversarial relations with respect to the State of Israel.

159. The State of Israel is within such Islamic thought an evil that has nestled itself in a territory that belongs to the Islamic sphere of influence.

160. This foresaid and required extermination of the Jewish people is a given in Islamic sources

The *kehilla* of the Messiah has no other choice than to openly choose against every kind of anti-Semitism, even when it clothes itself in the garb of anti-Zionism. This is so essential that it can be stated as a *"status confessionis,"* a positional choice that must be lived and stated as a "confession of faith," a position that is unrelinquishable.[161] In a world that follows more and more an anti-Zion direction, from secular, religious-nationalistic, and Islamic sides this choice brings suffering.

Serving God and His Messiah in Relation to the State of Israel

Jewish worship knows of thanksgiving and prayer for the State of Israel as "the first flowering of our redemption."[162] The canonical narrative as put forth in this book also leaves no room for a neutral evaluation of the return of the Jewish people to the land and the establishment of the state. Though it might remain hidden to us, the Holy One of Israel remains connected to His people. Therefore, the return of the people following the *Shoa* and also the State of Israel stand in relation to the kingship of its Messiah.[163]

The designation of the State of Israel as "the first flowering of our redemption" shows that even within Judaism the state does not coincide with all that God wishes for His people. Israel remains called to live the full calling of kingdom of priests in the midst of the earth. The Tora and the Tanakh are central to this as revelation of the will of the God of Israel. At the same time Israel is waiting for the *tikkun olam* which will restore the imperfection of (the State of) Israel measured against God's intentions.

Within the circle of Christian churches the question is often posed about the legitimacy of critiquing Israel as state. What churches and Christian organizations, however, should note is that the calling of believers from the nations is not in the first place to confront Israel with the Tora, but first of all to affirm God's election of Israel. Only he who has taken the plank (in this case the disregard of God's commands and

(both the Koran, the traditions and other religious literature) and can be listened to as a theme in today's actuality. A Dutch standard work (providing at page 167 a summary of sayings from the Koran) is Jansen, *Van jodenhaat naar zelfmoordterrorisme*. In Medieval traditions (Hadith 41, 6985) we read: "Abu Huraira reported Allah's Messenger (Peace be upon him) as saying: The last hour would not come unless the Muslims will fight against the Jews and the Muslims would kill them until the Jews would hide themselves behind a stone or a tree and a stone or a tree would say: Muslim, or the servant of Allah, there is a Jew behind me; come and kill him; but the tree Gharqad would not say, for it is the tree of the Jews." See https://muflihun.com/muslim/41/6985 (accessed 5th of April 2017).

161. *Status confessionis*, a Latin expression (originally from Lutheran theological origin), designating a situation which asks for a solid stance and confession of faith. This is derived from Matt 10:32–33, where *Yeshua* foresays that there will be situations in which one must confess Him if one wishes to be known by the Messiah before God. In World War II this designation was important in relation to the struggle for truth within the German churches. See http://brillonline.nl/entries/religion-past-and-present/status-confessionis-SIM_124963?s.num=4 (accessed 5th of April 2017).

162. See footnote 103 in this chapter. Jewish tradition values a situation of not-being-subjected to foreign powers as a token of the Messianic times (b. Berakhot 34b).

163. See paragraph 23.11.

Part III: Returning and Rethinking: Living in a "New" Canonical Narrative

promises) out of his own eye, can see clearly enough to help remove the speck out of his brother's eye.[164] To put very directly: there is no place for lecturing Israel about the theme of inhabiting the land without recognizing of the abiding calling of Israel to live and dwell in the land. Besides, it is in the first place the calling of the believers from the nations to confront the nations with God's words and will, even if this brings them into conflict with accepted opinions or political decision-making. This applies also to Arab or Palestinian Christians within the Body of the Messiah.

When churches or Christians do not take a clear position in distancing themselves from all forms of hatred against Israel and anti-Zionism, then their critique, although perhaps well-meant, appears in Jewish eyes and ears to just be an extension of the former "locking up of Jews," within limits determined by churches and governments, that has taken place during the centuries.[165] Within various coalitions regarding the conflict over the land, both international and sometimes also interreligious, motives radically opposed to God's intentions play a role.[166]

This does not mean, however, that the Body of Messiah can or should not contribute to the healing of the conflict over the land between Israel and its Palestinian inhabitants. Steps taken on a path of reconciliation are part of the service to Israel's God and His Messiah.[167] It makes a difference, however, whether this happens from the "old" canonical narrative that does not wish to know of God's abiding covenant with His people, land, and city, or from the perspective of the "alternative" canonical narrative described here.[168]

It is clear that this path described here will bring suffering and also separation between people, but this is a way of co-suffering with the Messiah as He makes His way toward the restoration of all things.

Speaking and Hearing, Listening and Answering

The faith community around Messiah *Yeshua* has also learned the command to speak the word heard from God.[169] For centuries "the Church" held the opinion that this

---

164. Matt 7:5.

165. This is also the case with the policies of the World Council of Churches. It can be postulated that the "old" narrative is still very much alive therein. Also through the influence of the churches from the Middle-East the policies of this organization are strongly anti-Zionist and therefore negatively toward the State of Israel.

166. Sometimes anti-Zionist Christians participate in overtly (sometimes Muslim-organized) anti-Jewish conferences about "the conflict." This can also be observed in the so-called international BDS (Boycot-Divestment-Sanctions) movement.

167. See par example footnote 116 in this chapter.

168. Contributions from the ecumenical movement focusing on reconciliation and ending the conflict (many initiatives could be named) often come forth from opinions marked by the "old" canonical narrative. As a result no real discussion is possible with those segments of Judaism that are serious about the eternal election of people, land and city.

169. Matt 28:20 speaks of "everything I have commanded you."

word of God did not leave any room for the abiding election and calling of Israel because Israel's role had been outplayed on God's stage, or because "the Church" had taken Israel's place. To obey this gospel then meant professing that God would no longer honor His promises to Israel. The "gospel of the Church" put Christ in direct opposition to Israel as God's *segula*-people. For Israel to say "yes" to this Christ meant saying "no" to the faithfulness of God toward His people.[170] Conversion to "Christianity," whether or not by force, was accompanied by the requirement to radically break with the Jewish community and way of living.[171] Thereby, missionary work also threatened the survival of Israel as a distinct people among the nations.[172] Reconsideration, partly started by the second World War and the *Shoa*, has rightly resulted in "Missions to the Jews"[173] and "Proclamation of the gospel among Israel,"[174] giving way to "seeking the encounter and dialogue with Israel."[175]

But for a real dialogue to happen, it is important first of all that the Christian community listens to God. The dialogue with Israel, namely, changes fundamentally when this dialogue is characterized by a new understanding of the canonical narrative of the Tanakh and the New Testament from the side of the faith community around Messiah Jesus, "the Church."

At the same time the right to be a dialogue partner, sharing something of one's own motivation, must be "earned" by a new practical involvement with and service to Israel.[176] In this, believers from the nations have a different position from Jewish Messianic believers, although the witness and life of Jewish believers sometimes still is determined by thoughts and customs coming forth from the old canonical narrative.

Following centuries of bad listening to the Scriptures, the first thing for believers from the nations to do now within the encounter with Judaism is to listen, and to learn to answer from a new understanding of Scripture.

170. Kinzer, *Postmissionary Messianic Judaism*, 223–26, postulates, following Paul van Buuren, that in a paradoxal manner the reverse was also true. The "no" of Jews to Jesus, stemming from the desire to cling to God's faithfulness and His election, actually was a "yes" to God.

171. See Introduction (I.4) and in this chapter paragraph 23.10.

172. This is the feeling on Jewish side: missions (leading to conversion) meant to many Jews so much as extermination of the Jewish people.

173. The designation "Mission to the Jews" stems from a time that there was little consciousness of the Christian guilt with respect to the evil done to Gods people though the centuries, and suggests—although this was often not the case in practice—that the Jewish people was just viewed as one of the nations.

174. Also this designation, that appears "softer" and started to be used in later times, presupposes a rather uncomplicated view on the relation with Judaism.

175. Article I of the Church Order of the Protestant Church in the Netherlands reads: "The church is called to give expression to its unrelinquishable solidarity with the Jewish people. As a Christ-confessing community of faith it seeks a dialogue with the Jewish people concerning the understanding of Holy Scripture, in particular as regards the coming of the Kingdom of God." https://www.protestantsekerk.nl/over-ons/protestant-church/church-order (accessed 7th of April 2017).

176. In the language of the Church Order of the Protestant Church in the Netherlands: without practical "unrelinquishable solidarity" there is no basis for dialogue.

Part III: Returning and Rethinking: Living in a "New" Canonical Narrative

Learning New Language and Thought Patterns

Much of our thinking and speaking moves along lines which we sometimes are hardly conscious of. Centuries-long influence of the traditional canonical narrative has created thought and language patterns, which contribute to continuation of this traditional narrative.

A well known example is the designation of Pentecost as "the birthday of the Church." Not only is *Shavuot* already severed from *Pessah* within the Christian ecclesiastical calendar,[177] but this designation discredits that the Spirit's descent in Jerusalem is the fulfillment of promises of salvation given to Israel.[178] At that specific time and place in Jerusalem, God gives a "fountain" from which *also* Gentiles may drink. The traditional designation "birthday of the Church" makes the presence of Israel invisible, and in doing so severs the gift of the Spirit from the context of the totality of God's promises to Israel.[179]

Another example, the anachronistic use of the designation "church" for believers from the Tanakh,[180] has the result that Israel disappears in "the Church" both prior to and after Abram's election.[181] Apart from the negative associations the word "church" carries, this way of speaking in relation to Israel is in every way connected to the old canonical narrative. The choice of the designation "Body of the Messiah" for the community of faith around the Messiah leaves more room to discern the continuity of Israel within this faith community, and to let it play its role.[182]

Not only must we, as the Christian faith community, endeavor to learn new manners of speech, we must also learn to develop a new sensitivity for the meaning of our terminology to the ears of Israel, and to understand what thoughts and images it arouses, and how our terminology can continue to harm.

---

177. See paragraph 23.10.

178. See chapter 14 (14.4); 15 (15.5); 16 (16.4); 17 (17.3); 19 (19.6 and 19.7); 20 (20.3) and paragraph 23.10 in this chapter.

179. Also the so-called "ecclesiastical year"—the Christo-centric feast calendar of the Christian churches (that begins with Advent and Christmas, and via Pentecost and "Eternity-Sunday" returns again to the beginning)—gives no place and voice to the embedding of the salvation of the Messiah within Israel.

180. So for example Calvin in his *Institutio* (*Institutes of the Christian Religion*), Book II, chapter 11,2 http://www.ccel.org/ccel/calvin/institutes.i.html (accessed 7th of April 2017); also the Confessio Belgica (article 27) and the Catechism of Heidelberg (Sunday 21). This "uncomplicated" use of the word "church/Church" will be caused too by the fact that the Greek word *ekklesia* (often used in the New Testament as a designation for the/a congregation of Christ) is used within the Greek translation of the Tanakh (Septuagint), rendering the Hebrew word *kahal*, to designate the community/congregation of Israel. The step toward the anachronistic use of "church/Church" (to designate the congregation of all true believers in all ages; unavoidably connected with all associations to what "the Church" has done or has been) is then made easily. Also see footnote 149 in this chapter.

181. Gen 12:1–3.

182. As stated above (23.4, footnote 21) carries the usual conceptual pairing of "Church-Israel" or "Israel-Church" associations of a contradistinction resulting from a history that did not recognize the connection with or even continuity of Israel "in the Messiah."

New insights ask for new language, like new wine needs new wineskins.[183] A language that reassesses insights and concepts and invites to walk new paths. Therefore this book uses other ways of putting thoughts into words, using Hebrew and Jewish expressions for that purpose. Thereby a certain, awareness-creating estrangement is invoked, as simultaneously the continuity within God's revelation is shown.

Seeking Unity

As already stated above we find within the Body of the Messiah frontrunners in many of these areas. People or organizations which make steps in prayer and service in the directions sketched above. Very often those in charge within churches or faith communities lack knowledge or appreciation of these endeavors. A reformation of thought and life, as pleaded in this chapter, needs, however, openness to ways of renewal that the Spirit of the Messiah wishes to walk. In this time of the Hebron-kingship of the Messiah, His Body is called to a real learning together.

23.14 Ongoing Reformation of Thought and Practice

This chapter shows how an "other" canonical narrative brings about an "other" reality. Reconsidering our ways requires, however, a willingness to be taught by God time and again. Never will Israel or the believers from the nations entirely accomplish their learning. To be a disciple of the LORD is part of the salvation of the *olam haba*.[184]

The Messiah wishes to instruct both Israel and the nations from the camp of Israel underway toward the full Eighth Day and the *tikkun olam*. This Messianic instruction stands under the promise of the Breath of God. The Spirit instructs and involves Israel and the nations in the ascent to Zion of the Holy One. The "other" canonical narrative is, at the deepest level, a narrative about God's desire for His Indwelling amidst His people in the midst of the earth.

---

183. Matt 9:17; Luke 5:37–38.
184. Isa 54:13.

Chapter 24

Accompanying the Holy God Underway Toward the *Tikkun Olam*

24.1 One Big Narrative

THE LAST CHAPTER. ONE big narrative has captured our attention. The ongoing narrative of the Tanakh and the Scriptures of the New Covenant. The big narrative in which the God of Israel calls His *segula*-people Israel and the nations to accompany Him underway toward the consummation. He Himself wishes to return to Zion to finally dwell in the midst of His re-created creation. With this return and this coming home the exile for God, Israel and creation will also come to an end. The *tikkun olam*, the perfection and restoration of all things, will be ushered in by Him. The full light of the Messianic Eighth Day will shine.

We live in a time in which many no longer believe in "big narratives" and "big words," and yet we are placed by God in a big narrative. The narrative of ONE, who desires to continually reveal His great love to His treasured possession, His people Israel. It is the narrative of the One God, who desires the nations to also share in the secrets of His love which He revealed in the camp of Israel.

The canonical narrative described in this book connects God and His desires, Israel, creation, the Messiah, the nations, the history of God's land, city and world, and the future of earth and heaven into one great narrative. In essential points it differs from the traditional version of the canonical narrative.[1] It is "the narrative of the heart

---

1. The contrast with the "old" canonical narrative is clearly shown in a passage by Dunn. Commenting on Romans 11:26 he writes: " (. . .) even though he (Paul, EJW) quotes the passage as a foundation or confirmation of his hope of Israel's salvation, he does not wish to rekindle the idea of Israel's national primacy in the last days (Zion either as the physical focus of or sole reason for the redeemer's coming)" (Dunn, *Romans 9–16*, 682). The designations "national primacy" and "sole reason" suggest that with the coming of Messiah Jesus there could and would be no room anymore for Zion as the physical center of God's intentions or of a special position of the people of Israel. Dunn reasons

of God" that runs from the great beginning, right through all sin and resistance, to the even greater and glorious end. It is also a narrative of God's deepening revelation of Himself.

It is a narrative of hope for people—even believers—without great ideals, for people living in a fragmentized world. It is a visionary narrative that wishes to orientate our individualistic focus on experience, self-preservation, or personal salvation again toward Zion in a very literal sense. It asks again for a focus of trust in the plans of God that span the ages. It asks for *emuna*.[2] And for a desire to know and follow the LORD God in all His ways. It is a narrative that is truth and will become reality:

> Look on Zion, the city of our festivals;
> your eyes will see Jerusalem,
> a peaceful abode, a tent that will not be moved;
> its stakes will never be pulled up,
> nor any of its ropes broken.
> There the LORD will be our Mighty One.
> It will be like a place of broad rivers and streams. (...)
> For the LORD is our judge,
> the LORD is our lawgiver,
> the LORD is our king;
> it is he who will save us. (. . .)
> No one living in Zion will say, "I am ill";
> and the sins of those who dwell there will be forgiven.[3]

24.2 Toward the Completion of the Priestly People's *Kedusha*

God's final return to His Indwelling in Zion is in every respect connected to the completion of the sanctification of the people of Israel called to be His priesthood. Thereby the LORD follows the structure we observed at the very first consecration of priests in Israel's midst.[4] Only after completing their seven-day long consecration[5] were the priests allowed to perform their duties in the Presence of the LORD. Also underway to the *olam haba*, perfected *kedusha* is conditional to the duty of the priestly people. According to the God-chosen pattern of the two-sided covenant relationship,[6] at some point in time all Israel will clothe itself in the sanctification as if in a holy garment, granted by God Himself in the Messiah. Israel's perfectly completed sanctification,

---

in a wrong manner from a strict contradistinction between salvation for Israel on the one hand and universal salvation on the other hand. The salvation of the Messiah, however, knows of both.

2. See the citation of HaRav Tzvi Yehuda HaCohen Kook (Preface, footnote 15).
3. Isa 33:20–24.
4. See chapter 8.
5. See chapter 8 (8.3).
6. For this see par example chapter 7 (7.2 and 7.7), 12 (12.4) and 16 (16.2).

Part III: Returning and Rethinking: Living in a "New" Canonical Narrative

together with its pure service to God, its *avoda*, will then be part of the manner by which God allows the dawning of the *olam haba*.

The LORD God longs for this perfected *kedusha* of Israel. Together with Him the Messianic firstlings from Israel, joined by the added believers from the nations—as *one* great priestly people—wait for the completion of the sanctification of the priestly Israel in the center of the earth.

The nearing of the full Messianic Day, a "Day" that began with the "enfleshment" of the Son within Israel,[7] is a process too, as is the nearing of the Day of the LORD. They also happen simultaneously.[8] And as both approach, we see both salvific revelation and an increasing darkness to occur. Just as the priests were unclothed every day during their seven-day consecration and then again were clothed and anointed, the Messianic priestly nation of the Messiah will become more and more sanctified and perfected through the darkest of times. A permanent "unclothing" and "clothing" will take place. When all Israel will have finally "entered" the Messiah, and—using the terminology of the priestly consecration[9]—will have "clothed itself with Him,"[10] then the Body of the Messiah will finally be priestly *kehilla* of God to the fullest.[11]

24.3 The Fight Over God's Vine: Zion and the Tribulations of the Messiah

Waiting for the perfected *kedusha* of Israel does not take place within a vacuum, but in the reality of the twenty-first century. Also today we see a resistance against God's plans that certainly is not less than when Israel was first called to be a kingdom of priests. The resistance still revolves in a very literal sense around the camp of Israel in the midst of the earth.

Israel's existence is as the existence of the vine in Psalm 80, planted amidst the nations that try to gnaw like boars at what God has planted there.[12] Messiah *Yeshua* lived this existence to the fullest and still shares in it as the First One of Israel.[13]

As King of the Jews He is connected to the whole of Israel. This not only applies to the part of Israel that, again in the terminology of the priestly consecration, has already sanctified and clothed itself in the Messianic priestly garments, but it applies as much to the part that will yet enter into this perfect eschatological sanctification, according to God's promise. Also the ever growing resistance against Israel's election as a priestly nation of the LORD is something that confronts the Messiah and those

---

7. See chapter 15.
8. See among others chapter 19.
9. See chapter 8.
10. Cf. Gal 3:27; Rom 13:14; Eph 4:24; Col 3:12, 14.
11. Cf. chapter 23 (23.12).
12. Ps 80:13.
13. See chapter 16 (16.6).

Accompanying the Holy God Underway Toward the Tikkun Olam

with whom He has connected Himself. Consequently, all Israel will therefore have to live the way of the vine in Psalm 80, again in our times. But we too as believers from all nations, grafted onto the root of Israel,[14] must increasingly share in this suffering caused by this hatred of Gods priestly nation.

Indeed, all nations will have to lift the "heavy stone" of Jerusalem.[15] Zion's place in the midst of the earth asks the nations to recognize the God-ordained priestly structures, of which His people and His city form the center.[16] The opposition of the nations against this center of the earth is at the deepest level also resistance to God's return to Zion. It is resistance against the ending of exile of the Holy One, His Messiah, and His people. This resistance from the nations, having demonic origins,[17] creates a night in which the increasing sanctification of the priestly nation and the return to Zion will take place.

It is the night in which the Song of Songs is learned, even while "the song of the prostitute" is heard over the earth. Israel with its God-granted *kedusha* is identified as "bride" in contrast to the *kedesha*, "the prostitute."[18] Ultimately the ongoing canonical narrative revolves around the "Song of Songs, the song of the love between God and Israel," while a false love song resounds.

Chapter 23 focused on the way that we, as believers from the nations, must walk in connection to the King of the Jews and His people. An intense love for God, His Messiah, and His desires compels us to share in "what is still lacking in regard to Christ's afflictions, for the sake of his body."[19] These afflictions will not be purely spiritual, but just like Paul describes will also involve our physical existence.[20] All who wish to live a godly life will be persecuted.[21] This God-required godliness, which evokes resistance and persecution, is in every way connected to all God's plans, words, and commands. Part of this godliness is not just the connectedness to Israel's God, the Creator, but also to His people, the bodily Israel of God.

The years in which the *Shoa* was conceived of and executed have shown that whoever through Messiah *Yeshua* remains connected in love to Israel's God and His people must face persecution. This is the same in our time. This path of persecution,

---

14. Rom 11:17–19.
15. Zech 2:3 (RSV).
16. See chapter 19.
17. For this see chapter 12.
18. *Kedesha* is the Hebrew word for a (shrine-)prostitute. See Gen 38:21; Deut 23:17 and Hos 4:14. It here shows that the contradistinction between bride and whore, so essential within the Book of Revelation, has its roots on the level of linguistics. Gen 38 tells the story of Judah who leaves the God-intended holy nation (*goy kadosh* or *am kadosh*) and (within this exile) only after a *kedesha*-like relation comes to repentance and returns. After this repentance and return the story of the intended deliverance of Israel continues along the way of Joseph. See also Poot, 167–76.
19. Col 1:24.
20. Cf. the "I fill up in my flesh" in Col 1:24.
21. 2 Tim 3:12.

Part III: Returning and Rethinking: Living in a "New" Canonical Narrative

however, offers us the opportunity to "accompany" God, His Messiah, and His people in love, service, and prayer that focuses on this return to Zion.[22] The "Next year in Jerusalem"[23] and the "Maranatha"[24] will join together.

24.4 The Ways Toward Unity in the Time of the Hebron-Kingship

The period of David's kingship in Hebron presented the tribes of Israel with the opportunity to reunite. God's choice of Hebron as center of this unification made it clear that unity within Israel was necessary.[25] Later on the prophets spoke of the Messianic unity of all Israel that would be part of God's salvation for His people.[26]

We observed earlier that also the present kingship of Messiah Jesus can be characterized as Hebron-kingship.[27] The theme of the unity of Israel is important within His life and prayer.[28] In Him this promised unity of Israel began, and in Him the nations are also called to unity with God's people.[29]

The Jerusalem-kingship of David could only begin when Israel had united itself under His kingship. God also works similarly today. The Messianic unity of all Israel and the eschatological unity of the nations with God's people will form the prelude to the dawning of the *olam haba*. At the same time they are part of the salvation of God in the full Messianic Eighth Day.

In this time of the Hebron-kingship of His Messiah, God calls Israel and the nations to unify in Him. The "great multitude that no one could count"[30] is not called away from Israel and Zion, but is gathered there. Historically the "harvest of the nations" has often been solely interpreted as a call to a kind of universal salvation, not as a reorientation toward Zion in order to participate in the salvation already revealed there. And yet, the history of missions within the Christian church is actually the history of "taking hold of the hem of the robe of a Jewish man" and joining Him while "God is with you."[31]

The call to unity within the Body of the Messiah, clearly sounding in John 17, is a call also for believers from the nations. But first of all, as discussed in chapter 23, it

22. See chapter 23 (23.13).

23. This is the wish with which the Jewish *Seder*-meal is ended. Thereby the participants at the meal look forward to the fulfillment of *Pessaḥ* in the great final of God's ways, implying also the ending of exile (cf. Luke 22:16–18).

24. 1 Cor 16:22 (KJV). NIV and RSV render this Aramaic exclamation respectively as "Come Lord!" and "Our Lord, come!"

25. See chapter 19 (19.11).

26. See chapter 12 (12.10).

27. See chapter 18, 19 and above (24.8).

28. Par example see John 10:1–17 and 17.

29. Cf. John 10:16; Eph 1:22 and 2:14–22.

30. Rev 7:9.

31. Zech 8:23.

is a call to unity with Israel. First to the unity with the Messianic firstlings from Israel, and then also a call to walk the paths of unity with respect to *all* Israel. Here suffices to say that these ways toward unity belong to the essence of this phase within God's history with Israel and the world.

After all, now is the time for the proclamation of the gospel of the kingdom among the nations.[32] The nations are called to unity under the kingship of God, to become one also with the vanguard of Israel and to share in God's desire to see the whole of his people come to unity under His kingship. God's mission among the nations and His mission with respect to His people have everything to do with the promise of the eschatological unity within the people of Israel and between Israel and the nations. This unity is a Messianic gift on the one hand, but on the other hand it involves a command within the two-sidedness of the covenant relation with Israel's God. The rising up of the firstlings of the nations and their unity belong to the ways which God and His Messiah walk while searching for and inviting all of Israel to join. This beginning of eschatological unity among the nations is also intended to make all Israel jealous. The gift of the Holy Spirit as foretaste and "guarantee"[33] of the *tikkun olam*, therefore, calls for orientation toward this unity. That the Spirit at the same time is also called the firstling gift, the "firstfruits"[34] (also of the salvation of unity), shows that we still await the full revelation of this unity within the *olam haba*.

The Divine call to unity in this time of the Hebron-kingship of the Messiah requires a reorientation from the side of the ecumenical movement. The same applies to the dialogue of the great Christian traditions and confessional families. God corrects our misguided search for unity, in and around a Christ, severed by us from Israel. He orientates the unity required by Him again to Zion. He calls denominational families to subject themselves to the King of the Jews as preparation for His kingship in Jerusalem. It is precisely because this reorientation is requested from all denominational families and believers from the nations, that this reorientation contributes to unity. When all have to discover and relinquish their false identities, then all are called to receive a newly discovered, identity-in-unity in Messiah *Yeshua*.

Since this reorientation requires such careful reconsideration, calling us to walk new and unknown ways, we must pray that models for reorientation, unity, and reconciliation will be given. Models in which the physical Zion and the return of God and His people to the land and His city will have a place. Since these ways of unity will have to be learned again, such models could be helpful.

---

32. Matt 28:18–20.
33. 2 Cor 1:22 (RSV; NIV renders "a deposit guaranteeing what is to come"); Eph 1:14.
34. Rom 8:23.

24.5 During the Hebron-Kingship: Israel Approaching the Second *Pessaḥ*

As previously discussed, a second *Pessaḥ* is being awaited for Israel.[35] The firstlings of Israel, who have recognized and accepted the *kedusha* of Messiah *Yeshua*, will at some time be followed by all Israel. The Messiah as the great First One of Israel is the guarantee of this priestly sanctification of all Israel.

When the whole priestly nation of Israel will be finally sanctified by God and will also have sanctified itself in obedience, the completion and fulfilled celebration of *Pessaḥ* will take place.

It is God's love, a God who—as was the case with Hosea—tries to win the love of all Israel for God's *Hoshea-Yeshua*.[36] The mystery of the estrangement and non-recognition will ultimately transform into recognition and encounter.[37] The Holy One of Israel is committed to this transformation. Perhaps God will make use of a faith community from the nations that has repented and been oriented anew toward Zion, yet His faithfulness guarantees the complete fulfillment of the calling of all Israel to be His kingdom of priests.

When this calling becomes perfectly fulfilled, then the world will, together with Israel, experience a great and foretold fulfillment of the Exodus from Egypt and the making of the covenant at Sinai that followed. It will be a grand feast of deliverance and resurrection from death in all its forms. A celebration of the fulfillment of the New Covenant, of which the Spirit has already been given as the first gift. A feast of entrance into the promised future of the coming age, the *olam haba*, as an entrance into the new land promised by God.

Since we believe in God's faithfulness, we look for His deeds within his people that are oriented toward this coming future.

24.6 Underway Toward the Last Trumpet and the Fulfillment of *Yom Kippur* and *Sukkot*

Both the Tanakh and the New Testament speak of the future in the language of the Feast of Tabernacles.[38] Just like *Pessaḥ*, *Sukkot* also has a history of fulfillment that reaches into the future world. Together with Israel, the whole Messianic faith community and ultimately the whole of creation is approaching this future world. Also the other feasts preceding *Sukkot* in God's feast calendar will yet enter into a final fulfillment.[39]

---

35. See chapter 19 (19.11).
36. See chapter 14 (14.3).
37. Zech 12:10–14; Rev 1:7.
38. See chapter 12 (12.17) and chapter 21 (21.6; 21.10 and 21.14).
39. Cf. chapter 23 (23.9).

The annual Day of Trumpets that precedes the ten Days of Awe leading up to the Day of Atonement,[40] will be fulfilled in the last trumpet that will announce the nearing judgment and the beginning of the kingship of God.[41]

The meaning of the Day of Atonement also has aspects connected to the future. Even when the meaning of *Yom Kippur* is thought of as a (predominantly) prophetic prefiguration of the death of Messiah *Yeshua*, as is the case in the Letter to the Hebrews, then this interpretation may still imply other aspects. This day can be interpreted as well as a prophecy promising that all iniquity will be taken away from Israel. Then *Yom Kippur* is a prophecy of a grand *Gilgal* for Israel.[42] A day on which, following the desert journey through the world, the complete purification takes place.[43] This day can also call the nations to purification before the kingdom of God begins.[44] In summary, *Yom Kippur* has a fulfillment history with multiple aspects.[45]

When we seek connection to Israel's yearly celebration of this day, God's future may not catch us by surprise.[46] On the contrary, a yearly day of remembrance, repentance, turning to God, and preparing ourselves to appear before the Throne of God may bring believers from the nations to a more conscious expectation of the appearance of God's royal power that will make everything right.[47]

24.7 Underway: The Body of the Messiah's Royal Prophetic Task

God has begun the restoration of all things in the Firstling of Israel and the faith community from Israel and the nations, sanctified in Him. Through the increasing darkness of the nearing Day of the LORD, the Body of the Messiah approaches the full morning of the Eighth Day.

The Body of the Messiah, meant to be a foretaste of God's eschatological salvation, is called to be a model of living and learning. God's original intention to create a house of learning in the center of the earth is approaching its full realization.[48] Instruction is available from the midst of Israel, and the nations may be blessed by learning alongside Israel. The mutual blessing between Israel and the nations thus

---

40. Lev 23:23–24; Num 29:1–6; cf. Neh 8:1. This day became later within Judaism the New Year's day (*Rosh HaShanah*).

41. Cf. 1 Cor 15:52; 1 Thess 4:16; Rev 11:15.

42. Cf. Joshua 5:9–10. *Gilgal* is derived from the verb *galal* that means "to roll away."

43. Cf. the circumcision of the uncircumcised generation of the people of Israel in Gilgal (Joshua 5:2–9).

44. Just like Israel repents and returns to God during the ten days preceding *Yom Kippur*.

45. Perhaps, in the Tanakh, the designation of this day (*Yom kippurim*, with *–im* as plural ending) points to these multiple atonements. Usually, however, the plural word *kippurim* is used to convey the concept of "atonement."

46. See chapter 23 (23.9).

47. Cf. 2 Cor 5:10–20; Heb 12:25–29.

48. See par example chapter 1 (1.10), 6 (6.8), 10 (10.7 and 10.8) and 12 (12.8).

becomes visible.⁴⁹ This mutual blessing had been God's intention from the beginning and will be perfected in the *olam haba*.

This existence is meant to model, albeit incompletely, what God intended when He called Israel to be a kingdom of priests. But at the same time the Body of the Messiah still awaits the perfection of this calling. This perfection is bound up with all Israel's entering into the Messianic *kedusha*. While it waits, the Body of the Messiah is called to share in God's inner involvement with all His people, described in the preceding chapter.

The Body of the Messiah is also the vanguard of God's future, and in that capacity also encounters the opposition against God and His plans. The increasing darkness which accompanies the nearing of the Day of the LORD, is also the hour of the lawless opponent of God.⁵⁰ For the Messianic community, to live in that hour of lawlessness implies drinking the bitter cup of suffering.⁵¹

The calling to be a kingdom of priests calls the Body of the Messiah to live as shining stars amidst "a warped and crooked generation."⁵² There will be those who resist the display of God's intentions and warning against disobedience toward Him and His commandments. At the same time, however, the Messianic priesthood is called to pray for the nations in this situation.

24.8 Temple Servants for the *Olam Haba*: The *Avoda* of All Israel—The Body of the Messiah Perfected—One *Kehilla* and the Twenty-four Elders

In the beginning of this study we learned how God, when He began creating heaven and earth, was already oriented toward the completion of His creation.⁵³ His blessing would be the driving force which would bring earth and heaven, animals and humankind, to that goal.⁵⁴ With humankind's obedience to its calling, the earth would finally be filled with the image of the LORD. God's good creation was ultimately intended to enter into sanctification. Within this *kedusha* of "the good" everything would be sanctified and dedicated to God.⁵⁵

We observed creation waiting for further instruction, one that God would give in the midst of and by means of Israel as the priestly house of learning.⁵⁶ The realization of God's great and cosmic intentions would occur by means of the election and

---

49. See chapter 2 (2.7) and 21 (21.14).
50. See chapter 21 (21.3 and 21.4).
51. Matt 20:22–23; cf. John 18:11.
52. Eph 2:15.
53. See chapter 1 (1.3 and 1.4).
54. See chapter 2 (2.1 and 2.2).
55. See chapter 2 (2.2).
56. See chapter 1 (1.4; 1.6; 1.9) and 2 (2.2).

Accompanying the Holy God Underway Toward the Tikkun Olam

calling of His people Israel and end in the *Shabbat* of the future, when all will be completed.[57]

Here we focus on the grand finale that Israel, the nations, and creation are heading for, while conscious of the fact that the reality of the future of the *olam haba* is only known to God.

> "What no eye has seen,
> what no ear has heard,
> and what no human mind has conceived"—
> the things God has prepared for those who love him.[58]

The salvation of the *tikkun olam* will be so grandiose that all human thinking, all imagination and every manner of expression, will fall short. In its full details neither the future has been revealed,[59] nor has Israel's calling as a kingdom of priests seen a complete fulfillment. But so much is clear, all Israel will be consecrated and sanctified to serve the Holy God in worship. It was to this that the people were called and God will not rest before all of His people share in this pure *avoda*. The whole of the people will be priestly in every respect.[60]

The afflictions of the Messiah[61] for the sake of His Body will have ended. All Israel, together with one great multitude from all nations and peoples, will be gathered into the Body of the Messiah, the First One of Israel. Yet the specific identity and calling of Abraham's offspring will still be present within it. The added multitude of priests from the nations may share in this Temple service for the LORD. Messiah *Yeshua* will be the head of these Temple servants.

One *kehilla* it will be. One great gathering called to holy service. Within the structure of the Temple service outlined in the Tanakh, the numbers twenty-four and 24,000 play an important role,[62] as all ministries in and around the Temple had to be fulfilled by a structure of twenty-four ministry groups.[63] Within the revelation granted to John, we find twenty-four elders at the Throne of God.[64] Are they, like the elders of Israel, who beheld the glory of God at Sinai,[65] in the proximity of God's glory the representatives (or "the elders") of Israel and the nations? Will the "elders" of Israel at the Throne ultimately be flanked by twelve representatives from the nations, who never were out of sight, because the twelve tribes of Israel in fact were meant to

---

57. See chapter 2 (2.2).
58. 1 Cor 2:9.
59. Rom 8:19 and 1 John 3:2.
60. Isa 61:6.
61. Cf. Col 1:24.
62. See respectively 1 Chr 24:18 and 25:31, and 1 Chr 23:4 and 27:1–5.
63. 1 Chr 24:19.
64. Rev 4:4, 10; 5:8; 11:16; 19:4.
65. Exod 24:1–2, 9–11.

Part III: Returning and Rethinking: Living in a "New" Canonical Narrative

be the bridge to them?[66] Is there a unity shown of two times twelve elders?[67] Will the enmity of the nations, that "settled over against"[68] the sons of Jacob, finally end? Will the hostility of Ishmael toward Isaac also come to an end?[69] Does it then become clear that the nations are allowed to share in the prerogatives of the sanctified Israel? Is that the reason for the mentioning of twenty-four thrones and twenty-four crowns?[70]

The end will be the holy *avoda* of God's Temple nation, of which the royal and priestly Israel is the inner circle, and to which priests of the nations have been added. Their life will be characterized by the words: "Holy to the LORD."[71] Throughout the centuries the *tefillin* on the forehead of Jewish men referred to this.[72] In this perfect *avoda* will the *Shema* become reality to the fullest. ONE God and *one* love of *one* Messianic *kehilla*!

24.9 Threefold Reflection of the Self-Revelation of the Holy One of Israel

We are nearing the end of the canonical narrative. It will, in fact, surpass all thoughts and words. The presentation that this book offers of the one and ongoing canonical narrative of the Tanakh and the Scriptures of the New Testament is nearly concluded. It is the narrative of the God of Israel—the God of Abraham, Isaac and Jacob—who is the Creator of everything that is, and who desires to bless everything beginning with and out of the camp of Israel in the midst of His creation. The canonical narrative of Scripture is the story of God's love that He has shown both through and within Israel. From there He wishes to ultimately bless all creation, including all nations.

The path He has taken is also a way in which He has revealed Himself more and more. Perhaps we can already recognize this deep self-revelation of the Holy One of Israel when He designates Himself as the God of Abraham, Isaac, and Jacob.[73] Perhaps we can interpret the way that the Eternal One walked with these patriarchs as a mirror that offers us, in the life of these three men, a reflection of unimagined depths in God's being and acting.

---

66. See chapter 7 (7.8), 9(9.6).

67. It might be possible to interpret also the two loaves that had to be presented to the LORD at Shavuot (Lev 23:17) as pointing to this multiplication.

68. Cf. Gen 25:18 (RSV) and 16:12 ("he shall dwell over against all his kinsmen," RSV).

69. Cf. the fact that also Ishmael had twelve sons (Gen 25:12–16).

70. Rev 4:4, 10; 19:4.

71. Cf. Exod 28:36; 39:30 and Zech 14:20.

72. Cf. Deut 6:8; Exod 13:9. *Tefillin* is the Hebrew word for the phylacteries that are worn on forehead (and arm) by Jewish men during morning prayers.

73. Par example see Exod 3:6, 15–16; 4:5; Matt 22:31–32.

Accompanying the Holy God Underway Toward the Tikkun Olam

In the history of Abraham, a father who binds his own son to be a sacrifice is shown, thus opening up the path to the fulfillment of God's ways.[74] In the life of Isaac we are confronted with a son who willingly allows himself to be bound in obedience to the Eternal God; a son who may live and sees two nations originating from himself.[75] In the ways which God walks with Jacob, we see how the blessing of God multiplies the 'promise-bearer-nation,' safeguards it in exile, brings it back to the center of the earth, and ultimately Israel becomes the blessing for the nations.[76]

Earlier in this book, when dealing with the theme of God's Indwelling in relation to the appearance of Messiah *Yeshua*, we observed how an unknown and unimagined self-revelation of the LORD took place.[77] We will not again discuss here these depths indicated within Scripture. We can, however, certainly state again that the ONE-ness of the Holy One of Israel apparently needs to be clarified by God Himself. Within this path of self-revelation, God's ONE-ness appears to be clarified in an unimagined manner in the revealed relations between God, the *Shekhina*, and the *Ruaḥ HaKodesh*. This threefold reality in relation to the one-ness of God is shown also in other places within the Scriptures.[78]

At the deepest level the canonical narrative of the Tanakh and the Scriptures of the New Testament therefore appears to be a narrative about God and by God as He reveals Himself more and more. At the deepest level it is *one* narrative of the love of the ONE—Father, Son and Holy Spirit—for His *segula*-people Israel in the midst of the nations. All nations and all creation may share in this love revealed there. A ceaseless "Holy, holy, holy" with covered faces[79] is a response befitting this threefold love.

24.10 The Indwelling and the *Shabbat* of God

The Messianic Eighth Day will be complete within the *olam haba*. Israel's election and its calling will be perfectly fulfilled, and the nations along with creation may share in

---

74. Cf. Gen 22. It is noteworthy that Abraham after the binding of Isaac receives word that his brother and his sister-in-law received eight sons. Bethuel—the eighth(!) son of his brother—begets Rebekah. Isaac will receive offspring through her. *Following* the fulfillment of Abraham's obedience, it becomes clear that also the promise of God begins to be fulfilled!

75. Cf. Gen 25:19–23. "Edom" (Esau's offspring) later becomes the summarizing designation for the hostile nations within Judaism.

76. The people of Jacob (numbering seventy people, Gen 46:27; cf. the seventy nations in Gen 10) becomes in Joseph, although again in exile, a blessing unto the nations.

77. See chapter 15.

78. An example: Observing the priority of the commands with respect to the ark-table-candelabrum within the totality of the building commands of the Holy One for His Dwelling (Exod 25:1–40), we can conclude that the ark (in the dark and inaccessible Most Holy Place), the table and the candelabrum (both in the illuminated and accessible Holy Place) form a threefold elaboration of the Unity of God's Presence, both transcendent and immanent, amidst His people. We can certainly observe here an indication of trinitarian nature relating to God's being. See also chapter 7 (7.8) and 8 (8.2).

79. Isa 6:2–3.

Part III: Returning and Rethinking: Living in a "New" Canonical Narrative

the salvation of the restoration of all things. God's intention with creation—the consummation, the *tikkun olam*—will be realized. His intended purposes will have been realized even more gloriously than imagined, through the ways of (dis)obedience and deliverance.

The Indwelling of God Himself will be the center and pinnacle. His will and desire to dwell in the center, in the camp of Israel, in order to press His creation (also in a very physical sense) to His heart, will then have been fully realized. In the "enfleshment" of Messiah *Yeshua* within Israel, the *Shekhina* not only pressed Israel to His heart, but in Israel also all creation. The Indwelling of God and the Lamb in the New Jerusalem will show this physical connection.

In every conceivable manner it will be the fulfillment of the Song of Songs. The search of God for His beloved will have ended. It will be said:

> He brought me to the banqueting house,
> and his banner over me was love.[80]
>
> My beloved is mine and I am his;
> he browses among the lilies.[81]

With this Indwelling, as seen from Zion, the exile of the Eternal One will belong to the past as well. His longing for Zion will be fulfilled. Even for the God of Israel it will no longer be: "Next year in Jerusalem!" but forever, eternally:

> The LORD is there.[82]

After the heat and toil of history, the rest of the ultimate *Shabbat* will begin for the Holy One of Israel as well. His love will then lead His people and all creation into the *kedusha* as intended as the goal of creation right from the beginning.

> See! The winter is past;
> the rains are over and gone.
> Flowers appear on the earth;
> the season of singing has come,
> the cooing of doves
> is heard in our land.
> The fig tree forms its early fruit;
> the blossoming vines spread their fragrance.[83]

---

80. Song 2:4 (RSV).
81. Song 2:16.
82. Ezek 48:35.
83. Song 2:11–13.

Accompanying the Holy God Underway Toward the Tikkun Olam

The God of Abraham, Isaac and Jacob, the God and Father of Messiah *Yeshua*, will come into His rest.[84] It will be an eternal *Shabbat Shalom* for Him.[85]

A book with twenty-four chapters: *one* ongoing canonical narrative given to us by God. A narrative in which the whole of the Tanakh and the Scriptures of the New Covenant sound together as one. One narrative that comes to us from the depth of the heart of God and that urges us, in Messiah *Yeshua,* to accompany Him. To long with Him. To wait with Him. To suffer with Him. To walk with Him. And to comfort Him along the way with our fellowship. To walk this way is "Learning Messiah." In order to ultimately enter with the LORD God's own *Shabbat*.

Coming home in the fullness of the Messianic Eighth Day . . .

---

84. Cf. Ezek 16:42.

85. Literally "*Shabbat* of Peace." Jewish people wish each other a blessed *Shabbat* with these words.

Epilogue

A JOURNEY THROUGH UNKNOWN terrain, such has been the writing of this book. This epilogue is a kind of a high place within the landscape, offering the possibility to look back and survey the road one walked. Looking back, you understand anew what choices you made and why. You see clearly why you set out on this journey in the first place, and what has been the consistent direction, apart from all choices made en route. You also realize even more why others sometimes took or take a different path.

The pathway of this book has been a search. A "learning to read God's way anew." But with "learning to read anew" comes a new gamut of experiences. The intense and joyful exploring of new roads, but also confusion and the question, *Where will this lead me?* An increasing understanding, but also an inner resistance, a denial of what is too dark, and new humility because of a collective past—it has happened to me. It can happen to anyone who reads this book.

Yet something has been constant: the voice of the Scriptures and the awareness of being called. This book belongs to the category of biblical theology, but whoever reads the Bible is plunged directly into the questions regarding the interpretation of the Scriptures. Therefore, as explained in the Introduction, my context has been the Tanakh and the Scriptures of the New Covenant, as they have been given to us from the camp of Israel and from the Christian faith community that originated there. These Scriptures speak of the desire of the God of Israel to reveal Himself to His people and the world. In line with this, I have read the Scriptures as the Word of God, and not as a purely human creation or a purely human concept. I have tried to read, and to learn to read anew with trust in the Holy Spirit, who has also been promised to us as *goyim* by the King of the Jews. My reading began and developed within the faith community that has originated through *Yeshua*, and in fellowship with the worldwide Body of Jesus rather than in opposition to it. At the same time, I also carry the Reformation-awareness, that we are in need of an ongoing reformation of our thought and life.

This book deals with the influence of paradigms that can hinder our understanding. And yet the Divine gift of the Tanakh and the New Testament has an inherent obstinacy, the Scriptures breaking (through) the hold of our paradigms. Although this book pleads a reformation in our understanding of God's ways with Israel and the nations, this does not mean that the whole of Christian theology is characterized as useless, and treated accordingly. What I designate as "the obstinacy of the Scriptures," has caused an abundance of exegetical and systematic-theological treasures to come forth from the reading of Scripture in spite of the paradigm of the traditional canonical narrative. Treasures with revelation-worth, although within the framework of the reorientation offered in this book they might, like gemstones, receive a new setting.

This book clearly shows that the reading of Scripture in close connection with Israel need not bring forth a "liberal" theology, or that such theology is a prerequisite.

A "high" view of Scripture, in which the Tanakh and the New Testament are fully revelation of the God of Israel, does not obstruct this close connection with Israel, but gives it a foundation that strengthens it.

A "high" Christology, in which the full Indwelling of God in the Son is central, is not necessarily incompatible with a reading in connection with Israel. Just as an emphasis on (the necessity) of the active obedience of the Messiah does not run counter to a theology of atonement-by-satisfaction. As already indicated, both elements play a role within the *kedusha* of the Messiah, this reality also being expressed within traditional systematic theology through the concepts of active and passive obedience (*oboedientia activa* and *oboedientia passiva*).

It is possible, however, that because of the new "setting," underlying structures will become visible with certain elements coming together like puzzle pieces. Additionally, our ways of systematizing within systematic theology can change or be revised by the new orientation within the other canonical narrative. The theme of God's longing for Zion, the end of the exile, and the return of the *Shekhina* have great impact on the doctrine of God within Christian theology and the Christian faith community. The ways of God Himself should determine, and if necessary, correct our thinking about Him.

The same applies to the basic structures of the theology of missions, and consequently of the doctrine of the church, and of the communication of the message within (missionary) preaching. The alternative to the traditional narrative offered in this book shows that both "the origin of the salvation" and the history of salvation's arrival are part of the message. Salvation is both from the Jews and from Jerusalem. This is not a fact that can be easily left out as a historic detail, within an eternally-spiritual preaching of salvation, but it is part of the proclamation of salvation that God has wrought within the circle of His people and also for the world. This origin simultaneously connects us with the real history of the world and the priestly nation in its midst. Preaching this message that is in alignment with God's desire to return to Zion in order to complete the *tikkun olam* there, also creates an abiding connection with the earth and its future.

That the whole of creation must enter into the *kedusha*, in which also the Name of the Holy One will be sanctified to the fullest, implies that we are called to live fully on this earth. Our lives are to be lived in the power of the Holy Spirit, who is the

Part III: Returning and Rethinking: Living in a "New" Canonical Narrative

firstling gift of the coming age. The Christian faith community must be re-oriented to live our earthly lives as covenant partners of the Eternal God, an orientation so much kept alive within Judaism. Our doctrine of creation and all themes related to it receive a new orientation. Our understanding of "God's council"[1] is thereby widened and deepened, affecting our learning, preaching, and living.

The aforementioned "obstinacy" of Scripture (or perhaps we should better speak of the sovereign and over-powering obstinacy of the Eternal God), has caused the worldwide propagation of the Name of Israel's God by the Christian faith community to bring blessing and to have salvific meaning. And in spite of wrong paradigms and sometimes wrongly-motivated theology, this remains true. After all, Paul also writes about wrongly motivated preaching[2] that, against all odds, still yields a good return. The shocking realization of our provisional[3] or even blatantly false knowledge,[4] with which the Christian faith community is confronted in the encounter with Judaism, is not intended for death, but for life. Has God has willed to confront us in this manner with the deepest depths of our hearts in order to deliver us from all haughty complacency and from all thinking that considers itself final?

In any case, all great theological and liturgical traditions within the Christian faith community, without exception, must learn to understand themselves as incomplete. We are all called to return and rethink.

No one can free himself from the whole of the Body of the Messiah. Just as Israel is *one*, both in the reception of God's salvation as well as in guilt,[5] this is true for the Christian faith community. No one can say, *I have no part in the dark history of the Church*. This unequivocally also applies to those whose eyes have already begun to open. Together we went astray, together we must be healed.[6]

The alternative to the traditional canonical narrative that this book offers shows that various historic ruptures did not originate from an inherent contradistinction between the Tanakh and the New Testament. It was much more about paradigms and convictions based on them that led to contradistinctions and ruptures between Judaism and the Church, but also between Judaism and Messianic Judaism, and between Messianic Judaism and the Church. Presupposed contradistinctions, thought of as necessary, have led to real ruptures. It is very special that in this current age we begin

---

1. Cf. Paul's use of the designation "council of God" for the whole of His plans, decisions and will (Acts 20:27).

2. See Phil 1:15–18.

3. 1 Cor 13:12.

4. Cf. 1 Cor 3:12–15, there it shows that there is a possibility of "work" that will perish in the fire, because it is not "purge-proof" within the purification that will precede the *olam haba*.

5. For this see Deut 29:14–15, but also Daniel 9 where Daniel humbles himself in a priestly manner under the guilt of all Israel.

6. Cf. Isa 64:6–9.

to understand the origins of these ruptures, and get a vision for reconciliation and healing. Within this period of what I have called the Hebron-kingship of the Messiah, this "unification"[7] is a matter of the heart of God and His Messiah, and preparation for the Jerusalem-kingship. Every prayer and every act oriented to this God-desired unity between Israel and the nations is also love and consolation for the Eternal One Himself. In this context the prayer of *Yeshua* in John 17 also appears to be much more than a prayer for denominational unity. At the deepest level this prayer is about the unity, so much desired by Jesus, between all who will ever put their trust in Him as the God-sent Messiah. And therefore it is also a prayer for both the ultimate unity of all Israel[8] *and* the fullness of the nations,[9] within the one herd of the one Shepherd.[10] May a clear insight into this one canonical narrative of the Tanakh and the Scriptures of the New Covenant serve this unification!

The *shofar* for the Hebron-kingship of the Messiah has sounded long ago, and will certainly sound for the kingship in Zion. Let us be hearing and *Learning Messiah*!

In the Preface I wrote about my encounter with living Judaism. Without that encounter, this book would never have come into existence. Therefore, first of all I wish to thank Michael Swirsky, my friend and rabbi in Jerusalem. Mike, I am thankful for what you have meant to me; you have been and still are a guide in so many respects. A coach, an endless well of new book titles, a man who listens with his heart time and again, both in Jerusalem and at a distance. It is a privilege to know you.

I did not need to make the journey of writing this book alone. A number of people have accompanied me, both close by and from a distance. Co-reading is also a form of co-traveling. Thanks to all the friends who took the effort to read either parts or the whole of the manuscript, coming with me on this journey. Without your support this journey would have been much more difficult. I am also thankful for the stimulus and possibilities that the church board and the congregation in Aalsmeer offered me.

Daniël Drost (connected to the Baptist Seminary in Amsterdam, the Netherlands), contributed in a special way, as did Aart Brons (stationed at that time in Jerusalem as consultant for the Center of Israel Studies[11] in Ede, the Netherlands). Thank you, Daniël and Aart, for reading the finished manuscript and for your worthwhile feedback and encouragement.

My friend Anton de Ruiter has meticulously checked and commented on the whole manuscript. Thank you, Anton, also for our very stimulating conversations.

---

7. See chapter 18 (18.8 and footnote 125) and 19 (19.9).
8. Cf. Rom 11:12.
9. Cf. Rom 11:25.
10. John 10:16.
11. For the aims and practice of this Dutch study center and some English publications see www.centrumvoorisraelstudies.nl.

Part III: Returning and Rethinking: Living in a "New" Canonical Narrative

I also mention here Dineke Houtman, now professor of Judaic Studies at the Protestant University in the Netherlands (especially focusing on the relation between Judaism and Christianity). Dineke, thank you for your attentive and meticulous reading of the manuscript and the treasure trove of remarks, suggestions, questions, and critical comments that I found time and again in the margins! You probably did not know what you took on when you promised to read the manuscript, but I am thankful for your commitment and your encouraging feedback.

Perhaps unnecessary, but I wish to state it here anyway: This book has been written from a desire to learn to know God's ways; any shortcomings and points that need correction, however, can only be credited to me.

A publisher causes a manuscript to become a book. Nico de Waal, thank you for your involvement, appreciative critical reading, and for the commitment of Boekencentrum Uitgevers.

Finally, the one who sacrificed most during the years in which this book took shape, that is you, Coby. Thereby it has become as much your book, and your contribution to a renewed learning within the Body of the Messiah. Thank you for your faithfulness and unconditional support during the whole writing process.

This book is for you, who shares in everything underway to Zion.

List of Hebrew Terms

(Following a modern system of transliteration of Hebrew words and terms)

Am kadosh	holy people
Akeda	the Binding (the near-sacrifice of Isaac, in Genesis 22)
Aleinu	literally: "upon us (is the obligation to praise God)." Opening word and name of a prayer said at the end of each of the daily service
Avoda	worship; as designation for the service/ministry to God in the Temple and as designation of the whole of life as service to God
Avoda zara	literally: "alien worship" – designation for idolatry
Bereshit	in the beginning; both the opening word and the Hebrew name of the book of Genesis
Bereshit bara	in the beginning (God) created
Brit	covenant
Brit am	covenant for/of the people; designation used in Isaiah 42:6 and 49:8
Brit ḥadasha	new covenant; also, modern Hebrew term for the New Testament
Ḥesed	loving-kindness, faithful (covenantal) love
Ḥuppa	wedding canopy, under which a Jewish couple stand during their marriage ceremony
Eḥad	one
Emuna	faith, trust in God
Eved	servant or slave (related to a*voda*)

List of Hebrew Terms

Galut	exile
Ger	alien, foreigner
Ger toshav	resident alien/foreigner, a non-Jew living in the Land of Israel
Gibbor	strong man, hero
Goël	redeemer; guardian-redeemer (NIV)
Goy	non-Jew, gentile
Goyim	(plural of *goy*) nations, also designation for non-Jews, gentiles
Ḥannuka	consecration; feast commemorating the reconsecration of the Temple following its desecration by Antioch IV Epiphanes
HaShem	literally: "the Name"; designation for God
Hoshana	exclamation: "Save [us]!" (Psalm 118:25), hosanna
Hoshana Rabba	literally: "the Great Hosanna" – the seventh day of the Feast of Tabernacles, at which the cry *Hoshana!* sounds many times during the liturgical prayers
Halakha (plural *halakhot*)	designation for the way of the commandments that has to be walked in obedience; the body of Jewish law; also, a particular law
Yeshua	salvation; a variant of the Hebrew name *Yehoshua* (Joshua), which, in turn, was the basis of the Greek name Jesus
Yom HaShoa	day when the Jewish people commemorates the *Shoa* (the Holocaust)
Yom Kippur	Day of Atonement
Kavod	honor, glory; also used to designate the appearance of God's majesty
Kedesha	(shrine) prostitute
Kedusha	holiness, sanctification
Kehilla	congregation or community
Ketuba	marriage contract
Ketuvim	the Hagiographa (third subdivision of the Tanakh)
Kohanim	priests (plural of *kohen*)

List of Hebrew Terms

Maḥane	camp
Makom	place, also: one of the names of God
Mashiaḥ	Messiah
Melakhim	kings (plural of *melekh*)
Menaḥem	comforter; a common masculine first name
Menora	the seven-branched candelabrum in the Tabernacle and Temple; sometimes mistakenly applied, as well, to the nine-branched Ḥannuka lamp (the proper name for which is *ḥannukia*)
Mikva	ritual bath
Mishpaḥa (plural *mishpaḥot*)	family
Mohel	circumciser, who performs a circumcision
Nevi'im	prophets; second subdivision of the Tanakh
Olam	world, age
Olam haba	the World to Come, the future age; designation for the time of the perfection and restoration
Olam haze	this World, the present age
Omer	sheaf; designation for the period of counting between *Pessaḥ* and *Shavuot*
Pessaḥ	Passover, the celebration of the Exodus and the deliverance from Egypt
Purim	literally: "lots"; cf. Esther 9:24–28 – the feast commemorating the deliverance of the Jewish people by the supplications of Queen Esther
Reshit	beginning
Rishon	first
Ruaḥ HaKodesh	the Holy Spirit
Rosh HaShana	literally: "the head of the year"; Jewish New Year day
Satan	(the) opponent (of God)
Seder	order; designation for the liturgical meal with which the celebration of *Pessaḥ* begins
Segula	most treasured possession

List of Hebrew Terms

Simḥat Tora	"Rejoicing of the *Tora*," a festive day at the end of the Feast of Tabernacles at which the reading cycle of the Torah is ended and started anew
Shabbat	day of rest, the seventh day of the week
Shalom	peace
Shavuot	"Feast of Weeks," the fiftieth day (seven weeks plus one day) counting from the second day of Passover
Shekhina	the Presence of God in the world (sometimes visible, but also in an invisible manner)
Shema	"Hear (O Israel)!" – designation of the central Jewish confession of faith (Deuteronomy 6:4–9)
Shemini Atzeret	literally: the Assembly of the Eighth (Day), a festival immediately following the Feast of Tabernacles
She'ol	realm of death
Shoa	literally: "destruction/devastation"; designation for the murder of six million Jews during World War II ("the Holocaust")
Shofar	ram's horn (sometimes rendered as "trumpet")
Sukka (plural Sukkot)	temporary dwelling, hut, tabernacle
Sukkot	Feast of Tabernacles
Tefillin	phylacteries
Tanakh	the Hebrew Bible ("Old Testament"); an acronym of the names of its three subdivisions: T[ora] (Pentateuch), N[evi'im] (Prophets), K[etuvim] (Hagiographa)
Terafim	small idols
Teshuva	repentance, returning to God
Tikkun olam	literally: "the perfecting of the world"; cf. the restoration of all things (Acts 3:21)
Tish'a Be'Av	the Ninth of (the month of) Av, a fast day commemorating the destruction of the Temples and other disasters in Jewish history
Tora	literally: "instruction"; the whole of the God-given revelation at Sinai; also, designation of the first five

	books of the Tanakh (the Pentateuch, i.e. Genesis through Deuteronomy)
Tov	good
Tzaddik	righteous (man/person)

Bibliography

Agnon, S.Y. *Present at Sinai. The Giving of the Law*. Commentaries selected by S.Y. Agnon. Translated by Michael Swirsky. Philadelphia: Jewish Publication Society, 1999.

Andel, C.P. van. *Jodenhaat & Jodenangst: Over meer dan twintig eeuwen antisemitisme*. Amersfoort: De Horstink, 1983.

Ateek, Naim Stifan. *A Palestinian Christian Cry for Reconciliation*. New York: Maryknoll, 2008.

Aumann, Moshe. *Conflict and Connection: The Jewish-Christian-Israel Triangle*. Jerusalem: Gefen, 2003.

Bacchiocchi, Samuele. *From Sabbath to Sunday: A Historical Investigation of the Rise of Sunday Observance in Early Christianity*. Berrien Springs, MI: Biblical Perspectives, 2000.

———. *God's Festivals in Scripture and History: Part 2: The Fall Festivals,* Berrien Springs, MI: Biblical Perspectives, 1995.

Beek, A. van de. *De kring om de Messias: Israël als volk van de lijdende Heer*. Spreken over God 1,2. Zoetermeer: Meinema, 2002.

Berlin, Adele, and Marc Zvi Brettler, eds. *The Jewish Study Bible*. Oxford: Oxford University Press, 2004.

Bialik, Hayim N., and Yehoshua H. Ravnitzky, eds. *The Book of Legends. Sefer Ha-Aggadah. Legends from Talmud and Midrash*. New York: Schocken, 1992.

Blois, Matthijs de. *Israël: Een staat ter discussie?* Heerenveen: Jongbloed, 2010.

Bockmuehl, Markus. *Jewish Law in Gentile Churches: Halakhah and the Beginning of Christian Public Ethics*. Edinburgh: T&T Clark, 2000.

Borowitz, E. B. *Renewing the Covenant: A Theology for the Postmodern Jew*. Philadelphia: Jewish Publication Society, 1991.

Bruce, F. F. *Commentary on the Epistle to the Hebrews*. The English Text with Introduction, Exposition and Notes. London: Marshall, Morgan & Scott, 1971.

———. *The Acts of the Apostles*. The Greek Text with Introduction and Commentary. Reprint 2nd ed. London: Tyndale, 1970.

Bruggen, Jakob van. *Mattheüs: Het evangelie voor Israël*. 2nd ed. Kampen: Kok, 1994.

———. *Paulus: Pionier voor de Messias van Israël*. Kampen: Kok, 2001.

Calvin, John. *Institutes of the Christian Religion*. http://www.ccel.org/ccel/calvin/institutes.i.html.

Campen, M. van. *Gans Israël, II. Voetiaanse en coccejaanse visies op de joden gedurende de zeventiende en achttiende eeuw*. Zoetermeer: Boekencentrum, 2006.

Campen, M. van., and G. C. den Hertog, eds. *Israël, volk, land en staat: Terugblik en perspectief*. Zoetermeer: Boekencentrum, 2005.

Campenhausen, Hans Fr. von. *Die Entstehung der christlichen Bibel*. Tübingen: Mohr, 1968.

Bibliography

Chill, Abraham. *The Mitzvot: The Commandments and Their Rationale.* Jerusalem: Keter, 2000.

Cohen Stuart, G.H. *Joodse Feesten en Vasten: Een reis over de zee van de Talmoed naar de wereld van het Nieuwe Testament.* 3rd ed. Baarn: Ten Have, 2004.

Le Cornu, Hilary, and Joseph Shulam. *A Commentary on the Jewish Roots of Acts.* Vol. I-II. Jerusalem: Academon, 2003.

———., and Joseph Shulam. *A Commentary on The Jewish Roots of Galatians.* Jerusalem: Academon, 2005.

Dächsel, K. Aug. *Bijbelverklaring.* Vol. 1–10, (photographic reprint). Utrecht: Den Hertog, 1981.

Drost, A.H. *Is God veranderd? Een onderzoek naar de relatie God-Israël in de theologie van K.H. Miskotte, A.A. van Ruler en H. Berkhof.* Zoetermeer: Boekencentrum, 2007.

Dunn, James D.G. *Romans 1–8.* Dallas: Word Books, 1988.

———. *Romans 9–16.* Dallas: Word Books, 1988.

———. *The New Perspective on Paul, Revised Edition.* Grand Rapids: Eerdmans, 2008.

Encyclopaedia Judaica. Original unedited edition: www.jewishencyclopedia.com; 1972 edition: http://www.bjeindy.org/resources/library/access-to-encyclopedia-judaica.

Flusser, David. *Jesus in Selbstzeugnissen und Bilddokumenten.* Reinbek bei Hamburg: Rowohlt, 1968.

Frymer-Kensky, Tikva, et.al. *Christianity in Jewish Terms.* Boulder, CO: Westview, 2000.

Goldhagen, Daniel J. *Hitler's Willing Executioners: Ordinary Germans and the Holocaust.* New York: Knopf, 1996.

Goldwurm, Hersh. *Succos—Its Significance, Laws, and Prayers: A Presentation Anthologized from Talmudic and Traditional Sources.* 2nd ed. New York: Mesorah, 1997.

Halevi, Judah. *The Kuzari (Kitab al Kazhari): An Argument for the Faith of Israel.* New York: Schocken, 1964.

Harvey, Richard. *Mapping Messianic Jewish Theology: A Constructive Approach.* Milton Keynes UK: Paternoster, 2009.

———. "Towards a Messianic Jewish Theology of Reconciliation in Light of the Arab-Israeli Conflict. Neither Dispensationalist nor Supersessionist?" In *The Land Cries Out. Theology of the Land in the Israeli-Palestinian Context*, edited by Salim. J. Munayer and Lisa Loden, 82–103. Eugene, OR: Cascade, 2012.

Hays, J.D. "Applying the Old Testament Law Today." *Bibliotheca Sacra* 158 (2001) 21–35.

Heschel, Abraham J. *The Sabbath.* New York: Farrar, Straus and Giroux, 2005.

Heschel, Susannah. *The Aryan Jesus: Christian Theologians and the Bible in Nazi Germany.* Princeton: Princeton University Press, 2008.

Hirsch, Samson R. *Bereishith/Genesis. Translation and Commentary,* 2nd revised ed. New York: Judaica, 1989.

———. *Shemoth/Exodus. Translation and Commentary,* 2nd revised ed. New York: Judaica, 1989.

Hocken, Peter. *The Marranos: A History in Need of Healing.* TJCII, 2006.

IP-nota (*Het Israëlisch-Palestijns conflict in de context van de Arabische wereld van het Midden-Oosten. Bijdrage tot meningsvorming in de Protestantse Kerk in Nederland*) accepted by the Generale Synode van de Protestantse Kerk in Nederland, 11th of April 2008. https://www.protestantsekerk.nl/actueel/dossiers/israel-en-palestina/kerkorde-en-ip-nota

Isaacs, Ronald H. *Mitzvot: A Sourcebook for the 613 Commandments.* Northvale: Jason Aronson, 1996.

Janicki, Toby. *God-Fearers, Gentiles & The God of Israel*. Marshfield, MO: First Fruits of Zion, 2012.

Jansen, Hans. *Christelijke theologie na Auschwitz. Deel I: Theologische en kerkelijke wortels van het antisemitisme*. 3rd ed. Den Haag: Boekencentrum, 1982.

———. *Van jodenhaat naar zelfmoordterrorisme: Islamisering van het Europees antisemitisme in het Midden-Oosten*. Heerenveen: Groen, 2006.

Jensen, Morten H. "The Galilean Cradle of Jesus and His Followers. All Roads Lead to Galilee." In *Chosen to Follow. Jewish believers through History and Today*, edited by Knut H. Høyland and Jakob W. Nielsen, 1–21. Jerusalem: Caspari Center, 2012.

Josephus, Flavius, *Antiquities of the Jews*. http://www.attalus.org/old/aj_14b.html.

Juster, Dan. *Jewish Roots: A Foundation of Biblical Theology*. Shippensburg: Destiny Image, 1995.

Kahan, Aharon Y. *The Taryag Mitzvos: A new concise compilation of all 613 commandments culled from Talmudic, Midrashic and Rabbinic sources*. New York: Keser Torah, 1987.

Katanacho, Yohanna. *Christ is the Owner of Haaretz*. http://katanacho.com/datadir/en-events/ev30/files/Christ%20is%20the%20Owner%20of%20Haaretz.pdf.

Keil C.F., *Jeremiah, Lamentations*. Vol. VIII. In: Commentary on The Old Testament by C.F. Keil and F. Delitzsch. Translated from the German. Grand Rapids: Eerdmans, 1977.

Kidner, Derek. *Psalms 73–150: A Commentary on Books III-V of the Psalms*. London: Inter-Varsity, 1975.

Kinzer, Mark S. *Postmissionary Messianic Judaism: Redefining Christian Engagement with the Jewish People*. Grand Rapids: Brazos, 2005.

———. *Israel's Messiah and the People of God: A Vision for Messianic Jewish Covenant Fidelity*. Edited by Jennifer M. Rosner. Eugene, OR: Cascade, 2011.

Klinken, Gert van. *Christelijke stemmen over het Jodendom: Zestig jaar Interkerkelijk Contact Israël*. Delft: Eburon, 2009.

Kook, HaRav Avraham Yitzhak HaCohen. *Lights on Orot: The Teachings of HaRav Avraham Yitzhak HaCohen*. Commentary by Rabbi David Samson and Tzi Fishman. Jerusalem: Torat Eretz Yisrael, 1996.

Kook, HaRav Tzvi Yehuda HaCohen. *Torat Eretz Yisrael: The Teachings of HaRav Tzvi Yehuda HaCohen Kook*. Commentary by HaRav David Samson. Translated and edited by Tzvi Fishman. Jerusalem: Torat Eretz Yisrael, 1991.

Levine, Amy-Jill, and Marc Zvi Brettler, eds. *The Jewish Annotated New Testament*. New York: Oxford University Press, 2011.

Loden, Lisa. "Towards Reconciliation. Messianic Jewish Believers and Palestinian Christians." In *Chosen to Follow. Jewish believers through History and Today*, edited by Knut H. Høyland and Jakob W. Nielsen, 217–225. Jerusalem: Caspari Center, 2012.

Locht, Gábor. *De Sabbat: Een wet van genade*. Zoetermeer: Boekencentrum, 2006.

Midrash Rabbah. Translated into English with Notes, Glossary and Indices under the Editorship of Rabbi dr. H. Freedman, and Maurice Simon. Vol. I-X. 3d ed. New York: Soncino, 1983.

Milgrom, Jacob. *Leviticus 1–16: A New Translation with Introduction and Commentary*. New York: Doubleday, 1991.

———. *Leviticus 17–22: A New Translation with Introduction and Commentary*. New York: Doubleday, 2000.

———. *Leviticus 23–27: A New Translation with Introduction and Commentary*. New York: Doubleday, 2001.

Bibliography

———. *Numbers: The traditional Hebrew text with the new JPS translation. Commentary by Jacob Milgrom*, Philadelphia: Jewish Publication Society, 1989.

Mishna, *Mishnayot*. Translated and Annotated by Philip Blackman, Vol. 1-6. New York: Judaica, 2000

Miskotte, K. H. *Als de goden zwijgen: Over de zin van het Oude Testament.* Amsterdam: Holland, 1956.

Munayer, Salim. "Theology of the Land, From a Land of Strife to a Land of Reconciliation." (edited by Joshua Korn). In *The Land Cries Out. Theology of the Land in the Israeli-Palestinian Context,* edited by Salim. J. Munayer and Lisa Loden, 234–264. Eugene, OR: Cascade, 2012.

Munayer, Salim. J. and Lisa Loden, eds. *The Land Cries Out. Theology of the Land in the Israeli-Palestinian Context.* Eugene, OR: Cascade, 2012.

Nirenberg, David. *Anti-Judaism: The Western Tradition.* New York: W.W. Norton, 2013.

Nouwen, Henri. *The Living Reminder, Service and Prayer in Memory of Jesus Christ.* New York: HarperCollins, 1977.

Oswalt, J.N. *The Book of Isaiah. Chapters 40–66.* Grand Rapids: Eerdmans, 1998.

Parkes, James. *The Conflict of the Church and the Synagogue: A Study in the Origins of Antisemitism,* 2nd ed. Cleveland: Meridian, 1964.

Paul, Mart-Jan. "Het Nieuwe Testament als voortzetting en voltooiing van het Oude Testament." In *Theologie van het Oude Testament. De blijvende boodschap van de Hebreeuwse Bijbel,* edited by Hendrik Koorevaar and Mart-Jan Paul, 387–412. Zoetermeer: Boekencentrum, 2013.

Poll, Evert W. van der. *De Messiaanse Beweging en haar betekenis voor christenen.* Putten: Shalom, 2001.

———. *Sacred Times For Chosen People: Development, Analysis and Missiological Significance of Messianic Jewish Holiday Practice.* Zoetermeer: Boekencentrum, 2008.

Poot, Henk. *Jozef: Een messiaanse geschiedenis.* Hoenderloo: Nova, 1998.

Ramban, Nachmanides. *Commentary on the Torah.* Translated and Annotated with Index by Rabbi Charles B. Chavel. 5 Volumes (Genesis–Deuteronomy). New York: Shilo, 2010.

Rashi (http://www.sefaria.org/texts; http://www.chabad.org/library/bible_cdo/aid/63255/jewish/The-Bible-with-Rashi.htm).

Ridderbos, Herman. *Paulus: Ontwerp van zijn theologie.* 2nd ed. Kampen: Kok, 1971.

Rosenbaum, Ron, ed. *Those Who Forget the Past: The Question of Anti-Semitism.* New York: Random House, 2004.

Rosner, Jennifer M. *Healing the Schism: Barth, Rosenzweig, and the New Jewish-Christian Encounter.* Minneapolis: Fortress, 2015.

Roukema, Riemer. *Jesus, Gnosis & Dogma.* London: T&T Clark, 2010.

Rudolph, David, and Joel Willitts, eds. *Introduction to Messianic Judaism, Its Ecclesial Context and Biblical Foundations.* Grand Rapids: Zondervan, 2013.

Runesson, Anders. "Who Parted from Whom? The Myth of the So-Called Parting of the Ways between Judaism and Christianity." In *Chosen to Follow. Jewish believers through History and Today,* edited by Knut H. Høyland and Jakob W. Nielsen, 53–72. Jerusalem: Caspari Center, 2012.

Sacks, Jonathan. *The Koren Siddur: with Introduction, Translation and Commentary by Rabbi Sir Jonathan Sacks.* Jerusalem: Koren, 2009.

Schmidt, Karl L. *Die Judenfrage im Lichte der Kapitel 9–11 des Römerbriefes.* Theologische Studien herausgegeben von Karl Barth, Heft 13. Zollikon: Evangelischer Verlag, 1943.

Sforno, *Commentary on the Torah.* Translation and explanatory notes by Rabbi Raphael Pelcovitz. 3d ed. New York: Mesorah, 2004.

Sherman, Nosson. *The Torah: Haftaros and Five Megillos with a Commentary Anthologized from the Rabbinic Writings.* 9th ed. New York: Mesorah, 1998.

Shulam, Joseph, and Hilary Le Cornu. *A Commentary on the Jewish Roots of Romans.* Baltimore, MD: Lederer, 1997.

Sizer, Stephen. *Zion's Christian Soldiers? The Bible, Israel and the Church.* Nottingham: InterVarsity, 2007.

Skarsaune, O., and R. Hvalvik, eds. *Jewish Believers in Jesus: The Early Centuries.* Peabody, MA: Hendrickson, 2007.

Skarsaune, Oskar. *In the Shadow of the Temple. Jewish Influences on Early Christianity.* Downers Grove, IL: InterVarsity, 2002.

———. "Who Influenced Whom? Contours of a New Paradigm for Early Jewish-Christian Relations." In *Chosen to Follow. Jewish believers through History and Today*, edited by Knut H. Høyland and Jakob W. Nielsen, 35–52. Jerusalem: Caspari Center, 2012.

Soulen, R. Kendall. *The God of Israel and Christian Theology.* Minneapolis: Fortress, 1996.

Stern, David H. *Jewish New Testament Commentary.* 5th ed. Clarksville, MD: Jewish New Testament Publications, 1996.

Strack, Hermann L., and Paul Billerbeck. *Das Evangelium nach Matthäus. Erläutert aus Talmud und Midrasch.* München: Oskar Beck, 1922.

Strathmann, H., and Meyer, R. "*laos*," In: Theologisches Wörterbuch zum Neuen Testament, edited by Gerhard Kittel. Vol. IV, 29–57. Stuttgart: Kohlhammer, 1942.

Tomson, Peter J. *Paul and the Jewish Law: Halakha in the Letters of the Apostle to the Gentiles.* Minneapolis: Fortress, 1990.

Urbach E. E. *The Sages: Their Concepts and Beliefs.* Translated from the Hebrew by Israel Abrahams. 4th ed. Cambridge, MA: Harvard University Press, 1995.

Vos, G. *Biblical Theology*: *Old en New Testaments*. Grand Rapids: Eerdmans, 1971.

Westerman, Edjan. *De Tora van de Messias en zijn twee kinderen.* Nijkerkerveen, 2004. http://www.messiasleren.nl/wp-content/uploads/2015/08/De-Tora-van-de-Messias-en-zijn-twee-kinderen-2004.pdf

———. *Hoofdlijnen van de interpretatie van Jeremia 4:19–22; 8:18–9:2(=9:3); 14:17–18 en 48:31–32,36.* Amsterdam, 1979. Final research paper doctoraal (drs.) examination, Free University, Amsterdam.

———. "The Messiah and His Two Children: A Midrashic Prophetic Interpretation of Isaiah 8,18" (contribution to a yet unpublished book on the occasion of the 80th birthday of dr. P. Hocken). http://www.messiasleren.nl/wp-content/uploads/2015/08/Artikel-Festschrift-Peter-Hocken-The-Messiah-and-His-two-children-definitief.pdf).

Westermann, C. *The Book of Isaiah, Cap. 40–66.* Philadelphia: Westminster, 1969.

Wolff, H.W. *Dodekapropheton 1. Hosea.* In: Biblischer Kommentar Altes Testament. Neukirchen: Neukirchener Verlag, 1961.

Wright, N.T. "Epilogue. The Holy Land Today." Originally published in: N.T. Wright, *The Way of the Lord. Christian Pilgrimage in the Holy Land and Beyond.* Grand Rapids: Eerdmans, 1999, 119–130. http://ntwrightpage.com/Wright_Holy_Land_Today.htm.

———. *Paul: Fresh Perspectives.* London: SPCK, 2005.

Wyschogrod, Michael. *Abraham's Promise: Judaism and Jewish-Christian Relations.* Edited by R. Kendall Soulen. London: SCM, 2006.

Bibliography

———. *The Body of Faith. God in the People Israel.* 2nd ed. Northvale, NJ: Jason Aronson, 1996.

Yakira, Elhanan. *Post-Zionism, Post Holocaust: Three Essays on Denial, Forgetting, and the Delegitimation of Israel.* Cambridge: Translated by Michael Swirsky. Cambridge University Press, 2010.

Yanover, Yori. "Maimonides. Islam Good, Christianity Bad, Muslims Bad, Christians Good." http://www.jewishpress.com/indepth/opinions/maimonides-islam-good-christianity-bad-muslims-bad-christians-good/2013/11/15/.

b. *Yoma,* Vol. I-II, Talmud Bavli, Schottenstein Edition. New York: Mesorah, 1998.

Young, E.J. *The Book of Isaiah,* Vol. III. Grand Rapids: Eerdmans, 1974.

Index of Scripture

Tanakh/Hebrew Bible

Genesis

1–11	11
1–2	5, 6, 63, 65, 252
1	4, 5, 12, 14, 15, 40, 169, 175
1:1	4, 84
1:2	226
1:3–5	246
1:4	12
1:11–13	5, 79
1:12	12
1:14–19	5
1:18	12
1:20–25	5
1:20–23	11
1:21	12
1:22	5, 193
1:24–25	11
1:25	12
1:26–28	36, 210, 279
1:26–27	11, 38, 170
1:26	5
1:27	5, 252
1:28	5, 12, 193, 213
1:31	12
2:1–3	218
2:2–3	12, 290
2:3	12, 193
2:7	114, 226
2:15	13
2:16–17	13, 36, 37
2:16	38
3	5, 14, 40, 94, 105
3:1–3	51
3:1	13
3:4–5	13
3:4	13
3:6–7	13
3:8	13, 77, 126
3:12–14	51
3:13	13
3:14–15	13
3:14	14
3:15	275
3:17	13, 14, 15
4	14, 42
4:7	210, 213
4:11	15
5	14
5:2	14
5:24	14
5:29	14, 15
5:32	14
6:1–2	14
6:3	14, 226
6:5	14, 15
6:6	15
6:8	14
6:9	14
6:11	14
6:12	14
6:18	15
7:4	68
7:10	68
8:11	68
9:1–7	37, 38
9:1	15
9:5–6	15
9:6	38
9:7	15
9:18–29	15
9:25	15
10	15, 17, 345
10:6	41
10:10	84
10:14	41
10:15–20	41

Genesis (continued)

10:21–31	99	17:19–21	37
10:25–27	41	17:20	32
11	16	17:22	33
11:1–9	278, 281	17:23	27
11:1	16	18:1–15	24
11:2	84	18:10–15	22
11:4	16	18:14	166
11:6–7	170	18:16–33	24, 84
12	83	18:18	235
12:1–3	17, 19, 21, 23, 237, 332	18:19	24, 25, 42
12:1	17	19:29	24
12:2	22	19:37–38	35, 99
12:3	24, 54, 128, 235, 315, 327	20	26, 84
12:4	26	20:7	25
12:7–8	27	20:17–18	24
12:10–20	21, 26	21:4	69
13	24	21:8–10	26
14:1–17	84	21:10	31
14:1	84	21:12	29, 31
14:11–17	84	21:22–34	26
14:18–20	84	22	119, 170, 353, 345, 353
14:17–20	212	22:3	20
14:18	212	22:8	28
15	25, 30, 37	22:11	170
15:1–5	22	22:13	177
15:4–6	25	22:14	28, 177
15:5	41	22:15	170
15:6	22, 119, 227	22:16–18	119
15:7	21	22:16	177
15:9–20	30	22:18	28, 235
15:10	199	23	33
15:12	25, 30, 199	23:6	83
15:13–16	25	24:6–9	29, 31
15:13	25	24:27	29
15:16	25, 30, 98	25:1–18	35
15:17–21	118	25:1–6	27, 32
15:17	175, 199	25:1–4	99
16	26	25:2–3	32
16:7–13	170	25:12–16	344
17	37	25:18	26, 32, 344
17:1–2	26	25:19–23	345
17:1	26	25:21	22
17:2–8	26	25:23–24	29
17:6	83	25:23	31, 32
17:7	50, 118, 142	25:24	31
17:9–14	37	25:28	31
17:9–13	260	25:29–34	31
17:9–11	26	26	84
17:10–14	26	26:2–5	31
17:12	69	26:2	21
17:16	83	26:23–24	31
17:18–22	29, 31	27	84
17:18–19	31	27:1–40	31
		28:3–4	31
		28:4	31

28:12	33	49:8–12	84
28:13–15	29, 31	49:8–10	78
28:14	235	49:10	84, 90, 154
28:20–22	33	50:15–21	294
29–31	32, 84	50:20	33, 34
29:34	42	50:24–26	35
31:3	32	50:25	35
31:30–35	32		
31:30	97		
31:34	97	## Exodus	
32	84		
32:1–3	32	1	41
32:9	32	1:7	35
32:22–32	32	1:8	85
32:30	33	2:1–10	42
33:18–20	33	2:1	42
33:20	33	2:11	42
34	33	2:24–25	42
34:2	33	3–4	171
34:16	33	3:1—4:17	48
34:22	33	3:2	170
34:30	33	3:6	344
35:2	33, 97	3:12	48
35:5	33	3:14	170
35:9	33	3:15–16	344
35:10	34	3:15	43
35:11	84	3:17	42
35:13	33	3:18	43, 44
35:19–20	35	4:1–9	44
36	34, 35	4:5	344
36:1	34, 99	4:10–17	43
36:12	99	4:22–23	43, 90
36:43	34	4:24	43
37–50	34, 84, 216	4:25–26	43
37:1	34	4:25	43
37:2	34	4:31	44
38	34, 337	5:1–18	44
38:21	337	5:3	43, 44
41:41	84	5:19–21	44
41:43	84	6:1–7	44
41:57	84	6:2–3	43
45:2	294	6:4	42
45:3	294	6:7	43
45:5	294	6:9	44
45:7–8	294	6:12	44
45:14–15	294	6:15–26	42
45:14	294	7–12	279
45:24	294	7:7	42
46:2–4	34	7:16	44
46:4	34	8:8	43, 44
46:27	17, 345	8:18	44
47:7	25, 35	8:22	44
47:10	25, 35	8:25–28	43, 44
48–49	35	8:25	44
49	90	10:7–11	43, 44

Index of Scripture

Exodus (continued)

10:11	44	17:8	47
10:21–23	161	17:9–10	47
10:24–26	43, 44	17:14	47
11:2–3	45	17:16	47
11:7	76	18	88, 158
12	85, 279	18:1	47
12:1–2	45	18:9–11	47
12:8–11	45	18:17–23	47
12:14–17	45	18:21–26	89
12:19	38	19:1–5	88
12:22	45	19:1	48
12:23	45	19:3–6	48
12:27	45	19:3	48, 50
12:29–30	44, 162	19:5–6	xxxiv, 23, 51, 79, 82, 85, 86, 90, 93
12:32	44	19:5	20, 42, 50, 80
12:35–36	45	19:9	169
12:38	63, 279	19:10–15	219
12:39	45	19:17–20	219
12:40–41	8	19:17	62
12:40	25	19:20	62
12:41	46	19:21–25	219
12:42	45, 199	19:21	206
12:48	38	19:22	57
13:2	57	19:24	57
13:9	344	20–24	57
13:12	45	20	130
13:13	45	20:1–21	219
13:17	46	20:2	21
14:3–4	46	20:5	96
14:5–9	46	20:6	220
14:10–12	46	20:8–11	12
14:14	46	20:10	38
14:15–18	46	20:18–21	170
14:25	46	20:18	50, 61
14:26–31	85	20:21	62
14:31	46, 50	20:22—23:33	61
15	122	20:22	50
15:1–21	85	22:30	69
15:1–18	46	23:19	4
15:1	222	23:20–23	170
15:13	46	24:1–2	343
15:17	47, 47	24:2	206
15:22–27	47	24:3–8	61
15:25–27	47	24:4	62
15:25	220	24:7	51, 62
15:26	47	24:8	50, 165
16	47	24:9–11	62, 130, 343
16:23–24	47	24:12	62
16:23	12	24:15–18	62
16:28	220	24:16	62
17:1–7	47	25	57
17:4	47	25:1–40	345
17:8–16	88, 99, 158, 278	25:1–9	57
		25:1–2	62
		25:8–9	207

25:8	62, 196	40:12–16	65
25:9	63	40:20	114
25:10—27:21	63	40:33	207
25:21	36		
26:11	234		
27:8	90	## Leviticus	
28–29	57, 63		
28	66	1:4	67, 74
28:1	57, 66	1:9	74
28:4	69	1:11	198
28:36	69, 344	4:6	116
28:38—30:10	63	4:17	116
28:40–43	66	6:9	59
28:42	69	6:13	75
29:1–37	65	6:14	59
29:37	68, 69	6:22	119
30:9	74	6:25	59
30:11–38	63	8–9	65, 74
30:11–16	178	8:3	65
30:15	178	8:6–9	66
30:34–38	74	8:6	66
31:1–11	63	8:9	66
31:12–17	63, 260	8:11	116
32:2–3	65	8:12	66
32:5	63	8:13	66
32:14	64	8:14	66
32:25–29	64	8:15	66
32:26–29	185	8:18–19	67
32:30–34	64	8:20–21	67
32:34	170	8:22–23	67
33:2–3	64	8:23–24	67
33:2	170	8:25–28	67
33:14	64	8:30	67
33:16	64	8:31–32	67
33:18–23	64	8:33–35	67
34:3	206	8:33	67
34:4–7	64	8:35	68
34:8–9	64	9:1	69
34:10–28	64	9:22	69
34:19–20	45	9:23	69
34:19	45	9:24	69, 75
34:20	45	10:1–7	74, 159, 219
34:29–35	64, 169	10:1	74
35:4–29	65	10:2	75
35:5	65	10:3	75
35:21–22	65	10:6	75
35:26	65	10:8–9	75
35:29	65	10:10	75
38:25–26	178	10:11	76
39:1–31	66	10:12–20	74
39:30	344	10:19	74
39:32—40:33	65	11	76
40	65, 74	11:47	76
40:1–2	207	12:1—13:46	76
40:2	78	12	76

Index of Scripture

Leviticus (continued)

12:3	69
13–14	160
13:47–59	76
14	76
14:7	116
14:10	69
14:23	69
14:33–53	76
15	76
15:14	69
15:29	69
15:31	76
16	197, 199
16:4	66
16:6	77
16:11–14	77
16:21	183
16:22	198
16:24	66
16:30	77
16:33	77
17:8–9	38, 249
17:8	38
17:10–16	38, 249
17:12–16	39
18	38, 249
18:5	76
18:24–30	39, 98, 107
18:24–28	76
18:28	99
18:29–30	199
19	77, 105
19:2	53, 76, 105, 220
19:37	220
20	38, 249
20:2–5	38, 249
20:2	39
20:22	76, 99
20:23	98
20:24–26	76
20:26	76
21–22	194
21	57
21:1–3	262
22	57
22:32	53, 77
23	131, 262
23:9–16	195
23:9–11	187
23:11	187
23:17	344
23:23–36	282
23:23–24	341
23:36	69, 282
23:39	69, 237
23:33–43	81
23:42–43	81
23:44	260
24:10–16	38, 249
24:16	39
24:17–22	38, 249
24:18	38, 249
24:21–22	39
25	233
25:8–55	77
25:23	19, 77
25:25	233
25:42	43
25:55	43
26:12	78, 299
26:34–35	124
26:41	31

Numbers

1–2	72
1:1	78
1:2–3	78
1:52–54	78
2	19, 57, 58, 78
2:2	78
2:3–4	78
2:17	78
3:44–51	45
4:2	181
4:3	181
4:23	181
4:30	181
5:11–31	96
5:12–31	59
6:1–21	59, 96
6:10	69
7:2–88	89
7:89	114
8:5–22	45
8:19	206
9:1–14	233
10:33–36	80
12:3	280
13	94
13:16	157
14	94
14:20	94
14:21–23	95
14:30–35	95
14:33	94
15:20	4

16:5–7	206	16:13–15	81
17:1–9	220	16:15–16	79
18:1	103	16:18–20	88
20:12	195	17	97
22:22–35	170	17:8–13	88, 247
25:1–18	42	17:14–20	88, 89, 91, 208
25:12	103	17:14	99
27:15–23	89	17:15	89
27:17	89	17:17	97
28–29	131	17:18–20	87
29:1–6	341	18:4	4
29:12–38	82	18:9–22	97
29:35	69	18:12–14	98
31:5	276	18:15–22	88
35:25	197	18:15–18	71
35:28	197	18:15	71, 89
35:32	197	18:18	119
35:34	21	21:22–23	199
36:13	183	23:1	130
		23:3–6	130
		23:7–8	130
		23:14	77, 80, 299
		23:17	337

Deuteronomy

		26:18–19	51
2:16–19	99	26:18	51
4:1–10	220	26:19	88
5:6–21	130	27	55
6:4–9	52, 95, 356	28	55, 93, 95, 180
6:4	27, 123, 132, 152, 169	28:1	88
6:8	344	28:13	88, 94, 105, 208, 214
7:1–6	98	28:15–63	102
7:3–4	96	28:25–26	94
7:6	51	28:28–29	94
7:7–8	44	28:32	94
7:21	222	28:36	94
8	181	28:44	88
8:2–3	54	28:47–57	94
8:16	54	28:63–65	94
9:4–6	44	28:63–64	235
9:6	56	29:14–15	118, 350
10:12–15	54	29:15	188
10:16	55	29:29	xxiii
10:17	222	30	31, 95
10:20	42	30:1–2	55, 179
11:12	19	30:2–3	95
11:26–28	55	30:3–10	118
11:29–32	55	30:3–5	55
12	8, 79	30:6	31, 55, 95, 113, 119, 179, 261
12:1	72	30:15–16	94
12:5	72, 79	32:1–43	55
12:11	79	32:5	55
12:14	79	32:6	21
14:2	51	32:8–9	16
14:23–25	79	32:8	17, 58
16	131	32:9	17
16:9	195		

371

Index of Scripture

Deuteronomy (continued)

32:10	51
32:15	85
32:16–17	55
32:17	94
32:21	55
32:24	12
32:36	43
32:39	55
32:43	56, 124
33:5	85
33:26	85
34	195

Joshua

5–6	171
5:2–9	341
5:9–10	341
5:13—6:5	170
7	105
8:30–35	55
9	98
11:19–20	98
13–21	80
18:1	80
18:8–10	80
22:19	107
23:6–13	98

Judges

1	98
2:2	98
2:1–5	96, 170
2:1—3:4	98
2:10—3:5	96
2:18	96
3:5–7	98
3:12–30	99
6–8	99
6	171
6:11–24	170
6:25	96
10–11	99
13–16	99, 106
13	171
13:3–23	170
13:7	96
17–18	97
17	100

18	101
18:30	101
19	106

1 Samuel

1–3	80
1:12	107
1:15	107
1:19	42, 107
1:22	107
2:12–25	97, 101
2:17–18	107
2:16	101
2:17	101
2:22	97
2:29	101
3:20	89
4:4	114
7:2–17	89
7:15	89
8	89
8:1–3	97
8:7	89
10:1	119
10:9	114
15:22–23	196
15:22	102
16:1	89
16:6	119
16:10	70, 89
16:12	89
17	92
17:12	70
17:37	240
18–31	92
19:13	97
22	157
22:20–23	101
26:19	107
28	97
30	92

2 Samuel

2–5	228
2–4	215
2:1–4	215
3:1	104, 215
5:1–12	234
5:1–3	215
5:1	217
5:4	181

5:5	215
5:6–10	215
6	207
7	90, 207
7:10	90, 124
7:11–16	90
7:13–14	119
7:13	206
7:14	91
7:15	206
7:23–24	209
7:23	213
8:5–8	99
8:5	99
8:10	99
8:18	86
10	99
11	91, 106
11:1	99
12	xxvii
12:7	293
12:13	294
12:26–31	99
13–20	106
15–20	92, 210
15:30	230
15:32	230
17:1	276
24	104
24:16	45

1 Kings

1:7	101
1:19	101
1:25	101
1:33–34	160
1:38–39	206
1:45	160, 206
2:26–27	101
4:26	276
7	207
8:66	69, 70
10:26—11:13	91
11:1–8	97
11:9–13	97
11:11–13	104
11:11–12	91
11:14	94
12	97, 104
12:25–33	101
14:25–26	99
17–18	105
18:13–15	105
18:20–46	75
18:24	75
18:39	97
19:13	170
19:18	98, 105
21	106

2 Kings

4:38–44	98
5:17	107
6:1–7	98
10:31	104
11–12	101
11	106
16	104
16:5	99
16:10–18	99
17–19	99
17:18	107
17:20	107
17:23	107
18	207
19:15	81, 114
22–23	101, 207
23:10	28
23:26–27	104
23:27	107
23:29—24:7	99
24:3–4	169
24:20	107

Isaiah

1:10	98, 106
1:1–17	102
1:16–17	106
1:23	106
2:1–5	9, 87, 126, 253
2:2–3	28
2:3–5	128
2:3	193, 208, 268
2:4	130
2:12	100, 183
2:17–18	100
2:18	183
3:16–23	106
4:3	54
4:5–6	287
5:7	106
5:8–25	106
6	106
6:2–3	345

Index of Scripture

Isaiah (continued)

Reference	Pages
6:9–10	296
7:1	99
7:14	120, 163
8:5–10	266
8:16	98
9:1–2	120, 230
9:6	120
9:7	119, 120
10:5–19	99, 266
10:23	21, 80
11:1–2	119
11:1	120
11:3–5	119
11:6–10	209
11:6–9	121, 130
11:9	120
11:10	120, 128
11:13	123, 217
12	122, 236
13–23	109
13–14	99
14:13–14	99
19:23–25	128, 130, 321
19:24	21, 58, 127
22:17	185
23	99
25	128
25:6	126, 130
25:7–8	189
25:7	128
25:8	129, 131
26:12	115, 169, 172, 282
26:19	129
28:5–6	115
28:7	102
29:9	106
30:1–17	99
31:1–9	99
32:1–2	121
33:5	126
33:15	221
33:20–24	335
35:5–6	131
35:8–10	131
35:9	12
37:16	81
40	325
40:1–2	125, 315, 325
40:1	xxxii, 157, 308
40:3	158
40:10	166
40:13–14	166
41:1	326
41:8–10	116, 123
41:8–9	115
42:1–7	116, 121
42:1	119, 120
42:4	116, 117, 120, 283, 310
42:6	xxii, 53, 105, 116, 117, 155, 179, 353
42:19	115
43:1–8	122
43:6–7	21
43:9	326
43:10	115, 266
43:13	266
43:21	116
44:2	85
44:3–5	116
45:1	119
45:4	115
45:21	248
48:11	169
48:12	266
48:20	115
49:1–9	116, 121
49:1	326
49:3	116
49:6	53, 105, 116, 117, 118, 155, 157, 179
49:8–13	122
49:8–12	180
49:8–9	118, 120
49:8	xxii, 116, 117, 118, 353
49:14–16	125
49:18	125
49:19–21	125
49:22–23	326
49:22	122, 128
50:4–10	116, 121
50:4	127
50:5–6	30
50:7–9	116
51:3	125, 126
51:4–7	119
52:7–9	125
52:8	125
52:12	122
52:13—53:12	116, 121, 182
52:15	116, 128, 183
53	119, 128, 213
53:4	160
53:5	183
53:6	183
53:8–11	116
53:8	27, 183, 185
53:10–12	183, 213
53:10	116, 183
53:11–12	118
53:11	183

Reference	Pages
53:12	225
54	128, 241
54:2–3	125
54:5	125
54:6–8	125
54:11–17	325
54:11–14	254
54:11–12	125
54:13	127, 193, 333
55:3–5	120
55:3	295
55:4–5	127, 129
55:6	128
55:7	295
55:8–9	166, 295
55:8	296
55:9	308
55:11–13	295
55:11	171, 308
55:12	122
56:1	221
56:3–5	130
56:4	129
56:5	129
56:6	129
56:7	128, 129
57:19	246
59:2	161
59:9	24, 161
59:19	241
59:20	233
59:21	116
60	241, 325
60:1–3	87, 125
60:4–11	125
60:4–9	122
60:4	128
60:8–9	128
60:10	128
60:13	165
60:14	128
60:15–18	125
60:19–21	286
60:19–20	126
60:21	127
61	156, 198
61:1–2	156
61:2	120, 222
61:6	49, 53, 71, 115, 121, 127, 194, 198, 343
61:9	21
61:10	71, 125
62	326
62:4–5	125
62:5	125
62:6–7	326
63:9	166, 171, 197, 232, 326
64:6–9	350
65:17	129
65:25	130
66:10–24	120
66:10–14	325
66:12	125
66:13	157
66:15–17	128
66:18–24	129
66:18–19	128
66:20	129
66:21	129, 202, 207, 252, 263
66:22	122, 129

Jeremiah

Reference	Pages
1:11–12	220
2–3	97
2:1–3	95, 297
2:2–3	61
2:2	96, 108
2:3	4
2:7	19, 96
3:1	97
3:16	130
3:19–22	181, 198
4:3–4	314
4:4	261
4:19–22	132
6:13	102
7:1–15	102
7:3–15	102
8	159
8–9	159, 161
8:4—9:26	65, 159
8:11	159
8:13—9:24	65, 98, 159
8:18–22	109
8:18–20	159
8:19	108, 159
8:20–22	159
8:21	159
8:22	159
9	159
9:1	159
9:2	108, 159, 231
9:7	159
9:10–12	231
9:16	231
9:23–24	109
9:26	31, 109
10:18	185

Index of Scripture

Jeremiah (continued)

Reference	Page(s)
12:9	297
12:16–17	79
12:16	128
14:17	161
16:13	185
16:14–17	122
16:16	128
16:18	19, 124
17:13	71
23:1–8	120
23:5–6	120
23:5	120, 207
23:6	115, 120
23:7–8	122
23:13	185
24:7	123
26:1–24	102
26:8–11	102
26:18	108
30–31	123, 124, 206
30	123
30:3	123
30:9	123
30:11	122
30:21–22	123
30:21	206
30:22	123, 132
31	123, 259
31:2	122
31:3	109, 132, 142, 180, 206
31:15–17	123
31:20	110, 132, 161, 166
31:22	297
31:31–34	114, 119
31:32	130, 259
31:33	81, 119, 177, 178, 201, 207, 311
31:34	127, 177, 201
31:35–37	142
33:15	207
33:16	126
33:25–26	123
36	87
45	110
46–51	109
46:26	128
46:28	122
48:30–32	161
48:47	128, 130
49:6	128, 130
49:39	128

Ezekiel

Reference	Page(s)
1–3	108
1	170
1:3	102
1:4–28	165, 170
1:28	170
4:13	107
5:5	21, 80
8	102
8:6	234
9:1–7	229
9:4–7	185
9:4	105
9:6	109
10–11	108
10:1–22	165, 170
10:15–22	108
11	108
11:16	126
11:19	123
11:20	123
11:22–25	165, 170
11:22–23	225, 230
11:23	108
16	97, 106
16:8	61, 95
16:42	347
16:46–52	98
18:32	25
20:6	96
20:7–8	213
20:9	112
20:12	260
20:14	112
20:32	99
20:37–38	123
20:40	96
23	97, 99
25–32	109
26:1–2	99
28	99
28:22	75
33:23–26	39
34	89, 123, 235
34:23–24	89, 120
34:24	124
34:26	126
36	113, 124, 323
36:5	19, 124
36:6	124
36:9–12	124
36:9	124
36:16–18	124
36:18–19	112

36:20	112	**Hosea**	
36:22–23	60		
36:22	112, 308	1–3	97
36:23	112	1:9	23
36:24–38	60	2:4	97
36:24–27	114	2:5	302
36:24	124	2:6	97
36:25–27	95	2:13	108
36:25–26	178	2:14–16	61
36:25	71, 177, 185	2:18–19	98
36:26–27	119	2:19–20	267, 296
36:26	177	3:1	96
36:27–28	124	3:3–5	267
36:27	81, 127, 311	3:3	98
36:28	123	3:5	277, 296
36:32	112	4:1–10	53
36:33–38	124	4:1–6	79, 102
36:35	124	4:2	106
36:38	113	4:3	102, 104, 124
37	284, 323	4:11	106
37:1–14	122	4:12	124
37:11	122	4:14	106, 337
37:12	122	6:1–3	129
37:13	122	6:6	102, 196, 221
37:14	127	9:3	107
37:15–28	97, 123, 217	10:12	314
37:22–23	123	11:1–4	48
37:22	124	11:1	90, 178, 181
37:24	121, 123, 124	11:8–9	56
37:25	125	11:8	110
37:27	123	13:5–6	108
38–39	100, 284	13:14	213
38:2	100		
38:12	21, 80		
38:16	19	**Joel**	
39:7	113		
39:12	107	1:6	19
39:14	107	2:23	195
39:16	107	2:27	59
39:25	113	2:28–29	127, 195
39:27	112	2:28	127, 129
39:29	127, 311	2:32	128
40–48	126	3:1–3	xxxi, 99
43:1–5	125, 165, 170	3:2–3	225, 299
43:1–4	230	3:2	19, 96
43:4	166		
43:7	125, 126, 165, 166		
43:26–27	69	**Amos**	
44:9	31		
47:1–12	126, 290	1–2	109
47:21–23	127	1:2	109
48:8	58	3:2	75
48:15	58	3:7	280
48:21	58	3:15	106
48:35	81, 126, 131, 165, 241, 346		

Amos *(continued)*

4:1	106
5:4	221
5:7–13	106
5:18–20	161
5:20	185
6:3–6	106
6:6	299
7:17	107
8:4–6	106
8:9–10	161
8:10	162
8:12	161
9:11–16	248
9:11–15	122
9:11–12	248

Micah

2:10	104
2:12–13	122
2:12	125
2:13	187
3:6–7	161
3:11	102
3:12	108
4:2	128
4:3	130
5:2	121, 173, 217
5:4	70, 276
5:7–8	80
6:1–3	107
6:8	37, 106, 196, 221
6:10–11	106
7:2–3	106

Habakkuk

2:4	221
2:14	12, 130, 187
3:17–19	302

Zephaniah

3:4	103
3:9	116, 128, 298
3:14–17	122
3:15–17	165
3:15	59
3:17	59, 132, 166

Haggai

2:1–9	121
2:6–9	108
2:20–23	108

Zechariah

1:11	241
1:12–17	266
1:15	266
2:3	337
2:8–9	295, 328
2:8	xxxii, 51, 297
2:9	xxxii
2:10–11	59
2:11	58
2:13	58
3:1	94
3:2	94
3:8	120, 121, 207
3:9	277
4:1–6	66
4:6	115
4:10	241
6:8	241, 272
6:9–15	53, 86, 207, 208
6:11	208
6:12	120, 120, 207
6:13	120
6:15	207
8:7–8	123
8:5	125
8:16–17	106, 221
8:23	79, 128, 268, 299, 338
9:9	120
9:10	120, 128
10:9	109
12:1–9	100
12:10–14	127, 277, 282, 340
12:10	162, 276
12:12–14	79
13–14	108, 109
13:1	71, 127, 277
13:2	124, 185
13:7	161, 225
14	131
14:1–7	100
14:2	109
14:3	276
14:4	276, 277
14:8	126
14:9	132, 277
14:11	222

14:16–19	277
14:16	132
14:17–18	79
14:20	131, 344

Malachi

1:6–14	102
1:11	241, 268
2:1–9	102
2:4	103
2:5–7	103
2:8–9	103
2:13–16	106
3:1–6	158
3:1–5	75, 170
3:1–2	109, 161
3:1	166, 275
3:3–5	161
3:3	166
3:5	107
3:12	103
3:13—4:6	109
3:17	51
4:1–2	75
4:1	103, 161
4:2	131
4:4–6	103
4:5	277
4:6	20

Psalms

1	79
2	92, 201, 207, 211, 214, 224
2:1–3	214
2:2	120
2:6–7	171
2:6	207
2:7	160, 207
2:12	224
8	211
11:4	241
11:5	27
15	221
16:10	54
19:14	xxv
22	162, 211
22:3	81
22:18	225
27:4–5	126
33:4	235
33:6	171
40	196
40:6–8	196
40:6	102
45	171, 211
45:6–7	171
48:2	155, 273
50:12–14	102
50:21	xxxii, 296, 297, 309
51:10–11	295
63:8	53, 105
63:9	297
67	xix, 79, 239
67:1–2	xix
67:2	54, 79
67:7	239
67:8	79
68:18	178, 187, 213
69:20	315
72	212
72:17	173
74:12	21, 58
77:13	9
77:19	9, 299
77:20	308
80	182, 210, 336, 337
80:1	81
80:6	182
80:8–11	182
80:8–9	46
80:8	98
80:13	182, 185, 336
80:15	182
80:16	185
80:17	182, 203
80:19	182
87	268, 321
89	212
89:27–29	207
89:27–28	171
89:27	208, 213
92:5	133
92:13–15	79
92:13–14	47
95:11	64, 80
96	212
97	212
98	212
99	114, 212
99:6	66
102:27	266
103:1	22
103:2	22
103:20–22	22
105:15	119
106:19–21	64

Psalms (continued)

106:37	94
107:20	171
110	158, 211, 212
110:1	120, 212
110:2–4	171
110:2	88, 120
110:4	120, 212
111:10	9, 168
113:3	xvii, 241, 268
115:16	12
118:22	208
118:25	354
119	xxiv
122:3	xix, 234
122:6	326
132	114
132:13–14	20, 126
134	43
134:1	27, 302
135:4	51
136:22	43
147	59
147:15	171
147:20	59

Proverbs

1:7	9, 168
8:22–31	171
8:22	4
8:23	207
9:10	9
10:22	32
18:10	33
30:4	171

Job

1–2	94
28:28	9
40:4	8

Song of Songs

2:4	346
2:11–13	346
2:16	223, 346
6:3	132, 223
7:10	223

Ruth

1:16	79

Lamentations

1:16	157
3:22–23	60
4:6	106
4:13	102
5:18	108

Ecclesiastes

2:8	51

Esther

3–8	278
9:18–32	263
9:24–28	355

Daniel

6:10–11	274
7	210, 212
7:10	212
7:13–14	121
7:14	53, 121, 158, 182, 209, 212
7:18	53, 121, 209
7:22	53, 209
7:25	145
7:27	53, 209
9	71, 324, 350
9:4–7	295
10:7–9	170
10:13–21	185
10:13	100
10:20–21	100
11:36	100
12:1–3	109
12:2–3	129
12:4	272
12:10	109

Ezra

6:21	102
7–10	102

Nehemiah

7:1	13
8–13	102
8:1	341
8:10	53
8:19	69

1 Chronicles

5:1–2	78
5:2	84
9	13
11:1–9	234
11:1–3	215
11:1	217
11:4–6	215
13	207
15	207
16:19–22	25
16:22	119
21	80, 104
21:1	94
21:26	75
22–29	97
22–26	207
22:1	80
22:6–10	207
22:10	207
23:4	343
24–25	279
24:18	343
24:19	343
25:31	343
26	13
27:1–5	343
28:2	114
28:3	91
28:5	91
28:8	90
28:19	63, 90
29:22	86

2 Chronicles

3:1	28, 80
5:3	81
6:2	81
6:41	81, 114
7:1–3	75
7:8–10	81
7:9	69
7:10	70
7:19–20	104
7:20	105
10–11	104
11:13–14	101
11:15	101
12	99
16:9	241
22:10—23:21	106
24:2–3	101
24:14–16	101
26:16–21	206
28	101, 104
29–31	207
29	101
29:17	70
30	233
30:2	233
30:3	228
30:13	233
30:15–20	228
30:17	228
32:25	104
33:1–9	101
33:6	28
33:7–9	104
33:9	104
33:15	101
34–35	207
34	101
34:1–7	101
34:3	70, 107
34:5	107
34:8	107
36:5–20	99
36:11–21	169
36:14	103
36:21	124
36:23	20

New Testament

Matthew

1:17	154
1:21	155, 156, 157, 160
1:23	163
2:1–2	155
2:2	205
2:6	155
2:15	178
2:22–23	167
2:22	230
3:2	156, 158

Index of Scripture

Matthew (continued)

Reference	Pages		Reference	Pages
3:3	158		11:19	172
3:10-12	161		11:20-24	161, 224
3:10	158		11:25-27	171
3:11-12	158		11:25	224
3:11	165		11:27	172, 222
3:13-17	181		11:28-30	222
3:13	160		11:30	222
3:15	161, 181		12:6-8	221
3:16	160		12:6	196
3:17	160, 171, 206		12:7	196
4:1-11	160		12:24	224
4:10-11	209		12:28	188, 209
4:11	181		12:49	211
4:15	230		13	161, 168
4:17	156, 158, 184, 255		13:10-17	265
4:23-25	202, 208		13:11-15	188
4:24-25	155		13:52	xxiv, 309
5-7	167, 195, 301		14:22-23	168
5	222		15:21-28	162
5:14	155		15:26	23
5:17-20	220		16:19	247
5:17-19	xxiv, 181		16:23	185, 224
5:17-18	195, 223, 277		17:5	160, 206
5:17	181, 189		17:10-13	277
5:22-24	211		17:24-27	178, 181
5:35	155, 273		17:26	178
5:40	301		17:27	177, 178
5:41	301		18	178
5:44	301		18:18	247
5:47	211		18:21-35	223
6:9	196		19:1-12	223
7:5	330		19:8	222
7:28-29	221		19:27-28	214
8:4	202		19:28	209
8:8	165		20:20-28	214
8:14-17	167		20:22-23	342
8:17	160, 181		21:12-17	161, 224
8:27	165		21:12-16	207
9:12-13	221		21:23-27	224
9:12	224		21:31-32	168
9:17	333		21:33-41	225
9:18-26	159, 167		21:42	208
9:34	224		22:31-32	344
10:1—11:1	202		22:40	221
10:1	209		23	161, 222, 223, 225
10:17-31	228		23:3	309
10:24-25	231		23:8	211
10:25	224		23:23-24	222
10:32-33	329		23:23	196, 222, 223, 309
10:34-36	161, 224, 228		23:35-36	229
11-12	168		23:37-39	216
11:2-6	188		23:38-39	225
11:3	168		23:38	274
			23:39	155, 234, 235, 274
			24	211, 230, 273

24:1	225	5:21–43	159, 209
24:3–28	230	6:3	168
24:3–14	229, 230	6:7	209
24:3	225, 231, 273	6:30–44	168, 209
24:4–5	280	6:45–52	168
24:8–13	272	7:7–13	309
24:9	238, 277	7:10–13	222
24:12	275, 280	7:19	261
24:14	233, 238, 272	7:24–30	155
24:15	273	8:1–10	168
24:16–20	273	8:31–38	210
24:21–22	273	8:31	210
24:23–24	280	8:38	209, 210
24:24	280	9:11–12	277
24:30–31	229, 279	9:30–32	210
24:37–42	279	9:47	209
25	211, 230	10:13–16	196
25:14–15	230	10:14–15	209
25:16	230	10:32–34	210
25:31–46	209, 211, 275	10:35–40	214
26:6–13	199	10:42–45	213
26:14–16	186	11:11–26	188
26:28	180, 188	11:11–25	207
26:30–32	225	12:10–11	208
26:31	161	12:28–34	171
26:69–75	224	12:29–31	235, 249
27:23	224	13	211, 273
27:37	205	13:4–23	230
27:45	185	13:9–11	233
27:46	162	13:18–19	273
28:10	211	14:24	180, 188
28:16–20	155, 162, 208	14:25	188
28:18–20	187, 339	14:27	161
28:18	187, 238, 314	15:33	161
28:19–20	202, 226	15:34	162
28:19	268, 310		
28:20	330		

Mark

Luke

		1	169
		1:16–17	168
1:9	160	1:32–33	156, 205
1:10	160	1:35	163, 194
1:13	181, 209	1:46–55	157
1:14–15	209	1:52	187
1:22	167, 221	1:68–75	157
1:27	167, 209	1:76	168
1:29–34	167	2:14	157
1:44	202	2:19	167
2:1–12	167, 196	2:25–38	326
2:10	168, 182, 210	2:25	157
3:13–19	155	2:29–32	157
4:10–11	209	2:30–32	162
4:35–41	209	2:32	117, 155, 179
5:6–13	209	2:34	159

Index of Scripture

Luke (continued)

2:35	223, 224
2:38	157
2:40–51	167
2:51	167
3:16	165
3:21	160
3:22	160
3:23	181
3:38	14
4:14–30	198
4:19	222
4:21	156, 220
4:22	168
4:43	209, 255
5:8	165, 221
5:14	202
5:37–38	333
6:20–49	301
6:27–28	301
6:29	301
7:11–17	167
7:29	168
7:30	168
7:35	172
8:10	209
8:25	165
8:40–56	159
9:1	209
10:1–20	202
10:1	209
10:17	209
10:34	326
11:2	235
11:20	188
13:16	159
13:34–35	274
15:13	216
17:14	202
17:21	188, 209, 243
19:11–27	209
19:11–12	216
19:11	211
19:41–44	266
19:41	161, 228, 231
19:42	224, 229, 282
19:45–48	207
21	211, 273
21:10–19	233
21:12–24	230
21:12	264
21:20–24	229, 273
21:21	273
21:23–24	155, 225, 229, 230, 232
21:24	229, 235, 273
22:16–18	338
22:16	188
22:20	180, 188
22:29–30	214
22:30	209
22:42	196
22:47–48	224
23:8–12	201
23:28	159
23:26–31	225
23:34	225
23:48	225
23:56	318
24:25–27	210
24:26	194
24:46–47	187, 202
24:50–51	196
24:53	202, 227

John

1	169
1:1–5	303
1:4–5	169
1:14	163, 169, 172, 220, 303
1:12	198
1:17	169
1:18	166, 228, 308
1:21	71, 89
1:25	71
1:29	197, 201
1:32–33	160
1:46	71
2:13–25	161
2:13–24	224
2:13–23	207
2:13–22	246
2:19	208
2:21	196, 202, 208
4:1–3	223
4:1–2	182
4:22	151, 162, 208, 273, 310
4:26	163
5:21	186
5:23	172
5:26–29	212
5:26	186
5:30	196
5:41	186
6:1–41	168
6:1–15	223
6:14	89
6:15	210

6:22–66	224	14:25–26	157, 171, 310
6:48	163	14:26	272
6:51	163	14:30	155
6:60	224	15:1–8	182
6:64	222	15:1	163
6:67	224	15:5	xxii
6:68–69	218	16:1–3	228
7:10—8:20	237	16:1–2	264
7:37–39	236	16:11	155
7:37–38	282	16:12–15	171, 310
7:40	89	16:13	272
7:53—8:11	222	17	338, 351
8:1–11	237	17:6	168, 196, 235
8:12	155, 163, 179, 282, 286	17:19	160, 194
8:26	222	17:24	168
8:30–36	198	17:26	235
8:31–36	213, 221	18:6	172
8:34–36	224	18:11	342
8:38	172	18:39–40	224
8:44	264, 283	19:14–15	205
8:53	168	19:15	210
9:5	155	19:20	225
9:39–41	296	20:17	171
9:40–41	224	20:28	172
10	235	20:29	172
10:1–17	338	21:22–23	10
10:7	163	21:22	205
10:11	163		
10:16	162, 239, 338, 351		
10:18	199	## Acts	
10:22–39	172, 317		
10:22	263	1:2	155
10:30–31	164	1:6–11	158, 204
10:30	168	1:6–8	204
10:31	168	1:6	214
11:49–52	199	1:7	8, 190
11:52	162	1:8	155, 214, 238
12:1–8	199	1:11	168
12:19	200	1:12–26	158
12:20–32	155	2	58, 61, 310
12:20–21	200	2:1–3	178
12:24–26	239	2:9–11	154
12:28	235	2:14–40	242
12:30–31	162, 213	2:23	201
12:31	155, 185, 187	2:27	54
12:32	155	2:31	186
13:23	166	2:32	186
14:2–3	289	2:33–36	211
14:6	118, 179, 198	2:33	186, 196, 210, 226
14:7–10	308	2:34–35	203
14:9	228, 235	2:36	209
14:16–17	157	2:41	228
14:16	157	3:1	227
14:23	172, 252	3:8	227
14:24	222	3:13–14	201

Index of Scripture

Acts (continued)

Reference	Page
3:14–15	186
3:14	225
3:21	20, 356
3:22	89
4:4	228
4:11	208
4:24–28	201
4:25–28	214
4:25–26	201
5:12	227
5:20–21	227
5:42	227
6–7	238
6:7	202
7–13	267
7:37	89
8:1–3	238
8:1	238
8:4–40	233
8:4	232, 233, 238, 239
8:5	239
8:9–25	302
8:9–11	240
8:12	239
8:14–17	239
8:18–24	240
8:26–40	239
8:30–31	243
9:4	232
9:8–9	240
9:15–16	244
9:23	264
10	239, 241
10:2	250
10:9–16	244
10:19–20	239
10:34–43	242
10:37	242
10:39	242
10:42	250, 284
10:43	242
10:44–46	239
10:44–45	244
11:1–18	244
11:16–17	257
11:19	232, 239
11:20	240
11:20–21	244
11:21–26	240
11:29–30	241, 267, 268
13–14	240
13:2–3	244
13:5	244
13:6–12	240
13:9	267
13:12	244
13:14	244, 262
13:23–41	242
13:33	207
13:38–39	197
13:45	264
13:46	244
13:47	117, 179
14:2	264
14:14–17	242
14:22	231, 238
14:27	244
15	39, 247, 257, 325
15:1–2	241
15:1	244, 245, 250
15:2–4	247
15:2	241
15:5	245, 247, 250
15:10	222
15:11	248
15:12	248
15:14–15	242
15:14	248, 250
15:18	242
15:20–21	249
15:21	250, 315
15:36—18:22	240
16:3	227, 261
16:13	262
16:16–18	240
17:2–3	262
17:22–31	242
17:26–28	16
17:31	284
18:4	262
18:10	250
18:12	264
18:23—21:14	240
19:8	262
19:21	241
20	268
20:7	263
20:16	241, 262
20:22	241
20:27	350
21–26	264
21	149, 268
21:17	241
21:20	144, 227, 228
21:26	241
22:21–33	264
24:17–18	227
26:12–18	244

26:17–18	242
26:18	213
26:19–23	242
28:16	240
28:24–27	265

Romans

1	37
1:1–2	243
1:4	186, 194, 196, 201, 218
1:5	190, 226, 250
1:13	240
1:16	187, 244, 326
1:18	255
2:1–3	255
2:1	255
2:6	255
2:16	213
2:17–29	255
2:28–29	260
2:29	178, 261
3:1–2	295
3:2	xxi
3:9–20	255
3:20	224
3:21	255
3:22	255
3:23–26	255
3:23–24	202
3:24	255
3:25	199
3:31	255
4:3	227, 255
4:9–10	255
4:13	256
5:1–11	256
5:1	202, 255
5:5	256
5:12–21	200, 213
6–8	256
6	179
6:15–23	256
7:7	224
7:12	257
8	150, 231, 264
8:1–17	256
8:1	202, 255
8:3–4	256
8:14–17	202
8:14–15	256
8:15	198
8:16–17	231
8:17	256
8:17–39	272
8:18–39	241
8:18–27	231
8:19–22	272
8:19	343
8:22–23	241
8:22	256, 272
8:23–27	272
8:23–26	203
8:23	186, 256, 272, 339
8:26–30	268
8:26–27	290
8:26	256
8:27	231
8:29	256
8:34	231, 232, 241, 256, 272, 290
8:36	231
8:37–39	290
9–11	xxx, 231, 241
9:1–3	264, 266
9:1–2	231, 257, 266
9:4–5	258, 261, 295
9:4	176, 183, 231
9:6	266
9:14	266
9:15–16	21
9:20–21	264
9:20	8
9:25–26	23, 266
9:30—10:3	257
10:4	223, 237
10:12	251
10:18	265
11:1–10	297
11:2–5	265
11:7–10	265
11:8	265
11:11	265, 268, 315
11:12	351
11:14	315
11:17–24	263
11:17–21	xxxi
11:17–19	337
11:17	264
11:18	264
11:20–21	278
11:20	xxxi, 263
11:21–22	264
11:22	xxxii
11:23	263
11:25–27	274
11:25–26	200, 233
11:25	235, 264, 351
11:26–27	265
11:26	231, 233, 234, 241, 257, 276, 334

Index of Scripture

Romans (continued)

11:28	307
11:29	xxxv, 21, 22, 237, 261, 265, 266
11:32	297
11:33–36	264
11:33	265
11:36	241
12:1–2	254, 264
12:1	176, 193
12:9–12	264
13:8–10	256
13:10	237
13:14	258, 336
14–15	257
14:1—15:1	262
14:10	284
15:8	181, 215
15:9	184
15:25–28	267
15:25–26	241, 268
15:27	268
16:5	244, 324
16:25–26	200
16:25	243
16:26	190, 226, 250

1 Corinthians

1:30–31	179
2:7	243
2:9	343
2:10–12	243
2:10	243
3:12–15	350
3:16–17	202, 252
4:5	213
5:6–8	197
6:2	209
6:19	202
7:17–24	247
7:17–20	257
7:21–24	250
8:4–6	187
10:2	117
10:4	173, 197, 308
10:11	242
10:18	287
10:19–22	187
13:12	272, 350
15:3–4	243
15:20–22	200
15:21–28	289
15:22	187
15:23–28	212, 230
15:25–27	189
15:25–26	214
15:28	276, 289
15:42–44	285
15:45–49	200
15:45	187
15:47	187
15:51–53	281
15:52	282, 341
15:54–55	213
16:1–4	268
16:1–3	241
16:15	244, 324
16:22	338

2 Corinthians

1:5–6	203, 231
1:20	183, 215
1:22	339
3:6	188
3:7–18	188
4:6	200
4:7–15	203, 231
5:10–20	341
5:10	212, 284
5:17	179, 189
5:18	184, 193
5:20	202
5:21	185, 186, 199
6:16	252
11:2	254

Galatians

1:2	257
1:16	200
2:1–10	59
2:3–5	257
2:3	261
2:7	250
3:2–5	257
3:2	257
3:6	227, 258
3:8–9	24, 237
3:8	235
3:10	258
3:11	258
3:14	237, 258
3:17–19	237
3:26–29	258
3:27	258, 336

3:28–29	251
4:4	181, 197
4:6	198
4:8	139
5:2–3	257
6:12–13	257
6:15	261
6:16	172, 258

Ephesians

1:9	200
1:13–14	173, 244, 256
1:14	339
1:17–18	200
1:17	243
1:20	212
1:22	338
2–3	242
2:1–3	213
2:10	227, 282
2:11–12	246
2:13	246
2:14–22	338
2:14–18	245
2:15–16	247
2:15	252, 253, 342
2:17	246
2:19	243, 251
2:20	208
2:22	202, 244, 252
3	280
3:1–12	200
3:3	243
3:4–6	184
3:4–5	243
3:4	243
3:5	9, 200, 243
3:6	243, 251, 299
3:8	243
3:9	9, 200
3:14–21	xxxv, 288
3:14–19	269
3:15	xxxv
3:19	243
3:20–21	269
4:7–13	187
4:8	213
4:20	xxiv
4:21–24	188
4:24	336

Philippians

1:15–18	350
2:5–11	173
3:5	261

Colossians

1:13	213
1:15–20	187
1:15–18	175
1:15–17	308
1:15	173
1:17	173
1:18	173, 187
1:19	173
1:20	173
1:24—2:3	280
1:24	203, 216, 231, 238, 267, 337, 343
1:25–26	184
1:26–27	200, 243
1:26	243
1:27	243
1:28	188
2:9	172, 173
2:11–14	261
2:11–12	113
2:13–15	209
2:15	187, 213
2:16–17	318
2:16	262
2:17	260, 262
2:19	262
3:1	212
3:11	240, 251
3:12	336
3:14	336

1 Thessalonians

2:14	264
2:15	264
4:13–17	281
4:16	282, 341

2 Thessalonians

2:3–10	273
2:3–4	145
2:3	273, 275, 277, 280
2:4	273, 277
2:13	226, 244

Index of Scripture

1 Timothy

2:5	173
3:16	173
4:1–5	280
4:1–3	275
5:24–25	190

2 Timothy

1:10	186, 189
3:1–5	275
3:12	337

Titus

2:14	250

Hebrews

1–2	211
1:2	174, 247
1:3	174, 308
1:5–9	211
1:5	174
1:8–9	174
1:13	212
2:5–9	209
2:15	189
3:6–19	259
4	80
4:9	318
4:11	259
5:4–10	195
6:4–5	195
6:9–12	259
6:9	201
7	212
7:2	212
7:3	212
7:4–10	84
7:10	23
7:11–14	212
7:16–28	212
7:19	201
7:22	201
7:28	195, 198
8:1–2	198
8:3–5	258
8:6	195, 201
8:12	201
8:13	259
9:1–10	197
9:10	260
9:12	198
9:15	174, 189, 197, 259
9:18	198
9:23	197, 201
10:5–10	196
10:12	212
10:18	198
10:19–39	259
10:19–22	259
10:19–20	202
10:20	198
10:36	177
10:37–38	260
12:1–17	259
12:10	226
12:14	226
12:23	284
12:25–29	341
12:27	195
12:28	259
13:9	260
13:10	258
13:12–13	185
13:12	225

James

1:17	308
1:18	238, 324
2:6	299
2:15–16	299
2:20–26	227
3:9–12	146
5:7	284
5:9	284

1 Peter

1:1–2	253
1:10	184
2:4–10	208
2:7	208
2:9–10	49, 202, 215, 253
2:10	23
2:21–25	182
3:20	70
4:17	185, 229
5:10	75

2 Peter

1:4	226
3:8–9	25

1 John

1:1–3	166
1:1–2	220
1:5	284
2:18–27	277
2:18–19	278
2:18	273
2:22	273
3:1	198
3:2	343
5:4–5	290

Revelation

1:1	214
1:5–6	49, 252, 253, 279
1:5	213, 215
1:6	xxxiv, 174, 215
1:7	274, 276, 287, 300, 340
1:9–20	278
1:9	275
1:12–20	174
1:12–13	278
1:18	174
2–3	174, 286, 288
2:1—3:22	278
2:9	146, 264
2:27	174
3:9	146, 264
3:12	174, 287
3:21	174
4–5	272
4:1—5:14	278
4:1	278
4:4	343, 344
4:10	343, 344
5–8	214
5:5–6	275
5:5	214, 279
5:6	174, 272, 279
5:8	343
5:9–10	49, 287
5:9	279
5:10	xxxiv, 215, 253
5:11–14	279
5:12–13	174
6	272
6:1	279
6:3	279
6:5	279
6:7	279
6:9–11	290
6:12	279
6:16–17	287
7	287
7:1–8	275, 276
7:9–17	277, 282, 287
7:9	287, 338
7:10–12	174
7:10	287
7:14	279
7:15	287
7:17	287
8–9	272
8:1	279
9	280
10:7	280
11	277
11:1–14	288
11:2	274
11:3–10	274
11:8	271
11:15–19	214, 288
11:15	281, 282, 341
11:16	343
11:17–18	282
12–13	214, 288
12	275
12:1–12	278
12:9	283
12:10	214
12:11	290
12:12	275
12:13–14	275
12:17	275
13	273, 275, 280
13:1	275
13:6	275, 278
13:11	280
13:18	278, 281
14	275
14:1–5	279, 287, 288
14:1	274, 275, 276
14:4	238, 324
14:6–13	288
14:6–7	288
14:8	273, 280
14:10	274
14:12–13	286, 287
14:13	288
14:14	279

Index of Scripture

Revelation (continued)

Reference	Pages
14:20	279
15	278
15:2–4	280
15:2–3	287
15:3–4	46, 287
16:1—18:24	278
16:13–14	281
16:14–16	274
17:1—19:5	280
17–18	273, 277
17:11	70
17:12–13	281
19:4	343, 344
19:6–21	230
19:6–10	280
19:6	281
19:7–8	278, 282
19:7	280, 281
19:9	280
19:11–16	276
19:13	174, 277
19:16	281, 284
19:19–20	281
19:19	274
20	282, 283
20:3	286
20:4–6	282
20:4	282, 283
20:6–7	284
20:6	xxxiv, 49, 283
20:7–10	214
20:7–8	283
20:7	283
20:8	274, 283, 284
20:9	271, 274, 283
20:10	285
20:11	284
20:12	284
20:14	285
20:16	274
21–22	241, 254, 274, 282
21:1—22:5	280
21:1–6	285
21:1	174, 276
21:2	276, 288
21:3	xxxiv, 174, 253, 285
21:4	276, 285
21:9–21	285
21:9–10	288
21:9	278
21:12	8, 18, 58, 286
21:14	289
21:16	276
21:22—22:5	286
21:22–27	8
21:22–25	286
21:22	276, 286
21:23	282, 286
21:24–26	18, 58, 288
21:24–25	286
21:24	268
22:1–2	274, 290
22:1	289
22:3	289
22:5	xxxiv, 253, 286, 290
22:17	272, 288, 290
22:27	278

www.ingramcontent.com/pod-product-compliance
Lightning Source LLC
Chambersburg PA
CBHW081146290426

44108CB00018B/2457